The Dictionary of Multimedia

The Dictionary of Multimedia
Terms & Acronyms

1999 Edition

Brad Hansen

Chicago · London

President and Publisher	Jim Leisy (jimleisy@fbeedle.com)
Manuscript Editor	Eve Kushner
Production	Tom Sumner
	Stephanie Welch
	Susan Skarzynski
Cover Design	Tom Sumner
Marketing Group	Cary Crossland
	Chris Collier
	Marc Chambers
	Jason Smith
Order Processing	Lois Allison
	Krista Hall
Manufacturing	Malloy Lithographing
	Ann Arbor, Michigan

© 1999 Franklin, Beedle & Associates Incorporated

For information, write to:

FITZROY DEARBORN PUBLISHERS
70 East Walton Street
Chicago 60611
USA

or

FITZROY DEARBORN PUBLISHERS
11 Rathbone Place
London W1P 1DE
ENGLAND

British Library and Library of Congress Cataloging-in-Publication Data are available.

ISBN 1-57958-084-X

First published in the United States and United Kingdom, 1999

Dedication

For my wife, Jani.

Contents

Contents: Tables
viii

Contents: Expanded Definitions
ix

Contents: Appendices
x

Preface
xi

The Dictionary of Computing and Digital Media
1

List of Appendices
347

Contents: Tables

ASCII Character Codes 12

Authoring Software 26

Data Rate Conversion 76

EBCDIC Characters 109

File Name Extensions 113

General MIDI Instrument Map 134

Hexadecimal Equivalents 144

Internet Country Codes 165

MIME Types 210

Contents:
Expanded Definitions

Asymmetric Digital Subscriber Line (ADSL) *21*

compact disc formats *59*

digital service levels *83*

Digital Video Disc; Digital Versatile Disc (DVD) *95*

Fibre Channel *118*

FireWire (IEEE 1394) *121*

Integrated Services Digital Network (ISDN) *156*

Internet Relay Chat (IRC) *162*

Java programming language *170*

Moving Picture Expert Group (MPEG) *203*

Open Systems Interconnection (OSI) *226*

Portable Network Graphics (PNG) *245*

recommended standards (EIA RS232, RS422, RS449) *269*

Small Computer System Interface (SCSI) *284*

standards based on RFCs (STD) *294*

Virtual Reality Modeling Language (VRML) *329*

Contents: Appendices

I. Hypertext Markup Language (HTML) 349
    1. Basic Tutorial on HTML 349
    2. New Features in HTML 4.0 373
    3. Table of HTML Tags and Attributes 379
    4. Cascading Style Sheets (CSS1) 392
    5. Server-Side Includes (SSI) 402
    6. HTML Color Codes 407
    7. HTML Coded Characters 410

II. JavaScript: Objects and Operators 412

III. Extensible Markup Language (XML) 447

IV. Unix/Linux Operating System Commands 492

V. Standards Organizations 504

VI. Requests for Comment (RFC) 513

VII. Copyright Issues 533

Preface

This book is for programmers, graphic artists, writers, video producers, audio engineers, network managers, hardware technicians, and telecommunications professionals who embrace the complex world of digital media and realize the need for a common language in which to communicate with one another. This book is unique in bringing together definitions of critical terms and concepts drawn from the diverse bodies of knowledge incorporated in the production of digital media. To complement the definitions, the extensive appendices explain how to prepare content for the World Wide Web and provide references on current standards and copyright law.

The terms defined in this dictionary were selected because of their relevance to the production and distribution of digital media with computers. A creative team builds graphic, audio, and video products that are digitized by computer hardware and programmed for interactive access. A server may deliver these products to clients over a telecommunications network, or they might be distributed on fixed media, such as a CD-ROM. For the production team to function, its members must have some common definitions for the words they use to communicate. The terms in this dictionary originate from the disciplines represented by those who develop and deliver digital content. The following list includes some of these disciplines and content pertaining to each:

- *Hardware*—computers, electronics, components, interfaces, media, physics
- *Software*—logic, programming, data, file structures, scripting, applications
- *Networking*—Internet, protocols, connections, standards, data transfer
- *Telecommunications*—telephony, broadcast, radio, television, cable, satellite
- *Human factors*—organizations, committees, individuals, ergonomics
- *Graphics*—imaging, animation, drawing, color theory, photography, semiology
- *Audio*—acoustics, engineering, music, MIDI, recording, signal processing
- *Video*—lighting, postproduction, editing, film, tape formats, compression

The development of digital media requires teamwork and the contribution of many minds and hands. Likewise, many individuals have contributed directly and indirectly to assembling the information in this book. Many members of computer-user groups and professional associations have shared their knowledge unselfishly, including the World Wide Web Consortium (W3C), the Association for Computing Machinery (ACM), the Institute of Electrical and Electronics Engineers (IEEE), the International Multimedia Association and the International MIDI Association (IMA), the National Center for Supercomputing (NCSA), the Audio Engineering Society (AES), and the International Television Association (ITVA).

The appendices contain current information regarding World Wide Web development and related topics. The HTML appendix includes a basic tutorial on HTML, courtesy of the NCSA. This appendix also covers all of the HTML 4.0 tags and attributes, and the new features in version 4.0 compared to version 3.2. A section explains Cascading Style Sheets, with examples of syntax for defining styles in HTML documents. Another section addresses Server-Side Includes, a method for dynamically generating content from a web server. Tables show how to specify the HTML color codes and coded characters.

Other appendices provide a reference for programming languages that are used to create dynamic HTML documents. The JavaScript appendix shows how the language is implemented and lists the objects and operators that are available. The properties, methods, and event handlers that may be used with each object are defined. The full Extensible Markup Language (XML) specification is provided in another appendix, courtesy of the World Wide Web Consortium.

The majority of web servers run on the Unix/Linux platforms, so we have included a general description of these operating systems and the function performed by common commands.

Because the standards used in computing and Internet applications are evolving rapidly, two appendices address the source and content of these standards. A list of selected Requests for Comment (RFC) that define Internet protocols is included. It gives the reader an interesting historical perspective on the development of Internet technologies. The title, author(s), date of submission, and status for each RFC are given. Another appendix discusses the primary organizations that establish international standards and the work they do, along with contact information for each.

The final appendix addresses the issues surrounding copyrights. In lay terms, it discusses current laws related to ownership and protection of intellectual property of all kinds and ramifications for digital media and the Internet. Thanks to Terrence J. Carroll, an attorney who specializes in copyright law, for support in developing the appendix.

Definitions in this dictionary are located beside spelled-out terms and phrases, rather than beside the acronyms that represent the terms and phrases. The reader is generally referred from an acronym to the term where it is spelled out for the definition. Words, symbols, and numbers are ordered alphabetically, as they would be spelled. For example, "C++" follows "courseware," and "16-bit" follows "site." To avoid confusion in quantifying data, one convention to which we adhere should be pointed out. The abbreviation for kilobits is Kb, while kilobytes is KB. A similar convention applies to megabits (Mb) and megabytes (MB). The need for accuracy, clarity, and precision in writing about this field has been a high priority in preparing this document.

Jim Leisy and all of the staff at Franklin, Beedle & Associates—Sue, Cary, Marc, Jason, Stacia, Chris, Lois, Krista, Stephanie, and Susan—have been extremely supportive in developing this reference book. In particular, Tom Sumner has been tireless in his pursuit of clarity, completeness, and consistency. Thanks to Jeff Ong and Bill DeRouchey for contributing the illustrations, and to Eve Kushner for her careful editing of the manuscript. I am deeply grateful to my wife Jani, son Graham, and daughter Claire, who shared their lives with my endeavor to research and present this information to you.

—Brad Hansen
brad@hansenmedia.com

A

AAL See *ATM Adaptation Layer.*

AAP See *Association of American Publishers.*

A:B:C notation (n.) The standard way to describe relationships between sample rates and color clock rates in digital video formats. Higher rates result in better resolution. Three numbers are used to represent ratios, as follows:

(A) The basic sample rate compared with the color clock rate.
(B) The color horizontal downsampling rate compared with the basic sampling rate.
(C) The color vertical downsampling rate plus 1.

A standard 4:2:2 format indicates that sampling is done at four times the color clock rate, which is 3.58 MHz; that two horizontal chroma samples are taken for every four luminance samples; and that there is no reduction in vertical color resolution (1 + 1).

abend (n.) Abnormal end; an error message indicating the unexpected termination of a program or signal that may be either recoverable or unrecoverable.

ABI See *Application Binary Interface.*

ABIOS See *Advanced Basic Input/Output System.*

ablation (n.) The use of a laser beam to burn pits into thin metal film for optical data storage. The process is used to create CDs.

abort (v.) To cancel a computing procedure while in progress.

ABR See *automatic baud rate detection.*

A-B roll (n.) An editing process in which videotape is played from two tape machines, A and B. As the tapes are rolled, portions of each are dubbed onto a third tape, the composite master. Video editors use this technique to import footage from multiple source tapes. The resulting product is often enhanced by placing transitions between segments from different sources and by using special effects.

ABS See *Alternative Billing Service.*

abscissa (n.) The x-coordinate, plotted on a graph in response to the input of a function. The y-coordinate is referred to as the *ordinate.* Pronounced "ab-SISS-a."

absolute time (n.) The time that elapses from the exact beginning of an audio CD or a digital audio tape (DAT) to any given point in the program material that follows. This information is used to determine the precise start and stop times of a recorded program.

abstract class (n.) In object-oriented programming, a class without instances. Instead, it has concrete classes as subclasses. Example: *mammal* is an abstract class, and *cow* is a concrete class.

abstraction (n.) 1. A process in which something is made into a function of something else, or is "parameterized." Bracket abstractions make a term into a function of a variable. 2. A process of hiding details or generalizing. Example: in abstract syntax, the details of the syntax are ignored.

abstract machine (n.) Software that executes an intermediate language used in a compiler or interpreter. This processor is not intended to be implemented in hardware. It has an instruction set, a register set, and a model of memory. It may be used to make a language implementation easier to port to various platforms. A virtual machine is an abstract machine for which an interpreter exists.

abstract syntax (n.) A form of data structure independent of machine-oriented encoding or language.

Abstract Syntax Notation One (ASN/1) (n.) Language used to encode Simple Network Management Protocol (SNMP) packets. It is also used by Open Systems Interconnection (OSI) protocols for describing abstract syntax, and it is defined in the ISO standard documents 8824.2 and 8825.2.

Abstract Windowing Toolkit (AWT) (n.) The independent windowing, graphics, and user interface toolkit in the Java programming environment.

AC See *alternating current.*

Accelerated Graphics Port (AGP) (n.) An interface specification developed in 1997 by Intel Corporation. It is based on the peripheral component interconnect (PCI) bus and was designed to facilitate three-dimensional graphics. AGP creates its own dedicated channel, so the graphics controller can directly access main memory, rather than use the PCI bus. This point-to-point channel is 32 bits wide. It runs at 66 MHz but supports data transmission at both the rising and falling ends of the clock cycle for increased speed. The total effective bandwidth is 533 Mbps at double speed (2X) throughput. Three-dimensional textures are stored in main memory, rather than in video memory. Among the requirements for implementing AGP are the OSR 2.1 version of Windows 95 or Windows 98 and a Pentium hardware system with an AGP bus slot. Optional features of AGP include the following:

- Direct Memory Execute mode, which allows textures to be stored in main memory.

- multiple throughput rates: 1X (266 Mbps), 2X (533 Mbps), 4X (1.07 Gbps).

- pipelining, which allows the graphics card to send multiple instructions at once, rather than one at a time.

- sideband addressing, which hastens data transfer by sending command instructions over a separate parallel channel.

accelerator card (n.) A circuit board inserted into a slot on the motherboard that increases the processing speed and performance of the CPU. Production artists use graphics accelerators to increase productivity because these artists must wait for the screen to redraw every time they edit an image.

Acceptable Use Policy (AUP) (n.) An Internet Service Provider's statement of permissible uses.

acceptance testing (n.) Formal testing conducted to determine whether a system satisfies the stated criteria for a customer.

access (v.) To seek and retrieve information from a hard disk, floppy disk, CD-ROM, or any other digital or analog storage medium.

Access (n.) 1. A relational database application integrated into the Microsoft Office Pro suite. 2. A query language similar to English used in Pick, an operating system developed by VMark Computer, Inc.

ACCESS.bus (n.) Developed by Digital Equipment Corporation, this bus format is based on the Inter-Integrated Circuit serial bus invented by Philips Semiconductors and Signetics. The ACCESS.bus Industry Group supports it as an alternative to the Universal Serial Bus (USB) from Intel Corporation. Software drivers are required to provide the interface between ACCESS.bus hardware and application programs. Physically, ACCESS.bus runs at a relatively low speed over limited distances. It replaces the limited number of specialized ports in a PC with one general-purpose port that supports multiple peripherals in a daisy chain. Pointing devices, modems, printers, a keyboard, and a monitor using the Video Electronics Standards Association (VESA) Display Data Channel (DDC) standard may all be connected on the same bus. It supports up to 125 devices, and each device may operate at a different data rate, up to 100 kilobits per second

(Kbps). The maximum cable length is eight meters. *Hot plugging,* which allows a device to be connected or disconnected without turning off power to a computer, and *auto-addressing,* which automatically identifies a unit attached to the bus and shakes hands without user intervention, are features of the standard.

Access Control List (ACL) (n.) List of the services available on a server. Each item on the list also has a list of the hosts permitted to use that particular service.

access line (n.) The connecting line between a customer's premises and the central office of a local telephone company.

access method (n.) The way in which network devices access a network. This method is determined by the Systems Network Architecture (SNA), which controls the flow of network information.

access node (n.) The connection point in a local telephone network at which numerous access lines are consolidated into fewer feeder lines. Access lines are normally multiplexed onto digital loop carrier (DLC) systems supporting T1 transmission. A private branch exchange (PBX) is another type of access node, as are cellular antenna sites and optical network units (ONUs).

access time (n.) The time required to locate and load data from storage after the seek command is issued. Typically, this measurement includes the time it takes the reading head to move between the most distant segments of the medium and to position itself radially. To begin reading or writing, the head must be positioned over the proper sector. This radial motion is called *seeking,* and the collection of sectors available under multiple heads is called a *cylinder.* The time it takes for a disk to rotate

3

until the proper sector is located under the heads is *rotational latency,* which combines with seek time to yield the total access time.

accounting management (n.) The control of individual and group access to network resources to ensure proper bandwidth and security or to assess charges to clients. It is one of five categories of network management defined by the ISO for management of Open Systems Interconnection (OSI) networks.

accumulator (n.) A register in the central processing unit (CPU) where intermediate results are stored. Access to main memory is not as fast as access to the accumulator, which typically has a direct path to and from the arithmetic and logic unit (ALU). Late-model CPUs generally have many registers that may be used as accumulators.

ACD See *Automatic Call Distribution* or *Automatic Call Distributor.*

ACI See *adjacent channel interference.*

ACID test (n.) A test of the atomicity, consistency, isolation, and durability of transaction processing. Passing the ACID test means having a high degree of resilience and recoverability. The term is derived from the process of testing metals with strong acid to determine gold content.

ACIS (n.) A geometric engine owned by Spatial Technologies that is named for its inventors (Andy, Charles, and Ian's System). It employs a sophisticated object-oriented approach to modeling and is used in several computer-aided design (CAD) programs.

ACK (n.) An acknowledgment character that is returned to a sending device by a receiving device to indicate that the data has been received correctly.

ACL See *Access Control List* or *Association for Computational Linguistics.*

ACM See *addressed call mode* or *Association for Computing Machinery.*

acoustic coupler (n.) Device that connects a modem to a telephone line with the use of a handset. It converts electrical signals from the modem into sound with a loudspeaker, against which the mouthpiece of the handset is placed. The earpiece is placed against a microphone. The sound from the connected circuit is converted into electrical signals. The signals are then returned to the modem. Although this device was popular in the 1970s, it is rarely used because modems now connect directly to telephone lines.

acquisition (n.) 1. The process of capturing assets or transferring information from an analog to a digital format. 2. In telecommunications, the process of locking tracking equipment onto a signal from a communications satellite and synchronizing with it.

Acrobat (n.) A program developed by Adobe for cross-platform document exchange in which files are created in the Portable Document Format (.pdf) from PostScript. The full complement of Acrobat tools consists of the Distiller, the Exchange package, the Catalog package, and the Reader. The Reader is freely distributed so that it may be installed and used on any computer to decipher an Acrobat document.

acronym (n.) An identifier derived from the letters or initials of a phrase and used as an abbreviation.

ACT See *annual change traffic.*

ActionMedia II (n.) One of the first video capture cards developed by Intel that employs their Digital Video Interactive (DVI) compression technology. It has been replaced by the Intel Smart Video Recorder.

active DBMS (n.) Active database management system; a conventional database management system combined with a means of event detection and condition monitoring. Event handling may be rule based, as it is in an expert system.

active matrix display (n.) A liquid crystal display (LCD) panel that has three transistors (red, green, and blue) for each pixel and that yields better color and resolution than a *passive matrix display.* Thin film transistor (TFT) technology makes this possible.

active monitor (n.) The process in an IBM token ring network that detects the presence of a token, removes circulating frames with invalid destinations, and performs introductions between nodes on the ring.

active object (n.) An object in programming that encompasses its own thread of control.

active video lines (n.) Video traces that are scanned on the screen between the horizontal and vertical blanking intervals. The lines are generated by the electron gun in a cathode-ray tube (CRT). About 483 lines are visible or active in the NTSC 525-line system used in the United States.

active window (n.) The portion of the screen that is prepared to accept input from an input device.

ActiveX (n.) Developed by Microsoft to compete with Java, ActiveX is an implementation of object linking and embedding (OLE) with reduced features. It is designed to run over low-bandwidth Internet connections.

actor (n.) Any object that exists as a concurrent process in object-oriented programming (OOP).

actuator (n.) The mechanism that moves the read and write heads of a disk drive across the platter surfaces.

Ada (n.) Named after Ada Lovelace, a programming language similar to Pascal that was designed at Honeywell in 1979. The Pentagon mandated its use for Department of Defense software projects. Ada is a complex, block-structured language intended for embedded applications.

Adaptable User Interface (AUI) (n.) A toolkit from Oracle used to write applications that are portable between different windowing systems. A single call-level interface is provided with a resource manager and editor for several graphical user interfaces (GUIs), including the Mac OS, Microsoft Windows, and X Window System.

adapter 1. (n.) In audio and video applications, an object that allows a different type of connector to be plugged into each end, making a connection despite incompatible termination. An example is a gender changer, which is used to connect two cables that both have male termination. 2. (adj.) Describes a type of interface card that connects to peripherals or a network.

adaptive answering (n.) A feature commonly found on a Class 1 faxmodem that allows it to answer an incoming call and to determine whether the signal is a fax or data call.

Adaptive Data Compression (ADC) (n.) A Hayes modem protocol.

adaptive differential pulse code modulation (ADPCM) (n.) A standard method endorsed by the Interactive Multimedia Association (IMA) for storing digital audio on a multiple-session CD-ROM XA or a CD-i. The procedure reduces the amount of data needed by examining previously encoded data and adaptively predicting future encoding, eliminating some redundancy, and storing the differences between successive digital samples rather than full values. It is an extension of the pulse code modulation (PCM) audio encoding format. Another version of this audio encoding process standardized by the CCITT for telecommunications applications can transmit a voice over a 32-kilobit-per-second (Kbps) digital channel. Each sample is defined by three or four bits that represent the difference between adjacent samples.

ADAT See *Alesis Digital Audio Tape.*

ADB See *Apple Desktop Bus.*

ADC See *Adaptive Data Compression* or *analog-to-digital converter.*

ADCCP See *Advanced Data Communications Control Procedures.*

A/D converter (n.) See *analog-to-digital converter.*

additive color mixing (n.) The process of creating hues by mixing colored light rather than pigments. Mixing the additive primary colors in equal proportions results in white. See figure.

additive synthesis (n.) In audio production, creating a composite waveform by summing

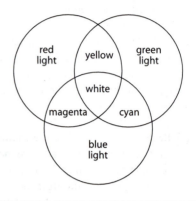

additive color mixing

multiple individual waveforms.

address 1. (n.) Any label that identifies the location of data in either static or dynamic memory, such as a frame number on coded videotape. 2. (n.) An unsigned integer used to select one fundamental element of storage, usually a word from a computer's main memory or another storage device. The central processing unit (CPU) outputs addresses on its address bus, which may be connected to an address decoder, a cache controller, a memory management unit, or some other device. 3. (n.) In computer networking, an email address, Internet address, or media access control (MAC) address on a network. 4. (n.) In telecommunications, a telephone number. 5. (v.) To send a message to a particular location.

addressability (n.) The existence of a method to control delivery of services to certain, select subscribers on a system. In the cable industry, this allows an operator to activate, disconnect, or scramble the signal received by a subscriber remotely from the headend. After a subscriber signals the service provider, the provider's computer addresses the subscriber's set-top box, temporarily allowing it to descramble the program so that it may be viewed. Any address-able set-top box may be controlled by this method.

addressable converter (n.) A device connected to a cable television receiver to give the program provider the capacity to transmit or to block services to an individual subscriber.

address bus (n.) The system of connections carrying a binary-coded address from the microprocessor through a computing system. The address bus is a subset of the processor and memory buses, which consist of the data lines, the address lines, and the control lines. The address bus indicates which particular addresses in the memory and system buses are to be used in a data transfer operation. It identifies the precise location where the next bus transfer or memory transfer will occur. The size of the memory bus controls the amount of memory that the central processing unit (CPU) can address directly.

address code (n.) 1. Time code stamped on a tape to identify each frame of video. The hour, minute, second, and frame numbers are expressed by eight digits in the format hh:mm:ss:ff. 2. The cue code placed in the vertical blanking interval (VBI) of a videodisc frame as a point of reference.

addressed call mode (ACM) (n.) In telecommunications, a mode that allows control signals to initiate and terminate calls under the V.25bis specification.

address mask (n.) In electronic messaging, a subnet ID that uses some of the most significant bits of the host address portion of an Internet Protocol (IP) address to divide the single network into smaller addressable portions. See also *subnet.*

address resolution (n.) The translation of an Internet address into the corresponding Ethernet address, or physical address, usually done with Address Resolution Protocol (ARP). It consists of a library routine and processes that convert hostnames into Internet addresses. See also *domain name system.*

Address Resolution Protocol (ARP) (n.) The method by which a host Ethernet address is determined from its Internet address. A server sends an ARP packet with the Internet address of another host and waits for it to send back an Ethernet address. Every host typically maintains a cache of address translations to expedite the process. ARP, defined in RFC 826, allows the Internet address to be independent of the Ethernet address. Hosts not compatible with ARP must perform constant mapping.

address space (n.) 1. The range of addresses (either physical or virtual) that a processor can access. It depends on the width of the processor's address bus and address registers. 2. The range of physical addresses or virtual addresses allocated to a process.

address track time code (ATTC) (n.) Longitudinal time code (LTC) recorded on a designated track of an analog videotape or in the center of an analog audio tape.

adjacent (adj.) In network technology, simple network access (SNA) nodes are adjacent if they are connected to a given node with no intervening nodes. In the Open Systems Interconnection (OSI) model, adjacent nodes are those that share a common segment, whether in Ethernet, Fiber Distributed Data Interface (FDDI), or token ring networks.

adjacent channel interference (ACI) (n.) Noise caused when two or more channels are present at frequencies that are too near one another in the spectrum.

ADN See *advanced digital network* or *Advanced Digital Network*.

Adobe Type Manager (ATM) (n.) A utility that extrapolates a screen resolution character at 72 dots per inch (dpi) from a PostScript character in order to display it cleanly on a monitor.

ADPCM See *adaptive differential pulse code modulation*.

ADR See *Automatic Dialog Replacement*.

ADSL See *Asymmetric Digital Subscriber Line*.

ADSP See *AppleTalk Data Stream Protocol*.

ADSR (n.) Attack, decay, sustain, release; a circuit that defines the shape of a synthesized sound over time. ADSR settings specify amplitude levels that change at various stages as a note sounds. These settings determine the package, or envelope of a sound, which is not related to the pitch. See figure.

ADSR curve

Advanced Basic Input/Output System (ABIOS) (n.) Service routines built into IBM-compatible computers that support multitasking.

Advanced Data Communications Control Procedures (ADCCP) (n.) A standard, bit-oriented, data link control protocol that the U.S. government uses for communications.

advanced digital network (ADN) (n.) In general, a group of computers, peripherals, or other equipment connected to one another for the purpose of passing information and sharing resources. Networks can be either local or remote. The topology of a network is the geographic arrangement of links and nodes, which may be arranged in the shape of a star, tree, or ring.

Advanced Digital Network (ADN) (n.) The brand name used by Pacific Telesis for its inexpensive, leased 56-kilobit-per-second digital network service.

advanced intelligent network (AIN) (n.) Telephone network architecture implemented by major telephone companies worldwide. These networks direct telephone calls according to criteria specified by the telephone company. The three core components of an AIN are listed below. These components communicate through out-of-band signaling or over a signaling network using Signaling System 7 (SS7) protocol.

1. Signal Control Points (SCPs): Computer databases that store customer-specific information used by the network to route calls.
2. Signal Switching Points (SSPs): Digital telephone switches that can talk to SCPs and ask them for customer-specific instructions about how the call should be completed.
3. Signal Transfer Points (STPs): Packet switches that shuttle messages between SSPs and SCPs.

Advanced Interactive Executive (AIX) (n.) The

IBM version of Unix.

advanced mobile phone service (AMPS) (n.) Cellular telephone technology or any equipment designed to work with common analog cellular telephones in the United States.

Advanced Power Management (APM) (n.) System that conservatively allocates power for essential functions in battery-operated notebook computers.

Advanced Research Projects Agency (ARPA) (n.) U.S. government organization that developed packet-switching techniques and created the network called ARPANET, which was the precursor to the Internet.

Advanced RISC Machine (ARM) (n.) Advanced reduced instruction set computing Machine; an inexpensive, power-efficient, 32-bit RISC microprocessor that has embedded control, computing, digital signal processing (DSP), consumer multimedia, and other applications. It is licensed for production by Cirrus Logic, Sharp, Texas Instruments, VLSI Technology, and others. It has a small orthogonal instruction set in which every instruction includes a four-bit code.

Advanced SCSI Programming Interface (ASPI) (n.) Advanced Small Computer System Interface Programming Interface; developed by Adaptec, a protocol used to configure devices and media on a Small Computer System Interface (SCSI) chain.

Advanced Streaming Format (ASF) (n.) Multimedia file format for data that must flow at a constant bit rate and must be decoded or realized in real time. It was designed by Microsoft to pass information over the Internet using Netshow. ASF files can deliver audio, video, or scripting commands to a client computer.

Advanced Technology Attachment (ATA) (n.) The name give to Western Digital's IDE disk interface by ANSI when it was standardized. *ATA-2* and *Fast-ATA* are names used for the EIDE interface.

Advanced WavEffect (AWE) (n.) A sound synthesis process employed by the EMU8000 music synthesizer integrated circuit (IC) located on the Sound Blaster AWE32 card.

AE See *automatic exposure.*

AECT See *Association for Educational Communications and Technology.*

aerial cable (n.) A wire suspended overhead from poles or buildings, as opposed to an underground cable. Cable television companies rent space on poles from the telephone companies and electric companies that own the poles.

AES/EBU See *Audio Engineering Society/European Broadcast Union.*

AF See *audio frequency.*

AFC See *automatic frequency control.*

affordance (n.) A tangible aspect of an object that allows action or manipulation. Examples: handles, buttons, and scroll bars.

AFK (adj.) Shorthand for "away from keyboard." See *shorthand.*

AFSK See *audio frequency shift keying.*

AGC See *automatic gain control.*

agent (n.) The portion of a system that prepares and exchanges information on behalf of a client or server. *Intelligent agent* refers to some automatic process capable of communicating

9

with other agents.

AGP See *Accelerated Graphics Port.*

AI See *artificial intelligence.*

AIFF See *Audio Interchange File Format.*

AIIM See *Association for Information and Image Management.*

AIN See *advanced intelligent network.*

AIX See *Advanced Interactive Executive.*

a-law (Pronounced "AY-law") (n.) Standardized in the ITU G.711 specification, a method of coding eight-bit companded audio with pulse code modulation (PCM) to yield a 64 dB dynamic range. It is used to transmit digital voice channels over telephone lines worldwide, except in North America, Japan, and South Korea, where μ-*law* coding is used. It is not interchangeable with μ-law coding. A converter must be used to translate between these two differently coded PCM voice messages. See also μ-*law* under *mu-law.*

Alesis Digital Audio Tape (ADAT, pronounced "AY-dat") (n.) Developed by Alesis Corporation, an eight-track audio recording format that uses S-VHS cassettes for recording media. This was the first practical, inexpensive, digital multitracking machine, and it became popular in project studios. The TASCAM DA-88 is another popular eight-track digital recorder that uses Hi-8 cassettes rather than S-VHS. The DA-88 format was adopted by Sony and is commonly used in feature film production. Pronounced "a-LEE-sis."

ALGOL 60 (n.) See *Algorithmic Language 1960.*

algorithm (n.) A type of formula that defines a sequence of steps necessary to perform a process.

algorithmic (adj.) Describes a program structured like a mathematical procedure that solves a problem with a limited number of steps.

Algorithmic Language 1960 (ALGOL 60) (n.) A compact, portable programming language developed in 1960 and designed for scientific computations.

alias (n.) 1. In the Mac OS 7.0 and higher, an icon that represents or points to the original file. Multiple aliases can be created and placed where they may provide convenient access to the original file. 2. A short name that is translated into a longer name or string to save space. Many command interpreters allow a user to define aliases for commands. The computer loads the aliases into memory when the interpreter starts and expands them without needing to refer to any file. 3. Another name for a host with the same Internet address as the original host. A hostname alias can indicate that the host provides a particular network service, such as Archie, FTP, or the web. With this provision, services to hosts can be changed by moving an alias from one Internet address to another without bothering the clients.

aliasing (n.) 1. The appearance of unwanted visual effects, known as *jaggies,* in digitized images. An example is the stairstep effect on raster display systems that do not have a high enough resolution to reproduce smooth diagonal lines or circles. 2. In audio sampling, a distortion-producing reflection caused by the fact that all frequency components higher than half the sampling frequency are reflected in the lower range. Aliasing creates artifacts. It can be avoided by processing the waveform to be sampled with a low-pass filter at half the sample rate before digitizing.

A

alignment (n.) 1. In a tape recorder, the positioning of the head in relation to the tape path. 2. In a word-processed or graphic document, the horizontal and vertical relationships of elements.

alpha blending (n.) A technique used to produce atmospheric effects in three-dimensional graphics. Alpha values determine how transparent a pixel will be.

alpha channel (n.) 1. In video production, a separate signal used to control visual effects such as overlay and transparency. 2. In a digital graphics environment, the bits that control the percentage of visibility between upper and lower layers, or foreground and background elements.

alphanumeric (adj.) Describes a combination of letters, numerals, and other symbols used for codes and computational expressions.

alpha test (n.) The initial testing on software to evaluate general functionality. It occurs before a beta test, in which software is field-tested by users.

alt (n.) 1. One of the Usenet newsgroup hierarchies founded by John Gilmore and Brian Reid in which anyone can create a new group without going through normal voting procedures. 2. Refers to the many free newsgroups available through Usenet. It is something of an icon for topics related to alternative culture.

Alt (n.) A modifier key on many computer keyboards, including the IBM PC and the Macintosh.

Altair 8800 (n.) The first microcomputer kit.

AltaVista (n.) A web site maintained by Digital Equipment Corporationm (DEC) with a very efficient web and Usenet search engine. It once held the distinction of being the largest web index, referencing millions of pages and articles.

ALTEL See *Association of Long Distance Telephone Companies.*

alternating current (AC) (n.) In the United States, 120-volt electricity delivered by utility companies. It changes polarity from positive to negative 60 times per second. In other countries, the rate of alternation is often 50 cycles per second (cps). Direct current (DC), by contrast, is a continuous stream of current in one direction with constant polarity. The regular pulse of AC can be picked up by audio systems that are not well grounded, introducing an undesirable 60-cycle hum. Compare *direct current.*

Alternative Billing Service (ABS) (n.) Intelligent network service enabling subscribers to charge a call to a telephone number other than the one they are using with a credit card or ID number.

ALU See *arithmetic and logic unit.*

AM See *amplitude modulation.*

ambient (adj.) Describes a natural state, such as room temperature. Ambient sounds are referred to as *environmental* because they exist in a natural environment.

American National Standards Institute (ANSI) (n.) A U.S. government body that approves standards in many areas, including computers and communications. ANSI is a member of the ISO. ANSI and ISO standards may be purchased from ANSI Sales, 1430 Broadway, New York, NY 10018. Telephone: (212) 642–4900.

American Society of Composers, Authors, and

ASCII Character Codes

Decimal	Hex	Symbol	Function	Decimal	Hex	Symbol	Function
0	0	^@	(NUL) Fill Character	52	34	4	Four
1	1	^A	(SOH) Start of Heading	53	35	5	Five
2	2	^B	(STX) Start of Text	54	36	6	Six
3	3	^C	(ETX) End of Text	55	37	7	Seven
4	4	^D	(EOT) End of Transmission	56	38	8	Eight
5	5	^E	(ENQ) Enquire (request response)	57	39	9	Nine
6	6	^F	(ACK) Acknowledge	58	3A	:	Colon
7	7	^G	(BEL) Bell (sound a tone)	59	3B	;	Semicolon
8	8	^H	(BS) Backspace	60	3C	<	Less-than Sign
9	9	^I	(HT) Horizontal Tab	61	3D	=	Equals Sign
10	A	^J	(LF) Line Feed	62	3E	>	Greater-than Sign
11	B	^K	(VT) Vertical Tab	63	3F	?	Question Mark
12	C	^L	(FF) Form Feed	64	40	@	At Sign
13	D	^M	(CR) Carriage Return	65	41	A	
14	E	^N	(SO) Shift Out (change character set)	66	42	B	
15	F	^O	(SI) Shift In (change character set)	67	43	C	
16	10	^P	(DLE) Data Link Escape	68	44	D	
17	11	^Q	(DC1) Data Control 1 (XON)	69	45	E	
18	12	^R	(DC2) Data Control 2	70	46	F	
19	13	^S	(DC3) Data Control 3 (XOFF)	71	47	G	
20	14	^T	(DC4) Data Control 4	72	48	H	
21	15	^U	(NAK) Negative Acknowledge	73	49	I	
22	16	^V	(SYN) Synchronous Idle	74	4A	J	
23	17	^W	(ETB) End of Transmission Block	75	4B	K	
24	18	^X	(CAN) Cancel (end a command)	76	4C	L	
25	19	^Y	(EM) End of Medium	77	4D	M	
26	1A	^Z	(SUB) Substitute (also end of file)	78	4E	N	
27	1B	^[	(ESC) Escape	79	4F	O	
28	1C	^\	(FS) File Separator	80	50	P	
29	1D	^]	(GS) Group Separator	81	51	Q	
30	1E	^^	(RS) Record Separator	82	52	R	
31	1F	^_	(US) Unit Separator	83	53	S	
32	20		(SP) Space Character	84	54	T	
33	21	!	Exclamation Mark	85	55	U	
34	22	"	Double Quotes	86	56	V	
35	23	#	Pound Sign	87	57	W	
36	24	$	Dollar Sign	88	58	X	
37	25	%	Percent Sign	89	59	Y	
38	26	&	Ampersand	90	5A	Z	
39	27	'	Single Quote	91	5B	[	Open Bracket
40	28	(	Open Parenthesis	92	5C	\	Backslash
41	29	)	Close Parenthesis	93	5D	]	Close Bracket
42	2A	*	Asterisk	94	5E	^	Caret
43	2B	+	Plus Sign	95	5F	_	Underscore
44	2C	,	Comma	96	60	'	
45	2D	–	Minus Sign, Hyphen	97	61	a	
46	2E	.	Period	98	62	b	
47	2F	/	Slash	99	63	c	
48	30	0	Zero	100	64	d	
49	31	1	One	101	65	e	
50	32	2	Two	102	66	f	
51	33	3	Three	103	67	g	

Decimal	Hex	Symbol	Function	Decimal	Hex	Symbol	Function
104	68	h		116	74	t	
105	69	i		117	75	u	
106	6A	j		118	76	v	
107	6B	k		119	77	w	
108	6C	l		120	78	x	
109	6D	m		121	79	y	
110	6E	n		122	7A	z	
111	6F	o		123	7B	{	Opening Brace
112	70	p		124	7C	|	Bar
113	71	q		125	7D	}	Closing Brace
114	72	r		126	7E	~	Tilde
115	73	s		127	7F		

Publishers (ASCAP) (n.) A licensing agency that controls the rights for the broadcast and performance of musical compositions.

American Society of Mechanical Engineers (ASME) (n.) An international body that has established hundreds of codes and standards for mechanical and electromechanical devices.

American Standard Code for Information Interchange (ASCII, pronounced "ASK-ee") (n.) The standard seven-bit code developed in 1965 by Robert W. Bemer to define text characters in a compatible format across different types of data processors. The original ASCII character set consisted of 128 numbers, ranging from 0 through 127, assigned to letters, numbers, punctuation marks, and a few very common special characters. IBM introduced the extended ASCII character set in 1981, an eight-bit code for its personal computers. This increased the number of characters represented to 256, allowing for special mathematical and graphical characters. The characters are referred to by names, such as ampersand, asterisk, backslash, caret, colon, comma, commercial at, Ctrl-C, dollar, dot, double quote, equals, exclamation mark, greater than, hash, opening brace, opening bracket, left parenthesis, less than, minus, percent, plus, question mark, closing brace, closing bracket, right parenthesis, semicolon, single quote, slash, space, tilde, underscore, vertical bar, and zero. The code works relatively well for English language text, but ASCII text is unable to represent many characters correctly in foreign languages. Software is described as "eight-bit clean" if it correctly handles character sets that use all eight bits. See table.

America Online (AOL) (n.) A large online Internet service provider based in Vienna, Virginia. It offers millions of subscribers electronic mail, conferencing, software libraries, and computing support. In 1994, AOL Internet FTP was made available to subscribers, and in May 1995 full Internet access included the WWW. Web access must be filtered through the AOL servers.

Amiga (n.) A line of microcomputers developed by Commodore Business Machines and used by consumers for games, video processing, and multimedia. Amigas are known for advanced graphics capabilities. Commodore Business Machines went bankrupt in April 1994, and the German company Escom AG bought it in April 1995.

A-mode (n.) The mode a video editing system is in while it assembles segments in the order specified on the edit decision list (EDL). This process usually involves multiple changes of source reels.

ampere (n.) A measurement of electrical current equal to 1 volt applied to 1 ohm of resistance.

ampersand (n.) ASCII character 38, "&."

amplifier (n.) An electronic device that boosts signal strength. Amplifiers, or amps, are required to drive speakers for audio output. They are also required at regular intervals in a cable television system between the headend and the subscriber, approximately every 1500 feet.

amplify (v.) To increase the amplitude or power of a given signal. In relation to audio, to increase the sound pressure level (SPL). Amplitude is the height of a waveform, or the measurement of a signal from trough to peak.

amplitude modulation (AM) (n.) The process of adding information to a constant carrier signal by modulating or changing its amplitude in direct correlation with another signal. See figure.

amplitude shift keying (ASK) (n.) A form of digital modulation in which discrete changes in the carrier signal's amplitude convey a digital signal.

AMPS See *advanced mobile phone service.*

analog (n.) A method of representing physical variables that flow and change continuously, such as voltage, pressure, or motion. Their values are expressed as the quantitative magnitude of the variables. Analog devices are often controlled by knobs and sliders, and their output is shown by dials, gauges, and meters. The output of an analog system is analogous to changes that it tracks or measures on a scale of infinite variety.

analog loopback (n.) A self-test process for modems in which keyboard data is sent to the transmitter, modulated into analog form, sent back to the receiver, demodulated into digital form, and returned to the screen to complete a verification loop.

analog RGB (n.) Analog red-green-blue; a video signal that sends separate signal lines for red, green, and blue picture information. Each of the signals is encoded as a proportional voltage rather than as digital bits. Video systems for most microcomputers employ this method of displaying images.

analog-to-digital converter (ADC, A/D converter) (n.) A circuit that converts changes in voltage, pressure, or motion over time into a stream of digits to define an event with time-based binary data.

analog video (n.) A continuous electronic signal generated by a camera or a videotape source

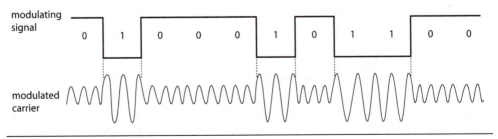

amplitude modulation

that represents an infinite number of smooth gradations between video levels. By contrast, a digital video signal assigns a finite series of steps in the gradations and is stored as data.

anchor (n.) An area (span, region, or button) in the content of a hypertext node that can serve as either the source or the destination of a hypertext link. The source anchor could be a word, phrase, image, or possibly the entire node. The destination anchor could be a node or a location within the node. Activating a source anchor by clicking on it causes the link to be followed and the anchor at the opposite end of the link to be displayed. Anchors are typically colored or highlighted in some way to make them stand out from the text around them. In HTML, anchors are created with the <A (anchor destination)> construct. The opening "A" tag of a source anchor has a hypertext reference (HREF) attribute giving the destination in the form of a URL or page. It is followed by the text that serves as the hypertext link in the referring document. Example: <A HREF="http://www.hanssenmedia.com/content"> The Knowledge Base Online</A>. See the section on linking in the appendix on HTML.

anchor point (n.) In a drawing program, the beginning or ending point of a Bezier curve.

AND (n.) Logic operator in an "if-then" proposition. If a series of statements is all true, the AND of those statements is true. If any statement in the series is false, the AND of those statements is false.

AND gate (n.) A logic gate whose output is 1 under the condition that all inputs are 1.

angle bracket (n.) One of two characters: < (less than), which is ASCII 60, or > (greater than), which is ASCII 62.

angry fruit salad (n.) Jargon for a graphic image with too many colors.

ANI See *automatic number identification.*

animatic (n.) A compilation of key scenes used to plan and lay out video spots and motion pictures.

animation (n.) The rapid display of a series of still images or objects that are repositioned in each frame to simulate movement on a still background.

annual change traffic (ACT) (n.) A small portion of the code in an application that a software developer modifies during a calendar year.

anonymous FTP (n.) Anonymous file transfer protocol; Internet hosts often provide this interactive service, which allows a user to transfer documents, files, programs, and other archived data using FTP. Users log in under the user name *ftp* or *anonymous* with their email address as the password. This grants access to a directory hierarchy containing publicly accessible files, normally in the *pub* subdirectory. A reference to a file available by FTP may also take the form of a URL beginning with the letters *ftp* and followed by a colon.

anonymous remailer (n.) System that disguises the identity of the sender of email over the Internet. It can be used to post to Usenet newsgroups anonymously.

ANSI See *American National Standards Institute.*

anti-aliasing (n.) Software alterations in the representation of data to help diagonal or curved lines appear smooth and continuous when displayed from computer-generated sources. In audio applications, the smoothing of steps between discrete samples to reduce the undesirable effects of low bit-rate capture. See figure.

anti-aliased letters on left, aliased letters on right

AOL See *America Online.*

Apache (n.) A popular HTTP server for Unix that anyone can use for free. Developed in 1995, it is based on Hypertext Transfer Protocol daemon (HTTPd), a program written at the National Center for Supercomputing Applications (NCSA). Apache was the most widely used HTTP server on the Internet in 1998, running on more than a third of all web servers. Among its features are authentication databases, content negotiation, and configurable error messages, all based on a database management system (DBMS). It is available at *http://www.apache.org.*

APD See *avalanche photodiode.*

APDA See *Apple Programmers and Developers Association.*

APDU See *application protocol data unit.*

aperture (n.) The opening in a camera lens that regulates the amount of light that can enter. The size of the aperture is measured in f-stops. See also *f-stop* or *iris.*

API See *Application Programming Interface.*

APM See *Advanced Power Management.*

apogee (n.) Point in a satellite's orbit that is farthest from Earth's center.

Apple Desktop Bus (ADB) (n.) The standard input/output (I/O) port and protocol used on a Macintosh to connect the keyboard, mouse, and other devices.

Apple Programmers and Developers Association (APDA) (n.) The source for all the tools needed to conduct high-level multimedia development using the Macintosh platform. APDA can be contacted at (800) 282–2732 in the United States or (800) 637–0029 in Canada.

Apple Remote Access (ARA) (n.) A communications protocol through which a user can dial up a host Macintosh from a remote modem and share the host's desktop on the remote computer. Files can be downloaded or uploaded between the two connected computers.

AppleScript (n.) An object-oriented shell language for the Macintosh, comparable to an extended version of HyperTalk, the scripting language developed for HyperCard.

applet (n.) A small Java program that can be attached to an HTML document for the WWW and executed by a Java-enabled browser running on any platform with a virtual machine that handles Java bytecode. A full Java application runs outside the browser. Before Java, the term referred to any small application that performed a specific task.

AppleTalk (n.) A local area network (LAN) protocol developed by Apple Computer for connecting peripherals and computers. It is a part of the system software that Apple Computer provides, and it operates over a variety of wiring types. Technically, it is a carrier sense multiple access with collision detection (CSMA/CD) network running at 230 kilobits per second (Kbps) that can connect up to 32 devices using shielded twisted-pair cable for a distance of approximately 1000 feet.

AppleTalk Data Stream Protocol (ADSP) (n.) A protocol that provides a simple transport method for networked data.

Apple Unix (A/UX) (n.) A version of Unix that runs on networked Apple computers.

Apple Video Compressor (n.) Developed by Apple Computer, the original compression and decompression CODEC used for QuickTime. Early versions of the CODEC have been updated.

application (n.) 1. A software program that creates or reads a data file. 2. The set of data and program software contained on a CD.

Application Binary Interface (ABI) (n.) The emulation in software of a hardware-software platform other than the native one, allowing foreign applications to run. An example would be running a Windows application under the Unix operating system.

application layer (n.) In the OSI model, this top layer provides the functionality that allows software programs to run and files to be accessed.

application program (n.) A complete stand-alone program that performs a specific function directly for the user, as opposed to system software such as the operating system kernel, server processes, and libraries, which support applications. Word processors and spreadsheets are common examples of applications. A client or browser is a networking application. Applications run in *user mode,* whereas operating systems and utilities run in *supervisor mode.* The short form is *app.*

Application Programming Interface (API) (n.) The interface or conventions by which an application program accesses the operating system and other services. It is defined at the source code level and provides a level of abstraction between the application and the kernel to ensure the portability of the code.

application protocol data unit (APDU) (n.) The highest-level view of communication in the OSI seven-layer model, this packet of data is exchanged between two application programs across a network. An individual packet exchanged at this level could be transmitted as several packets at a lower layer, in addition to containing headers for routing.

Application-Specific Integrated Circuit (ASIC) (n.) An integrated circuit that performs a particular function. The basic circuit building blocks provided by the circuit manufacturer are configured and interconnected for a specific use. They are used in automobiles and microwave ovens.

ARA See *Apple Remote Access.*

arbitration (n.) The bidding of multiple devices attached to a single bus to control the bus.

Archie (n.) Available as a Unix command via

17

Telnet, a tool that allows users to search a database of anonymous FTP sites.

architecture (n.) The general design of a computer hardware and software system. A system with *open architecture* allows the addition of internal cards and external peripherals.

archival (adj.) Describes a storage medium that preserves data for an extended period. Archival media must remain stable without degrading over time.

archive (v.) To record information in long-term storage.

archive site (n.) An Internet host where program source, documents, email, or news messages are stored for public access via anonymous FTP, gopher, the WWW, or another document distribution system. It is also referred to as an *FTP archive*.

archiving (n.) The process of moving data from online storage to nearline (optical disc) or offline (tape) storage. A directory is stored along with the data.

ARCnet See *Attached Resource Computer Network*.

area code (n.) A three-digit number designating a toll center in the United States, Canada, or Mexico. Area codes are distributed according to the North American Numbering Plan (NANP).

areal density (n.) *Bits per inch (bpi)* x *tracks per inch (tpi)*. This calculation indicates how many bits per square inch exist on the surface of a disk. *Bit density* x *track density* = *areal density*.

argument (n.) In programming, a value or reference assigned to a function, command, or procedure. In the function square(a) = a * a, *a* is the formal argument. Normally, arguments to a program are given after the command and are separated by spaces. In the example "run thisfile," *run* is the command and *thisfile* is the argument.

arithmetic and logic unit (ALU) (n.) The portion of a central processing unit (CPU) that performs mathematical functions, including multiplication, addition, subtraction, and Boolean operations. Most often, floating-point operations are done by a separate unit.

ARJ (n.) Archive program used by IBM-compatible computers to compress data and to store or transfer smaller files. See also *tape archive* or *ZIP*.

ARM See *Advanced RISC Machine* or *asynchronous response mode*.

ARP See *Address Resolution Protocol*.

ARPA See *Advanced Research Projects Agency*.

ARQ See *automatic request for retransmission*.

array (n.) 1. A set of coordinates that define rows and columns. A two-dimensional array is described with x- and y-coordinates, whereas a three-dimensional array requires x-, y-, and z-coordinates. 2. A group of identically typed data items distinguished by their subscripts. An array typically has any number of dimensions. A single variable, or *scalar*, might be considered an array. An array with one dimension might be considered a *vector*. An array might be represented as X[a,b,c,d], where *X* is the array name and *a, b, c,* and *d* are the subscripts, or *indexes*. Each index is written in separate brackets in the C language. Arrays are more useful for storing data to be accessed later in an unpredictable order than they are for storing items that will be sequentially called.

artifact (n.) Evidence of undesirable distortion that appears in digitized audio or video files as a result of inaccurate information introduced during capture or compression. Artifacts may take the form of new, unwanted data or the degradation of existing content.

artificial intelligence (AI) (n.) Software that makes decisions based on accumulated experience and information. The software features functions normally associated with human intelligence, such as learning, adapting, reasoning, and self-correcting.

artificial light (n.) In a video production or camera shoot, this is indoor or outdoor illumination from a man-made source, such as fluorescent bulbs, quartz lamps, or car headlights.

artwork (n.) Any type of graphics prepared for computer display, printing, or video. This may include drawings, paintings, photographs, maps, graphs, charts, captions, titles, and all elements in which artistic design considerations are of primary concern.

AS See *autonomous system.*

ASCAP See *American Society of Composers, Authors, and Publishers.*

ASCII See *American Standard Code for Information Interchange.*

ASF See *Advanced Streaming Format.*

AS/400 (n.) An IBM minicomputer released in 1988 and still produced in 1997. It provides multiuser support and is used by many small businesses. Programming for the system may be done in assembly language, C, Cobol, SQL, BASIC, and RPG.

ASIC See *Application-Specific Integrated Circuit.*

ASK See *amplitude shift keying.*

ASME See *American Society of Mechanical Engineers.*

ASN/1 See *Abstract Syntax Notation One.*

aspect ratio (n.) Resolution expressed in relative height and width values. The standard ratio for computer screens is 4:3. This is the basis for the standard resolutions of 240:180, 320:240, 640:480, 800:600, 1024:768, and 1600:1200, all of which are used in digital video. The aspect ratio for television monitors is wider, and the problem of *overscan* introduces variables related to the safe viewing area around the edges. The ratio of modern motion pictures varies from 5:3 to 7:3, creating a problem when a wide-format motion picture is transferred to a 4:3 ratio screen. A 35 mm photograph has dimensions of 36 mm x 24 mm, resulting in a 3:2 ratio. A letterbox effect occurs when photos are ported to the computer screen. See figure on the following page.

ASPI See *Advanced SCSI Programming Interface.*

assemble editing (n.) Placing video sequences back-to-back on a videotape without providing a constant reference signal or uninterrupted time code. This process is prone to minor timing errors. *Insert editing,* or placing sequences on top of an existing reference track, is more stable.

assembly (n.) The conversion of instructions and data written in a computer programming

aspect ratios

language into lower-level machine code.

assembly language (n.) A lower-level programming language that consists of words and phrases used to control a microprocessor. An assembler converts the subroutines of assembly language into machine code that a computer can read.

asset (n.) Any piece of data (such as an audio, graphic, text, or video file) used in a multimedia program.

assigned numbers (n.) The RFC standard (STD) 2, which identifies the currently assigned values from several series of numbers used in network protocol implementations. STD 2 is periodically updated, and the latest values may be secured from the Internet Assigned Numbers Authority (IANA). Anyone developing a protocol or application that requires the use of a link, socket, or port should contact the IANA for a number assignment.

Association for Computational Linguistics (ACL) (n.) International professional society for people addressing issues that involve language and computing. The ACL publishes a quarterly journal, *Computational Linguistics*, and sponsors special interest groups (SIGs). The ACL has more than 2000 members.

Association for Computing Machinery (ACM) (n.) The established international scientific and educational computer society. ACM was established in 1947 by mathematicians and electrical engineers, and it offers computer scientists a forum for sharing knowledge.

Association for Educational Communications and Technology (AECT) (n.) Professional group that promotes the study of how current technologies are applied in education, particularly at the institutional level.

Association for Information and Image Management (AIIM) (n.) A global organization of users and providers of information and document management technologies. Their expanded definition of the term *document* includes content in a variety of formats, such as print, email, voice messages, film, and video. The focus is on helping users apply technology to improve critical business processes. There are more than 650 corporations and 9000 individuals among its members. AIIM originated as the National Microfilm Associa-

A

tion in 1945 and changed its name in 1983. AIIM provides a forum for information exchange and works to advance worldwide standards of interoperability in cooperation with the American National Standards Institute (ANSI).

Association of American Publishers (AAP) (n.) Industry group whose members represent major publishers of print materials, as well as associated professionals. The organization has worked to define standards for document preparation and other issues that affect digital content developers.

Association of Long Distance Telephone Companies (ALTEL) (n.) Trade association whose members are alternative long distance carriers and service resellers.

Association of Visual Communicators (AVC) (n.) Group of graphics professionals dedicated to communicating effectively by using images.

asymmetrical compression (n.) Any video or audio compression process in which more time and resources are required to encode than to decode.

asymmetrical modulation (n.) Duplex data transmission technique that divides a link into two channels, one fast and one slow. During transmission between two modems, the one transmitting the most data uses the faster channel. The modem transmitting less data is given the slower "back" channel (450 bps). The channels may be dynamically reversed during a connection if the volume of data changes in either direction.

Asymmetric Digital Subscriber Line (ADSL) (n.) Method of transmitting data at a high rate over existing twisted-pair wiring from a telephone company's central office to a business or residence. In this method, the downstream rate is faster than the upstream rate—hence, the "asymmetric" qualifier. The ADSL standards are defined in the ANSI T-1.413 specification. The standards define two categories of digital transmission. Category I specifies a basic feature set for ADSL systems with various options. Category II is designed for higher data rates over longer distances and allows for greater noise immunity than Category I. Category II requires the use of Trellis-coded modulation, echo cancellation, and forward error correction, all of which enable simultaneous transmission upstream and downstream sharing a frequency spectrum. A line-encoding scheme using carrier amplitude and carrier phase modulation provides a one-way data channel to the subscriber at up to 6.4 megabits per second (Mbps), which is adequate for full-motion, full-screen video in the MPEG-2 format. That scheme also provides for an upstream flow of 640 kilobits per second (Kbps), divisible into channels to offer several services simultaneously. The maximum length of the copper single twisted pair used for transmission is 18 000 feet and varies widely depending on line conditions. With this technology, a standard telephone drop to a home can deliver compressed video that exceeds cable in quality, voice service, and fast modem connections to the Internet. The Universal ADSL Working Group (UAWG) Consortium is a group of network operators, computer companies, and telecommunications providers that developed a standard for splitterless ADSL, or ADSL Lite, referred to as G.lite by the International Telecommunications Union–Telecommunications Standardization Sector (ITU-T). Splitterless ADSL lowers the speed of service from a maximum of 8 Mbps to 1.5 Mbps, greatly reducing the risk of interference between voice and data signals. The ADSL Forum has a web server at *http://www.sbexpos.com/sbexpos/associations/ adsl/home.html.*

Terms related to ADSL:

- **Access Node** (n.) Concentration point for broadband and narrowband data that may be located at a central office or a remote site.

- **ATU-C** (n.) ADSL transmission unit–central; located at the central office end of a network, this unit can be integrated with an access node.

- **ATU-R** (n.) ADSL transmission unit–receiver; located at the customer premises end, this unit can be integrated with a Service Module (SM).

- **loop** (n.) Twisted-pair copper telephone line with a wide range of transmission characteristics based on diameter, distance, age, and connections.

- **Premises Distribution Network** (PDN) (n.) System for connecting the ATU-R to SMs. It may be passive or active, point-to-point, or multipoint.

- **Service Module** (SM) (n.) Unit that performs terminal adaptation functions, taking the form of a local area network (LAN) router, PC interface, or set-top box.

- **Single-Line Digital Subscriber Line** (SDSL) (n.) High-Data-Rate DSL over a single telephone line. A nonstandard implementation using plain old telephone service (POTS) for symmetric services to individual users.

- **splitter** (n.) Filter that separates high-frequency (ADSL) and low-frequency (POTS) signals at the network end and at the premises end.

- **Synchronous Transfer Mode** (STM) (n.) Transmission of data at a constant rate.

- **T-SM** (n.) Interface between the ATU-R and the Premises Distribution Network.

- **U-C** (n.) Interface between the loop and the POTS splitter on the network side. The asymmetry of the signals on the line requires that both ends of the loop be interfaced separately.

- **U-C2** (n.) Interface between the POTS splitter and the ATU-C.

- **U-R2** (n.) Interface between the POTS splitter and the ATU-R.

- **VA** (n.) Logical interface between the ATU-C and the Access Node.

- **VC** (n.) Logical interface between the Access Node and the network.

asynchronous (adj.) 1. Describes the performance of computer operations in sequential stages, rather than in a continuous variable stream. 2. The opposite of realtime conferencing in email applications. In realtime conferencing, more than one person can participate in a conversation at the same time from different locations; in asynchronous communication, they must take turns. 3. In telecommunications, a mode in which two devices are free to send data in a continuous stream at any time. Each byte begins with a start bit and ends with a stop bit. This is the most common mode of communication between computer modem users.

asynchronous response mode (ARM) (n.) In an unbalanced data connection, a mode in which the secondary station may begin transmitting to the primary station without obtaining permission.

Asynchronous Transfer Mode (ATM) (n.) A means of transmitting data. This mode combines different data types (audio, video, or text) with a sophisticated formula for allocating bandwidth and shuttling packets, or cells, of a fixed length (53 bytes). It provides a common means of transporting all types of data, some of which exist as streams that are reassembled on reception.

asynchronous transmission (n.) Method of transferring data in which each packet of information is individually synchronized by means of start and stop elements in the header.

ATA See *Advanced Technology Attachment.*

Atari (n.) A company that manufactured 16- and 32-bit microcomputers with built-in MIDIs in the 1970s and 1980s. They currently manufacture stand-alone video game hardware and software for use with television sets.

ATDT See *Attention Dial Tone.*

ATM See *Adobe Type Manager* or *Asynchronous Transfer Mode.*

ATM Adaptation Layer (AAL) (n.) Protocol used on top of Asynchronous Transfer Mode (ATM) to support high-level service requirements, converting non-ATM bit streams into ATM cells. The five adaptation layer levels provide both connection-oriented and connectionless services for data transfer. Layer 5 for computer networking provides error recovery and retransmission of undelivered or corrupted packets.

Attached Resource Computer Network (ARCnet) (n.) A local area network (LAN) configuration that operates at 2.5 megabits per sec-

ond (Mbps) over coaxial cable using a token-passing protocol. It features a distributed star topology and is reliable and easily expanded.

attachment (n.) Any file linked to an email message that can be opened and viewed with an application on the recipient's computer.

attachment unit interface (AUI) (n.) A 15-pin connector used to couple computers on an Ethernet network.

ATTC See *address track time code.*

Attention Dial Tone (ATDT) (n.) A modem command required to make an initial connection with another modem.

attenuate (v.) To reduce the strength of a signal. In audio applications, attenuators often appear as faders or sliding potentiometers that control the decibel levels of individual channels on mixing boards.

audio (n., adj.) Any item related to sound, as in *audio tape, audio track,* or *audio file.*

audio bridge (n.) An electronic device that controls multiple telephone lines connected for two-way audio and data transmission. This device is commonly used for audioconference applications.

audioconference (n.) A meeting over telephone lines with participants in different geographic locations who speak with one another simultaneously. Full-duplex systems allow users to hear other voices while they speak into their headsets. Half-duplex systems allow either reception or transmission of a signal at any given moment but not synchronous two-way communication.

audio dub (n., v.) Replacing all or part of a

videotape's sound track without affecting pre-recorded images.

Audio Engineering Society/European Broadcast Union (AES/EBU) (n.) Two groups that developed similar digital audio transmission standards, specifying transmission of data in a stream with encoded stereo audio signals, along with optional information. The signals are in the high-frequency range, and 110-ohm balanced cables should be used to connect devices.

audio frequency (AF) (n.) Sounds within the normal range of human hearing, approximately 20 Hz to 20 kHz.

audio frequency shift keying (AFSK) (n.) In telecommunications, a method of modulating a carrier wave with audio frequencies (AFs) to send digital signals.

audiographics (n.) A hardware and software system that permits computer users in different locations to connect over telephone lines and to share data, graphics, and voice signals in real time. With an audiographic connection, users can work on the same application or document simultaneously, see the data on their computer screens, and discuss their progress over a voice channel. In the most basic application, the term refers to any single-frame transmission of graphics with audio signals.

audiographic teleconferencing (n.) A realtime conference over telephone lines, typically ISDN, using both an audio and a data connection. A computer screen may be shared at multiple sites and used as an electronic whiteboard. One powerful feature of this type of teleconferencing is that it allows users to share an application. In this way, users at remote sites can dynamically update a shared document.

Audio Interchange File Format (AIFF) (n.) A sound file format defined by Apple Computer and others that can include both sampled sound and MIDI data. The AIFF-C variation stores the data in compressed form. AIFF files can be imported by most multimedia authoring programs for the Macintosh and by some programs running on IBM-compatible computers. The raw sample data in an AIFF file is identical to that in a .wav file, but it is packaged differently.

audiotex (n.) Interactive voice response (IVR) equipment and services. Audio information services include many 900-number services.

audio track (n.) The section or layer of an audio tape, videotape, or videodisc containing the sound signal that accompanies the video signal. Systems with two separate audio tracks can produce stereo sound or two independent monophonic tracks.

Audio-Video Interleaved (AVI) (n.) A digital video architecture that can be used in Microsoft Windows. Known as *Video for Windows,* it is a common standard for synchronized audio/video delivery on IBM-compatible computers. In this file format, blocks of audio data are woven into a stream of video frames.

AUI See *Adaptable User Interface* or *attachment unit interface.*

AUP See *Acceptable Use Policy.*

author 1. (v.) To create an interactive computer program with the use of an authoring language or system. Developers without formal programming skills can use scripting commands to prepare applications for computer systems or CD-ROMs. Authoring requires a disciplined approach to preparing the elements of a multimedia program with careful planning and design. 2. (n.) A person who participates in the creation of a multimedia program or an interactive CD-ROM.

authoring software (n.) A program that facilitates the development of interactive multimedia. Systems vary widely in their capabilities, and factors such as the platform, audience, and desired results should be taken into consideration when selecting the appropriate tool. It requires less time to develop interactive multimedia with the aid of an authoring system than it does to program it in compiled code. The methods used to develop graphics, text, video, audio, animation, and other media objects generally are not affected by the choice of an authoring system. Software designed for creating and editing specific media types is used to refine objects to be imported into the authoring environment, although an authoring tool may have some rudimentary editing features. Here are descriptions of the primary types of authoring paradigms:

- **flow control with icons** (n.) An approach characterized by rapid prototyping and short development time. A palette of icons presents the tools for interaction, and a flowline connects the icons. Runtime speed may be slower than that of other development tools.

- **frame-based system** (n.) An approach that uses screens, frames, or cards as the workplace and that brings media types onto each frame. This system generally provides a way to control the timing of a presentation and the layering of assets. An icon palette is available, and conceptual links are made between objects that represent media types, such as graphics, audio, and video files. A scripting language is provided to set up interaction. With this type of tool, it is diffi-

cult to see the connections while building a program. Some frame-based systems provide a matrix, or a *score,* that shows the progression of frames on the horizontal axis and the media channels, or *tracks,* on the vertical axis.

- **hierarchical object** (n.) A system that defines relationships with metaphors represented by embedded objects (media types or events) and iconic properties (controls or conditional statements), similar to an object-oriented programming language.

- **hypermedia linking** (n.) A tool that allows conditional relationships to be built between elements and that gives the author a means to direct traffic. Most programs show the relationship between elements but do not offer a visual map of the connections.

- **scripting language** (n.) An approach similar to traditional programming. File names identify multimedia elements, sequencing, and hot spots. An object-oriented version of the scripting language is usually implemented.

The accompanying table lists widely used authoring programs, identifies the publisher, indicates the platforms on which programs may be developed or run, and describes the authoring paradigm and prominent features. Programs that offer a cross-platform player require that the authoring be done in the original environment. After development, the program can be ported to the player platform as a self-contained module.

auto-assembly (n.) In video postproduction, the use of an edit decision list (EDL) as well as a computerized edit controller to automate the process of making a final edited master tape.

autobaud See *automatic baud rate detection.*

autochanger (n.) An optical media system that can store and retrieve data from multiple CDs, similar to a jukebox that plays phonograph records.

Autodesk Animator (n.) Developed by Autodesk, a collection of PC animation tools that create files in the Autodesk proprietary FLC and FLI formats.

autoexec.bat (n.) A batch file, or command set,

Authoring Software

Tool	Platform	Features
Apple Media Tool, Apple Computer	Macintosh, Windows player	Frame-based; powerful and extensible.
Authorware, Macromedia	Macintosh, Windows	Flow control with icons; broad external media support; optimal for CBT and rapid prototyping; ports to Shockwave for the WWW.
CourseBuilder, Discovery Systems Int'l.	Macintosh, Windows player	Flow control with icons; creates interactive courseware without scripting.
cT, Carnegie Mellon University & WorldWired	Macintosh, Windows, Unix	Scripting system with web player; handles video, hot-text, and response tracking.
Digital Chisel, Pierian Spring	Macintosh, Windows	Frame-based; instructional tool ported to Java for the WWW.
Director, Macromedia	Macintosh, Windows	Frame-based with scripting; animation; object-based scripting language; creates Shockwave files for the WWW.
Grasp, Paul Mace Software	DOS	Scripting language.
HyperCard, Apple Computer	Macintosh	Frame-based with scripting; the original card metaphor; HyperTalk language.
HyperWriter, Ntergard	DOS, Windows	Frame-based, document metaphor; CBT uses.
IconAuthor, AimTech	Windows, OS/2, NT, Unix, Macintosh player	Flow control with icons; data-handling features are a plus for CBT tracking; portable to the WWW.
MediaForge, Strata	Windows	Iconic; extensible with Visual Basic adaptation; flexible and powerful.
mTropolis, mFactory	Macintosh, Windows player	Hierarchical object system; visual environment; no longer in production.
Oracle Media Objects, Oracle	Macintosh, Windows	Frame-based with scripting.
Quest, Allen Communications	Windows	Frame-based with scripting; language is ANSI C.
Scala MM100, Scala, Inc.	DOS, Windows	Interface is event list with timing controls.
ScriptX, Kaleida Labs	Macintosh, Windows player	Scripting language; powerful, but out of production.
SuperCard, Allegiant	Macintosh, Windows player	Frame-based with scripting; hypertext; external media handling.
Toolbook, Asymetrix Corporation	Windows	Frame-based with scripting; database linking; MCI compliant; macros perform interactive functions; ports to the WWW, outputs Java; optimized for CBT.

that is automatically executed by a PC running MS-DOS whenever the system is turned on or booted.

autofeed (n., adj.) A mode in which a scanner can operate continuously. A new page is loaded automatically when the previous page has been scanned.

automatic baud rate detection (ABR, autobaud) (n.) Performed by a receiving device, this process determines the code level, speed, and stop bits of incoming data by reading a predetermined initial character. ABR permits a receiving device to accept data flexibly from a variety of transmitting devices operating at different speeds.

Automatic Call Distribution (ACD) (n.) A method of routing and tracking telephone signals.

Automatic Call Distributor (ACD) (n.) Telephone system that handles a high volume of incoming and outgoing calls. This technology is used increasingly by telemarketers. An ACD can answer an incoming call, search a database for handling instructions, and send the call to a recorded message or to the appropriate person. These systems can automatically dial a series of numbers and transfer the call to an operator if a human voice answers the call.

Automatic Dialog Replacement (ADR) (n.) An automated process for substituting a new voice track for the original, often to eliminate unwanted sounds from production audio tracks. ADR systems play short segments of actors' dialog repeatedly in a constant rhythm so that they can hear it through headphones and recreate their original performance, improving synchronization with the picture. This process is also referred to as *looping*.

automatic exposure (AE) (n.) Circuitry in a video recorder or still camera that monitors light levels and adjusts the iris or shutter speed to compensate for changing light conditions.

automatic frequency control (AFC) (n.) The process of locking a receiver to a television station's or FM radio station's frequency.

automatic gain control (AGC) (n.) A limiting circuit used in audio playback systems to prevent damaging high-volume levels. It is also used in consumer-level recording devices to boost the recording level during quiet passages or to reduce the level when loud sounds occur.

automatic number identification (ANI) (n.) Caller ID service provided by local exchange carriers in which the caller's number is sent to the receiving number before the second ring. It is one of several Custom Local Area Signaling Services (CLASS), all of which require Signaling System 7 (SS7) interoffice signaling.

automatic request for retransmission (ARQ) (n.) In data communications, a situation in which the receiver asks the transmitter to resend a frame or a block of information, generally as a result of error correction.

autonomous system (AS) (n.) Collection of routers operating under a single administrative authority using a common Interior Gateway Protocol (IGP) for packet routing.

AutoPlay (n.) A CD-ROM standard developed by Microsoft that allows Windows 95 to detect a disc and load its program automatically.

auto repeat (n.) A feature of many media playback devices, this mode allows program material to be continuously replayed until it is interrupted.

A/UX See *Apple Unix.*

auxiliary data field (n.) A 288-byte field that precedes the data field in a CD-ROM sector. It contains error correction codes in a mode 1 disc, but it may contain data on a mode 2 disc.

avalanche photodiode (APD) (n.) Device that detects light and converts it to electrical signals.

avatar (n.) 1. The name of the superuser account on numerous Unix systems. Some people prefer this name to the conventional name, which is *root*. 2. An object on the screen that graphically represents the user in an interactive multiuser dimension (MUD). The user can move around and control this object.

AVC See *Association of Visual Communicators.*

AVI See *Audio-Video Interleaved.*

AWE See *Advanced WavEffect.*

awk (n.) Developed in 1978, an interpreted language for manipulating text that has been included with many versions of Unix. The name is derived from the initials of its authors, Alfred Aho, Peter Weinberger, and Brian Kernighan. The GNU version is called *gawk.* Perl was inspired in part by awk.

AWT See *Abstract Windowing Toolkit.*

B

backbone (n., adj.) In relation to networks, the primary trunk or high-speed connection within a network that connects shorter, often slower, stub and transit networks. It carries the heaviest traffic and is the top level in a hierarchical network. Stub and transit networks that connect to the same backbone are guaranteed to be interconnected.

backbone site (n.) A major Internet, Usenet, or mail site that processes a great deal of third-party traffic. Important backbone sites since early 1993 include UUNet, the mail machines at the University of California at Berkeley, and the Western Research Laboratories of Digital Equipment Corporation (DEC).

back channel (n.) Return connection in a two-way data circuit, such as a coaxial cable or satellite circuit. This upstream channel usually has lower bandwidth than the forward channel.

backdoor (n.) A breach that designers or maintainers purposely leave in the security of a system. Some operating systems are shipped with privileged accounts, or backdoors, intended for use by field service technicians or the maintenance programmers. Also referred to as a *trapdoor* or *wormhole*.

back end (n.) Software that performs the last stage of a process, executing a task that is transparent to the user. The term refers to network applications that run on a server without making the client aware of their operations.

background (n.) 1. The area of a screen or frame over which images or objects are placed; the most distant element in composite layering. 2. The place where less critical events or operations are conducted during shared processing in a multitasking environment. Print spooling while a document is being edited is an example, as is the ability to receive a facsimile while performing other computing functions.

back light (v.) To illuminate a subject from behind in a video production or camera shoot, creating a sense of depth by separating the foreground from the background. This process can result in silhouetting if done improperly.

backplane (n.) High-speed communications bus to which individual components are connected, such as expansion cards on a PC.

back up (v.) To record an archival copy of data on a storage medium.

backup (n., adj.) The copy of data that is recorded and stored for archival purposes, typically offline.

29

Backus-Naur form (BNF) (n.) High-level syntax that can be used to express context-free grammars formally. This type of notation is rarely documented but is commonly used to specify the syntax of programming languages. The BNF for a city, state, and zip code would appear as follows:

```
<address> ::= <city-name> "," <state-code>
<zip-code> <end-of-line-character>
```

In translation, this would yield the name of a city followed by a comma, a state code, and a zip code followed by an end-of-line (EOL) character.

bad sector (n.) Area on the surface of a disk that is unable to hold data reliably due to damaged formatting or a flaw in the medium itself.

bad track table (n.) Label attached to a hard disk drive case identifying flawed tracks. The low-level formatting program initially used to define tracks and sectors on the disk contains this information.

balanced line (n.) A grounded line with two conductors that carry equal voltages that are opposite in polarity. In a balanced-to-ground line, the impedance-to-ground levels in both conductors are equal in strength. Audio connections made with this type of line are less susceptible to interference and radio frequency (RF) noise.

balun (n.) A transformer situated in a circuit between a balanced load and an unbalanced load. A balanced line has two conductors, with equal currents in opposite directions, whereas an unbalanced line consists of one conductor with a common ground.

band (n.) Frequency range between two defined limits. The audio band of frequencies that can be detected by the human ear lies between approximately 20 Hz and 20 kHz.

bandpass filter (n.) A device that blocks all frequencies that are not in a specified range. It can be used to process audio signals.

bandwidth (n.) 1. The transmission capacity of an electronic medium, such as network wiring, fiber-optic cable, or microwave links. 2. The range of signal frequencies in which a piece of audio or video gear can operate. 3. The difference between high and low limiting frequencies. See the accompanying table for commonly accepted definitions of bandwidths in telecommunications and broadcasting. The public telephone system has a bandwidth of about 3 kHz. See figure and table.

Definitions of Bandwidths in Broadcasting and Telecommunications

Acronym	Definition	Frequency Range
ELF	Extremely Low Frequency	under 300 Hz
ILF	Infra Low Frequency	300 Hz–3 kHz
VLF	Very Low Frequency	3 kHz–30 kHz
LF	Low Frequency	30 kHz–300 kHz
MF	Medium Frequency	300 kHz–3 MHz
HF	High Frequency	3 MHz–30 MHz
VHF	Very High Frequency	30 MHz–300 MHz
UHF	Ultra-High Frequency	300 MHz–3 GHz
SHF	Super High Frequency	3 GHz–30 GHz
EHF	Extremely High Frequency	30 GHz–300 GHz

B

bandwidth between 1K and 5K is shaded

bang path (n.) A specified series of machine names through which a mail message from one user to another will pass. It is possible to identify an explicit Unix-to-Unix CoPy (UUCP) path through which email is to be routed. See also *mail path* or *Unix-to-Unix CoPy*.

banner (n.) 1. Any title page automatically added to a print job by a print spooler. 2. In relation to the Internet, this is a rectangular box that appears on a web page and which is linked to a site. It typically contains a logo and a marketing blurb intended to attract visitors to the site.

bar code (n.) A pattern of parallel lines whose variable thickness and separation encode a message that an optical scanner or wand can read and that a computer can then decode. Many businesses use a bar code as a universal product code (UPC) on retail items, and libraries use it to catalog books. It can be used to control videodisc playback as well. See figure.

barker channel (n.) Cable TV channel dedicated to promoting pay-per-view events, most often by displaying crawling text.

barn doors (n.) A set of folding flaps that cover

bar code

the front of a video light and are adjusted to control dispersion.

barrel distortion (n.) The situation in which the vertical sides of a video display area curve outward. Compare *pincushion distortion*. See figure.

barrel distortion

baseband (n., adj.) A method of transmitting digital information over short distances. The cable's complete bandwidth is used to transmit a single signal. The signals are not modulated, and they are transmitted individually. It is possible to transmit signals simultaneously using time division multiplexing (TDM). This is a less expensive, simpler means of transmitting information than broadband transmission. Compare *broadband*.

base multitimbral specification (n.) A synthesizer subsystem standard that Multimedia Personal Computer (MPC) audio board manufacturers follow in implementing MIDI playback. According to this specification, three pitched tones are available at once to play up to six notes, and two percussive timbres can play two percussive notes.

BASIC See *Beginners' All-Purpose Symbolic Instruction Code.*

Basic Encoding Rules (BER) (n.) Standard method of encoding data units. This method is described in Abstract Syntax Notation One (ASN/1), which refers to the abstract syntax description language used to encode data, not a specific encoding technique.

Basic Input/Output System (BIOS) (n.) A file that contains system control instructions for a microcomputer. Instructions in the ROM of the BIOS help start up a system and define the existing input and output connections.

Basic Rate Interface (BRI) (n.) One of the common interfaces used in an Integrated Services Digital Network (ISDN). It consists of two full-duplex bearer B-channels at 64 kilobits per second (Kbps), along with a data D-channel at 16 Kbps. The B-channels can accommodate videoconferencing, voice, or facsimile data, whereas the D-channel handles private data. The BRI "U" interface uses two wires, whereas the BRI "T" interface uses four wires.

batch file (n.) In MS-DOS, a text-based file with the file name extension .bat that carries out commands when executed. Batch files can be used to avoid retyping commands, to load other programs, or to change a computer's parameters. Batch processing consists of the continuous execution of a series, or batch, of commands.

baud (n.) A communication channel's capacity, as measured in symbols or transitions per second. This measurement is equivalent to bits per second (bps) only for two-level modulation with no framing or stop bits. A symbol is a unique state of the communication channel, distinguishable by the receiver from all other possible states. The term *baud* was originally a unit of telegraph signaling speed, set at one Morse code dot per second. It was proposed at the International Telegraph Conference of 1927 and named after J.M.E. Baudot (1845–1903), the French engineer who constructed the first successful teleprinter. The term *baud* causes much confusion and is usually best avoided. The use of bits per second (bps), bytes per second (Bps), or—more accurately—characters per second (cps) is recommended.

Baudot code (n.) Data transfer code used for teletype (TTY), radio teletype (RTTY), and telecommunications devices for the deaf (TDD). This 5-bit code has undergone numerous revisions.

bay (n.) In the physical frame of a microcomputer case, a space for installing an internal drive or a peripheral.

Bayonet-Neill-Concelman (BNC) (n.) A round connector attached to the end of a co-axial cable and used in video applications. It is pushed onto the receptacle and then locked with clockwise twisting. See figure.

BNC connectors

B

BBS See *bulletin board system.*

BCC See *blind carbon copy* or *block check character.*

BCD notation See *binary-coded decimal notation.*

B-channel (n.) An ISDN user channel that carries digital data at 64 kilobits per second (Kbps). It can carry a mixture of data types, including voice data that is encoded with pulse code modulation (PCM).

Because It's Time Network (BITNET) (n.) Network that was widely used by educational institutions in the 1980s and that had nodes on hundreds of college campuses. It was officially discontinued in 1996.

Beginners' All-Purpose Symbolic Instruction Code (BASIC) (n.) An algebraic computer programming language that was designed by John G. Kemeny and Thomas E. Kurtz at Dartmouth College in 1963. The language employs "if-then" logic statements and other English commands as well as mathematical formulas. BASIC interpreters became standard features in mainframes and minicomputers.

Bellcore (n.) Bell Communications Research; a company owned by the seven Regional Bell Operating Companies (RBOCs) that was formed in 1984 with the divestiture of AT&T. Its mission was to provide centralized research and development services for the RBOCs. It has also coordinated communications for the federal government. Bellcore was purchased in 1996 by Science Applications International Corporation (SAIC).

Bell 43401 (n.) A publication from Bell that defines the requirements for data transmission over DC-continuous, private metallic circuits provided by the telephone company, primarily for limited-distance applications.

Bell Operating Company (BOC) (n.) The name of any of the 22 regulated telephone companies formed by the divestiture of the former AT&T Bell System. They were created in December 1983 by a consent decree between AT&T and the U.S. government. As part of this agreement, they were permitted to carry local (intraLATA) traffic exclusively and forced to hand off long-distance (interLATA) traffic to competitive exchanges (interexchange carriers, or IXCs). The seven Regional Bell Operating Companies (RBOCs) are known as *Baby Bells.* These holding companies are made up of some, but not all, of the 22 BOCs. The RBOCs are Ameritech, Bell Atlantic, BellSouth, NYNEX, Pacific Telesis, SBC Communications, and US West. RBOCs are generally known as *local exchange carriers* (LECs).

Bell standards (n.) A set of standards defined by AT&T for modem communications, numbered as follows:

- Bell 103: Any AT&T 300-bps modem that provides asynchronous transmission with both originate and answer capabilities. Frequency shift keying (FSK) type.

- Bell 113: Any AT&T 300-bps modem that provides asynchronous transmission with either originate or answer capabilities, not both. FSK type.

- Bell 201, 201B, and 201C: Any AT&T 2400-bps modem that provides synchronous transmission. 201B applies to full-duplex public telephone line operation; 201C applies to half-duplex public telephone line operation. Differential phase shift keying (DPSK) type.

- Bell 202: Any AT&T 1800-bps modem that provides asynchronous transmission and uses a four-wire circuit for full-duplex operation. Also describes an AT&T 1200-bps modem that provides asynchronous transmission and that uses a two-wire circuit for half-duplex operation. FSK type.

- Bell 208, 208A, and 208B: Any AT&T 4800-bps modem that provides synchronous transmission. Bell 208A refers to leased-line applications, whereas 208B was designed for public telephone line operation. Phase shift keying (PSK) type.

- Bell 209: Any AT&T 9600-bps modem that provides synchronous transmission and that uses a four-wire leased-line circuit for full-duplex operation. Combined PSK and amplitude shift keying (ASK) type or quadrature amplitude modulation (QAM) type.

- Bell 212 and 212A: Any AT&T 1200-bps modem that provides synchronous transmission and that uses a public telephone line for full-duplex operation. PSK type.

benchmark (n.) A task or series of tasks used to test the capabilities of a processor or system for speed and performance.

bending radius (n.) The least amount of curvature that can be put into a cable under a specified degree of tension. It affects the size of bends in conduits and the size of openings at pull boxes where loops can form. It is a critical aspect of cable deployment, particularly in hybrid fiber networks and fiber-optic cable systems.

BER See *Basic Encoding Rules* or *bit error rate*.

Berkeley Internet Name Domain (BIND) (n.) Domain name system (DNS) developed and distributed by the University of California at Berkeley. It is commonly used by Internet hosts.

Berkeley Software Distribution (BSD) (n.) Implementation of the Unix operating system and utilities developed by the University of California at Berkeley. The version number of the distribution is typically used to identify it; 4.3 BSD is version 4.3 of the Berkeley Unix distribution. It is commonly used on machines that serve as an Internet host.

Bernoulli principle (n.) The airfoil principle named for the Swiss mathematician Daniel Bernoulli (1700–1782). This principle states that pressure in a fluid decreases with the rate of flow. It has been applied to the design of removable media and disk drives.

bespoke (adj.) Describes custom-made computer-based training software or courseware.

best effort (n.) A phrase used to identify low-priority network traffic on the Internet. Real-time communication, such as video and audio streams that require a minimum bandwidth and latency, is given a higher priority. Email can tolerate an arbitrary delay, so it is classified as a best-effort service.

betacam (n.) A professional-quality 0.5-inch video recording and playback format developed by Sony. Betacam is portable and provides video quality comparable to 1-inch videotape. Betacam SP is a higher-quality version that uses true component video signals.

Betamax (n., adj.) A consumer videotape format developed by Sony, sometimes referred to as *Beta*. The format calls for 0.5-inch (12.65 mm) tape in a 6-inch x 3.75-inch

(155 mm x 95 mm) cassette. Although the format offers superior resolution, it was eclipsed in popularity by the VHS system developed by Matsushita and JVC.

beta test (n.) A second and final test for a software product, usually done by actual users in real-world situations with the *beta release*.

bezel (n.) The housing that encases the front of a video monitor. Touch screens usually have a large bezel for their controlling electronics. Pronounced "BEHZ-ul."

Bézier curve (n.) A graphic element defined by a formula consisting of two anchor points and two vector values, as opposed to a bitmap. See also *vector data*. Pronounced "behz-ee-yah." See figure.

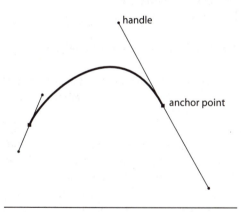

Bézier curve

BGP See *Border Gateway Protocol*.

BGs (n.) Background sounds that are mixed in an audio production. Typically, they are environmental sounds, such as crowds or outdoor noises, edited to fit the length of a scene or spot. Pronounced "BEE-gees."

bid (v.) To vie for connectivity or access among other competing lines that address the same bus.

bidirectional (adj.) 1. Describes the capability to transmit data in two directions, both sending and receiving, but not necessarily the capability to do so simultaneously. 2. Describes a microphone pattern that picks up sounds equally well on the two opposing sides. See *microphone patterns*.

big-endian (adj.) Describes the method of storing and transmitting binary data so that the most significant bit (or byte) is at the head, or beginning of a packet. The term is adapted from the Lilliputians in *Gulliver's Travels* by Jonathan Swift; they debated whether soft-boiled eggs should be opened at the big end or the little end. Compare *little-endian*.

big iron (n.) Fast, powerful computers. The term originally described Cray supercomputers and some IBM mainframes.

bilinear filtering (n.) A means of predicting the most appropriate pixel value in a three-dimensional texture on the screen, based on interpolation from the four adjacent pixels in the texture.

binary code (n.) A code in which each element has one of two possible values, a 1 or a 0, expressed by the presence or absence of a pulse or a high- or low- voltage level in the circuitry.

binary-coded decimal notation (BCD notation) (n.) A binary number system in which each digit in decimal notation is represented by adding four digits in binary notation. Multiple sets of four-digit groupings are used to represent larger decimal numbers. The weighting of binary digits in each column is 8, 4, 2, 1. The number five, 0101, is the result of adding 4 plus 1. Here are more examples:

0 = 0000	9 = 1001		
1 = 0001	10 = 0001	0000	
2 = 0010	11 = 0001	0001	
3 = 0011	23 = 0010	0011	
4 = 0100	48 = 0100	1000	
5 = 0101	76 = 0111	0110	
6 = 0110	99 = 1001	1001	
7 = 0111	213 = 0010	0001	0011
8 = 1000	952 = 1001	0101	0010

binary digit (bit) (n.) A numeral in the base-two binary notation system; a 1 or a 0.

binary file (n.) A file that contains nontextual data, such as an image or an application.

binary notation (n.) The base-two numbering system that uses the digits 1 and 0. This system can be used to represent any type of data. Logic circuits can define these two digits as different states in many ways. Binary notation is not divided into discrete groups of four digits like binary-coded decimal notation. The value of each column increases by a power of two, from right to left (1, 2, 4, 8, 16, 32, 64). Here are examples:

0 = 0000	10 = 1010
1 = 0001	11 = 1011
2 = 0010	12 = 1100
3 = 0011	13 = 1101
4 = 0100	14 = 1110
5 = 0101	16 = 10000
6 = 0110	32 = 100000
7 = 0111	37 = 100101
8 = 1000	64 = 1000000
9 = 1001	74 = 1001010

binary phase shift keying (BPSK) (n.) Digital modulation scheme used for upstream signaling on hybrid fiber-coax (HFC) networks.

binary synchronous communication (BSC; bisync, pronounced "BYE-sink") (n.) An industry-standard IBM communications protocol that is character- or byte-oriented. A defined set of control characters is used to synchronize the transmission of binary-coded data between two stations, both of which must be synchronized prior to data transmission.

binary transfer (n.) A method of transferring information between computers that involves the use of error correction protocol, such as XModem or Systems Network Architecture (SNA). This method is useful if the data is not purely text-based ASCII characters.

binaural audio (n.) Two audio tracks that are recorded with special microphone placement for each track to give the listener a perception of depth, or three-dimensional sound, when the tracks are played back together. This is different from simple stereo audio.

BIND See *Berkeley Internet Name Domain.*

BinHex (n.) Process that converts an eight-bit file into a seven-bit ASCII code with the file name extension .hqx. A file is converted to lines of letters, numbers, and punctuation. BinHex files can be sent through email systems and stored on any type of computer, because they consist exclusively of text and do not require that a system be "eight-bit clean." Converting a file to text makes it larger, so it takes longer to transmit a BinHex type of file.

BIOS See *Basic Input/Output System.*

bipolar transmission (n.) A signaling method used in digital transmission in which a signal carrying a binary value alternates between positive and negative polarities. The signal amplitude can represent a 0 or 1 at either polarity, and the spaces with no value are represented by zero amplitude.

bis (n.) The second version of an original CCITT standard. In common usage, the term appears after the "V.x" designation, as in "V.42bis," which refers to a modem specification. The third version in a succession is referred to as "V.xter," as in "V.27ter."

B-ISDN See *Broadband Integrated Services Digital Network.*

bisync See *binary synchronous communication.*

bit (n.) Binary digit; representing a single unit (either 0 or 1) of data, it is the smallest unit in computer information handling. Computer processing capability is evaluated by the number of bits handled at once. PCs use 8-, 16-, 32-, or 64-bit microprocessors.

bit-block transfer (n.) A technique for moving pixel blocks in memory onto a monitor. More efficient than moving individual bits or bytes, this method is referred to as *blitting.*

bit depth (n.) On computer monitors, each pixel can be represented by a variable number of bits used to describe the pixel's color. Bit depth is the number of bits used in this capacity. A bit depth of two means that only black or white pixels can be shown, a bit depth of four allows the display of 16 colors, a bit depth of eight allows 256 colors, a bit depth of 16 represents 65 536 colors, and 24-bit color yields 16.7 million colors.

bit error rate (BER) (n.) A unit of measurement defining the number of bit writing errors compared with the total number of bits received during a transmission, or the percentage of bits in error found in a given volume or area of storage medium.

bitmap (n.) 1. An image defined by discrete values that are assigned to each pixel. 2. A common PC graphics file format in which the image is stored as a pattern of dots with the file name extension .bmp.

BITNET See *Because It's Time Network.*

bit rate (n.) The speed at which data is moved, expressed in bits per second (bps). If a file size is known and the data transfer rate at which it streams is known, it is possible to determine the duration of time that an audio or video file will play, based on its size. To calculate the duration of playback for an existing MPEG file of known size and bit rate, divide the file size by the data transfer rate. A 5-MB (megabyte) file equals 5000 KB (kilobytes). If the data transfer rate is 150 KBps, the 5000-KB file contains 33 seconds of running video (5000 divided by 150). A bit rate expressed in megabits per second (Mbps) is a factor of 8.192 times the same rate expressed in kilobytes per second (KBps), because a kilobyte is equal to 1024 bits times 8.

bits per inch (bpi) (n.) The number of units of binary data that can be written within the area of a square inch on the surface of a disk or other type of storage medium.

bits per second (bps) (n.) A rate of data transfer, not to be confused with Bps, which refers to bytes per second.

bitstream transmission (n.) The transmission of characters at a fixed rate of speed. No stop and start elements are used, and there are no pauses between bits of data in the stream.

black box (n.) An electronic circuit or assembly that can be isolated from a system in order to perform a special function, such as controlling an external peripheral.

blackburst (n.) Also known as *house sync,* a timing signal or clock reference consisting of a video signal without a picture or any positional information.

blanking interval (n.) 1. In a video display, the short duration at the end of a scan line when the signal is suppressed and when the beam repositions itself. 2. The time it takes a video player to locate the next frame to display. See figure.

blanking interval between scan lines

bleed (n.) The blurring of color borders in a video image or in printed graphics. The result is color that overruns its defined boundary.

blending (n.) The combination of two pixels in the context of a graphic.

blind carbon copy (BCC) (n.) Part of an email header that lists addresses to which a message should be sent but that will not be seen by all recipients. It is defined in RFC 822 and supported by many mail systems.

blinkenlights (n.) Humorous jargon for front-panel lights found on electronic equipment.

block (n.) 1. In a CD-ROM or CD-i, the user data portion of a logical sector. 2. Any group of bits transmitted as a unit or packet. It contains control delimiters at the beginning and end, a header, a data stream, and check characters used for error correction.

block check character (BCC) (n.) A control

character appended to each packet of data that is transmitted in blocks. The BCC allows the receiver to check for errors and request retransmission if necessary.

block diagram (n.) Rough graphical layout of a system's logical structure.

block error correct (v.) To add 276 bytes of error correction code to the end of each block of data while premastering a CD-ROM, allowing errors in the user data block to be corrected.

Blue Book standard (n.) 1. The format used by CDs that are designed for laser disc players. 2. One of the four standard references from Adobe Systems on the page-layout and graphics-control language PostScript. The other guides are known as the Green Book, the Red Book, and the White Book.

blue screen (n.) A solid blue background used when shooting video with special lighting so that the background can be "keyed" out, leaving only the subject, which may be placed over any background of the compositor's choice. This is the technique used by television weather forecasters, who appear with a map juxtaposed behind them.

blue screen of death (n.) Jargon for the condition of a monitor after a Windows NT system suffers an error from which it cannot recover.

BMP (n.) A three-character MS-DOS extension at the end of a file name that identifies the file as containing a bitmapped pattern (for example, filename.bmp).

BNC See *Bayonet-Neill-Concelman.*

BNF See *Backus-Naur form.*

board (n.) Short for printed circuit board; an

internal plug-in unit with printed circuit wiring and components. It can control some essential function of the computer's central processor or provide a special feature, such as telecommunications, audio, or video control and display. Also known as a *card*.

boat anchor (n.) Jargon for obsolete hardware.

BOC See *Bell Operating Company.*

bomb (n., v.) Synonym for crash, referring to the failure of software or the operating system.

bookmark (n.) A pointer or reference to an HTML document. In Netscape Navigator, a user can archive a bookmark. In MS Internet Explorer, a bookmark is stored in the *Favorites* directory.

Boolean algebra (n.) Named for the logician George Boole (1815–1864), this term means two-valued logic in computer science. Boole's work, which inspired the descriptive term in mathematics, concerned the algebra of sets, involving the operations of intersection, union, and complement of sets.

Boolean operator (n.) A qualifying term that refines a definition. Examples include "AND" (items that include both terms that appear in a query), "NOT" (items that contain one term but not another), and "OR" (items that are derived from either class defined). In general, a Boolean operator is a variable that can accept only true or false values.

Boolean search (n.) A type of search for information in which qualifiers such as "AND," "OR," and "NOT" are used.

boot (v.) To start a computer and prepare it to process commands by loading the operating system.

boot record (n.) Under the ISO 9660 standard, the record that identifies the location of a boot file on a CD-ROM. This file contains an operating system that can be loaded.

boot sequence (n.) The sequence in which a microprocessor receives instructions from ROM to check its circuits and then tries to load files from a disk drive. It initially tries the A: (floppy) drive, and if the necessary files are not found, it tries to read from the C: (first hard disk) drive.

boot virus (n.) An MS-DOS virus that infects the boot record program on hard disks and floppy disks or that infects the master boot record on hard disks and that is loaded into memory before MS-DOS. The virus takes control of the computer, infecting any floppy disks subsequently inserted.

Border Gateway Protocol (BGP) (n.) Exterior gateway protocol defined in RFCs 1267 and 1268 by the Internet Engineering Task Force (IETF).

bot (n.) Truncation of *robot;* a term most often found in multiuser dimensions (MUDs) and Internet Relay Chats (IRCs). It refers to a character that is not a person but rather a collection of responses from a computer program.

bounce (v.) 1. To mix two or more audio tracks into one. Also called *ping-ponging.* 2. To return a piece of email because of a delivery error.

bound variable (n.) In programming logic, a quantified variable. It is a formal argument in a function that is replaced by the actual argument when the function is applied.

Bourne shell (n.) The first command line interpreter shell and script language for Unix, written by S. R. Bourne of Bell Laboratories in

1978. The Berkeley C shell is more widely used today.

bpi See *bits per inch.*

bps See *bits per second.*

Bps See *bytes per second.*

BPSK See *binary phase shift keying.*

branch (v.) To leap from one location in a program to another, based on programmed responses to user input.

branching point (n.) A path that a user can choose, given two or more directions or destinations.

branch prediction (n.) A function that a microprocessor with "instruction pre-fetch" performs by guessing whether or not a branch will be taken and by fetching the anticipated code in advance from its location. A branch instruction and the instruction that immediately follows it are stored in the *branch target buffer.* Based on this pattern, the microprocessor predicts which way the instruction will branch the next time it is executed. A pipeline break is avoided when a branching prediction is correct.

break (v.) 1. To stop a program in progress temporarily to debug. The point at which it stops is the *breakpoint.* 2. To send an RS-232 break of two character widths over a serial line.

BRender (n.) A three-dimensional Application Programming Interface (API) provided by Argonaut, a British game developer. Pronounced "BE-render."

BRI See *Basic Rate Interface.*

bridge (n.) A connecting device between two or more subnetworks, or local area networks (LANs), that run similar cabling and protocols. It uses the bottom two layers of the Open Systems Interconnection (OSI) model to create an extended network on which workstations on different subnetworks can share data.

bridge disc (n.) A technique for storing data on a CD-ROM XA disc that allows the data to be played back on several platforms. A Photo-CD is a type of bridge disc that can be played on a CD-i or Photo-CD player, as well as on a multiple-session CD-ROM drive.

bridge/router (n.) A sophisticated networking device that performs the functions of a bridge, a router, or both simultaneously. It can route multiple protocols, such as TCP/IP and XNS, while bridging other traffic.

broadband (adj.) Describes any transmission medium that supports a wide frequency range, including audio and video frequencies. It can be multiplexed to carry several independent channels, each in its own bandwidth. Broadband transmission is often in the range of 1 MHz or more. At the minimum, the term refers to bandwidth greater than that required for voice, which telecommunications standards have set at 4 kHz. ISDN is considered a broadband medium. Cable television employs broadband techniques to send multiple channels over a single cable. Compare *baseband.*

Broadband Integrated Services Digital Network (B-ISDN) (n.) The second generation of the CCITT ISDN standard. The network is designed to transmit realtime multimedia via plain old telephone service (POTS).

broadcast (v.) 1. To transmit television and radio programs through the air. 2. In network applications, to forward a message to numerous destinations.

broadcast quality (n.) Loosely defined, the level of quality at which television stations will transmit, adhering to the NTSC format in the United States. This format calls for 525 lines of video at a rate of 60 fields per second, with the appropriate levels of brightness and color (luma and chroma).

browse (v.) To scan networked information with no particular target in mind.

browser (n.) 1. Software that allows a user to search through information on a server. The term usually refers to a universal client application, such as Netscape Navigator or MS Internet Explorer, that interprets HTML documents. 2. The name Eastman Kodak uses on Photo-CDs for the database program that lets users search for images by keyword or title.

brute force (n.) A way of programming that relies on a computer's processing power instead of elegant technique or useful abstraction.

BSC See *binary synchronous communication.*

BSD See *Berkeley Software Distribution.*

B-spline (n.) A basic spline from which an approximated curve is derived, typically used in the creation of wire-frame models for a dimensional figure. See figure.

bubble memory (n.) A filmlike storage device made of materials that are easily magnetized in just one direction, either upward or downward. When a magnetic field is imposed on the film, the areas in opposite alignment to the field shrink to bubbles. Bubble memory is nonvolatile and requires very low power levels but

torus formed by a bicubic B-spline surface

is not as fast as electrically erasable programmable read-only memory (EEPROM).

buffer (n.) 1. Memory space that temporarily stores a small amount of data to help compensate for differences in the rate at which one device transfers data to another. A buffer can also be used to store small bits of data that are used repeatedly (such as a digitized beep or some other sound). Most CD-ROM drives have buffers. 2. A storage space in which data is held temporarily until it is passed to or from a host computer or peripheral device.

buffer overflow (n.) A condition that occurs when an attempt is made to store more data in a buffer than it can handle. This results from using a buffer too small to hold all the data that must accumulate before a piece of it can be processed. The overflow may be caused by a mismatch in the processing rates of the producing and consuming processes.

bug (n.) An undesirable aspect of a software or hardware system that may cause it to malfunction.

build (n.) An interim version of software in which bugs are resolved and features are refined prior to release.

bulletin board system (BBS) (n.) An accessible

computing system that provides an electronic database. Users can log into the BBS and leave messages for a group, or they can download files. Topic groups are usually established, allowing any user to submit or read a message. A BBS often offers users archives of files, personal email, and other services, depending on the preferences of the system operator, or *sysop*. There are thousands of local bulletin board systems run by hackers from their homes.

bulletproof (adj.) Describes an extremely robust, crash-resistant software development with great powers of recovery. Synonymous with *armor-plated*.

bump (v.) To adjust the timing between audio and video tracks in precise framing units while both are running. Frequently used to fine-tune lip sync and to position sound effects.

bump map (n.) A texture map that can be applied to the surface of a three-dimensional image to simulate natural surfaces, patterns, or imperfections.

bundled title (n.) A CD-ROM that is packaged with hardware components, peripherals, or entire systems and that is not priced separately from the other items.

burn-in (n.) An initial period of operation in which a manufacturer or reseller screens equipment and circuits for problems and establishes that components are stable.

burst (n.) In color television reception, a signal that provides a reference for the 3.58-MHz oscillator. The signal is sent during the vertical blanking interval (VBI).

burst EDO DRAM (n.) Burst Extended Data Out Dynamic Random Access Memory; a type of EDO DRAM in which read or write cycles are batched in bursts of four. Burst EDO bus speeds range from 40 MHz to 66 MHz, much faster than the 33 MHz that is available with the use of fast page-mode RAM or EDO DRAM.

burst error (n.) An error that contains a group of consecutive bits, often because of scratches on the surface of a CD-ROM.

bus (n.) 1. The connection or path between the CPU and the input/output (I/O) devices or the connection between two processors. Types of buses that have traditionally been used in IBM-compatibles include ISA, VESA, and PCI. The NuBus system was used on older Macintosh computers. In 1995, Apple Computer replaced the NuBus with the 64-bit PCI bus in selected Power Macintosh models. 2. A signal- or power-transmitting conduit that allows two or more lines to be connected and their signals to be mixed.

bus architecture (n.) A set of connections between functional units in a computer. Buses exist within the central processing unit (CPU), connecting it to external memory and peripheral devices. The width of the bus determines the size in bits of the largest data unit it can carry. The bus width and the number of data units transmitted per second determine a computer's performance. Most microprocessors have 32-bit buses both internally and externally. The internal bus in most microcomputers is wider than the external bus.

bus master (n.) In a microcomputer, this device drives both the address bus and bus control signals at some point in time. In a simple architecture, only the central processing unit (CPU) can be the bus master, so all communications between input/output (I/O) devices (slaves) must involve the CPU. Advanced architectures allow other capable devices or processors to control the bus. Direct memory access (DMA) is a basic form of bus mastering, in which the CPU sets up the I/O device to read from contiguous blocks of memory and to signal the CPU when it has done so. Full bus mastering indicates that an I/O device is capable of performing complex sequences without CPU intervention.

button (n.) A graphic component of an interface that represents some embedded function. When clicked, a button can branch the user to another location in the program.

buyout music (n.) Audio tracks sold with a license that allows the purchaser to duplicate and use them in productions without paying royalties.

by hand (adv.) Describes a way of performing a repetitive or tedious operation that could be done automatically by a computer but that a programmer performs step by step. For example, HTML can either be created by an editing program or coded by hand.

bypass mode (n.) An operating mode on ring networks, such as Fiber Distributed Data Interface (FDDI), and on token ring networks. In this mode, an interface is removed, or bypassed, from the ring.

byte (n.) A measurable number of consecutive bits that are usually treated as a unit. Bytes of eight bits usually represent either one character or two digits. A computer's storage capacity or memory is figured in kilobytes (KB). One KB equals 1024 bits, or 2 to the 10th power.

byte aligned (adj.) Describes information in memory that is located an exact multiple of eight bits from the starting point.

bytecode (n.) A portable file format into which Java programs are compiled. The bytecode is distributed to a computer that interprets it into native processor instructions on the fly as the Java program is executed.

bytecode compiler (n.) A translator that outputs a Java program in bytecode intended for interpretation by a bytecode interpreter. The same bytecode can be executed on any processor on which the bytecode interpreter runs, which is an advantage over outputting machine code for each particular processor on which the code will run. The Java engine compiles bytecode for the Java Virtual Machine (JVM).

bytes per second (Bps) (n.) A rate of data transfer, not to be confused with bps, which refers to bits per second.

B

C

C (n.) Programming language created by Dennis Ritchie at AT&T Bell Labs in 1972. It was intended for systems programming on the PDP-11 computer and was used to reimplement Unix. C is a terse, low-level, permissive language. It is the dominant language in systems and microcomputer applications programming because it is transportable and easily adapted to new environments. The original C has been standardized and modified to become ANSI C.

cable 1. (n.) Any kind of wire or cord used to transmit signals or connect equipment. Cables can contain single or multiple wires and are shielded to reduce interference. Most cables allocate at least one wire as a ground. Coaxial cable is used for video applications. 2. (adj.) Describes local television service delivered over cable rather than broadcast through the air.

cable loss (n.) Attenuation of a signal's strength as it travels through a cable. Higher frequencies suffer from greater loss than lower frequencies in coaxial cables.

cable modem (n.) A device that enables a user to connect a computer to the coaxial cable provided by a cable television (CATV) network. A special type of modem must be installed at the cable provider's site, or headend, which turns the cable system into a local area network (LAN) that can serve digital programming as well as access to digital services, such as a web server. Cable modems are capable of multimegabit data transfer and do not require connection and disconnection to the network for each session, since they are always online. The service is asymmetric, with a downstream rate of transfer to the user that is faster than the upstream rate. A different modulation scheme is used for traffic in each direction. Available bandwidth from the cable provider is shared by all users on a circuit, and data throughput is reduced as the number of users increases.

A group of cable television providers has formed a working group, Data Over Cable Service Interface Specifications (DOCSIS), to formalize standards in this emerging technology.

One type of cable modem uses Intel's "Intercast" technology. In this model, a receiving unit mounted on a circuit board in a PC can access digital services inserted into a television signal's vertical blanking interval (VBI). Each interval can carry about as much data as a 9600-baud modem carries. Transmission from the cable provider is one-way and is not interactive unless a modem on a telephone line is connected simultaneously.

cable tap (n.) In an Ethernet network, a device that connects a transceiver to the main cable.

cable television (CATV) (n.) Local television

service delivered over cable rather than broadcast through the airwaves. It was called *Community Antenna Television* before the installation of cable.

cache (n.) A portion of processor memory that holds recently accessed data, designed to speed up subsequent access to the same data. When data is read from or written to main memory, a copy is saved in the cache, along with its address in main memory. The cache monitors the address of subsequent reads to determine whether the data requested is already in the cache. If it is, the situation is referred to as a *cache hit,* and the instruction to read the data from main memory is aborted. If a *cache miss* occurs, the data is fetched from main memory and saved in the cache. Typically, a cache is constructed with faster memory chips than those in the main memory, so a cache hit returns data much more quickly than normal memory access does. When a processor writes to main memory, the data is first written to the cache on the assumption that it will be read again soon. In a *write-through cache,* data is written to main memory at the same time as it is cached. In a *write-back cache,* data is written to main memory only when it is forced out of the cache.

cache line (n.) The smallest unit of memory than can be transferred between main memory and a cache. A whole line is read and cached at once from main memory, rather than just a single word or byte. This takes advantage of page-mode Dynamic RAM (DRAM), permitting faster access to consecutive locations.

caching (n.) The use of memory or disk storage to speed data processing. Frequently used data is temporarily stored where it can be quickly accessed later.

CAD/CAM See *computer-aided design/computer-aided manufacturing.*

caddy (n.) The case or cartridge that protects CD-ROMs while they are inserted in the drive. Late model drives are typically caddiless, so the CD rests in an open tray.

CAI See *computer-aided instruction.*

CAL See *computer-aided learning.*

call (n., v.) In computer programming, to invoke a procedure or subroutine and to transfer control to it. Ordinarily, control is returned to the program at the instruction immediately after the point from which the call was made.

callback modem (n.) A modem that returns a call and opens a connection if the security code input during a dialup session is authorized for access. A callback modem is often used to verify a caller's identity before granting access to secure information.

CAM See *computer-aided manufacturing.*

camcorder (n.) Contraction of *camera* and *recorder;* portable videotaping gear. The usual formats are VHS and 8 mm, along with their higher-resolution versions, S-VHS and Hi-8. VHS-Compact (VHS-C) is a smaller version of VHS.

cameo lighting (n.) Illumination of foreground subjects with a directional light on a stark black background.

CAP See *competitive access provider.*

capacitance (n.) 1. The degree to which a substance or device conducts or passes electricity. 2. The ability to store an electric charge, measured in farads.

capacitor (n.) One of the components in a circuit that stores voltage, acting like a holding tank. The charge is released when it is triggered.

capacity (n.) In telecommunications, the quantity of traffic a facility can carry. The measurement depends on the type of facility. Data lines are measured in bits per second (bps). Switch capacity is measured by the maximum number of calls a facility can switch in an hour or the number it can maintain simultaneously. Coaxial cable and wireless communications systems are measured in bandwidth.

capstan (n.) A roller or spindle that controls the speed and movement of magnetic tape through a recorder or player. See figure.

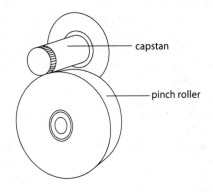

capstan

carbon-based life form (n.) Jargon for human being. Compare *silicon-based life form*.

card (n.) Short for printed circuit board; an internal plug-in unit with connections between components traced on the surface of the board. A card can control some essential function of the computer's central processor or provide a special feature, such as telecommunications, audio, or video control and display. Also known as a *board*.

cardinality (n.) According to set theory, the number of elements in a set. Two sets with the same number of elements have the same cardinality, which is known as *bijection*.

carpal tunnel syndrome (n.) The swelling of tendons in the wrist, compressing the median nerve and causing pain and numbness in the hand. Poor posture at a computer terminal may result in strain and could contribute to this ailment.

carriage return (CR) (n.) A control character in EBCDIC or ASCII code that positions the cursor at the left margin.

carrier band (n.) Frequency range that can be modulated to carry information on a given transmission system.

carrier detect signal (n.) Signal that tells attached data terminal equipment (DTE) that a modem is receiving a signal from another modem. Also called a *received line-signal*.

carrier sense multiple access with collision detection (CSMA/CD) (n.) A network protocol.

carrier signal (n.) A constant sine wave that can be modulated with a second signal that contains data. The high-pitched tone that a modem emits is an audible carrier signal. Changes, or modulation, in the carrier's amplitude, frequency, or phase can convey information.

carrier wave (n.) Generated at a transmitting station, a radio frequency wave on which signal information is modulated.

cascade (v.) With reference to hardware, to connect numerous multiple-port devices in order to expand the number of ports or available input/output (I/O) lines.

Cascading Style Sheets (n.) A World Wide Web Consortium (W3C) recommendation that provides a method of defining the layout and presentation features of a Hypertext Markup Language (HTML) document. Specifications about how a page should look in terms of headings, indents, margins, fonts, and all matters related to appearance may be placed in a single location and are referenced by the page. Alternatively, a style feature, such as colored text, may be designated before each tag it affects in an *inline style sheet*. In the example below, the heading "Welcome to our site" would appear in blue letters:

```
<H1 style="color:blue">Welcome to our site</H1>
```

It is more efficient to embed all style definitions at the head of a document, defining what color each level of headings should be. This is called an *embedded style sheet*. A style class can be invented and applied to any tag. Class names begin with a period, and their function is enclosed in braces. Here is a simple example of an embedded style sheet:

```
<STYLE type="text/css"> H1 { color: blue }
H1.yellow { color: yellow } </STYLE>
```

In this example, first-level headings (H1) appear in blue letters, and headings of the new class called H1.yellow appear in yellow letters.

A style sheet can be linked to a page yet stored in a file by itself. When a text file contains all the information that would be included in an embedded style sheet and when the <LINK> tag is used, the file (named style.css, for example) will behave as though it were embedded. The page can reference this style sheet if the following line is placed at the head of the document:

```
<LINK rel="stylesheet" href="style.css"
type="text/css">
```

The cascading function arises from a hierarchy in which the browser follows directions. Browser defaults are the most general style rules, which are overruled by definitions in a style sheet. Inline rules stated at the tag level take precedence, followed by an embedded style sheet, followed by a linked style sheet. A class definition overrules the default presentation for a tag, and inline style definitions overrule everything else. The level of control is really what cascades.

case (n.) The distinction between capital (uppercase) or small (lowercase) letters or characters.

case-sensitive (adj.) Describes a text-matching operation that distinguishes capital letters from lowercase ones. Neither MS-DOS file names nor Internet domain names are case sensitive. Unix file names are case sensitive, as are RFC 822 local mailbox names.

cast (n.) 1. The actors who appear in a production. 2. The overemphasis of one hue or tint in an image.

Category 4 (n.) A standard for wiring that must be met when connecting a network with a bandwidth of 20 megabits per second (Mbps) and a 16-Mbps token ring network.

Category 3 (n.) A standard for wiring that must be met when connecting 10-megabit-per-second (Mbps) 10BASE-T Ethernet and a 4-Mbps token ring network.

cathode-ray tube (CRT) (n.) A graphic display that produces an image by directing a beam of electrons to activate a phosphor-coated surface in a vacuum tube. The technology is used in both television and computer video monitors.

CATNIP See *Common Architecture for Next Generation Internet Protocol.*

CATV See *cable television.*

CAV See *constant angular velocity.*

CB See *Citizens Band.*

C-band (n.) A high-frequency spectrum between 4 GHz and 8 GHz used for Fixed Satellite Service (FSS). Uplink occurs at approximately 6 GHz; downlink occurs at a rate of 3.7 GHz to 4.2 GHz.

CBEMA See *Computer and Business Equipment Manufacturers Association.*

CBI See *computer-based instruction.*

CBL See *computer-based learning.*

CBT See *computer-based training.*

CCD See *charge-coupled device.*

CCIR See *Consultative Committee for International Radio.*

CCIRN See *Coordinating Committee for Intercontinental Research Networks.*

CCIR-656 See *Consultative Committee for International Radio.*

CCIR-601 See *Consultative Committee for International Radio.*

CCITT See *Comité Consultatif International de Télégraphique et Téléphonique.*

CCITT Group IV See *Comité Consultatif International de Télégraphique et Téléphonique.*

CCITT Group III See *Comité Consultatif International de Télégraphique et Téléphonique.*

CCL See *Connection Control Language.*

CCS See *Common Command Set.*

CD See *compact disc.*

CDA See *Communications Decency Act.*

CD-DA See *compact disc.*

CDDI See *Copper Distributed Data Interface.*

CDEV See *control panel device.*

CD+G See *compact disc.*

CD-i See *compact disc.*

CD-i audio levels See *compact disc.*

CDMA See *Code Division Multiple Access.*

CD+MIDI See *compact disc.*

CDPD See *Cellular Digital Packet Data.*

CD-plus See *compact disc.*

CD-R See *compact disc.*

CD-ROM See *compact disc.*

CD-ROM drive (n.) Compact disc–read-only memory drive; any reader or playback device for data encoded on a CD-ROM. A CD-ROM drive performs more error correction than an audio CD player. Usually controlled by a computer to read text, graphic, video, and audio files, it also reads the Red Book audio format.

See figure.

CD-ROM extended architecture (CD-ROM XA) (n.) Compact disc–read-only memory extended architecture; an extension of the Yellow Book standard, generally consistent with the ISO 9660 format. It is designed to add better audio compression and to stream interleaved video with audio for multimedia applications. CD-ROM XA provides compatibility with ADPCM audio, multisession discs, Photo-CD, and CD-i. CD-ROM XA relies solely on Cross-Interleaved Reed-Solomon Code (CIRC) for error correction.

CD-ROM extensions (n.) Compact disc–read-only memory extensions; software routines that connect MS-DOS with specific CD-ROM drivers and compatible computers to read discs in the ISO 9660 and High Sierra formats.

CD-ROM upgrade kit (n.) Compact disc–read-only memory upgrade kit; a package with software, an interface card, cables, and the drive for installing a CD-ROM drive in a computer.

CD-ROM XA See *CD-ROM extended architecture.*

CD-RW See *compact disc.*

CDTV See *Commodore Dynamic Total Vision.*

CD-WO See *compact disc.*

laser beam path on a CD-ROM player

cel (n.) In animation, a transparent piece of film onto which images are drawn.

cell (n.) 1. In a spreadsheet, the point at which a row and a column intersect. 2. In data transmission, a packet of information containing some bytes of address information combined with data. 3. In telecommunications, the basic geographic unit of a wireless telephone system.

Cello (n.) The trademark name of a freeware Internet browser. Cello allows access to the World Wide Web, gopher, and file transfer protocol (FTP). It does not, however, accommodate email messages to newsgroups.

cellular (adj.) Describes a means of dividing an area into regions, or cells, so that each region becomes a network in which every point is located within the range of a central transmission facility.

Cellular Digital Packet Data (CDPD) (n.) Open standard that allows cellular transmission of wireless data. CDPD divides data files into packets and transmits them on idle channels of existing cellular voice networks. It specifies 19 200 bps data communications over unused analog cellular voice channels.

central office (n.) The physical site at which a telephone company terminates customer lines and locates switching equipment that can connect those lines with other networks.

Central Office Classes (n.) The classes of telephone company central offices, which are as follows:

Class 1 = regional switching center
Class 2 = sectional switching center
Class 3 = primary switching center
Class 4 = toll center
Class 5 = end office or local exchange

central processing unit (CPU) (n.) The primary computing device, or the brain, of a computer system in which data is manipulated and in which calculations take place. It consists of a single microprocessor chip.

centrex (n.) Contraction of *central exchange;* business telephone service provided by a local exchange carrier (LEC) from its central office. Services include call forwarding, call transferring, call restricting, least-cost routing, intercom, and call holding. Centrex is an alternative to a private branch exchange (PBX).

Centronics parallel (n.) A standard 36-pin parallel interface that permits printers and other peripherals to be connected to a computer.

ceramic substrate (n.) Flat slice of ceramic, typically beryllium oxide or aluminum oxide, that holds an integrated circuit (IC).

CERN See *Conseil Européen pour la Recherche Nucléaire.*

CGA See *Color Graphics Adapter.*

CGI See *Common Gateway Interface.*

CGM See *Computer Graphics Metafile.*

channel (n.) 1. Either of two independent signals in a stereo audio system, designated right and left. Most audio, video, and computer playback devices provide two channels for stereo sound. 2. In an Internet Relay Chat (IRC) network, a unit of connected users. Every word each person types is read by others on the same channel. 3. A communications pathway between a host server and a client through which information (data requested by the user) is multicast.

channel service unit (CSU) (n.) An interface used to connect a computer to a digital medium in the same way that a modem is used to connect to an analog medium. A communications carrier provides a CSU to customers, who may use their own equipment to retime and regenerate the incoming signals. A digital service unit (DSU) supplies all of the transmit logic, receive logic, and timing recovery, whereas a customer must provide this information to the carrier in order to use a CSU.

channel service unit/data service unit (CSU/DSU) (n.) Hardware that performs the functions of both a channel service unit (CSU) and a data service unit (DSU). The CSU is used to terminate a telecommunications line for data transmission. It performs line conditioning, protection, loopback, and timing functions. The DSU terminates the data circuit to the data terminal equipment (DTE) and converts the customer's data stream into a suitable transmission format.

chapter (n.) Each independent segment on a videodisc.

chapter cue (n.) A signal in the vertical blanking interval (VBI) of a master tape identifying the first frame of a new chapter. On a videodisc pressed from this master tape, a chapter stop is encoded on the corresponding disc frame.

chapter number (n.) A number displayed on a screen to identify videodisc chapters.

chapter stop (n.) A code embedded in a videodisc to signal the break between two separate chapters, allowing access to a specific chapter.

character (n.) A data component that represents a single letter or symbol of input/output (I/O). Letters are normally represented by the ASCII character set, using the least significant seven bits of a byte or word.

character set (n.) A standard collection of characters, such as ASCII or Unicode. It may include letters, digits, punctuation marks, mathematical symbols, control codes, or other symbols. Every character in a set is represented by its own character code, a binary number used for storage and transmission. In the ASCII set, the letter *A* is represented by code 65.

characters per second (cps) (n.) Data transfer rate estimated by dividing the bit rate by the total character length. At 2400 bits per second (bps), eight-bit characters with start and stop bits (making 10-bit characters) are transmitted at approximately 240 cps. Advanced protocols, such as V.42bis, use longer transmission frames and data compression to increase cps.

character user interface (CUI) (n.) An interface in which only characters are displayed on the screen, as opposed to graphics in a graphical user interface (GUI). MS-DOS is an example.

charge-coupled device (CCD) (n.) A light-detecting component used by digital cameras.

chat (n., adj.) An online forum for realtime, text-based discussion by participants who are logged on simultaneously. The virtual space in which such a discussion takes place is a *chat room*.

check disc (n.) A prototype videodisc or compact disc (CD) produced prior to mass replication to confirm the data's accuracy and integrity.

checksum (n.) A number representing the sum of a set of data bytes. The number is sent with the data set, and error correction schemes use it to determine whether the data has been accurately received.

chew (n.) Jargon for network lag. The percentage of lost packets compared with the total number sent over a network.

child directory (n.) In MS-DOS, the directory that resides within a parent directory in the logical format or hierarchy.

child record (n.) A record that is logically located lower in the hierarchical tree than a parent record and that is directly linked to the parent.

Chimera (n.) A modular, X Window System–based web browser for Unix. It runs on SunOS 4.1.x and Linux 1.1.x. Chimera supports forms, inline images, FTP, HTTP, local file access, proxy servers, and gopher.

chip (n.) A silicon wafer onto which circuit paths are etched or printed photographically in layers, connecting active and passive devices within the solid structure. See figure.

chip set (n.) A combination of integrated circuits (ICs) designed for a particular purpose.

chorus (n.) An audio effect created by the simultaneous production of tones at slightly different frequencies, resulting in a shimmering sound in the upper overtones. A violin section playing in unison creates a characteristic natural chorus effect.

chroma See *chrominance*.

chroma key (n.) A video effect created by shooting objects against a monochrome background, the color of which is "keyed" out so it can be replaced with images from another source. Foreground objects appear to be juxtaposed over the new background in the composition. This color-based video matting (overlay) technique drops all areas of a selected color (usually blue) from the foreground im-

chip formats

age and substitutes corresponding areas of the new background.

Chrome (n.) Multimedia technology developed by Microsoft that acts as an interface to DirectX, using a set of Extensible Markup Language (XML) tags. It can script animations through the DirectX hardware interface so that the host does more work than the server. It requires a 350-MHz Pentium II, 64 megabytes (MB) of RAM, and Accelerated Graphics Port (AGP) graphics with at least 4 MB of video memory.

chrominance (chroma) (n.) The color and saturation information in a video signal. Luminance must be present to make it visible. Low chroma levels appear to be washed out, whereas high levels are too vivid, causing bleeding between different colors. See also *luminance.*

chunk (n.) A block of a type of data used in Tagged Image File Format (TIFF) and Resource Interchange File Format (RIFF) standards.

Chyron (n.) 1. A manufacturer of video character generators. 2. In the computer industry, a word applied to any character generator or to lettering on the screen. Pronounced "KIE-ron."

CIDR See *Classless Inter-Domain Routing.*

CIF See *Common Image Format* or *Common Intermediate Format.*

CinePak (n.) A video compression algorithm that was developed by SuperMac and that was previously called *Compact Video.* Updated in 1998, CinePak is one of the most popular CODECs for QuickTime video.

CIRC See *Cross-Interleaved Reed-Solomon Code.*

circuit switching (n.) A network configuration in which a continuous connection is established between two devices, providing an uninterrupted flow of information. A telephone call is an example of circuit switching. Compare *packet switching.*

CISC See *complex instruction set computing.*

Citizens Band (CB) (n.) One of two bands used for low-power radio transmission in the United States (26.965–27.225 MHz and 462.55–469.95 MHz). CB radios are limited by the Federal Communications Commission (FCC) to 4 watts of power, limiting their range to only a few miles. CB radios became popular among truck drivers in the United States in the late 1970s.

CIX See *Commercial Internet Exchange.*

cladding (n.) A material that surrounds the core of a fiber-optic cable, providing insulation and protection.

clapboard (n.) A hinged slate with diagonal stripes for identification of a scene or shot. It is slapped together to cue the beginning of on-camera action. Clapboards were originally used to synchronize pictures with sound.

class (n.) 1. A set of objects that share a common structure and behavior. The structure is determined by the variables that represent the state of an object in the class, whereas the behavior is established by a set of methods associated with the class. Classes are related in a class hierarchy. One class could be a subclass of a superclass, or it could be composed of other classes. It may be abstract or concrete. 2. One of three types of Internet addresses, distinguished by their most significant bits.

CLASS See *Custom Local Area Signaling Services.*

class hierarchy (n.) A set of classes and their interrelationships.

Classless Inter-Domain Routing (CIDR) (n.) Technique supported by the Border Gateway Protocol 4 (BGP-4) that facilitates routing between multiple independent networks.

class library (n.) A collection of reusable classes for use with an object-oriented programming language such as Java.

clean boot (n., v.) Bypassing the config.sys and autoexec.bat files on startup.

cleanroom (n.) A room in which semiconductors are manufactured and CDs are pressed. It is kept virtually dust-free to reduce particle contamination. A "class 100" room has fewer than 100 particles larger than 0.5 microns in diameter per cubic foot.

clear channel (n.) A transmission path in which the full bandwidth is available to the user because it is not shared.

clear to send (CTS) (n.) A control signal used in a switched half-duplex circuit in an RS-232 modem interface to notify the computer that it has line control. In a full-duplex circuit, this is a constant signal.

CLF See *common log file.*

CLI See *Command Line Interface.*

click (v.) To press and release a mouse button rapidly, usually over a hot spot or icon in a graphical user interface (GUI).

client (n.) In the client/server model, the system that initiates requests to the server, database, or processing engine. The client uses its own intelligence as it further processes the results for display. An example of a client application is a web browser, referred to as a *universal client.*

client error (n.) In relation to the Internet, a problem that occurs due to an invalid request by the client's browser. Possible errors include the following:

- 400 = Failed: Bad Request. The server could not understand the request because of incorrect syntax.

- 401 = Failed: Unauthorized. Either the request required user authorization or the authorization was refused.

- 402 = Failed: Payment Required. A successful transaction must take place before the request is fulfilled.

- 403 = Failed: Forbidden. The server understood the request but refused to fulfill it.

- 404 = Failed: Not Found. The server did not find anything matching the client's request. The URL requested may not exist.

client/server (adj.) A type of network architecture that distributes computing responsibility between a front-end and a back-end program. Prior to implementation of the client/server model, the burden of data processing fell on either the client (early PC environments) or the server (a typical mainframe). In the client/server model, clients share data and processing functions with the server.

Client To Client Protocol (CTCP) (n.) A protocol that permits structured data, such as font information, to be exchanged between Internet Relay Chat (IRC) users. A query may also be sent from one user to another using this protocol. Commands include FINGER, PING, ECHO, VERSION, DCC CHAT, DCC SEND, TIME, and CLIENTINFO.

clip art (n.) Illustrations or artwork files that are made available for use in productions and projects. Catalogs of clip art categorized by subject are widely distributed, and those who purchase them are typically granted permission to use the images without concern about copyright infringement.

Clipboard (n.) A memory location in which data copied or cut from a document resides until it is pasted or cleared. This form of memory buffer is available in most graphical user interface (GUI) systems.

clipping (n.) Operating an audio device, such as an amplifier, in an amplitude region in which signals cannot be processed linearly. Peaks of waveforms are cut off and distortion is produced. Clipped waveforms consist mostly of odd harmonics.

clock rate (n.) The number of cycles per second (cps) at which a computer performs its most basic operations, such as transferring a value from one register to another, as determined by the frequency of an internal crystal-based oscillator. Common clock rates, or processor speeds, for Intel Pentium-based chips are 133, 166, 200, 233, 266, 300, 350, 400, and 450 MHz.

clock reference (n.) A timing signal with which audio and video devices can synchronize during recording and playback.

clock speed (n.) The shortest amount of time required for a central processing unit (CPU) to perform a single instruction. A computer clock generates regular timing pulses in a range from 25 to 400 MHz.

clone (n.) A computing system based on the IBM design that runs software such as Microsoft DOS and Windows.

closed architecture (n.) A system whose software and hardware are compatible with only one manufacturer or developer, possibly preventing the system from being freely extensible. By contrast, *open architecture* uses widely adopted standards, ensuring compatibility.

close-up (n.) Tightly framed video or still shot in which the subject is viewed at close range and dominates the screen. The terms *medium close-up* and *extreme close-up* define how closely the subject is framed.

Clover key (n.) The Macintosh Command key, also known as the *Feature key*.

cluster (n.) On a disk, an allocation unit consisting of at least one physical block. A file is composed of several clusters, or logical units, which may not be contiguous.

CLUT See *color look-up table*.

CLV See *constant linear velocity*.

CMOS See *complementary metal-oxide semiconductor*.

CMRS See *Commercial Mobile Radio Service*.

CMYK (adj.) Describes a type of color representation based on the cyan (C), magenta (M), yellow (Y), and black (K) inks used in color printing. With subtractive color mixing, one can produce all available colors from the first three inks. Black is used to add tonal range and to define edges. Cyan is a blue, and magenta is a red.

CNAME (n.) A query that asks a domain name system (DNS) server on the Internet for a host's official hostname.

coaxial cable (coax, pronounced "KOH-acks") (n.) A standard video cable with a single center conductor surrounded by insulation and with an outer conductor made of woven metal. If the cable is run underground or exposed to water, it is enclosed by another layer of insulation. See figure.

coaxial cable construction

Cobol See *Common Business-Oriented Language*.

code (n.) Any representation of information using numbers, letters, or symbols.

CODEC See *compression-decompression*.

Code Division Multiple Access (CDMA) (n.) A method of concurrent transmission in which a packet of data is coded to differentiate it from other packets. This is comparable to Time Division Multiple Access (TDMA), a popular but slower transmission technique.

coded order (n.) In video compression, the order in which frames are stored and decoded. This order is not necessarily the same as the order in which they are displayed.

COFF See *Common Object File Format*.

coherent light (n.) A light beam made up of a single frequency in which the light waves are in phase with one another. It is the type of light emitted from a laser.

colocation (n.) 1. Placement of one telephone operator's equipment on premises owned by another to facilitate a direct connection between networks. 2. The placement of a web server at the facility of an Internet Service Provider (ISP).

color balance (n.) The process of matching the strength of red, green, and blue signals in an additive color system to make an accurate shade of white and color tones from the mixture.

color bars (n.) A video test signal consisting of solid blocks of the three primary colors (red, green, and blue) and their combinations. The blocks are referred to as *bars*. Most frequently, the Society of Motion Picture and Television Engineers (SMPTE) version is used.

color cycling (n.) An animation technique in which a special effect is created by swapping colors in and out of a color look-up table (CLUT).

Color Graphics Adapter (CGA) (n.) One of the early IBM PC graphics standards.

color look-up table (CLUT) (n.) A selection of colors assigned a digital value and held in a table. A program decodes a color picture for display by matching the code stored for each pixel with the associated color value in the look-up table. This process is also called *indexed color*, and the table is referred to as a *color map*. See figure.

color look-up table components

color model (n.) A means of defining the color of an image with components in three or four dimensions. The most frequently used systems include RGB (red, green, and blue light), HLS (hue, luminance, and saturation), HSV (hue, saturation, and value) and CMYK (cyan, magenta, yellow, and black).

color perception (n.) The sensation of hues created by the human eye as it discerns the frequencies of electromagnetic waves. The accompanying graph illustrates the color perceived by waves in each frequency band of the spectrum, measured in nanometers. See figure.

color spectrum nanometers

color temperature (n.) The relative amount of red and blue in a "white" light, measured in degrees of kelvin (K). Typical readings for video production are 5600 K outdoors and 3400 K indoors.

colorYCC (n.) Developed by Eastman Kodak for Photo-CD, a device-independent color-encoding process. Each color pixel is separated into two 8-bit chroma components (C) and one 8-bit luma component (Y), for a total of 24 bits. The process can also convert RGB color to YCC and vice versa. It provides image compression and high resolution for video or print graphics.

COM See *Component Object Model*.

Comité Consultatif International de Télégraphique et Téléphonique (CCITT, International Telephone and Telegraph Consultative Committee) (n.) A worldwide standards organization that defines communications protocols. The recommendations enable global compatibility for voice, data, and video transmission over telecommunications devices. The CCITT has been replaced by the International Telecommunications Union (ITU). The following recommendations are among those made by the CCITT:

* **CCITT Group III** (n.) A compression standard used for facsimile transmission.

* **CCITT Group IV** (n.) A compression standard widely used for storing images on optical discs. It is based on a two-dimensional compression scheme in which every scan line is the reference line for the next scan line, and only the changes, or deltas, are stored.

command interpreter (n.) A resident program that reads and executes textual commands. When BIOS loads on a PC, it immediately runs the MS-DOS command interpreter command .com. The commands that it recognizes are internal, such as DIR, COPY, and PRN, unlike executables, which are external commands. Some commands may be executed within the interpreter itself, such as control constructs.

Command interpreters in Unix are referred to as *shells*.

Command key (n.) On a Macintosh keyboard, a special key with a flower-shaped symbol that performs functions when combined with other keys. It is also known as the *Feature key* and the *Clover key*. Common functions are global menu choices:

Command-A	Select all
Command-C	Copy selected material to Clipboard
Command-F	Find
Command-G	Find again
Command-I	Get information
Command-M	Make alias
Command-N	New folder or document
Command-O	Open
Command-P	Print
Command-Q	Quit application
Command-S	Save file to current folder
Command-V	Paste from Clipboard
Command-W	Close file or folder
Command-X	Cut to Clipboard
Command-Z	Undo last command or typing

command line (n., adj.) In an operating system that requires keyboard characters for instructions, such as MS-DOS or Unix, a display line that prompts the user to input keyboard instructions.

Command Line Interface (CLI) (n.) An environment in which the user can only communicate with a program through textual input and output. Input, or keyboard commands, are interpreted and executed by the program, which provides output in the form of text or graphics on a monitor. A CLI can provide more control than a graphical user interface (GUI).

comment out (v.) To mark a line or section of program code with delimiters, which prevents it from being compiled or interpreted. Comments in the delimited section often give other programmers information about the program.

Commercial Internet Exchange (CIX) (n.) A group of Internet Service Providers who provide a backbone service free from Acceptable Use Policies (AUPs) and dedicated to commercial use.

Commercial Mobile Radio Service (CMRS) (n.) A regulatory classification that the Federal Communications Commission (FCC) uses to govern all commercial wireless service providers, including personal communications services (PCS), cellular, and Enhanced Specialized Mobile Radio (ESMR).

Commodore Dynamic Total Vision (CDTV) (n.) Interactive multimedia system designed for consumer use. It reads programs on special CD-ROMs. The system is obsolete.

Common Architecture for Next Generation Internet Protocol (CATNIP) (n.) A proposed standard for IP version 6 (IPv6), also known as IP Next Generation (IPng). One of the problems addressed by this new architecture is the need for more Internet addresses. IPv6 is defined in RFC 1752.

Common Business-Oriented Language (Cobol, pronounced "KOE-ball") (n.) A widely used programming language developed by the Conference on Data System Languages (CODASYL) Committee between 1959 and 1961.

common carrier (n.) A private company that offers public telecommunications services.

Common Command Set (CCS) (n.) Small Computer System Interface (SCSI) commands specified in the SCSI-1 Standard X3.131–1986

Addendum 4.B, governing the communication between all SCSI devices.

Common Gateway Interface (CGI) (n.) A widely used set of standards designed to run external programs from a World Wide Web HTTP server. CGI defines a set of environmental variables and specifies how to pass arguments to the executing program as part of the HTTP request. It may exist as any program that accepts command line arguments. Perl is often used to write CGI scripts. A script can access information in a database, format the results as HTML, and return this information to the browser. When a server receives a CGI execution request, it creates a new process to run the external program, which can create problems if the process fails to terminate. Microsoft developed the Internet Server Application Programming Interface (ISAPI) standard, and Netscape devised NSAPI; both standards allow CGI-like tasks to run as part of the main server process, making it unnecessary to create a new process for each CGI request.

Common Image Format (CIF) (n.) Standard sample structure used to represent the picture information in a single frame in digital video, independent of frame rate and synchronization or blanking structure. The uncompressed bit rate for transmitting CIF at 29.97 frames per second (fps) is 36.45 megabits per second (Mbps).

Common Intermediate Format (CIF) (n.) A videoconferencing standard with a resolution of 352 pixels x 288 pixels.

common log file (CLF) (n.) A log file format developed by the National Center for Supercomputing Applications (NCSA) that has become the standard logging format for the majority of web servers.

Common Object File Format (COFF) (n.) The executable and object file format used by Unix System V, Release 3.

Common Object Request Broker Architecture (CORBA, pronounced "KORE-bah") (n.) A network architecture specified by the Object Management Group (OMG), it provides the standard interface definition between OMG-compliant objects.

Communications Decency Act (CDA) (n.) An amendment to a federal telecommunications bill that went into effect in February 1996. The law attempted to make it criminal to post indecent language on the Internet anywhere that a minor could read it. In June 1996, a three-judge panel in Philadelphia ruled the amendment unconstitutional.

communications port (com port) (n.) The connector on a microcomputer for a communications interface, typically a serial port.

compact disc (CD) (n.) Originally the common term for a compact audio disc, now used freely to refer any optical disc 4.75 inches (12 cm) in diameter containing information encoded digitally in the constant linear velocity (CLV) format. The official designation for an audio CD is compact disc–digital audio (CD-DA). The accompanying illustration shows the evolution of compact discs and the relationship between different types of compact discs. See figure.

The following terms refer to specific types of CDs and CD formats:

- **CD-DA** (n.) Compact disc–digital audio; the format used for high-fidelity music that offers a 90+ decibel signal-to-noise ratio and 74 minutes of digital sound. The

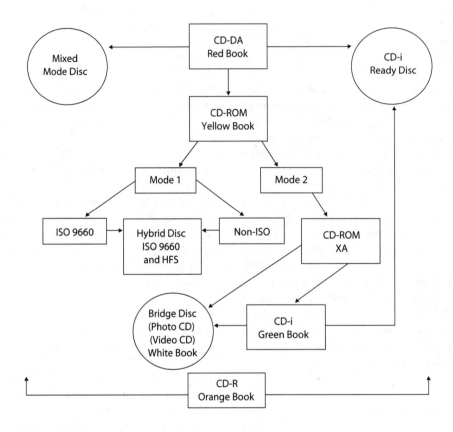

compact disc family

standard for this format is the Red Book. Audio files are uncompressed 16-bit, 44.1-kHz samples.

- **CD+G** (n.) Compact disc + graphics; developed by Warner New Media, this CD format is not readable by standard CD-ROM players. It includes extended graphics capabilities, as well as some limited video graphics written to the CD subcode area. The primary use is for karaoke, in which song lyrics are displayed

and the music is played without vocals to accompany a person who sings the song. Pronounced "see-DEE plus GEE."

- **CD-i** (n.) Compact disc–interactive; developed in 1991 by Philips, a CD-ROM format that holds audio, digital data, still graphics, and MPEG video. These discs adhere to the Green Book standard. An infrared remote control device, a mouse, or a trackball allows users to interact with the content on the disc by clicking a cursor over hot spots on the video display.

- **CD-i audio levels** (n.) Compact disc–interactive audio levels; levels of audio encoding that are part of the Green Book specification. Level A is a method of recording audio that offers fidelity comparable to that of standard CD audio, but it compresses the data to about half as much space on a disc. Level B is used in both the CD-i and CD-ROM XA formats; this method of recording audio offers medium fidelity but is more highly compressed than level A. Used in both the CD-i and CD-ROM XA formats, level C is a method of recording audio that offers fidelity sufficient for speech. It is highly compressed.

- **CD+MIDI** (n.) Compact disc + Musical Instrument Digital Interface; developed by Warner New Media, this CD format adds MIDI information to the digital audio data. Pronounced "see-DEE plus MID-ee." See also *Musical Instrument Digital Interface.*

- **CD-plus** (n.) A CD-ROM format from Sony and Philips that plays Red Book audio, written on the first tracks, and that includes graphics and data files readable by a microcomputer on later tracks. Windows 95 supports the CD-plus format.

- **CD-R** (n.) Compact disc–recordable; developed in 1990 by Philips and Sony, it adheres to the Orange Book standard. It permits a CD recorder to write CD-DA, CD-ROM, CD-ROM XA, and CD-i block structures to a blank CD-ROM disc. The primary applications are for prototype production discs, or *one-offs,* and for archiving data. In 1992, a second generation of CD recorders became standard.

They are capable of *multisession* recording, or writing additional information to a disc without deleting existing data. To read a multisession disc, readers must be able to identify a complex table of contents (TOC), but not all readers can do this. The original ISO 9660 logical file structure does not handle multisession discs, because it was created before their invention. See figure.

CD-R layers

- **CD-ROM** (n.) Compact disc–read-only memory; a 4.75-inch (12 cm) disc on which optical memory storage is encoded. CD-ROMs hold about 650 megabytes (MB) of data. The standards for this format are called the Yellow Book. The logical level standard is called ISO 9660. The Unix extension is called the *Rock Ridge Format.*

- **CD-ROM XA** (n.) Compact disc–read-only memory extended architecture; an evolution of the standard CD-ROM format that provides for ADPCM audio, multisession discs, Photo-CD, and CD-i compatibility. This format relies solely on Cross-Interleaved Reed-Solomon Code (CIRC) for error correction.

- **CD-RW** (n.) Compact disc–rewritable; a recordable CD-ROM that may be written over many times. It uses a different medium from a CD-R, which may be recorded only once.

• **CD-WO** (n.) Compact disc–write once; another name for *CD-R*.

Compact Video (n.) Developed by SuperMac, this CODEC can compress QuickTime movies in 320 x 240 pixel resolution at high frame rates for CD-ROM playback.

companding (n.) The process of compressing data for transmission and expanding it on reception.

compatibility (n.) In relation to compact discs (CDs), the extent to which different types of discs can be read by various types of disc drives or players. For example, all CD-DA discs are fully compatible with all CD-DA players, so any such player can interpret and reproduce music from any such disc, regardless of the manufacturer.

compatible (adj.) Capable of running the same software, such as MS-DOS, on various hardware configurations.

competitive access provider (CAP) (n.) A telecommunications carrier that bypasses a local network to connect to long-distance carriers. A CAP provides high-capacity lines to business customers and interexchange carriers and may offer switched services. Also known as *alternative access providers*.

compiled language (n.) Unlike an interpreted language, which is translated into machine code every time it is run, a compiled language is converted into machine language once. This code is stored and called each time the program is run. The collection of symbols used to write the program is called *source code*. The

translated machine language is called *object code*. Examples of compiled languages are Pascal and C++.

compiler (n.) A computer program that translates higher-level language instructions into machine code that a computer can read.

complement (n.) The value that must be added to a number to yield a specified sum.

complementary metal-oxide semiconductor (CMOS) (n.) A metal-oxide semiconductor (MOS) device containing both N-channel and P-channel MOS active elements. CMOS is one of two basic processes (MOS and bipolar) used to fabricate integrated circuits (ICs).

complex instruction set computing (CISC) (n.) A type of microprocessing in which each instruction can perform several low-level functions, such as arithmetic operations, memory access, and address calculations. It is the predecessor of a reduced instruction set computing (RISC) processor. Common CISC processors are the Motorola 680x0 chips used in the Macintosh and in the Intel 80x86, including the 486 and Pentium.

Component Object Model (COM) (n.) An implementation of object linking and embedding (OLE) developed by Microsoft for interoperation of distributed objects in a network. Some of the capabilities it provides are similar to those defined in Common Object Request Broker Architecture (CORBA). In the same way that OLE provides services for a compound document, COM provides services for interface negotiation and makes networked objects available in response to an event.

component video (n.) A video signal in which the chrominance (color) and the luminance (brightness) components have been recorded separately. The result is better picture quality. S-VHS and Hi-8 offer two-part component, or Y/C. This format offers higher resolution than composite video (which mixes the Y and C components), because it yields increased bandwidth in the luminance portion of the signal. *Color-under,* or limited color bandwidth, is a process used in Y/C. The common betacam component system further divides color into three components (Y, R-Y, B-Y), which provide better luminance and color accuracy, and lower noise than Y/C.

com port See *communications port.*

composite 1. (v.) To build the final version of a production with layers drawn from video, graphics, and audio content, which are integrated according to the production plan. 2. (n.) In telecommunications, the output of a concentrator or multiplexer that includes the multiplexed data.

composite video (n.) A video signal in which all the information about color, brightness, line, field, sync, and blanking is mixed together. Cross-color artifacts are apparent in composite video, compared with component video, which has great clarity. Compare *red-green-blue.*

composition (n.) In video production, the visual makeup of a picture or scene. It includes such variables as balance, framing, field of view, texture, and other aesthetic considerations.

compound document (n.) A collection of multiple data types, each linked to the application that created it, connected by a navigable interface.

Comprehensive Perl Archive Network (CPAN) (n.) Internet archives with information about Perl. These archives are available at *ftp://*

ftp.funet.fi/pub/languages/perl/CPAN or *ftp:// uiarchive.cso.uiuc.edu/pub/lang/perl/CPAN.*

compress (v.) To make a file significantly smaller without altering the substantive information. Compression eliminates redundant data. With analog audio files, compression limits the bandwidth and reduces the differences in amplitude between the softest and loudest sounds in a program. In most multimedia applications, digital video must be compressed in order to stream smoothly at an acceptable frame rate.

compressed audio (n.) In relation to digitally encoded sounds, a special processing technique that reduces the quantity of data required to define the sounds.

Compressed SLIP (C-SLIP) (n.) Compressed serial line Internet protocol; version of SLIP that uses Van Jacobson TCP header compression. It has no effect on the data in a packet and has nothing to do with compression by modem. It reduces a TCP header from 40 bytes to 7 bytes.

compressed video (n.) A video clip that is digitally encoded with computer algorithms to reduce the amount of data needed to define the video content.

compression (n.) The conversion of digital data, typically video and audio, into a more compact form by using complicated algorithms.

compression-decompression (CODEC) (n.) This may be either a software-only or a hardware-assisted scheme that is used to process digital video or audio files. The amount of data required to represent moving pictures with sound is reduced by a CODEC, which normally discards redundant data on compression.

Some of the more widely used CODECs are Indeo, MPEG, CinePak, and the Sorenson CODEC.

compression ratio (n.) The size of an uncompressed data file divided by the size of the compressed version, expressing the degree to which a compression algorithm can reduce file size. The MPEG video compression algorithm typically achieves a ratio of 180:1. JPEG still-picture compression formulas achieve ratios of less than 20:1; at higher ratios, or with greater compression, they exhibit noticeable artifacts and blockiness.

compulsory license (n.) A license that permits the use of copyrighted work without the owner's specific consent, provided the user complies with legal formalities and pays a legislatively prescribed fee to the owner. Cable systems and other media distributors use copyrighted materials for a fee set by the government. There is no need for negotiation between the copyright holder and the licensee.

CompuServe (n.) An online Internet service provider founded in 1969 and purchased by America Online (AOL) in 1998. It is widely used internationally, with strong technical forums. The full name is CompuServe Information Service (CIS).

computer (n.) Programmable digital equipment that performs computations and manipulates data.

computer-aided design/computer-aided manufacturing (CAD/CAM) (n.) Software applications used by engineers for the graphic design of components and systems. Once components are built, they may be manipulated on screen and evaluated. CAM applications extrapolate manufacturing specifications from the CAD designs and may be used to control manufacturing processes.

computer-aided instruction (CAI) (n.) The use of computers to facilitate learning. Also called *computer-aided learning (CAL), computer-based instruction (CBI), computer-based learning (CBL)*, and *computer-based training (CBT)*.

computer-aided learning (CAL) (n.) The use of computers to facilitate learning. Also called *computer-aided instruction (CAI), computer-based instruction (CBI), computer-based learning (CBL)*, and *computer-based training (CBT)*.

computer-aided manufacturing (CAM) (n.) Applications that use manufacturing specifications from computer-aided designs (CADs) to control the manufacturing processes. See also *computer aided design/computer-aided manufacturing*.

Computer and Business Equipment Manufacturers Association (CBEMA) (n.) A trade association with a rich history. Founded in Chicago as the National Association of Office Appliance Manufacturers in 1916, the organization changed its name to Office Equipment Manufacturers Institution in 1929, then to Business Equipment Manufacturers Association in 1961. In 1973 the organization became CBEMA, recognizing the importance of computers in business. In 1994 the association was reorganized and renamed the Information Technology Industry (ITI) Council. It continues to represent companies involved in the development of technology and promotes the global competitiveness of its member companies.

computer-based instruction (CBI) (n.) The use of computers to facilitate learning. Also called *computer-aided instruction (CAI), com-*

puter-aided learning (CAL), computer-based learning (CBL), and computer-based training (CBT).

computer-based learning (CBL) (n.) The use of computers to facilitate learning. Also called computer-aided instruction (CAI), computer-aided learning (CAL), computer-based instruction (CBI), and computer-based training (CBT).

computer-based training (CBT) (n.) The use of computers to facilitate learning. Also called computer-aided instruction (CAI), computer-aided learning (CAL), computer-based instruction (CBI), and computer-based learning (CBL).

computer graphics (n.) Any image a computer generates digitally. IBM-compatible PCs require graphics adapter cards to produce images generated by the computer on a screen. Some of the common standards for PC graphics are Color Graphics Adapter (CGA), Enhanced Graphics Adapter (EGA), Video Graphics Array (VGA), Super Video Graphics Array (SVGA), and Extended Graphics Adapter (XGA).

Computer Graphics Metafile (CGM) (n.) An object-oriented graphic file format used by many software applications.

Computer-Telephony Integration (CTI) (n.) The combination of digital systems, data networks, and telecommunications infrastructure to provide communications solutions.

concatenate (v.) In programming, to combine character strings.

concentrator (n.) A type of multiplexer for telecommunications signals. It allows numerous signals to be input and output simultaneously, using fewer outgoing lines than incoming lines. A concentrator may be used

to connect as many as 24 individual 2400-bit-per-second (bps) lines to a host using a single 57 600-bps channel.

concrete class (n.) In object-oriented programming, a class that may be instantiated. Compare abstract class.

condenser microphone (n.) A microphone that translates acoustical signals into electrical ones by using a variable capacitor. Power must by supplied to the capacitor, either by a battery or by a phantom power supply.

conditional branching (n.) In computing, after a specified set of conditions is satisfied, the process by which previously programmed instructions take a user to a different location in the program. The destination to which the program branches is conditional, depending on the nature of a user's input. If specific conditions are not met, the computer follows the normal sequence without branching.

conference (n.) In networked communications, an asynchronous online discussion area to which a user may post information and comments for others with access. During an audio- or videoconference, all users are able to communicate in real time, or synchronously.

confetti (n.) Small, colored dots on a video screen caused by signal dropouts or video noise. See also noise.

config.sys (n.) A text file located in the root directory of an MS-DOS computer with system configuration commands. The operating system reads this file as the computer boots, after reading the setup file from the CMOS RAM and before running autoexec.bat. Common config.sys file commands are shown here with an explanation:

65

DEVICE=C:\DOS\HIMEM.SYS /testmem:off
(Load the expanded memory manager, or EMM.)

DEVICE=C:\DOS\EMM386.EXE RAM
(Load the expanded memory manager, or EMM.)

BUFFERS=10,0
(Specify memory for disk buffers.)

FILES=70
(Set the number of files that may be open simultaneously.)

DOS=UMB
(DOS is located in upper memory block, or UMB.)

LASTDRIVE=Z
(Disk drives are A: to Z:.)

FCBS=16,0
(Set the number of file control blocks, or FCBs.)

DEVICEHIGH /L:1,12048=
C:\DOS\SETVER.EXE
(Report the version of DOS to older programs.)

DOS=HIGH
(Maintain a link between DOS and UMB.)

COUNTRY=358,437 C:\DOS\COUNTRY.SYS
(Set the country code for some programs.)

STACKS=9,256
(Set dynamic stacks for hardware control.)

SHELL=C:\DOS\COMMAND.COM
C:\DOS\ /E:1024 /p
(Set the location of the command interpreter.)

Connection Control Language (CCL) (n.) A set of commands used to identify and manage data connections.

connectionless (adj.) A type of communication in which data transfer occurs between hosts without previous setup. Packets may take different routes because each is independent of the other. User Datagram Protocol (UDP) is a connectionless protocol.

connection-oriented (adj.) Describes communication in which data transfer moves through three phases: establishment of connection, data transfer, and release of connection. TCP is connection oriented.

Conseil Européen pour la Recherche Nucléaire (CERN, European Laboratory for Particle Physics) (n.) The Swiss research center at which the World Wide Web was developed.

constant (n.) In programming, a value that does not change. Compare *variable*.

constant angular velocity (CAV) (n.) The constant speed at which certain videodisc players spin a disc, regardless of the reading head's position. The tracks near the center pass under the reading head more slowly than the tracks near the perimeter. Each frame is separately addressable. The standard speed for CAV discs is 1800 rpm (NTSC) or 1500 rpm (PAL), and the disc makes one revolution for each frame. The maximum program duration is approximately 30 minutes per side on a 12-inch disc. Compare *constant linear velocity*.

constant linear velocity (CLV) (n.) The variable rate at which certain optical disc or videodisc players spin a disc so that all data sectors pass under the reading head at the same rate. The disc rotates faster when the head is closer to the center of the disc and more slowly as the head moves away from the center of the disc. Videodiscs of this type are *extended-play discs;* they play twice as long per side as CAV discs, or up to one hour. The CLV format loses some of the control features of a CAV disc, such as freeze-frame capability. Compact discs (CDs) of all types spin at a constant linear velocity and exhibit a constant sector size. Compare *constant angular velocity.*

Consultative Committee for International Radio (CCIR) (n.) 1. A European committee that sets radio and television standards. 2. The standard for the 625-line television system used in Western Europe, commonly referred to simply as CCIR.

The following standards are among those recommended by the committee:

- **CCIR-601** (n.) The standard for digital component video that specifies component color difference coding (Y, R-Y, B-Y) and the 4:2:2 format.

- **CCIR-656** (n.) The standard for digital component electrical interfaces that defines synchronizing signals and blanking, as well as parallel and serial interface specifications.

consumer market (n.) Also called the *domestic market,* the segment of the market in which audio-video equipment is mostly used in homes and in which software consists of movies and games. The professional market uses industrial gear.

content (n.) The story, information, graphics, audio, and video material that is incorporated in a digital production.

contention (n.) In telecommunications, a method of access used by private branch exchange (PBX) or public telephone systems in which a limited number of ports serve numerous devices on a first-come, first-served basis.

content provider (n.) Owner or licensee of program material. Paramount and Viacom are content providers. Microsoft is both a software developer and a content provider.

context-sensitive (adj.) Depending on a user's actions, a context-sensitive program responds with help or prompts that are specifically related to activities in which the user is engaged.

contiguous (adj.) Describes a data storage file whose elements are grouped together, as opposed to being fragmented in separate locations on a disk. If a file is fragmented, it may not stream smoothly because the heads of the drive have to move around during transmission. Video files will drop frames on playback if they are not contiguous. To make all the files on a disk contiguous, one must execute the "defrag" command in MS-DOS, the "defragment" command in Windows, or the "optimize" command with a Macintosh utility.

continuity (n.) 1. A condition that exists in an uninterrupted circuit or signal path. A continuity test determines whether a circuit is complete by measuring 0 ohms of resistance, whereas a broken circuit shows infinite ohms of resistance. 2. In video production, a logical succession of events that requires a video producer to position characters consistently and to place props in scenes that are meant to appear as a natural progression in time. 3. Directional consistency in camera angles from shot to shot.

continuous branching (n.) A feature of an interactive program that modifies the environment constantly in response to the user, rather than only at predetermined branching points or menus.

contrast (n.) The range between the darkest and brightest components in an image. Displays often provide hardware adjustments for controlling contrast, and scanners permit software controls. Adjusting contrast in a selective manner can make relatively light or dark areas of an image visible while increasing detail.

control code (n.) One of the 32 ASCII codes reserved for issuing hardware control commands, such as advancing a printer page.

Control-L (n.) A one-way communication system in consumer model camcorders and VCRs that is used to approximately coordinate tape transport commands for automated editing.

controller (n.) 1. In computer hardware, a processing component that manages the flow of data between the computer and peripheral devices. 2. The input device for a video game that moves and manipulates objects on the screen. A mouse is a controller for a computer with a graphical user interface (GUI).

control panel (n.) In a graphical user interface (GUI), a utility program that may be used to adjust parameters for system settings, such as volume, color, and the rate of response to input devices.

control panel device (CDEV, pronounced "SEE-dev") (n.) A piece of system code used in the Mac OS to extend functionality.

Control Program for Microprocessors (CP/M) (n.) A specific microcomputer operating system (OS) developed by Digital Research Incorporated.

Control-S (n.) Bidirectional communication system that allows an external edit controller or compatible deck to issue tape transport commands to a slave unit VCR or camera.

control track (n.) 1. A track on video recorders that is imprinted with pulses to set timing and to align the tape with the recording and playback heads. 2. A rudimentary method of video positioning that counts pulses on the tape rather than reading time-stamped data to identify a frame's location.

convergence (n.) In a computer monitor, the alignment of the red, green, and blue light beams aimed at phosphors in a triad. The simultaneous firing of the red, green, and blue beams excites the three corresponding phosphors to generate the color white. Slight deviation of the beams due to magnetic misalignment of the electron trajectory causes colored shadows around pixels, giving the beams poor convergence. If the beams are perfectly aimed at the pixels on the screen, the monitor has good convergence.

cookie (n.) A handle, transaction ID, or other token of agreement between programs. The purpose of a cookie is to relate a later transaction to the current one. When a web server places a cookie on a client's hard disk, it can use that information in a subsequent connection to determine how information should be sent to that particular client. Netscape originated the concept. The decision of whether to accept a cookie offered by a web server is entirely up to the client. There is nothing inherently harmful or dangerous in accepting cookies, except that the client has no idea what information is transferred in the process. See also *HTTP cookie*.

Coordinating Committee for Intercontinental Research Networks (CCIRN) (n.) A committee that includes the United States Federal Networking Council (FNC) and similar agencies in Europe. The executive directors of the FNC and the European Association of Research Networks (RARE) are co-chairs of the committee. The CCIRN provides a forum for planning among North American and European research networking groups.

copper (n.) Network cable with a core conductor of copper or aluminum.

Copper Distributed Data Interface (CDDI) (n.) The implementation of Fiber Distributed Data Interface (FDDI) network protocols using twisted-pair copper wiring instead of fiber.

coprocessor (n.) Frequently referred to as a *math coprocessor,* a chip that was designed to execute floating-point calculations and other mathematical functions rapidly. Many spreadsheets and computer-aided design (CAD) applications are constructed to take advantage of a coprocessor's presence in a microcomputer's circuitry.

copyright (n.) The ownership rights to an idea, document, graphic, sound, or other reproducible event or object. This right belongs to the creator unless creation is done under a work-for-hire contract. A copyright may be transferred to another party, or it may be licensed with limitations or contractual conditions.

copy stand (n.) A table or flat surface with a photographic or video camera stationed overhead. Lamps are mounted on the sides to illuminate an image or object placed on the stand, which is the focal point of the camera.

CORBA See *Common Object Request Broker Architecture.*

core (n.) In fiber optics, the center part of an optical waveguide through which light passes. In single-mode fiber, the core diameter is 8 to 12 microns, whereas in multimode fiber, the diameter may range up to 100 microns.

corrupted data (n.) Data that has lost its integrity and that is partially damaged. The loss of any data can cause an entire file to become corrupted and can render it unreadable.

Cosmo Player (n.) A special browser developed for the SGI platform that interprets virtual reality modeling language (VRML) commands.

cost per megabyte (n.) A measure of the price for each megabyte of usable storage. The common formula is to divide the cost of the drive or of the medium by the number of megabytes. This measure alone ignores performance, which is a more significant factor in evaluating storage devices.

courseware (n.) The aggregate of discs, books, illustrations, tapes, and computer programs required for the delivery of an instructional module. The name implies that there is a software component.

CPAN See *Comprehensive Perl Archive Network.*

CPE See *Customer Premises Equipment.*

C++ (n.) A superset of the C language developed by Bjarne Stroustrup at AT&T Bell Laboratories in 1986. C++ is one of the most popular object-oriented languages. In C++, a *class* is a user-defined type. Constructors and destructors are member functions called to create or destroy instances. C++ allows implicit type conversion and default function arguments. It permits the overloading of both operators and function names. In May 1989, version 2.0 added such features as multiple inheritance, type-safe linkage, pointers to members, and abstract classes.

CP/M See *Control Program for Microprocessors.*

cps See *characters per second* or *cycles per second.*

CPU See *central processing unit.*

CR See *carriage return.*

cracker (n.) Jargon for a person who gains unauthorized access to a computing system with malicious intent.

crash (n., v.) Usually refers to a system crash, caused by a software malfunction and remedied by rebooting the machine. A head crash on a hard disk drive causes physical damage.

crawl (n., v.) The steady, controlled display of text, horizontally or vertically. Rolling credits at the end of a movie are an example of text crawl. Sometimes used as slang for thin undulating lines along the edge of a video monitor that appear to "crawl" like a snake. This may be due to the alignment of video heads or to timing errors.

crawler (n.) A robot, typically one that searches sites on the web.

CRC See *cyclic redundancy check.*

crop (v.) To cut off one or more sides of an image to make it smaller or to eliminate unnecessary material.

cross-compiler (n.) A compiler that runs on one type of processor and that generates code for another type of processor.

cross-hatching (n.) Filling or shading an area

cross-hatching

of a graphic with evenly spaced intersecting lines. See figure.

Cross-Interleaved Reed-Solomon Code (CIRC) (n.) The first level of error correction that is used in every compact disc (CD), and the only one that is used for audio CDs. CIRC consists of two Reed-Solomon Codes interleaved crosswise.

cross-platform (adj.) The capacity of software to run on different operating systems and hardware. Cross-platform development means that an asset is captured or prepared on a different platform from the one on which it is delivered.

cross-polarization (n.) Use of two transmitters, with both operating on the same frequency. In this configuration, one transmitter-receiver pair is vertically polarized, and the other is horizontally polarized.

cross-post (v.) To place an article on Usenet that is copied to more than one newsgroup simultaneously.

crosstalk (n.) Undesirable sound that bleeds into a connection or into an isolated track on an audio tape from an adjacent track. On an optical disc, crosstalk is the adjacent track data that the laser head picks up as it attempts to hold the desired signal track being played; this is possibly caused by inaccurate focus or a warped disc.

CRT See *cathode-ray tube.*

C-SLIP See *Compressed SLIP.*

CSMA/CD See *carrier sense multiple access with collision detection.*

CSU See *channel service unit.*

CSU/DSU See *channel service unit/data service unit.*

CTCP See *Client To Client Protocol.*

CTI See *Computer-Telephony Integration.*

CTS See *clear to send.*

C2 (n.) A Cross-Interleaved Reed-Solomon Code (CIRC) that corrects burst errors and detects other errors.

CUA Architecture (n.) A style of user interface developed by IBM and used in OS/2 and Microsoft Windows.

cucalorus (n.) Lighting accessory with random cutouts that is used to simulate shadows, known as "cookie shadows" in the jargon of video producers.

cue (n.) 1. An identifying element placed in the vertical blanking interval (VBI) of video. Frame numbers, picture codes, chapter codes, flags, and closed captions are examples. 2. A signal given by the producer or director that influences performers' actions during video or audio recording.

cue inserter (n.) A specialized device used with videodisc mastering equipment to identify the field in which to place the frame ID code when recording from video. The cue inserter places cues in the vertical blanking interval (VBI) of the master tape for transfer to disc.

cue, still (n.) A signal in the vertical blanking interval (VBI) of a master tape that identifies a still frame on a videodisc.

CUI See *character user interface.*

cursor (n.) An image, arrow, or I-beam on a computer screen that shows where information may be entered or where a mouse or light pen are located on the screen. It may be represented by any icon.

CU-SeeMe (n.) Developed at Cornell University in 1992, a shareware videoconferencing application for the web. It facilitates audiovisual connections between clients and supports multiuser conferencing by using servers called *reflectors* to distribute the video and audio signals between multiple clients. It is available at *http://cu-seeme.cornell.edu.* Pronounced "SEE-you-SEE-me."

Customer Premises Equipment (CPE) (n.) Computers and household telephone equipment, fax machines, or modems that interconnect with the network at the customer's premises or that are owned by someone other than the telephone company that provides services.

Custom Local Area Signaling Services (CLASS) (n.) Enhanced telephone services that rely on the Signaling System 7 (SS7) channel to carry data about a call. CLASS enables services such as call forwarding and caller ID.

cut 1. (n.) In audio and video, a segment or scene taken from a production. 2. (n.) Command from the director to stop acting and recording immediately. 3. (v.) In video editing, to change scenes abruptly without using a transition.

cut and paste (v.) To lift and reposition a segment of a document or an image to another location on screen, to another document, or to a file created by a different application. Clips are usually stored on the clipboard during a cut and paste.

cutaway (n.) In video, a shot of something that is not the principal subject or action but that is related to it in some way. The technique is often used to provide transitional footage or to avoid a jump cut.

cuts-only editing (n.) A method of videotape editing in which shots are connected from one scene to another directly without transitions, such as *wipes* or *dissolves*. See also *cut* or *edit*.

cyber- Jargon used by newbies and outsiders as a prefix to refer to the world of networked computers. An example is *cyberspace,* first used by William Gibson in his book *Neuromancer.*

cybernetics (n.) The study of nervous system controls in the brain as a basis for developing information-processing and communications technologies.

cyberspace (n.) Jargon used by newbies to refer to an environment made possible by a network of computers designed for exploration and communication with both data structures and other humans. This term was introduced in *Neuromancer* by William Gibson.

cycles per second (cps) (n.) Number of times that a regularly repeating waveform completes its motion in the time span of one second. A complete cycle includes movement through both the peak and the trough of a wave. In the case of a square wave, a cycle includes both positive and negative states.

cyclic redundancy check (CRC) (n.) An error detection scheme in reading, writing, or transmitting data. The value of the CRC character in a block of data received must match the value transmitted.

cylinder (n.) The set of tracks that are aligned vertically on platters and that are not accessible without head movement in a hard disk drive. Units of data that are related to one another are placed in cylinders so that they may be read faster and so that they require less head movement, or *seek time.*

Cyrix 6x86 (n.) A 64-bit 80x86-compatible microprocessor designed by Cyrix and manufactured by IBM. It combines aspects of both reduced instruction set computing (RISC) and complex instruction set computing (CISC) chips. Cyrix 6x86 has a superscalar, superpipelined core and performs register renaming as well as speculative execution. It is socket-compatible with the Pentium P54C processor.

D

DA See *distribution amplifier.*

D/A See *digital-to-analog.*

DAC See *D/A converter.*

D/A converter (DAC, pronounced "DACK") (n.) Digital-to-analog converter; a microprocessor chip or circuit that converts numerical data represented by a string of discrete numbers into analog information represented in continuous form, such as a signal that speakers may render into sound.

daemon (n.) A program that lies dormant waiting for certain conditions to occur. Unix systems run daemons to handle requests for services from other network hosts. Examples included ftpd and nfsd (file transfer), rlogind and telnetd (remote login), cron (local timed command execution), and rshd (remote command execution). Pronounced "DEE-mun."

daisy chain (n.) A pattern of bus wiring in which all devices receive identical signals, unless a device in the chain modifies the signal before passing it on. The Apple LocalTalk protocol (RS-485) and Thin Ethernet (10BASE2) are examples. In a more general sense, the term refers to connecting electronic devices, such as peripherals, in a series.

daisy-wheel printer (n.) An impact printer that prints individual letters arranged around the edge of a disk, which serves as the print head. The disk resembles a daisy with many petals or a wheel with spokes. See figure.

daisy wheel from a printer

DAP See *Directory Access Protocol.*

dark fiber (n.) Inactivated fiber-optic line with

73

no associated opto-electronics. The term refers to the physical cable itself, rather than a certain amount of bandwidth or transport capacity. Telephone and utility companies are deploying large quantities of dark fiber to meet anticipated future demand. The opto-electronics may be added as needed.

DARPA See *Defense Advanced Research Projects Agency.*

DAT See *digital audio tape.*

data (n.) In the digital realm, information processed or produced by computers. In general, any collection of numerals, letters, and symbols that define something, whether it be an idea, document, image, condition, situation, or event.

data area (n.) According to ISO 9660, the space on a CD-ROM where user data is written, immediately following the system area. The data area begins at 00:02:16 absolute time.

database (n.) A file of information assembled in an orderly manner by a program designed to record and manipulate data. A telephone directory is an example of output from a database.

database management system (DBMS) (n.) A suite of programs that are used to manage structured sets of persistent data and that offer users query facilities. Oracle and Sybase are examples. A DBMS controls the organization, storage, and retrieval of fields, records, and files in a database, in addition to controlling the security and integrity of the database. Data security prevents unauthorized users from viewing or altering information in the database. A DBMS can maintain database integrity by not allowing more than one user to update the same record at the same time and by keeping duplicate records out of the database. Query languages allow users to interrogate the database interactively and to analyze its data.

Database design is the process of deciding how to organize data into record types and how the record types should relate to one another. An information system is made up of subjects (customers, employees, vendors) and activities (orders, payments, purchases). A DBMS mirrors an organization's data structure and processes the transaction volume efficiently. Hierarchical, network, and relational databases are common methods of organizing data. *Hierarchical databases* link records together as in an organization chart, and a record type has only one owner. In *network database* structures, a record type can have multiple owners. *Relational databases* do not link records together physically, but the design of the records provides a common field to allow for matching. A relational database is the most flexible, but it may be too slow for heavy transaction processing.

database query language (n.) The type of programming language employed by database users to formulate requests and generate reports. A widely used example is Structured Query Language (SQL).

database server (n.) In a local area network (LAN), the computer that holds and manages a database. Unlike a file server, which acts as a remote disk drive, the database server performs management tasks.

data bus (n.) Circuitry for transferring data between computer components, connecting the ports, the memory, the controllers, and the microprocessor. A *system bus* is the pathway on which data travels between components within a computer. Types of PC buses are the processor bus, the address bus, the memory bus, and the input/output (I/O) bus. Two distinct types of *I/O buses* are the serial bus and the parallel bus. A *serial bus* sends one bit of data at a time and is used to send data over longer distances than the parallel bus. Some common examples of serial buses are a local area network (LAN) using 10BASE2 Ethernet, the ACCESS.bus, and the Universal Serial Bus (USB). A *parallel bus* is more limited in the distance it covers because it sends data in synchronized chunks over multiple lines, rather than bit by bit. A parallel bus can send 8,16, 32, or 64 bits at once, along with control and address signals. The SCSI bus and IEEE 488 graphics bus are common examples of parallel buses that move data over cables and connectors to and from external components. Several internal parallel buses exist on the motherboard of a PC. The internal parallel bus as a whole moves data within a computer with a combination of connectors, voltages, and timing signals.

data capture (n.) A process by which analog material is read, often by an optical sensor, and converted to digital data that a computer can process. The original captured content comes from a graphic, video, or text source. In audio applications, the capture device is a sampler. To capture data is to digitize it.

data channel (n.) The path through which data travels between the input/output (I/O) devices and computer memory. More than one I/O operation may be performed concurrently, and the flow of information is bidirectional. On an ISDN line, whether Basic Rate Interface (BRI) or Primary Rate Interface (PRI), the data channel carries control information and sets up connections on associated bearer channels.

data communications equipment (DCE) (n.)

An intermediary device in a serial RS-232C communication system that receives, modulates, and parses a signal.

data encryption key (DEK) (n.) Private information used to encode message text securely and to verify signatures.

Data Encryption Standard (DES) (n.) A security scheme for data communications specified by Federal Information Processing Systems (FIPS) publication 46 and approved by the National Bureau of Standards (NBS).

Data Exchange Format (DEF) (n.) A format for computer-aided design (CAD) programming files developed by Autodesk for its AutoCAD program. It is platform-independent and is also called *Drawing Interchange Format (DXF)*.

data fork (n.) The portion of a Macintosh file that contains pure data, exclusive of proprietary system data. Compare *resource fork*. See also *Macintosh file system*.

data glove (n.) A specialized input device that senses the position of a user's hand and then manipulates objects in a virtual reality scenario in a manner that corresponds to the hand movements.

datagram (n.) A self-contained block of data with sufficient information to be routed from the source to the destination computer without needing a previous exchange to have established a context for the data.

data jack (n.) A connector mounted in the wall for data cables, usually accepting a wide telephone-style eight-pin RJ-45 plug.

Datakit (n.) A circuit-switched digital network, such as X.25. It supports host-to-host and

D

RS-232 connections for terminals and printers. Email functions (Unix-to-Unix CoPy, or UUCP) and remote login functions are performed on Datakit transport service. The version of Datakit supported by AT&T Information Systems is ISN (Information System Network).

data link control (DLC) (n., adj.) Characters that perform various transmission functions in data communications, including connection, initiation, termination, and error checking.

data link layer (n.) The second-lowest layer in the OSI model responsible for assembling and disassembling data packets sent over a network.

data processing (n.) Performing a systematic sequence of operations on data for future use, output, storage, or analysis.

data rate (n.) The speed at which data flows. This is often a critical measurement when dealing with streams of audio or video information that require high bandwidth and that must not be interrupted. See Data Rate Conversion Table.

data service unit (DSU) (n.) A converter that translates digital data from an RS-232 interface or a V.35 interface on a router into an encoded format that may be transmitted over a T1 line connecting a wide area network. It allows connection of data terminal equipment (DTE) to digital services.

data set (n.) 1. Synonym for *modem.* 2. Another term for *file.*

data stream (n.) A flow of digital information that is time-stamped. An audio sample be-

---

Data Rate Conversion Table

The following table shows the conversion of data rates between Kilobytes per second (KBps) and Megabits per second (Mbps). To compute the Mbps, multiply KBps times 0.008192.

Kilobytes/sec	Megabits/sec	Kilobytes/sec	Megabits/sec
30 KB/sec	.2458 Mb/sec	220 KB/sec	1.802 Mb/sec
40 KB/sec	.3277 Mb/sec	230 KB/sec	1.884 Mb/sec
50 KB/sec	.4096 Mb/sec	240 KB/sec	1.967 Mb/sec
60 KB/sec	.4915 Mb/sec	250 KB/sec	2.048 Mb/sec
70 KB/sec	.5734 Mb/sec	275 KB/sec	2.253 Mb/sec
80 KB/sec	.6554 Mb/sec	300 KB/sec	2.458 Mb/sec
90 KB/sec	.7373 Mb/sec	325 KB/sec	2.662 Mb/sec
100 KB/sec	.8192 Mb/sec	350 KB/sec	2.867 Mb/sec
110 KB/sec	.9011 Mb/sec	375 KB/sec	3.072 Mb/sec
120 KB/sec	.9830 Mb/sec	400 KB/sec	3.277 Mb/sec
130 KB/sec	1.065 Mb/sec	450 KB/sec	3.686 Mb/sec
140 KB/sec	1.147 Mb/sec	500 KB/sec	4.096 Mb/sec
150 KB/sec	1.229 Mb/sec	600 KB/sec	4.915 Mb/sec
160 KB/sec	1.311 Mb/sec	700 KB/sec	5.734 Mb/sec
170 KB/sec	1.393 Mb/sec	800 KB/sec	6.554 Mb/sec
180 KB/sec	1.475 Mb/sec	900 KB/sec	7.373 Mb/sec
190 KB/sec	1.556 Mb/sec	1000 KB/sec	8.192 Mb/sec
200 KB/sec	1.638 Mb/sec	1200 KB/sec	9.830 Mb/sec
210 KB/sec	1.720 Mb/sec	1500 KB/sec	12.288 Mb/sec

comes a data stream when it is played back in real time. Streaming media types include animations and video clips.

data striping (n., v.) Segmenting logically sequential data so that it may be written to multiple disk drives in a round-robin fashion. If a processor is capable of reading or writing data faster than a single disk can supply or accept it, data striping speeds up data transfer. While data is moved from the first disk, the second disk locates the next segment. Data striping is used in redundant arrays of independent disks (RAID).

data suit (n.) A body suit with electrodes that a user wears when exploring a virtual world. This is an extension of the data glove idea.

data terminal equipment (DTE) (n.) Any computer or device that sends and receives data and that is connected to a modem or to some other data communications equipment

(DCE). The designation as either DTE or DCE determines the role of the device on the network.

data warehouse (n.) A system that stores, retrieves, and manages large quantities of data. In business applications, this often refers to a vast accumulation of information that may be used to project or assess business activities comprehensively.

daughterboard (n.) An auxiliary circuit board that plugs into a connector on a motherboard or adapter card, adding functionality.

DAVIC See *Digital Audio Visual Council.*

dB See *decibel.*

DB connector (n.) Data bus connector; a data bus hardware link that is available in a variety of configurations. The initials *DB* are followed by a number that indicates how many pins, or

Male   Female

DB connectors

wires, may be connected. Common types of connectors are DB-9, DB-15, DB-19, DB-25, DB-37, and DB-50. Standards have been established that define pin assignments to ensure compatibility among hardware manufacturers. See figure.

DBMS See *database management system.*

DB-9 plug (n.) A nine-pin RS-232C serial port, such as the one found on an IBM-compatible computer or a Sony videotape deck.

DBS See *Direct Broadcast Satellite.*

DC See *direct current.*

DCC See *Direct Client-to-Client.*

DC-continuous (adj.) Describes metallic circuits provided by a telephone company with direct current continuity. The Bell 43401 publication defines requirements for transmission over this type of circuit.

DCE See *data communications equipment* or *distributed computing environment.*

D-channel (n.) The channel that carries control signals and call data in a packet-switched mode via an ISDN interface. It typically operates at 16 kilobits per second (Kbps) over a Basic Rate Interface (BRI), with 9600 bits per second (bps) available for a voice link.

DCI See *Display Control Interface.*

DCT See *discrete cosine transform.*

DCT coefficient (n.) Discrete cosine transform coefficient; output amplitude of an input signal in video capture. An eight-block-by-eight-block sample is translated into 64 two-dimensional spatial frequencies that define the spectrum of the input signal. The value of each coefficient is defined by the 64-point input signal and can be regarded as the relative amount of the two-dimensional spatial frequencies contained in the signal.

DDC See *Display Data Channel.*

DDE See *dynamic data exchange.*

DDP See *distributed data processing.*

DDR See *digital disk recorder.*

DDS See *Digital Dataphone Service.*

dead tree edition (n.) Jargon for the paper version of a publication available in an electronic format.

debug (v.) To isolate and correct errors or malfunctions in computer software or hardware.

DEC See *Digital Equipment Corporation.*

DEC Alpha (n.) Digital Equipment Corporation Alpha; a reduced instruction set computing (RISC) microprocessor made by DEC with a minimum clock speed of 200 MHz used in workstations.

decibel (dB) (n.) 1. In acoustics, a unit used to measure the amplitude of sound. 2. In audio engineering, a unit that expresses the difference in intensity between two signals. The dB system provides information about the ratio of two powers. If the ratio between the power of two signals is two to one, there is a difference of 3 decibels between them. In 1939, the electronics industry adopted a standard value for 0 dB—a 1-milliwatt reference signal at

1000 Hz in a 600-ohm line. This .001-watt reference, known as *dBm,* represents a level of 0.7746 volts.

decimate (v.) To discard portions of a signal in order to reduce the amount of information to be encoded or compressed. Lossy compression algorithms ordinarily decimate while subsampling.

decoder (n.) Any hardware or software system that translates data streams into video or audio information.

decompression (n.) The process of restoring compressed data to its original condition.

decrement (v.) To decrease one step at a time.

decryption (n.) A procedure used in cryptography to translate encrypted data into readable text.

dedicated (adj.) Describes any computing system that performs one function exclusively.

dedicated line (n.) A telephone line leased to connect two users permanently. The line could be a voice-grade connection over ordinary public switched circuits, or it could be specified for encoded digital signals at faster rates. It is different from a dialup connection, which is only opened when either end requests service.

DEF See *Data Exchange Format.*

default (n.) The standard setting of an optional parameter. Factory defaults are the original settings for most equipment.

Defense Advanced Research Projects Agency (DARPA) (n.) A U.S. government agency that funded research for the ARPANET and the Internet.

defragment (defrag) (v.) To place all data on a hard disk in contiguous sectors, avoiding gaps between parts of a file or pieces of files spread geographically on the disk. When audio or video is digitized directly to a disk, the disk must be defragmented so that a continuous stream of data may be recorded on it.

degauss (v.) To remove a magnetic field.

DEK See *data encryption key.*

delete (v.) To make a file inaccessible. Data in the file allocation table (FAT) is all that is usually removed. The file's contents still exist on the storage medium and can often be recovered.

delimiter (n.) Any character or symbol that marks the beginning or end of a data segment. The angle brackets that surround HTML tags (<...>) are delimiters.

delivery system (n.) Combined hardware and software used to present or play back media, whether they be audio, video, text, images, or a combination of data types in an interactive environment.

delta (n.) A small quantitative change; the difference between two states.

delta modulation (n.) A process for converting analog audio to a digital form, similar to pulse code modulation (PCM). Delta modulation is the sampling of an audio signal at 32 Kbps at 1-bit resolution, as opposed to creating eight 8-bit samples per second in PCM at the rate of 64 Kbps.

delta YUV (DYUV) (n.) A digital video compression format that measures the differences between adjacent pixels, rather than differences between consecutive frames. If the contrast between adjacent pixels is high, definition is lost. CD-i employs DYUV compression. Because normal vision is less sensitive to color than to intensity, DYUV encodes luminance (Y) information at full bandwidth and encodes chrominance (UV) information at half bandwidth, then stores the difference, or delta, between adjacent values.

demarcation point (n.) Point of interconnection between telephone company communications facilities and terminal equipment or wiring on the customer's premises. Carrier-installed facilities at the demarcation point consist of a wire or a jack. From that point on, the wiring and equipment are the customer's responsibility.

demodulation (n.) Process of retrieving an original signal from a modulated carrier wave. This is the technique used in data sets to make communications signals compatible with machine signals. See also *modem*.

demonstration right (n.) The right to display a copyrighted work publicly. Contractors who create work for hire can preserve these rights for the purpose of showing their work to prospective clients.

demo reel (n.) An audio tape or videotape with samples of a performer's work.

demultiplex (v.) To separate two or more signals previously combined by compatible multiplexing equipment. The device that pulls the streams of data out of a larger data stream is called a *demultiplexer,* or *DEMUX*.

DEN See *Directory Enabled Network.*

Dense Wave Division Multiplexing (DWDM) (n.) A protocol for transmitting data over optical connections.

density (n.) In reference to storage, the degree to which data is spatially distributed on a storage medium. Higher density indicates more compact storage.

depth cueing (n.) In three-dimensional graphics creation, a process that creates the illusion that objects fade into the distance.

depth of field (n.) A range in which all objects located at different distances from the camera appear in focus in the viewfinder. This range varies with the distance between camera and subject, the focal length of the camera lens, and the aperture setting.

dequantization (n.) A process that reverses quantization, in which many points are mapped to one point. Information lost in that mapping cannot be completely recovered in dequantization.

derivative product (n.) A work that adapts material from a previous creation. The original creator owns and may license the rights to derivative products.

DES See *Data Encryption Standard.*

desktop (n.) In a graphical user interface (GUI), the background screen on which icons and menus appear.

desktop computer (n.) A microcomputer that fits on top of a desk. Desktop systems have become popular for publishing and for audio or video production because of the miniaturization and proliferation of peripherals.

Desktop Management Task Force (DMTF) (n.) Industry consortium that sets standards for defining and controlling components on a network.

desktop publishing (DTP) (n.) A broad term for the use of a microcomputer with software to create text and graphics for print. Desktop publishing implies the use of page-layout programs.

desktop video (n.) Video that is created, edited, produced, or viewed on a microcomputer system.

destructor (n.) A function provided by a class in the C++ programming language that is used to delete an object.

Deutsche Industrie Norm (DIN, pronounced "DIHN") (n.) A type of connecting plug and mating socket with numerous pins that enables a single connector to handle more than one function or channel. A MIDI cable has a five-pin DIN plug on each end. See figure.

five-pin DIN plug

developer (n.) A person or company that creates an entertaining, educational, or informational product, such as a game, a web site, or a reference CD-ROM.

device control character (n.) Typically refers to one of four ASCII characters: DC1, DC2, DC3, or DC4. The characters are usually paired, such as DC1/DC3 to switch a device off and on (quit/start).

device driver (n.) A software program that

controls data transfer between a computer and a peripheral device, such as a printer, CD-ROM, or cartridge drive. It may control internal system features, such as digital video or audio playback.

device-independent bitmap (DIB) (n.) An image format with universal transportability. In this format, the sequence in which pixels appear and their bit depth are not specifically related to their layout in a specific device. A device-dependent bitmap (DDB) image may be converted to the DIB format without loss of information.

DFT See *Discrete Fourier Transform.*

DHCP See *Dynamic Host Configuration Protocol.*

Dhrystone (n.) Benchmarking program that evaluates all aspects of a computer system's performance except for floating-point math performance. The program is used for measuring the processor's performance, and because it makes no operating system calls, measurements of hardware performance are not influenced by system configuration.

diagnostic (n.) 1. A procedure for evaluating software and hardware performance in order to troubleshoot computer systems. 2. An application that automates the scheduled maintenance and repair of complex systems.

dialog (n.) A question-and-answer session between an operator and a computer program that occurs in a *dialog box* in which the user chooses an option or enters data. Interaction between an operator and technology is called a *dialog.*

dialup (adj.) Describes the connection made between computers via phone lines and modems. In general usage, the term refers to the kind of connection made when using a terminal emulator and a regular modem (switched character-oriented asynchronous communication). The term also describes a port that accepts dialup connections. A dialup connection is referred to as a *dialup line.* Likewise, an online service or Internet Service Provider that offers dialup connectivity is said to offer *dialup service.* Any line or connection that can be addressed by modem and that is established by a switched-circuit connection using the telephone system fits this description.

DIB See *device-independent bitmap.*

die (n.) 1. A rectangular piece of semiconductor material onto which electronic circuits have been fabricated. 2. A semiconductor that is not yet packaged.

differential line (n.) A two-wire electrical connection in which one wire carries the original signal (+) and the other wire carries an inverted version (-) of the signal. The receiver of a signal sent over this type of line subtracts the inverted signal from the normal signal, resulting in a signal proportional to the original. Transmission noise induced in the wires is canceled in this process. The RS-422 standard specifies differential drivers and receivers, but the RS-232 standard does not.

differential phase shift keying (DPSK) (n.) A modulation technique used in modems.

digerati (n.) Analogous to *literati,* jargon that refers to computer-savvy individuals.

digital (adj.) Describes anything that uses discrete numerical values to represent data or signals (as opposed to a continuously fluctuating flow of current or voltage). A computer processes digital data representing text, sound, pictures, animations, or video content. Compare *analog.*

digital audio (n.) Audio program material represented by binary code rather than by an analog recording. Analog audio is converted to digital audio using sampling techniques that store a numerical definition of the signal in an ordered sequence of discrete samples. An acoustic waveform is sampled thousands of times each second when it is stored digitally. This value is the *sample rate.* Each sample represents the intensity or pressure of the wave at that instant. Another parameter is the number of bits used to sample, or the *bit rate.* Audio may be encoded in linear, logarithmic, or mu-law formats. Common file name extensions for audio are .wav or .snd (MS Windows or DOS), .au (Unix), and AIFF (Macintosh). Higher sampling rates and bit rates result in a more accurate digital representation of the signal. In order to reproduce digital audio, a digital-to-analog converter (DAC) is required.

digital audio tape (DAT, pronounced "DAHT") (n.) Developed through a collaboration between Sony and Philips in the mid-1980s, a format for storing digital audio files on magnetic tape. The complete name is *R-DAT,* where *R* stands for rotary heads in the recorder or player. In addition to storing music, the DAT format records subcode information, such as the track number and absolute time calculated from the beginning of the tape. Up to 120 minutes of signal may be recorded on a single tape. Recording studios use DAT tapes for masters because the signal-to-noise ratio is so high and because duplicates can be made with no degradation. The DAT specification defines the following modes and characteristics:

1. Two channel, 48-kHz or 44.1-kHz sample rate, 16-bit linear encoding, 120 minutes,

frequency response 2–22 kHz (±0.5 dB), SN = 93 dB, DR = 93 dB

2. Two channel, 32-kHz sample rate, 12-bit nonlinear encoding, 240 minutes, frequency response 2–14.5 kHz (±0.5 dB), SN = 92 dB, DR = 92 dB

Digital Audio Visual Council (DAVIC) (n.) An international group of approximately 250 companies developing an "end-to-end" standard for interactive digital media, including interfaces and requirements for applications, systems, and networks. The group includes members of the original MPEG Joint Technical Committee (JTC).

digital carrier (n.) Any medium that transmits digital signals, similar to the physical layer of the OSI network model. Carriers may be baseband or broadband.

digital compositing (n.) The art of combining video frames as digital signals rather than as analog signals. This allows computer images to be applied to video frames. Most current offline systems incorporate digital video frames and animations.

Digital Dataphone Service (DDS) (n.) A telecommunications network that typically transmits synchronous data at 56 kilobits per second (Kbps), requiring special interface equipment at both ends.

digital delay (n.) An audio effects processor that samples sounds, stores them digitally, and outputs them at a user-specified duration after the input. It has an effect similar to reverb when a short delay (less than 100 milliseconds) is selected. It can be used to repeat words or entire phrases when a delay of several seconds is selected.

digital disk recorder (DDR) (n.) A device that postproduction studios often use to record frames of video or animation because they have hardware that is capable of capturing a large field of data at once. Abekas is a popular brand of DDR.

Digital Equipment Corporation (DEC, pronounced "DECK") (n.) Makers of the VAX computer and VMS operating system.

digital linear tape (DLT) (n.) A magnetic tape storage technology developed by Digital Equipment Corporation (DEC) and later sold to Quantum. DLT reads and writes half-inch, single-hub cartridges that hold up to 35 gigabytes (GB). Since 1995, DLT has been employed widely as a backup system for large local area networks (LANs).

digital loop carrier (DLC) (n.) The optical fiber component of the local telephone network. DLC systems are deployed between central offices and access nodes from which copper lines run to end users. More than 50 percent of all new lines built each year are DLCs. The capacity to integrate Asymmetric Digital Subscriber Line (ADSL) into a DLC makes this service available to a much wider range of customers.

Digital Multiplexed Interface (DMI) (n.) A voice and data private automatic branch exchange (PABX) standard for the use of T1 transmission with 64-kilobit-per-second (Kbps) channels, allowing a more open ISDN architecture.

digital satellite system (DSS) (n.) Marketed to consumers as an alternative to cable television, a satellite-receiving system with a dish about 18 inches in diameter that can be used to tune into a wide range of microwave frequencies.

digital service (DS) (n.) A level and framing

83

specification for synchronous data streams sent over circuits in the North American digital transmission hierarchy. This generally refers to T1, with a transmission rate of 1.544 kilobits per second (Kbps). The transmission is bipolar with a 50 percent duty-cycle signal. Telecommunications lines for data transmission have rates of data transfer specified at predetermined levels. Examples of the common transfer rates for various levels of service are shown in the following list:

DS-0   64 kilobits per second (Kbps), the standard speed for one channel.

DS-1   1.544 megabits per second (Mbps) in North America, 2.048 Mbps elsewhere.

DS-1C   3.152 Mbps in North America over T1.

DS-2   6.312 Mbps in North America over T2.

DS-3   44.736 Mbps, equal to 28 T1 channels, over T3.

DS-4   273 Mbps over a T4 facility.

Selected terms are defined in the following list:

- **DS-0** (n.) A digital service (DS) level zero, the standard specification for digitizing voice at 64 kilobits per second (Kbps) using pulse code modulation (PCM). DS-0 is multiplied in DS-1 and higher levels.

- **DS-1** (n.) A digital service (DS) level and a framing specification for digital signals in the North American digital transmission hierarchy over a T1 line. A DS-1 signal carries 24 voice channels encoded at 64 kilobits per second (Kbps) at a transmission rate of 1.544 megabits per second (Mbps).

- **DS-1C** (n.) A digital service (DS) level and a framing specification for digital signals

in the North American digital transmission hierarchy carried on T1. A DS-1C signal uses 48 pulse code modulation (PCM) channels and has a transmission rate of 3.152 megabits per second (Mbps), twice that of DS-1. DS-1C uses two DS-1 signals that are combined and sent on a 3.152-Mbps carrier, which allows 64 kilobits per second (Kbps) for synchronization and framing using "pulse stuffing." The channel 2 signal is logically inverted, and a framing bit is stuffed in two out of three code words, resulting in 26-bit information units. The channels are interleaved and then scrambled by the addition modulo 2 of the signal with the previous bit. Finally, the bitstream is combined with a control bit sequence that permits the demultiplexer to function by preceding every 52 bits with one DS-1C framing bit. A series of 24 such 53-bit frames forms a 1272-bit "M-frame."

- **DS-2** (n.) A digital service (DS) level and a framing specification for digital signals in the North American digital transmission hierarchy. A DS-2 signal uses 96 pulse code modulation (PCM) channels and has a transmission rate of 6.312 megabits per second (Mbps), twice that of DS-1C.

- **DS-3** (n.) The third digital service (DS) level and a framing specification for digital signals in the North American digital transmission hierarchy. A DS-3 signal has a transmission rate of 44.736 megabits per second (Mbps). DS-3 is used on T3 synchronous ISDN lines, for example.

digital service unit (DSU) (n.) Hardware that provides digital transmission between a channel service unit (CSU) and data terminal equipment (DTE), such as a modem that connects analog devices. The DSU transmitter processes the signal into bipolar pulses suitable for transmission over a digital facility. The DSU receiver extracts timing information and data from the bipolar signal.

digital signal processor (DSP) (n.) An integrated circuit (IC) that performs complex operations on data. The data processed is usually an audio signal in the form of a digitized waveform. Effects processors, which are common types of DSPs, perform functions such as digital delay, reverb, filtering, equalization, and stereo chorusing. The term is not limited to audio processing; it also applies to the treatment of video and other data types.

digital signature (n.) Data added to a message that authenticates the sender's identity through public key encryption. The sender uses a one-way hash function to generate a hash code of about 32 bits from the message data. The sender then encrypts the hash code with a private key. The receiver recomputes the hash code from the data and decrypts the received hash code with the sender's public key. If the two hash codes are equal, the receiver can be sure that data has not been corrupted and that it came from the given sender.

Digital Subscriber Line (DSL) (n.) A twisted-pair copper wire connection with a special modem at either end that filters out background noise and interference and allows high-speed data transfer. It is limited to a transmission distance of 18 000 feet. ISDN is a DSL application with a transfer rate of 160 kilobits per second (Kbps), which far exceeds the peak rate of 33.6 Kbps upstream that analog modems can achieve. Typically, High-Data-Rate DSL (HDSL) is used to implement T1 connections. The Asymmetric DSL (ADSL) application is a further advance in this technology, supporting up to nine megabits per second (Mbps) throughput, compared with

the maximum of 2.048 Mbps handled by ISDN.

digital switching (n.) A connection in which binary-encoded information is routed between an input and an output port by means of time division multiplexing (TDM) rather than with a dedicated circuit.

digital-to-analog (D/A, pronounced "DEE-to-AY") (adj.) A circuit that interprets data that represents changes in motion, pressure, or light over time and that converts such data into voltages that change over time.

Digital Versatile Disc See *DVD*.

digital videocassette (DVC) (n.) 1. A consumer tape format that records video and audio signals digitally for high resolution and lossless dubbing to another tape. This video data may be stored on a hard drive for nonlinear editing and transferred directly over the FireWire interface. 2. A video storage medium that uses 0.25-inch metal tape with a digital format similar to that of CCIR-601, combined with an adapted form of JPEG compression.

Digital Video Disc See *DVD*.

Digital Video Interactive (DVI) (n.) Developed at RCA's David Sarnoff Research Center and subsequently purchased and marketed by Intel Corporation, a technology that allows realtime compression-decompression and display of full-motion video with audio using hardware assistance on desktop computers. The highest video quality, known as Production Level Video (PLV), is achieved by using offline, nonrealtime compression on powerful parallel processing computers. Lesser-quality Real-Time Video (RTV) compression may be achieved on a desktop computer. Although the quality of DVI is high and although it is ca-

D

pable of 100:1 compression ratios, the proprietary hardware decoder board is not in widespread use and is not expected to be a platform of future development.

digitize (v.) 1. To encode images or sound in a format that may be processed by a computer. 2. To convert analog information, such as an audio signal, into digital data.

DIMM See *dual in-line memory module.*

DIN See *Deutsche Industrie Norm.*

DIP switch (n.) Dual in-line package switch; a miniature two-position switch mounted on a circuit board to set parameters or control functions. Pronounced "DIP." See figure.

DIP switch

Direct Broadcast Satellite (DBS) (n.) 1. System of transmitting digital video directly to the home via a 200-watt, high-powered satellite for reception by a small, relatively inexpensive antenna. The programming is transmitted or broadcast by satellite directly to the subscribers' premises. Ground distribution or reception equipment is only used in the uplink process to the satellite or at the subscribers' premises. Also called *Direct Satellite Service (DSS)* or *Direct-to-Home Satellite Service.* Hughes Electronics DirecTV is a well-known DBS service provider. 2. A receiver, repeater, or regenerator for microwave signals in geosynchronous orbit typically 22 300 miles above the surface of Earth. The footprint at this distance is approximately one-third of the globe.

Direct Client-to-Client (DCC) (n.) A feature of Internet Relay Chat (IRC) client software that allows users to bypass the server, sending and receiving messages and files directly. This protocol protects users from being monitored by an IRC server operator. DCC commands include DCC CHAT, DCC SEND, and DCC GET.

direct current (DC) (n.) A flow of electrons that moves in one direction at a relatively constant rate through a wire or a circuit. Batteries deliver DC voltage. See also *alternating current.*

direct draw (n.) A graphics feature of Windows 95 that permits rapid calls to the display, rather than routing the calls through the graphical device interface.

direct memory access (DMA) (n.) In computing, the process of moving data to and from memory without routing it through the central processing unit (CPU).

directory (n.) A listing of information about data files and their locations on a storage medium. In the logical format of a hard disk, a floppy disk, or a CD-ROM, this "branch" of the information tree contains other directories (subdirectories) and files.

Directory Access Protocol (DAP) (n.) Based on the X.500 standard, a protocol used for communication between a Directory User Agent (DUA) and a Directory System Agent (DSA).

Directory Enabled Network (DEN) (n.) A framework for storing information about routers, switches, and other network components within a centralized directory. It is useful for managing network equipment, controlling traffic, and setting security and usage policies. Microsoft and Cisco Systems collaborated on the DEN proposal for Windows NT 5.0.

directory service (n.) Networking software that has the capacity to provide information about resources available on the network, including files, printers, data sources, applications, or other users. It provides users with access to resources and information located on extended networks.

Directory System Agent (DSA) (n.) Software that provides directory service for a portion of an organization's directory information.

Directory User Agent (DUA) (n.) Software that accesses directory services for the directory user or for a search engine.

Direct Satellite Service (DSS) (n.) Broadcast of signals straight from a satellite source to a dish, commonly used as an alternative to cable television (CATV). DSS offers a wide variety of programming choices, as well as high-resolution video and audio.

Direct3D (n.) The three-dimensional Application Programming Interface (API) that is part of the DirectX package for multimedia applications. Direct3D was developed by Microsoft.

DirecTV (n.) A dish and decoding system that receives television channels by satellite transmission rather than by cable. See also *Direct Broadcast Satellite*.

DirectX (n.) A software developers kit (SDK) for the Microsoft Windows 95 programming interface standard. It gives programmers a standard way to access enhanced hardware features directly without using the Windows 95 Graphics Device Interface (GDI). DirectX improves performance in graphics with DirectDraw, in audio with DirectSound, and in handling input from devices with DirectIn. It improves multimedia performance, provided that all of the hardware and software involved supports DirectX.

disc (n.) Any thin, round platter that stores various types of information in analog or digital formats. It is often used as the short form for CD-ROM, laser disc (analog videodisc), or compact disc–digital audio (CD-DA). The data is written in a spiral from the center to the edge. Data on a disc is read by an optical sensor that picks up reflections from a laser beam. Not to be confused with the magnetic storage medium, which is called a *disk*.

disc geography (n.) The relative location of files, applications, or media assets and data on discs. Closer proximity of related segments results in faster access time. See figure on following page.

discrete (adj.) In digital applications, describes separate and distinct pieces of data, each of which may be part of a larger stream of information.

discrete access (n.) In network technology, an access method that requires each workstation to have a separate, individual connection to the host. Compare *shared access*.

discrete cosine transform (DCT) (n.) A video-encoding technique that uses the same approach that Fourier transform uses for audio encoding. DCT reduces the data required to represent color or grayscale levels in a video signal, applying equations that require very few pieces of information to identify the content.

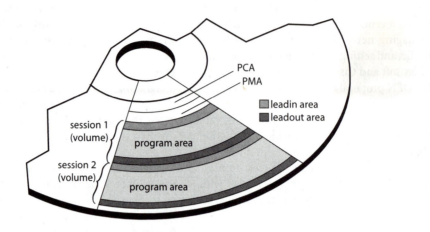

session 1
(volume)

session 2
(volume)

program area

program area

PCA
PMA

leadin area
leadout area

geography of a multisession disc

Discrete Fourier Transform (DFT) (n.) A Fourier transform frequently used in signal processing, particularly in analyzing and compressing video and audio files. One implementation of the DFT is the Fast Fourier Transform (FFT). See also *discrete cosine transform*.

Discrete Multi-Tone (DMT) (n.) A digital modulation scheme that uses digital signal processors (DSPs) to transfer more than 6 megabits per second (Mbps) of data over a single copper twisted pair.

discrete wavelet transformation (DWT) (n.) A video compression algorithm in which spatial data is converted to frequency data and assigned to quadrants.

disk (n.) A circular, enclosed magnetic storage medium on which information may be accessed randomly, as opposed to sequentially. Floppy disks are small, portable storage vehicles; hard disks, or fixed disks, are capable of storing more data. Not to be confused with the optical storage medium, which is called a *disc*.

disk cache (n.) A segment of RAM that speeds up access to data on a disk drive. It holds a copy of recently read data from the disk, including sector information, anticipating that it will be needed again soon.

disk mirroring (n.) The process of writing a pair of disks simultaneously, providing a mirror-image backup if one disk fails. Both disks attach to a host controller.

Disk Operating System (DOS, pronounced "DOSS") (n.) 1. A computing environment designed for use with a floppy or hard disk. It permits data to be transferred between a computer's memory and disk storage. 2. The Microsoft DOS (MS-DOS) designed for the IBM PC and compatibles.

disk spanning (n.) The method of attaching multiple drives to a single host adapter whereby all of the drives appear as a single, contiguous, logical unit.

disk striping (n.) The writing of data across

multiple disks rather than on one drive. Data is divided into segments, each of which is written to successive drives. Disks are striped when used in an array, and this allows data to be written faster.

display (n.) A video monitor device, or cathode-ray tube (CRT), which presents numbers, characters, graphics, video, or any other visual information.

Display Control Interface (DCI) (n.) In an IBM-compatible computer video system, an enhancement that moves graphic data directly to the video card, bypassing the processor.

Display Data Channel (DDC) (n.) Standard proposed by the Video Electronics Standards Association (VESA) for bidirectional communication between computer monitors and video adapters. According to this specification, a video monitor sends an Extended Display Identification (EDID) message continuously to the video adapter. The EDID contains information about the monitor's characteristics. This information includes bandwidth, refresh rates for screen resolutions, dot pitch, support for Display Power Management Signaling (DPMS), and identifying data. This standard is intended to allow a video card to support the monitor as well as possible. Standard software utilities are implemented to control the monitor's settings. DDC uses the ACCESS.bus to communicate with the card, and some models offer an extra port on this bus for connecting other peripherals.

display order (n.) The order in which digital video frames should be shown. It is usually the same as the order of input to the encoder, which is typically sequential.

dissolve (n., v.) The gradual disintegration of a video image, or a means of transition to an-other frame. Fade-outs and fade-ins are examples of dissolves to and from a black screen. Dissolves between two video clips require two source VCRs in an A-B roll configuration.

distance learning (n.) Any learning that occurs at a site other than the classroom where an instructor is located. The term is often associated with the transmission of satellite or cable television courses for education and training. The meaning has expanded to encompass many training activities and other technologies. It is assumed that guidance and coursework are specified by an instructional program and that the activity is structured, as opposed to being a self-motivated independent study without external influence. Other terms for this type of education are *flexible learning, student-based learning,* and *student-centered learning.* The latter is particularly accurate, in that it identifies the student's location as the learning site. It is common for student-centered learning activities to occur on a campus where classroom activities are enhanced by network access and other learning technologies that students access in a library or computer lab.

distance vector protocol (n.) A protocol that runs on a local area network (LAN) router to minimize the number of link-level connections, or hops, a data packet must make as it travels between originating and terminating devices.

distortion (n.) Any alteration in an audio waveform, causing frequencies at the output of a signal-processing device that were not present at input. It typically occurs when a signal is digitally processed or amplified.

distributed computing environment (DCE) (n.) Standard conventions and server functionalities as established and promoted by

D

the Open Software Foundation (OSF), a consortium led by IBM, Digital Equipment Corporation (DEC), and Hewlett-Packard. It offers an architecture of standard programming interfaces for distributing applications over heterogeneous networks.

distributed database (n.) A combination of multiple databases that appears to a user to be one database. The Internet domain name system (DNS) is an example.

distributed data processing (DDP) (n.) The use of more than one networked computer to run an application at multiple sites simultaneously.

distributed file system (n.) A file system that accesses data from remote locations across a network. It recognizes multiple servers, manages itself, and can be accessed from any location on the network.

distribution amplifier (DA) (n.) In video postproduction, a device that delivers a signal to multiple receiving machines.

distribution segment (n.) A television cable that extends from a trunk to a feeder cable. Homes that are within 500 feet of a distribution segment may have a direct drop, which leads from a tap on the feeder to the home.

dithering (n.) A form of smart conversion from a higher bit depth to a lower bit depth used in audio and graphics files. The process attempts to improve the perceived quality of onscreen graphics when the color palette is reduced. In the conversion from 24-bit color to 8-bit color (in which millions of colors are reduced to 256 colors), dithering adds patterns of different-colored pixels to simulate the original color. The technique is also known as *error diffusion* and is applied to both audio bit rate reduction and graphics resolution. See figure.

dithered image

DLC See *data link control* or *digital loop carrier.*

DLL See *dynamic link library.*

DLS See *downloadable sound.*

DLT See *digital linear tape.*

DMA See *direct memory access.*

DMA channel (n.) Direct memory access channel; a logical pathway in a microcomputer for exchanging data between peripherals and memory or just between peripherals without passing the data through the central processing unit (CPU).

DMI See *Digital Multiplexed Interface.*

DMT See *Discrete Multi-Tone.*

DMTF See *Desktop Management Task Force.*

DNS See *domain name system.*

docking station (n.) A base unit into which a notebook computer may be inserted, providing access to desktop peripherals and accessories.

documentation (n.) Materials, such as an instruction manual, that explain how to operate software or hardware. There is a trend toward putting documentation online.

Document Type Definition (DTD) (n.) A refinement of the Standard Generalized Markup Language (SGML) stating the official rules by which a particular type of document is to be interpreted. The HTML DTD was designed by Tim Berners-Lee and Dan Connolly to identify the unique features of HTML.

dolby noise reduction (n.) A process that increases the signal-to-noise ratio by raising the volume of quiet passages during recording and by lowering them to their original levels during playback. The lowering reduces noise, such as tape hiss, that may be introduced during recording. See figure.

dolly (n.) In video production, a camera support mounted on wheels that permits smooth movement in any direction.

domain (n.) In an Internet address, the part of the naming hierarchy that consists of a sequence of characters separated by dots. The five most common types of domains are .com for company, .org for nonprofit organization, .edu for educational institution, .net for network operations, and .gov for government agency. The domains are administered by Internet Network Information Center (InterNIC), and each has a primary and secondary domain name server associated with it. The primary domain name system (DNS) is located on a machine in the associated network, and the server may be determined through the "nslookup" command. Country domains are common, such as uk (United Kingdom) and au (Australia). See *Internet country code* for a complete listing.

domain name (n.) The text name corresponding to the numeric Internet Protocol (IP) address of a computer on the Internet. For example, *www.hansenmedia.com* is a domain name.

Loud sounds overpower the inherent noise and hiss on an audio tape. However, during soft passages the noise is much stronger in relation to the signal.

On recording, dolby processing increases the level of quiet sounds in the high-frequency range, but it does not alter loud sounds.

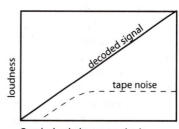

On playback the tape noise is reduced along with all the high-frequency quiet sounds that are restored to their original levels in the decoding process.

dolby signal processing

domain name lookup (n.) The process of converting a numeric Internet Protocol (IP) address into a text name. For example, 192.030 .001.002 is converted to *www.thisdomain.com.*

domain name system (DNS) (n.) A distributed database and data query service used on the Internet to translate hostnames into Internet addresses, defined in RFC 1034, STD 13 and RFC 1035. Referred to as *resolution,* the translation enables users to keep their domain names, even though the server's Internet Protocol (IP) address could change. DNS may be configured to use a sequence of name servers in a query, predicated on domains in the name for which it is searching, until it finds a match. DNS may be queried interactively using the command "nslookup." The phrase refers to naming conventions for hosts, servers, and clients on the Internet.

domestic market (n.) The consumer market in a particular country or geographic area, as opposed to the industrial or professional markets.

D1 format (n.) Developed by the Society of Motion Picture and Television Engineers (SMPTE), a component digital videotape format that is a professional recording standard based on the CCIR-601 recommendation. The format separates the signal into one brightness channel and two color channels (Y, R-Y, B-Y). The tape is 19 mm wide and a single cassette holds up to 94 minutes of program material. Using this format, it is possible to dub multiple copies without a noticeable loss of quality in successive generations.

dongle (n.) 1. Jargon for *server key,* a small piece of hardware connected to the serial port that permits a secure application to run. 2. An adapter or connector that interfaces video monitors or peripherals. 3. A small DB-25 connector shell that contains EPROM and drivers. The dongle must be connected to an I/O computer port while the program that requires

it is running. A dongle provides security and copy protection for commercial software.

DOS See *Disk Operating System.*

DOSKey (n.) Disk Operating System key; a utility program that permits a user to customize MS-DOS commands, create stored macros, type more than one DOS command on a line, and personalize the computing environment.

DOS Protected Mode Interface (DPMI) (n.) The required method by which a DOS program accesses extended memory in the Microsoft Windows environment. The service is provided by the HIMEM.SYS driver.

dot matrix 1. (n.) A two-dimensional pattern of dots that defines graphic elements. 2. (adj., dot-matrix) Describes a type of computer printer that uses pins to print dots on paper. The combined dots form text characters and graphic images.

dot pitch (n.) The smallest distance between adjacent points of color on a monitor. A small dot pitch means that the image is sharp.

dots per inch (dpi) (n.) A measurement of resolution that defines the output of a display or printer. A screen font usually appears at 72 dpi, whereas a laser printer usually prints at 300 dpi minimally.

double buffering (n.) The process of writing a graphical frame into memory at the same time that another frame is being displayed. It allows smoother transitions between frames in an animation.

double-speed (adj.) Describes second-generation CD-ROM drives that transfer data at twice the rate of single-speed drives. Double-speed drives should technically be capable of a data transfer rate of approximately 300 kilobytes per second (KBps), whereas single-speed drives transfer data at 150 KBps.

downlink 1. (n.) A transmission link from a satellite to an Earth station. 2. (v.) To receive signals from a satellite broadcast with a microwave dish.

download (v.) To transfer data or code from one computer to another, typically from a large host or server to a smaller client.

downloadable sound (DLS) (n.) A specification that enables a common playback experience on different delivery platforms when a General MIDI file is played. The DLS file, consisting of samples, is transmitted along with a MIDI sequence, so that a wavetable synthesizer can use the sample provided rather than one resident in its memory. Only sound cards and equipment with RAM available for storing samples to be played with a sequence can take advantage of this technology. Level 1 of the specification supports hardware with a wavetable engine that plays samples with loops. It provides 24 voices minimally at a sample rate of 22 kHz, with 512 kilobytes (KB) of storage reserved for samples. A full package may include up to 120 melodic instruments, eight sound effects (SFX), and 47 percussion sounds in a set on MIDI channel 10. This standard is implemented by the Yamaha XG and Roland GS formats.

downsample (v.) To reduce the amount of data in a stream by selecting only a percentage of the original signal, and to throw out some data to reduce the size or to meet narrow bandwidth requirements. Video signals are often downsampled during encoding.

downstream (adv.) The direction in which a signal travels from the transmitter, or origina-

tion point, to the receiving site.

downward compatible (adj.) Describes software that can be used on older computing systems and that can read files created with an earlier version of a software application.

dpi See *dots per inch.*

DPMI See *DOS Protected Mode Interface.*

DPSK See *differential phase shift keying.*

drag and drop (n.) A means of manipulating icons, text, or objects in a graphical user interface (GUI). By holding a mouse button down while moving an icon over a directory or application program and by releasing the button, a user can open a file or deposit it in the directory.

DRAM See *Dynamic RAM.*

Drawing Interchange Format (DXF) (n.) A format for computer-aided design (CAD) files developed by Autodesk for its AutoCAD program. It is platform-independent and is also called *Data Exchange Format (DEF).*

drawing program (n.) A program that produces graphical objects rather than bitmaps, which are created by painting programs. Drawing programs use mathematical formulas to define lines that can be scaled and resized without distortion.

drift (n.) Unwanted motion in horizontal lines of video. Drift occurs when an electronic component, such as a capacitor, becomes unstable, causing the image to scroll up slowly.

drill-down map (n.) A series of progressively more detailed graphics that enlarge an area of a map or of a large image. An example is an interactive city map that displays a neighborhood when the user clicks on it. A subsequent click might show a square mile in part of the neighborhood. A click on that map might bring up a square block.

drive (n.) Any hardware component of a computer system that spins and reads floppy disks, fixed disks, tapes, CD-ROMs, laser discs, or other media.

drive letter (n.) A letter of the alphabet used to identify a disk drive or peripheral connected to a microcomputer. The primary hard disk drive is generally called the *C drive,* floppy disk drives are usually *A* and *B,* and a CD-ROM drive might be *D.*

driver (n.) A software control program that integrates with the computer operating system to give instructions to and interface with a device such as a CD-ROM player or a video card.

drop (n.) Typically a copper twisted-pair or coaxial cable running from a branch of a telecommunications network to an individual customer's premises. In a cable system, a co-axial drop connects a branch of coaxial cable to a set-top box on the customer's premises or even directly to a cable-ready television set.

drop-down menu (n.) A window that pops up below a topic selected from the menu bar, offering additional choices or functions.

drop frame (n.) A time code format for video that periodically skips a pulse to account for the difference between the 30 frames per second (fps) standard and the actual 29.97 fps rate found in the NTSC format. Correction for this inconsistency is accomplished by dropping two frames each minute. Any frame can be dropped except for every tenth frame.

dropout (n.) 1. The temporary loss of signal in data transmission. By technical telephony standards, a dropout is a period of at least 4 milliseconds during which a signal has dropped more than 12 decibels. 2. Impaired signal from an analog tape playback device caused by blank spots in the tape coating, which show up on a monitor as streaks and white specks.

drop shadow (n.) A graphic effect used with typefaces to create the illusion that a light source is shining on an object or a letter from above and that a shadow is cast behind and below.

drum scanner (n.) A data-capturing device that incorporates a cylindrical drum for mounting original images.

DS See *digital service.*

DSA See *Directory System Agent.*

DSL See *Digital Subscriber Line.*

DS-0 See *digital service.*

DS-1 See *digital service.*

DS-1C See *digital service.*

DSP See *digital signal processor.*

DSS See *digital satellite system* or *Direct Satellite Service.*

DS-3 See *digital service.*

DS-2 See *digital service.*

DSU See *data service unit* or *digital service unit.*

DTD See *Document Type Definition.*

DTE See *data terminal equipment.*

D3 format (n.) The telecommunications digital service (DS) Level 1 format with 24 eight-bit channels, each of which has a bandwidth of 8 kHz. Its data rate of 1.544 megabits per second (Mbps) is an old Bell standard in North America, not the CCITT standard of 2.048 Mbps used elsewhere.

DTMF See *Dual Tone Multi-Frequency.*

DTP See *desktop publishing.*

D2 format (n.) A digital videotape composite format for mastering that permits multiple generations of dubbing without an apparent loss of picture quality. It is based on an eight-bit digital version of NTSC or Phase Alternation Line (PAL) composite video. Because D2 format is composite, it does not have the pristine quality of D1 format, which is a component digital format. The tape itself is 19 mm wide and can record up to 208 minutes of programming.

DUA See *Directory User Agent.*

dual-channel audio (n.) A system with two audio channels that can play them simultaneously or independently.

dual in-line memory module (DIMM) (n.) A high-density RAM package, similar to a single in-line memory module (SIMM), but with dual rather than single connections to the motherboard.

dual in-line package switch See *DIP switch.*

dual ported (adj.) Describes memory circuits that can be accessed simultaneously through two independent address and data buses. Such circuits are often used in video display hardware in conjunction with video RAM (VRAM).

Video display hardware can read memory to display the contents on screen while the central processing unit (CPU) writes data to other areas of memory through a different port simultaneously.

Dual Tone Multi-Frequency (DTMF) (n.) The way in which a telephone system communicates what keys are pressed when a number is dialed on a touchtone device. Each key on the telephone's numeric pad generates two tones, one defining its row and the other defining its column on the pad. The exchange decodes these to identify the key pressed.

dub (v.) 1. To copy a tape, producing a second generation. 2. To insert and combine new video or audio elements on an existing tape to produce a composite master tape.

dump (v.) 1. To transfer digital data from one source to another. 2. To remove data or to empty a container.

duplex (adj.) Describes a transmission line capable of communication in two directions simultaneously.

DVC See *digital videocassette.*

DVD (Digital Video Disc, Digital Versatile Disc) (n.) Term that loosely refers to numerous configurations that define the physical structure and the data contained on a 12 cm disc. A DVD in any of several formats contains MPEG-2 video with either AC-3 (Dolby) audio or MPEG-2 audio (common in Europe). The term *Digital Versatile Disc* was originally used to indicate that the medium may contain any type of data, not just audio and video files in a proprietary format. *DVD-ROM* is the term most often used to describe a disc formatted with a larger capacity than a CD-ROM. A DVD-ROM does not necessarily contain video data, as the words would imply.

DVD generally refers to an optical disc with multiple data layers that exceeds the capacity of a standard CD-ROM and that may contain video, audio, or any other type of digital data. In the areas of home entertainment and computer data storage, it has the capacity to replace all existing audio tape, videotape, CD-ROM, and video game formats.

The storage capacity of a DVD is greater than that of a CD-ROM because it has a laser beam with a shorter wavelength, smaller pits on the disc surface, a denser track pitch, and more efficient channel encoding. A visible red laser with a wavelength of 635 to 650 nanometers was chosen for DVD when the specification was unified from competing technologies developed by Toshiba, Sony, and Philips. The DVD specifies a laser beam of smaller diameter than the 780-nanometer infrared laser diode used by a CD-ROM. The smallest CD-ROM pits are 1.1 micrometers in diameter. The pits on a DVD are 0.4 micrometers in diameter on a single layer disc and about 10 percent larger when a second layer is used. Because a DVD has smaller pits and narrower laser beams, the tracks can be closer together. Track pitch is 0.74 micrometers on a DVD, compared with 1.6 micrometers on a CD-ROM. The modulation and encoding scheme was also modified in the DVD format to increase the density of data.

A single-layer DVD spins at a constant linear velocity (CLV) of 3.4 meters per second, approximately the same speed as an 8X CD-ROM. At this velocity, data may be extracted at a rate of 11.08 megabits per second (Mbps). The sustained audio-video media delivery rate is 9.8 Mbps, deducting overhead (formatting and private data).

DVD Configurations

- **DVD-ROM (Book A)** A high-capacity read-only optical disc capable of rapid data transfer that may be used as a general-purpose computer storage device. A DVD-ROM may hold any type of digital data and is readable by a DVD-ROM drive connected to a computer. This type of drive is basically an 8X CD-ROM drive with seven times the storage capacity. Files are stored in the Micro UDF/ISO 9660 Bridge format. DVD-ROM is an extension of the CD-ROM specification with a maximum file size of 1 gigabyte (GB).

- **DVD-Video (Book B)** A high-capacity read-only optical disc capable of rapid data transfer that is used for the interactive playback of movies and games or of other video, audio, and graphic content using the MPEG-2 video compression format. The DVD-video Book B type is played on a DVD player and viewed on a television monitor. It has become one form of a "set-top box." These discs may also be played on a computer with a special hardware decoder and supporting software.

- **DVD-Audio (Book C)** A high-capacity read-only optical disc capable of rapid data transfer that may be used for the playback of high-quality audio using 24-bit linear pulse code modulation (LPCM) sampled at 48 or 96 kilobytes per second (KBps). A widely agreed-upon audio standard among manufacturers had not yet been defined in 1998.

- **DVD-R (Book D)** A new high-capacity write-once optical disc with rapid data transfer rates that can be used as a general-purpose computer storage device. It may be recorded but not erased. It is able to read and write up to 3.9 gigabytes (GB) of data.

- **DVD-RAM (Book E)** A high-capacity read-write optical disc capable of rapid data transfer that may be used as a general-purpose computer storage device. This format allows reading, writing, and erasing. Because phase change technology is used, the capacity for data is approximately half of that of a read-only device. A DVD-RAM disc will read and write 2.6 gigabytes (GB). It is presumed that a DVD-RAM disc will be readable on both the DVD-R and DVD-ROM drives built in the future. Rewritable DVD equipment is expected to be commercially available in 1999.

DVD Capacity

A DVD disc may contain two data layers on each side, or four total, for a maximum capacity of 17.08 GB on a 12 cm disc. Two 0.6 mm thick substrates are bonded to form a 1.2 mm thick disc with data in the middle, similar in form factor to a CD-ROM. The most commonly produced are single-layer, single-sided discs with a 4.70-GB capacity.

A standard CD-ROM holds about 650 megabytes (MB), approximately 0.65 GB. The following list shows the capacity of the various DVD formats, with one or two sides and one or two layers. The DVD-R is a recordable format, the DVD-RAM a rewritable format. (SS/DS = single-sided/double-sided; SL/DL = single-layer/double-layer)

Sides	Layers	Capacity
1	1	4.7 GB
1	2	8.5 GB
2	1	9.4 GB
2	2	17.0 GB

DVD SS/SL: 4.7 GB of data, 2+ hours of video
DVD SS/DL: 8.5 GB of data, 4 hours of video
DVD DS/SL: 9.4 GB of data, 4.5 hours of video
DVD DS/DL: 17 GB of data, 8+ hours of video

DVD-R SS/SL: 3.95 GB of data
DVD-R DS/SL: 7.9 GB of data

DVD-RAM SS/SL: 2.58 GB of data
DVD-RAM DS/SL: 5.16 GB of data

DVD File Structure Hierarchy

A DVD contains two separate types of information: navigation data, which controls the media, and presentation data, which consists of the objects themselves. Control data points to the audio-video object files on a DVD in the same way a file allocation table (FAT) points to files on a disk drive. Presentation and navigation data packets are separated at the track buffer in the DVD player model. Control data can be expressed as a series of nested layers, hierarchically listed below.

- **Title** Descriptor that distinguishes multiple movies or episodes on one disc. Each title is either a single program chain (One_Sequential_PGC_Title) or a collection of different program chains (Multi_PGC_Title).

- **Part of Title** (POT) A set of links to one or more program (PG) units on a disc. As with a Program Chain (PGC), this is a means of creating different camera angles, outcomes, or versions of the same PGC. POTs can also be used to mark scenes.

- **Program Chain** (PGC) A collection of programs with integrated or related content.

- **Program** (PG) Usually a scene consisting of multiple cells.

- **Cell** Preceded by a navigation packet and alternating video and audio packets, typically all the audio-video data associated with several Groups of Pictures (GOPs).

- **Video Object Unit** (VOBU) A related Group of Pictures (GOP).

- **Group of Pictures** (GOP) 1. The smallest unit of random access on a disc (a GOP includes a coded intraframe). 2. The largest interframe-dependent coding unit. Interframe compression is bounded within a GOP, minimally 15 frames of data (0.5 seconds in duration) in the NTSC video format (525 frames per 60 fields).

- **Packet** A block of data containing 2048 bytes, which is the sector payload size. A packet contains data from a single MPEG program stream.

- **NAV Packet** Block of data defining the playback behavior of the current cell, containing the optional Button Command.

Logical Structure of Video Manager and Video Title Set

A disc volume may contain up to 99 different titles, each with a navigation menu that allows the user to select a version of the title. The root menu that branches to all titles on the disc is coded within the Video Manager (VM). Each title is organized as a Video Title Set (VTS).

- **Video Manager** (VM) An object that sets up menus for a series of titles.

- **Video Manager Information** (VMGI) A menu that includes Attributes for Menu, Title Search Pointers, and PGCI for Menu.

- **Video Title Set** (VTS) A collection of video objects (VOBs). The control data

(VTSI, or Video Title Set Information) for the title (VTS) includes Attributes for Menu, Attributes for Title, Part of Title Search Pointer, Time Map Table, PGCI for Menu, and PGCI for Title.

- **Program Chain Information** (PGCI) Defines the playback order of Program Chains (PGCs).

- **Video Object** (VOB) Objects that contain the actual Program Chains (PGCs), Parts of Titles (POTs), Programs (PGs), and any other program material.

DVI See *Digital Video Interactive.*

Dvorak keyboard (n.) A keyboard layout designed for speed. The most commonly used letters in the English language are positioned on the center row of keys. It was designed in the 1930s by August Dvorak and William Dealy as an alternative to the QWERTY keyboard layout. Pronounced "da-VOR-ack." See figure on the following page.

DWDM See *Dense Wave Division Multiplexing.*

DWT See *discrete wavelet transformation.*

DXF See *Drawing Interchange Format.*

dye polymer (n., adj.) A compound made of similar molecules that are linked together. A dye polymer layer that can be altered by exposure to lasers is used in optical disc recording systems.

dynamic binding (n.) The arrangement in which code executed to perform a given operation is determined at run time by an object-oriented programming (OOP) language. Several different classes of objects may receive a particular message.

Dvorak keyboard

dynamic data exchange (DDE) (n.) An exchange format that allows two or more programs running simultaneously in Microsoft Windows or OS/2 to communicate with one another. Multitasking is enhanced by the use of programs that can take advantage of this access to data across applications.

dynamic execution (n.) Several processes that work together in the Intel Pentium Pro central processing unit (CPU), including multiple branch prediction, data flow analysis, and speculative execution.

dynamic filtering (n.) A process that eliminates the electronic emissions of a computing system, which are picked up by sensitive circuitry and can appear as noise in the sound board output.

Dynamic Host Configuration Protocol (DHCP) (n.) A MS Windows NT server protocol that provides a means of dynamically allocating Internet Protocol (IP) addresses to IBM PCs running on a local area network (LAN). A range of IP addresses are assigned to DHCP, and each client on the LAN has its TCP/IP software configured to request an IP address from the DHCP server.

dynamic link library (DLL) (n.) A library of programming code linked to application programs at the time that they are run rather than as a phase of their compilation. One block of library code can be shared between multiple tasks rather than duplicated. The version of a DLL must be compatible with its executable program. Dynamic linking is used in the Sun and the Microsoft Windows operating systems.

dynamic microphone (n.) A type of transducer and circuit that converts an acoustical signal into an electrical signal by using a coil moving in a magnetic field. This type of microphone is generally less sensitive than a condenser microphone and has a narrower frequency response.

Dynamic RAM (DRAM, pronounced "DEE-ram") (n.) Dynamic random access memory; a type of memory component in which the memory cells require periodic recharging. Information stored in the memory cells as positive or negative charges may be accessed randomly. DRAM consists of an integrated circuit (IC) that uses a charged capacitor.

dynamic range (n.) In an audio program, the difference between the lowest and the highest levels of amplitude, or loudness, expressed in decibels.

dynamic storage allocation (n.) While a program that uses storage space is running, a process that reserves space for data that the program may generate. The data will be stored in allocated blocks.

DYUV See *delta YUV.*

E

Earth station (n.) Antenna and related equipment that receive or transmit satellite signals.

Easter egg (n.) An often humorous message buried in an application by its programmers with no documented access for the user.

EBCDIC See *Extended Binary-Coded Decimal Interchange Code.*

EBU See *European Broadcast Union.*

EBU time code (n.) European Broadcast Union time code; standard for time-stamping data on audio tape or videotape. Similar to Society of Motion Picture and Television Engineers (SMPTE) time code.

ECC See *error correction code.*

echo (n.) In telecommunications, the reflection of a signal back to the sending station.

echo cancellation (n.) The process of isolating and filtering unwanted signals caused by echoes from the primary transmitted signal.

EDAC See *error detection and correction.*

EDC See *error detect code.*

EDFA See *Erbium-Doped Fiber Amplifier.*

EDI See *Electronic Data Interchange.*

edit (v.) 1. To combine and integrate audio or video segments from multiple media sources, creating a composite master tape. 2. To remove undesirable content from a recorded program or file.

edit controller (n.) A complex system that controls video and audio recording or playback machines, positioning them at appropriate points and changing modes as needed in order to assemble an edited production.

edit decision list (EDL) (n.) In the offline, nonlinear, video editing process, a record of the edits made. The list identifies beginning and ending frames in Society of Motion Picture and Television Engineers (SMPTE) code. It consists of a series of entry and exit points in tapes that will be combined. Those points allow the user to recreate or modify a video program. The EDL includes the time code where cuts are to be made and where special effects are to be introduced. The list can be logged from a window dub, an offline editing system, or a computer.

editor (n.) 1. Any program on any operating system used to create or modify pure text files. In the Mac OS, SimpleText is the default editor, and in Microsoft Windows it is Notepad.

Common editors in Unix are vi, ee, and pico. 2. A person who refines an audio or video program or text file by cutting and modifying existing data and integrating new content.

EDL See *edit decision list.*

EDO DRAM See *Extended Data Out Dynamic Random Access Memory.*

EDO RAM See *EDO DRAM.*

edutainment (n.) Entertaining and educational digital media products.

EEPROM See *electrically erasable programmable read-only memory.*

effects processor (n.) An audio production tool that performs operations such as reverb, delay, equalization, compression, and filtering. It may take the form of an outboard unit through which signals are routed, or it may exist as a software plug-in to an editing program.

EFM See *eight-to-fourteen modulation.*

EGA See *Enhanced Graphics Adapter.*

EGP See *Exterior Gateway Protocol.*

EHF See *extremely high frequency.*

EIA See *Electronics Industries Association.*

EIAJ See *Electronics Industries Association of Japan.*

EIDE See *Extended Integrated Drive Electronics.*

EIDS See *Electronic Information Delivery System.*

eight-bit audio (n.) A sound file that is digitized or played back using an 8-bit sample size. The quality is inferior to that of a 16-bit sample. It is adequate for spoken words and some sound effects but too noisy and limited in frequency range for high-quality music. Two factors significantly affect the quality of digital audio. These are the bit depth and the sample rate, or the frequency at which a sound is sampled. Common sample rates are 11.025, 22.050, 44.1, and 48 kilobits per second (Kbps).

eight-bit color (n.) A monitor setting or graphic file format that allocates eight bits of memory to each pixel and yields up to 256 different colors simultaneously.

8 mm videotape (n.) An eight-millimeter-wide videotape format used in camcorders. Hi-8, which employs S-video separation of color and luminance, is a higher quality version.

eight-to-fourteen modulation (EFM) (n.) The process that turns each eight-bit byte of data into 14 "channel" bits during the mastering of a compact disc.

EISA See *Extended Industry Standard Architecture.*

EJB See *Enterprise Java Beans.*

electrically erasable programmable read-only memory (EEPROM) (n.) A special type of programmable read-only memory (PROM) that can be erased with an electric current before being reloaded. Pronounced "ee-EE-prom." See also *programmable read-only memory.*

electroluminescence (n.) The process of subjecting solid phosphor to an alternating current field, causing it to emit light. This technology is implemented in flat-panel displays for notebook computers because it is energy-efficient.

electromagnetic interference (EMI) (n.) Emissions from electronic devices and lighting that interfere with the performance of other devices, often introducing noise or distortion.

Electronic Data Interchange (EDI) (n.) A networking protocol that allows encrypted data to be sent between two parties over the Internet securely.

Electronic Information Delivery System (EIDS) (n.) A microcomputer- and videodisc-based audio-video training system contracted by the United States Army in November 1986 as the designated, standard, stand-alone, computer-based training (CBT) system. EIDS refers to both the hardware configuration, provided by Matrox Electronics under the initial contract, and the standard for courseware (i.e., it must be EIDS-compatible). With 14 000 units installed, EIDS is the largest videodisc implementation.

electronic mail (email) (n., adj., v.) Messages transmitted between computer users through networks or via modems and telephone lines. A mail user agent (MUA) is used to compose a message, which is then sent to a message transfer agent (MTA) program, which delivers it locally or passes it to another MTA on a network typically using Simple Mail Transfer Protocol (SMTP). Email messages adhere to the RFC 822 standard. They begin with the appropriate headers, which identify the name and email address of the sender and recipient(s), the time sent, the date sent, and a subject field. Headers are followed by a blank line and the body of the message. Most email systems support standard multipurpose Internet mail extensions (MIME), which allow the sender to attach various file types in addition to ASCII text. A signature is usually placed at the end of the body.

electronic publishing (n.) The creation and distribution of computer-generated media. Electronic publishing is similar to traditional print publishing, but the product is in the form of digital data. Content is distributed on storage devices or over networks for computer-based delivery.

Electronics Industries Association (EIA) (n.) A professional organization whose recommendations are identified by the prefix *RS-*, as in RS-232 and RS-422.

Electronics Industries Association of Japan (EIAJ) (n.) The EIAJ was founded in 1948 as a nonprofit national trade organization to develop Japan's electronics industry and represent its views. The mission of the EIAJ is to represent the Japanese electronics industry in working on the challenges it faces. The industry is being called upon to further its social commitment in areas such as the environment, safety, and product liability. Other important issues include advancing international technical standardization, supporting the creation of emerging markets, fostering technological development, and enhancing international industrial cooperation. The EIAJ offers programs with the cooperation of related organizations and associations worldwide. The EIAJ has approximately 560 full and associate members, including manufacturers in the consumer electronics, industrial electronics, and electronic components and devices sectors.

electronic whiteboard (n.) A device that allows users to share data, text, and images simultaneously over a telephone connection. Typically, PCs with special hardware and software are

E

connected by an ISDN line, and a session similar to a video conference is conducted with a whiteboard. Users may draw or write on their whiteboard with markers, and a living document may be updated simultaneously by multiple users who share access to it. Some systems also allow voice messages to be sent among those connected.

electrostatic discharge (ESD) (n.) A sudden burst of electrical flow that occurs when static electricity is grounded, or the rapid transfer of voltage between any two objects with different electrical potentials. It is a common cause of damage to integrated circuits.

ELF emission (n.) Extremely low frequency emission; generated by monitors and other common appliances, a magnetic field that may be hazardous to frequent computer users.

Emacs (n.) Editing macros or extensible macro system; a screen editor written in C and widely used on Unix and VMS systems. Originally written at MIT, Emacs is distributed by the Free Software Foundation. Emacs offers online help and features a WYSIWYG display. A version exists for most operating systems, and modes are available for editing text in many programming languages. Pronounced "EE-maks."

email See *electronic mail.*

email address (n.) Electronic mail address; the source or destination of an email message identified by a string of characters, such as *johndoe@corporation.com.* The RFC 822 standard for email addresses is used for the majority of Internet communications. *johndoe* is the local portion, or mailbox, on the destination computer. It is the only address name required on a local area network (LAN). *corporation.com* is the host portion or domain name, and it must be included after the symbol @. Mail is

stored on a server and is read whenever the user logs on.

EMI See *electromagnetic interference.*

emitter (n.) Laser or light-emitting diode (LED) used to convert an electrical signal into an optical signal for transmission by an optical waveguide.

EMM See *expanded memory manager.*

emoticon (n.) A face made with keyboard characters. Also called a *smiley* :-)

emphasis (n.) In imaging, a midrange control that can cause tones to be exaggerated or minimized. It is the equivalent of a loudness control in an audio amplifier. If parts of an image are too dark and too bright, the middle tones become subdued. The detail of an image becomes clearer as the middle tones are enhanced.

EMS See *Expanded Memory Specification.*

EMU8000 (n.) A hardware and software subsystem providing music synthesis sound effects to 32-voice MIDI playback. It is widely distributed as the Advanced WavEffect MIDI synthesizer chip used on the Sound Blaster AWE32 (SB AWE32) card.

emulator (n.) A computer system used to test programs under development and simulate their performance.

Encapsulated PostScript (EPS) (n.) The graphic format designed by Aldus to describe an image in Adobe's PostScript Page Description Language (PDL). A bitmapped thumbnail version of the image is generally placed in the header of the file in TIFF format for indexing and previewing.

encapsulation (n.) 1. The addition of layers containing header information to a protocol data unit (PDU) from the layer above. The headers may be combined from the physical layer, the network layer (IP), and the transport layer (TCP). 2. In object-oriented programming (OOP), the way in which data structures and their methods, or procedures, are kept together.

encode (v.) 1. To translate images or sound into a digital format. Encoding is the final step in converting an analog signal into a data representation. Other steps are sampling and quantizing. 2. To combine three-color signals into one composite video signal.

encoder (n.) 1. A microprocessor-based hardware system that converts analog video signals into a series of binary numbers that define the signal content. 2. A device that transforms original RGB video signals into a luminance signal (Y) and a chrominance signal for NTSC transmission.

encryption (n.) A process used to encode data. Encryption makes it difficult to decode without proprietary software, thus protecting data from unauthorized access. Encrypted data is usually created by applying an algorithm that must be reapplied to translate it.

end of file (EOF) (n.) 1. The out-of-band value returned by sequential character-input functions in the C programming language when the end of a file has been reached. 2. The keyboard character (usually Ctrl-D, which is the ASCII end-of-transmission character) that a Unix terminal driver maps into an end-of-file condition. 3. A character placed at the conclusion of a data set or data stream informing the reader or receiver that it has ended.

end of message (n.) A control character that identifies the last bit of data in a message.

Energy Star (n.) An energy-efficiency guideline established by the Environmental Protection Agency (EPA) to identify an upper limit for wattage that an inactive computing device may draw. Compliance is voluntary, and manufacturers whose equipment meets the guidelines may display the Energy Star logo.

engine (n.) In software, a program (such as a database engine or search engine) that performs a function. It is usually transparent to the user. An interface is provided that allows the user to interact with the data or media.

Enhanced Graphics Adapter (EGA) (n.) An IBM PC display adapter that supports 16 colors from a palette of 64 colors at 640 x 350 pixels, as well as several other resolutions. See the Graphics Adapter Resolutions table. Pronounced "ee-jee-AY."

Enhanced Small Device Interface (ESDI, pronounced "EHZ-dee") (n.) An interface for transferring data between a mass storage device (or some other peripheral) and a microcomputer. An ESDI board has a buffer and can transfer data at 10 to 24 megabits per second (Mbps).

Enhanced Specialized Mobile Radio (ESMR) (n.) Developed by Nextel and Geotek Communications, an advanced two-way radio service that competes with wireless telephone service in some areas.

ENQ (n.) Enquire; an online convention for querying a user's availability. It is also the ASCII character 5.

Enterprise Java Beans (EJB) (n.) Customized Java components typically used on the Internet to solve problems across a wide area network (WAN).

entropy (n.) The degree of disorder or randomness in a system. The entropy of a system is related to the amount of information it contains and the ways in which the information can be structured. An ordered system can be defined with fewer bits of information than a disordered one.

entropy encoder/decoder (n.) A type of encoder/decoder that compresses and decompresses quantized DCT coefficients compactly based on spatial characteristics.

envelope (n.) In audio engineering, a curve created by connecting the amplitude parameters of a sound over time. A simple envelope might consist of the attack, decay, sustain, and release levels, or ADSR. Changing the ADSR settings alters the shape of a tone but not its basic pitch. An *envelope generator* is a device used to shape these four elements.

environment (n.) In programming, a list of variable bindings. To evaluate a variable is to look up its value in the environment. The environment is extended with new bindings when new variables are declared or when a function's parameters are bound to its actual arguments. In most block-structured procedural languages, the environment consists of a linked list of activation records.

EOF See *end of file.*

EPROM See *erasable programmable read-only memory.*

EPS See *Encapsulated PostScript.*

equalization (n.) In audio recording and processing, the use of filters or attenuators to adjust output levels in specified frequency ranges. See figure.

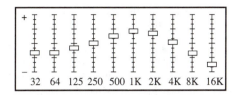

graphic equalizer

erasable programmable read-only memory (EPROM) (n.) A storage device that uses electrical charges stored in an isolated (floating) metal-oxide semiconductor (MOS) transistor gate to simulate data. Because of the isolation, an EPROM can retain a charge for more than 10 years without an external power supply. An EPROM is programmed when a charge is injected into the floating gate. The floating gate can be discharged when ultraviolet (UV) light is applied through a window in the package. This procedure erases the stored data and prepares the device to be reprogrammed. Pronounced "EE-prom."

erase (v.) To delete previously recorded data from a storage medium, such as a floppy disk. Data is not actually removed from the medium, but rather the pointers to it are rendered invisible. Most data can be recovered after being erased, unless the medium has been reformatted.

Erbium-Doped Fiber Amplifier (EDFA) (n.) The first optical amplifier that uses a portion of fiber-optic cable doped with the rare-earth element erbium and that is optically pumped with a laser diode. It can amplify a range of different wavelengths simultaneously. Erbium-Doped Amplifiers are being deployed in submarine cables.

erlang (n.) Named after Danish telephone engineer A. K. Erlang, a unit of measurement for traffic on telecommunications systems. One erlang equals one full hour of continuous use on one phone line.

error control (n.) The application of procedures to check the reliability of characters or blocks of data. Some error-control protocols, such as V.42, Microcom Networking Protocol (MNP), and U.S. Robotics High Speed Technology (HST), employ cyclic redundancy check (CRC) and automatic request for retransmission (ARQ).

error correction code (ECC) (n.) In CD-ROM writing, a system of scrambling data and recording redundant data onto a disc as it is premastered. During playback, this redundant data helps detect and correct errors that arise in data transmission. See also *block error correct.*

error detect code (EDC) (n.) On a CD-ROM, a code that consists of 32 bits of information per sector. The code is used to detect errors in the data of a sector.

error detection and correction (EDAC, pronounced "EE-dak.") (n.) An encoding technique that detects and corrects bit errors in digital data.

escape sequence (n.) A series of keystrokes that performs a function, such as moving a cursor on the screen.

ESD See *electrostatic discharge.*

ESDI See *Enhanced Small Device Interface.*

ESMR See *Enhanced Specialized Mobile Radio.*

establishing shot (n.) A scene used in video to acquaint the viewer with the environment.

etch (v.) In semiconductor manufacturing, to remove specific portions of a layer through a chemical reaction.

Ethernet (n.) Developed at Xerox PARC in 1976, this coaxial cable local area network (LAN) standard (IEEE 802.3) was specified by Digital Equipment Corporation, Intel, and Xerox and is widely implemented throughout the industry. Packets of data are transmitted over 50-ohm coaxial cable with multiple shielding using the carrier sense multiple access with collision detection (CSMA/CD) algorithm until they arrive at the destination without colliding with other packets. The first contention slot following transmission is reserved for an acknowledge packet. A node on Ethernet is either transmitting or receiving data at any point in time. The bandwidth of 10BASE-T is about 10 megabits per second (Mbps), and 100BASE-T is capable of moving data at 100 Mbps. A gigabit (Gb) Ethernet standard has been introduced, which allows much faster data rates. The typical disk-Ethernet-disk transfer rate with TCP/IP is 30 kilobytes per second (KBps). Version 2 specifies that the collision detection of the transceiver must be activated during the interpacket gap. In addition, it requires that when transmission finishes, the differential transmit lines are driven to zero volts. Version 2 also specifies certain network management functions, such as reporting collisions, retries, and deferrals.

Ethernet address (n.) The identifying hexadecimal number for an individual Ethernet controller board. It is a 48-bit number (aabbccddeeff) in which the first 24 bits (aabbcc) identify the manufacturer of the controller. Most addresses may be changed with software commands, although some are hard-wired on the controller or stored in ROM. The six hexadecimal numbers are normally written in pairs with a colon between each pair, as in 06:00:20:05:44:DC. Also known as a *MAC address.*

EtherTalk (n.) The Ethernet protocol used by Apple computers.

Eudora (n.) A popular electronic mail software package developed by QUALCOMM for communicating over TCP/IP with microcomputers. Both commercial and shareware versions are available.

European Association of Research Networks (n.) Reseaux Associés pour la Recherche Européenne (RARE); a body of researchers representing companies that are engaged in the study of Internet-related topics.

European Broadcast Union (EBU) (n.) A group of organizations that work together to coordinate joint technical interests and to advise on the establishment of standards. Pronounced "ee-bee-YOU."

European Laboratory for Particle Physics See *Conseil Européen pour la Recherche Nucléaire.*

event-driven (adj.) Describes a program or user interface with a main loop that waits for events to occur. An *event handler* passes details of an event to the operating system. A typical event might be a mouse click over a certain screen location.

exception (n.) A condition that arises because of error checking and that alters the normal behavior of a program. An exception could be generated by either hardware or software. A reset, an interrupt, or a signal from a memory management unit (MMU) are examples of hardware exceptions.

exchange (n.) In telecommunications, a coordination point established by a common carrier in a geographical area. The central office support and the equipment for communications services are provided at the exchange.

exchange access (n.) The use of telephone exchange services or facilities for the origination or termination of telephone toll services. One telephone company gives exchange access to another.

executable program (n.) A type of computer program that performs a function or carries out a series of commands. It is identified by the file extension .exe in MS-DOS.

execute (v.) To carry out software commands.

exit strategy (n.) The means by which capital investors may receive a return on their investment. Acquisition by another company and the sale of shares in a public offering are two common strategies.

expanded memory manager (EMM) (n.) In MS-DOS, the emm386.exe program that converts extended memory into expanded memory.

Expanded Memory Specification (EMS) (n.) Bank switching in early IBM-compatible systems that permits 8088 chips to use more than 1 megabyte (MB) of physical memory. It has been replaced by extended memory.

expansion bus (n.) A circuit or pathway that allows components to interact with a computer's CPU. Types of buses are identified in the Expansion Bus Types table on the following page, along with the width of the data path and the clock speed. See also *I/O bus.*

expansion slot (n.) A socket on a microcomputer motherboard into which an expansion board may be inserted. Half-sized circuit boards fit into an eight-bit ISA slot, whereas full-sized boards use a 16-bit slot. PCI boards pass 64 bits of data simultaneously and require a special type of socket for their edge connec-

---

Expansion Bus Types

Bus	Processor	Data Path	Clock Speed
ISA	(PC/XT)	8-bit	8.33 MHz
	(PC/AT)	16-bit	8.33 MHz
EISA	(PC/80486)	32-bit	8.33 MHz
MCA	(IBM PS/2)	32-bit	10 MHz
NuBus	(Mac)	32-bit	10 or 20 MHz
VESA	(PC/80486)	32-bit	40 or 66 MHz
PCI	(PowerPC/Pentium)	32/64-bit	131 MHz

---

tor. Examples of expansion boards that fit into slots include sound cards, video adapters, internal modems, and host controllers. The slots in multimedia computers are often filled with cards that perform special digitizing functions.

expert system (n.) A program that calls on information stored in a knowledge base to make decisions using an inference engine. Data is processed in a manner similar to human reasoning, and problems are solved by accessing "if-then" statements in the knowledge base.

exponent (n.) In mathematics, a function that raises a given constant, or base, to the power of its argument. A number that is increased by orders of magnitude has grown exponentially.

extended architecture (XA) (n.) An evolution of the standard CD-ROM format that provides for adaptive differential pulse code modulation (ADPCM) audio, multiple session discs, Photo-CD, and CD-i compatibility. This CD format relies solely on Cross-Interleaved Reed-Solomon Code (CIRC) for error correction.

extended attribute (n.) Data that identifies a file in Windows NT and OS/2 with more information than a simple attribute contains. Information is added about the original application that created the file and the names of other related files.

extended attribute record (XAR) (n.) Adhering to ISO 9660 standards, a record that has attributes not listed in the directory record, including information about escape sequences, dates, permissions, and other private data.

Extended Binary-Coded Decimal Interchange Code (EBCDIC, pronounced "EHB-suh-dik") (n.) Code that can identify 256 eight-bit characters, as opposed to the 128-character set available in ASCII code. See table.

Extended Data Out Dynamic Random-Access Memory (EDO DRAM, pronounced "EE-dee-oh DEE-ram") (n.) A type of DRAM available since 1995 that accesses nearby memory locations faster than normal DRAM can. EDO DRAM allows the data outputs to be accessed and controlled more easily. In pipelined systems, it is useful for overlapping accesses in which subsequent cycles are begun before the data from the previous cycle is removed from the bus. EDO DRAM is used with Intel's Pentium processors. A compatible chipset, such as Triton, must be used to take advantage of EDO DRAM. Since early 1995, EDO DRAM has been available for computers. See also *burst EDO DRAM.*

Extended Graphics Adapter (XGA) (n.) An IBM PS/2 graphics standard that provides a resolution of 1024 pixels x 768 pixels with eight-bit color. See the Graphics Adapter Resolutions table.

EBCDIC

Decimal	Hex	Acronym	Function	Decimal	Hex	Acronym	Function
0	0	NUL	Null	53	35	TRN	Transparent
1	1	SOH	Start of Heading	54	36	NBS	Numeric Backspace
2	2	STX	Start of Text	55	37	EOT	End of Transmission
3	3	ETX	End of Text	56	38	SBS	Subscript
4	4	SEL	Select	57	39	IT	Indent Tab
5	5	HT	Horizontal Tab	58	3A	RFF	Required Form Feed
6	6	RNL	Required New Line	59	3B	CU3	Customer Use 3
7	7	DEL	Delete	60	3C	DC4	Device Control 4
8	8	GE	Graphic Escape	61	3D	NAK	Negative Acknowledge
9	9	SPS	Superscript	62	3E		(Not Assigned)
10	A	RPT	Repeat	63	3F	SUB	Substitute
11	B	VT	Vertical Tab	64	40	SP	Space
12	C	FF	Form Feed	65	41	RSP	Required Space
13	D	CR	Carriage Return	66	42		(Not Assigned)
14	E	SO	Shift Out	67	43		(Not Assigned)
15	F	SI	Shift In	68	44		(Not Assigned)
16	10	DLE	Data Length Escape	69	45		(Not Assigned)
17	11	DC1	Device Control 1	70	46		(Not Assigned)
18	12	DC2	Device Control 2	71	47		(Not Assigned)
19	13	DC3	Device Control 3	72	48		(Not Assigned)
20	14	RES/ENP	Restore/Enable Presentation	73	49		(Not Assigned)
21	15	NL	New Line	74	4A	¢	Cent Sign
22	16	BS	Backspace	75	4B	.	Period
23	17	POC	Program-Operator Communication	76	4C	<	Less-than Sign
24	18	CAN	Cancel	77	4D	(	Open Parenthesis
25	19	EM	End of Medium	78	4E	+	Plus Sign
26	1A	UBS	Unit Backspace	79	4F	|	Logical OR
27	1B	CU1	Customer Use 1	80	50	&	Ampersand
28	1C	IFS	Interchange File Separator	81	51		(Not Assigned)
29	1D	IGS	Interchange Group Separator	82	52		(Not Assigned)
30	1E	IRS	Interchange Record Separator	83	53		(Not Assigned)
31	1F	IUS	Interchange Unit Separator	84	54		(Not Assigned)
32	20	DS	Digit Select	85	55		(Not Assigned)
33	21	SOS	Start of Significance	86	56		(Not Assigned)
34	22	FS	Field Separator	87	57		(Not Assigned)
35	23	WUS	Word Underscore	88	58		(Not Assigned)
36	24	BYP/INP	Bypass/Inhibit Presentation	89	59		(Not Assigned)
37	25	LF	Line Feed	90	5A	!	Exclamation Point
38	26	ETB	End of Transmission Block	91	5B	$	Dollar Sign
39	27	ESC	Escape	92	5C	*	Asterisk
40	28	SA	Set Attribute	93	5D	)	Close Parenthesis
41	29	SFE	Start Field Extended	94	5E	;	Semi-colon
42	2A	SM/SW	Set Mode/Switch	95	5F		Logical NOT
43	2B	CSP	Control Sequence Prefix	96	60	–	Minus Sign, Hyphen, Dash
44	2C	MFA	Modify Field Attribute	97	61	/	Forward Slash
45	2D	ENQ	Enquire	98	62		(Not Assigned)
46	2E	ACK	Acknowledge	99	63		(Not Assigned)
47	2F	BEL	Bell	100	64		(Not Assigned)
48	30		(Not Assigned)	101	65		(Not Assigned)
49	31		(Not Assigned)	102	66		(Not Assigned)
50	32	SYN	Synchronous Idle	103	67		(Not Assigned)
51	33	IR	Index Return	104	68		(Not Assigned)
52	34	PP	Presentation Position	105	69		(Not Assigned)

E

Decimal	Hex	Acronym	Function	Decimal	Hex	Acronym	Function
106	6A	¦	Broken Pipe	161	A1	~	Tilde
107	6B	,	Comma	162	A2	s	
108	6C	%	Percent Sign	163	A3	t	
109	6D	_	Underscore	164	A4	u	
110	6E	>	Greater-than Sign	165	A5	v	
111	6F	?	Question Mark	166	A6	w	
112	70		(Not Assigned)	167	A7	x	
113	71		(Not Assigned)	168	A8	y	
114	72		(Not Assigned)	169	A9	z	
115	73		(Not Assigned)	170	AA		(Not Assigned)
116	74		(Not Assigned)	171	AB		(Not Assigned)
117	75		(Not Assigned)	172	AC		(Not Assigned)
118	76		(Not Assigned)	173	AD		(Not Assigned)
119	77		(Not Assigned)	174	AE		(Not Assigned)
120	78		(Not Assigned)	175	AF		(Not Assigned)
121	79	`	Grave Accent	176	B0		(Not Assigned)
122	7A	:	Colon	177	B1		(Not Assigned)
123	7B	#	Number Sign	178	B2		(Not Assigned)
124	7C	@	At Sign	179	B3		(Not Assigned)
125	7D	'	Single Quote	180	B4		(Not Assigned)
126	7E	=	Equal Sign	181	B5		(Not Assigned)
127	7F	"	Double Quote	182	B6		(Not Assigned)
128	80		(Not Assigned)	183	B7		(Not Assigned)
129	81	a		184	B8		(Not Assigned)
130	82	b		185	B9		(Not Assigned)
131	83	c		186	BA		(Not Assigned)
132	84	d		187	BB		(Not Assigned)
133	85	e		188	BC		(Not Assigned)
134	86	f		189	BD		(Not Assigned)
135	87	g		190	BE		(Not Assigned)
136	88	h		191	BF		(Not Assigned)
137	89	i		192	C0	{	Opening Brace
138	8A		(Not Assigned)	193	C1	A	
139	8B		(Not Assigned)	194	C2	B	
140	8C		(Not Assigned)	195	C3	C	
141	8D		(Not Assigned)	196	C4	D	
142	8E		(Not Assigned)	197	C5	E	
143	8F		(Not Assigned)	198	C6	F	
144	90		(Not Assigned)	199	C7	G	
145	91	j		200	C8	H	
146	92	k		201	C9	I	
147	93	l		202	CA	SHY	Syllable Hyphen
148	94	m		203	CB		(Not Assigned)
149	95	n		204	CC		(Not Assigned)
150	96	o		205	CD		(Not Assigned)
151	97	p		206	CE		(Not Assigned)
152	98	q		207	CF		(Not Assigned)
153	99	r		208	D0	}	Closing Brace
154	9A		(Not Assigned)	209	D1	J	
155	9B		(Not Assigned)	210	D2	K	
156	9C		(Not Assigned)	211	D3	L	
157	9D		(Not Assigned)	212	D4	M	
158	9E		(Not Assigned)	213	D5	N	
159	9F		(Not Assigned)	214	D6	O	
160	A0		(Not Assigned)	215	D7	P	

Decimal	Hex	Acronym	Function	Decimal	Hex	Acronym	Function
216	D8	Q		236	EC		(Not Assigned)
217	D9	R		237	ED		(Not Assigned)
218	DA		(Not Assigned)	238	EE		(Not Assigned)
219	DB		(Not Assigned)	239	EF		(Not Assigned)
220	DC		(Not Assigned)	240	F0	0	Zero
221	DD		(Not Assigned)	241	F1	1	One
222	DE		(Not Assigned)	242	F2	2	Two
223	DF		(Not Assigned)	243	F3	3	Three
224	E0	\	Reverse Slash	244	F4	4	Four
225	E1	NSP	Numeric Space	245	F5	5	Five
226	E2	S		246	F6	6	Six
227	E3	T		247	F7	7	Seven
228	E4	U		248	F8	8	Eight
229	E5	V		249	F9	9	Nine
230	E6	W		250	FA		(Not Assigned)
231	E7	X		251	FB		(Not Assigned)
232	E8	Y		252	FC		(Not Assigned)
233	E9	Z		253	FD		(Not Assigned)
234	EA		(Not Assigned)	254	FE		(Not Assigned)
235	EB		(Not Assigned)	255	FF	EO	Eight Ones

E

Extended Industry Standard Architecture (EISA, pronounced "EE-sah") (n.) An evolved version of Industry Standard Architecture (ISA). Announced in September 1988, it was developed primarily by Compaq in response to the IBM Micro Channel Architecture (MCA) bus. The EISA bus provides 32-bit slots for use with 386DX or higher systems. It supports adapter cards created for the older ISA standard but offers greater system expansion, fewer adapter conflicts, and a maximum bandwidth of 33 megabytes per second (MBps). Another advantage over ISA is an automated setup for adapter board interrupts and addressing issues. EISA setup software recognizes potential conflicts and automatically configures the system to avoid them through interrupt request (IRQ) sharing; in other words, multiple bus cards can share a single interrupt. This feature has also been implemented in peripheral component interconnect (PCI) bus cards. See also *Industry Standard Architecture* or *Micro Channel Architecture*.

Extended Integrated Drive Electronics (EIDE) (n.) An improved version of the ATA hard drive controller with faster data rates, 32-bit transactions, and (in some cases) direct memory access (DMA). Named by Western Digital in 1994, EIDE is also referred to as *Fast ATA-2*. An EIDE interface can simultaneously control up to four storage devices connected to a computer. See also *Advanced Technology Attachment* or *Integrated Drive Electronics.*

extended memory specification (XMS) (n.) The provision for memory located after the first megabyte (MB) of address space in an IBM-compatible computer with an 80286 or later processor. It is not directly available in real mode, just through EMS, UMB, XMS, or HMA (High Memory Area, the first 64 kilobytes of memory above the 1-MB limit accessible by DOS); only applications executing in protected mode can use extended memory directly. In protected mode, the extended memory is provided by a supervising protected mode operating system such as Microsoft Windows. The processor makes this memory available through the use of global and local descriptor tables. Memory assigned to a local descriptor cannot be accessed by another program without causing a hardware trap, so it is considered protected. A protected mode OS such as Windows can also provide expanded memory to real mode programs. DOS Protected Mode Interface is Microsoft's prescribed method for having an MS-DOS program access extended memory in a multitasking environment.

Extended Multitimbral Specification (n.) A synthesizer subsystem standard followed by Multimedia PC audio board manufacturers. It permits 16 melodic notes and 16 percussive notes to sound at once, and provides a palette of nine different melodic tones and eight percussive tones.

Extensible Markup Language (XML) (n.) A subset of Standard Generalized Markup Language (SGML) ISO 8879, upon which Hypertext Markup Language (HTML) is also based. The objective of XML is to enable generic SGML to be served, received, and processed on the web in the same way that HTML is handled. Unlike HTML, it allows new tags to be defined and transmitted along with the content of a document.

The XML specification, recommended by the World Wide Web Consortium (W3C), describes a class of data objects called XML documents and describes how computer programs should process them. It is a restricted form of SGML and fully conforms to the SGML standard. Development was begun in 1996 by the XML Working Group of the W3C, and the standard was approved in 1998.

XML documents are comprised of storage units called entities, which contain either parsed or unparsed data. Parsed data consists of characters, some of which identify character data, and some of which identify markup.

Markup defines a document's storage layout and logical structure, and XML provides a mechanism to control these elements. An XML processor is a software module that is required to read XML documents and to provide access to their content and structure. The XML processor works in conjunction with an application. The XML specification describes the required behavior of an XML processor, how it must read XML data, and the information it must provide to the application.

The XML Version 1.0 specification provides the information needed to create XML documents and to process them on the Internet. Associated standards referenced in the specification are Unicode and ISO/IEC 10646 for characters, Internet RFC 1766 for language identification tags, ISO 639 for language name codes, and ISO 3166 for country name codes. The complete XML Version 1.0 specification may be found in the appendix on XML.

extension (n.) 1. Any small program that plugs into a larger one and provides increased functionality. Extensions allow operating systems to control CD-ROM drives. 2. The letters that appear after the dot (.) in the name of an MS-DOS file to classify and identify the file type. Extensions for some of the frequently used multimedia file types are .avi (Video for Windows), .gif (compressed graphics), .jpg (compressed graphics), .mid (MIDI), .mov (QuickTime), .mpg (MPEG video), and .wav (Windows audio). The Macintosh file-naming system uses two hidden extensions called file attributes that are each four letters long. One is for the file type, and the other is for the creator. See table.

extent (n.) A contiguous set of sectors on a disk, or blocks on a CD-ROM, that are occupied by a particular file or section of a file and

File Name Extensions

File descriptions marked with * are ASCII; all other file types are binary. VMS files are marked ** because they are variable.

.ext	Description	File Usage	.ext	Description	File Usage
.acr	image file (medical)	image viewer	.euc	Japanese (Kanji)	Japanese reader
.aif(c)	sound (Apple, SGI)	sound player	.exe	executable file	type the file name to run
.aif(f)	sound (Apple, SGI)	sound player	.exe	self-extracting file	type the file name to run
.arc	compressed archive	pkunpak, WinZip, ARCE	.f	Freeze for Unix	unfreeze (freeze)
.arj	compressed	arj (DOS)	.fac	picture	picture viewer
.art	First Publisher clip art file	First Publisher	.fit(s)	image	image viewer
.asc	image	image viewer	.flc	animated picture	picture viewer
.au	audio	u-law player	.fli	animated picture	picture viewer
.avi	video (MS Windows)	Media Player	.flx	image	image viewer
.avr	sound	sound player	.fssd	sound	sound player
.avs	animation	image viewer	.gb	Chinese	Chinese viewer
.bac	binary backup	restore	.gds	image	image viewer
.bas	BASIC source	run in QBasic	.gif	picture	picture viewer, browser
.bbm	image	image viewer	.gl	animated picture	picture viewer
.bck	**VMS backup	restore	.gry	picture	picture viewer
.big	Chinese (old version)	Chinese viewer	.gz	compressed	decompress (gzip124)
.big5	Chinese (old version)	Chinese viewer	.gzip	compressed	decompress (gzip124)
.bmf	image	image viewer	.h	*C/C++ header file	text editor
.bmp	picture (bitmap)	picture viewer	.ha	compressed	decompress
.boo	image	image viewer (msbpct.exe)	.ham	image	image viewer
			.hlb	**VMS help libraries	various
.cgm	computer graphics metafile	CGM viewer	.hlp	**VMS help files	various
.clp	picture	picture viewer	.hpk	compressed	decompress (hpack78.zip)
.cmf	music	music player (Playcmf)	.hqx	Macintosh compressed	decompress
.com	compressed	decompress			
.com	MS-DOS executable file	type the file name to run	.hrz	image	image viewer
			.htm(l)	*HTML document	text editor, HTML editor
.com	**VMS DCL command file	command	.hyp	compressed	decompress (hyper25.zip)
.cpt	Macintosh compressed	decompress	.hz	Chinese	Chinese viewer (CWD)
.cur	image	image viewer	.ibm	picture	picture viewer
.cut	image	image viewer	.ice	archive	decompress
.dat	**VMS data file	various	.ico	image	image viewer
.dcs	image	image viewer	.ief	image	image viewer
.des	*text	word processor	.iff	binary data (various types)	image viewer
.dib	picture (bitmap)	picture viewer	.img	picture	picture viewer
.dig	*text	word processor	.ish	compressed	decompress (ish200.lzh)
.dl	animated picture	dl viewer	.jas	image	image viewer
.dlg	image	image viewer	.jbig	image	image viewer
.dms	compressed	decompress	.jfi	image	image viewer
.doc	*text (MS Word)	word processor	.jis	Japanese	Japanese reader
.dvi	*special TeX text	word processor	.jpc	picture	picture viewer
.dwc	archive	decompress (zzap)	.jpeg	picture	picture viewer, browser
.dwg	image	image viewer	.jpg	picture	picture viewer, browser
.dxf	*ASCII Drawing Interchange	AutoCAD	.lbm	image	image viewer
			.lbr	archive	decompress (lue220)
.eps	Encapsulated PostScript image	PostScript viewer	.lha	compressed	decompress (lha213)
			.lis	*program listing	DOS editor
			.lm8	picture	picture viewer

.ext	Description	File Usage	.ext	Description	File Usage
.lzh	compressed	decompress (lha213)	.ppt	PowerPoint presentation	MS PowerPoint
.lzs	compressed	decompress (larc333.zip)	.ps	*laser printer file	word processor
.lzw	LHWarp	archive decompress	.psid	picture, text	picture viewer
.lzx	compressed	decompress	.ra	RealAudio	RealMedia player
.mac	MacPaint picture	picture viewer	.ras	picture	picture viewer
.mag	picture	picture viewer	.raw	animated picture	picture viewer
.man	*text manual	word processor	.rax	image	image viewer
.map	image	image viewer	.rgb	picture	picture viewer
.mat	sound	sound player	.rle	picture	picture viewer
.md	compressed	decompress (zzap)	.rmi	sound	sound player
.mgf	image	image viewer	.rol	sound	sound player
.mhg	multimedia	multimedia player	.scx	image	image viewer
.mid	music	MIDI player	.sdn	shell archive	decompress (zzap)
.mki	picture	picture viewer	.sea	self-extracting archive (Macintosh)	run to extract
.mod	music	mod player (MOD4WIN)			
.mov	multimedia	QuickTime player	.sf	sound	sound player
.mpa	audio	MPEG audio player	.sgi	picture	picture viewer
.mpg	multimedia	MPEG player	.shar	*shell archive	unshell (unshar)
.mps	multimedia	MPEG player	.shg	image	image viewer
.mp2	audio	MPEG audio player	.shk	compressed (Macintosh)	decompress
.mp3	audio	MPEG audio player	.sit	compressed (Macintosh)	decompress
.mrb	image	image viewer	.snd	music	music player
.msp	image	image viewer	.s3m	sound	sound player
.mtm	sound	sound player	.stm	sound	sound player
.mtv	picture	picture viewer	.tar	tape archive	untar (DOS)
.nff	image	image viewer	.tar.gz	compressed tar	decompress, untar
.nst	sound	sound player	.tar.Z	compressed tar	decompress, untar
.off	image	image viewer	.tdo	compressed	decompress (teled121)
.omf	image	image viewer	.tga	picture	picture viewer
.pak	compressed	decompress (zzap)	.tif(f)	image	image viewer
.pbm	picture	picture viewer	.txt	*text	word processor
.pcc	image	image viewer	.uc2	compressed	decompress (uc2ins)
.pcd	Kodak Photo-CD	picture viewer	.ul	sound	sound player
.pcm	sound	sound player	.utl	sound	sound player
.pct	picture	picture viewer	.uud	uudecode	application
.pcx	picture (Paintbrush)	picture viewer	.uue	*uuencode	decode (uudecode)
.pdf	image	Acrobat Reader	.vic	picture	picture viewer
.pds	picture	picture viewer	.vik	picture	picture viewer
.pgm	picture	picture viewer	.vis	picture	picture viewer
.pic	picture	picture viewer	.voc	sound	sound player
.pict	picture (Macintosh)	picture viewer	.wav	sound	sound player
.pit	Macintosh compressed	decompress	.wmf	Windows Metafile	image viewer
.pm	picture	picture viewer	.xbm	picture (X Window System)	picture viewer
.png	image (Portable Network Graphics)	image viewer, browser			
.pnt	MacPaint	image viewer	.xm	sound	sound player
.pol	music	music player	.xpm	picture	picture viewer
.pp	Amiga compressed	decompress (PPLib)	.xwd	image	image viewer
.ppm	portable pixelmap	picture viewer	.y	compressed	decompress (yabba)
			.zip	compressed	decompress (unzip)

that are numbered consecutively in ascending order. Multiextent files on a CD-recordable disc are recorded at different locations if the disc has been written in multiple sessions.

Exterior Gateway Protocol (EGP) (n.) Standard used to communicate routing information to the routers that connect autonomous network systems.

external command (XCMD) (n.) A program written to extend the functionality of the HyperCard authoring environment. It is created in another programming language and called from within HyperCard.

eXternal Data Representation (XDR) (n.) Developed by Sun Microsystems, a standard for machine-independent data structures. It is similar to Abstract Syntax Notation One (ASN/1).

external functions (XFCN) (n.) A program written to provide new features for the HyperCard authoring environment, similar to an external command (XCMD).

extract (v.) To decode a file encoded for network transmission. The term is usually used in reference to the uuencode/uudecode Unix utility.

extranet (n.) A wide area network (WAN) version of an intranet. An extranet supports and controls external access. It makes portions of a company's intranet available to the Internet, allowing customers, vendors, and remote workers to access the company's data with a web browser. Although such a facility requires high security, it is a valuable means of delivering services and communicating efficiently.

extremely high frequency (EHF) (n.) Frequency in the 30- to 300-GHz range.

extrude (v.) To give two-dimensional objects a three-dimensional look by extending solid shadows from two-dimensional lines and shapes. This graphic effect may be applied to boldfaced print to attract attention.

e-zine (n.) Electronic magazine; online periodical.

E

F

face (n.) In three-dimensional animation, a plane in a wireframe model.

facility (n.) 1. In telecommunications, the line and all equipment required to furnish a completed circuit. 2. A capability offered by hardware or software that provides functionality for the user.

facsimile (fax) (n.) Procedure for the analog transmission of images over telephone lines. The majority of fax machines adhere to the Group III standard, which allows for sending 200-dot-per-inch (dpi) black-and-white images. Group IV fax machines can send data at up to 64 kilobits per second (Kbps) over ISDN or leased lines and offer grayscale images at resolutions of up to 400 dpi.

fade (v.) In editing or production, to gradually reduce or increase visual or audio intensity, moving to or from blackness and silence. Commonly used phrases are *fade in, fade out,* and *fade to black.* To *fade in* is to bring the levels up gradually from blackness or silence to a normal brightness and volume, and to *fade out* is to reverse this process. In compressed video, very slow fades often create undesirable artifacts and "blockiness." Quick cuts are preferred for this reason.

fader (n.) A sliding volume control, or potentiometer, often used to control the amplitude of signals on a mixing board.

fallback (n.) When two modems experience data corruption, perhaps resulting from line noise, a feature of their protocol that allows them to renegotiate to a lower-speed connection.

fall forward (n.) When two modems have fallen back to a lower speed because of data corruption, a feature that allows them to return to a higher speed as the connection improves.

FAQ See *frequently asked questions.*

farad (n.) A unit of electrical capacity, measured across the terminals of a capacitor, when a charge of 1 coulomb at the input produces a change in the output of 1 volt.

Fast ATA (n.) Fast Advanced Technology Attachment; implementations by Seagate and Quantum of the ATA-2 interface. Also referred to as *Fast ATA-2.*

Fast Ethernet (n.) A version of Ethernet that allows transmission at 100 megabits per second (Mbps), compared with the 10-Mbps rate of standard Ethernet. It requires that wiring, hubs, and network cards be upgraded from standard Ethernet.

Fast Fourier Transform (FFT) (n.) An algorithm that computes the Fourier transform of a set of discrete data values. Given a finite set of data points, such as an audio sample, FFT expresses the data in terms of its component frequencies. It can reconstruct a signal from frequency data.

FAT See *file allocation table.*

fat binary (n.) An executable file format for distributing software that may be used on either a PowerMac or a Macintosh with a Motorola 680x0 processor. It is termed *fat* because it contains two versions of the code, one for each type of processor. Fat refers to the excess baggage. In most cases the computer itself automatically chooses the appropriate version of the code at run time. The Mac OS supports fat binaries for both 680x0 and PowerPC native code.

fat client (n.) A networked computer with some processing capability of its own, independent from the host.

fault-tolerant (adj.) Describes a system that resists failure. An example is a RAID 1 mirrored system, which is fault tolerant because it provides disk input/output (I/O) even if one of the drives fails.

fax See *facsimile.*

faxmodem (n.) A device that performs the functions of both a fax machine and a modem.

FC See *Fibre Channel.*

FCB See *file control block.*

FCC See *Federal Communications Commission.*

F-connector (n.) A threaded coaxial cable connector used with video equipment. See figure.

female   male

F-connectors

FCS See *frame check sequence.*

FDDI See *Fiber Distributed Data Interface.*

FDHD See *floppy drive high-density.*

FDI See *Feeder Distribution Interface.*

FDISK (n.) The original MS-DOS utility program used to format a hard disk to serve as a boot disk containing system files. Pronounced "EHF-disk."

FDM See *frequency-division multiplexing.*

feature connector (n.) On a graphics adapter for a PC, a connector with 20 to 26 pins that permits access to the video signal path and that allows video signals to be mixed, or "overlayed," with computer graphics.

FED See *field emission display.*

Federal Communications Commission (FCC) (n.) The U.S. government agency that regulates telephone services, radio, and satellite communications. Regarding electronic devices, a "Class A" certification is required for equipment used in industrial applications, whereas home electronics must comply with a "Class B"

F

certification, which specifies lower levels of radiation.

Federal Networking Council (FNC) (n.) Group of representatives from U.S. government agencies that coordinates and manages the development of communications networks, including the Internet. Among the members are representatives from the DARPA, Department of Defense, NSF, and NASA.

feed (n.) Signals received from a satellite downlink, or signals supplied to a satellite uplink terminal.

feedback (n.) 1. The electronic signal that occurs when the output of a system becomes its own input in real time. An example is the high-pitched squealing that occurs when a microphone is placed in front of a loudspeaker. 2. In an interactive instructional system, the positive or negative reinforcement of the user's responses.

feeder (n.) That part of a cable television or telecommunications network to which subscribers are connected. With cable television, the feeder is a group of wires, usually 25-pair or multiples thereof, in a single cable sheath. Feeder cable is synonymous with *backbone wiring*. Bellcore defines it as a large loop cable emanating from a central office, typically underground, with periodically placed access points.

Feeder Distribution Interface (FDI) (n.) An interface that distributes signals from an optical fiber trunk into multiple fiber feeders.

Ferroelectric RAM (FRAM, pronounced "EFF-ram") (n.) Ferroelectric random-access memory; nonvolatile semiconductor memory that features fast read/write random access. A ferroelectric memory cell consists of a ferro-

electric capacitor and a metal-oxide semiconductor (MOS) transistor, similar in construction to a DRAM.

FET See *field-effect transistor.*

Fetch (n.) Developed by Jim Matthews at Dartmouth College, a Macintosh program for transferring files using FTP.

FFT See *Fast Fourier Transform.*

Fiber Distributed Data Interface (FDDI) (n.) A standard for transmitting high-bandwidth traffic via fiber optics at 100 megabits per second (Mbps). A local area network (LAN) specification from ANSI, FDDI uses token ring topology. FDDI-II is an advanced, 200-Mbps version of FDDI.

Fiber in the Loop (FITL) (n.) In telephony, networks in which some fiber-optic cable is used between the central office and a customer's premises.

fiber miles (n.) The length in miles of actual fiber strands deployed in a network.

fiber optics (n.) The transmission of signals or data in the form of light pulses through a strand of glass fiber.

Fiber to the Curb (FTTC) (n.) Broadband architecture in which fiber-optic lines are extended past every home. Copper twisted-pair or passive coaxial drops carry signals between the fiber-optic lines and houses. An optical network unit (ONU) performs optical-to-electrical signal conversion for clusters of 8 to 12 homes.

Fibre Channel (FC) (n.) Defined by the ANSI X3T11 standard, a data transfer protocol capable of moving data at speeds up to 1 gigabit per second (Gbps). It was invented in 1988 by Hewlett-Packard and became an open standard in 1991 with the involvement of IBM and Sun Microsystems. In 1995 ANSI adopted the basic FC standards.

At the physical level, Fibre Channel is a serial bus that may connect 126 storage devices on a single data path. Copper twisted-pair wiring up to 30 meters long may be used between nodes, and distances of 10 kilometers may be connected with fiber-optic media. This network technology was designed for storage and server clustering. It is possible to daisy chain individual FC components, and devices are hot-swappable. The rate of data transfer is 100 megabits per second (Mbps) on a single loop and 200 Mbps over a dual loop. The dual-loop feature provides high resilience for the storage data path and overall application-processing environment. If one loop becomes unavailable, the second loop takes over. Disk storage can be safely placed more than six miles away from the host and still be online. FC maps common transport protocols, including IP and SCSI, allowing FC to merge high-speed input/output (I/O) and networking functionality in a single technology.

Fibre Channel-Arbitrated Loop (FC-AL) is the most widely accepted implementation that shares bandwidth. Designed for server clusters, a switched version of Fibre Channel gives each node a 100-Mbps dedicated channel in a "fabric" of switches and ports. A gigabit linking module (GLM) is a generic transceiver unit that integrates the key functions needed for installation of a Fibre Channel interface on a host system. The GLM provides the drivers, transmit/receive optics, serializer/deserializer, and laser safety features.

Optical Fiber Control (OFC) lasers have been specially designed for use with Fibre Channel.

To protect users from eye damage, these high-powered lasers are controlled with a handshake; they turn off when unplugged. Non-OFC optics use a lower-powered laser that is safe for the eye. The industry trend is toward safer, non-OFC lasers for local area connection. Both OFC and non-OFC lasers are currently specified for use in Fibre Channel products.

Abbreviations for the ANSI X3T11 Fibre Channel standards and draft standards are as follows:

FC-PH: FC–Physical
FC-AL: FC–Arbitrated Loop
FC-GS: FC–Generic Services
FCP: FC Protocol for SCSI
FC-LE: FC Protocol for 802.2LE
FC-FP: FC Protocol for HIPPI

Two industry associations support Fibre Channel technology: the Fibre Channel Association (FCA) and its working group, the Fibre Channel Loop Community (FCLC). They may be reached at *http://www.fcloop.org*. Applications that are prime candidates for FC solutions include Internet/intranet serving, data warehousing, providing online services, streaming video, and medical imaging.

Fidonet (n.) Management software for a private bulletin board system (BBS) that provides procedures and data exchange standards for email, file transfer, conferencing, and other functions.

field (n.) 1. The horizontal lines created during one pass of an electronic beam from the top to the bottom of a screen. A field is the same as a frame in computer video because the lines are drawn sequentially. However, two interlaced fields are used to draw each frame in broadcast video formats. A single field fills only every other horizontal line of resolution.

This equals one-half of a complete television scanning cycle (1/60 of a second NTSC, 1/50 of a second PAL/SECAM) per frame. 2. In a database application, the location of data within a record.

field dominance (n.) The order in which video fields are recorded on a videotape during edits or transfers. There are two fields per frame; field-1 dominance places a new picture in the first field of each frame, whereas field-2 dominance places it in the second.

field-effect transistor (FET) (n.) A board-level component in which voltage applied between the gate and the substrate controls the flow of current between the source terminal and the drain terminal. The two types are MOSFETs and Junction FETs. Both are used in circuits that require very low power consumption because a small amount of current flows through the gate of an FET.

field emission display (FED) (n.) A flat-panel electronic monitor that employs a matrix of cathodes, control electrodes, and phosphor elements to produce an electronic image on its screen.

field frequency (n.) The rate of display for each field in a video format, typically 59.94 times per second in NTSC. In general descriptions of the format, this number is rounded off to 60 fields. Two fields combine to make a frame.

field of view (n.) The portion of a shot, or vista, that is visible through a camera lens. The image seen in the viewfinder on many cameras does not exactly match the actual field recorded on tape or film.

FIFO See *first-in-first-out.*

file (n.) 1. Any collection of information that is recorded and given a unique name. It may contain text, images, sound, or an application. 2. In computing terms, a container for data.

file allocation table (FAT) (n.) A map of a hard disk or CD-ROM that defines the exact location of tracks, sectors, and clusters on the storage medium. Windows 98 provides FAT32, an advanced 32-bit file system that allows drives with a capacity of more than two gigabytes (GB) to be formatted as a single partition. It updates the original 16-bit FAT by creating smaller disk cluster sizes, allowing more data to be stored on a hard disk. Pronounced "FAT."

file control block (FCB) (n.) In MS-DOS, the collected data about any file currently open.

File Manager (n.) In Microsoft Windows 3.1, an application program that allows the user to organize and view the files and directories on a disk. It typically resides in the "Main" program group located in the Program Manager application. In Windows 95 this function was replaced by Explorer.

file server (n.) A hardware and software system that provides file-handling and storage functions for multiple users on a local area network (LAN). The most common commercially available file server packages are Sun Microsystems' Network File System (NFS) for Unix and Novell Netware for IBM PC compatibles. Storing files on a file server eliminates the need to store multiple copies on individual computers.

file transfer (n.) Moving a file between two networked computers.

file transfer protocol (FTP) (n.) A client-server protocol that allows a user on one computer to transfer files to and from another computer over a TCP/IP network. It is defined in

RFC 959, STD 9.

fill 1. (n.) A supplementary light source that softens shadows and brings out the background missed by the key light in a video shoot. 2. (n.) A color or pattern occupying a graphic region. 3. (v.) To place a color or pattern in a graphic region.

film chain (n.) Referred to as *telecine,* a collection of equipment used to transfer frames of film to electronic frames or videotape, including projectors, multiplexers, and cameras.

FILO See *first-in-last-out.*

filter 1. (n.) In a visual context, a partially transparent material that passes or blocks light of a particular color or orientation. 2. (n.) In an audio context, an electronic circuit that passes or blocks signals of a specified frequency. 3. (n.) Any device that shapes or conditions a signal, including anti-aliasing, diffusing, equalizing, and sharpening filters applied in the process of editing digital images. 4. (v.) To narrow the scope of a search by specifying ranges or types of data to exclude.

Finder (n.) In the Mac OS, the application that manages the graphical user interface (GUI). It is used to open, copy, delete, and move files, which are represented by icons.

finger (n.) A software program that may be used to detect information about a user on a Unix network, including information about patterns of usage.

firewall (n.) On a local area network (LAN) connected to a larger network, the security system that prevents outside intrusion and that keeps internal information from getting out. Typically, all traffic must pass through the machine on which the firewall is implemented.

FireWire (IEEE 1394) (n.) An interface standard that specifies a transmission method, medium, and protocol. This high-performance serial bus defines a point-to-point cable-connected virtual bus and a backplane physical layer. The cable version supports data rates of 100, 200, and 400 megabits per second (Mbps) over a cable medium supported by the standard. The backplane version operates at 12.5, 25, or 50 Mbps. Both versions are fully compatible at the link layer and above. Features include multimaster capabilities, live connection and disconnection (hot plugging), and transmission speed scalable from 100 to 400 Mbps.

The technology was developed by Texas Instruments to address the need for mass information transfer. Ordinary networks do not provide connection capabilities and bandwidth that can meet future demands. Parallel high-speed communications, such as SCSI, are not suited to long-distance transmission and do not support live connection and disconnection of peripherals, such as digital video cameras, scanners, or printers. This capability is provided by the 1394 standard. The cable version integrates I/O connectivity in personal computers using a scalable, high-speed serial interface.

The standard is a transaction-based packet technology for both chassis and peripheral devices. The serial bus behaves as though it were memory space interconnected between devices or as if devices resided in slots on the main backplane. Device addressing is 64 bits wide, allocating 10 bits for network IDs, 6 bits for node IDs, and 48 bits for memory addresses. It is capable of addressing 1023 networks with 63 nodes on each. The memory capacity for each device on the chain is 256 terabytes (TB).

Memory-based addressing views resources as

F

registers or as memory that can be accessed with processor-to-memory transactions. A bus entity is referred to as a *node,* which may be individually identified, addressed, and reset. Multiple nodes may be in a single module, and multiple ports may be in a single node.

The distance between each node should not exceed 4.5 meters, and the maximum number in a chain is 16, for a total maximum end-to-end distance of 72 meters. Cable distance between each node is limited primarily by signal attenuation. A cable with 28-gauge signal pairs may be up to 4.5 meters long, whereas a cable with 24-gauge signal pairs may be 14 meters long. A maximum of 16 cable hops is allowed between the most widely separated nodes. The end-to-end distance may vary from 72 to 224 meters, depending on the configuration.

Signals transmitted on cable and backplane environments are non-return-to-zero (NRZ) with Data-Strobe (DS) encoding. DS encoding allows only one of the two signal lines to change each data bit period, doubling the tolerance jitter. DS encoding is licensed from SGS-Thompson/INMOS.

The FireWire IEEE 1394 standard supports asynchronous and isochronous data transfers. The asynchronous format transfers data and transaction layer information to a specific address, whereas the isochronous format broadcasts data based on channel numbers rather than on specific addressing. Both nonrealtime critical applications (such as scanners and printers) and realtime critical applications (such as video and audio) can operate on the same bus because the interface provides both formats.

The serial bus 1394 could replace other peripheral connection communication methods in use today, such as the Centronics parallel,

RS-232, SCSI, and Apple Desktop Bus (ADB). It would enable a single high-performance serial bus. New interfaces, such as direct connect video I/O, will employ this technology because of its advantages. Memory space addressing is a good solution for "slotless" systems, such as personal digital assistants (PDAs). Communications at different speeds between 100 and 400 Mbps may occur simultaneously on one medium. The "hot-plugging" and dynamic reconfiguration abilities make it a user-friendly environment. This standard will allow a user to connect an expansion system with communications on demand without having to shut down and reconfigure whenever devices are added or removed.

firmware (n.) A device or machine component with a microprocessor on board. It is characterized by data in ROM that controls hardware components.

first-in-first-out (FIFO, pronounced "FIE-foe") (n.) A queue, or hardware buffer, from which data is taken out in the same sequence in which it was inserted. A FIFO can buffer a stream of data that is transmitted at different rates between an unsynchronized sender and receiver. The opposite of a FIFO is a *last-in-first-out (LIFO),* also known as a *stack.*

first-in-last-out (FILO, pronounced "FIE-low") (n.) A queue, or hardware buffer, from which data is taken out in the opposite order in which it was inserted.

FITL See *Fiber in the Loop.*

fixed disk (n.) A circular, enclosed magnetic storage medium on which information may be accessed randomly, as opposed to sequentially. Floppy disks are small, portable storage vehicles; hard disks, or fixed disks, can store more data by using multiple rigid platters.

fixed repetition (n.) An instructional design feature that repeats a lesson or module without alteration.

Fixed Satellite Service (FSS) (n.) Radio communications between Earth stations located at specified fixed points using one or more satellites. This service may include links between satellites. Compare *Mobile Satellite Service.*

flag (n.) A bit of data set to 0 or 1 that represents a particular piece of information, position, or status.

flame (v.) To criticize or heap indignities on an individual in a public email message, often resulting from an inappropriate or uninformed remark made by the individual who is flamed.

flare (n.) The result of excessive light beaming into a camera lens and reflecting off of internal glass elements. A picture with flare may either show bright flashes or spots of extreme contrast reduction.

flash memory (n.) An EPROM module that is nonvolatile, has a fast access rate, and can be erased with ultraviolet light. The term also refers to EEPROMs, which are electronically erased. They provide data to equipment that can accept and read a small EPROM card.

Flash ROM (n.) An integrated circuit (IC) that contains nonvolatile, erasable, rewritable memory.

flat (adj.) 1. Describes an image of low contrast. 2. Describes an image with objects shaded in uniform color and brightness for each small polygon, rather than with varied shading at edges or across the polygon.

flat-file database (n.) A type of database that holds records in a single file. These databases are not as fast or as powerful as relational databases.

flatten (v.) To remove proprietary or structural information from a data file or to filter system-related data. Mapping to a "flat" ASCII file, rather than to formatted text, is an example. In multimedia the term is frequently applied to the removal of the Macintosh data fork from a QuickTime movie to prepare it for playback in Windows. After being flattened, the file must be renamed to conform to MS-DOS conventions, with up to eight legal characters followed by the .mov extension.

FLC (n.) A sophisticated version of the Autodesk Animator FLI animation file format that supports 640-by-480-pixel images in up to 8-bit color. Viewers for FLC files are available for most computers. Pronounced "FLICK."

FLI (n.) The acronym for the original Autodesk Animator animation file format. This file format supports 320-by-240-pixel images in up to eight-bit color. FLI viewers are available for most computers. Pronounced "FLEE."

flicker (n.) An "interfield" flicker, also known as *jitter,* which is caused when two fields that comprise a single video frame are not identical. Two different pictures will alternate 60 times per second when viewed in a still-frame mode. A flicker is also introduced by low vertical refresh rates in a TV screen, which prevent the eye from retaining a continuous perception of successive images.

floating-point arithmetic (n.) The way in which a computer keeps track of the decimal point when performing calculations. Floating-point notation is used to express a quantity with a reduced number of digits. Typically, a *mantissa* consisting of several digits is qualified by a two-digit *exponent*. Example: the number 0.0057 is represented in scientific notation by 5.7×10^{-3}, and in floating-point notation by .57E - 3.

floating-point operations per second (FLOPS) (n.) A measurement of the speed of a scientific computer, often rated in millions (MFLOPS).

floating-point unit (FPU) (n.) A math coprocessor chip that performs floating-point arithmetic and by doing so offloads this computationally intensive function from the CPU. Programs that are optimized to take advantage of a math coprocessor run much faster when an FPU is present.

floppy disk (n.) Short for floppy diskette, a storage medium commonly used in all types of microcomputers. Physically, it consists of a paper-thin flexible disk coated with magnetic material and mounted in a plastic enclosure 3.5 or 5.25 inches in diameter. The 3.5-inch disks have replaced the larger size, and they hold up to 1.44 megabytes (MB) of uncompressed data. The capacity of the diskette is determined by whether the medium is single-sided (SS), double-sided (DS), double-density (DD), or high-density (HD). See figure on the following page.

floppy drive high-density (FDHD) (n.) A disk drive used in Macintosh computers that can read from and write to 3.5-inch disks in both double-density and high-density formats and that can accept DOS-formatted disks for cross-platform applications.

FLOPS See *floating-point operations per second.*

flowchart (n.) In an interactive design, a map of the user's options and corresponding responses to input. It outlines branching and shows program segments and decision points.

flow control (n.) Processes applied in serial communications that stop the sender from sending more data until the receiving unit is prepared to receive it. The sender continues with transmission when the receiver signals to resume. It may be accomplished in either software or hardware.

flower key (n.) The Macintosh Command key, or the Feature key.

fluid head (n.) Camera tripod mount that moves smoothly, filled with a viscous fluid that dampens friction and lubricates.

flush (v.) 1. To delete data or to abort an output operation. 2. To force buffered data to be written to permanent memory.

fly-by (n.) In a 3-D virtual reality scene, the act of navigating over a map, a building, or terrain as though the user were flying an aircraft. The user assumes the role of a pilot and controls the perspective and motion with a mouse or other controls. It is useful as a tool for experiencing architecture from different viewpoints before it is constructed.

flying erase head (n.) In a helical scan video recorder, an erase head that rotates along with the recording heads so that it can erase a single line of video. With this technology, new segments can be added seamlessly to existing footage.

FM See *frequency modulation.*

FMV See *full-motion video.*

FNC See *Federal Networking Council.*

3.5-inch floppy disk

focal length (n.) With a camera lens set to infinity, the distance between the focal point (optical center) of a lens and its focal plane, the place where the image falls on the imaging chip or film. Short focal lengths result in a wide-angle view, whereas long focal lengths offer a narrow field of view. Zoom lenses provide variable focal lengths.

fold case (v.) To treat uppercase and lowercase text exactly the same. Case in file names should be preserved, because some operating systems, such as Unix, are case sensitive. Most text editors permit the user to specify whether a text search should be case sensitive or whether the editor should fold case.

folder (n.) Equivalent to a directory in a graphical user interface (GUI), an image that represents a container for documents or applications.

Foley (n.) Named after Jack Foley, a Hollywood director and sound engineer active in the 1940s, the process of generating sound effects by duplicating the movements of an actor onscreen. Foley artists in a sound studio watch a scene, then recreate and synchronize a new sound track with the picture.

folio (n.) A page number in a printed and bound document.

font (n.) A typeface or family of alphanumeric

characters and symbols in a single style, such as Times Roman or Helvetica. The concept was originally used to define print and has been applied to computer-generated characters.

foo (n.) Word used by programmers to name many things, especially scratch files. Most commonly, it serves as a metasyntactic variable used in examples of syntax. It is akin to *qux, baz, garply, corge,* and *plugh* in the language of hackers.

foobar (n.) A metasyntactic variable that hackers use, just as they use *foo.* It is not related to the military expression "f****** up beyond all recognition."

footprint (n.) 1. The amount of space on a desktop or table required for the base of a computer or peripheral. 2. In satellite communications, the territory covered by the transmitting beam of the satellite.

fork (n.) One of two parts in a Macintosh file. The *resource* fork contains executable code and items used by the system, whereas the *data* fork contains user data.

format 1. (v.) To prepare a storage medium by defining tracks and sectors where data will be placed in compliance with a specific operating system's requirements. Disks formatted for the Macintosh are not readable in Microsoft DOS or Windows without a cross-platform utility that translates data. 2. (n.) The specifications of a particular software-hardware platform, or a unique means of configuring data for that platform. 3. (n.) The physical and technical design feature that differentiates between types of video and audio equipment, such as 8 mm, Hi-8, S-VHS, and VHS.

formatted capacity (n.) Maximum amount of data that a formatted disk may contain. It is equivalent to the unformatted capacity minus the defined boundaries between sectors.

form factor (n.) Physical attributes of a hardware device, particularly regarding shape and size.

Formula Translator (FORTRAN) (n.) Developed by IBM, a computer compiling language that was originally invented to solve scientific problems but that is also used for commercial applications. The syntax consists of algebraic expressions and arithmetic statements.

FORTRAN See *Formula Translator.*

forum (n.) The generic term for a discussion group on a bulletin board system (BBS), on a mailing list, or in a Usenet newsgroup. Users submit postings for everyone with access to the forum to read whenever they log on. The forum often revolves around a thread, or topic. It differs from point-to-point personal email or a realtime chat in these ways.

Fourier transform (n.) Named after J. B. Joseph Fourier, a mathematical process capable of expressing a waveform as a weighted sum of sines and cosines. Discrete Fourier Transform is generally the type used in multimedia.

4:2:2 (n.) In A:B:C notation, the ratio of the sampling rates used to translate three components of an analog video signal into a digital signal. These ratios are used to define CCIR-601, the standard used for professional video production equipment and D-1 format digital videotape. See also *A:B:C notation.*

fps See *frames per second.*

FPU See *floating-point unit.*

FQDN See *Fully Qualified Domain Name.*

fractal (n.) A set of points, or coordinates, with a fractional dimension. In digital compression, a fractal model may be applied to an image to preserve its original shape. The model can later be used to generate repetitive features found in the image.

fractional T1 (n.) A telecommunications service that offers customers the use of one or more channels in a T1 connection, as opposed to all 24 channels. Customers are billed according to the number of channels used.

FRAD See *Frame Relay Access Device.*

fragment (n.) 1. A portion of a packet. When a router forwards an Internet Protocol (IP) packet to a network with packet size limitations, it may break up a packet into fragments that the IP layer reassembles at the destination host. 2. A portion of a file stored on a hard disk drive that is separated from other parts of the same file. The "defragment" function eliminates fragmented files and places whole files in contiguous disk space.

fragmented file (n.) A file that has been written to a disk in discontiguous sectors.

FRAM See *Ferroelectric RAM.*

frame 1. (n.) A single video image that belongs to a stream of moving pictures. In an interlaced system, such as NTSC, it consists of two interlaced fields. A video frame in NTSC consists of 525 lines, whereas a frame in SECAM or PAL consists of 625 lines. In multimedia applications, a frame may refer to a still image on the screen that is not part of a video stream. 2. (n.) In telecommunications, a transmission block or encapsulated packet in the data link layer. 3. (n.) A feature of the later releases of Netscape Navigator that displays different parts of a web page in the same window. An example is a list of terms in a frame on one side of the active window and a graphic image or a paragraph defining the term on the other side of the window in a frame. 4. (v.) To compose a video shot with desired content, angle, and field of view.

frame-accurate (adj.) Describes professional video-editing equipment that can locate and process a specific individual image or frame. Consumer products generally can locate only approximate locations.

frame address code (n.) Time-stamped data that identifies a frame of video by its location. The code is placed in the vertical blanking interval (VBI) prior to the frame.

frame buffer (n.) 1. A RAM allocation dedicated to storing a frame of digital video and used to refresh a raster image. The buffer may include some processing ability. As with all digital video descriptors, the number of bits per pixel determines picture quality. 2. A component that records and stores the lines of a video frame and functions as a time base corrector.

frame check sequence (FCS) (n.) A 16-bit field containing error-checking information that appears at the end of a frame in a bit-oriented protocol.

frame dropping (n.) A condition caused by the inability of a decompression system to play all the encoded frames in a stream of digital video. Because playback algorithms preserve the integrity of the audio track at the expense of video frames, some frames may not be displayed on playback in order to sustain the audio track.

frame grabber (n.) A device that captures and

stores a single video frame to be edited or printed later.

frame rate (n.) The number of times per second a video image is redrawn, scanned, or displayed on a monitor. The rate for NTSC format is 29.97(nearly 30) frames per second (fps). For PAL/SECAM format it is 25 fps. Film runs at 24 fps.

Frame Relay (n.) A data terminal equipment–data communications equipment (DTE-DCE) interface specification based on Link Access Procedure–D (LAPD, defined in Q.921), the ISDN version of Link Access Procedure–Balanced (LAPB) (X.25 data link layer). It is a form of packet switching with small packets and comparatively little error checking. A consortium of companies including StrataCom, Cisco Systems, Digital Equipment Corporation (DEC), and Northern Telecom jointly developed the specification. Frame Relay can connect dedicated lines and X.25 to Asynchronous Transfer Mode (ATM), switched multimegabit data service (SMDS), Broadband ISDN, and other "fast-packet" technologies. Frame Relay is compatible with current X.25 hardware, but it adds addressing and some control bits. Any network layer protocol may be used over the data link layer frames.

Frame Relay Access Device (FRAD) (n.) A telecommunications unit with hardware and software that turns packets from TCP or Systems Network Architecture (SNA) sources into frames that can be sent over a Frame Relay wide area network (WAN).

frames per second (fps) (n.) In video or animation, the number of times each second a new picture appears on the screen.

framework (n.) In object-oriented programming, a set of classes that embodies an abstract design for solutions to several related problems.

framing (n.) An error-control procedure in which bits are inserted into packets so that a receiver can identify the time slot allocated to each channel in a multiplexed digital transmission line, such as T1.

framing specification (n.) The standard that prescribes protocol bits surrounding the data bits on a communications channel in order to allow the data to be framed into chunks, such as start and stop bits in RS-232. It allows a receiver to lock in and synchronize at points along the data stream while data is being transmitted.

Free Software Foundation (FSF) (n.) Founded by Richard Stallman, an organization committed to the creation and dissemination of software that is free from licensing fees or restrictions. It supports the GNU project, which developed the GNU Emacs editor and a C compiler.

freewheel (n.) 1. An action that an audio-video synchronizing device takes when it continues to generate time code after encountering dropouts in the time code source. 2. A situation in which an audio device continues to generate audio without responding to a time code input or controls.

freeze-frame (n., adj.) 1. The motionless display of a single frame or image selected from video or film footage. 2. An image drawn from a longer motion sequence.

frequency-division multiplexing (FDM) (n.) A process in which the available bandwidth of a circuit is divided by frequency into narrower bands, each of which is used for a separate voice or data transmission channel. FDM was once the most common method of multiplexing long-haul connections transmitted by analog microwave signals. Modern fiber-optic trunks employ time-division multiplexing (TDM).

frequency modulation (FM) (n.) Change in the frequency of a carrier signal that expresses information based on the rate and degree of change. FM has been a common technique for sound synthesis since it was proposed by John Chowning in 1971. The Yamaha DX-7 family of synthesizers used FM synthesis exclusively to generate sounds. See figures.

frequency response (n.) The range of frequencies, from low to high, that can be processed or reproduced by an audio system.

frequency shift keying (FSK) (n.) In telecommunications, the assignment of different audio frequencies to binary digits. Transmission of tones that change in pitch, each tone represented by a 0 or a 1, provides a receiving unit a means of identifying and keying in on information carried by the changing tones.

frequently asked questions (FAQ, pronounced "FACK") (n.) On the Internet, a list of commonly asked questions and answers about specific topics.

front end (n., adj.) Software that provides an interface to another program. An example is the visual interface used to access information in a database or in a menu-driven multimedia program. Ideally, a front-end application is user friendly.

FSF See *Free Software Foundation.*

FSK See *frequency shift keying.*

carrier wave (signal to be modulated)

sound signal (modulator signal)

FM signal (modulated signal)

FM broadcast signal

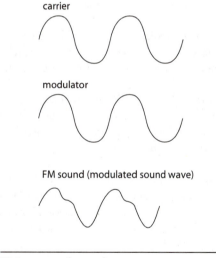

carrier

modulator

FM sound (modulated sound wave)

FM-generated waveforms

FSN See *Full-Service Network.*

FSS See *Fixed Satellite Service.*

f-stop (n.) In photography, a number that represents a logarithmic value for the intensity of light in a given lens. It is a factor of the ratio between the focal distance and the diameter of the iris, or lens opening. A lens with a focal distance of 70 mm and a diaphragm diameter of 20 mm has an f-stop value of 7:2, which may be reduced to 3.5:1. This is expressed as an f-stop of f3.5. Lower ratios indicate larger lens openings and shorter focus depths. The f-stop is initially set for the depth of field. Each increasing stop doubles the amount of light emitted.

FTP See *file transfer protocol.*

FTTC See *Fiber to the Curb.*

fulfillment (n.) Services that include warehousing, order processing, and shipping of products, such as CD-ROMs. Fulfillment is typically performed by a duplicator or manufacturer.

full-duplex (adj.) Describes bidirectional, simultaneous, two-way communication over telephone lines, preferably on a four-wire circuit.

full-frame ID (n.) Full-frame identification; a code placed in a video stream to identify the first video field of a new film frame. Also referred to as a *white flag.*

full-frame time code (n.) Society of Motion Picture and Television Engineers (SMPTE) code on videotape that accounts for all frame numbers chronologically. Also known as *non-drop-frame time code.*

full-motion video (FMV) (n.) Moving pictures that play back at the full resolution and frame rate in which they were encoded, resulting in a smooth, continuous display. According to broadcast video standards, this is usually considered 30 frames per second (fps) in the NTSC format and 25 fps in the PAL format.

Full-Service Network (FSN) (n.) A broadband network that supports a range of interactive services, including switched video-on-demand (VOD). The phrase was first used by Time Warner to define the high-profile advanced hybrid fiber-coax (HFC) network trial in Orlando, Florida. Numerous FSN applications are available on the Internet.

Fully Qualified Domain Name (FQDN) (n.) The complete name of an address in the domain name system, as opposed to only a hostname. The hostname is just the first part of an FQDN.

function (n.) In programming, an equation that yields a value when it is executed or when it is invoked. This value may be used as an operand in an expression. For example, the function *square* yields the value of X squared when it is invoked as the expression *square(X).*

fundamental (n.) In a compound waveform, the lowest frequency of regular vibration. It is on this pitch that all harmonics in an overtone series are based; the first partial in the series.

fuzzy logic (n.) A set of principles introduced by Dr. Lotfi Zadeh in the 1960s. Fuzzy logic provides a means to model the uncertainty of natural language. It employs a superset of Boolean logic with references to partial truth, or values that lie between absolute true and false statements. Fuzzy logic supplements Boolean truth values with degrees of truth that are similar to probabilities.

G

GaAs See *gallium arsenide.*

gaffer (n.) A stagehand who constructs and dismantles sets for film or video productions.

gain (n.) In audio, the increase in signal provided by an amplifier between input level and output level. It may be positive, negative, or null (unity gain).

gallium arsenide (GaAs) (n.) Semiconductive material used to build circuits that are three to ten times faster than those made of silicon and that use as little as one-tenth of the power. GaAs can detect, emit, and convert light into electrical signals, facilitating the creation of integrated opto-electronic chips.

game port (n.) A serial connection on a computer that is used for interfacing input devices such as joysticks.

gamma (n.) A value that identifies the degree of contrast in a photograph or electronic image according to a gradation curve. A steep curve indicates a high gamma value and high contrast. Gamma may be adjusted by components, colors, halftones, or highlights, or it may be adjusted across an entire image. *Gamma correction* is the adjustment of contrast in an image.

gamma correction (n.) A procedure employed by graphics display systems to compensate for decay in the phosphor of a monitor. As the gamma value varies, some display adapters adjust the video signal accordingly. Gamma correction is used along with other techniques to achieve color matching.

gamma ratio (n.) Graphic displays, scanners, and most electronic cameras have nonlinear characteristics in their signal-to-light intensity. Using a mathematical power function, most of these devices transfer image data with the equation *output = input ∧ gamma*. In this equation, ∧ represents the exponent *gamma* (the Greek letter), the exponent of the power function. The power function is described by a number showing the ratio between the input and output, which is the exponent *gamma*. Input and output are both scaled to a range between 0 and 1, with 0 representing black and 1 representing maximum white or a color. If a power function is applied to this measured transfer function and if the exponent is extracted, it is referred to as *gamma.*

The output of a device can be measured as a function of its input. This function is the *gamma ratio.* The output of a device with a gamma of 2.5 is two and one-half times greater than the intensity of its input. A gamma factor can also be applied to the output of a look-up table in a frame buffer, as long as the input and output are related by the same power-law expression. If all the components in an imaging system have transfer characteristics that are power functions, then the transfer function of the entire system is also a power function. The exponent, or gamma, of a system's transfer function is the product of all of the individual exponents (gammas) of the separate stages in the system. If the overall gamma of an imaging system is 1.0, its output is linearly proportional to its input. This means that the ratio between the intensities of any two areas in the reproduced image will be the same as in the original scene. Characteristics of the human eye and the differences in how devices capture and display light dictate that gamma be a variable function in systems that reproduce images.

gamut (n.) The range of colors that can be displayed on a video monitor.

garbage collection (n.) A process that reclaims storage space during the evaluation of an expression in a memory system. In systems that use dynamic storage allocation and in which expressions are represented as graphs containing pointers to data structures, garbage collection reclaims space used by subexpressions that do not point to a meaningful destination. The Java language is noted for its automatic garbage collection.

GAS See *GNU assembler.*

gate (n.) In electronic circuitry, a pathway that may be open or closed, depending on the source of the input, the strength of a signal, or the conductivity of chemicals used in semiconductors. Logic gates are programmed to correspond to related "if-then" statements. The

state of an open or closed gate is analogous to the binary state of a 0 or a 1. The application of this analogy allows computing machinery with millions of gates to respond conditionally and to perform logical functions.

gated (n.) Short form of gatedaemon, pronounced "GATE-dee"; used for network routing, a program that supports multiple protocols and protocol families. It is free and available by anonymous FTP from *gated.cornell.edu.*

gateway (n.) A dedicated computer that connects to two or more networks and that routes information between them. Networks connected to a gateway may be running different protocols, such as TCP/IP and SNMP, and the gateway converts between protocols operating in the top three layers of the Open Systems Interconnection (OSI) model. The term *gateway* has generally been replaced by the word *router.*

gauge (n.) The diameter of a cable or a wire. Even numbers are used to identify thickness in the American Wire Gauge (AWG) scale, which rates nonferrous conductors. Smaller numbers reflect thicker wires. Greater diameter results in better conductivity and less resistance, making it possible to run thicker cables over longer distances without signal degradation. Telephone wires are thin, usually #22, #24, or #26. Standard appliance cables are #16 or #18, and house wiring is usually #12 or #14. Heavy industrial applications use #2 wiring.

gawk (n.) GNU awk; a superset of standard awk that includes Plan 9 features. It has been ported to Unix, MS-DOS, and the Mac OS.

Gb See *gigabit.*

GB See *gigabyte.*

Gbps See *gigabits per second.*

GBps See *gigabytes per second.*

GCC (n.) See *GNU C compiler.*

GDI See *Graphical Device Interface.*

General MIDI (n.) General Musical Instrument Digital Interface; a standard configuration for MIDI systems. It refers to the assignment of particular sounds to specified preset locations. General MIDI sequencer files should sound roughly equivalent when executed by a variety of sound cards or synthesizers. This is not always the case, given the extreme differences between the sound of FM synthesizers and wavetable sample players.

Specifically, MIDI is a mapping structure that assigns instrument sounds, or voices, to each of the 128 different presets, programs, or patch locations. In a multitimbral MIDI sequence, each musical part or voice is sent to a different preset according to a "patch map." General MIDI defines the type of sound that resides at each patch location. There are 16 groups of eight instrument types. MIDI programs may be assigned to MIDI channels, and a sequence of note-on and note-off events may be sent to each discrete channel. The determination of which voice responds to which channel is controlled by a system message that sets up the receiver.

General MIDI specification sets the first 9 channels for instruments and the 10th for percussion. The remaining channels, 11 through 16, are left open for user configuration. Because early generations of sound cards were unable to support all 16 channels, Microsoft devised a proprietary system for assigning MIDI voices

in Windows. In this scheme, *Basic MIDI* devices use MIDI channels 13 through 16. In a more evolved system called *Extended MIDI,* devices use channels 1 through 9 for instruments and channel 10 for percussion; no assignments are possible for channels 11 through 16.

The first of two accompanying tables shows the General MIDI instrument program map. In addition to the 128 instruments listed in this table, the General MIDI specification assigns 47 drum sounds to a "key map." The second table shows the General MIDI percussion key map. The percussion instrument assigned to each note number is named. For your reference, middle C is note number 60. See tables on the following pages.

General MIDI mode (n.) General Musical Instrument Digital Interface mode; the mode in which a Microsoft Windows audio system operates if its MIDI Mapper matrix sets patches and channels to default MIDI Manufacturers Association (MMA) standards.

general protection fault (GPF) (n.) An error message that occurs when software tries to read from or write to memory that it does not own or to which it has no access.

generation (n.) 1. In storage media, particularly magnetic tape, the number of times a dub is removed from the master. A copy of the first copy is second-generation. The quality of each successive generation on magnetic tape declines. With digital formats, there is no difference between generations. 2. In hardware, a stratification reference to major evolutionary stages in development. Successive generations incorporate significant improvements and changes.

generational loss (n.) Reduced quality in audio or video clarity as a result of successive

G

133

General MIDI Map to Instrument Locations

Program	Family	Instrument Name	Program	Family	Instrument Name
1	Piano	Acoustic Grand	53	Ensemble	Choir Aahs
2	Piano	Bright Acoustic	54	Ensemble	Voice Oohs
3	Piano	Electric Grand	55	Ensemble	Synth Voice
4	Piano	Honky-tonk	56	Ensemble	Orchestra Hit
5	Piano	Electric Piano I	57	Brass	Trumpet
6	Piano	Electric Piano 2	58	Brass	Trombone
7	Piano	Harpsichord	59	Brass	Tuba
8	Piano	Clav	60	Brass	Muted Trumpet
9	Pitch Perc	Celesta	61	Brass	French Horn
10	Pitch Perc	Glockenspiel	62	Brass	Brass Section
11	Pitch Perc	Music Box	63	Brass	Synth Brass I
12	Pitch Perc	Vibraphone	64	Brass	Synth Brass 2
13	Pitch Perc	Marimba	65	Reed	Soprano Saxophone
14	Pitch Perc	Xylophone	66	Reed	Alto Saxophone
15	Pitch Perc	Tubular Bells	67	Reed	Tenor Saxophone
16	Pitch perc	Dulcimer	68	Reed	Baritone Saxophone
17	Organ	Drawbar Organ	69	Reed	Oboe
18	Organ	Percussive Organ	70	Reed	English Horn
19	Organ	Rock Organ	71	Reed	Bassoon
20	Organ	Church Organ	72	Reed	Clarinet
21	Organ	Reed Organ	73	Pipe	Piccolo
22	Organ	Accordian	74	Pipe	Flute
23	Organ	Harmonica	75	Pipe	Recorder
24	Organ	Tango Accordian	76	Pipe	Pan Flute
25	Guitar	Acoustic Guitar (nylon)	77	Pipe	Blown Bottle
26	Guitar	Acoustic Guitar (steel)	78	Pipe	Shakuhachi
27	Guitar	Electric Guitar (jazz)	79	Pipe	Whistle
28	Guitar	Electric Guitar (clean)	80	Pipe	Ocarina
29	Guitar	Electric Guitar (muted)	81	Synth Lead	Lead 1 (square)
30	Guitar	Overdriven Guitar	82	Synth Lead	Lead 2 (sawtooth)
31	Guitar	Distortion Guitar	83	Synth Lead	Lead 3 (calliope)
32	Guitar	Guitar Harmonics	84	Synth Lead	Lead 4 (chiff)
33	Bass	Acoustic Bass	85	Synth Lead	Lead 5 (charang)
34	Bass	Electric Bass (finger)	86	Synth Lead	Lead 6 (voice)
35	Bass	Electric Bass (pick)	87	Synth Lead	Lead 7 (fifths)
36	Bass	Fretless Bass	88	Synth Lead	Lead 8 (bass + lead)
37	Bass	Slap Bass 1	89	Synth Pad	Pad 1 (new age)
38	Bass	Slap Bass 2	90	Synth Pad	Pad 2 (warm)
39	Bass	Synth Bass I	91	Synth Pad	Pad 3 (polysynth)
40	Bass	Synth Bass 2	92	Synth Pad	Pad 4 (choir)
41	Strings	Violin	93	Synth Pad	Pad 5 (bowed)
42	Strings	Viola	94	Synth Pad	Pad 6 (metallic)
43	Strings	Cello	95	Synth Pad	Pad 7 (halo)
44	Strings	Contrabass	96	Synth Pad	Pad 8 (sweep)
45	Strings	Tremolo Strings	97	Synth FX	FX 1 (rain)
46	Strings	Pizzicato Strings	98	Synth FX	FX2 (soundtrack)
47	Strings	Orchestral Strings	99	Synth FX	FX 3 (crystal)
48	Strings	Timpani	100	Synth FX	FX 4 (atmosphere)
49	Ensemble	String Ensemble 1	101	Synth FX	FX 5 (brightness)
50	Ensemble	String Ensemble 2	102	Synth FX	FX 6 (goblins)
51	Ensemble	Synth Strings I	103	Synth FX	FX 7 (echoes)
52	Ensemble	Synth Strings 2	104	Synth FX	FX 8 (sci-fi)

Program	Family	Instrument Name	Program	Family	Instrument Name
105	Ethnic	Sitar	117	Perc	Taiko Drum
106	Ethnic	Banjo	118	Perc	Melodic Tom
107	Ethnic	Shamisen	119	Perc	Synth Drum
108	Ethnic	Koto	120	Perc	Reverse Cymbal
109	Ethnic	Kalimba	121	Sound FX	Guitar Fret Noise
110	Ethnic	Bagpipe	122	Sound FX	Breathing Noise
111	Ethnic	Fiddle	123	Sound FX	Seashore
112	Ethnic	Shanai	124	Sound FX	Bird Tweet
113	Perc	Tinkle Bell	125	Sound FX	Telephone Ring
114	Perc	Agogo	126	Sound FX	Helicopter
115	Perc	Steel Drums	127	Sound FX	Applause
116	Perc	Woodblock	128	Sound FX	Gunshot

G

MIDI Drum Sounds

Note #	Instrument Name	Note #	Instrument Name	Note #	Instrument Name
35	Acoustic Bass Drum	51	Ride Cymbal 1	67	High Agogo
36	Bass Drum 1	52	Chinese Cymbal	68	Low Agogo
37	Side Stick	53	Ride Bell	69	Casaba
38	Acoustic Snare	54	Tambourine	70	Maracas
39	Hand Clap	55	Splash Cymbal	71	Short Whistle
40	Electric Snare	56	Cowbell	72	Long Whistle
41	Low Floor Tom	57	Crash Cymbal 2	73	Short Guiro
42	Closed Hi-hat	58	Vibraslap	74	Long Guiro
43	High Floor Tom	59	Ride Cymbal 2	75	Claves
44	Pedal Hi-hat	60	High Bongo	76	High Wood Block
45	Low Tom	61	Low Bongo	77	Low Wood Block
46	Open Hi-hat	62	Mute High Conga	78	Mute Cuica
47	Low-mid Tom	63	Open High Conga	79	Open Cuica
48	High-mid Tom	64	Low Conga	80	Mute Triangle
49	Crash Cymbal 1	65	High Timbale	81	Open Triangle
50	High Tom	66	Low Timbale		

duplication. See also *generation*.

generic courseware (n.) Educational material that appeals to a broad market, rather than custom courseware for a specific audience.

genlock (n.) Abbreviation for synchronization generator lock; a machine that aligns the data rate of a video image with that of a digital device to ensure accurate timing in the digital copy.

Geographic Information System (GIS, pronounced "jee-eye-ESS") (n.) A computer system for capturing, storing, integrating, manipulating, analyzing, and displaying maps and other data related to positions on the surface of Earth. Uses for GIS include planning, marketing, managing resources, and engineering.

geosynchronous satellite (n.) A satellite that orbits at the same rate as Earth rotates, so that the satellite remains stationary in relation to a given point on Earth.

GFLOP See *gigaflop*.

GHz See *gigahertz*.

giant magnetoresistive (GMR) (adj.) Describes a type of hard disk head developed by IBM. Traditional hard disks read the electrical pulse induced in a coil as a magnetized region on the disk rotates under the head. A magnetoresistive (MR) head reads the change in resistance in a special magnetic material as the magnetized region passes under the head. The giant MR head employs quantum tunneling of electrons to produce a more sensitive head that reads from and writes to smaller regions on the disk, allowing up to 10 gigabytes (GB) per square inch of storage.

GIF See *Graphic Interchange Format.*

giga- Prefix meaning one billion. In the decimal system, 1 000 000 000 is expressed as 10 to the 9th power. In the binary system, it is expressed as 2 to the 30th power, or 1 073 741 824.

gigabit (Gb) (n.) One billion bits.

gigabits per second (Gbps) (n.) A measurement of data transfer in billions of bits per second.

gigabyte (GB) (n.) One billion 8-bit bytes, or 1 073 741 824 bytes.

gigabytes per second (GBps) (n.) A measurement of data transfer in billions of bytes per second.

gigaflop (GFLOP) (n.) One billion floating-point operations per second, or one million megaflops.

gigahertz (GHz) (n.) One billion cycles per second.

GIS See *Geographic Information System.*

GKS (n.) A standard that specifies a system for generating and storing computer graphics. It primarily addresses object-oriented graphics, but also supports bitmaps. GKS works on the program-interface level, rather than on the user level. It is defined in the ANSI X3.124–1985 specification.

glark (v.) Jargon meaning to understand a term from its context.

glass master (n.) The mold from which optical discs, such as CD-ROMs, are stamped. It is made of glass, and the data is stored as pits in the mold.

glitch (n.) Jargon for either a momentary disturbance in a signal or corrupted data.

global file specification (n.) A special character that matches any character or group of characters in a string comparison. In the Unix system, "?" matches any single character, and "*" matches any string of characters.

global index (n.) The file name extension (.gid) of a Windows 95 file. A .gid file is created by the help browser in Windows 95 for Winhelp files (.hlp), and it stores user preferences.

global key (n.) A keyboard character that performs a specific global function, regardless of program context. The Escape key (Esc) is an example.

Global Positioning System (GPS) (n.) A U.S. government satellite system targeted to include 21 satellites orbiting at 10 900 miles from Earth. With data from GPS satellites, inexpensive receivers can provide accurate positioning information anywhere in the world.

Global Security Service (GSS) (n.) A network protection protocol that provides features such as a single login to multiple services.

GMR See *giant magnetoresistive.*

GND See *ground.*

GNU (n.) GNU's not Unix; a project managed by the Free Software Foundation to provide a free replacement for Unix. Emacs and the GNU C compiler (GCC) are software tools designed for this project. Pronounced "guh-NOO."

GNU assembler (GAS) (n.) A program offered by the GNU Project of the Free Software Foundation that translates assembly language code into machine language that a computer can run.

GNU C compiler (GCC) (n.) GNU's not Unix C compiler; a portable compiler for C and C++ created by Richard Stallman. It supports multiple front ends and back ends by translating instructions first into Register Transfer Language and then into assembly code for the target architecture.

gold disc (n.) Jargon for a CD-recordable (CD-R). The blank disc has a lower layer of polycarbonate with a preformed track spiral, which the recording laser beam follows and inscribes. A translucent layer of green recordable material adheres to the polycarbonate, and there is a reflective layer of gold on top. These resilient discs are coated with lacquer.

gopher (n.) A distributed document retrieval system defined in RFC 1436. It has been replaced by the World Wide Web, which is itself a document retrieval system that provides access to gopher documents. Gopher originated at the University of Minnesota, where the mascot is a gopher.

GOSIP See *Government OSI Profile.*

GOTO (n.) A command or keyword used in FORTRAN, Cobol, BASIC, and C to cause an unconditional jump or transfer of control from one point in the program to another.

Gouraud shading (n.) An efficient three-dimensional rendering algorithm that averages the luma and chroma values at each corner of a polygon.

Government OSI Profile (GOSIP) (n.) Government Open Systems Interconnection Profile; a refined subset of OSI standards used by U.S. government procurements to increase the efficiency of the original OSI standards. Pronounced "GAH-sup."

GPF See *general protection fault.*

GPS See *Global Positioning System.*

gradient (n.) A method of filling or shading an object that blends different shades, patterns, or intensities across the surface of the object.

grammar (n.) In programming, a formal definition of the syntactic structure of a computer language. It is usually stated in terms of production rules, which specify the order of elements in a properly formed string. A grammar can be used to parse a sentence or to generate one. Parsing assigns a terminal syntactic category to each input token and a nonterminal category to each appropriate group of tokens. Parsing is generally preceded by lexical analysis.

Graphical Device Interface (GDI) (n.) A software interface between a video adapter or printer and the MS Windows operating system. It provides hundreds of functions for drawing geometric shapes and rendering fonts in Windows. This set of Application Programming Interfaces (APIs) provides instructions to a generic video driver and does not support proprietary adapters and accelerators. The Display Control Interface (DCI) superceded GDI, providing direct access to the video adapter. It has been superceded by *DirectDraw*, a component of *DirectX*.

graphical user interface (GUI, pronounced "GOO-ey") (n.) An environment in which icons represent objects that an operator can manipulate with a pointing device. Initially designed by Xerox, a GUI serves as the basis for the Mac OS and has been used in a similar context by Microsoft Windows. See also *user interface*.

Graphic Interchange Format (GIF) (n.) Defined in 1987 by CompuServe Information Service (CIS), a standard for digitized images compressed with the Lempel-Ziv-Welch (LZW) algorithm. *Graphic Interchange Format* and *GIF* are service marks of CIS, as a result of a 1994 legal action by Unisys Corporation against CIS for violating Unisys's LZW software patent. GIF 89A is an open, fully supported, nonproprietary specification available to the entire online community and used primarily on the World Wide Web. The file name extension for any GIF format is .gif. It was originally pronounced "JIFF" by its developers, but many new users who have begun working with web graphics in recent years pronounce it "GIFF" with a hard G. Both are commonly used.

graphics (n.) The visual content prepared for a production. Computer-generated letters, symbols, drawings, photographs, scans, slides, and all other still visuals belong to this broad category.

graphics accelerator (n.) A specialized circuit board containing a coprocessor that enhances the graphical performance of a computer by

Graphics Adapter Resolutions

Adapter	Resolution	Simultaneous Colors/Mode
EGA	640 x 350	16/text
	720 x 350	4/text
	320 x 200	16/graphics
	640 x 200	16/graphics
	640 x 350	16/graphics
VGA	720 x 400	16/text
	360 x 400	16/text
	640 x 480	16/graphics
	320 x 200	256/text
Super VGA	800 x 600	16 777 216/graphics
(Macintosh)	832 x 624	16 777 216/graphics
XGA	1024 x 768	16 777 216/graphics
(IBM 8514/A)	1024 x 768	256/graphics
	1152 x 864	16 777 216/graphics
Super XGA	1280 x 1024	16 777 216/graphics
Ultra XGA	1600 x 1200	16 777 216/graphics
	1800 x 1440	16 777 216/graphics
	1920 x 1200	16 777 216/graphics
	2040 x 1664	16 777 216/graphics

relieving the central processing unit (CPU) from graphics processing. A graphics accelerator is inserted in an expansion slot.

graphics adapter (n.) A specialized circuit board that provides a monitor with all the information it needs to display graphics. Some graphics adapters are built into the computer circuitry, but a third-party graphics card is more commonly inserted in an expansion slot. The peripheral component interconnect (PCI) bus is frequently used for this type of adapter. An advanced type of adapter for IBM compatibles is the Accelerated Graphics Port (AGP). The graphics adapter determines the resolution and refresh rate, or frequency, of the signal sent to the monitor. See Graphics Adapter Resolutions table.

graphics input (n.) The use of a peripheral, such as a drawing tablet, mouse, touch screen, or light pen, to create or alter a graphics display.

graphics input device (n.) Any digitizer that feeds a computer x- and y-coordinates and in some cases color data.

graphics output device (n.) Any device that displays or records an image. Monitors and printers are examples.

graphics tablet (n.) A type of drawing surface, often with pressure sensitivity, that feeds a computer data defining x- and y-coordinates from a handheld input device, such as a light pen.

grayscale (n.) In a computer graphic, the number of levels of gray that exist between black and white. With a minimum of 256 levels, resolution comparable to that of a black-and-white photograph can be achieved.

Green Book standard (n.) The specification for CD-i developed in 1991 by Philips. Discs that adhere to this CD-ROM format contain audio files, digital data, still graphics, and MPEG video. An infrared remote control device, a mouse, or a trackball allows users to interact with the content on the disc by clicking a cursor over hot spots on the video display.

grep (n.) A Unix command that searches files for lines matching a given regular expression. It is named for the subcommand "g/re/p," which means Global Regular Expression Print.

grip (n.) In a film or video production, the person who mounts or positions the camera according to the director's instructions. The camera itself may be mounted on a dolly, a crane, or on any other surface that provides a desirable camera angle.

grok (v.) Jargon meaning to understand, pronounced "GRAWK."

ground (GND) (n.) An electrical connection between equipment and a zero voltage point. A ground loop occurs when equipment is grounded at more than one point.

GSS See *Global Security Service.*

guard band (n.) A narrow bandwidth of dead space between two adjacent channels. A guard band is space inserted between tracks of recorded material on audio tapes or videotapes to prevent crosstalk between tracks.

GUI See *graphical user interface.*

gzip (n.) A GNU utility that reduces the size of a file using Lempel-Ziv LZ77 compression. The original file is replaced by one with the file name extension .gz or .z. Compressed files may be restored by using gunzip, a companion applet that uncompresses. Gzip works on Unix systems, and versions exist for VMS and MS-DOS.

G

H

H See *henry.*

hacker (n.) A person with sophisticated programming skills who can break codes and access restricted data without access privileges.

HAL See *Hardware Abstraction Layer.*

half-duplex (HD) (adj.) Describes a telecommunications circuit that provides data transmission in two directions but that can transmit in only one direction at a time.

half-height (adj.) Describes a floppy disk drive, CD-ROM drive, or other peripheral that is 1.625 inches tall and that may be mounted in a short drive bay. It may be either 4 or 5.75 inches wide and either 4 or 8 inches deep.

half-inch (n.) Jargon for the 0.5-inch videotape used in betacam, S-VHS, and VHS video formats.

halftone (n.) With regard to a graphical display or a printed document, a color value created with dots. The degree of color intensity is determined by the density and diameter of the dots. Printers, scanners, and monitors use halftone graphic techniques. This method of depicting color is different from grayscale, which defines actual shades of gray. See figure.

halftone image

handle (n.) In a graphical environment, the corner or edge of an object onto which the user may click and drag to reposition or resize an image.

handshake (n.) As part of the communications protocol, the exchange of signals between two devices to establish a connection.

handwriting recognition (n.) A hardware-software system that converts handwritten letters into text files. It can be implemented on the touch screen of a personal digital assistant (PDA), with a light pen on a graphics tablet, or by using a scanner with optical character recognition (OCR) software.

hang (v.) Jargon that means to wait for an event that will not occur. A system that is hung may also be referred to as *wedged* or *frozen.*

HARC-C See *Houston Advanced Research Center–C.*

hard copy (n.) Documents and images in printed, concrete form, such as pages of text, slides, prints, transparencies, graphs, and plots.

hard disk (n.) A fixed magnetic disk drive that stores large amounts of data. Winchester is a common type. A hard disk consists of a stack of rigid platters with multiple read/write heads. See figure.

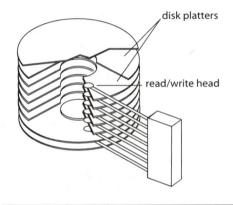

hard disk mechanism

hard effect (n.) A production sound that is difficult to produce live. Hard effects are typically pulled from an effects library or created for a particular project. Also known as a *spot effect*.

hardware (n.) The electromechanical portion of a data processing system. Computer machinery, circuit boards, monitors, peripheral devices, cables, and connectors are all hardware components.

Hardware Abstraction Layer (HAL) (n.) In the Microsoft Windows NT operating system, the place where the assembly language code is isolated.

hardware key (n.) A small connector that plugs into the parallel port of a computer. It typically contains code that the computer needs

in order to perform a certain function, such as running proprietary software. Sometimes referred to as a *dongle*.

harmonic (n.) A tone whose frequency is a multiple of the lowest tone in the harmonic series, the fundamental. Musical sounds consist of a fundamental and a number of harmonic overtones. The exception to this is the sine wave, which is devoid of harmonics. See figure.

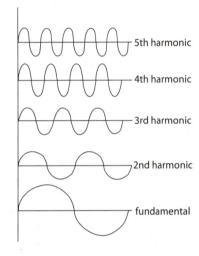

harmonics

Hayes AT command set (n.) A standard developed by Hayes Corporation to control intelligent modem parameters. This set of commands has become the de facto standard in the industry.

HBI See *horizontal blanking interval.*

HD See *half-duplex.*

HDLC See *High-Level Data Link Control.*

HDSL See *High-Data-Rate Digital Subscriber Line.*

HDT See *Host Digital Terminal.*

HDTV See *high-definition television.*

head (n.) An electromagnetic assembly that reads and writes data to any type of medium, such as magnetic tape, an optical disc, or the platter in a hard disk drive. See figure.

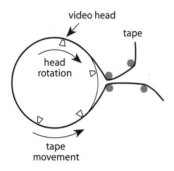

read and write head in a VCR

headend (n.) The site in a cable system or broadband coaxial network where the programming originates and the distribution network starts. Signals are usually received off the air from satellites, microwave relays, or fiber-optic cables at the headend for distribution.

header (n.) 1. In telecommunications and computing, information recorded at the beginning of a packet of transmitted data to identify what follows. On a CD-ROM it is recorded at the beginning of a sector, containing the address of the sector (the logical block number) and the mode in which the sector is recorded. 2. With reference to hardware, a row of pins on a circuit board that will accept a connector.

header field (n.) In CD-ROM terms, the address of a sector (the logical block number). It consists of four bytes recorded at the beginning of each sector that identify the address of

the sector and the mode in which the sector is recorded.

head parking (n.) Automatic repositioning of the heads in a hard drive to move them to an unused track when a computer system is shut down, so that they will not damage data in the event of a failure.

headroom (n.) The amount of excessive amplitude that an analog tape recorder can accept past the point where the meters peak and before distortion occurs. Headroom is valuable when recording live sounds that could peak the meters unexpectedly.

head slot (n.) A small aperture in the jacket, or casing, of a floppy disk that exposes the medium to read/write heads.

heap (n.) In programming, the dynamic memory allocation space where blocks of memory are allocated and freed in an arbitrary order and where the pattern of allocation and the size of blocks are unknown until run time. A heap is required by languages in which functions can return arbitrary data structures.

heartbeat (n.) 1. In network terms, the signal emitted by a Level 2 Ethernet transceiver at the end of each packet to show that the collision-detection circuit remains connected. 2. Used by software or hardware, a regular synchronization signal that may take the form of a bus clock or a periodic interrupt.

heat sink (n.) A piece of metal connected to an electronic device. The heat sink dissipates heat and radiates it to the environment to prevent the device from overheating. A heat sink often has fins to increase its surface area. A gelatinous compound is frequently applied between the device and the heat sink to improve thermal conduction.

Heidi (n.) An Application Program Interface (API) developed by Autodesk that supports the rendering and output of three-dimensional images.

helical scan (n.) A tape playback system with two video heads mounted on opposite sides of a revolving drum. The head drum spins at a single frame per revolution, so each head scans one field, or half a frame, per revolution. The system achieves high tape speeds by moving the tape and the heads. The tape moves in a spiral path as it winds around the video head drum.

helper application (n.) A program that enables a web browser to play multimedia file types, such as audio, video, or animation. This is analogous to an application that reads a file attached to an email message if the correct MIME type is specified and if it is available on the system.

henry (H) (n.) A unit of inductance named for American physicist Joseph Henry (1797–1878). A single henry is the inductance of a closed loop in which the induced voltage is 1 volt if the current flowing through it changes at the rate of 1 ampere per second.

hertz (Hz) (n.) A unit of frequency measurement named for German physicist Heinrich Rudolf Hertz (1857–1894); 1 Hz equals 1 cycle per second (cps), 1 kilohertz (kHz) equals 1000 cps, and 1 megahertz (MHz) equals 1 000 000 cps.

heuristic (adj.) Describes a trial-and-error method of solving problems by evaluating the progress made at various steps in a process.

heuristic routine (n.) A software methodology that solves problems by trial and error

rather than by an algorithmic procedure. A computer may be said to engage in learning during this process.

Hewlett-Packard Graphics Language (HPGL) (n.) A bitmapped graphic file format used by IBM-compatible graphics programs.

hexadecimal (n.) A numbering system with numbers 0 through 9 and letters *A* through *F,* which together are called *hex digits.* See table on the following page.

HFC See *hybrid fiber-coax.*

HFS See *Hierarchical File System.*

hidden attribute (n.) A feature that prevents files from being displayed in the directory list while MS-DOS or Windows is running.

hidden file (n.) A file whose attributes are set so that it is not normally shown in a directory listing. Hiding system files in MS-DOS prevents the user from accidentally deleting them.

Hi-8 video (n.) An improved version of the Sony 8 mm format. Hi-8 video yields higher luminance levels and better quality than standard 8 mm and provides Y/C component S-video connections.

Hierarchical File System (HFS) (n.) The directory structure used in the Mac OS that defines a pattern of nested folders and determines how they are stored on formatted media.

hierarchical link (n.) In object-oriented programming, a "parent-child" relationship between two objects. Changes made to the parent are automatically inherited by the child, but changes made to the child will not necessarily be reflected in the parent.

Hexadecimal Equivalents

Hexadecimal	Decimal	Binary	Hexadecimal	Decimal	Binary
01	1	00000001	15	21	00010101
02	2	00000010	16	22	00010110
03	3	00000011	17	23	00010111
04	4	00000100	18	24	00011000
05	5	00000101	19	25	00011001
06	6	00000110	1A	26	00011010
07	7	00000111	1B	27	00011011
08	8	00001000	1C	28	00011100
09	9	00001001	1D	29	00011101
0A	10	00001010	1E	30	00011110
0B	11	00001011	1F	31	00011111
0C	12	00001100	20	32	00100000
0D	13	00001101	21	33	00100001
0E	14	00001110	22	34	00100010
0F	15	00001111	23	35	00100011
10	16	00010000	24	36	00100100
11	17	00010001	25	37	00100101
12	18	00010010	26	38	00100110
13	19	00010011	27	39	00100111
14	20	00010100	28	40	00101000

hierarchical routing (n.) Division of a network into a hierarchy of smaller networks in which each level is responsible for its own routing. The three levels of hierarchy in the Internet are backbones, midlevel networks, and stub networks.

hierarchical structure (n.) A system of tree-structured directories that is built in layers and based on pathways between root directories and subdirectories.

High-Data-Rate Digital Subscriber Line (HDSL) (n.) Telecommunications transmission technology developed by Bellcore that uses a special DSL modem in T1 applications to filter out background interference in twisted-pair copper wires. A send-receive unit is required at each end of the connecting wire, and the transmission distance is limited.

high-definition television (HDTV) (n.) A video format with higher resolution than the NTSC, PAL, and SECAM broadcast standards it will replace. HDTV formats range from 655 to 2125 scanning lines and display in a 16:9 aspect ratio. The HDTV format has a video bandwidth of 30 to 50 MHz, which is more than five times greater than that of standard NTSC. The most typical implementation of HDTV provides 1125 lines of horizontal resolution rather than 525 in NTSC, partially because of the wider aspect ratio. HDTV is also equipped with dolby AC-3 surround-sound and CD-quality audio.

High-Level Data Link Control (HDLC) (n.) Standard ISO protocol for communications devices and software applications operating in synchronous environments. HDLC defines how data frames should be formatted for exchange between modems.

high-level language (HLL) (n.) Any programming language in which a single statement may be translated into numerous assembly language or machine code instructions. High-level languages are designed to be machine-independent, in contrast to an assembly language.

C++, BASIC, Pascal, and FORTRAN are examples of high-level languages.

High-Performance Parallel Interface (HIPPI) (n.) ANSI standard X3T9.3 that increases the speed of a computer bus between routers, peripherals, and other computers at speeds of 800 megabits per second (Mbps) over 32 twisted pairs of copper wiring, and 1600 Mbps over 64 twisted pairs. Cable lengths are limited to 25 meters over copper wire and 300 meters over multimode optical fiber. HIPPI is a common interface for supercomputers.

high-performance serial bus (IEEE 1394) (n.) A serial bus interface standard that provides high-speed communication and isochronous realtime data services. It can transmit data at 100 megabits per second (Mbps), 200 Mbps, or 400 Mbps. As many as 16 cables up to 4.5 meters long may be connected in a daisy chain to a single computer. IEEE 1394 allows peer-to-peer device communication without taxing the processor or using system memory. It supports plug and play (PnP) and can supply up to 60 watts of power over a standard inexpensive six-wire cable. See also *FireWire*.

High Sierra format (n.) A standard CD-ROM format for file and directory placement. It was developed by computer vendors, software developers, and CD-ROM system integrators. Twelve companies began work on the format proposal in 1985 at the High Sierra Hotel in Lake Tahoe, Nevada. The ISO 9660 format is a revised version of the High Sierra format adopted by the ISO.

High-Speed Serial Interface (HSSI, pronounced "HISS-ee") (n.) A data communications protocol that can support serial transfer of data at a rate of 52 megabits per second (Mbps). The most common connections are wide area network (WAN) routers and leased lines, such as DS-3, which transmits at up to 44.736 Mbps.

High Speed Technology (HST) (n.) A high-speed modem protocol with error control, developed by U.S. Robotics.

High Split (n.) Broadband cable system in which the upstream signaling bandwidth is about 6 MHz to 180 MHz and the downstream bandwidth is about 220 MHz to 400 MHz. A guard band between upstream and downstream signals prevents interference between the two.

HIPPI See *High-Performance Parallel Interface*.

hit (n.) Any action or event that takes place on a web server, such as when a user views a page or downloads a file.

HLL See *high-level language*.

HLS See *hue, luminance, and saturation*.

hologram (n.) An image with a layered, three-dimensional appearance that is produced by a laser-based system rather than by lenses.

home page (n.) A document that is accessed via the World Wide Web by using a browser, or universal client. A home page, or web page, is typically written in HTML, which provides the capacity to link "hot" words to other words, graphics, or pages. The home page is usually the point of entry for a web site, with hyperlinks to the other pages.

hop (n.) In relation to routing, each step in a path through routers from origin to destination on a network.

horizontal blanking interval (HBI) (n.) The length of time required for the beam of a cathode-ray tube (CRT) to return from the right side of a line of pixels to the left side of the next line while scanning. The interval is included in the signal for each of the 525 lines in an NTSC picture. See also *vertical blanking interval.*

horizontal resolution (n.) The number of lines measurable across the width of a video monitor or screen. This number determines the degree of discernible detail. More lines of resolution result in better picture quality.

host adapter (n.) A controller card, such as a SCSI adapter, that routes data between the CPU and peripherals, such as CD-ROM drives, printers, or disk drives.

host computer (n.) Any computer that provides the processing power for the terminals and for the peripherals connected to it.

Host Digital Terminal (HDT) (n.) Interface point for information transmitted to and from an optical network unit (ONU). The HDT manages signal traffic and provides the interconnection point for local switching.

hostname (n.) A unique name that identifies a computer on a network. An Internet hostname is an ASCII string, such as *hansenmedia .com*. The hostname is translated, or resolved, into an Internet address by the domain name system (DNS). A single computer may have several hostnames (aliases), but only one is designated as its canonical name, in which each facet of the complete address is defined.

hot (adj.) 1. Describes a defined region on the monitor that responds to a mouse click or to pressure in the case of a touch screen when an interactive program is running. Activating the defined area initiates an action or causes a process to be performed. 2. In audio terms, describes a tape recorded at the maximum possible signal level. 3. In video production, describes a camera that is in use, or "on air."

hot fix (n.) The replacement of a failed disk drive in a multiple drive system with a "hot spare" while the remaining drives are online. Also called a *hot swap.*

HotJava (n.) The Sun Microsystems web browser that can execute programs written in Java. Java applets can be included in HTML pages. Applets run on any platform that supports HotJava, including Solaris 2, Windows 95, and Windows NT.

hot link (n.) 1. A connecting point manifested as text, buttons, or icons that are specially tagged in an interactive program, making it possible to connect instantly to information in another location or to execute instructions simply by clicking on them or by otherwise activating the links. 2. A connection between two or more programs that updates data in linked programs automatically when it is changed in one of the associated programs. For example, making a change in a database file linked to a graph representing the data will cause a corresponding change in the graph.

hotlist (n.) A term that the NCSA Mosaic web browser uses to describe the list of URLs that a user has visited and chosen to add to the list. The hotlist is equivalent to *Bookmarks* in Netscape Navigator or *Favorites* in MS Internet Explorer.

hot spot (n.) An area or region on the computer screen that responds to mouse clicks. An image map on a page of HTML is an example of a hot spot that provides a link to another location.

hot swap (n.) The replacement of a failed disk

drive in a multiple drive system with a "hot spare" while the remaining drives are online. Also called a *hot fix*.

house sync (n.) The timing signal, typically SMPTE code, that is supplied to all audio and video recording and playback equipment in a postproduction house. A common timing source ensures rock-solid tracking between different machines.

Houston Advanced Research Center–C (HARC-C, pronounced "hark-SEE") (n.) A video compression algorithm based on wavelet theory and programmed in C.

HPGL See *Hewlett-Packard Graphics Language.*

HQX (n.) A Macintosh program that converts binary files into the seven-bit BinHex format so they can be transferred to another user as text. The file name extension for a BinHex format file is .hqx.

HSSI See *High-Speed Serial Interface.*

HST See *High Speed Technology.*

HSV See *hue, saturation, and value.*

H.320 (n.) Standard for conferencing over network or telephone lines integrating voice, digital video, and control messages into an interleaved signal over one or more 64-kilobit-per-second (Kbps) channels. Video formats specified are Common Intermediate Format (CIF) at a resolution of 352 x 288 pixels and Quarter CIF (QCIF) at a resolution of 176 x 144 pixels. Both resolutions are specified at 30 frames per second (fps) with interleaved audio. Any type of circuit may be used, including ISDN, Switched 56, or fractional T1.

HTML See *Hypertext Markup Language.*

HTML 4.0 (n.) Hypertext Markup Language version 4.0; a Document Type Definition (DTD) that is a subset of Standard Generalized Markup Language (SGML) and that extends HTML version 3.2 with additional commands and features. Even the 4.0 version of popular browsers is unable to interpret some of the features in HTML 4.0. This version's new elements include the OBJECT element, the BUTTON element, and the INS and DEL elements for marking edited text. Also see the appendix on HTML.

HTTP See *Hypertext Transfer Protocol.*

HTTP cookie (n.) Hypertext Transfer Protocol cookie; a packet of data that is sent by an HTTP server to a web browser, is stored on the client computer, and is returned by the browser each time it accesses the server that sent the cookie. Cookies may contain any kind of data that the server chooses to send, but they are primarily used to inform the server of the state of the browser and the configuration of the client. A cookie can be used by a server to identify a registered user of a site in order to avoid asking for a password on each visit.

HTTPd (n.) Hypertext Transfer Protocol daemon; developed by Rob McCool at the National Center for Supercomputing Applications (NCSA), HTTP 1.0 server software that makes HTML and other document types available to web browsers. It is compact and fast, and it works with most browsers. It allows a server to handle HTML forms and to execute searches.

HTTP 1.1 (n.) Hypertext Transfer Protocol version 1.1; a revision of the original HTTP that improves performance. Under HTTP 1.0, a new connection via TCP is required for each piece of data transferred from a web page. This means that an individual connection is made for each graphical object, then thrown away.

The revised version employs "persistent connections," maintaining a single connection through multiple downloads and taking advantage of TCP algorithms to avoid congestion. Another important new feature is "pipelining," which allows an ordered series of HTTP requests to be made at one time and received in order. The updated HTTP 1.1 must be running on both the server and the client. New versions of Netscape and Microsoft client software include the upgrade, and it is being built into server software. Traffic on the Internet will be reduced substantially, because the number of packets sent (such as TCP "open/close" packets) will be controlled.

HTTPS See *Hypertext Transfer Protocol, Secure.*

H.261 (n.) A video compression standard developed by the International Telecommunications Union (ITU) for ISDN transmission. Data is compressed at $64P$ kilobits per second (Kbps), where P ranges from 1 to 30, depending on the number of ISDN channels used. Developed primarily to support videoconferencing, H.261 is referred to as P x 64, pronounced "P-TIMES-64."

hub (n.) A network repeater that does not provide retiming functions.

hue (n.) A color, such as cyan, yellow, magenta, or green.

hue, luminance, and saturation (HLS) (n.) Three parameters of a computer graphic. *Hue* refers to the specific color. Rose, crimson, and burgundy are all red hues. *Luminance* defines the brightness, or amount of light. *Saturation* refers to the strength of a color, compared with neutral gray. Saturation is also called *intensity, depth,* or *chroma.*

hue, saturation, and value (HSV) (n.) A system of defining colors.

Huffman coding (n.) A data compression technique outlined in a paper by D. A. Huffman in 1952. Huffman coding varies the length of an encoded symbol in proportion to its information content. The more frequently a symbol or token is used in a data file, the shorter the binary string must be that represents it in the compressed stream. Huffman codes can be properly decoded because they obey the prefix property, which means that no code can be a prefix of another code. Therefore the complete set of codes can be represented as a binary tree, known as a *Huffman tree.*

hybrid disc (n.) 1. A CD-ROM that is in the logical disc format and that contains both ISO 9660 and Hierarchical File System (HFS) data structures, so that it is readable by both Windows and the Mac OS. 2. A multisession disc. *Hybrid disc* is the term usually used for a CD-ROM in the Orange Book format. Developed by Philips and Eastman Kodak, this format allows information to be added to previously recorded data. A Kodak Photo-CD is an example.

hybrid fiber-coax (HFC) (n.) Network topology for cable television that consists of combined fiber-optic feeders and traditional coaxial cables with amplifiers in the branch lines. Several telecommunications companies have implemented the HFC broadband network topology because it is affordable and scalable.

HyperCard (n.) An interactive authoring environment developed by Apple Computer. HyperTalk is HyperCard's scripting language that consists of English language commands and that creates links between words, buttons, and diverse media. HyperCard programs (stacks) consist of frames (cards) with routines (scripts). External commands (XCMDs) and external functions (XFCNs) are used to extend functionality.

hyperlink (n.) Often simply called a *link,* a connection between two points in a hypertext document or between different documents. A browser displays a hyperlink with colored or specially formatted text. When a hyperlink is activated by a mouse click, the browser immediately seeks and displays the target of the link.

hypermedia (n.) Another word for *multimedia, new media,* or *digital media.* It refers to a dimensional environment with text, graphics, audio, animation, and video elements that are all linked to other elements.

HyperTalk (n.) The scripting language used in HyperCard.

hypertext (n.) Indexed words that are linked to graphics, audio, or other words not located nearby. Theodore Nelson is credited with the first usage of the term in 1965. Like the strands of a spiderweb, hypertext links connect HTML pages on the World Wide Web.

Hypertext Markup Language (HTML) (n.) A set of commands for marking a document so that it can be read by a web browser, such as Netscape Navigator. All home pages on the World Wide Web are HTML documents. HTML is a subset of Standard Generalized Markup Language (SGML). HTML codes, or tags, specify the function of a text string (title, heading, body, etc.), but they do not instruct a parser on how to display information. As a result, various browsers format documents differently. See also the appendix on HTML.

Hypertext Transfer Protocol (HTTP) (n.) The client-server TCP/IP used for exchanging HTML documents on the World Wide Web. Version 1.1, defined by RFC 2068 in May 1997, offers major improvements over the original, which was version 1.0.

Hypertext Transfer Protocol, Secure (HTTPS) (n.) The Netscape variation of HTTP used to process secure transactions. The Navigator browser supports HTTPS, which is a special URL access method for connecting to HTTP servers using Secure Sockets Layer (SSL). The Internet Assigned Numbers Authority (IANA) has designated the default HTTPS port number as 443.

Hz See *hertz.*

I

IAB See *Internet Architecture Board.*

IANA See *Internet Assigned Numbers Authority.*

IAP See *Internet Access Provider.*

I-beam (n.) The cursor shape in a graphical user interface (GUI) that identifies the location on the screen where characters will appear in a text-entry mode.

IBM-compatible (adj.) Describes a personal computer that runs MS-DOS and that is often referred to as a PC, as opposed to a Macintosh.

IBM PC (n.) International Business Machines Personal Computer; generic term for any microcomputer based on the Intel family of microprocessors: 8086, 8088, 80286, 80386, 80486, Pentium, or Pentium II. The speed of the central processing unit (CPU) is the most significant factor in performance, determined by clock rate and the number of bits the CPU can process internally.

IBM PC AT (n.) A version of the IBM PC released in August 1984 with an Intel 80286 processor, a 16-bit bus, a 1.2-megabyte (MB) floppy disk drive, and a larger case than the original PC had.

IBM PC XT (n.) An IBM-compatible personal computer that was released in March 1983 with an Intel 8088 processor. The XT 286 version was released in September 1986 with an Intel 80286 processor and an eight-bit bus.

IBM PS/2 (n.) IBM Personal System/2; an IBM-compatible personal computer that replaced the IBM PC series in 1987. It used 8088, 80286, or 80386 processors and implemented IBM's Micro Channel Bus. It ran MS-DOS and OS/2 operating systems, and was compatible with most PC programs at the time.

IC See *integrated circuit.*

ICIA See *International Communications Industries Association.*

ICMP See *Internet Control Message Protocol.*

icon (n.) Any graphic symbol that represents an object, function, or task. Most often, it represents a file or application in a graphical user interface (GUI). When the cursor appears on top of an icon, a mouse click will generally initiate an action.

ICT See *Integrated Computer Telephony.*

ICW See *interactive courseware.*

ID (n.) Abbreviation for identification.

I-D See *Internet-Draft.*

IDE See *Integrated Drive Electronics.*

IEC See *International Electrotechnical Commission.*

IEEE See *Institute of Electrical and Electronics Engineers.*

IEEE 802 (n.) A set of standards commonly used for local area networks (LANs) and metropolitan area networks (MANs). The 802 standards divide the data link layer into two sublayers. The first of these is the medium access control (MAC) layer, defined in 802.3, 802.5, and 802.6. MAC defines specific methods by which access may be gained to a LAN, including Ethernet random access and IBM token ring. The second sublayer is the Logical Link Control (LLC) layer, defined in 802.2. LLC addresses the processes of establishing and terminating services as well as data transfer. The three types of links described in LLC are the acknowledged connectionless link, the unacknowledged connectionless link, and the connection-mode link. The 802 specifications refer to the following network features:

- IEEE 802.1: The general architecture of LANs and internets, known as the spanning tree algorithm.

- IEEE 802.11: The standard for wireless LANs and networks.

- IEEE 802.2: The standard for frames of data sent over Ethernet, token ring, and other types of LANs.

- IEEE 802.3: The standard for carrier sense multiple access with collision detection (CSMA/CD) used in 10-megabit-per-sec-

ond (Mbps) Ethernet.

- IEEE 802.4: The standard for the physical layer of a LAN with token-passing access on a bus topology.

- IEEE 802.5: The standard for the physical layer of a LAN with token-passing access on a ring topology using unshielded twisted-pair wiring.

- IEEE 802.6: The standard for metropolitan area networks (MANs), also known as distributed queue dual bus (DQDB).

IEEE 802.3 (n.) The standard defining the hardware layer and transport layer of Ethernet. The maximum packet size is 1518 bytes, and the maximum segment length is 500 meters. The maximum total length is 2.5 km, and the maximum number of hosts is 1024.

IEEE 488 (n.) An eight-bit parallel bus that allows up to 15 intelligent devices to share a single bus. Used primarily for test equipment, the IEEE 488 has a maximum data rate of about 1 megabit per second (Mbps). Also known as *General Purpose Interface Bus (GPIB)* or *Hewlett-Packard Interface Bus (HP-IB).*

IEEE 1394 See *FireWire* or *high-performance serial bus.*

IESG See *Internet Engineering Steering Group.*

IETF See *Internet Engineering Task Force.*

IFF See *Interchange File Format.*

IGES See *Initial Graphics Exchange Specification.*

IGP See *Interior Gateway Protocol.*

IIA See *Information Industry Association.*

IICS See *International Interactive Communications Society.*

illegal character (n.) A character that may not be used in a command or statement because it is reserved for another use. For example, an MS-DOS file name may not contain a period, because the operating system uses that character to separate the file name from its extension.

IMA See *Interactive Multimedia Association* or *International MIDI Association.*

image (n.) A collection of graphical data representing a two-dimensional scene. An image is composed of pixels arranged in an array. The pixels contain information representing the brightness and color of the image at that point, most often encoded as RGB triplets. The term is generally applied to a representation of existing objects that have been photographed and scanned digitally.

image map (n.) A graphic in an HTML document. When the mouse is clicked inside active areas of the image map, they act as links to other locations in the same way that hypertext links function.

image processing (n.) The manipulation of data to produce a display or to alter a previously defined graphic using digital means.

imaging (n.) 1. The process of digitizing graphics captured by a camera. 2. The process of recording images digitally on film, tape, CD-ROM, or disk.

IMAP See *Internet Message Access Protocol.*

impedance (n.) The combined effect of capacitance, inductance, and resistance on a signal.

According to Ohm's law, voltage is the product of current and resistance at a given frequency. Microphones are differentiated by whether they operate on a high- or low-impedance circuit. A low-impedance condenser microphone is more sensitive than a high-impedance dynamic microphone. A low-impedance microphone requires phantom power or a battery.

import (v.) To move data into an open file from memory. The data may be any compatible file type, such as a graphic, and it may be exported from a different application. For example, an AIFF sound file may be imported into a Macromedia Director movie and either linked to the movie or combined with all the other assets in the movie file.

in-band signaling (n.) In telecommunications, a type of signaling consisting of tones within the voice frequency band that are carried along the same circuit as the voice path. Most telephone signals, such as request for service, dialing, and disconnect, are in-band signals.

in-betweening (n.) A function incorporated in some computer animation programs that automatically draws images on the screen to simulate motion between two coordinates. Also called *tweening.*

inches per second (ips) (n.) The running speed of an audio tape player, such as 3.75, 7.5, or 15 ips.

incremental backup (n.) An archival procedure that copies only files that have changed since the last backup was performed. It is a common way to save recent work from a hard disk to a floppy disk without saving information that has been archived in a full backup.

Indeo (n.) A software-based digital video compression-decompression (CODEC) standard developed by Intel Corporation. Frequently used to facilitate and improve delivery in the Video for Windows or QuickTime formats, it can achieve software decompression with a 320 x 240 pixel resolution at 12 to 15 frames per second (fps) on a 486DX66 processor. Much better resolution and frame rates can be achieved on faster processors. The individual video display system, particularly the video card drivers installed, will greatly affect the frame rate during decoding. Indeo is software based, so the quality improves with processor speed and computing power.

indexed color system (n.) A procedure for defining color information that obtains data from a descriptive file and that points to a table of output colors called a *color look-up table (CLUT)*.

individualized instruction (adj.) Describes software that modifies the teaching approach or content based on student feedback in order to optimize learning.

inductance (n.) The ability of a coil of wire, or inductor, to block high-frequency signals from flowing through it. Inductance is measured in henrys (H).

industrial market (n.) The segment of video and multimedia markets that addresses training, marketing, sales, and communications for businesses rather than for home consumers. Compare *consumer market* or *domestic market*.

Industry Standard Architecture (ISA, pronounced "EYE-suh") (n.) The name of the common expansion bus architecture in an IBM-compatible PC.

inference engine (n.) A program that infers new information from known facts using inference rules. An expert system or a knowledge-based system usually includes such an engine.

inference rule (n.) A method of combining known facts to arrive at new facts. For example, if Spot is a dog, and if all dogs have four legs, we can infer that Spot has four legs. It is possible to express the rule in Boolean algebra as $(A \& A => B) => B$. This is to say that if proposition A is true, and if A implies B, then proposition B is also true. An inference rule can also be used to imply conditional status. For example, either the sun is shining or it is dark outside. If the sun is not shining, we can infer that it is dark. This rule may be written $((A \text{ OR } B) \& \text{ NOT } B) => A$. This is to say that if either A is true or B is true (or both), and if B is false, then A must be true.

infinite loop (n.) In programming, a segment of a program that is executed repeatedly without stopping. This type of program is used to control an embedded system that is intended to run continuously until it is stopped or interrupted.

Information Industry Association (IIA) (n.) Established in 1968, the IIA is an organization that represents more than 550 companies involved in creating, distributing, and facilitating the use of information in print and digital formats. The IIA addresses the industry's interests in government policy and regulatory matters; promotes the industry and provides advance information about new developments and emerging technologies; and provides a business development forum for interaction among top executives in the information industry.

infotainment (n.) Interactive CD-ROM programs that blend entertainment with informational, educational activities.

153

infrared (n.) A spectrum of electromagnetic radiation with wavelengths that are longer than visible light waves but shorter than microwaves. The infrared bandwidth lies between 0.75 and 1000 microns. This spectrum is used for fiber-optic transmission and for through-the-air transmission for short distances. Remote control devices typically rely on infrared technology.

inheritance (n.) In object-oriented programming (OOP), the capacity to derive new classes from existing classes. A derived class (subclass) inherits the instance variables and methods of the base class (superclass), and it may add new instance variables and methods of its own. New methods may be defined with the same names as those in the base class; in that case, the new methods override the original ones.

in-house (adj.) Describes production or development conducted in a company or organization without external resources, facilities, or consultants. Developing media in-house is the opposite of outsourcing production.

INI file (n.) A file with the extension .ini that contains data specific to a certain application in Microsoft Windows, usually defining the configuration and default settings for the application. Pronounced "IH-nee FILE."

INIT (n.) In the Mac OS, a utility program that initializes on startup. Conflicting INITs may cause the mouse to freeze and the system to crash. To avoid this, a user can start a Macintosh while holding down the Shift key, which disables all INITs. They may be enabled one by one until the conflict is isolated. Pronounced "ih-NIT."

Initial Graphics Exchange Specification (IGES) (n.) A cross-platform format for computer-aided design (CAD) programming.

IGES is an industry standard defined by the American National Standards Institute (ANSI).

initialization (n.) A set of routines run by a device or program. Blank media must be initialized for the platform on which they will be used. If media with data stored on them are initialized, the data is eliminated. Printers on a network must be initialized for access. Microcomputers set up registers and memory locations on initialization.

injection molding (n.) The process of forcing melted plastic (polycarbonate) into a precast form. This is the method used to create the substrate of a compact disc.

inline image (n.) A graphic image displayed as a component of an HTML document among lines of text. Images are compressed in the GIF, JPEG, or PNG format. The image is called by a statement in HTML text similar to the following:

<IMG SRC=Image.gif>

in-point (n.) The first frame of a video segment or the beginning of an audio track that is chosen for editing.

input 1. (v.) To send information to a computer or processor. 2. (n.) The data sent to a processor or storage device. 3. (n.) A terminal, jack, or receptacle provided for the introduction of an electrical signal into a device.

insert editing (n.) Postproduction technique in which new video or audio material is inserted into preexisting material on a master tape. The time code is not altered. Compare *assemble editing.*

insertion point (n.) The position on a screen

where a cursor is blinking and where characters are entered when typed.

inside wiring (n.) Connecting cables that belong to a telephone company customer, located between the demarcation point and the telephone equipment in a home or office. It typically consists of copper twisted pairs.

instantiation (n.) 1. In programming, the production of an object by replacing variables with new values or other variables. 2. In object-oriented programming (OOP), the production of a particular object from its class template. This means that a structure is allocated with the types specified by the template and that instance variables are initialized with either default values or those provided by the class's constructor function.

Institute of Electrical and Electronics Engineers (IEEE, pronounced "eye-triple-EE") (n.) The largest technical professional society in the world. Founded in 1884 and based in the United States, it has more than 325 000 members in 147 countries. Technical conferences and symposia are sponsored around the world in electrical, electronics, and computer engineering, as well as in computer science. Disciplines include aerospace, computers, communications, biomedical technology, electric power, and consumer electronics.

instructional design (n.) Computer-aided methods of teaching material. Designers of interactive instructional programs address such issues as questioning strategy, levels of interaction, reinforcement, and branching routines.

instructional designer (n.) A developer of educational training programs.

Instructional Systems Design (ISD) (n.) The planning and pedagogy employed to develop an effective student-centered learning program. System components include computer hardware, software, and networks.

Instructional Television Fixed Service (ITFS) (n.) A broadcast system that operates in a specified band of microwave frequencies exclusively established by the Federal Communications Commission (FCC) for educational programs. ITFS operates when the transmitter and receiver are within the "line of sight," a radius of approximately 20 miles. A special converter is required to receive and translate the broadcast audio, video, or data into standard television signals.

integrated circuit (IC, pronounced "eye-SEE") (n.) A self-contained circuit module that passes electric current along predetermined paths. The circuit is created by arranging chemicals on the surface of a semiconductor, such as crystalline silicone. ICs may contain transistors, resistors, and many other types of processing components in their circuitry. There are several levels of ICs, categorized as follows:

- small-scale integration (SSI): 2–9 circuits

- medium-scale integration (MSI): 10–99 circuits.

- large-scale integration (LSI): 100–999 circuits.

- very large-scale integration (VLSI): 1000–9999 circuits.

- ultra large-scale integration (ULSI): more than 10 000 circuits.

Integrated Computer Telephony (ICT) (n.) A system that combines data communications with telecommunications. It involves the convergence of technologies such as Voice over IP (VoIP), call centers, and combined voice/data/video/fax transmission over broadband networks.

Integrated Drive Electronics (IDE) (n.) An interface standard based on the IBM PC ISA 16-bit bus for fixed disks that identifies the power and data signal interfaces between the motherboard and the integrated disk controller and drive. The IDE bus supports two devices, a master and a slave. Compaq invented the IDE bus in 1986 in collaboration with Western Digital, Imprimis, and Conner Peripherals. The first draft of a codified specification appeared in March 1989, and a finished version known then as the Advanced Technology Attachment (ATA) was sent to ANSI for ratification in November 1990. In multimedia applications, SCSI is preferred over the IDE interface, because SCSI is faster and allows more devices to be connected than IDE.

Integrated Services Digital Network (ISDN) (n.) An international digital telecommunications standard that accommodates voice, data, and signaling and that brings high bandwidth to the microcomputer desktop. The typical Basic Rate Interface (BRI) uses two common twisted pairs, unshielded, to deliver two 64-kilobit-per-second (Kbps) bearer B-channels and one data-signaling D-channel at 16 Kbps. The two bearer channels may be used simultaneously. The telephone connection may be approximately one mile away from the central office switch, which limits access to those in proximity of a switch. The Primary Rate Interface (PRI) carries 24 bearer channels and a 64-Kbps data channel with a capacity of nearly two megabits per second (Mbps). Among European countries, a Memorandum of Understanding (MOU) has been established that defines "Priority 1" ISDN facilities and services as follows:

- CLIP   Calling line identification presentation (displays the caller's number)

- CLIR   Calling line identification restriction (prevents the caller's number from displaying)

- DDI   Direct dialing in (to an individual user on a private exchange)

- MSN   Multiple subscriber number

- TP   Terminal portability

"Priority 2" ISDN facilities and services are defined as follows:

- AOC   Advice of charge

- CCBS   Completion of calls to busy subscriber

- CD   Call deflection

- CFB   Call forwarding busy

- CFNR   Call forwarding no reply

- CFU   Call forwarding unconditional

- COLP   Connected line identification presentation

- COLR   Connected line identification restriction

- CONF   Add-on conference call

- CUG   Closed user group

- CWL   Call waiting

- ECT   Explicit call transfer

- FPH — Freephone supplementary service

- HOLD — Call hold

- MCID — Malicious call identification

- MMC — Meet me conference

- SUB — Subaddressing

- 3PTY — Three-party service

- UUS — User-to-user signaling

intellectual property (n.) Content or knowledge that may be protected by copyright. Protection of the owner's rights to intellectual property has become a significant concern in multimedia, given the ease with which content can be digitized and transferred.

interactive courseware (ICW) (n.) The term used by the U.S. military for software used with computer-based training. ICW relies on interaction with the trainee to determine the pacing and sequence of a course of instruction.

interactive laser disc levels (n.) Three degrees of interactivity that were proposed by the Nebraska Videodisc Design/Production Group in 1980. They are as follows:

- Level 1: A consumer-model player with freeze-frame, picture stop, chapter stop, frame address, and dual-channel audio, but with limited memory and processing power.

- Level 2: An industrial-model player with Level 1 features plus programmable memory and faster access time.

- Level 3: A Level 1 or Level 2 player interfaced with a computer or a peripheral.

interactive media (n.) Analog or digital programs that allow users to control the flow of program material. The media may consist of any combination of audio, graphic, video, or animated content. Media may be produced with varying degrees of interactivity.

Interactive Multimedia Association (IMA) (n.) A group of corporations that create products used in the multimedia industry. The home office of the IMA is in Arlington, Virginia.

interactive services (n.) Services that allow a subscriber to send messages to a programming source or content provider, to control the flow of information, and to engage in two-way communications such as polling, shopping, and banking.

interactive television (n.) A system that can send information to a broadcast television provider via some communications device, such as a telephone, keypad, or touch screen, allowing viewers to transmit messages to the televised source.

interactive video (n.) Digital technology that lets the viewer control the flow of video content. In interactive video, the user's choices and decisions determine how a program is presented.

interactive voice response (IVR) (n.) Feature of an Integrated Computer Telephony (ICT) system that enables voice to be transmitted over an Internet connection. IVR provides transaction processing, which interacts via Internet Protocol (IP) Telephony with a database. IP Telephony includes services that allow two computers to communicate or that permit voice signals and computers to com-

157

municate. Digitally synthesized voice may be used in a telephone system to interact with callers. In addition, IVR systems perform voice recognition of simple commands and can facilitate voice dialing.

interactivity (n.) Reciprocal communication between a user and a playback device or a digital media system.

Intercast (n.) Technology developed by Intel Corporation that enables a cable television signal to include digital information in the vertical blanking interval (VBI). This information is typically a web broadcast from the cable provider, which a computer can read with a standard browser while displaying a television program in the Audio-Video Interleaved (AVI) digital video format. The interactive content delivered is intended to enhance the particular television program being viewed, such as a web page with statistics on players participating in a sporting event.

Interchange File Format (IFF) (n.) A chunk-based, hierarchical file format originally developed for the Amiga computer by Electronic Arts. File types are generally known by a four-character designation. Audio is AIFF, and animation is ANIM. Microsoft .wav and .avi file types are based on a similar scheme known as RIFF.

interchange levels (n.) Under the ISO 9660 standard, the three nested levels at which a CD-ROM file may be named and recorded. Many operating systems and their extensions that read discs require Level 1 restrictions to be observed. The levels may be described as follows:

- Level 1: The files consist of a single file section in one extent. They are recorded

as a continuous stream and not interleaved. File and directory names must adhere to the strict ISO 9660 naming conventions.

- Level 2: The files consist of one file section in one extent with no interleaving, but no naming restrictions apply.

- Level 3: The files are not restricted.

interconnect (n.) In cable television, a microwave circuit, or cable, that links headends or distribution hubs so that they can exchange programs or services.

interexchange carrier (IXC) (n.) Long-distance telephone company that provides telephone service between Local Access and Transport Areas (LATAs), or exchanges.

interface 1. (n.) A device that connects two pieces of hardware, such as the link between a computer processor and a peripheral. 2. (n.) In programming, the means by which a computer user gives instructions to and receives information from a computer. 3. (v.) To transfer data or signals by means of a connector or by using a circuit that decodes or translates.

interference (n.) Undesirable energy that is received with a signal and that may appear as noise caused by electromagnetic fields.

interfield frames (n.) Frames that result from 3:2 pulldown, the film-to-tape conversion process in which a video frame contains two fields from different film frames. See figure on the following page. See also *3:2 pulldown*.

interframe coding (n.) A method of video compression in which an encoder eliminates a portion of the data that defines a stream of

interfield frames

images, discarding redundant data shared between consecutive frames. Compare *intraframe coding*.

Interior Gateway Protocol (IGP) (n.) Within an autonomous system, a protocol that distributes routing information to the routers.

interlace (v.) To combine two field scans to form a single video frame. In a video stream, the first field contains even-numbered scan lines, whereas the second field consists of odd-numbered lines. The two complementary fields lace together to form a single, complete frame. This practice, common to most video systems, is based on the concept of video persistence. The human eye holds the image of the first field while the second field is displayed, and it blends the two.

interlaced GIF (n.) Interlaced Graphic Interchange Format; used on the web, a type of streaming graphic in which scan lines have been rearranged. The graphic initially appears quickly in low resolution. Definition gradu-

ally improves as the complete image is loaded incrementally. Users catch a glimpse of the image before it is entirely loaded without having to wait for the entire image to be rendered to perceive it.

interLATA (adj.) Describes a telecommunication service that originates in one Local Access and Transport Area (LATA) and terminates in another. Regional Bell Operating Companies (RBOCs) cannot legally provide interLATA service.

interleaving (n.) 1. The nonsequential storage or transmission of information in an alternating series of frames or chunks. A sequence is reassembled on playback to present a continuous flow in the original order. Data files are not always stored in one contiguous block of memory. On a compact disc, files may be split so that small image and audio chunks are discrete but located near each other. With interleaving, the laser reading head moves smoothly between the file locations. Without interleaving, gathering information alternately from the two files would require many seeks and excessive head movement. 2. A method of error detection and correction for CD-ROMs in which a sequence of data is read into a grid vertically and read out again horizontally so that wrong lines are rearranged into individual wrong bits. This process facilitates the isolation and correction of errors.

International Communications Industries Association (ICIA) (n.) A professional organization that provides its worldwide membership with education, training, and certification in communications technologies to enhance their ability to conduct business successfully, profitably, and competently. The ICIA represents individuals and organizations that derive revenue from the commercialization or utilization of communications technologies. The ICIA seeks to ensure the quality of its members' products and services by representing the communications industry to the public, to business, to education, and to the government. The ICIA engages in workforce development activities, industry technology updates, and international expositions. It offers publications, market research, and industry certification programs.

International Electrotechnical Commission (IEC) (n.) The original international organization that set standards for electronic devices, formed in 1906 in Europe.

International Interactive Communications Society (IICS) (n.) A grassroots organization of multimedia developers that has supported the growth of the multimedia industry since its inception. Local chapters have been formed in many cities around the world.

International MIDI Association (IMA) (n.) The policy-setting group that establishes the standards incorporated in the MIDI specification.

International Telecommunications Union (ITU) (n.) A Geneva-based organization that addresses standards used globally, such as those for video teleconferencing. The three sectors that the ITU addresses are Telecommunications Standardization (ITU-T), Radio-communications (ITU-R), and Telecommunications Development (ITU-D).

International Telecommunications Union–Telecommunications Standardization Sector (ITU-T) (n.) An international body that makes technical recommendations regarding telephone and data communications systems. Prior to March 1993, ITU-T was known as Comité Consultatif International de Télégraphique et Téléphonique (CCITT). Plenary sessions are held every four years, and new standards are adopted. Having been held in 1992 and 1996, the next session is set for 2000. Study Group XVII of the ITU-T recommends standards for data communications over telephone networks, as well as V.x standards and X.n protocols.

International Telephone and Telegraph Consultative Committee See *Comité Consultatif International de Télégraphique et Téléphonique* or *International Telecommunications Union–Telecommunications Standardization Sector.*

International Television Association (ITVA) (n.) A professional organization of producers, technicians, engineers, and others who participate in the fields of broadcast, video, and film.

Internet (n.) A packet-switched network developed by the Advanced Research Projects Agency (ARPA) of the Department of Defense to give researchers access to databases and computers. The Internet dates from 1969, when the ARPANET was started. The Internet has grown into a large, diverse community of online users that is self-governing and that develops its own procedures. Physically, it is the interconnection of many small "stub" networks at campuses, research institutes, corporations, and military installations that have middle-level networks and backbones operating with multiple protocols. Nodes on the Internet share a common TCP/IP addressing interface. The Internet spans most countries, consists of several thousand networks, and has millions of users. It is expected that distributed multimedia over the Internet will rapidly increase, allowing the delivery of sounds and video over the network as bandwidth increases for more users. Internet activities include sending messages over email, conducting group discussions over Usenet, accessing databases, and "surfing" World Wide Web documents, or pages, that are linked to one another.

Internet Access Provider (IAP) (n.) An organization that gives commercial and residential consumers access to the Internet. An IAP purchases an Internet link from another company with a direct link to the Internet and resells portions of that bandwidth to the general public. An IAP might buy one or more T1 links (1.544 megabits per second, or Mbps) and resell that bandwidth over ISDN lines (64 or 128 kilobits per second , or Kbps) and analog modems (14.4, 28.8, or 56 Kbps). An Internet Service Provider (ISP) may also be an IAP.

Internet address (n.) The 32-bit host address defined by the Internet Protocol (IP) in RFC 791, STD 5. An Internet address is usually expressed in dotted-decimal notation, such as 128.121.103.76. The term should not be confused with the Fully Qualified Domain Name belonging to a host. The Internet address must be translated into an Ethernet address either by Address Resolution Protocol (ARP) or by constant mapping. The address can be split into a network address and a host number unique to each host on the network, and it can sometimes be split into a subnet address as well. Also known as an *IP address.*

Internet address classes (n.) A categorization of Internet address types, based on the assignment of units, or digits, to the four portions of each address that are separated by periods in dotted-decimal notation. The three types of Internet address classes are as follows:

- Class A address: The first three units are assigned by InterNIC, and the remainder are allocated by the organization to which they were assigned.

- Class B address: The first six units are assigned by InterNIC, and the remainder are allocated by the organization to which they were assigned.

- Class C address: The first nine units are assigned by InterNIC, and the remainder are allocated by the organization to which they were assigned.

Internet Architecture Board (IAB) (n.) Technical group that manages the Internet Engineering Task Force (IETF) and the Internet Research Task Force (IRTF). These task forces delineate and recommend Internet protocols.

Internet Assigned Numbers Authority (IANA) (n.) The central registry for assigned numbers, or Internet Protocol (IP) parameters, such as port, protocol, and enterprise numbers and options, codes, and types. The currently assigned values are listed in the assigned numbers document STD 2. A number assignment may be obtained from the email address *iana@isi.edu.*

Internet backbone (n.) A high-capacity telecommunications network carrying a large volume of traffic. Usually SONET-based fiber-

161

optic connections, these links form major arteries within the national public switched telephone network (PSTN). The term *Internet backbone* generally refers to the NSFNET, a National Science Foundation–funded series of links operating at very high data rates.

Internet Control Message Protocol (ICMP) (n.) An extension of the Internet Protocol (IP) defined in RFC 792, STD 5 that permits the generation of error messages, test packets, and informational messages related to IP.

Internet country code (n.) A country abbreviation that identifies the top-level domain of a machine. See table on page 165.

Internet-Draft (I-D) (n.) A working document of the Internet Engineering Task Force (IETF). Such a draft typically precedes an RFC and is valid for only six months.

Internet Engineering Steering Group (IESG) (n.) A body that consists of the Internet Engineering Task Force (IETF) area directors and the IETF chair. The IESG performs the initial technical review of Internet standards and manages the IETF.

Internet Engineering Task Force (IETF) (n.) An international community of network administrators, vendors, and researchers who coordinate the operation of the Internet. The U.S. government funds the IETF, and the Corporation for National Research Initiatives participates.

Internet Explorer (n.) A universal client, or browser, developed by Microsoft for accessing HTML documents on the World Wide Web.

Internet Message Access Protocol (IMAP, pronounced "EYE-map") (n.) The method by which a client can access electronic mail messages on a server. IMAP permits manipulation

of remote mailboxes but does not specify a means of posting mail. This function is handled by a mail transfer protocol such as Simple Mail Transfer Protocol (SMTP).

Internet Protocol (IP) (n.) The network layer for the TCP/IP protocol used on Ethernet networks, defined in RFC 791, STD 5. It is a connectionless, best-effort packet-switching protocol. It provides packet routing, fragmentation, and reassembly through the data link layer.

Internet Protocol next generation (IPng) (n.) An Internet Engineering Task Force (IETF) proposal to update the current version of Internet Protocol. Portions of IPng address CATNIP, TUBA, and SIPP.

Internet Registry (IR) (n.) The place where domain names are recorded by the Defense Data Network Information Center.

Internet Relay Chat (IRC) (n.) A global multiuser chat system that allows people to discuss topics over "channels" on the Internet. Written in 1988 by Jarkko Oikarinen, IRC is constantly evolving as the conventions pertaining to its use change. To access an IRC, a user must run a client program that connects to an IRC network; Telnet cannot be used. Source code for an IRC client is available by anonymous FTP to the following sites:

Windows	*cs-ftp.bu.edu:/irc/clients/pc /windows*
Unix	*ftp.funet.fi/pub/unix/irc*
Macintosh	*ftp.funet.fi/pub/unix/irc/mac*
MS-DOS	*ftp.funet.fi/pub/unix/irc/msdos*

Here are a few of the many IRC servers avail-

162

able for connection:

United States   *irc.bu.edupiglet.cc.utexas.edu*

Canada   *irc.mcgill.ca*

Europe   *irc.funet.ficismhp*
    .univlyon1.frstork.doc.ic.ac.uk

Australia   *troll.elec.uow.edu.au*

Japan   *endo.wide.ad.jp*

All IRC commands start with /, and most are one word. Typing "/help" calls for help information. Typing "/names" calls for a list of names. A user may limit the list of names by typing "/names -min 20"; only a list of channels with 20 or more people on it will be called. The output of "/names" appears as follows:

Pub: #hack   @brillo rascal mon

Pub: #Nippon   @jellyroll @molli_R

Pub means public (or visible) channel, # is the prefix, and *hack* is the channel name. An @ indicates the channel operator, who controls the channel.

To join a particular channel, type "/join #channelname". New users benefit from visiting the channel "#irchelp". To join a conversation, type a line of text and send it by striking the Enter key. IRC will automatically insert <nickname> before all channel messages. To leave a channel, type "/part #channelname". To access a list of channels and topics, type "/list -min 30", which will show channels with 30 or more members. Many IRC operators visit #Twilight_Zone frequently. Here are some widely used foreign-language channels:

#nippon   Japanese channel, with kanji characters

#espanol   Spanish channel

#russian   Russian channel

An IRC users' manual is available from *cs-ftp.bu.edu:/irc/support*. It is recommended that this IRC primer be read prior to joining any list. Addresses for IRC-related mailing lists are shown here:

"operlist"   Discusses server code, routing, and protocol. To join, send mail to *operlist-request@kei.com* with Subject: subscribe.

IRC Servers

Port	Address	Country
6667	iapp.netscape.com	United States
6667	austin.tx.us.undernet.org	United States
6667	sanjose.ca.us.undernet.org	United States
6667	washington.dc.us.undernet.org	United States
6667	oxford.ok.eu.undernet.org	United Kingdom
6667	Montreal.qu.ca.undernet.org	Canada
6667	caen.fr.eu.undernet.org	France
7000	xgw.dal.net	Finland
7000	liberator.dal.net	United Kingdom
7000	uncc.dal.net	United States
7000	skypoint.dal.net	United States
7000	cin.dal.net	United States

"ircd-three"   Discusses protocol revisions of the ircd (IRC server). To join, send mail to *ircd-three-request@kei.com* with Subject: subscribe.

For more technical information, refer to the IRC RFC (RFC 1459), which is available at all RFC FTP sites, such as *cs-ftp.bu.edu:/irc/support/rfc1459.txt*. Here are other online IRC information sources:

- *cs-ftp.bu.edu:/irc/support/alt-irc-faq*

- *ftp.kei.com:/pub/irc/alt-irc-faq*

- *http://www.kei.com/irc.html*

If the Netscape Navigator 2.0 browser or a later is used to access the Internet, the Netscape Chat plug-in, which is an IRC client, is available. A copy of this plug-in can be downloaded from *ftp://ftp20.netscape.com/pub/chat*. It should be placed in a separate directory before it is installed. More IRC servers are listed in the IRC Servers table on the previous page.

Internet Research Steering Group (IRSG) (n.) The body that governs the Internet Research Task Force (IRTF).

Internet Research Task Force (IRTF) (n.) A group of researchers who advise the Internet Architecture Board (IAB) on issues that affect the Internet. The IRTF is chartered by the IAB to consider issues and discuss solutions.

Internet Server Application Programming Interface (ISAPI, pronounced "eye-SAP-ee") (n.) A programming interface between an application and the Microsoft Internet Server. Active servers created with ISAPI extensions can be complete applications themselves or can connect to other services. ISAPI is used for the same sorts of functions as Common Gateway Interface (CGI), but ISAPI uses Microsoft Windows dynamic link libraries (DLL) for greater efficiency. The server loads a DLL the first time a request is received. The DLL then stays in memory, ready to service other requests until the server decides it is no longer needed. This minimizes the overhead associated with executing such applications many times. An HTTP server can unload ISAPI application DLLs to free memory, or it can preload them to speed up the first access. Applications may be enhanced by ISAPI filters.

Internet Service Provider (ISP) (n.) A company that delivers Internet access to other companies and to individuals.

Internet Society (ISOC) (n.) A nonprofit professional organization that supports technical developments for the Internet, promotes new applications, and educates about Internet operation and use. Technical standards are developed under the auspices of the ISOC, which publishes the *Internet Society News Quarterly* and holds the annual INET conference. ISOC is supported by the U.S. government and the Corporation for National Research Initiatives.

Internetwork Packet eXchange (IPX) (n.) Developed by Xerox Corporation and made popular by Novell, the basic protocol in the Novell Netware file server system. IPX is a network layer protocol. A router with IPX routing can interconnect local area networks (LANs) so that Netware clients and servers can communicate. The Sequenced Packet eXchange (SPX) transport layer protocol runs on top of IPX.

InterNIC (n.) Internet Network Information Center; the name of the three organizations that the National Science Foundation (NSF) selected in 1992 to receive cooperative agree-

Internet Country Codes

Country	Code	Country	Code	Country	Code
Afghanistan	af	French Southern Territories	tf	Norway	no
Albania	al	Gambia	gm	Oman	om
Algeria	dz	Georgia	ge	Pakistan	pk
Angola	ao	Germany	de	Palau	pw
Antarctica	aq	Ghana	gh	Panama	pa
Argentina	ar	Gibraltar	gi	Papua New Guinea	pg
Armenia	am	Greece	gr	Paraguay	py
Australia	au	Greenland	gl	Peru	pe
Austria	at	Grenada	gd	Philippines	ph
Azerbaijan	az	Guam	gu	Poland	pl
Bahamas	bs	Guatemala	gt	Portugal	pt
Bahrain	bh	Guinea	gn	Puerto Rico	pr
Bangladesh	bd	Guyana	gy	Qatar	qa
Barbados	bb	Haiti	ht	Romania	ro
Belarus	by	Honduras	hn	Russian Federation	ru
Belgium	be	Hong Kong	hk	Rwanda	rw
Belize	bz	Hungary	hu	Samoa	ws
Bermuda	bm	Iceland	is	Saudi Arabia	sa
Bolivia	bo	India	in	Senegal	sn
Bosnia	ba	Indonesia	id	Singapore	sg
Botswana	bw	Iran	ir	Slovakia	sk
Brazil	br	Iraq	iq	Slovenia	si
Bulgaria	bg	Ireland	ie	Solomon Islands	sb
Burundi	bi	Israel	il	Somalia	so
Cambodia	kh	Italy	it	South Africa	za
Cameroon	cm	Jamaica	jm	Spain	es
Canada	ca	Japan	jp	Sri Lanka	lk
Cayman Islands	ky	Jordan	jo	Sudan	sd
Central African Republic	cf	Kazakhstan	kz	Surinam	sr
Chad	td	Kenya	ke	Swaziland	sz
Chile	cl	Korea, Democratic	kp	Sweden	se
China	cn	Korea, Republic of	kr	Switzerland	ch
Colombia	co	Kuwait	kw	Syrian Arab Republic	sy
Congo	cg	Laos	la	Taiwan	tw
Congo, Democratic Republic	cd	Latvia	lv	Tanzania	tz
Costa Rica	cr	Lebanon	lb	Thailand	th
Croatia (Hrvatska)	hr	Liberia	lr	Trinidad & Tobago	tt
Cuba	cu	Lichtenstein	li	Tunisia	tn
Cyprus	cy	Lithuania	lt	Turkey	tr
Czech Republic	cz	Luxembourg	lu	Uganda	ug
Denmark	dk	Macau	mo	Ukraine	ua
Dominica	dm	Macedonia	mk	United Arab Emirates	ae
Dominican Republic	do	Madagascar	mg	United Kingdom	uk
Ecuador	ec	Malaysia	my	United States	us
Egypt	eg	Marshall Islands	mh	Uruguay	uy
El Salvador	sv	Martinique	mq	Uzbekistan	uz
Equatorial Guinea	gq	Micronesia	fm	Vatican City State	va
Estonia	ee	Monaco	mc	Venezuela	ve
Ethiopia	et	Mongolia	mn	Vietnam	vn
Falkland Islands (Malvinas)	fk	Morocco	ma	Virgin Islands (British)	vg
Fiji	fj	Mozambique	mz	Virgin Islands (U.S.)	vi
Finland	fi	Namibia	na	Western Sahara	eh
France	fr	Nepal	np	Yemen	ye
France (Metropolitan)	fx	Netherlands	nl	Yugoslavia	yu
French Guiana	gf	New Zealand	nz	Zambia	zm
French Polynesia	pf	Nicaragua	ni	Zimbabwe	zw

ments in the areas of information services, directory and database services, and registration services. General Atomics provides information services, AT&T provides directory and database services, and Network Solutions, Inc., (NSI) provides registration services.

interoperability (n.) The capacity of software and equipment from different vendors to be successfully integrated.

interpolation (n.) Related to graphics, the process of computing intervening values within a numerical range and applying those values to fill the spaces between given values. When a picture is enlarged, this process accomplishes higher resolution.

interpreted language (n.) Program code that is converted into a machine-readable format and processed simultaneously. Interpreted language is slower than a compiled language because of the translation that occurs at run time, but it is more flexible. Java is an interpreted language.

interpreter (n.) Any software program that executes other software programs. By contrast, a compiler does not execute its input program, or source code, but translates it into executable machine code, which is output to a file for later execution. The same source code may be run directly either by interpreting it or by compiling it and then by executing the machine code produced. It takes longer to run a program under an interpreter than to run compiled code, but it may take less time to interpret such a program than to compile and run it.

interrupt request (IRQ) (n.) A computer instruction that momentarily stops the normal operation of a routine. The operation can usually be resumed later from the interruption point. As the peripheral devices interface with the central processing unit (CPU), they frequently send signals to indicate that a software routine or circuit needs attention from the CPU. The term also refers to a signal line or channel used to carry the interrupt signal from hardware devices to the PC's interrupt controller chip. The original PC provided eight such lines, whereas later models provide 16. IRQ lines cannot ordinarily be shared, and each peripheral device is assigned an IRQ number. Conflicts result when two or more channels are assigned the same IRQ number on a personal computer. Installing a sound card in a PC is a situation that would require one or more interrupt channel assignments. The best choice for the sound card interrupt is usually the Sound Blaster (SB) default, IRQ 5. MS-DOS reserves this channel for a second printer port. If another device is assigned to IRQ 5, an eight-bit sound card interrupt may be moved to IRQ 7. A 16-bit sound card interrupt may be moved to any available IRQ be-

Standard Interrupt Assignments

Number	Function
IRQ 0	Timer Output 0
IRQ 1	Keyboard (buffer full)
IRQ 2	Cascade from IRQ 9
IRQ 3	Serial Port 2; Serial Port 4; SDLC Communications; BSC Communications; Cluster Adapter; Network (alternate); 3278/79 (alternate)
IRQ 4	Serial Port 1; Serial Port 3; SDLC Communications; BSC Communications; Voice Communications Adapter
IRQ 5	Parallel Port 2, Sound Blaster Default
IRQ 6	Floppy Disk Controller
IRQ 7	Parallel Port 1; Cluster Adapter (alternate)
IRQ 8	Realtime Clock
IRQ 9	Software Redirected to INT OA (hex); Video; Network; 3278/79 Adapter
IRQ 10	Reserved
IRQ 11	Reserved
IRQ 12	Reserved
IRQ 13	Coprocessor
IRQ 14	Hard Disk Controller
IRQ 15	Reserved

tween 8 and 15. The standard interrupt assignments are listed in the Standard Interrupt Assignments table.

intracoded frame (n.) In digital video, a frame with self-referential information, devoid of data that is related to previous or future frames in the sequence. Also known as an *I-frame*.

intraframe coding (n.) In video compression, a technique that allocates more data to the coding of highly detailed parts of a single frame at the expense of less detailed areas. Compare *interframe coding*.

intraLATA (adj.) Describes telecommunications services that originate and end within a single Local Access and Transport Area (LATA).

intranet (n.) A local area network (LAN) that uses a dedicated web server running TCP/IP to provide HTML documents and other files that clients access when using a web browser as their interface. The intranet may provide users with an external connection to the Internet, facilitating communication with both local and distant web servers. The advantages of an intranet are the speed with which streaming data can be delivered locally, the security of an internal LAN with a firewall, and the use of a single user-friendly interface for both internal and external communications.

intuitive (adj.) Describes user-friendly software that automatically gives the user options or information.

inverted tree structure (n.) A method of providing access to a wide range of data pages, offering a series of menus until the desired page of information is reached.

I/O bus (n.) Input/output bus; the interface through which data or instructions are transmitted to and from a computer. Peripherals such as scanners and printers use I/O buses.

IP See *Internet Protocol.*

IP address (n.) Internet Protocol address; a unique 32-bit number that identifies a specific Internet server. It is formatted in dotted decimal notation as a series of four sets of digits separated by periods. IP addressing is defined by RFC 791, STD 5. Also known as *Internet address.*

IP multicasting (n.) Internet Protocol multicasting; one-to-many broadcast of data by a server using IP.

IPng See *Internet Protocol next generation.*

ips See *inches per second.*

IPSec See *IPSecurity.*

IPSecurity (IPSec) (n.) A suite of protocols that provide authentication and encryption over the Internet. IPSec works at Layer 3, rather than Layer 4, because the Secure Sockets Layer (SSL) provides services in Layer 4.

IP Telephony (n.) The use of networks running Internet Protocol (IP) to send and receive messages, such as voice data, to replace traditional telephone company services. The public switched telephone network (PSTN) may be used to transmit the data between modems, or a local area network (LAN) may be used.

IPv6 (n.) Internet Protocol version 6; the next generation of IP developed by the Internet Engineering Task Force (IETF). IPv6 increases the maximum number of user addresses and provides IPSecurity, among other enhancements.

IPX See *Internetwork Packet eXchange.*

IPX/SPX (n.) The transport protocol used in most Novell Netware environments. In client-server environments in which the server engine is a network loadable module (NLM), communication between the client and the server is generally conducted over IPX/SPX.

IR See *Internet Registry.*

IRC See *Internet Relay Chat.*

iris (n.) A diaphragm in the lens of a video camera that controls the size of the aperture, regulating the amount of light that may enter the camera. The size of the iris is measured in f-stops.

IRIX (n.) An operating system used on Silicon Graphics systems. Pronounced "EYE-rix."

IRQ See *interrupt request.*

IRSG See *Internet Research Steering Group.*

IRTF See *Internet Research Task Force.*

ISA See *Industry Standard Architecture.*

ISA bus (n.) Industry Standard Architecture bus; a durable interface implemented since 1981 on all PC-compatible computers. The ISA bus still takes its place beside the newer, faster PCI technology, however. The ISA 16-bit bus replaced the eight-bit bus in 1984. The 16-bit bus has a maximum standard speed of 8.33 MHz and a maximum throughput of about eight megabytes per second (MBps). This is adequate for most common system peripherals, sound cards, and network adapters.

ISAPI See *Internet Server Application Programming Interface.*

ISAPI filter (n.) Internet Server Application Programming Interface filter; a replaceable dynamic link library (DLL) that the server calls when an HTTP request is made. Upon loading, the ISAPI filter communicates to the server what sort of notifications will be accepted. After that, whenever a selected event occurs, the filter processes the event. Examples include authentication schemes, compression, encryption, logging, and traffic analysis.

ISD See *Instructional Systems Design.*

ISDN See *Integrated Services Digital Network.*

ISINDEX (n.) An HTML tag that tells the browser to display a text entry box on the current page. Text that a user enters into the box is appended to the current URL as a URL-encoded query string and sent to the server by the GET method. This functionality allows simple user input to search a document. The server must map the query URL to an appropriate process and is only useful if the server has access to a search engine.

ISMAP (n.) An attribute of the inline image HTML tag <IMG> that specifies that if the image is selected, the browser will generate a request indicating the coordinates of the point that was clicked. This request is interpreted by a server that has mapped certain regions of the image to predetermined actions.

ISO (n.) Greek for "the same as" or "equal to." The de facto name of the International Organization for Standardization. It is not an acronym, but a play on words. This organization, founded in Geneva in 1946, is involved in the development and definition of worldwide standards. In multimedia, they have defined CD-ROM formats, compression algorithms, communications specifications, and standards for a wide range of technical software applications. They serve most fields except electrical or electronic applications, which are dealt with by the International Electrotechnical Commission (IEC). Together, the ISO and the IEC form the Joint Technical Committee (JTC), which is staffed by members from 80 countries. Pronounced "EYE-soh."

ISOC See *Internet Society.*

isochronous (adj.) Describes a type of data transmission in which characters are separated by a whole number of bit-length intervals. Timing information is embedded in the data stream. In asynchronous transmission, by contrast, characters may be separated by random-length intervals.

ISODE See *ISO Development Environment.*

ISO Development Environment (ISODE, pronounced "EYE-so-DEE-ee") (n.) Software that allows Open Systems Interconnection (OSI) services to use a TCP/IP network.

ISO image (n.) An exact representation of the entire set of data and programs as they will appear on a CD-ROM, including content and logical format. An ISO image is simulated on another medium, such as an optical cartridge, data tape, or CD-R. It is sent to a disc manufacturer for premastering and mastering. It is also referred to as a *CD-ROM image* or a *disc image.*

ISO 9735 (n.) The ISO standard that defines application layer syntax. Set forth in 1988, it was amended and reprinted in 1990. Governing electronic data interchange for administration, commerce, and trade, it is known as *EDIFACT.*

ISO 9660 (n.) An international standard that specifies the logical file format for CD-ROM files and directories. It is directly derived from the High Sierra Group Proposal. ISO 9660 discs can be read by most PC CD-ROM drives if the proper software driver has been loaded into the system.

ISO 9000 (n.) Standards for quality management and assurance adopted by more than 90 countries. ISO 9000 standards apply to all types of organizations in many industries. A standard language for documenting quality control processes, systems to manage evidence that these practices are instituted, and third-party auditing to review and maintain certification are all parts of ISO 9000. Products are classified into generic categories: hardware, software, processed materials, and services. Documentation is central to ISO 9000 conformance.

ISO 11172 (n.) Defined by ISO, the international standard for MPEG-1 video compression.

ISO 13818 (n.) Defined by ISO, the international standard for MPEG-2 video compression. This is the same as ITU H.222.

ISP See *Internet Service Provider.*

ITFS See *Instructional Television Fixed Service.*

ITU See *International Telecommunications Union.*

ITU-T See *International Telecommunications Union–Telecommunications Standardization Sector.*

ITVA See *International Television Association.*

IVR See *interactive voice response.*

IXC See *interexchange carrier.*

J

jack (n.) Related to audio, video, or computing gear, a connecting point that accepts a plug on a cable or a line. A jack is usually a female connector.

jaggies (n.) Jargon for undesirable artifacts that appear in a graphic display or a printout as a result of inadequate resolution. Jaggies portray lines that are not horizontal or vertical. See also *aliasing.*

jargon (n.) Slang and other terms used in a particular field.

Java (n.) An interpreted programming language similar to C++ that is optimized for object-oriented, multithreaded, distributed computing. The interpreter—the runtime system on which Java is dependent—may either exist as a separate application or operate within another program, such as a web browser. Java allows a client computer with its own runtime environment to execute dynamic applications independently from a networked host. A Java program may be downloaded and run dynamically from a web server. The language is a secure, high-performance, portable development environment for distributing dynamic content over the Internet. Using Java eliminates the need to port an application to each different platform because the same executable runs on any computer with the proper interpreter, or "virtual machine," and with the necessary class objects. Java provides its own memory management in the form of an automatic garbage collector, which runs as a separate thread. When there are no references to an object, the garbage collector tags it for removal.

The development of Java began in 1991 by James Gosling, an employee of Sun Microsystems, who was charged with building a programming language that would operate on any platform. He began by attempting to extend the C++ compiler, but soon realized that he needed to create a new language. It eventually became known as Java, after failing a trademark search under the name of "Oak." Originally it was intended for consumer electronic devices, and prototypes were built in 1993. The World Wide Web was growing in significance, and in 1994 Sun developed a Java-capable browser called WebRunner. It later became known as HotJava.

Early in 1995 Arthur Van Hoff, who had joined the Sun team a year before, implemented the Java compiler in Java itself. Gosling's original compiler had been implemented in C. Sun Microsystems officially announced the Java Environment at SunWorld in May 1995.

Java consists of three interdependent components. The first is a programming language in which the code needed for applications is written. The second is the run-time environment, or Java Virtual Machine, which provides the architecture for applications. The third is the set of tools with which to build, compile, and run applications: the Java compiler, the Java interpreter, and the HotJava browser. The compiler lets programmers create machine-independent *bytecode,* which runs under the interpreter and browser environments.

At the heart of the Java package is a set of class libraries for the browser and the interpreter, the routines that programmers use to perform basic functions. These class libraries are a package of predeveloped and pretested code, which can be linked to create individual applications. Some of the common libraries are as follows:

- Applets: Utilities needed for interaction with any Java-enabled browser.

- AWT: Abstract Windowing Toolkit; the graphic interface tools including fonts, buttons, controls, and scrollbars.

- I/O: Standard provision for input and output, along with file utilities.

- Language Foundation: Classes for strings and arrays, part of the basic structure of Java.

- Network: Utilities for accessing network protocols like FTP, Telnet, and the web.

- Utility: Provision for stacks, vectors, encoding/decoding, and hash tables.

Although Java is similar in many ways to C++, it does not allow a procedural approach, since it is thoroughly object-oriented. In addition to the capabilities of C++, Java adds automatic boundary checking by eliminating pointers, and it performs automatic garbage collection. Due to its multithreading features, it can take care of these memory management functions in the background.

In Java the fundamental unit, or object, is referred to as a *class.* A class is a grouping of code that models the behavior of an object in software. A faucet is an example of an object in real life. All objects have a state, and the state of the faucet could be on or off, or perhaps hot or cold. The state of an object is described by *instance variables.* Variables that are controlled by a class are inaccessible to any other class, except under special conditions. The flow of water is controlled by turning a faucet on or off. In Java, a *method* is used to control a class, or object. A method is a small body of code that performs a function that can be reused. The functions of a class are limited to what is prescribed by its methods. In the plumbing of a building there are many faucets, but they are identical in function. Each faucet (class) many be either on or off (instance variable) by turning it (method). A class (faucet) must only be created once, after which it may be reused many times. Another *instance* of the faucet may be created, or reproduced, without reinventing the object. A method is all that is needed to control any number of instances of a class.

Another important aspect of an object is that each instance *inherits* the characteristics or properties of the original object. Some aspects of a new class may be changed, while the new class retains all the properties of the old class. The new faucet could be made of brass instead of chrome. The new class becomes a *subclass* of the original *superclass.* A class is simply a template for future instances of an object.

In Java a *package* is a single compilation unit which is a collection of similar classes, and *access modifiers* control access to methods and variables. Four levels of access are defined:

Public, Private, Protected, and *Friendly.* Public methods are freely accessible. Private methods are accessible only to the class itself. Protected variables are accessible only through methods in a given class and its subclasses. Friendly methods and variables are accessible to any classes in the same package. A program is written by creating a class, and a class is automatically a subclass of the superclass *Object.* Other superclasses are *Applet* and *Thread.*

Java is very different conceptually from C++. There are no pointers, no *goto* statements or individual functions, no multiple inheritance, and no type definitions. There are no structures or unions. Instead of header files, Java uses *interfaces.* The interface is the means by which other classes see what methods a class may implement. Java keeps track of all references to an object, and when there are no longer any references to it, Java removes it with the garbage as a low-priority thread in the background.

Java provides portability by compiling *bytecode,* which is interpreted on each platform by the run-time environment, or Java Virtual Machine (JVM). The bytecode is an executable for the Virtual Machine, which exists only in software. The code is then interpreted and executed on the target hardware itself. All code will run on any computer for which an interpreter has been ported, including an Intel Pentium, an Apple Macintosh, or a Sun SPARCstation. Memory layout problems are solved by deferring symbolic reference to the interpreter at run time.

The robustness of Java is due in large part to its automatic memory management and strict compile-time and run-time checking. In C++, memory is addressed by the use of pointers, or variables that hold the address of the memory range used. A pointer could be misdirected to the wrong location. Java eliminates the pointer and encapsulates memory usage into classes. The syntax is strictly checked for errors upon compilation and again as it is interpreted at run time.

Multithreading is included at every level in Java, beginning at the syntactical level with synchronization modifiers in the language. Multitasking is the act of running two or more applications at once in an operating system. Multithreading is the act of executing more than one thread at once while running a single application.

Java is a secure environment for several reasons. The first stage in the interpreter is a bytecode verification to test whether code conforms to Java specification as it is received. Then the interpreter provides a distinct name space for each class that is uploaded, preventing accidental name references. Since there are no pointers when it is compiled, Java is immune to memory allocation problems. At run time it does not allow illegal processes, incorrect parameters, or violation of access restrictions.

Information about Java may be found at these web sites:

- *http://java.sun.com*

- *http://www.javasoft.com*

- *http://www.gamelan.com*

- *http://www.javaworld.com*

JavaBeans (n.) The trademarked component architecture of the Java programming language, developed by Sun Microsystems, IBM, and others. JavaBeans may be parts of Java programs, or it may be a group of self-contained applications. JavaBeans may be assembled to make complex applications. These applicaitons are capable of running within other component architectures, such as ActiveX and OpenDoc.

Java Database Connectivity (JDBC) (n.) An Application Programming Interface (API) that is a subset of the Open Database Connectivity (ODBC) API, which allows Java classes and objects to simplify programming for Structured Query Language (SQL) databases.

Java Open Language Toolkit (JOLT) (n.) A project aimed at providing a freely available and redistributable implementation of the Java language and tools. Related information is available at *http://www.redhat.com/linux-info/jolt.*

JavaScript (n.) A web scripting language developed by Netscape that was originally named LiveScript. The source code is freely available, and the language is easy to learn. The syntax is similar to that of C, yet not as complex. Java is intended to enhance forms and simple database front ends on the World Wide Web. JavaScript code is embedded in an HTML document with the tag <script language= "JavaScript">. It is interpreted by recent versions of Netscape Navigator and MS Internet Explorer. See the appendix on JavaScript for details.

Java Virtual Machine (JVM) (n.) The specification for a hypothetical processor that runs Java code. It is for this machine that the Java compiler creates an executable program from source code. It compiles to an intermediate stage, converting the source code to bytecode. This bytecode is more efficiently translated into native code for the processor on each particular platform. The JVM must be installed on a machine in order for any Java bytecode to run.

Jaz drive (n.) A removable cartridge drive from Iomega Corporation. A Jaz drive accepts disks

that hold 1 gigabyte (GB) of data. An average transfer rate of 330 megabytes (MB) per minute is possible with a high-speed SCSI configuration.

JDBC See *Java Database Connectivity.*

JEDEC See *Joint Electronic Devices Engineering Council.*

jewel box (n.) The plastic box in which audio CDs and CD-ROMs are packaged. The enclosed printed matter usually consists of a booklet and a tray card.

jitter (n.) In relation to video, a shift in the phase of pulses during transmission or playback, causing a lack of synchronization and unstable video signal reception.

J-lead (n.) On a chip carrier, an electrical lead curved in the shape of a *J*. This type of lead may be surface mounted on a PC board or plugged into a socket.

jog (v.) To move from one frame to another in a video clip, or to shuttle the clip by a single frame, or by a small number of frames, when editing.

Joint Electronic Devices Engineering Council (JEDEC) (n.) A group that defines standards for the electronics industry.

Joint Photographic Expert Group (JPEG, pronounced "JAY-peg") (n.) 1. An international consortium of hardware, software, and publishing interests. Under the auspices of the International Organization for Standardization (ISO), JPEG was defined as a universal standard for the digital compression and decompression of still images for use in computer systems. 2. The format that the group defined. JPEG is a lossy compression scheme. It uses discrete cosine transform (DCT) and quantization to encode still images. The technique may be used to compress images with moderate detail up to about a 15:1 ratio before visible degradation occurs. An 800-kilobyte (KB) file may be compressed to approximately 80 KB with the application of JPEG compression, and relatively little necessary data will be lost in this 10:1 ratio. When the same 800-KB file is reduced to 40 KB, which is a 20:1 ratio, artifacts may be noticeable. In the process, a single numeric chroma *descriptor* is used to identify a block of pixels that are all approximately the same color. That descriptor is multiplied by a factor that defines the area of the block. High compression ratios produce a "blocky," or pixelated, look. Simple images with little detail and few gradients lend themselves to higher compression ratios.

Joint Technical Committee (JTC)(n.) A working group of the ISO that defines universal standards.

JOLT See *Java Open Language Toolkit.*

joystick (n.) An input device that rotates on an axis and controls the position of a cursor. A joystick may be equipped with a button that sends messages for a program to interpret. Video and arcade games are often enabled by the use of a joystick.

JPEG See *Joint Photographic Expert Group.*

JTC See *Joint Technical Committee.*

JTC1/SC24 (n.) The ISO/IEC group responsible for creating the GKS, PHIGS, and Computer Graphics Metafile (CGM) standards. JTC1/SC24 was recently involved in standardizing multimedia presentation technologies.

jukebox (n.) An optical or magnetic storage unit that holds multiple discs, any of which may be selected and automatically loaded into the play station. The term usually refers to a stack of CD-ROMs.

jump (v.) To branch to another location in an interactive program, depending on user input.

jump cut (n.) An abrupt type of video edit that shows a new camera angle, a different frame size, or a notable change in the placement of the subject. This causes the subject to appear to jump. Jump cuts are generally avoided, or they are replaced with a cutaway to a related scene.

jumper (n.) A small clip that slips over pins on a circuit board to complete or break a circuit, thus serving as a hardware switch.

Junction FET (n.) A field-effect transistor without an insulated gate.

justification (n.) The process of allocating space in a line of text so that the left and right margins will align evenly.

JVM See *Java Virtual Machine.*

K

K See *Kelvin.*

Ka-band (n.) Electromagnetic waves in the radio frequency spectrum between about 33 and 36 GHz. This upper portion of the microwave range is used primarily by satellites and for mobile voice transmission. Pronounced "KAY-AAY band." Compare *Ku-band.*

Kaleida (n.) The name adopted by collaborators from Apple Computer and IBM who sought to develop and promote new cross-platform multimedia software technologies with applications for computers, personal electronics, and communications. The Kaleida project was ended in 1995, after several years without results. See also *ScriptX.*

karaoke (n.) "Empty orchestra" in Japanese; the act of singing into a microphone while a laser disc or video CD plays an accompaniment track without vocals. Karaoke equipment displays the lyrics to a song as subtitles on a video monitor and mixes the input of a microphone with the recorded accompaniment. An entertainer reads the lyrics and sings into the microphone along with the recording. Karaoke is popular in homes and nightclubs in Japan. Pronounced "KAR-ah-OH-kay."

Kb See *kilobit.*

KB See *kilobyte.*

Kbps See *kilobits per second.*

KBps See *kilobytes per second.*

Kelvin (K) (n.) Temperature scale used to define the color of a light source.

Kermit (n.) A file transfer protocol and terminal emulation program used to download files from a host to a local computer by modem. Kermit can transfer binary files over Telnet and over other connections without corrupting data.

kern (v.) To control the spacing between letters in a document. Certain letter combinations require more or less space between them to become legible and pleasing to the eye. For example, the letter combination *AV* is an example of negative spacing. This allows the characters to nest without excessive white space between them.

kernel (n.) 1. In programming, an essential subset of a language that defines all the constructs in the language. It is also known as a *core language.* 2. A basic part of any operating system responsible for resource allocation, hardware interfaces, security, and other low-level operations.

key 1. (n.) A button on an input device that sends data to the computer program to which

175

it is connected. 2. (n.) Jargon for *key frame,* an image used at the beginning or end of an animation sequence. 3. (n.) Jargon for *key light,* often the brightest light shining on the main character in a scene of a video or film production. 4. (v.) To switch between two or more video sources, based on a control signal. The control signal itself may be referred to as the key. An example is *chroma keying,* in which a color is used as a key to eliminate or to block objects of that color in a video composition. 5. (n.) A string or a value required by an algorithm that decodes encrypted data. Some encryption schemes use a private key, whereas others use a public key. 6. (n.) A value that identifies a record in a database, based on a fixed function applied to that record. The set of keys for all records forms an index.

keyboard (n.) 1. Any device that contains alphanumeric, symbol, and function keys that can input text or give instructions to a computer. The version that resembles a typewriter is referred to as a *QWERTY* keyboard because of the layout of the keys. 2. A piano, synthesizer, or MIDI keyboard with black and white keys used to perform music.

keyer (n.) In video editing, a video switcher that cuts a hole in the background and fills it with material from another source. Text and graphics are frequently "keyed" over NTSC video. The keyer superimposes two or more images by alternating among inputs during the scans across the screen that define the video image. With the aid of this technique, a weather forecaster appears to be standing in front of a map but is actually in front of a blue screen.

key frame (n.) 1. An image used at the beginning or end of an animation sequence or as a reference point in a video stream. 2. In compressed video, a frame that contains a complete description of itself, rather than just data about differences between it and the previous frame.

keypad (n.) A small keyboard that typically consists only of numeric and function keys. A keypad is found on the right side of most computer keyboards and on calculators.

keystoning (n.) Distortion caused when a projection angle that is not perpendicular displays graphic images or video on a flat surface. A projection that exhibits keystoning is not rectangular, because one side is longer than the opposing side. Also called *parallax.*

keyword 1. (n.) In a high-level computing language, a word that calls subroutines. 2. (adj.) Describes a type of test in some training applications that helps evaluate a learner's comprehension.

kHz See *kilohertz.*

kilo- Prefix meaning one thousand. In the decimal system, 1000 is expressed as 10 to the 3rd power. In the binary system used to quantify data, this is expressed as 2 to the 10th power, or 1024.

kilobit (Kb) (n.) In reference to binary data, 2 to the 10th power, or 1024 bits.

kilobits per second (Kbps) (n.) A measurement of data transfer or movement in thousands of bits per second.

kilobyte (KB) (n.) 2 to the 10th eight-bit bytes, or 1024 bytes. MS-DOS can allocate a maximum of 640KB of data in RAM to conventional memory.

kilobytes per second (KBps) (n.) A measurement of data transfer or movement in 2 to the 10th bytes per second.

kilohertz (kHz) (n.) One thousand cycles per second.

kiosk (n.) A freestanding, interactive multimedia system that typically has a touch screen for input. It is often located in a public area, and it may be used to convey information or to collect data.

kluge (n.) Jargon for a software patch that solves a problem expediently, although not elegantly. Pronounced "KLOOJ."

knockout (n.) The removal of an element in a multilayered graphic so that the underlying color does not tint overlapping layers. See figure.

knockout

knowbot (n.) Program that scouts the web collecting information about sites, descriptive text in metatags, and URLs to be indexed by a search engine. Also known as a *spider* or a *bot*. Most of the major indexes employ knowbots, including Yahoo!, WebCrawler, Infoseek, and AltaVista.

knowledge (n.) The concepts and relationships assumed to exist in an artificial intelligence (AI) system. Knowledge is different from raw data, because new knowledge may be created from existing knowledge using logical inference by an AI system. Knowledge is information about a particular topic, and this information may be processed according to the rules of AI, allowing new information to be inferred.

knowledge base (n.) A collection of knowledge represented by a rule-based inference engine.

Korn shell (ksh) (n.) Written by David Korn of Bell Labs, a standard Unix shell. It is a command line interface available in a public domain version called *pdksh*.

ksh See *Korn shell*.

Ku-band (n.) A range of the electromagnetic spectrum used by satellites. Ku-band is between 12 and 14 GHz. Pronounced "KAY-YOU band." Compare *Ka-band*.

K

177

L

lag (n.) Delay in the transfer of data caused by a slow connection between two machines, often resulting from errors. One of the causes of lag is chew.

Lambert shading (n.) A method of applying a graduated shade to a surface by filling small polygons with different colors, or shades, resulting in a faceted appearance. Also called *faceted shading*. See figure.

Lambert-shaded cylinder

LAN See *local area network.*

LANC See *Local Application Numerical Control.*

land (n.) The space between pits on the surface of a compact disc.

landing zone (n.) The cylinder number at which the head is parked when a hard disk drive is idle or off.

landscape (n.) A layout in which the width of a printed page is greater than the height. In a portrait layout, the height is greater than the width. See figure.

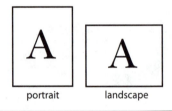

portrait   landscape

landscape and portrait layouts

language (n.) In programming, a set of instructions specified by a programmer that can be carried out by a computer. BASIC, Cobol, Pascal, FORTRAN, and C++ are common languages.

LAPD See *Link Access Procedure–D.*

LAPM See *Link Access Protocol for Modems.*

laptop (n.) Any portable computer. Because portables are becoming smaller and lighter, it is increasingly common to call them *notebook* computers.

large-scale integration (LSI) (n.) In a microprocessor, an integrated circuit (IC) that generally contains more than 100 and fewer than 1000 circuits.

laser (n.) Light amplification by stimulated emission of radiation; a device that generates and amplifies energy in the optical spectrum into a beam. The focused beam consists of a single wavelength of light. When it passes over an uneven surface (such as the data spiral of a compact disc), changes in the wavelength of reflections can be detected and converted into a stream of binary data.

laser disc (LD) (n.) A reflective optical medium, also called a *videodisc*. Laser Disc is a trademark of Pioneer, USA, and the term has been used freely to describe any thin, round platter that stores various types of information in analog or digital formats. A laser disc is an analog medium but provides a high degree of interactivity because a user can jump instantly to different points, or chapters, on a disc. The data is written in a spiral from the center to the edge. Data on a disc is read by an optical sensor that picks up reflections from a laser beam.

laser pickup (n.) A mechanical subsystem in an optical disc player that holds and positions the laser.

laser printer (n.) Any printer that uses laser optics to produce text and images on photosensitive paper. Desktop laser printers require toner cartridges and typically have a resolution ranging from 300 dots per inch (dpi) to 600 dpi.

laser rot (n.) The degradation of an optical disc caused by the use of contaminated raw materials or improper process controls.

Laservision (LV) (n.) A trade name for the videodisc format supported by manufacturers such as Pioneer, Philips, and Sony.

Laservision read-only memory (LV-ROM) (n.) A laser disc format that combines analog video with digital data and audio on a 12-inch laser disc. Philips developed LV-ROM in 1986, and Pioneer reintroduced an updated version in 1990. The Pioneer version provides for digital data in the ISO 9660 (High Sierra) CD-ROM format to be encoded along with analog stereo audio and video information on a standard 12-inch videodisc. Also called *Advanced Interactive Video (AIV)*.

last-in-first-out (LIFO) (n.) A method of organizing data in a queue. The order in which it was received and stored is reversed, so that the last piece of data received is the first to be processed. Compare *FIFO*.

LATA See *Local Access and Transport Area*.

latency (n.) 1. Time spent waiting for a response. 2. A component in the measurement of access time in hard disk drives and in CD-ROM drives.

Latin-1 (n.) An eight-bit, single-byte coded graphic character set capable of representing up to 256 characters. It contains letters for English, German, French, Spanish, and most Scandinavian languages, but does not support Greek, Hebrew, Arabic, or Cyrillic languages.

layer (n.) 1. The level in a network at which a certain protocol is in effect. Direct communication between two hardware hosts is at the bottom level. User applications make up the top level, or layer. Upper layers build on those under them. At each layer, programs use different protocols to communicate. The Open Systems Interconnection (OSI) network model has seven layers of protocols, whereas TCP/IP has five. 2. In graphics production, a page that may be placed above or below others in a stack. A layer may be transparent to varying degrees, so that those beneath it are visible. To *composite* graphics is to layer them. One example of compositing layers is the placement of titles over frames of video.

layering (n.) A concept applied in multimedia production to create dimensionality. In sound design, a mix may have numerous channels, or layers, with different audio tracks on each channel. A layered graphic design typically shows objects in the foreground with others in the background. When a video production is edited, materials from various sources are layered. Complex three-dimensional animations employ a high degree of layering.

Layer Two Tunneling Protocol (L2TP) (n.) The Internet Engineering Task Force (IETF) protocol used to create a Virtual Private Network (VPN) over the Internet. L2TP is a combination of Point-to-Point Tunneling Protocol (PPTP) from Microsoft and L2F technology from Cisco. L2TP also supports protocols other than IP, such as Internetwork Packet eXchange (IPX) and AppleTalk, as well as non-IPSecurity protocols.

lay up (v.) To transfer production sound from an edited videotape to an audio medium for sweetening. The final mix is "laid back" to the video master.

LBA See *Logical Block Addressing.*

L-band (n.) A segment of the electromagnetic spectrum that lies in the range between 390 and 1550 MHz. It is used for satellite transmission and microwave applications, such as the Global Positioning System (GPS).

LCC See *Leadless Chip Carrier.*

LCD See *liquid crystal display.*

LD See *laser disc.*

LDAP See *Lightweight Directory Access Protocol.*

leader (n.) In the process of storing analog recordings on magnetic tape, a clean, blank segment of tape-like material that is spliced before the first cut and between programs. Sometimes the term is used loosely to refer to a few seconds of blank tape at the head of a reel. Pronounced "LEE-der."

lead-in (n.) In videodisc programs, the 40 seconds of video black preceding the active program. Pronounced "LEE-din." Compare *lead-out.*

lead-in area (n.) A space reserved at the beginning of a recordable compact disc (CD-R) that is left blank for the disc's table of contents (TOC). The table is recorded in this space when the disc is filled or when it is permanently closed and finalized.

leading (n.) In electronic text or on the printed page, the distance between the type on two lines. Leading is measured from the baseline on which type rests to the next baseline. It is therefore composed of the height of the characters plus the space between the lines. Pronounced "LED-ding."

Leadless Chip Carrier (LCC) (n.) An integrated circuit (IC) package with input and output pads instead of leads around the edges.

lead-out (n.) In videodisc programs, the 30 seconds of video black with no audio following the active program. Compare *lead-in.*

lead-out area (n.) A space reserved at the end

of a session on a recordable compact disc (CD-R) indicating that the data has ended and that the session has been finalized.

leased access (n.) Local cable television system channels that the Federal Communications Commission (FCC) requires to be reserved for lease by independent video programmers.

leased line (n.) A dedicated telephone connection that links two or more points without passing through switching equipment. Such lines are often used to connect a local area network (LAN) with an Internet Service Provider (ISP).

LEC See *local exchange carrier.*

LED See *light-emitting diode.*

legacy system (n.) A hardware-software package that remains in use because of the expense or difficulty of upgrading or replacing it with newer, more functional equipment.

Lempel-Ziv-Welch (LZW) (n.) Developed by Terry Welch in 1984, a lossless compression scheme used to reduce file size. A variant of Lempel-Ziv compression, LZW maintains a table that maps input strings, or recurring byte sequences, to their associated output codes. It works by identifying similarities between character codes and then recording that data in an abbreviated format. Unisys Corporation patented LZW compression and decompression in 1984.

letterbox (v., adj.) To crop the top and bottom of the screen while displaying video. Programs recorded in the original aspect ratio of film, which is proportionately wider than the aspect ratio of a computer or television monitor, will often appear with black bands above and below the viewing area. These bands are

called the *letterbox effect*. The two formats whose framing shares a native aspect ratio of 16:9 are film and digital video. When high-definition television (HDTV) signals are viewed on a standard television tube with an approximate aspect ratio of 4:3, the letterbox effect results, unless a considerable amount of the picture is cropped from the sides. See figure.

letterbox effect

level (n.) In audio terminology, the amplitude or strength of a signal, usually expressed in decibels related to a reference signal. In video, levels are measured in IRE units, a scale named after the Institute of Radio Engineers. IRE measures video levels. Peak video level is 100 IRE units

lexical analysis (n.) In programming, the first stage of processing a language. Characters that comprise the source program are read one at a time and grouped into *lexemes,* which are constructs such as keywords, identifiers, literals, and punctuation. These lexemes are then passed to the parser. The process is also known as *linear analysis* or *scanning.*

LFO See *low-frequency oscillator.*

library (n.) In programming, a list of procedures or functions that can be accessed and implemented. A library is a collection of previously built code or routines.

LIFO See *last-in-first-out.*

light-emitting diode (LED, pronounced "el-ee-DEE") (n.) A semiconductor diode that emits light when current passes through it. The most common LED application is the alphanumeric display on a calculator. A laser is a type of LED that can serve as the source for optical data transmission.

lightguide (n.) Jargon for optical fiber, or a bundle of fibers.

light pen (n.) A stylus that controls the position of a cursor on a monitor. It has a light-detecting tip and is used either for graphics input on a drawing tablet or as a user interface (UI) device.

lightwave (n.) Synonym for fiber optics. Also refers to optical communications not transmitted by fibers.

Lightweight Directory Access Protocol (LDAP) (n.) A relatively simple protocol for updating and searching directories that run on TCP/IP. An LDAP directory entry is a collection of attributes with a distinguished name. Each of the entry's attributes has a type, such as "mail," and one or more values. A mail attribute might contain a value such as *brad @hansenmedia.com.* LDAP directory entries are arranged in a hierarchical structure that reflects political, geographic, or organizational boundaries. Countries reside at the top of the tree, followed by entries for states and organizations.

linear (adj.) Describes a medium in which content is arranged sequentially and in which the user must move through the material by going forward or backward, as opposed to enter-

ing a data stream at any point. A videotape is linear, whereas digital media is nonlinear.

linear audio (n.) On a videotape, the use of a separate track dedicated to recording audio. This technique may result in low fidelity, but the audio may be edited separately from the video. It is used to replace wild sound on a field tape with narration and sound effects.

line art (n.) Images that contain only black-and-white information with no grayscale or blended tones. This category includes halftone images that appear gray but that consist of tiny black dots on a white background.

Linear Tape Open (LTO) (n.) A new open standard proposed by IBM, Seagate Technology, and Hewlett-Packard for increasing the areal density, access speed, and transfer rate in midrange tape storage systems. LTO competes with DLT technology, the de facto standard.

line conditioning (n.) Alteration of the conductive properties of wires used to transmit power or signals. Transformers, resistors, capacitors, and other components are inserted into a line, which may be a twisted pair of copper wires, to adjust and correct signal levels. Analog voice lines are typically loaded, which means that inductors are inserted at regular intervals. Dry lines, or those lacking either inductors or the DC voltage used for telephone voice transmission, are best for transmitting digital data.

line extender (n.) An amplifier that compensates for loss in the strength of a signal over distribution lines.

line level (adj.) Describes an audio signal that ranges from 100 millivolts (mV) to approximately 1 volt for full signal. A line level signal is typically the output of a preamplifier rather than the low-level signal that comes directly from a microphone.

line noise (n.) Electrical interference picked up in a communications link, such as an RS-232 serial connection, that may cause spurious characters to appear. Line noise may be induced by poor connections, crosstalk from other circuits, electrical storms, or other electromagnetic sources.

line printer port (LPT) (n.) On an IBM-compatible computer, a parallel port through which a printer is often interfaced with a 25-pin connector. See also *parallel port*.

Lingo (n.) A scripting language used for authoring in Macromedia Director. Lingo is similar to HyperTalk, the language used in HyperCard scripting.

link (n.) 1. A connection between two pieces of data. An example of a link is the relationship between a hypertext anchor and the URL to which it refers. 2. A connection between network nodes.

Link Access Procedure–D (LAPD) (n.) A link-level protocol for the D channel in ISDN connections. LAPD has a different framing sequence from the LAP-Balanced (LAPB) protocol.

Link Access Protocol for Modems (LAPM) (n.) The automatic request for retransmission (ARQ) system with cyclic redundancy check (CRC) that is part of the V.42 protocol.

link layer (n.) Layer 2, the data link layer, in the Open Systems Interconnection (OSI) reference model.

link rot (n.) Jargon for the condition of links on a web page that point to locations that have changed or no longer exist.

Link State Routing Protocol (n.) A routing protocol such as Open Shortest-Path First (OSPF) that allows a router to exchange information with other routers about accessing external networks. It assesses the link speeds, number of hops, traffic congestion, and other features in a network connection. Link state routers calculate the shortest path for a message and update other routers when their own routing tables change. Link state routing normally requires more processing but less transmission overhead than distance-vector routing protocols, such as RIP, which typically use a single metric and which exchange all of their table information with other routers on a regular schedule.

Linux (n.) Short for Linus Unix; an implementation of the Unix kernel that runs on Intel and Alpha hardware in the general release. Versions of Linux for SPARC, PowerPC, and SGI are in active development. Versions that are ported to microcomputers support networking and shells. Linus Torvalds, the primary copyright holder, coordinates development of the Linux kernel. The whole kernel is available under the GNU general public license. See the appendix on Unix and Linux commands. Pronounced "LEE-nucks."

liquid crystal display (LCD) (n.) An array of liquid crystal cells that are turned on and off electronically, modulating light that shines from behind the display. When they are used with an overhead projection system, large LCD panels can simulate computer graphics output. Because LCDs consume very little power, they are often used for numbers and letters on calculators, watches, and handheld games.

LISP (n.) Abbreviated form of List Processor; a programming language developed by John McCarthy consisting of expressions that are lists of instructions to a computer. The lists establish relationships among themselves, and the values created by the relationships become part of the data in a LISP program. LISP is commonly used in artificial intelligence (AI) applications.

listserv (n.) A program that automates mailing lists on the Internet or on any large network.

lithography (n.) The transfer of a pattern or image from one medium to another, such as from a mask to a silicon wafer.

little-endian (adj.) Describes a format for storing or transmitting binary data in which the least significant byte or bit is placed at the head, or beginning of a packet. The term is adapted from the Lilliputians in *Gulliver's Travels* by Jonathan Swift; they debated whether soft-boiled eggs should be opened at the big end or the little end. Compare *big-endian*.

LLC See *logical link control*.

LMDS See *Local Multipoint Distribution Service*.

load (v.) 1. To transfer a computer program from storage into RAM. 2. To introduce electrical current into a line or circuit.

Local Access and Transport Area (LATA, pronounced "LAH-tah") (n.) A contiguous geographical area consisting of a state or metropolitan region served by a Bell Operating Company (BOC). There are 161 local telephone service areas in the United States. Calls made point to point within a single LATA are the responsibility of the local telephone company. InterLATA calls are processed by an interexchange carrier.

Local Application Numerical Control (LANC, pronounced "LANK") (n.) Developed by Sony, a machine control protocol for videotape recorders and players that carries Control-S data. It is implemented by a variety of camcorders in the 8 mm and S-VHS format and can transfer information in the hours:minutes:seconds:frames (hh:mm:ss:ff) format to and from digital controllers.

local area network (LAN) (n.) Any physical network technology that operates at high speeds over short distances, such as several thousand yards. Technologies that play roles in a LAN include Ethernet, token ring, Asynchronous Transfer Mode (ATM), Fiber Distributed Data Interface (FDDI) II, 10BASE-T, and Systems Network Architecture (SNA). The system of cables and interfaces controlled by a communications protocol that connects microcomputers for sharing resources and peripherals is all part of the LAN. Connection is also possible with an infrared link. Compare *wide area network*.

local bus (n.) In microcomputer architecture, a data bus with a short signal path between the main processor and input/output (I/O) processors. A local bus is frequently used for fast video functions. Popular local bus standards are the VESA and PCI buses.

local exchange (n.) A telecommunications provider's central office, which is where a subscriber's line is terminated.

local exchange carrier (LEC, pronounced "LEHK") (n.) An organization that provides intraLATA telephone service or exchange access. It may be any local telephone company in the United States, either a Bell Operating Company (BOC) or an independent, such as GTE.

localize (v.) To tailor the content of piece of media to fit the cultural requirements of a specific region or population.

local loop (n.) In telecommunications, the circuits between a telephone subscriber's residence or business site and switching equipment at the telephone company's central office.

Local Multipoint Distribution System (LMDS) (n.) Wireless cable service that offers multiple channels of video programming in the 27.5- to 29.5-GHz microwave spectrum. An antenna 4.5 inches in diameter is required to receive LMDS signals. Broadcast antennas serve cells that overlap in a radius of three to six miles. The first commercial LMDS operator was Cellular Vision in New York City.

LocalTalk (n.) The hardware used to connect Macintosh computers and peripherals for AppleTalk communications.

location (n.) 1. The address where data is recorded in computer memory. 2. A place where a film is shot, usually outdoors or in a "real-world" environment as opposed to in a studio with fake backgrounds.

log (v.) To record time code numbers that correspond to selected frames of video on tape, used by editors to identify segments for future reference.

log file (n.) A record created by a web server that contains all the access information, which documents activity on a web site.

logic (n.) 1. Philosophy that addresses the formal principles and methods of reasoning and knowledge. Logic is concerned with knowing truth. Symbols are used to formalize logical arguments and proofs representing propositions and logical connectives. Boolean algebra is applied to the basic operations of truth values using combinations of "AND," "OR," and "NOT." Predicate logic expresses the progression from premises to conclusions, or the process of deduction. 2. Formulas used to control the operation of integrated circuits (ICs) that apply relational propositions to gated circuits.

logical (adj.) Describes a conceptual object that serves a function or has meaning. In programming, a physical device is often referred to by a logical name. *Logical* is similar to *virtual*, because logical objects do not necessarily reside in any physical place.

Logical Block Addressing (LBA) (n.) A procedure that IBM-compatible microcomputers use to increase the size limit for a single Integrated Drive Electronics (IDE) hard disk from 528 megabytes (MB) to 8.4 gigabytes (GB). Addressing conversion takes place on the IDE disk controller card. Older Basic Input/Output System (BIOS) versions allow the user to select LBA mode manually.

logical block number (n.) A sequential address for accessing blocks of data on storage media. Blocks are numbered sequentially, beginning with 0.

logical code (n.) A tag that provides general directions in an HTML document. For example, the tag <EM> means "emphasis," which could be translated as either italic or bold. By contrast, a physical code indicates exactly how text should be displayed. The physical tag <B> indicates bold, and not any other general type of emphasis.

logical device (n.) Data in the logic of a computer that describes a peripheral or external equipment, whether or not the equipment is physically connected or even exists. It is a virtual representation of the features of a device, useful for mapping information that is passed to and from the physical device.

logical expression (n.) In computer logic, a comparison between two variables or values that yields a true or false answer. For example, the statement 1 > 0 is true.

logical file format (n.) In reference to data stored on a compact disc or on a hard drive, a structure shaped like a virtual tree of directories and files. This structure facilitates access to information. Also called *logical format*.

logical link control (LLC) (n.) In networking, the top portion of the data link layer in the OSI reference model. The specification is defined by IEEE 802.2. The LLC sublayer provides an interface for the data link service user with error checking. Directly below the LLC sublayer is the media access control (MAC) sublayer.

logical unit number (LUN, pronounced "el-yoo-EHN") (n.) Identifier for a device directly attached to a SCSI physical unit and not directly attached to the SCSI bus. A logical unit typically references a single physical unit, though not always. A SCSI hard drive is assigned a physical unit number (SCSI ID), and its controller is assigned an LUN.

logic gate (n.) An integrated circuit (IC) with inputs and outputs that represent binary values as voltages. The standard amount of voltage that transistor-transistor logic (TTL) uses is 0 volts for 0 (false) compared with 5 volts for 1 (true). Gates implement Boolean functions, such as AND, OR, NAND, NOR, NOT, and XOR. Gates with *state* can hold a temporary condition or status. A *flip-flop* gate holds state, and is capable of feeding certain outputs

back to certain inputs.

login (n., adj.) The identification and authentication process performed by users when accessing a computer system or network. A login script is run by the host computer.

log off (v., adj.) To end an online session with a computer or network. This is usually accomplished by typing *logoff* or *logout*.

log on (v.) To enter a networked multiuser environment, typically by submitting a user name and password to the host computer.

longitudinal redundancy check (LRC) (n.) A procedure that tests the completeness of networked data or information stored on a data tape. LRC is based on comparing a block check character (BCC) between sender and receiver, to see if the block of data has accumulated to the same size on both ends. If they are equal, then transmission is assumed to be complete.

longitudinal time code (LTC) (n.) Time code information that is recorded, or "stamped," in the form of an audio signal on an available linear track of a videotape. LTC provides a means of precisely locating any point on a tape, which enables frame-accurate machine control.

long shot (n.) A camera view from a distance showing a broad perspective of a subject or scene.

loop 1. (n.) A complete, self-contained electrical connection. 2. (n.) The uninterrupted, repeated display of a series of still frames, an audio file, a video segment, or the execution of a series of instructions. 3. (v.) To cause a segment of media to repeat.

loopback (n.) A diagnostic test in which a signal is returned to the transmitting device from the receiving device for comparison.

loop through (n.) A feature of an audio, video, or data circuit that provides an output connector, which sends the same signal that the unit receives as input. This enables an auxiliary unit to receive the signal at approximately the same time as the original unit receives the input signal.

lossless compression (n.) A compression technique that reduces the storage requirements of a file yet completely preserves the original information contained in images or in other data. Compare *lossy*.

lossy (adj.) Describes encoding or compression methods that do not preserve all the original data in a file, making that data impossible to recover later. Lossy compression can greatly reduce the quantity of data required to define an object by discarding redundant and unnecessary information in images and data files while maintaining the basic content. Data lost in the quantization of high-frequency components of an image is virtually imperceptible to the human eye, however, so the discarded data may be relatively insignificant. Discrete cosine transform is a type of lossy compression. Compare *lossless compression*.

low-frequency oscillator (LFO) (n.) In sound synthesis, a device capable of subsonic frequency generation, used most often as a controller for other functions, such as vibrato or tremolo.

low-level language (n.) An assembly language that translates each statement into a single machine instruction.

LPT See *line printer port*.

LRC See *longitudinal redundancy check*.

LSI See *large-scale integration*.

LTC See *longitudinal time code*.

LTO See *Linear Tape Open*.

L2TP See *Layer Two Tunneling Protocol*.

luma (n.) Brightness of a transmitted video signal.

lumen (n.) A unit of luminous flux emitted by a light source. Lumens are measured in candelas; 1 candela indicates the intensity radiated by a single candle.

luminance (n.) Degree of brightness or intensity. One of the three image characteristics coded in a component video signal (represented by the letter Y) and measured in lux or foot-candles. Luminance is the black-and-white portion of a video signal. The other two components of a video signal are the red and blue chroma factors.

luminance bandwidth (n.) The frequency range representing the degree of brightness that a video system can record or transmit. Shape detail is determined largely by this factor.

luminance key (n.) A signal that a switcher uses to alternate between two or more video images based on the brightness of one of the signals.

LUN See *logical unit number*.

lurker (n.) Jargon for a subscriber to a mail list or newsgroup who does not post often but who reads group postings regularly.

lux (n.) A unit of measurement equal to one lumen over a one-square-meter surface.

LV See *Laservision.*

LV-ROM See *Laservision read-only memory.*

Lynx (n.) Text-mode universal client, or browser, developed at the University of Kansas, primarily used on the Unix and MS-DOS platforms.

LZW See *Lempel-Ziv-Welch.*

M

MAC See *media access control.*

MAC address (n.) Media access control address; a hardware address belonging to any device connected to a shared media network via the MAC protocol. A MAC address may refer to the low-level address assigned to a device on an Ethernet; such an address would be translated to an Internet Protocol (IP) address via Address Resolution Protocol (ARP). Each network interface card (NIC) is assigned a unique address when manufactured. Also known as *Ethernet address.*

MacBinary (n.) A representation of the data and resource forks belonging to a Macintosh file, along with relevant Finder information, expressed in eight-bit words. A Macintosh terminal emulator will recognize a MacBinary file, use file transfer protocol (FTP) to separate the file into forks, and appropriately modify the desktop to display icons and other Macintosh-compatible constructs.

machine code (n.) Another term for *machine language.*

machine cycle (n.) The four steps a processor carries out for each machine language instruction: fetch, decode, execute, and store. Performed by the control unit, the steps may be fixed in the logic of the CPU or programmed

as microcode. The *fetch* cycle places the current program counter contents on the address bus and reads the word at that location into the instruction register (IR). The *decode* cycle uses the contents of the IR to determine which gates should be opened in the CPU's various functional units and buses. In the *execute* cycle, values are passed between the various functional units and buses, and the arithmetic and logic unit (ALU) is operated. During the *store* cycle, the result of the instruction is written to its destination, either a register or a memory location.

machine-independent (adj.) Describes software designed to perform similarly on more than one kind of computer. Java bytecode is meant to be machine-independent; the Java Virtual Machine (JVM) can be loaded on any type of computer.

machine language (n.) Binary code that expresses computer instructions and data in an executable form at the lowest level. No further translation is required for computer processing.

Macintosh (n.) Developed by Apple Computer in 1984, a popular microcomputer originally based on the Motorola 68000 series CPU. It evolved into the Power Macintosh in 1994 based on the PowerPC RISC processor. Its operating system is known as the Mac OS, a graphical user interface (GUI) originally designed by Xerox. Multimedia features such as sound generation, QuickTime video, and interactive icons have been built into the hardware and software of Macintosh computers since their inception, establishing a model in this regard for other systems designers.

Macintosh file system (n.) A logical construct with two parts, or forks, proprietary to the Mac OS. The *data fork* contains data that, on other operating systems, is typically stored in a file. The *resource fork* contains a collection of arbitrary attribute-value pairs, including program segments, icon bitmaps, and parametric values required by the Finder. Additional information regarding Macintosh files is stored by the Finder in a hidden file called the *Desktop Database*. It is difficult to store the different parts of a Macintosh file in other file systems that handle only consecutive data. For this reason, the data fork is often the only part sent when a file is transferred to a computer that uses another operating system. Alternatively, a Macintosh file may be converted into some other format before it is transferred.

Macintosh Programmer's Workshop (MPW) (n.) The environment in which applications are developed for the Macintosh system.

Mac OS (n.) Macintosh operating system; the proprietary operating system used by the Macintosh family of microcomputers.

macro (n.) A small block of code, or a series of commands, batched together and executed by a keystroke or by a combination of function keys. A macro is used to replace or automate frequently performed tasks.

magnetic storage (n.) Any medium used to save information encoded as variations in magnetic polarity. Common examples of magnetic storage are audio tapes, videotapes, magnetic tapes, and floppy diskettes.

magnetic tape (mag tape) (n.) Typically made from a mylar base, a thin, inelastic tape. It is coated with a ferromagnetic emulsion and used to record and store audio tracks, video programs, and computer data.

magneto optical (MO) (n.) The use of a laser beam to heat a special magnetic recording medium and to reduce its resistance to the reversal of magnetic polarity while a magnet is used to change polarity in selected spots. The medium becomes stable at normal temperatures, makes a relatively permanent record, and is housed in a protective cartridge. Most rewritable optical drives employ MO technology.

magneto-optical disc (n.) A high-density, read/write optical storage medium. In access speed, it is slower than a hard disk but faster than a CD-ROM. A disc is written by a laser that heats a spot on the disc surface. The spot is polarized by an electromagnet from the other side of the disc. When the disc is read, the change in polarity alters the reflection of light from the reading laser at that spot, and the difference is interpreted as a data value. A magneto-optical disc may be written and read many times, as if it were a large floppy disk.

mag tape See *magnetic tape.*

mailbox (n.) A file that is the property of a user on a particular computer in which email messages are received and stored for a user to read. It may simply be an email address to which messages are sent.

Mail Exchange (MX) (n.) Used to define a host computer, a domain name system (DNS) record that can accept mail.

Mail Exchange Record (n.) A domain name system (DNS) resource record type that indicates which host can process electronic mail for a particular domain.

mail exploder (n.) Feature of an email delivery system that implements mailing lists. An exploder takes messages sent to a single address and delivers them to all mailboxes on a list.

mail gateway (n.) A connection between multiple electronic mail systems that transfers mail between them. Machines that bridge dissimilar systems on different networks use mail gateways to translate messages.

mailing list (n.) An alias email address that a mail exploder expands to yield other email addresses. Some mailing lists are simple reflectors that redirect mail to a list of recipients. Others are moderated, or filtered, by humans. A request to subscribe to a mailing list or to be removed from one should be sent to the administrator's address, not to the list, to prevent it from going to all recipients on the list.

mail path (n.) The route that a message takes through one or several mail servers from the sending point to the destination.

mail server (n.) Any program that distributes files or information in response to requests received through electronic mail.

mail user agent (MUA) (n.) A program with which a user reads and composes electronic mail messages. It provides an interface between the user and the message transfer agent (MTA). Outgoing mail is sent to an MTA for delivery, and incoming mail is picked up from the MTA. Agents running on single-user machines may

pick up mail using POP. Pine is a common MUA for Unix.

mainframe computer (n.) The primary framework of a large computer's central processing unit (CPU).

main loop (n.) In an event-driven program, the top-level construct, which receives and operates on user input.

main memory (n.) The primary random access storage area in a computer where files and applications reside while controlled by the central processing unit (CPU).

main processing unit (n.) The computational core of a system. The main processing unit provides the logical, arithmetic, and control functions that access, process, and output data.

MAN See *metropolitan area network*.

management information system (MIS) (n.) Computing hardware and software designed to perform business functions, such as retrieving information, representing a database, projecting and forecasting, communicating, tracking accounts, and assisting in decision making about resource allocation.

Mandelbrot set (n.) A subset of a complex plane whose boundary is a fractal with great detail and variety. It is named for Benoit Mandelbrot, who performed the first research on the subject in the 1970s. See figure on following page.

mapping (n.) In graphic design, the process of specifying how a texture is applied to the surface of an object. In three-dimensional animation, the way a texture follows an object is a function of its mapping; it is also a function of the

Mandelbrot set

scale and orientation of the surface image.

markup (n.) The instructions embedded in a text document that specify general formatting features, such as headings and paragraphs. Many proprietary versions exist, but Standard Generalized Markup Language (SGML) is the universal standard.

martian (n.) Jargon referring to a packet that appears unexpectedly on the wrong network because of incorrect routing data.

mask (n.) 1. The area on a graphic screen on which nothing may be displayed. 2. In the photolithography process, a pattern of chrome and glass used to etch a layer of silicon in chip manufacturing.

master 1. (n.) The final edited version of a program, recorded on high-quality audio tape, videotape, or film, that is intended for broadcast or as the source for duplication. 2. (v.) To produce stamper molds used for replication. 3. (v.) In CD manufacturing, to create a glass master from which copies are reproduced. A laser beam "engraves" the pits, which represent binary data, into a photo-resistant surface.

matrix (n.) A predetermined array of quantities or elements.

Matrix Math eXtensions (MMX) (n.) An advancement in the Pentium microprocessor designed and manufactured by Intel Corporation. It is best described when it is contrasted with a non-MMX Pentium processor, such as the Pentium or the Pentium Pro. The Pentium Pro and the Pentium II MMX are both 32-bit processors with 64-bit data paths. Both have 7.5 million transistors in the microprocessor (not including the cache). The original Pentium has two 64-bit register sets: the integer register and the floating-point register. The Pentium MMX adds a third 64-bit MMX register, which has 57 new instructions. The MMX central processing unit (CPU) also adds 16 kilobytes (KB) of Level 1 (L1) cache to the chip. The MMX register loads multiple data with simultaneous processing, working on the single-instruction, multiple-data (SIMD) processing principle. In the original non-MMX Pentium, color images are processed individually, first red, then green, then blue, to display an image. The MMX processes all colors at once without a video accelerator card. MMX uses a branch prediction algorithm and logic similar to that of the Pentium Pro. MMX is available only in speeds of 166 MHz and higher. Starting at 223 MHz, the Pentium II integrates MMX technology on the chip with a standard 32KB of L1 cache and 512KB of Level 2 cache. It uses dynamic execution and speculative execution of code. MMX technology enhances the quality of audio and video by processing these types of data more efficiently and rapidly. The Pentium II incorporates dynamic execution and MMX technology in a single package.

matte (n.) In video production, an upper layer in a composition through which layers that lie beneath are visible through a hole cut in the matting layer. This video effect is used to frame a selected portion of the underlying layer in the same way that a matte frames a mounted painting.

Mb See *megabit.*

MB See *megabyte.*

M-bone See *multicast backbone.*

Mbps See *megabits per second.*

MBps See *megabytes per second.*

MCA See *Micro Channel Architecture.*

MCI See *Media Control Interface.*

MCI driver (n.) Media Control Interface driver; a software component that directs the recording and playback of multimedia objects. The syntax requires an MCI command to "open" a device, give it instructions, and "close" it. For basic functions all MCI devices share a set of commands, such as "play" and "stop." Microsoft originally defined 11 MCI devices that drivers control, including an undefined classification. See table.

MDI See *multiple-document interface.*

MDS See *Multipoint Distribution Service.*

mean time between failure (MTBF) (n.) A measure of how long a computer peripheral, such as a hard drive, can be expected to function before it fails.

media access control (MAC) (n., adj.) The lower sublayer of the data link layer in the Open Systems Interconnection (OSI) model.

MCI Drivers

MCI Device	Command Syntax
Animation player	MCI_DEVTYPE_ANIMATION
Audio CD player	MCI_DEVTYPE_CD_AUDIO
Digital audio tape	MCI_DEVTYPE_DAT
Video in a window	MCI_DEVTYPE_DIGITAL_VIDEO
Undefined	MCI_DEVTYPE_OTHER
Video overlay	MCI_DEVTYPE_OVERLAY
Image scanner	MCI_DEVTYPE_SCANNER
MIDI sequencer	MCI_DEVTYPE_SEQUENCER
Videocassette recorder	MCI_DEVTYPE_VCR
Videodisc player	MCI_DEVTYPE_VIDEODISC
Waveform player	MCI_DEVTYPE_WAVEFORM_AUDIO

It consists of the interface between the logical link control and the physical layer of the network. Different types of MAC are employed on different physical media.

Media Control Interface (MCI) (n.) A platform-independent multimedia specification published in 1990 by Microsoft and others. It provides a consistent way to control devices such as CD-ROMs and video playback units. See also *Resource Interchange File Format.*

media-independent (adj.) Describes any software program that delivers the same content on different playback systems.

Media Player (n.) A viewer for all types of audio and video data streams located in the *Accessories* directory of Microsoft Windows. If the drivers are loaded for a particular media type, such as Video for Windows (.avi), this applet provides a way to view and hear a stream of data. This is an easy way to access any type of multimedia on a Windows-based system. Version 5.0, released in 1998, plays a wide variety of file types, including MPEG, MIDI, and compressed video for the web.

medium (n.) In a digital context, a substance or an object on which information is stored or

M

transmitted, such as a disk or a network. In telecommunications, examples of transmission media include fiber optic cable, wire, air, and water. The plural form is *media*.

medium shot (n.) A camera perspective somewhere between a long shot and close-up in which subjects are viewed from a midrange distance.

mega- Prefix meaning one million. In the decimal system, 1 000 000 is expressed as 10 to the 6th power. In the binary system, mega- is expressed as 2 to the 20th power, or 1 048 576.

megabit (Mb) (n.) One million bits.

megabits per second (Mbps) (n.) A measurement of data transfer in millions of bits each second.

megabyte (MB) (n.) One million 8-bit bytes, or more precisely 1 048 576 bytes.

megabytes per second (MBps) (n.) A measurement of data transfer in millions of bytes each second.

megaflop (MFLOP) (n.) One million floating-point operations per second. A megaflop is the unit used in measuring the speed of a workstation or of a mainframe. A 25-MHz 486 computer can sustain approximately 1 MFLOP.

megahertz (MHz) (n.) One million cycles per second.

Memorandum of Understanding (MOU, pronounced "em-oh-YEW") (n.) A European agreement for telephone companies that provide ISDN services. The MOU specifies the facilities required for "Priority 1" service. See also *ISDN*.

memory (n.) The place in which data is recorded and stored, either permanently or temporarily. Memory is usually measured in kilobytes, megabytes, or gigabytes. It is placed in tracks and sectors on formatted media. See figure.

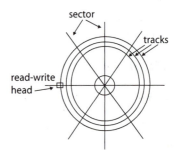

memory configuration on a magnetic disk

memory bus (n.) In a computing system, the means by which information is transferred between the central processing unit (CPU) and the main memory, or RAM. A dedicated chip set transfers information between the processor and the memory bus, so that the memory bus may be manipulated separately from the processor bus. The memory bus transfers information much more slowly than the processor bus. Slots for memory, or single in-line memory modules (SIMMs) and dual in-line memory modules (DIMMs), are connected to the memory bus in the same way that expansion slots are connected to the input/output (I/O) bus.

memory management unit (MMU) (n.) Circuitry that translates virtual addresses into physical addresses to support virtual memory and paging.

menu (n.) A list of options from which users may choose. The options are often available through a drop-down menu bar at the top of a graphical user interface (GUI) screen.

menu bar (n.) A set of icons or words graphically displayed across the top of a screen or window to give the user choices. When the user clicks on an item in the menu bar, a drop-down menu appears.

menu-driven (adj.) Describes a type of interface that allows the user to navigate by selecting from a menu of options on the screen rather than by typing characters on a command line.

mesh (n.) In three-dimensional modeling, an object defined by a series of points between which planes are defined.

meta- Greek prefix denoting "with." The term indicates that new meaning or functionality is added to something. For example, the Ctrl key is a *metakey* if used in combination with another key to change the function of that other key.

metafile (n.) A file that contains both bitmap and vector data, providing a means of storing objects by defining their shapes mathematically in a file. An example of a metafile is the Windows graphics file type with the extension .wmf. The format is useful when moving graphics between applications, such as Microsoft PowerPoint and Macromedia Director.

metal-oxide semiconductor (MOS, pronounced "MOSS") (n.) A silicon wafer with channel transistors that is used to create integrated circuits (ICs) or discrete components.

metal-oxide semiconductor field-effect transistor (MOSFET, pronounced "MOSS-fet") (n.) A transistor with a layer of metal-oxide insulation between the current channel and the gate. MOSFETs draw very little power and are commonly used in audio amplifier circuits.

metatag (n.) An HTML tag that belongs in the <HEAD> portion of a document, providing information about a page that is not displayed in the browser when the page is viewed. The type of editing program used to create a page is often identified in the metatag. Information placed in the metatag of the home page of a site is used by search engines to classify the site. Capturing metatags from all the sites on the web is the work of spiders and bots.

method (n.) 1. In object-oriented programming (OOP), the name given to a procedure or routine associated with one or more classes. An object of a certain class knows how to perform actions, such as creating a new instance of itself. Different classes may define methods with the same name (polymorphism). 2. The code a specific class provides to perform an operation associated with one or more classes.

metropolitan area network (MAN) (n.) Several local area telephone networks connected over a maximum distance of 50 kilometers. They often give business customers an alternative connection to long-distance carriers and are usually high-capacity fiber-optic networks.

MFLOP See *megaflop*.

MHz See *megahertz*.

Micro Channel Architecture (MCA) (n.) A revised bus for PC architecture that is incompatible with the original PC/AT architecture. IBM introduced MCA in its PS/2 series of microcomputers. Other vendors opposed MCA, with Compaq in the lead.

Microcom Networking Protocol (MNP) (n.) An asynchronous communications protocol

M

195

that permits packet retransmission, data compression, and speed negotiation between two modems. The CCITT V.42 standard specifies the four classes of MNP as a backup error correction scheme for the Link Access Protocol for Modems (LAPM).

microcomputer (n.) A self-contained computer system with a microprocessor, input devices, display, and memory. Also called a *desktop computer* or *personal computer*.

micron (n.) One-millionth of a meter. Also known as a *micrometer*.

microphone pattern (n.) The sensitivity of a microphone to the direction of sound sources in relation to the axis of the microphone body. Sounds that originate directly in front of the microphone's diaphragm have greater intensity and fuller frequency response than sounds that emanate from the side. The cardioid microphone has excellent off-axis rejection, which is desirable in some recording situations. See figure, and note the patterns illustrated.

microprocessor (n.) Any integrated circuit (IC) containing the CPU of a small computer. Intel has manufactured 80286, 80386, 80486, and Pentium chips for IBM compatibles, and Motorola has made 68000, 68020, 68030, and 68040 chips for the Macintosh. These are all complex instruction set computing (CISC) chips. Apple Computer, Motorola, and IBM designed a new generation of chips based on reduced instruction set computing (RISC); they are used in PowerPC and Power Macintosh computers.

microsecond (n.) One-millionth of a second.

Microsoft Compact Disc Extension (MSCDEX) (n.) A driver for a CD-ROM reader connected to a computer.

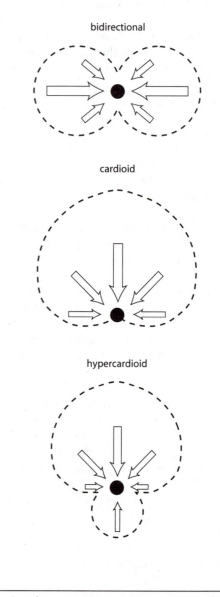

bidirectional

cardioid

hypercardioid

microphone patterns

Microsoft Disk Operating System (MS-DOS, pronounced "em-ess-DOSS") (n.) A single-user operating system that runs one program at a time and that is limited to working with one megabyte (MB) of memory, 640 kilobytes (KB) of which are usable for an application program. Special hardware permits EMS-compliant software to exceed the 1-MB limit, and some programs that run on top of DOS, such as Microsoft Windows 3.1, allow the user to load multiple applications at once and to switch between them. Features added to MS-DOS 2.0 and to subsequent versions resulted in two or more incompatible versions of many system calls, the instructions that interface an application with the operating system. MS-DOS is used on the Intel 16- and 32-bit microprocessors in IBM-compatible microcomputers.

Microsoft Network (MSN) (n.) A host for Internet activity. Microsoft supports MSN.

Microsoft Windows (MS Windows, Windows) (n.) A graphical user interface (GUI), or operating system, patented by Microsoft for use with personal computers running MS-DOS. MS Windows is loosely based on the point-and-click, icon-based interface invented by Apple Computer and deployed on all Macintosh computers. Windows 3.1 incorporates device drivers needed for multimedia functionality. Windows 95 and 98 are the second generation, leaving behind most of the dependence on MS-DOS. Windows NT is designed for networked computing applications, although the workstation version is commonly used on stand-alone computers.

microwave (n.) A bandwidth of high-frequency radio waves that lies between 890 MHz and 20 GHz. Microwaves are used for line-of-sight, point-to-point, and omnidirectional transmission of audio, video, and data signals within a terrestrial range of 20 to 30 miles.

microwave radio (n.) A high-frequency radio transmission system that operates point-to-

point. Repeaters are normally required to amplify the signal between parabolic antennas used for transmission and reception.

middleware (n.) Software that operates at the level between an application program and a network. It can mediate the interaction between separate applications across heterogeneous computing platforms on a network. Object request broker (ORB) software, which manages communication between objects, is an example.

MIDI See *Musical Instrument Digital Interface.*

MIDI Manufacturers Association (MMA) (n.) Musical Instrument Digital Interface Manufacturers Association; the organization of digital synthesis and studio equipment makers. MMA members collaborate on MIDI standards and related issues.

M

MIDI mode (n.) Musical Instrument Digital Interface mode; one of the four ways in which MIDI equipment may be configured. The modes determine which channels will be read and how many notes can be played at once. Mode 1 is OMNI ON/polyphonic, mode 2 is OMNI ON/monophonic, mode 3 is OMNI OFF/polyphonic, and mode 4 is OMNI OFF/monophonic. Channel mode messages set an instrument's mode to OMNI ON or OMNI OFF; OMNI ON means that all channels will be read, and OMNI OFF means that just one assigned channel will be read. Channel mode messages further set the equipment to respond polyphonically, playing more than one note at a time, or monophonically, playing only one note at a time. In monophonic modes no chords are possible.

MIDI 1.0 specification (n.) Musical Instrument Digital Interface 1.0 specification; the original specification for the use of MIDI communications defined by the International MIDI Association (IMA) in collaboration with manufacturers of digital synthesizers. The specification defines a protocol for transmitting information about musical performance, not about sound itself. The five types of messages in the specification can be divided into two groups: system messages and channel messages. *System messages* send information to an entire MIDI system, whereas *channel messages* send it to selected channels. Channel messages are most common, and they follow a status byte in the data stream that identifies which of the 16 MIDI channels will receive the data. There are two kinds of channel messages: channel voice and channel mode messages. *Channel voice messages* carry information such as "note-on" or "note-off" signals for any given key number with velocity values.

MIDI system message (n.) Musical Instrument Digital Interface system message; a message read by all devices connected to the system, unlike a channel voice or a mode message. The three types of MIDI messages—System Common, System Realtime, and System Exclusive—are defined as follows:

- System Common: Messages include *MIDI time code* (MTC) or *Quarter Frame*, *Song Position* and *Song Select* to control sequences, and *Tune Request*.

- System Realtime: Messages include the *MIDI Clock* timing pulse; *Start*, *Stop*, or *Continue* a sequence; *Active Sensing* to confirm a connection; and *System Reset* to return all devices to their default statuses.

- System Exclusive: Messages carry a manufacturer ID that only one brand of equipment recognizes. This type of message

includes the *Sample Dump Standard,* which allows nonexclusive descriptions of waveforms; these can be edited and played back on different brands of sample players. It also includes MTC messages, which can be used to synchronize with SMPTE devices. The MIDI file standard allows a sequence to be read by any type of MIDI device, regardless of the platform. The file format is the Standard MIDI File (SMF).

MIDI time code (MTC) (n.) A regular serial voltage transmission emitted by all MIDI devices at a rate of 31 250 times per second. This allows events in a MIDI sequence to be synchronized in time.

midlevel network (n.) In relation to a three-level Internet hierarchy, a second-level regional network, or a transit network, that connects stub networks to the backbone.

migration (n.) Automatic or program-controlled movement of data between slower storage media and faster storage media. The rules of migration determine when objects are moved.

mil (n.) One-thousandth of an inch, or 25.4 microns.

millions of instructions per second (MIPS, pronounced "MIPPS") (n.) A measurement of computer processing speed.

millisecond (n.) One-thousandth of a second.

MIME See *multipurpose Internet mail extensions.*

mimencode (n.) A part of the multipurpose Internet mail extensions (MIME) protocol that replaces uuencode for use in email and news.

Mimencode implements the encodings that were defined for MIME as uuencode replacements and is more robust for email applications. The term is a contraction of "mime" and "encode," pronounced "MY-men-code."

minicomputer (n.) A parallel binary system. A minicomputer has more storage and a faster processor than a microcomputer does, but its processor is smaller and less costly than that of a mainframe computer.

minidisc (n.) An audio CD format developed by Sony for use with its Data Discman portable system. Invented in 1991, a minidisc holds 200 megabytes (MB) of data. The format was revised in 1992 and introduced as a rewritable magneto-optical disc format for music. The medium resembles a small floppy disk.

minimize (v.) In a graphical user interface (GUI), to reduce an open window to an icon or to a very small representation of the file contents.

mip mapping (n.) The storage of several different resolutions of a texture map to avoid recalculating texture images as a viewer zooms closer to or farther away from a textured surface.

MIPS See *millions of instructions per second.*

mirror site (n.) An FTP site on the Internet that contains the same information held by another site so that demand on the original site is distributed.

MIS See *management information system.*

mission-critical (adj.) Describes system resources that, in the event of a failure, would seriously impair the ability of an organization to function.

mixed-mode disc (n.) A CD including computer data and CD-DA tracks. Typically, the computer data is placed in the first track, and the audio data is placed in one or more of the following tracks.

mixing board (n.) Used in audio production, a device with multiple input channels that permits a user to combine signals from various sources, vary the level of each, and bus the aggregate signal to the main outputs.

M-JPEG See *motion-JPEG.*

MMA See *MIDI Manufacturers Association.*

MMC See *Multimedia Marketing Council.*

MMDS See *Multichannel, Multipoint Distribution Service.*

MME See *multimedia extensions.*

MMU See *memory management unit.*

MMX See *Matrix Math eXtensions.*

MMX technology (n.) Matrix Math eXtensions technology; a process developed by Intel for integration with their Pentium processor. The process facilitates the presentation of multimedia content, such as animation, audio, and video.

MNP See *Microcom Networking Protocol.*

MO See *magneto optical.*

Mobile Satellite Service (MSS) (n.) Communication by satellite connection that serves ships, aircraft, and terrestrial vehicles. MSS satellites operate in the 1.6- to 2.4-GHz frequency ranges. A single MSS satellite can serve the entire United States.

Mobile Telephone Switching Office (MTSO) (n.) The central computer that connects cellular calls to the public telephone network. The MTSO controls all the operations of a cellular telephone system, including billing and monitoring.

mode (n.) 1. With reference to CDs, the method of storing code and data. There are two basic modes. In mode 1, used with CD-ROM applications, 288 bytes of each sector are used to store error correction code, and the remaining 2048 bytes per sector store data. Mode 2, used in CD-i and CD-ROM XA, has two forms. Form 1 is similar to mode 1 in that it has Red Book error correction. Form 2 discs allow 2336 bytes per sector of non–error corrected data for information storage; this capacity is used most commonly for graphic and audio content. 2. Oscillation that may be propagated in an electromagnetic field within a waveguide. Laser-generated light exhibits modes in an optical fiber.

model (n.) A simplified description of the behavioral characteristics of a system. A model is often used as a basis for simulation.

modeling (n.) 1. In three-dimensional animation, the first step in creating a 3-D object. 2. An educational process in which a computer system simulates a process. A user can input values and learn from the resulting changes in the process.

modem (n.) Contraction of modulator/demodulator; a device that converts digital data into audio signals for transmission over telephone lines and that translates the audio signals back into data on reception.

moderator (n.) An individual who manages an online discussion, sending submissions to a mailing list or newsgroup after determining their appropriateness.

modular (adj.) Composed of individual components that can stand alone or work together.

modular code (n.) A logic program in which each element, or object, is self-contained, stands alone, and holds all the data and instructions related to a particular task. Any element can call up any other object or element, and the recipient can perform the task for itself. The paradigm provides for object classes, methods, and inheritance. Also known as *object-oriented programming,* where the modules are independent and easily cross-linked.

modulation (n.) A change in the characteristics of a signal. When a carrier signal is modulated by or mixed with another signal, it is encoded with information that is analogous to information contained in another signal. The carrier transmits both signals. If the original carrier signal is of a constant level, changes in the composite signal represent the signal it is carrying. The opposite process is *demodulation,* or decoding of the data. A modem modulates a signal to transmit, and demodulates it to receive.

moiré pattern (n.) In a display with limited resolution, an undesirable optical effect created by overlapping grids and lines. For example, when a striped shirt is displayed on a television monitor, the scan lines may not align with the stripes, producing a moiré pattern on the screen. Pronounced "mwah-RAY."

monitor (n.) A picture tube or screen that can display video signals and/or computer graphics. See figure.

monochrome display (n.) A black-and-white monitor capable of displaying shades of gray but no colors.

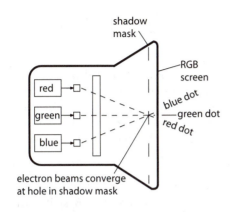

RGB monitor

monospaced font (n.) A set of letters and symbols in which each character has the same fixed width, or pitch, as opposed to those in a proportional font.

MOO See *MUD Object-Oriented.*

Moore's law (n.) An adage credited to Gordon Moore of Intel in 1964. He stated that the speed of integrated circuits (ICs) doubled every 12 months and predicted that the pattern would continue in the future. In reality, processing power has steadily doubled about every 18 months.

morph (v.) To melt one image into another by smoothly moving points from their original positions to new locations in another image. Morphing is done with graphic effects software packages that create a smooth transition from one image to another.

MOS See *metal-oxide semiconductor.*

Mosaic (n.) Developed at the National Center for Supercomputing Applications (NCSA), the first popular browser, or universal client, for the World Wide Web. It has evolved into Netscape Navigator.

mosaic filter (n.) An image-processing technique that divides an existing graphic into small squares, each of a single hue.

MOSFET See *metal-oxide semiconductor field-effect transistor.*

most significant bit (MSB) (n.) In a string of digits that store or transmit binary data, the first bit, or the bit farthest to the left, when the string is written in the usual way. If the MSB is not the first bit, it is the one with the greatest weighting.

motherboard (n.) The main printed circuit board in a computer, with sockets for additional boards or add-on cards. In a microcomputer the motherboard contains the bus, the microprocessor, and the chips used for interfacing with basic peripherals such as the keyboard, the display, the serial and parallel ports, and the mouse.

Motif (n.) Term for the standard X Window System graphical user interface (GUI) and the window manager from Open Software Foundation (OSF).

motion blur (n.) A blending or streaking effect added to images to simulate the appearance of moving objects. It is commonly used in animation sequences to show the path of an object.

motion choreography (n.) In animation and computer graphics, the process of determining the displacement, or change in position, of each object over time.

motion compensation (n.) A video compression scheme used in MPEG. Motion vectors are used to increase efficiency in predicting pixel values. These vectors are used to provide offsets based on the positioning of objects that move between intracoded frames (I-frames) and predictive-coded frames (P-frames). The information encoded is just the difference between the actual image and the predicted image. See also *MPEG frame type.*

motion-JPEG (M-JPEG, pronounced "em-JAY-peg") (n.) Motion–Joint Photographic Expert Group; a proprietary extension of the JPEG compression standard for still images that adapts it for moving images. Used to compress a stream of moving pictures at a constant frame rate, M-JPEG provides much lower compression ratios than do video compression standards, such as MPEG, which capitalize on similarities between successive frames. M-JPEG files are editable but generally are not transportable to different hardware platforms for playback. M-JPEG is implemented differently depending on the hardware used to encode it, but QuickTime version 3.0 translates M-JPEG from most proprietary formats and may be used to decode common M-JPEG files.

motion video (n.) 1. A video sequence with a high enough frame rate (number of pictures per second) that the sequence appears to be a continuous moving picture, not successive still images. 2. The progression of video images produced by a video camera. Motion video differs from video stills, animation, or computer graphics.

Motorola 68000 family (n.) A succession of 16- and 32-bit microprocessors designed and built by Motorola.

- 68000 features: 32-bit architecture internally, 16-bit architecture externally; 24-bit addressing and a linear address space; or-

thogonal instruction set and 16 registers that are split into data and address registers.

- 68020 features: 32-bit data and address buses; 256-byte instruction buffer.

- 68030 features: Instruction and data caches on the chip; an on-chip memory management unit (MMU).

- 68040 features: On-chip floating-point unit (FPU); 4-kilobyte (KB) split instruction and data caches. Used in Macintosh Quadra computers.

- 68060 features: Processing speeds two to three times higher than those of the 68040; the last development from Motorola in the high-performance 68000 series.

Motorola 680x0 (n.) Any member of the Motorola 68000 family of microprocessors. The variable *x* stands for 0, 1, 2, 3, 4, or 6.

MOU See *Memorandum of Understanding.*

mount (v.) To make a file system available for access. Unix does this by associating a file system with a directory. The "root" file system is mounted on the root directory. This places data in a position to be manipulated.

mouse (n.) An input device for a computer. A mouse rolls on a smooth surface and determines the location of the cursor on the screen. A mouse has one or more buttons, which are used to "click" on icons or hot spots on the screen. The computer interprets these mouse clicks as instructions. See figure.

MoviePlayer (n.) An applet used by the Macintosh to view QuickTime movies. The

cross-section, mechanical mouse

user interface is a standard Play Bar Controller, which allows one to start, stop, and pause a movie, adjust the volume, and watch the progress on a slider.

Moving Picture Expert Group (MPEG, pronounced "EM-peg") (n.) The working committee that, under the auspices of the ISO, defines standards for the digital compression and decompression of motion audio-video for use in computer systems. These standards consist of MPEG-1 (ISO/IEC 11172), MPEG-2 (ISO/IEC 13818), and later versions. The MPEG-1 standard delivers decompressed data at any rate between approximately 0.5 to 5.0 megabits per second (Mbps), allowing CD players to stream full-motion color movies at 30 frames per second (fps). MPEG-1 compression ratios as high as 200:1 are attainable. Source Image Format (SIF) is the reduced resolution obtained in MPEG-1 by decimating the 720-by-480-pixel input to 360 by 240 pixels prior to compression. The final resolution of MPEG-1 is 352 by 240 pixels. For compression bit rates lower than 3.5 Mbps, MPEG-1 SIF resolution is preferable to higher resolutions that require greater bandwidths. Captured from an NTSC source, MPEG-1 operates at 30 frames per second (fps) and 30 fields per second. MPEG-1 processes audio in 16-bit stereo at 44.1 kHz, the same rate as CD audio, or at higher rates. MPEG-2 builds on the MPEG-1 standard, extending to the higher data rates (6–15 Mbps) needed for broadcast-quality signals. MPEG-2 is designed to support a range of picture aspect ratios, including 4:3 and 16:9. It adheres to the CCIR-601 standard of 720 by 486 and 60 fields per second, as opposed to 30 fields in MPEG-1. To pass such a large amount of data, MPEG-2 needs a bit rate of at least 5 Mbps to achieve high resolution. As the compressed bit rate is reduced, output video quality declines.

MPC See *Multimedia Personal Computer.*

MPC-1 See *Multimedia Personal Computer.*

MPC-3 See *Multimedia Personal Computer.*

MPC-2 See *Multimedia Personal Computer.*

MPEG See *Moving Picture Expert Group.*

MPEG compression (n.) Moving Picture Expert Group compression; the conversion of an analog videotape or a live video source into a stream of digits. These digits represent the original product in the MPEG digital video format. MPEG compression is a complex combination of video and audio compression techniques that reduce the size of a data file at ratios up to 200:1.

MPEG frame type (n.) Moving Picture Expert Group frame type; one of the three basic types of frames created by an MPEG encoder. The frame types are as follows:

1. Intracoded frame (I-frame): A picture coded using only information drawn from itself. Like a key frame, an I-frame provides an access point in the data stream.
2. Bidirectionally predictive frame (B-frame): A picture coded using motion-compensated prediction from previous and future reference frames. B-frames provide an efficient means of coding but require a memory buffer for future reference frames.
3. Predictive-coded frame (P-frame): A pic-

ture coded using motion-compensated prediction from the previous reference frame.

MPEG layers (n.) Moving Picture Expert Group layers; levels in an MPEG file that hold information about moving pictures. The levels are in hierarchical order and deal with a series of frames at the top level down to details about regions of a frame. From bottom to top, the different layers in an MPEG stream are as follows:

- Block: An eight-row-by-eight-column (8 x 8) block of pixels. A block is the unit to which discrete cosine transform (DCT) is applied.

- Macroblock: The four 8 x 8 blocks of luminance data and the corresponding 8 x 8 blocks of chrominance data coming from a 16 x 16 section of the luminance component of the picture. A macroblock is the basic unit for motion-compensation prediction.

- Slice: A series of macroblocks that serves as the synchronizing unit for reconstruction of the image data. Typically, a slice is all the blocks in one horizontal picture interval, as well as 16 lines of the picture.

- Picture: Source image or reconstructed data for a single frame consisting of three rectangular matrices of eight-bit numbers that represent the luminance and chrominance signals.

- Group of pictures (GOP): A self-contained sequence of pictures that starts with an I-frame and contains a variable number of P-frames and B-frames. SMPTE time code may be added to mark the first picture in a group at this layer.

- Sequence: A video sequence beginning with a "sequence header," which is followed by one or more groups of pictures, and ending with a "sequence end" code.

MPEG-1 (n.) Moving Picture Expert Group–1; a version of the MPEG compression method. MPEG-1 is optimized for data transfer rates in the 1-to-1.5-megabit-per-second (Mbps) range, such as the transfer rate of CD-ROM drives and T1 communications links. See *Moving Picture Expert Group.*

MPEG-2 (n.) Moving Picture Expert Group–2; a form of MPEG compression that is optimized for data transfer rates faster than five megabits per second (Mbps) and that is intended for such applications as DVD and broadcast video. See *Moving Picture Expert Group.*

MPOA See *Multiprotocol Over ATM.*

MPW See *Macintosh Programmer's Workshop.*

MSAU See *Multistation Access Unit.*

MSB See *most significant bit.*

MSCDEX See *Microsoft Compact Disc Extension.*

MS-DOS See *Microsoft Disk Operating System.*

MS-DOS CD-ROM extensions (n.) Microsoft Disk Operating System compact disc–read-only memory extensions; a set of routines that connect MS-DOS with the driver routines for specific models of CD-ROM players. The extensions allow machines running this operating system to read CD-ROM discs formatted in the ISO 9660 and High Sierra formats.

MSN See *Microsoft Network.*

MSO See *Multiple System Operator.*

MSS See *Mobile Satellite Service.*

MS Windows See *Microsoft Windows.*

MTBF See *mean time between failure.*

MTC See *MIDI time code.*

MTSO See *Mobile Telephone Switching Office.*

mu Prefix meaning one-millionth. The origin is the Greek letter μ; a *u* is the ASCII character nearest in appearance. Pronounced "MY-cro."

MUA See *mail user agent.*

MUD See *multiuser dungeon.*

MUD Object-Oriented (MOO, pronounced "MOOH") (n.) Multiuser dungeon Object-Oriented; a visual version of a MUD.

μ-law (**mu-law** or **micro-law**) (Pronounced "MEW-law") (n.) Standardized in the ITU G.711 specification, a method of coding eight-bit companded audio with pulse code modulation (PCM) that yields a 72-dB dynamic range. It is used for digital voice channels over telephone lines in North America, Japan, and South Korea. It is not interchangeable with a-law coding, which is used for digital audio over telephone lines in the rest of the world. A converter must be used to translate between these two differently coded PCM voice messages. Compare *a-law.*

multicast (n., v.) In relation to networking, a packet with a destination address that multiple nodes on the network may receive. Simultaneously broadcasting news updates, stock quotes, or compressed video programs to a list of users is an example of the one-to-many process of multicasting.

multicast backbone (M-bone) (n.) An Internet provision for video transfer.

Multichannel, Multipoint Distribution Service (MMDS) (n.) A wireless cable application operating in the 2.5-to-2.7-GHz bandwidth. A single antenna can transmit over a 30-mile radius. A dish 12 inches in diameter receives the signal, and a set-top box descrambles it. MMDS is a cost-effective transmission method, and digital systems using MPEG-2 compression have the capacity to broadcast many programs simultaneously.

multifrequency monitor (n.) A display unit that can respond to a fixed number of video signal frequencies and that supports various resolutions and standards.

multi-homed domain (n.) The domain name, or Internet Protocol (IP) address, of one site in a multi-homed log file.

multi-homed host (n.) A server with numerous connections to a network. This server is capable of receiving or sending data over several links but incapable of routing traffic.

multi-homed log file (n.) A single log file that contains access information for multiple web sites.

multi-homed web server (n.) A single computer that hosts more than one web site.

multimedia (n., adj.) A synthesis of digital media types combining text, graphics, audio, animation, and video. Interactivity is a feature of most multimedia, which is also referred to as *digital media, new media,* or *hypermedia.*

M

multimedia extensions (MME) (n.) A set of software routines and specifications for running multimedia programs in Microsoft Windows 3.0. These routines and specifications were incorporated into Windows 3.1.

Multimedia Marketing Council (MMC) (n.) A group that owns the Multimedia Personal Computer (MPC) trademark. Composed of hardware vendors, the group collaborates with Microsoft. The MMC's specifications are marked with the MPC trademark.

Multimedia Personal Computer (MPC) (n.) A specification originally developed by Tandy Corporation and Microsoft as the minimum platform capable of running multimedia software. In 1993, the Multimedia Marketing Council introduced an upgraded MPC-2 standard; at that time, MPC was renamed MPC-1. MPC-2 was followed by a list of expectations for a third level, MPC-3. When these specifications were written, computers were much less powerful than current models are. Pentium MMX computers designed to deliver multimedia are many times more powerful than the MPC-3 specification requires. Specifications for these three standards are as follows:

- **MPC-1** (n.) Multimedia Personal Computer–1; a specification that defines the following minimum standard requirements for a multimedia computing system:
  - a 386SX or 486 central processing unit (CPU)
  - 2 megabytes (MB) of RAM
  - a 30-MB hard disk
  - a Video Graphics Array (VGA) video display
  - an eight-bit digital audio subsystem
  - a CD-ROM drive
  - system software compatible with Windows 3.1 or higher APIs.

- **MPC-2** (n.) Multimedia Personal Computer–2; a specification that defines the following minimum standard requirements for a Level 2 multimedia computing system:
  - 25-MHz 486SX with 4 megabytes (MB) of RAM
  - a 160-MB hard disk
  - a 16-bit sound card
  - a 16-bit video display capable of 65 536 colors
  - a double-speed CD-ROM drive
  - system software compatible with Windows 3.1 or higher APIs.

- **MPC-3** (n.) Multimedia Personal Computer–3; a specification that defines the following minimum system functionality for Level 3 compliance in a multimedia computing system:
  - a 75-MHz Pentium central processing unit (CPU) with 8 megabytes (MB) of RAM
  - a 520-MB hard disk
  - a 16-bit, wavetable-capable sound card with multitimbral MIDI playback
  - a 24-bit color display with MPEG-1 playback capability in hardware or software with a resolution of 352 x 240 pixels at 30 frames per second (fps)
  - a quad-speed CD-ROM drive with a 600-kilobyte-per-second (KBps) sustained transfer rate capable of playing all common CD-ROM formats, including Photo-CD and Video-CD
  - stereo speakers
  - system software compatible with Microsof Windows 3.1 and Microsoft DOS 6.0 or higher APIs.

multimedia platform (n.) Computing system or device used to deliver diverse media types—

including text, graphics, audio, animation, and video—in an interactive environment.

multimode fiber (n.) An optical waveguide that permits the propagation of more than one mode. Fiber that is graded-index or step-index may be used for multimode applications.

multiplatform (adj.) Describes the ability of software to perform on more than one hardware platform. Such software is sometimes referred to as *cross-platform,* particularly if it has been ported to run with a different operating system and equipment than those on which it was created.

multiple-document interface (MDI) (n.) A feature of Microsoft Windows that permits more than one document to be open simultaneously. The borders of the application window contain all open documents. Program Manager is a typical MDI application in Windows 3.1.

multiple inheritance (n.) In object-oriented programming (OOP), the capacity for a subclass to be derived from multiple parents that are themselves not derived from one another.

Multiple System Operator (MSO) (n.) A cable company that operates more than one cable television (CATV) system. The largest MSO in the United States is Tele-Communications, Inc. (TCI).

Multiple Virtual Line (MVL) (n.) Developed by Paradyne Corporation, a version of Digital Subscriber Line (DSL) technology that offers many advantages over other implementations, such as Asymmetric Digital Subscriber Line (ADSL). MVL features customer installation, is compatible with existing home wiring, and operates over greater distances. It uses a lower frequency signal and requires less power. An advantage of the lower frequency is that the signal does not interfere with existing telephone service, which is a serious problem for ADSL. MVL offers 768-kilobit-per-second (Kbps) bandwidth in both directions over distances of up to 24 000 feet. The existing North American standard, based on Discrete Multi-Tone (DMT) technology, competes with MVL as a basic format for high-speed digital services.

multiplex (MUX, pronounced "MUCKS") (v.) 1. To combine audio and video program data along with private data in layers that provide timing information, similar to the process of interleaving. 2. To deliver two or more distinct signals combined on a single channel.

multiplexer (n.) In broadcast and telecommunications, a device used to divide a transmission facility into multiple subchannels. This division is accomplished by alternately allocating a common channel to several different transmitters or by splitting the total frequency bandwidth into narrower bands and transmitting different signals simultaneously.

Multipoint Distribution Service (MDS) (n.) The Canadian version of Multichannel, Multipoint Distribution Service (MMDS), it provides line-of-sight transmission of television signals.

multiprocessor (n.) A computer that combines two or more similar microprocessors, providing more speed and power for complex procedures and for multitasking than a computer with a CPU does.

Multiprotocol Over ATM (MPOA) (n.) Multiprotocol Over Asynchronous Transfer Mode; developed by the ATM Forum, a standard that defines an architecture. This architecture will integrate packet forwarding with router-based virtual local area networks (LANs) that implement the forum's earlier LAN Emulation (LANE) standard.

multipurpose Internet mail extensions (MIME, pronounced "MIME") (n.) The standard method of sending and receiving attachments to email and web documents over the Internet. Most email attachments are not text (ASCII) files. They may be graphical, audio, video, or word-processed files. A binary attachment must be converted by mimencode to a type of ASCII file. Otherwise it will not be supported by Internet email. The following steps are involved in the exchange of email attachments using MIME:

1. The sender specifies the name of the file to be attached to the mail message and may choose to identify the file type (graphics, video, sounds, etc.). As a rule, the receiving mail program will automatically identify the file type if it is not specified. The file name extension indicates the format, such as .jpg, .doc, or .wav.
2. If the attachment is binary or contains something other than ASCII characters, the sending program automatically converts it to ASCII. This process increases the size of the attachment, which is then sent along with the mail message to the recipient.
3. If the recipient's mail program supports MIME, it converts the attachment back to its original binary format and pastes an icon or a line of text in the received mail message to represent the attached file. If the recipient selects that icon while in the mail program, the application program will run and will automatically display the attached file.

MIME, an Internet format defined by the Internet Engineering Task Force (IETF), prescribes a simple standardized way to represent and encode a variety of media types for transmission via Internet mail, including textual data in non-ASCII character sets. MIME extends RFC 822 in a manner that is simple, backward-compatible, and flexible.

RFC 822, the Internet standard for message formats, is used widely beyond the boundaries of the Internet itself. Most email traffic is limited to ASCII text, which is unable to define characters found in non-English text, audio, or graphical information. To use multimedia mail on the Internet, extensions to RFC 822 are required. The RFC 822 message format and the RFC 821 Simple Mail Transfer Protocol (SMTP) transport method limit message content to seven-bit ASCII characters. RFC 822 defines a message as a structured header followed by a single, monolithic text body. This format creates problems for multipart mixed-media mail. SMTP limits the length of lines within message headers and bodies. RFC 1049 defines a mechanism for single-part nontext mail, and RFC 1154 provides a mechanism for multipart mail.

An RFC 822–compliant Internet message consists of two parts: the header and the body. The header consists of a series of field names and field bodies. A blank line marks the end of the header and the beginning of the body, which may consist exclusively of US-ASCII text.

RFC 1049 introduced a new header field, *content-type*, which marked the entire message body as containing a certain type of data. If a content-type field is not present, the body is assumed to be US-ASCII text. A problem with RFC 1049 is the lack of support for multipart mail. A message body can contain only one item other than text.

MIME defines a new content-type, *multipart*. It may be used to encapsulate multiple body parts within a single RFC 822 message body. MIME describes the set of allowable content-types, defines a subtype mechanism for content-types, and provides for standardized encoding of non-ASCII data.

The MIME format defines seven valid content-types. In this way it differs from RFC 1049, which allowed users to define new content-types freely. The seven defined content-type values are as follows:

1. Text: The default subtype is plain text, with other subtypes associated with particular rich text formats. MIME defines the subtype *richtext* for formatted email.
2. Image: Subtypes are image format names, *image/gif* and *image/jpeg*. A mail reader that does not identify an image format will at least recognize that the content is an image.
3. Audio: Subtypes are audio format names; *audio/basic* is the default. *Audio/basic* denotes single-channel 8-kHz μ-law audio data, which is the equivalent of pulse code modulation (PCM), for telephone-quality audio attached to email.
4. Video: Subtypes are video format names; *video/mpeg* is the default.
5. Message: This content-type is used to encapsulate an entire RFC 822 format message. There are two message subtypes: *message/partial* for dividing a message into several pieces for transport and *message/external-body* for passing a very large message body by reference, rather than including its entire contents within the message.
6. Multipart: This content-type is used to pack several parts of various types and subtypes into a single RFC 822 message body.
7. Application: This content-type is used for most other kinds of data that do not fit these categories.

If Internet mail transport (SMTP, as described by RFC 821) were upgraded to permit arbitrary binary data of unlimited length in message bodies, encoding a message for transport would not be necessary. The Internet Architecture Board (IAB) RFC 1341 defining MIME has been superseded by RFC 1521.

The MIME Types table lists MIME content-types supported by most web servers and identifies their file extensions.

multiscan monitor (n.) A video display that accepts a range of horizontal and vertical timings, including those that correspond to VGA and RGB computer graphics. Some multiscan monitors automatically adjust to the appropriate timing based on the video source.

multisession (adj.) Contraction of multiple session; describes a CD-ROM format that allows information to be recorded incrementally in different recording sessions. During each session, the table of contents (TOC) is updated.

Multistation Access Unit (MSAU) (n.) A wiring concentration in an IBM token ring network that connects as many as eight nodes to a ring.

MultiSync (n.) A registered trademark of NEC Technologies, Inc., for their class of monitors designed to work with a wide range of video input frequencies and formats.

multitask (v.) To process more than one job at a time, typically with two or more applications running at once, and to transfer information between them. Both Microsoft Windows and the Mac OS can multitask.

MIME Types

MIME content-types supported by most web servers, identified with file extensions, are listed in the following table.

MIME Type	Identification	File Extension
application/acad	AutoCAD	dwg
application/arj	compressed archive	arj
application/astound	Astound	asd, asn
application/clariscad	ClarisCAD	ccad
application/drafting	MATRA Prelude drafting	drw
application/dxf	DXF (AutoCAD)	dxf
application/i-deas	SDRC I-DEAS	unv
application/iges	IGES graphics format	iges, igs
application/java-archive	Java archive	jar
application/mac-binhex40	Macintosh binary BinHex 4.0	hqx
application/msaccess	Microsoft Access	mdb
application/msexcel	Microsoft Excel	xla, xls, xlt, xlw
application/mspowerpoint	Microsoft PowerPoint	pot, pps, ppt
application/msproject	Microsoft Project	mpp
application/msword	Microsoft Word	doc, word, w6w
application/mswrite	Microsoft Write	wri
application/octet-stream	uninterpreted binary	bin
application/oda	ODA	oda
application/pdf	Adobe Acrobat	pdf
application/postscript	PostScript	ai, eps, ps
application/pro_eng	PTC Pro/ENGINEER	part, prt
application/rtf	Rich Text Format	rtf
application/set	SET (French CAD)	set
application/sla	stereolithography	stl
application/solids	MATRA Prelude Solids	sol
application/STEP	ISO-10303 STEP data	st, step, stp
application/vda	VDA-FS Surface data	vda
application/x-bcpio	binary CPIO	bcpio
application/x-cpio	POSIX CPIO	cpio
application/x-csh	C-shell script	csh
application/x-director	Macromedia Director	dcr, dir, dxr
application/x-dvi	TeX DVI	dvi
application/x-dwf	AutoCAD	dwf
application/x-gtar	GNU tar	gtar
application/x-gzip	GNU ZIP	gz, gzip
application/x-hdf	NCSA HDF Data File	hdf
application/x-javascript	JavaScript	js
application/x-latex	LaTeX source	latex
application/x-macbinary	Macintosh compressed	bin
application/x-midi	MIDI	mid
application/x-mif	FrameMaker MIF	mif
application/x-netcdf	Unidata netCDF	cdf, nc
application/x-sh	Bourne shell script	sh
application/x-shar	shell archive	shar
application/x-shockwave-flash	Macromedia Shockwave	swf
application/x-stuffit	StuffIt archive	sit
application/x-sv4cpio	SVR4 CPIO	sv4cpio
application/x-sv4crc	SVR4 CPIO with CRC	sv4crc
application/x-tar	4.3BSD tar format	tar

MIME Type	Identification	File Extension
application/x-tcl	TCL script	tcl
application/x-tex	TeX source	tex
application/x-texinfo	Texinfo (Emacs)	texi, texinfo
application/x-troff	Troff	roff, t, tr
application/x-troff-man	Troff with MAN macros	man
application/x-troff-me	Troff with ME macros	me
application/x-troff-ms	Troff with MS macros	ms
application/x-ustar	POSIX tar format	ustar
application/x-wais-source	WAIS source	src
application/x-winhelp	Microsoft Windows help	hlp
application/zip	ZIP archive	zip
audio/basic	BASIC audio (u-law)	au, snd
audio/midi	MIDI	mid, midi
audio/x-aiff	AIFF audio	aif, aifc, aiff
audio/x-mpeg	MPEG audio	mp3
audio/x-pn-realaudio	RealAudio	ra, ram
audio/x-pn-realaudio-plugin	RealAudio plug-in	rpm
audio/x-voice	Voice	voc
audio/x-wav	Microsoft Windows WAVE audio	wav
image/bmp	Bitmap	bmp
image/gif	GIF image	gif
image/ief	Image Exchange Format	ief
image/jpeg	JPEG image	jpe, jpeg, jpg
image/pict	Macintosh PICT	pict
image/png	Portable Network Graphic	png
image/tiff	TIFF image	tif, tiff
image/x-cmu-raster	CMU raster	ras
image/x-portable-anymap	PBM Anymap format	pnm
image/x-portable-bitmap	PBM Bitmap format	pbm
image/x-portable-graymap	PBM Graymap format	pgm
image/x-portable-pixmap	PBM Pixmap format	ppm
image/x-rgb	RGB image	rgb
image/x-xbitmap	X Bitmap	xbm
image/x-xpixmap	X Pixmap	xpm
image/x-xwindowdump	X Window System dump	xwd
multipart/x-gzip	GNU ZIP archive	gzip
multipart/x-zip	PKZIP archive	zip
text/html	HTML	htm, html
text/plain	plain text	C, cc, h, txt
text/richtext	MIME Richtext	rtx
text/tab-separated-values	text with tabs	tsv
text/x-setext	Structurally Enhanced Text	etx
text/x-sgml	SGML	sgm, sgml
video/mpeg	MPEG video	mpe, mpeg, mpg
video/msvideo	Microsoft Windows video	avi
video/quicktime	QuickTime video	mov, qt
video/vdo	VDO streaming video	vdo
video/vivo	VIVO streaming video	viv, vivo
video/x-sgi-movie	SGI Movieplayer format	movie
x-conference/x-cooltalk	CoolTalk	ice
x-world/x-svr	Virtual reality	svr
x-world/x-vrml	VRML Worlds	wrl
x-world/x-vrt	Virtual reality	vrt

multithreading (n.) A program execution environment that interleaves instructions from multiple independent execution messages. Multithreading differs from multitasking in that these messages, or threads, typically share more of their environment with each other than do tasks in the process of multitasking. When sharing a single address space and a set of global variables, threads may be distinguished only by the value of their program counters and stack pointers. Threads are switched very quickly, because there is so little state to save and restore.

multitimbral (adj.) Describes the capacity for more than one instrument, or MIDI timbre, to play simultaneously. A sequence of MIDI tracks may be created, and a different voice may be assigned to each track for multitimbral playback.

multiuser (adj.) Describes a networked computing environment that may be accessed by more than one person simultaneously. Unix was designed to support such an environment.

multiuser dungeon (MUD, pronounced "MUD") (n.) A type of multiplayer interactive game that is accessible through the Internet. A MUD is like an adventure game in a structured realtime chat forum, and it may include combat, traps, puzzles, and magic. The MUD community uses a mixture of Usenet and Internet emoticons, along with shorthand such as BBL, BRB, LOL, b4, BTW, WTF, TTFN, and WTH. Abbreviations specific to MUDs include FOAD (F*** off and die), ppl (people), TNX (thanks), UOK? (Are you OK?), and JAM (just a minute). Also called *multiuser dimension* or *multiuser domain*. See also *shorthand*.

Musical Instrument Digital Interface (MIDI, pronounced "MIH-dee") (n.) An industry-standard hardware/software system for microprocessor control of musical instruments and devices. It defines a protocol for the interchange of musical information between computers, digital musical instruments, and sound boards. MIDI is a simple serial communications bus, like a SCSI bus. The signal is a serial voltage transmission at the rate of 31 250 bits per second (bps). The messages are bytes encoded to define status (the type of message) and data (information about the preceding status byte). The cable is a shielded twisted pair of wires connected to pins 4 and 5 of a five-pin DIN plug. Pin 2 is the ground. Any device with a MIDI port can communicate with another one with similar connections. Only a MIDI interface and software are needed for a computer to control MIDI-compatible digital instruments. The file extension is .mid. See also *General MIDI*.

mute (v.) To silence an audio track.

MUX See *multiplex*.

MVL See *Multiple Virtual Line.*

MX See *Mail Exchange.*

N

NAB See *National Association of Broadcasters.*

NAK (n.) Negative acknowledgment; a code returned by a receiving unit when the data sent to it is corrupt.

named pipe (n.) An interprocess protocol used by OS/2 and Unix. A named pipe acts as a temporary file on disk or in memory and can be accessed by multiple processes to exchange information.

name resolution (n.) The process of mapping a name into its corresponding address. See also *domain name system.*

Name Server Lookup (NSLookup) (n.) The interactive query program implemented on the InterNIC domain name server that provides information about hosts in a domain.

name space (n.) The logical rule set that defines a directory's naming conventions. These conventions identify legal characters, the number of characters allowed, and the structure of a directory (flat versus hierarchical). Levels of the hierarchy are usually separated by a delimiter, such as \, ., or @. The X.500 standard allows unlimited hierarchies in the name space.

NAMM See *National Association of Music Merchants.*

nano- Prefix meaning one-billionth.

nanosecond (n.) One-billionth of a second.

NANP See *North American Numbering Plan.*

NAP See *Network Access Point.*

NAPLPS See *North American Presentation Level Protocol Standard.*

narration (n.) An audio commentary, or a voice-over, frequently used in multimedia productions to provide instructions, explain concepts, and "host" interactive programs.

narrowband (adj.) Describes any transmission link, such as a 4-kHz voice channel, that is limited to a low data rate. Compare *broadband.*

narrowcast 1. (v.) To direct a program toward a small, well-defined portion of the potential audience. 2. (n.) A program directed toward a specific audience.

NAT See *network address translation.*

National Association of Broadcasters (NAB) (n.) A large organization of professionals working in the fields of radio and television production and postproduction. The annual NAB conference attracts thousands of participants and vendors interested in new media technologies.

National Association of Music Merchants (NAMM) (n.) The organization of vendors and suppliers of musical instruments and electronic equipment for audio applications. Their annual conference attracts a wide range of participants, both consumers and professionals, who are interested in audio and music technologies, such as MIDI.

National Bureau of Standards (NBS) (n.) The original name for a group that makes recommendations to the U.S. government about federal data communications specifications and other issues related to computers and electronics. This agency is now called the *National Institute of Standards and Technology (NIST)*.

National Center for Supercomputing Applications (NCSA) (n.) Located at the University of Illinois at Champagne, Urbana, the birthplace of the universal client *Mosaic* in 1993. This program evolved into Netscape Navigator.

National Information Infrastructure (NII) (n.) The broad interconnection of computer, telephone, and cable networks. Often referred to as the *information superhighway.*

National Institute of Standards and Technology (NIST) (n.) A U.S. government body that assists in the development of standards for data communications, electronic devices, and computers. Originally known as the *National Bureau of Standards (NBS).*

National Research and Education Network (NREN, pronounced "EN-ren") (n.) A project that the U.S. Congress approved in 1991 to combine federal agency networks into a single high-speed network that serves as a central part

of the Internet backbone.

National Science Foundation (NSF, pronounced "en-ess-EFF") (n.) A U.S. government agency that funds research and infrastructure development for science. The NSFNET, a backbone network that spans North America, is funded by the NSF.

National Television Standards Committee (NTSC) (n.) A committee of the Electronics Industries Association (EIA) that prepared the standard specifications approved by the Federal Communications Commission (FCC) in December 1953 for commercial color broadcasting in the United States. The specifications define a color television format as having 525 scan lines, a field frequency of 59.94 Hz, a broadcast bandwidth of 4 MHz, a line frequency of 15.75 kHz, a frame frequency of nearly 1/30 of a second, and a color subcarrier frequency of 3.58 MHz.

native signal processing (NSP) (n.) A type of computing in which a powerful microprocessor performs the work of a digital signal processor (DSP) chip in real time, allowing such activities as video decoding to be integrated with other functions in a single processing system.

natural light (n.) Illumination from the sun, moon, or stars, whether indoors or outdoors. Natural light has a blue tint and a higher color temperature than most artificial light.

navigation (n.) The means by which a user explores and controls graphic, text, audio, and video elements in a multimedia program.

Nawk (n.) New awk; an enhanced version of awk. Nawk is a pattern-scanning and pattern-processing language that features dynamic regular expressions, additional operators, and user-defined functions.

NBS See *National Bureau of Standards.*

NC See *network computer.*

NCD See *network computing devices.*

N-connector (n.) A threaded coaxial cable connector named after Paul Neill.

NCSA See *National Center for Supercomputing Applications.*

NDA See *nondisclosure agreement.*

NDIS See *Network Driver Interface Specification.*

nearline (adj.) Describes a data storage system somewhere between online, or immediately accessible, and offline, which may be very time-consuming to locate. A digital tape cartridge that stores data sequentially and provides slow access is an example of a nearline storage medium.

nest (v.) To embed instructions, data, or subroutines sequentially within another structure.

Net (n.) Common abbreviation for the Internet.

NetBIOS See *Network Basic Input/Output System.*

netiquette (n.) Contraction of network etiquette; the conventions of politeness observed on Usenet, in mailing lists, and in Internet communications in general. Guidelines include not posting to inappropriate groups and refraining from commercial advertising. Personal messages to one or two individuals should not be posted to newsgroups. When responding to an earlier posting, the minimum necessary context should be quoted. Lines should be less than 70 characters long. Before asking a question, a user should read the existing messages in the group's frequently asked questions (FAQ).

NetMeeting (n.) A component of Windows 95 and 98 software that provides a video-conferencing environment. A camera, a digitizing card, a microphone, and a modem are required for audio-video communication with a limited number of other users in real time.

Netscape Navigator (n.) A popular universal client, or browser, used to access the World Wide Web.

Netscape Server Application Programming Interface (NSAPI) (n.) The application development environment for the Netscape web server.

NetShow (n.) Technology developed by Microsoft for streaming media. The NetShow media player plays content in most standard audio and video formats, as well as content generated by a NetShow server. The user can conveniently resize video windows on the fly. The encoder has built-in streaming capabilities.

NetWare (n.) Developed by Novell, an operating system for a local area network (LAN).

NetWare Link State Protocol (NLSP) (n.) Networking protocol that is a companion protocol to the Novell Internet Packet Exchange (IPX) for exchange of routing information in a Novell network. NLSP supersedes earlier Novell routing information protocols.

NetWare loadable module (NLM) (n.) An application program that can be dynamically

N

loaded and unloaded on a Novell NetWare 3.x or 4.x server. Examples of NLMs are Lotus Notes, Sybase's SQL Server, and Oracle Server.

network (n.) A group of computers, peripherals, or other equipment connected to one another for the purpose of passing information and sharing resources. Networks can be local or remote. The topology of a network is the geographic arrangement of links and nodes, which may be arranged in the shape of a star, a tree, or a ring.

network access control (n.) Circuits in a local area network (LAN) that determine when individual workstations may transmit messages.

Network Access Point (NAP) (n.) A high-speed connection to the Internet used by Internet Service Providers (ISPs). NAPs operate at the link layer of the OSI model.

network address (n.) The network portion of an Internet Protocol (IP) address, which varies by the class of network in the following way:

- Class A network: The first byte of the IP address.

- Class B network: The first 2 bytes of the IP address.

- Class C network: The first 3 bytes of the IP address.

In all cases, the remaining portion of an IP address is the host address. Assigned Internet network addresses are globally unique.

network address translation (NAT) (n.) System that provides a single Internet Protocol (IP) address for all hosts behind a firewall. It allows an internal client to open a connection to a remote site but does not allow a translated

machine to accept new connections directly from an external server.

Network Basic Input/Output System (NetBIOS, pronounced "NET-bye-ose") (n.) Software developed by IBM that interfaces between an individual computer's operating system and an IBM token ring network.

network computer (NC) (n.) On a network node, a workstation that is similar to a scaled-down personal computer. An NC depends on the server for software applications, upgrades, and maintenance. Also known as a *thin client.*

network computing device (NCD) (n.) A thin client.

Network Driver Interface Specification (NDIS) (n.) A standard created by Microsoft for writing hardware-independent drivers.

Network File System (NFS) (n.) A method of sharing data files on a local area network (LAN) or on the Internet. As an extension to TCP/IP, NFS lets files on remote network nodes appear to be connected locally. Sun Microsystems' NFS is defined by RFC 1094.

Network Information Service (NIS) (n.) A client-server protocol developed by Sun Microsystems known as the Yellow Pages, which is licensed to most Unix vendors. It is used to distribute user names and hostnames as well as other configuration data among networked computers. The commands and functions in NIS begin with the letters "yp." Examples of NIS commands in Unix are "ypmatch" and "ypwhich."

network interface card (NIC, pronounced "NICK") (n.) A printed circuit board installed in an expansion slot on a computer to allow the computer to be connected to a network.

network layer (n.) The third layer in the Open Systems Interconnection (OSI) model responsible for network routing of information packets. The network layer adds a header to define the routing addresses.

network management (n.) Manner of controlling the operation of a network to enhance efficiency and productivity. Network management may be divided into five categories: fault management, accounting management, configuration management, security management, and performance management.

Network Service Provider (NSP) (n.) A company that provides high-speed connections to the Internet for Internet Service Providers (ISPs) and other enterprises.

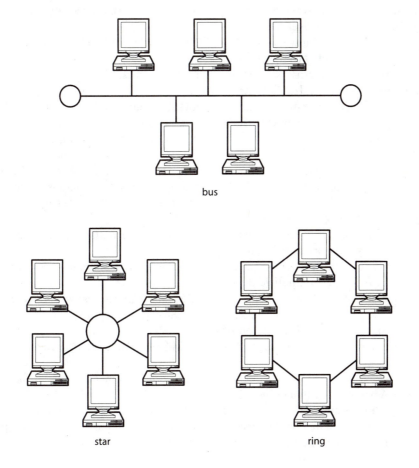

bus

star   ring

N

network topologies

network topology (n.) The logical and physical relationship between nodes on a network, defined by the layout of links and nodes. The topology is often similar in shape to a star, a tree, or a ring. See figure on preceding page.

network user identification (NUI, pronounced "en-you-EYE") (n.) A combination of the user's address and password on an X.25 packet-switched network.

neural network (n.) A processing device or a hardware-software system modeled on the design of the human brain. Most use training rules that adjust the weight of connections on the basis of presented patterns. Neural networks learn from examples and exhibit a structural capability for generalization. Neurons that make up the network may consist of simple threshold discriminators.

newbie (n.) Jargon for a person who is new to computing and to the Internet.

newsgroup (n.) A topic group or a forum on Usenet. Groups may or may not be moderated. Some moderated groups are distributed as a single large posting with an index. Examples of popular groups are *talk.politics.misc, comp.lang.c,* and *rec.arts.sf-lovers.*

New Technology (NT) (n.) The version of Microsoft Windows specified in the term *Windows NT.*

Newton (n.) A handheld computer manufactured by Apple Computer. Information is entered with a stylus, and handwriting recognition is built into the operating system. Known generically as a *personal digital assistant (PDA).*

NeXT computer (n.) A desktop workstation based on the Motorola 68030 processor developed in 1985 by Steve Jobs, after he left Apple Computer. Although the computer was discontinued, the Unix-based NeXTSTEP operating system survives on other platforms.

NeXTSTEP (n.) A Unix-based object-oriented operating system developed for the NeXT computer and ported to the Intel Pentium family of processors.

NFS See *Network File System.*

NIC See *network interface card.*

NiCad See *nickel cadmium.*

nickel cadmium (NiCad, pronounced "NYE-cad") (n.) A compound used in rechargeable batteries for notebook computers and for portable devices. This type of battery suffers from the "memory effect," wherein a battery recharged after only partial discharge will lose the capacity to hold a full charge.

NII See *National Information Infrastructure.*

NIS See *Network Information Service.*

NIST See *National Institute of Standards and Technology.*

NLM See *NetWare loadable module.*

NLSP See *NetWare Link State Protocol.*

node (n.) 1. A point of connection on a network. 2. The equipment attached at a point of connection on a network.

noise (n.) A burst of interference that is not part of the signal. In video, continuous noise may produce *snow,* a random salt-and-pepper pattern on the picture. In audio, radio frequency (RF) noise produces unwanted hiss or a disturbance in the signal.

nondisclosure agreement (NDA, pronounced "en-dee-AY") (n.) A common legal instrument used to keep a contractor from sharing confidential information with competitors or from making public any information discussed after a contractor signs the agreement.

noninterlaced (adj.) Describes a video system that draws all the horizontal lines across the screen in succession, as opposed to interlaced scanning in which even and odd lines are drawn alternately in two sweeps. A noninterlaced scan is also known as a *progressive scan.* Computer monitors are typically noninterlaced. By contrast, television video monitors are interlaced, and their signal content contains two fields for each frame.

nonlinear (adj.) In digital media, describes files or events that are indexed and that a user may therefore access immediately. In linear media, such as an audio tape or a videotape, the user must shuttle forward or backward to reach an event or a frame. Nonlinearity is a key distinction between digital and analog media. It is leveraged in well-conceived multimedia programs.

nonlinear editing (n.) A method of digital video editing that records source clips on a hard disk, allowing an editor to jump directly to any segment without shuttling through other clips.

nonlinear quantization (n.) In MPEG compression, the process of assigning more bits to define low-frequency data than to define high-frequency data. The human eye is more sensitive to lower frequencies. Some data is lost in the high-frequency spectrum, but the technique is extremely efficient in reducing the amount of data needed to define images. In general, this type of quantization attaches priorities to data based on its relative value during decoding and then discards less significant information.

nonrecalibrating (adj.) Describes a hard drive that does not pause periodically for a few milliseconds to perform a thermal recalibration, or a cooldown. Many hard disk drives are unsuitable for capturing video files direct to disk because they have thermal sensors that interrupt the process when the drive reaches a certain temperature. Special "AV" drives designed for audio and video capture are nonrecalibrating.

non-return-to-zero (NRZ) (adj., n.) Describes a recording process that encodes ones and zeros as a fluctuation between two values. Each time a one occurs in a stream of digits, the value changes. The value does not change when a zero occurs. The value representing zero is not equal to the reference value, it is simply a different value than is used to represent a one. See figure on the following page. In the top example, the magnetized value changes only on ones. In the bottom example, both ones and zeros are represented by a change in the value.

Non-Uniform Rational B-Spline (NURBS, pronounced "NERBS") (n.) A basic spline function used to construct curves from a set of control points that do not share the periodic properties of a uniform B-spline.

nonvolatile memory (n.) A ROM whose contents are maintained by batteries when the main power is switched off. Nonvolatile memory is useful for keeping the boot sequence and the Basic Input/Output System (BIOS) instructions constantly accessible. Generally, all storage mediums other than Dynamic

N

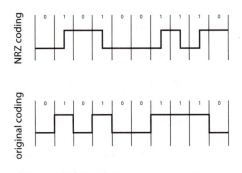

non-return-to-zero recording

RAM (DRAM) are nonvolatile.

normalize (v.) In audio engineering, to expand the highest peaks of amplitude to their greatest allowable levels, raising the amplitude of softer sounds proportionally. This expansion is a standard procedure in processing digital audio. It lends presence to a track and improves the signal-to-noise ratio.

North American Numbering Plan (NANP) (n.) A set of rules for the assignment of telephone area codes and the method by which calls are routed. The plan defines a three-digit area code, a three-digit exchange, and a four-digit subscriber code. The latest version was instituted in 1995, which allows the area code to be any combination of three digits. The plan previously restricted the second digit of an area code to a one or a zero. The new plan provides for 792 area code combinations and over 6 billion telephone numbers.

North American Presentation Level Protocol Standard (NAPLPS) (n.) A videotext protocol that permits pictures to be compressed into small blocks of data for low-bandwidth storage and transmission.

NREN See *National Research and Education Network.*

NRZ See *non-return-to-zero.*

NSAPI See *Netscape Server Application Programming Interface.*

NSF See *National Science Foundation.*

NSFNET (n.) National Science Foundation Network; the national backbone network funded by the NSF. The NSFNET is connected by a 45-megabit-per-second (Mbps) facility that spans North America. The NSFNET is part of the Internet and is also connected to networks in Europe and in the Pacific Rim.

NSLookup See *Name Server Lookup.*

NSP See *native signal processing* or *Network Service Provider.*

NT See *New Technology.*

NTSC See *National Television Standards Committee.*

NuBus (n.) A 32-bit bus architecture developed by Apple Computer for use in the Macintosh series of computers. Pronounced "NEW-bus."

NUI See *network user identification.*

null modem (n.) A cable used instead of a modem to connect serial ports on two computers directly. According to the RS-232C specification, both computers should transmit on pin 3 of their connectors and should receive on pin 2. A null modem cable has male connectors at both ends and connects pin 2 to pin 3 at opposite ends.

NURBS See *Non-Uniform Rational B-Spline.*

nybble (n.) Half a byte, or four bits.

Nyquist frequency (n.) In digitizing audio, a sample rate equal to twice the speed of the highest-frequency component in the content being sampled, including harmonics. The rate must be at least this high to avoid aliasing, or foldover, in the sampled audio file.

221

O

object (n.) In programming, a corporal body or an abstraction with well-defined constituents and interpretations. An object is an identifiable, encapsulated entity that provides one or more services requested by a client. In object-oriented programming (OOP), an object is an instance of a class. In general multimedia terms, an object is a stored data element, such as a video clip, an audio file, or a graphic representation of an object.

object code (n.) The machine language code that is output by a compiler or an assembler. Source code is converted into object code, so that a computer can read and respond to it. Object code can stand alone if a library of functions is available for linking.

object identity (n.) The property of an object that distinguishes it from other objects. In an object-oriented system, a property is independent of content, type, and addressability. Object identity is the only property of the object that is maintained irrespective of time or modifications.

object linking and embedding (OLE, pronounced "oh-LAY") (n.) Developed by Microsoft in 1990 in collaboration with other software companies, a software specification that allows developers to integrate information created by different applications. It accomplishes this by making simple extensions to existing graphics applications running under Microsoft Windows, Macintosh System 7.0, or OS/2 Presentation Manager. OLE is a standard that defines how objects interact, and it provides a software channel for passing objects. A program called *storage.dll* manages the OLE files as well as the links between originators and users. In Windows, the clipboard is a handy way to implement OLE capabilities. In any application that supports OLE, the copy-and-paste operations will transparently link objects to documents. An embedded voice annotation in a text document is a practical application of OLE that results in a crude but effective form of multimedia. Audio files must be packaged as objects because OLE does not work with raw files. The Object Packager application found in the *Accessories* directory is required to process raw files into objects for use with OLE.

object management (n.) The storage, retrieval, and archiving of objects in an object-oriented system.

Object Management Group (OMG) (n.) An organization that has developed standards and products associated with object management in a distributed networked environment. OMG has been recognized for its work on Common Object Request Broker Architecture (CORBA).

object-oriented database (OODB) (n.) A user interface that provides database management facilities in an object-oriented programming (OOP) environment. Data is stored as objects and can only be interpreted with the methods specified by its class. The relationship between similar objects is preserved, as are references between objects. Queries are extremely rapid, because the joins required by a relational database are not needed by an OODB. Without a search, a user can retrieve an object directly by following its object identifier.

object-oriented programming (OOP) (n.) A logic program in which each element, or object, is self-contained, stands alone, and holds all the data and instructions related to a particular task. Any element can call up any other object or element, and the recipient itself can perform the task. The paradigm provides for object classes, methods, and inheritance. OOP is also known as *modular code* because its modules are independent and easily cross-linked.

Object Packager (n.) A small application that is part of the Microsoft Windows system software and that is used to process raw files into objects for use with OLE. Object Packager is located in the *Accessories* directory and permanently links an object icon to the file name with which it is associated.

object reference (n.) An object name that reliably denotes a particular object in the Common Object Request Broker Architecture (CORBA).

object request broker (ORB, pronounced "ORB") (n.) An implementation of a common interface that allows multiple clients to access services provided by multiple objects. The standard, Common Object Request Broker

Architecture (CORBA), has been defined by the Object Management Group (OMG), an industry association.

object server (n.) An object-oriented networked database server that provides for the storage and retrieval of objects.

OC See *optical carrier.*

OCLC See *Online Computer Library Catalog.*

OCR See *optical character recognition.*

octet (n.) Term for eight bits of data. *Octet* is used instead of *byte* to refer to data words with eight-bit bytes.

OC x (n.) Optical Carrier x; an OC whose rate of data transmission is a multiple of 51.84 megabits per second (Mbps). An OC 12 connection moves digital data at 622 Mbps.

ODBC See *Open Database Connectivity.*

ODI See *Open Data-Link Interface.*

OEM See *original equipment manufacturer.*

OEM Service Release 2 (OSR-2) (n.) A collection of updates and bug fixes from Microsoft for the Windows 95 operating system. It was released in August 1996, and made available primarily to personal computer makers, or original equipment manufacturers (OEMs), to be installed on new machines.

off-axis rejection (n.) The pickup pattern for a microphone has a central axis that represents maximum sensitivity to sounds. When sounds are introduced from the sides of this axis, the sensitivity and frequency response of the microphone is much lower. Off-axis rejection is the term for the lower signal level the microphone produces in response to sounds that emanate from the sides rather than from the "sweet spot" in the center of the pickup pattern. See also *microphone patterns*.

offline (adj.) 1. Describes the processing of information while disconnected from a network. The data can be distributed when the connection is made. 2. Describes an operation that occurs independently and that is not under the control of a computer. 3. In video post-production, describes a type of editing that occurs separately from the final assembly and mastering process. 4. In video postproduction, describes a system that can make an edit decision list (EDL) or simple cuts only, rather than one that performs a full range of edits and video effects.

offset (n.) The difference in the time codes recorded on two videotapes. Editors usually begin a program at 01:00:00:00 (in the hours:minutes:seconds:frames format) to provide room up front for color bars and a slate. If an audio engineer begins the audio program on the same tape at 00:45:00:00, the sound track has a −15-minute offset. A small offset may be useful, depending on the audio equipment.

ohm (n.) The unit used to express electrical resistance. When 1 volt of electromotive force is applied, 1 ohm of resistance allows 1 ampere of current to flow.

OLE See *object linking and embedding*.

OMDR See *Optical Memory Disc Recorder*.

OMF See *Open Media Framework*.

OMG See *Object Management Group*.

ONA See *Open Network Architecture*.

one-off (n.) A CD-recordable (CD-R) on which program data has been written.

ONI See *Optical Network Interface*.

online (adj.) 1. Describes the situation in which computers and peripherals have direct, interactive communication with one another on a network. 2. A traditional video-editing term that describes a comprehensive system that can edit, record, and add special effects. Online systems are expensive, so rough edits or edit decision lists (EDLs) are typically compiled using offline systems. In video postproduction, the online edit is the final editing process that integrates all the elements created and specified during the offline edit.

Online Computer Library Catalog (OCLC) (n.) A nonprofit organization that provides their members, mostly libraries, with services such as reference searching, cataloging, interlibrary loan, and bibliographic verification. More than 10 000 libraries worldwide use these services.

online service (n.) A provider that offers dialup electronic mail, conferences, information resources, Internet access, and other communication services to users who have a computer, a modem, and a telephone line. Examples are America Online (AOL), CompuServe, Prodigy, and Microsoft Network (MSN). Each of these services has millions of users whose computers can be connected to a central file server and who can then exchange information among themselves.

ontology (n.) The hierarchical structuring of knowledge about things; this structure is created by categorizing things according to their essential qualities. In artificial intelligence (AI), an explicit formal specification of a way to represent the objects and the concepts that are assumed to exist in some area of knowledge and the relationships that exist among them. When the knowledge about a domain is represented in a declarative language, the set of objects that can be represented is called the *universe of discourse.* The ontology of a program may be defined by a set of representational terms.

ONU See *optical network unit.*

OOB signal See *out-of-band signal.*

OODB See *object-oriented database.*

OOP See *object-oriented programming.*

open architecture (n.) Related to microcomputers, a hardware configuration that allows circuit boards to be added in order to expand the system's functionality. The circuit boards are typically plugged into slots on a motherboard. Functionality is enhanced by connecting outboard gear or peripherals to internal expansion buses or to external ports. Software that integrates the expanded hardware with existing features is required.

Open Database Connectivity (ODBC) (n.) A standard for accessing diverse database systems. ODBC has interfaces for SQL, Visual Basic, and Visual C++, and it has drivers for dBASE, Access, Paradox, and other databases. ODBC 1.0 was released in September 1992. It is based on the call-level interface and was defined by the SQL Access Group.

Open Data-Link Interface (ODI, pronounced "oh-dee-EYE") (n.) A network card API developed by Novell that provides media and protocol independence. It allows the sharing of a single card by multiple transport layer protocols, and it resolves conflicts.

OpenGL (n.) Open Graphics Language; an Application Programming Interface (API) developed by Silicon Graphics as an open standard for three-dimensional computer-aided design (CAD) applications and for computer-aided visualization of images.

Open Media Framework (OMF) (n.) A de facto standard developed by Avid Technologies and a group of partners for specifying multimedia data types and controlling playback across different platforms for digital editing of video and audio.

Open Network Architecture (ONA) (n.) Telephone switches and circuits that enable unbundling, or separation of features, which facilitates interconnection with services provided by other vendors.

OpenScript (n.) The scripting language used by the Asymetrix ToolBook multimedia authoring program for Microsoft Windows.

Open Shortest-Path First (OSPF) (n.) A link state routing protocol, as opposed to a distance vector routing protocol. Defined in RFC 1247, OSPF is one of the Internet standard Interior Gateway Protocols (IGPs).

Open Software Foundation (OSF) (n.) An association of nine computer vendors to promote "open computing." Apollo, Digital Equipment Corporation (DEC), Hewlett-Packard, IBM, Bull, Nixdorf, Philips, Siemens, and Hitachi formed the foundation. The group plans to release common operating systems and interfaces, based on developments of Unix and the X Window System, for a wide range of

Intranet Protocols Defined by the OSI Network Reference Model

Across the top of the chart are the seven layers of the OSI Network Reference Model. Internet and Intranet protocols are shown at each layer.

1. Physical Cabling	2. Data Link Frame Format	3. Network Addressing	4. Transport Protocols	5. Session Port Number	6.1 Data Transmission	6.2 Data Organization	6.3 Data Format	7. Application Programs
802.3 Coax, CAT5	Ethernet II			RPC Portmapper	NFS	File Path	Binary	File Services
			UDP	161, 162	SNMP	SNMP Msg.	ASN/1	Network Mgmt.
802.5 CAT3	802.2 SNAP			53	DNS	DNS Msg.	DNS Text	Directory Services
				23	Telnet	ASCII	Text Stream	Host Sessions
FDDI, Fiber, Coax, CAT5		IPv4/6		20, 21	FTP	File Path	Binary	File Transfer
			TCP	80	HTTP	File Path	WWW Binary	Web Hypertext Apps.
				532	Usenet	ASCII, UUC	News Binary	Newsgroup Msg.
ISDN CAT1				POP2=109, POP3=110	POP	ASCII, UUC, MIME	Text, Binary	Email User Agent
	SLIP, PPP			25	SMTP	SMTP Msg.	Text, Binary	Email Msg. Xfer.
RS-xxx, CAT1								

Notes:

UDP: User Datagram Protocol
TCP : Transmission Control Protocol
IPv4/6: Internet Protocol version 4 or version 6
FDDI: Fiber Distributed Data Interface
SNAP: Systems Network Architecture Protocol

hardware architectures. In 1990, the OSF announced the release of OSF/1, the industry's first open operating system.

Open Systems Interconnection (OSI, pronounced "oh-ess-EYE") (n.) A standard and a model for data communications. OSI has the following seven layers (see table):

1. Physical layer (hardware, medium of connection). Specifies electrical and mechanical connections and the media access control (MAC). The physical layer is used by the data link layer directly above it. Two common physical layer protocols are CSMA/CD and token ring.

2. Data link layer (linking protocols). Splits data into frames, transmits the frames over the physical layer, and receives acknowledgment frames. The data link layer performs error checking and retransmits frames received incorrectly. It provides a channel to the network layer directly above it. The data link layer is divided into the upper sublayer, logical link control (LLC), and the lower sublayer, media access control (MAC).

3. Network layer (type of network). The third lowest layer, which determines routing of data packets from sender to receiver via the data link layer. The network layer

is used by the transport layer directly above it. The most common network layer protocol is Internet Protocol (IP).

4. Transport layer (protocol for transfer). Determines how the network layer is used to provide point-to-point connections between hosts. It establishes and releases connections between hosts and is also referred to as the host-to-host layer. The transport layer is used by the session layer directly above it. The most common transport layer protocol is Transmission Control Protocol (TCP).

5. Session layer (means of communication). Uses the transport layer to establish a connection between processes on different hosts. It handles the creation and security of each session. The session layer is used by the presentation layer directly above it.

6. Presentation layer (adaptation of connections). Performs functions such as text compression and format conversion to facilitate communication between hosts. The presentation layer allows incompatible processes in the application layer above it to communicate using the session layer below it.

7. Application layer (specific implementation of defined facilities). Handles resource allocation and problem partitioning. The application layer delivers the user interface. The presentation layer below it provides this layer with a local representation of data independent of the format used on the network.

Open Video System (n.) Term used in the Telecommunications Act of 1996 to describe the setup in which a video carrier provides common carrier services. Operators of open video systems are required to make a large percentage of their channels available to other programmers. By doing so, operators are not required to obtain a local cable franchise.

operating system (OS) (n.) Software loaded into RAM when a computer boots up, controlling fundamental processes such as saving and retrieving files. An OS may have a command line interface, like DOS. Alternatively, it may have a graphical user interface (GUI), as do the Mac OS and OpenLook for Unix (developed by Sun Microsystems).

operator (n.) Any character that represents an operation, or an action, performed on a number or a variable. Common operators include (+) addition, (-) subtraction, (*) multiplication, and (/) division. In query languages that can locate information in databases, Boolean operators (AND, OR, NOT, and NOR) are used. Another type is the relational operator, such as less than (<) and greater than (>).

OPL (n.) Developed by Yamaha, a type of synthesizer chip used in the Creative Labs Sound Blaster and in other popular sound boards. These chips use frequency modulation (FM) synthesis.

optical carrier (OC) (n.) A Synchronous Optical Network (SONET) signal.

optical character recognition (OCR) (n.) Software used with a scanner to convert printed pages into text files.

optical disc (n.) A disc that stores digital data, which can be read with reflected laser light that bounces off the surface of the disc. All CDs are optical discs.

optical disc player (n.) Any playback device that can read data from optical media by using reflected laser light.

optical fiber (n.) A glass or plastic filament that is used to transmit information using infrared or visible light. An optical fiber is typically a laser-driven carrier. The beam of light is an electromagnetic signal transmitted at an extremely high frequency. Optical fiber is less expensive than copper wire, and it is less susceptible to interference than other media. The light beams do not escape from the medium because of the total internal reflection. Fiberoptic connections provide extremely high bandwidth and security.

optical memory (n.) Any technology incorporating storage devices that use laser light to record or read data.

Optical Memory Disc Recorder (OMDR) (n.) A Matsushita/Panasonic write-once analog videodisc recorder that writes to 8-inch or 12-inch blanks. The format is incompatible with laser videodisc players from Pioneer, Philips, or Sony.

Optical Network Interface (ONI, pronounced "oh-en-EYE") (n.) In telecommunications, a device that performs electrical-to-analog conversion. An ONI provides the interface between an optical network and telephone equipment on the customer premises if the network delivers fiber to the home.

optical network unit (ONU) (n.) In telecommunications, a device that converts transmitted signals onto a single band of distribution frequencies. An ONU is a type of access node that translates optical signals into electrical signals and vice versa, enabling signals to be transmitted to and from customers over coaxial and copper-twisted pairs.

optical read-only memory (OROM) (n.) Medium that can be read by an optical reader but

that may not be written to.

optical storage (n.) Refers to any media that uses laser technology to store data, including CD-ROMs and magneto-optical cartridges.

opto-electronic device (n.) Any equipment or component that responds to light waves in the visible, infrared, or ultraviolet spectrums. The category includes devices that emit or modify incoherent or coherent electromagnetic radiation, as well as those that use light waves for their internal operation.

opto-electronics (n.) All types of electrical devices that detect light, such as photodiodes, as well as those that generate, control, or amplify light, such as lasers and light-emitting diodes (LEDs).

opto-isolator (n.) A miniature device that converts electrical signals into light, transmits the light across a small gap, and converts it back into electrical signals. An opto-isolator makes a circuit immune to interference and ground-loop problems because no electricity flows across the gap.

Orange Book standard (n.) The specification for compact disc–recordable (CD-R) systems, developed by Philips and Sony. It includes specifications for the hybrid disc technology on which Eastman Kodak's Photo-CD is based.

ORB See *object request broker.*

ordinate (n.) The y-coordinate, plotted on a graph in response to the input of a function. The x-coordinate is referred to as the *abscissa.*

original equipment manufacturer (OEM) (n.) A manufacturer of hardware that may be modified or included in a system marketed by a value-added reseller (VAR).

originate mode (n.) A transmission state in which an originating modem transmits at the low frequency defined by a communications channel and receives at the designated high frequency. The transmit and receive frequencies are the opposite of those of the called modem, which is in answer mode.

OROM See *optical read-only memory.*

orthogonal (adj.) Separate, mutually independent, and at times irrelevant. The term describes complete sets of primitives or capabilities that span the entire range of possibilities in a system and do not overlap. In logic, the set of operators NOT and OR is orthogonal. The set NAND, OR, and NOT is not orthogonal, because one of these can be expressed in terms of the others.

orthogonal instruction set (n.) In programming, an instruction set in which instructions all have the same format and register and can therefore be used interchangeably. The choice of register to use is orthogonal to the choice of instruction.

orthographic projection (n.) The visible outline of an object projected onto a surface in which the projection vector is parallel to the z-axis.

OS See *operating system.*

oscillator (n.) Any device that vibrates internally to generate a signal at a specified frequency, such as an audible tone. Usually used for test purposes, oscillators also produce musical tones.

OSF See *Open Software Foundation.*

OSI See *Open Systems Interconnection.*

OS-9 (n.) Operating System–9; developed by Microware Corporation in 1978, a realtime operating system that has been ported to the Motorola 68000 family, Intel 80386, Intel 80486, Pentium, and the PowerPC. The kernel can exist in ROM, is modular, and has a scalable unified file system.

OSPF See *Open Shortest-Path First.*

OSR-2 See *OEM Service Release 2.*

OS/2 (n.) Operating System/2; a multitasking, higher-level operating system. OS/2 was developed by IBM and Microsoft for those microcomputers in the PS/2 series that are equipped with 80386 or later microprocessors. See also *IBM PS/2.*

outboard (adj.) Describes external, rackmounted, audio signal processing equipment, such as an equalizer, a compressor, a limiter, an aural exciter, or a digital delay.

outline font (n.) A typeface with lines and curves defined by mathematical vectors, as opposed to a bitmap font, which is defined by individual pixels. An outline font can be scaled to any size and transformed more easily than can a bitmap font. PostScript and TrueType are both outline fonts, which are also known as *vector fonts.*

out-of-band signal (OOB signal) (n.) Content transmitted over a circuit that is separate from the channel carrying the voice, data, video, or other primary information. A filter is used to separate the signals. The OOB signal often contains dialing, supervisory, or other information controlling the primary signal.

out-of-band signaling (n.) Separation of a signal from the channel carrying information about the signal. See also *Signaling System 7.*

out-point (n.) The final frame of an audio or a video segment to be edited or dubbed.

output 1. (v.) To send data from a computer or processor to another device, such as a printer or disk drive. 2. (n.) The digital data sent from memory for display or transfer. 3. (n.) Any signal that is generated or passed on by any means.

outside plant (adj.) Describes any part of a telephone system that is exterior to a telephone company's buildings. Utility poles, access lines, load coils, and conduits are all included in this description.

outsource (v.) To hire specialists, consultants, or an external production company to produce segments of media types.

outtake (n.) Footage excluded from the final version of an audio or video production.

overdub (v.) To add new content or a new channel to an existing audio mix, such as a new vocal or instrumental track.

overflow error (n.) A buffer overrun in which data is received too fast to be captured completely and accurately. An overflow error may also occur when the memory allocation is not large enough to accept a unit of data sent to it.

overlay 1. (n.) The superimposition of text or graphics onto still or motion video by digital means, such as with a character generator. 2. (v.) To show one video image positioned on top of another. If two analog video signals are to be overlaid cleanly, they must be genlocked, or synchronized to the same timing signal.

overrun (n.) A condition in which data is transmitted from the send unit faster than the receiving unit can accept and process it. If the buffer is overrun when recording data on a CD-R, errors will occur, and the session will fail.

oversample (v.) To digitize audio or video data faster than normal to produce more samples, resulting in more accurate results.

overscan (n.) A condition in which a video signal bleeds off the edges of a monitor. When computer images are sent to a monitor in the overscan mode, up to 20 percent of the content around the edges may be lost. See figure.

safe viewing area
overscan area

overscan

overwrite (v.) To record data on top of existing data, rendering the original data unreadable.

P

PABX See *private automatic branch exchange.*

package 1. (n.) Any software application or set of computer programs needed to perform a task. 2. (n.) A combination of hardware and software that constitutes a complete multimedia delivery system. 3. (v.) To combine media, printed matter, and casing for the purpose of distributing a product.

packet (n.) A unit of binary information organized in a block for transmission, including control data about the type of information and the length of the packet, the data itself, and error detection and correction bits.

Packet InterNet Groper (Ping) 1. (n.) A program that sends an echo request to a destination on a network and waits for a reply. The request is in the Internet Control Message Protocol (ICMP) format. 2. (v.) To send an echo request to a destination on a network, as in "to ping the host computer."

packet switching (n.) A method of transferring data by addressing blocks of information, occupying a channel only while data is being transmitted. After transmission, the channel is free to transfer other packets. The data network determines the routing during the transfer of a packet. In *circuit switching,* by contrast, the routing is determined prior to transfer. In packet switching, packets do not always arrive in the order in which they are sent. Therefore, circuit switching is used when data such as audio files must stream over a network in order.

packet-switching data network (PSDN) (n.) A network in which data is transmitted in packets that can be routed individually over network connections and reassembled at the destination.

page (n.) A predetermined segment of expanded memory that can be swapped in and out of the page frame. The *page frame* is the physical location in conventional memory where expanded memory pages are stored.

Page Description Language (PDL) (n.) A programming language used to control the formatting and layout of a printed page. PDL sends instructions that a printer with processing capabilities can interpret. An example of a PDL is Adobe PostScript.

Paged Memory Management Unit (PMMU) (n.) An integrated circuit (IC) that supports virtual memory by helping the processor locate needed data, either on a hard disk or in physical memory.

page-mode RAM (n.) A static RAM chip that can hold information without being constantly refreshed by the central processor in a computer system. It allows faster memory performance than Dynamic RAM, which requires constant updating.

pagination (n.) The division of a document into pages. A word-processing program can paginate automatically or manually.

paging (n.) In programming, a process for increasing the available memory space by moving seldom-used parts of a program's working memory from RAM to a local disk drive. The unit of transfer is called a *page*. A memory management unit (MMU) monitors accesses to memory and splits each address into a page number and an offset within the page. Page numbers are entered in a page table for lookup. Paging permits the memory requirements of all running tasks to exceed the amount of physical memory. Swapping simply allows multiple processes to run concurrently, providing that each process on its own fits within physical memory.

paired cable (n.) Any cable consisting of conductors that are all twisted pairs. Paired cable is the most common communications wiring because the twist reduces the likelihood of interference between the lines.

PAL See *Phase Alternation Line.*

palette (n.) 1. In digital imagery, the number of predefined colors available for display or printing. 2. Within a software application, the onscreen selection of tools, options, or modes available to the user. A palette is most often displayed in a rectangular grid.

palette flash (n.) An undesirable event in which an application is instructed to change the current palette, causing a momentary bright flash to occur. For example, if consecutive frames in a Multimedia Director movie contained different palettes, a flash would appear on the monitor between the two frames while the movie played.

palmtop (n.) A compact personal computer, typically used to store contact information, telephone numbers, and meeting times and dates. Windows CE, a graphical user interface (GUI), allows the larger palmtops to use a scaled-down version of Microsoft Office applications. The Pilot, developed by PalmOS and marketed by U.S. Robotics, is a popular example.

Palo Alto Research Center (PARC) See *Xerox Corporation Palo Alto Research Center.*

pan (v.) 1. In video and film production, to rotate a camera horizontally across a panorama, changing the angle of view. 2. In computer graphics, to move in one direction along the plane of the drawing, keeping the same scale and orientation. 3. In audio production, to shift the position of a sound between the right and left stereo channels.

panic (v.) To malfunction, as the Unix operating system does when a critical internal consistency check fails in such a way that the system cannot continue. The kernel tries to print a message to the screen and write an image of memory into the swap area on disk for analysis later.

Pantone Matching System (PMS) (n.) A standard trademarked system of identifying more than 500 colors by number. PMS colors are created by an exact mixture of special base colors in specific proportions. Also known as *PMS color.*

PAP See *Password Authentication Protocol.*

Paradox (n.) Developed by Borland International, the first multi-user relational database for microcomputers with multitasking capabilities. It allows connectivity to Structured Query Language (SQL) data on a database server.

parallel (adj.) 1. Describes a method of transmitting data by sending a byte or a group of bits simultaneously. This contrasts with *serial data transfer,* in which bits are sent one at a time. 2. Describes the simultaneous processing of individual parts of a larger job in a computer application.

parallel port (n.) Interface from a computer system through which multiple bits of data are transferred in or out. This type of interface carries one bit on each wire, thereby multiplying the transfer rate obtainable over a single wire. A typical example of a parallel port is a printer port. The widely used Centronics port transfers eight bits at a time. SCSI and Integrated Drive Electronics (IDE) are special types of parallel ports.

parallel processing (n.) Method of using more than one computer simultaneously to process data. Flynn's taxonomy classifies both parallel and serial computers according to whether their processors execute the same instructions at the same time (single-instruction, multiple-data, or SIMD) or whether each processor executes different instructions (multiple-instruction, multiple-data, or MIMD). A *processor farm* is a group of computers cooperating on a problem or running under the control of another processor that distributes work and collects results.

parallel processor (n.) An integrated circuit that can perform different operations simultaneously.

Parameter RAM (PRAM, pronounced "PEE-ram") (n.) Parameter random-access memory; a portion of RAM used to store system configuration and startup settings on a Macintosh computer. PRAM is powered by a battery and will automatically default to factory settings if the battery is removed from the computer for a few minutes. This procedure, called *zapping the PRAM,* is a last resort when solving system problems.

PARC See *Xerox Corporation Palo Alto Research Center.*

parent directory (n.) In MS-DOS, a directory that lies one step above the child directory.

parity (n.) A technique used to determine whether errors were introduced in data transmission. A parity bit is appended to an array of bits to make the sum of all the bits always odd or even, and the result is checked on reception.

parser (n.) A computer program that determines the syntactic structure of a sentence or string of symbols in a computer language. As input, the parser takes a sequence of tokens generated by a lexical analyzer. The output from the parser might be an abstract syntax tree. Yacc is an example of a parser generator.

particle animation (n.) An animation technique used to depict natural forces, such as wind or gravity, as controlling the movement of small objects in a sequence.

partition (n.) A section of storage separately addressed by the operating system. Drives may be divided into multiple partitions.

Pascal (n.) A programming language designed by Niklaus Wirth in 1970 and named after the French mathematician Blaise Pascal (1623–1662). The language was designed for teaching programming because it is simpler to grasp than other languages in use at that time. Pascal is based on Algorithmic Language (ALGOL) and emphasizes structured programming constructs, data structures, and strong typing. The language C has displaced Pascal from the niche it acquired in applications and systems programming.

passive matrix display (n.) A type of liquid crystal display (LCD) that uses one transistor for each row of pixels and one for each column. By contrast, an *active matrix display* uses a transistor for each pixel. The quality of a passive matrix display is much lower than that of an active matrix.

password (n.) Any string of characters or numbers that a user enters in a computing system to gain access to protected files or to receive privileges.

Password Authentication Protocol (PAP) (n.) An authentication scheme that Point-to-Point Protocol (PPP) servers use to validate the identity of the originator of a connection. PAP involves two-way handshaking. When a link is established, the originator sends a password pair to the server. If authentication succeeds, the server sends back an acknowledgment. If authentication fails, the server either terminates the connection or gives the originator a second chance. PAP is not a robust authentication method. Passwords are sent in the open, and there is no protection against hackers. PAP is best applied if a plain text password must be available to simulate a login at a remote host. PAP is defined in RFC 1334.

paste (v.) To retrieve text or a graphic from the Clipboard or memory buffer and to insert it into a document.

patch 1. (v.) To connect circuits with a patch cord or a cable, typically on a patch bay. 2. (n.) A last-minute instruction or command added to a software program to make it run. A patch is not part of the formal plan.

path (n.) 1. A set of descriptors in MS-DOS that identifies the location of a file. For example, the path *C:\graphics\project\filename.bmp* leads to *filename.bmp,* a specific graphics file on the C: drive. 2. Linked curves in a vector-oriented image. 3. The route that a message, an instruction, or a datagram takes as it passes through a network.

path name (n.) The full identifier for a file or a directory in a hierarchical file system, including the drive letter followed by a colon and the nodes from the root directory. An example might be: *C:\MyStuff\documents\Joememo.doc.* The directories are separated by a path name separator, which is the backslash symbol, \, in MS-DOS. A path name may be absolute or relative. The part of a path name that follows the last separator is called the *base name.*

path name separator (n.) A character that separates elements of a path name. The backslash (\) is used in MS-DOS, while the forward slash (/) is used in Unix. No directory name or file name may contain this character.

PBX See *private branch exchange.*

PC See *personal computer.*

PCA See *program calibration area.*

PC/AT See *Personal Computer/Advanced Technology.*

PC/AT architecture (n.) Personal Computer/ Advanced Technology architecture; architecture of the IBM 80286-based computer, which uses a 16-bit data bus. As the PC/AT architecture evolved from the 8088-based PC/XT with an eight-bit bus, it retained compatible hardware features.

PCB See *printed circuit board*.

PCD See *Photo–Compact Disc*.

PC-DOS See *Personal Computer–Disk Operating System*.

PCI See *peripheral component interconnect*.

PCM See *pulse code modulation*.

PCMCIA See *Personal Computer Memory Card International Association*.

PCS See *personal communications services*.

PC Speaker Driver (n.) Personal computer Speaker Driver; a Microsoft Windows program that produces sounds using software and the computer's onboard speaker. A PC Speaker Driver is not a substitute for a sound board, but it can function in that way.

PCX (n.) A common graphics format in Microsoft Windows. ZSoft developed PCX for the PC Paintbrush program.

PC/XT (n.) Early IBM personal computer based on the Intel 8088 processor with an eight-bit bus.

PDA See *personal digital assistant*.

PDF See *Portable Document Format*.

PDL See *Page Description Language*.

PDS See *Processor Direct Slot*.

PDU See *protocol data unit*.

pedestal (n.) 1. In video production, the vertical plane in which a video camera moves as it is raised or lowered, without being tilted. 2. In telecommunications, an above-ground enclosure in which buried cables are spliced and terminated.

peer (n.) A computer that resides on the same protocol layer of a network as another and that is connected on the lowest level.

peer-to-peer network (n.) A network in which each computer is independent and can serve the others or act as a workstation. Peripherals connected to any computer networked in this fashion are available to any of the other peer computers connected.

pel See *picture element*.

Pentium (n.) An Intel microprocessor made with superscalar complex instruction set computing (CISC) architecture. The original Pentium had two 32-bit 486-type integer pipelines and a 64-bit data bus. It offered dependency checking and branch prediction and had more than 3 million transistors and a clock rate of 66 MHz.

Pentium Pro (n.) Developed in 1995, an Intel microprocessor that improves on the Pentium processor. The Pentium Pro has an internal reduced instruction set computing (RISC) architecture with a CISC-RISC translator, three-way superscalar execution, and dynamic execution. It also features branch prediction and register renaming and is superpipelined. A Level 2 cache has been added, with 256 kilobytes (KB) or 512KB on a separate die. The chip has a built-in float-

P

ing-point unit (FPU). The 1995 version of the Pentium Pro had a clock frequency of 133 MHz, consumed about 20 watts of power, and was about twice as fast as a 100-MHz Pentium. The Pentium Pro was optimized for 32-bit software and actually runs more slowly with 16-bit software than the original Pentium.

Pentium II (n.) The microprocessor that Intel introduced as the successor to the Pentium Pro. There are several versions, each intended for a different market. The standard Pentium II was designed for mainstream home and business users. The Celeron is an inexpensive version that lacks the cache of the standard Pentium II. The Xeon is intended for high performance and servers. The mobile version is used in portable computers.

Pentium II is a superscalar CPU with approximately 7.5 million transistors.

First-generation Pentium II processors, code named "Klamath," were manufactured using wafers 0.35 microns thick. They support clock rates of 233, 266, 300, and 333 MHz with an internal a bus speed of 66 MHz. Second-generation Pentium II processors, code named "Deschutes," are made using 0.25-micron wafers. They support rates of 350, 400, and 450 MHz with an internal bus speed of 100 MHz.

The Pentium II is packaged on a special daughterboard that plugs into a card-edge processor slot on the motherboard. The daughterboard is housed in a Single Edge Contact (SEC) cartridge. The standard Pentium II requires a 242-pin slot (Slot 1), while the Zeon fits in a 330-pin slot (Slot 2). Slot 1 is referred to as SEC-242, and Slot 2 is referred to as SEC-330. The daughterboard holds support

chips and cache memory chips as well as the Pentium II processor.

Every type of Pentium II processor features Multimedia Extensions (MMX), integrated Level 1 and Level 2 cache controllers, Dynamic Execution and Dual Independent Bus Architecture. Each operates with a 64-bit system bus and a separate 64-bit cache bus.

performance objective (n.) In computer-based training (CBT), a goal that is narrowly defined and clearly stated for students in an interactive environment.

peripheral (n.) A device that is controlled by a computer but that is a separate unit interfaced with the computer, such as a printer, a scanner, or an external modem.

peripheral component interconnect (PCI) (n.) A local bus standard that supports up to 16 physical slots. Intel Corporation led an industry group in developing the specification, which was released in 1992 and updated in 1993. Both 32- and 64-bit implementations are defined. PCI uses bridges to insert a bus between the CPU and the native input/output (I/O) bus to address weaknesses in the Industry Standard Architecture (ISA) and Extended Industry Standard Architecture (EISA) buses. A new set of controller chips was developed to extend the processor bus rather than to tap into it directly.

The PCI bus is referred to as a *mezzanine bus,* because it adds a layer to the traditional configuration. It bypasses the standard I/O bus and uses the system bus to increase the bus clock speed, taking advantage of the CPU's data path. Most computing systems built since 1993, including the DEC Alpha and the Macintosh PowerPC, integrate the PCI bus.

The PCI bus moves data at 33 MHz, capitalizing on the full data width of the CPU. When the PCI bus is used with a 64-bit processor, data can transfer at speeds of up to 264 megabytes per second (MBps). The PCI bus operates concurrently with the processor bus, which can process data in an external cache while the PCI transfers information between other system components. PCI supports bus mastering direct memory access (DMA).

PCI adapter cards use a special type of connector. The specification identifies three different board configurations: a 5-volt specification for stationary computer systems, a 3.3-volt specification for portable machines, and a universal specification for either type of system.

PCI cards are configured through software and do not have jumpers or switches. PCI was the model for the Intel plug and play (PnP) specification, and a PnP Basic Input/Output System (BIOS) enables automatic PnP configuration of components connected through the PCI bus. In addition to automatic configuration, PCI boards support parity checking of the data and the address bus signals. It is anticipated that the specification will be enhanced to operate at 66 MHz.

Perl (n.) An interpreted computer language developed by Larry Wall. Perl is a general-purpose language often used for scanning text and printing formatted reports. Many web developers use Perl. Common Gateway Interfaces (CGIs) and Perl libraries exist for several platforms. The flexibility of Perl makes it well suited for form processing. Perl5 is a major rewrite and enhancement of the widely distributed version 4. Short for Practical Extraction and Report Language or, as some would have it, Pathologically Eclectic Rubbish Lister.

Perl5 (n.) A significant enhancement of Perl version 4. It adds real data structures, subroutine calls, and method inheritance.

persistence (n.) The length of time a phosphor dot on the screen of a cathode-ray tube (CRT) remains illuminated after an electron beam has energized it.

personal communications services (PCS) (n.) Intelligent, portable, digital wireless two-way communications systems. Using frequencies between 1.5 MHz and 1.8 MHz with low-power transmitters, it serves buildings or neighborhoods known as *microcells.*

personal computer (PC) (n.) A relatively low-cost, portable computer system for business and home use that IBM and Apple Computer popularized. Strictly speaking, only an IBM-compatible model is called a *PC.*

Personal Computer/Advanced Technology (PC/AT) (n.) A personal computer introduced by IBM in 1984 featuring a tall case containing the Intel 80286 processor with a 16-bit bus, a 1.2-megabyte floppy disk drive, and a hard disk drive.

Personal Computer–Disk Operating System (PC-DOS) (n.) The IBM version of an operating system for personal computers.

Personal Computer Memory Card International Association (PCMCIA) (n.) Industry group that developed the specification for *PC cards,* which are credit card–sized plug-in cards for laptop computers. All types have a 68-pin connector, consisting of two rows of 34 pins. A card is 85.6 mm deep and 54 mm wide. The height of a PC card varies with its type and application.

P

Type	Height	Application
I	3.3 mm	Memory (RAM or Flash RAM)
II	5.0 mm	Network interface card (NIC) or modem
III	10.5 mm	Hard disk
IV	5.5 mm	Hard disk

A Type II slot will accept a Type I or a Type II card because a shorter card may be plugged into a slot that will accommodate a taller card. The original interface for PC cards only supported one interrupt, limiting the use of multiple-function cards.

There are several versions of the specification. The original specification defined Type I cards with no input/output (I/O) capability or software drivers because they were memory cards. Version 2.0 defined I/O but did not specify software drivers, which the vendors provided for their cards. The interface in this version is a 16-bit data path with a 6-MHz bus speed.

Version 2.1 was a major advance in the standard, allowing the cards to work in any type of computer with a PCMCIA slot and introducing "card services," a higher-level Application Programming Interface (API). Version 2.1 also introduced plug and play (PnP), hot swapping, and Execution in Place (XIP). XIP refers to programs that can read directly from the card's own ROM. A BIOS-level interface, "socket services," gave the PC card its own standard calls, which were independent of different vendor implementations. These standard software interfaces made PC cards easier to use.

The February 1995 release of the PC card standard added specifications for 32-bit bus mastering direct memory access (DMA) support, known as *CardBus,* at speeds of up to 33 MHz. It also provided for multiple-function adapters, so an Ethernet card and a modem card could be combined in one unit. The voltage requirement was reduced from 5 volts to 3 volts, which saves battery power. The Card Information Structure (CIS) on every card specifies the manufacturer, the model number, the voltage requirements, and the input/output (I/O) configuration.

personal digital assistant (PDA) (n.) 1. A term Apple Computer initially used to describe its Newton technology. 2. Any battery-powered handheld device that provides digital information management and communications and that is capable of calculating, scheduling, taking notes, maintaining address files, transferring data via a modem, and other similar activities.

Personal System/2 (PS/2) (n.) The second generation of personal computers built by IBM. The PS/2 series introduced 3.5-inch 1.44 megabyte (MB) floppy disks, the VGA display standard, and Micro Channel Architecture.

perspective correction (n.) A technique in three-dimensional texture mapping that evaluates the appearance of a texture from different points of view and then draws and illuminates the texture automatically.

PERT/CPM See *project evaluation and review technique/critical path method.*

peta- Prefix meaning a quadrillion (10 to the 15th power), an SI unit represented by an uppercase *P.* In the binary system, it is expressed as 2 to the 50th power.

PGA See *pin grid array.*

PGP See *Pretty Good Privacy.*

phantom power (n.) The direct current (DC) signal sent to a condenser microphone over audio lines. Phantom power is usually between 12 volts and 48 volts.

Phase Alternation Line (PAL) (n.) The European standard for color television, which operates at 25 frames per second (fps) with a resolution of 768 pixels by 625 scan lines per frame. See also *National Television Standards Committee* or *Sequentiel Couleurs à Mémoire.*

phase modulation (n.) A method of modifying the phase of a sine wave carrier signal so that it contains modulating signal information.

phase shift (n.) The degree to which the starting point of a waveform is early or late in relation to a reference point or to another waveform.

phase shift keying (PSK) (n.) A form of digital modulation in which discrete phases of the carrier signal convey a digital signal.

PHIGS See *Programmer's Hierarchical Interactive Graphics System.*

phone plug (n.) A male audio connector with a 0.25-inch diameter. A phone plug is used to terminate the cables connecting most high-impedance and line level instruments and signal processors, such as electric guitars, synthesizers, and amplifiers. The monophonic (mono) version allows two wires to be connected to a tip and a sleeve. A stereo version permits connection of three wires that have a tip, ring, and sleeve configuration. A female receptacle for this type of plug is called a *phone jack.* On consumer audio equipment, such as portable CD players and cassette decks, this style of connector has a 0.125-inch diameter and is called a *miniature (mini) phone plug.* See figure.

Phong shading (n.) A method of specifying

.25-inch phone plug

the color of each pixel in a three-dimensional model. It offers high quality but is incapable of reflection, transparency, or other advanced effects. See figure.

Phong-shaded cone

phono plug (n.) A male connector used in consumer audio gear and in composite video connections. It has a small pin in the center of a ring. Not to be confused with a phone plug, it is also called an *RCA plug.*

Photo-CD See *Photo–Compact Disc.*

Photo–Compact Disc (PCD, Photo-CD) (n.) Developed by Eastman Kodak, a compact disc format based on the hybrid disc specification and used to store scanned photographic images. Photo-CD media can be recorded in multiple sessions; in this regard the format adheres to the Orange Book specification. Film scanners are generally used to capture the graphic con-

P

239

tent for Photo-CDs. In a basic Photo-CD format, five different resolutions, or "image pacs," appear for each of the 100 images that a Photo-CD can hold. Expressed in pixels, these resolutions are 192 x 128, 384 x 256, 768 x 512, 1536 x 1024, and 3072 x 2048. Note that the aspect ratio is 3:2, as in a photograph, rather than the computer display ratio of 4:3. Images on a Photo-CD are defined in Kodak's proprietary YCC format. In MS-DOS, the extension for this file type is .pcd.

The Portfolio version of the Photo-CD format can accommodate higher-level programming with buttons that can branch to other images or a sequence of frames. An audio clip can be attached to each frame, but it will not play continuously if different images are displayed.

photoconductor (n.) In fiber optics, a transducer that emits current in proportion to the amount of light it receives.

photodiode (n.) A component in a laser disc player that translates variations in the light reflected from the surface of a disc into the electronic signals that define the audio, video, and control tracks.

photolithography (n.) A process for transferring a pattern from a mask to a silicon wafer using a photosensitive emulsion and light.

photon (n.) In physics, a unit of light energy. Photons travel through an optical fiber the same way electrons travel through a wire cable.

photo-realism (n.) Computer representation or imaging that seems as faithful to detail as a photograph.

physical code (n.) A tag that defines exactly how text should be displayed in an HTML document. Compare *logical code.*

physical format (n.) The standard for the way information is physically recorded on compact discs.

physical layer (n.) The lowest layer of the Open Systems Interconnection (OSI) model. The physical layer governs hardware connections, bytestream encoding for transmission, and physical transfer of information between network nodes.

physical media (n.) Any physical means of transferring signals between two systems. This term is typically used for media connecting the physical layer, which is the lowest layer of the Open Systems Interconnection (OSI) reference model.

physical sector (n.) The location in which data is placed on a compact disc or on other digital media. For example, the Yellow Book specification requires that each compact disc be divided into 270 000 physical sectors of 2336 bytes each.

PIC See *Picture file.*

pickup (n.) 1. An electronic transducer that sends a low-level signal corresponding to the sound produced by a musical instrument, such as an electric guitar or a bass. 2. Related to video or film production, a shot or sequence recorded after the initial shoot. The pickup is used during editing to update content. 3. Jargon for a microphone.

pico- A prefix meaning one-trillionth.

PICS (n.) A Macintosh-specific "multimedia" format developed in 1988 by Macromedia and others for exchanging animation sequences. A

PICS file is a sequential assembly of several Picture format (PICT) frames.

PICT See *Picture format.*

picture cue (n.) A signal in the vertical blanking interval (VBI) of a master tape that identifies the beginning of a frame. Each cue is encoded as a frame number on a videodisc pressed from the master tape.

picture depth (n.) The number of bits used to store picture data, or the number of shades of color that can be represented by that number of bits. Settings can be 1-bit color (black and white), 8-bit color (256 shades), 16-bit color (65 536 shades), or 24-bit color (16.7 million shades).

picture element (pel, pixel) (n.) The smallest unit defined on a display. See also *pixel.*

Picture file (PIC, pronounced "PICK") (n.) A bitmapped graphic file format developed by Lotus Corporation for IBM-compatible programs.

Picture format (PICT, pronounced "PICKED") (n.) Developed by Apple Computer in 1984, a standard format for storing and exchanging black-and-white graphics files. PICT2 (1987) supports eight-bit color and grayscale. Current PICT specifications do not limit color bit depth.

picture stop (n.) An index point on a laser disc that allows the user to stop at a particular frame. The picture stop is encoded in the vertical blanking interval (VBI).

PIF See *Program Information File.*

pincushion distortion (n.) Image distortion caused when the vertical sides of a displayed image curve inward to form concave edges. Most monitors are equipped with controls that minimize this. Compare *barrel distortion.* See figure.

pincushion distortion

PIN Diode See *Positive Intrinsic Negative Diode.*

Ping See *Packet InterNet Groper.*

ping-pong (v.) To mix several audio tracks on a multitrack tape recorder onto an unused track on the same tape. Ping-ponging increases the number of individual recorded layers. It is not possible to alter the mix between the tracks that are bounced onto an open track after the original tracks are erased or replaced by new program material.

pin grid array (PGA) (n.) A square integrated circuit (IC) with connecting pins surrounding the bottom edges on all four sides. PGA is the form factor frequently used for microprocessor chips.

pink noise (n.) An audio signal with an equal amount of intensity distributed throughout the frequency spectrum.

pinout (n.) A diagram that indicates how wires are terminated to pins in a connector.

pipeline (n.) In microprocessor design, a sequence of stages, or functional units, that per-

P

form a task in several steps. Each unit takes inputs and produces outputs that are stored in its output buffer. The output buffer of one stage is the input buffer of the next stage. A pipeline works at full efficiency when it is filled and emptied at the same rate at which it processes.

pipeline burst cache (n.) A block of synchronous memory constructed from pipelined SRAM. In pipeline burst cache, reading from or writing to a new location takes multiple cycles, but subsequent locations are accessed in a single cycle. A Pentium microprocessor uses pipeline burst cache as a secondary cache. The first 8 bytes of data are transferred in three CPU cycles, and the next three 8-byte blocks are transferred in one cycle each.

pit (n.) A physical indentation in the information layer of a CD or a laser disc. Pits determine how a laser beam is reflected. In transmissive discs, pits either block the beam or allow it to pass through the disc. Pits on JVC laser discs cause a detectable change in electrical capacitance. The ones on a CD-R differ from those on a mastered disc because CD-R pits are actually mounds that the laser beam creates in the dye polymer layer. A pit may also be referred to as the space between "lands" along the data spiral of a CD.

pixel (pel, picture element) (n.) An abbreviation of *picture element;* the smallest raster display element represented as a screen coordinate with a specified color and intensity level. Picture resolution is measured by the number of pixels used to create an image. A common resolution is 640 x 480 pixels.

PKUNZIP (n.) A freely distributed decompression program for PKZIP.

PKZIP (n.) A file compression utility created by PKWare for use in MS-DOS. WinZip is a Microsoft Windows version with a graphical user interface (GUI).

placeholder (n.) In a multimedia production, an item used as a surrogate for the finished product until the final version is completed. The placeholder may be a graphics file or an audio file.

planar (n.) The flat capacitor between silicon and polysilicon layers in a semiconductor.

plasma display (n.) A flat display with a grid of electrodes in a gas-filled panel. The gas emits light when ionized by the electrodes, yielding high-quality images.

plastic leaded chip carrier (PLCC) (n.) A type of semiconductor package.

platform (n.) A particular hardware and software operating system, such as the IBM-compatible/DOS platform or the Macintosh platform.

platter (n.) A disk in a hard drive onto which data is written.

playback (n.) The realization of recorded images or sound on any kind of audio or video equipment.

Playstation (n.) A hardware device created by Sony Corporation for playing games.

PLC See *programmable logic controller.*

PLCC See *plastic leaded chip carrier.*

plenum cable (n.) Wiring, typically for networking, installed in the space between a ceiling and the floor above it. In some cases the cable must meet certain code requirements.

plotter (n.) An output device similar to a printer that draws or plots a two-dimensional image on paper. Varieties include pen plotters, electrostatic plotters, photograph plotters, ink-jet plotters, and laser plotters.

plug (n.) The male connector in a plug-and-jack system.

plug and play (PnP) 1. (n.) The ability of an operating system to identify peripherals or other interfaced components, such as speakers or a CD-ROM reader, and to configure the system transparently to incorporate them. 2. (adj., plug-and-play) Describes hardware and peripherals that an operating system automatically identifies and installs.

plug-in (n.) A program that extends the utility of another program. Plug-ins for Netscape Navigator allow enhanced media types, such as RealMedia, to be employed.

PLV See *Production Level Video.*

PMA See *program memory area.*

PMMA See *polymethyl methacrylate.*

PMMU See *Paged Memory Management Unit.*

PMS See *Pantone Matching System.*

PNG See *Portable Network Graphics.*

PnP See *plug and play.*

PNP (n.) A bipolar transistor with an N-doped semiconductor as a base between two P-doped layers, the collector and the emitter. Doping refers to coating with a type of dopamine.

POE See *PowerOpen Environment.*

point (n.) A unit of measurement used in typography and graphic design that defines the height of text characters, the thickness of lines and borders, the size of leading, and the dimensions of other elements. Given that 1 point equals 1/72 inch, 12-point printed text is about 1/6 inch high.

pointer (n.) In programming, an address that identifies a location in a data structure.

pointing device (n.) A mouse, a pen, or a trackball that inputs spatial data to a computer. A graphical user interface (GUI) lets a user control the computer by pointing, clicking, and dragging. Movements of the pointing device are echoed on the screen by movements of the cursor.

Point of Presence (PoP) (n.) A collection of leased lines, routers, modems, and other telecommunications equipment located at a site. Internet Access Providers (IAPs) operate PoPs that subscribers can reach with a local telephone call. This interface connects to interLATA carriers.

point-of-sale (POS, pronounced "pee-oh-ESS") (adj.) Describes the place where shoppers make a buying decision. Multimedia kiosks running interactive programs that engage observers and promote or explain a product are often placed nearby to influence that decision.

point of view (POV, pronounced "pee-oh-VEE") (n.) In video production, a shot perspective in which the camera assumes the subject's viewpoint, giving audience members the illusion that they are looking through the subject's eyes.

P

point-to-point (adj.) Describes an uninterrupted connection between two pieces of equipment. A private telephone circuit and a satellite transmission are examples of point-to-point networks. See figure.

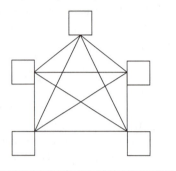

point-to-point network

Point-to-Point Protocol (PPP) (n.) Defined in RFC 1171, the Internet standard for transmitting Internet Protocol (IP) packets over serial point-to-point links. In contrast to SLIP, PPP can operate over both asynchronous connections and bit-oriented synchronous systems, dynamically configure connections with a remote network, and test that a link is usable. PPP can be configured to encapsulate AppleTalk, IP, and Internetwork Packet eXchange (IPX) protocols.

polarity (n.) The identification of a positive or a negative charge on one side of an electrical circuit or a conductor.

polarization (n.) The state in which the magnetic field of an electromagnetic wave oscillates linearly in only one direction. The direction of this magnetic field is referred to as the *polarization direction*.

polling (n.) 1. Connecting to a remote computer system to look for email or access information. 2. A method of controlling the sequence of transmissions with devices on a multipoint line. Polling requires each device to wait until the controlling processor clears it for transmission.

polycarbonate (n.) A resilient plastic used to manufacture compact discs.

polymer See *dye polymer*.

polymethyl methacrylate (PMMA) (n.) The rigid, transparent acrylic plastic used to manufacture optical media.

polymorphism (n.) In object-oriented programming (OOP), variables that may, at run time, refer to objects of different classes.

PoP See *Point of Presence*.

POP See *Post Office Protocol*.

Popmail (n.) A program that uses the Point of Presence (PoP) protocol to read email remotely across a network, usually implemented with SLIP.

port 1. (n.) A logical connection or channel for data flow in a communications system. Transmission Control Protocol (TCP) and User Datagram Protocol (UDP), which are transport layer protocols for Ethernet, use port numbers to demultiplex messages. 2. (v.) To translate software so that it runs on different platforms. 3. (n.) The product that results from translating software for a different platform. 4. (n.) A socket for connecting peripheral cables to a computer.

portability (n.) The ability to use the same software on different hardware systems or across platforms. A high degree of portability reduces the need to modify programs for delivery on different hardware.

Portable Document Format (PDF) (n.) A document type created by Adobe Acrobat that virtually any type of computer can access. PDF Writer converts existing graphics and text files into the .pdf format. Adobe Distiller converts existing PostScript documents. PDF provides a cross-platform method to transfer information. If Acrobat Reader, a freely distributed program, has been installed on a computer, it can effectively read and manipulate this universal document type.

Portable Network Graphics (PNG, pronounced "PING") (n.) An extensible file format for lossless, compressed storage of images. PNG is recommended by the World Wide Web Consortium (W3C) as an Internet Media Type (image/png) to replace GIF, and it may effectively replace TIFF as well. PNG supports indexed-color, grayscale, and true color images, along with an optional alpha channel. The sample depth may vary from 1 to 16 bits. PNG may be streamed on the Internet with a progressive display option. It provides file integrity checking and simple detection of common transmission errors. PNG stores gamma and chromaticity for color matching on heterogeneous platforms.

Like GIF, PNG can index up to 256 colors, streaming progressive display, transparent layers, platform independence, and totally lossless compression. The unique features of PNG are true color (up to 48 bits per pixel), grayscale (up to 16 bits per pixel), full alpha channel (general transparency masks), image gamma information, and detection of file corruption.

GIF is copyrighted and lacks some desirable features. PNG provides a new image format in the public domain that exceeds the limitations of GIF. PNG exhibits highly flexible transparency, compression efficiency, and resistance to transmission errors. Images transferred on the Internet are sometimes processed as text by mistake, which may cause file corruption. PNG is designed so that such errors can be detected quickly and reliably.

The PNG specification exhibits some carefully calculated limitations of its own. There is neither lossy compression nor an uncompressed variant of PNG. The format does not support multiple images in one file or CMYK color space. There is not a standard chunk specified for thumbnail views. Such features could be accomplished if the basic specification were extended. PNG uses network byte order consistently, so that files may be converted on any platform that supports TCP/IP and on all PC platforms.

PNG uses a two-dimensional interlacing scheme that is more complex than the linewise interlacing of GIF. The PNG file is slightly bigger, but it draws an initial image eight times faster than GIF. Although that initial image is coarser, PNG completely renders it more quickly. Horizontal and vertical resolution never differ by more than a factor of two, and

Values Always Contained in the First 8 Bytes of a PNG File

	Byte 1	Byte 2	Byte 3	Byte 4	Byte 5	Byte 6	Byte 7	Byte 8
decimal	137	80	78	71	13	10	26	10
hexadecimal	89	50	4e	47	0d	0a	1a	0a
ASCII C Notation	\211	P	N	G	\r	\n	\032	\n

text in an interlaced PNG is readable much sooner than in an equivalent GIF image.

The variety of images and display systems used for the web creates images that are too dark or light. PNG assumes that image viewing software will compensate for image gamma whenever the image is displayed. The viewer will appropriately adjust images with no gamma or with an incorrect recorded gamma for the delivery system. PNG employs "unassociated" or "nonpremultiplied" alpha, so that images with separate transparency masks may be stored without loss of data.

Filtering can reduce the compressed size of true color and grayscale images, so PNG includes a filtering capability. The filter algorithms operate on bytes rather than on pixels because filtering is usually ineffective on images with fewer than eight bits per sample. The encoder is allowed to change filters for each new scan line because adaptive filtering outperforms fixed filters and adds very little to the compressed file size. This process maximizes the quality of each scan line.

PNG allows some textual information to be stored along with the graphical data. Textual information should be stored in standard tEXt chunks with suitable keywords. Use of tEXt tells a PNG viewer that the chunk contains related text. Latin-1 is the recommended text format for these chunks because it is a direct subset of character sets commonly used on popular platforms such as Microsoft Windows and X Window System.

The values in the first 8 bytes of a PNG file are shown in the table on the previous page.

This byte order allows common file transfer problems to be detected immediately. The first 2 bytes distinguish PNG files on systems that expect the first 2 bytes to identify the file type uniquely. The first byte is a non-ASCII value, which reduces the probability that a text file may be incorrectly identified as a PNG file. The byte order also catches bad file transfers that clear bit 7. Bytes 2 through 4 name the format. The carriage return line feed (CRLF) sequence catches bad file transfers that alter new-line sequences. The Ctrl-Z character stops file display under MS-DOS. The final line feed checks for the inverse of the CRLF translation problem.

Chunk length is limited to avoid problems for systems that cannot handle four-byte unsigned values. A separate cyclic redundancy check (CRC) is provided for each chunk in order to detect transfer errors rapidly and to validate data. If a viewer does not provide as many colors as are listed in the palette belonging to an image, a palette histogram provides the information needed to select a target palette.

Current versions of browser software, such as Netscape Navigator and Microsoft Internet Explorer, can process and view PNG files. Current graphics-processing packages are capable of encoding in this new and highly recommended format. It is assumed that web developers will embrace PNG as superior to GIF.

Portable Operating System Interface in Unix (POSIX, pronounced "pah-ZICKS") (n.) An Institute of Electrical and Electronics Engineers (IEEE) standard that defines operating system services based on Unix but that other systems can implement easily.

portmapper (n.) A server that converts TCP/IP protocol port numbers into Remote Procedure Call (RPC) program numbers.

portrait (n.) A layout in which the height of a

printed page is greater than the width. In a "landscape" layout, the width is greater than the height. See figure under *landscape* for portrait and landscape layouts.

POS See *point-of-sale.*

positional reference (n.) A signal that feeds a receiving device information about a location point. Audio and video equipment can use this signal to synchronize during recording or playback.

Positive Intrinsic Negative Diode (PIN Diode) (n.) A photodetector that converts optical signals to electrical signals in a receiver.

POSIX See *Portable Operating System Interface in Unix.*

post 1. (n.) Jargon for postproduction. 2. (v.) To send a message to a mailing list or to a group of users, as opposed to sending it to an individual recipient.

POST See *power-on self test.*

posterize (v.) To convert an image to a more elementary form by lowering all tonal values, creating a surrealistic, stark result.

posting (n.) A message sent to a newsgroup or a mailing list. This message is broadcast rather than sent point-to-point.

postmaster (n.) A contact point or address for email to be sent to an Internet site or to a UUCP network site. The Internet email standard (RFC 822) requires every machine to have a postmaster address, which is usually aliased to the system administrator.

Post Office Protocol (POP, pronounced "POP") (n.) The protocol that allows indi-

vidual computers to retrieve electronic mail from a server.

postproduction (n., adj.) In the creation of video programs and multimedia productions, a phase that occurs after the original footage is shot. It includes offline and online editing, compositing, sweetening, and the final mix.

PostScript (n.) An interpreted, stack-based, page description language implemented by Adobe Systems in 1982. PostScript describes the appearance of text, graphical shapes, and images on printed or displayed pages in a device-independent way. PostScript has become the language of choice for printers and for cross-platform graphical output.

potentiometer (n.) A component in a circuit that provides varying degrees of resistance. It may take the form of a knob, a thumbwheel, or a slider. In audio equipment, a variable potentiometer is often called a *pot,* an example of which is a fader (a sliding volume control) on a mixing board. See figure.

potentiometers

POTS (n.) Plain old telephone service.

POV See *point of view.*

power-cycle (v.) To turn off and turn on the

247

power to a device with the intention of clearing an undesirable state.

PowerMac See *Power Macintosh.*

Power Macintosh (PowerMac) (n.) Based on the PowerPC chip, a microcomputer developed by Apple Computer and introduced in March 1994. A PowerMac system can emulate existing 680x0 code, as long as the code is provided in a fat binary version of an application along with native PowerPC code.

power-on self test (POST) (n.) A startup routine run by a computer. A POST scans circuits, and if the system is performing as expected, it sounds a beep.

PowerOpen Association (n.) An organization formed to promote the PowerOpen Environment and to support software developers. Founding members include Apple Computer, Bull Systems, Harris Computer Systems, IBM, Motorola, Tadpole Technology, and Thomson CSF. See also *PowerOpen Environment.*

PowerOpen Environment (POE) (n.) Specifications for PowerPC-based Application Programming Interface (API) and Application Binary Interface (ABI). The presence of the ABI specification in the POE allows it to have platform-independent binary compatibility, typically limited to particular hardware. Derived from AIX, the POE is an open standard that conforms to industry open standards.

PowerPC (n.) Developed by Apple Computer, IBM, and Motorola in a collaborative effort, a highly evolved microprocessor chip released in 1994 that replaces the 68000 series as the CPU for the Macintosh series. The PowerPC is based on reduced instruction set computing (RISC) processing. This family of processors from the PowerPC alliance includes the 32-bit 601, 603,

and 604; and the 64-bit 620, which contains 7 million transistors. The second generation of this chip is the PowerPC 750, used in Apple G3 computers.

PowerPoint (PPT) (n.) An application developed by Microsoft for electronic presentations, speaker support, and slide shows. Although it is capable of incorporating a variety of file types, it is not a robust multimedia authoring environment. PowerPoint has become a popular tool for creating presentations because it is bundled with the Microsoft Office suite. Files created by PowerPoint have the extension .ppt. Unfortunately, frames created in PowerPoint are not easily converted to other graphical file types, which makes it difficult to export content to other authoring environments.

PPP See *Point-to-Point Protocol.*

PPT See *PowerPoint.*

PRAM See *Parameter RAM.*

preamplifier (preamp) (n.) An electrical device that increases the strength of a signal so that it is powerful enough to drive a main amplifier. A preamp is generally required to boost the signal of a microphone to an adequate level for mixing and recording.

predictive encoding (n.) In MPEG compression, the storing of the difference between a prediction of the data and the actual data in subsequent frames. Encoding only these differences results in higher compression ratios.

pre-groove (n.) The spiral track molded into the polycarbonate substrate for the recording laser beam to follow when writing data onto recordable compact discs.

premastering (n.) The process of creating a

tape, a hard disk drive, or a CD-R containing data in the proper format. This data will be recorded onto a master from which compact discs will be replicated. Typically, premastering includes adding error correction and location data. The disc is reviewed and evaluated before the master disc is made.

Premiere (n.) A nonlinear video editing program developed by Adobe. Premiere is used in multimedia development, usually for creating and processing QuickTime movies.

preproduction (n., adj.) A phase that occurs before a video program or a multimedia authoring program is created. Preproduction includes preparatory tasks such as flowcharting, storyboarding, scriptwriting, and designing graphics.

preroll (n.) In video production, the process of rewinding tape to a point that precedes the beginning of a scene or to a specific frame identified by a time code. In order to bring the tape up to speed from a dead start, it is necessary to begin rolling slightly ahead of the first frame of a segment that is to be dubbed or encoded.

presentation layer (n.) An Open Systems Interconnection (OSI) layer that determines how application data is encoded while it is in transit between two end systems.

Presentation Manager (n.) A graphical user interface supported by the IBM OS/2 operating system that can multitask between existing MS-DOS and Windows applications.

Pretty Good Privacy (PGP) (n.) A public key encryption application written by Philip R. Zimmermann in 1991 for MS-DOS, Unix, and other platforms. It uses an encryption algorithm claimed by U.S. patent number 4,405,829. PGP facilitates the exchange of files

or messages with privacy and authentication. Secure channels are not required for the exchange of keys between users.

pretzel key (n.) Another name for the Macintosh Command key.

PRI See *Primary Rate Interface.*

primary key (n.) The most important data field used to identify a body of information, an object, or a record in a relational database.

Primary Rate Interface (PRI) (n.) An ISDN interface to primary access that operates at 1.544 megabits per second (Mbps). It consists of 23 B-channels at 64 kilobits per second (Kbps) and one D-channel at 64 Kbps. An additional eight Kbps is used for framing. Specifications for the system vary in Europe, where 30 B-channels are provided along with a 64-Kbps D-channel and where 64 Kbps is used for framing. Data and voice information may be transmitted simultaneously over all channels.

primitive (n.) 1. A simple graphical shape. Examples of two-dimensional primitives include squares, triangles, and circles. Examples of three-dimensional primitives include blocks, spheres, and tubes. 2. A function built into a programming language or an operating system that could not be written in the language. Primitives include arithmetic and logical operations and are implemented efficiently in machine language.

printed circuit board (PCB) (n.) A piece of a thin, nonconductive substance with lines for circuitry embedded and with components soldered on at connecting points. Also known as a *board* or *card.*

printer (n.) A common output device that

prints computer-generated graphics and text on paper. A daisy-wheel printer uses a disk with characters around the outer edge. A dot matrix printer makes a pattern of small dots. A laser printer produces high-quality graphics, up to 1200 dots per inch (dpi), though commonly 300 to 600 dpi, using technology similar to that of a copy machine.

print spooler (n.) Software that schedules printing tasks. Rather than committing all cycles of a computer during printing whenever a print command is issued, it allows the user to be productive and perform other tasks while the printer is addressed in the background.

private automatic branch exchange (PABX) (n.) An automatic telephone exchange that a user owns and that routes calls to and from the public telephone network.

private branch exchange (PBX) (n.) A phone system that internally connects lines in a business and provides a link to an outside line. Users must dial 9 to access the outside line.

proc amp (n.) Processing amplifier; a video image processor that alters the luminance, chroma, and sync in a signal. A proc amp is typically used to correct problems of poor color saturation, low light levels, or incorrect tint. Pronounced "PRAHK amp."

procedural language (n.) A programming language in which an explicit sequence of steps is specified to produce a result. Common procedural languages are BASIC, Pascal, and C.

processing (n.) 1. The manipulation of data from one state to another, usually at the request of an operator or a user. This is the basic function that computers perform. 2. The photographic development of a film negative.

processor audio (n.) Sound created and played back by computer data manipulation rather than sound digitized from an acoustical environment for playback with standard digital-to-analog (D/A) converters.

processor bus (n.) The routes over which data moves between the CPU and its chip set, the immediate support chips. Data moves among the CPU, the main system bus, and the external memory cache on the processor bus. Its purpose is to allow information to move to and from the CPU as fast as possible. An external cache for the CPU is usually employed in all systems with Pentium, Pentium MMX, Pentium Pro, and Pentium II chips. The bus provides circuits for data, for addresses, and for control purposes. The processor bus in a Pentium system has 64 data lines, 32 address lines, and several associated control lines. The Pentium Pro and Pentium II have 36 address lines but are identical to the Pentium and Pentium MMX in other respects. The transfer rate for the processor bus is calculated by multiplying the data width (64 bits = 8 bytes) by the clock speed of the bus, which is the same as the clock speed of the CPU. A Pentium with a 66-MHz clock transfers data at 528 megabytes per second (MBps). This is the maximum bandwidth of the bus.

Processor Direct Slot (PDS) (n.) A local bus connection in a Macintosh computer.

production (n.) In video terms, the activity that takes place while video or film footage is being shot. See also *postproduction* or *preproduction*.

production audio (n.) The sound track, including any dialog, recorded in the field while a video is shot. Production audio could be recorded on the videotape or, for better quality, on a separate field digital audio tape (DAT).

Production Level Video (PLV) (n.) The high-quality compression format applied to Digital Video Interactive (DVI) files.

professional market (n.) The segment of the population that purchases software or production equipment for use on the job, as opposed to the consumer market. See also *industrial market.*

program 1. (v.) To plan and define a series of computations or processes to be executed by a computer. Developing a software program includes writing code and specifying output formats. 2. (n.) Software instructions that control a computer's processes in solving problems and performing tasks. 3. (n.) Any kind of audio or video material on a tape or a disc that is prepared for an audience.

program calibration area (PCA) (n.) The section on a CD-R reserved so that the CD-R drive can calibrate the laser power for recording on the disc.

Program Information File (PIF) (n.) A file that defines how a non-Windows application program should be handled in Windows. A PIF includes such information as requirements for memory allocation and the configuration of the graphics interface. PIF has the file name extension .pif.

programmable logic controller (PLC) (n.) A microprocessor-based device used to automate industrial machinery.

programmable read-only memory (PROM, pronounced "PEE-rom") (n.) A type of non-volatile, semiconductor ROM component that the user can program once and that can only

be read thereafter.

Program Manager (n.) In Microsoft Windows 3.1, the primary application that controls the graphical user interface. This application displays groups of icons that represent applications and utility programs the user may select.

program memory area (PMA) (n.) The place on a CD-R where information about tracks and sessions is stored temporarily. Information in the PMA eventually becomes the table of contents (TOC) for a session.

programmer (n.) Someone who writes code for computers, defining the computational processes.

Programmer's Hierarchical Interactive Graphics System (PHIGS) (n.) A three-dimensional graphics and modeling support system that controls how graphical data is defined and displayed on computers.

programmer's switch (n.) A small push-button switch on the front or the side of a Macintosh that causes a command line prompt to appear. It supplies access to a debugger. If the computer crashes, the user can push the switch and input a code in response to the prompt, which may revive the system.

programming language (n.) The formal system of syntax and semantics with which computer programs are written. A language may be low-level and close to machine code, or it may be high-level if a single statement corresponds to numerous machine code instructions. A distinction is also made between *imperative languages* and *declarative languages.*

progressive scan (n.) A video system that creates an image by painting each successive hori-

P

zontal line across the screen in a *noninterlaced* scan rather than by painting alternate sets of lines in two sweeps down the screen in an *interlaced* scan.

progressive/sequential coding (n.) A type of image compression used in a JPEG file in which an image coded with progressive coding may be decoded sequentially.

project evaluation and review technique/critical path method (PERT/CPM, pronounced "pert-see-pee-EM") (n.) A complex project management process for determining the effectiveness of a system or a program.

PROM See *programmable read-only memory.*

prompt (n.) A request displayed on the computer monitor for action by the user. In MS-DOS a prompt includes a symbol for the internal hard disk or the external memory device currently being addressed.

proof of concept (n.) A prototype of a piece of media used to prove the viability of the project and to attract interest in a full-blown production.

proportional font (n.) A set of characters with a variable amount of horizontal space allocated to each. Narrow letters and symbols take up less space than wide ones. Compare *monospaced font.*

proprietary (adj.) Describes material that is unavailable for use without permission from the owner, whether an individual or an entity. Production companies may either produce proprietary products or perform "work for hire" in which the producer is not the owner. Proprietary software typically runs only on specific hardware platforms.

Prospero (n.) A distributed file system accessible over the Internet via FTP or Network File System (NFS). Clients and servers use Prospero to communicate in the Archie system. Prospero lets a user create views of a collection of files spread out over many servers on the Internet and provides a file-naming system.

prosumer (adj.) Describes high-tech production gear with output quality that falls between the professional and the consumer markets. The term is used in reference to camcorders and mixers that have specifications below broadcast grade but above those of equipment purchased for home use.

protected mode (n.) The mode in which Intel processors run, beginning with the 80286. Software written or compiled to run in protected mode may only use segment register values given to it by the operating system. Protected mode is the opposite of *real mode,* in which addresses are generated by adding an address offset to the value of a segment register shifted to the left 4 bits. The segment register and the address offset are 16 bits long, so adding the shift creates a 20-bit address. This is the origin of the 1-megabyte (MB) limit in real mode. Protected mode must be enabled by software. Compare *real mode.*

protocol (n.) A standard procedure or a set of rules with which software and hardware systems must comply in order to be compatible. All users must observe network protocol in order to have successful data communications. Protocols govern error handling, framing, and line control in transmitting and receiving packets. An example of a telecommunications protocol is XModem.

protocol converter (n.) A device for translating the data transmission code of one network or device to the corresponding code of another. A protocol converter enables pieces of equipment with different conventions to communicate with one another.

protocol data unit (PDU) (n.) A common term for *packet*.

protocol stack (n.) A layered set of protocols working together to provide network functions.

prototype (n.) A working model of a product used to demonstrate the product, test design ideas, or secure financing for a complete version.

proxy gateway (n.) A computer that passes a request for a URL from a web browser to an outside server and that returns the results. Clients on a network with a proxy gateway may be sealed off from the Internet with an agent that can access the Internet on their behalf, providing security for the users.

proxy server (n.) A web server that can accept URLs with a particular prefix. When it receives a URL with the special prefix, it strips off the prefix and seeks the URL in its local cache. If the document is found, it is returned immediately. If it is not found, it is fetched from a remote server, copied to the local cache, and returned to the requester.

PSDN See *packet-switching data network*.

PSK See *phase shift keying*.

PSTN See *public switched telephone network*.

PS/2 See *Personal System/2*.

public access 1. (n.) A block of time allocated for independent producers to air their programs on cable television. 2. (adj.) Describes

multimedia kiosks used by the general public or by a wide range of visitors, often with touch screens for input.

public domain (n., adj.) Intellectual property that is free of a copyright or a patent and that may be duplicated or used without permission. The use of public domain software is unrestricted and free for everyone.

public key encryption (n.) A system devised to keep data secure. In this system, a public key is used to encrypt data, and a private key is required to translate it.

public network (n.) Any network that is operated by a common carrier and that provides packet-switched, circuit-switched, and leased-line circuits to the public.

public switched telephone network (PSTN) (n.) The global voice telephone network, including local exchanges and long distance providers.

publish and subscribe (n.) The ability to establish links between documents in the Macintosh 7.0 operating system or in a later one. Subscribing documents are updated automatically when changes are made to the publishing document.

pull down/pull up (v.) In synchronizing audio with video tracks, to speed up or slow down the audio rate clock deliberately to correspond with speed differences in the video track. When film footage at 24 frames per second (fps) is transferred to NTSC videotape at 29.97 fps, the audio is "pulled up" to match the higher frame rate.

pull media (n.) In response to a user's request for content, a media file sent on the World Wide Web directly to the user via HTTP. In this sense, the user "pulls" the content. This contrasts with

253

push media, which is broadcast from a server.

pulse code (n.) An audio signal recorded on each frame of a videotape. A pulse code allows easy access to individual frames.

pulse code modulation (PCM) (n.) A standard means of encoding audio information in a digital format by sampling the amplitude of the audio waveform at regular intervals and by representing that sample as a digital numerical value. Current standards are based on CCITT Recommendation G.711, which specifies more codes for low-frequency components and fewer codes for high-frequency components. Telephone systems in the United States and Japan use μ-law encoding, whereas Europe and the rest of the world use a-law encoding. See also *adaptive differential pulse code modulation.*

push 1. (v.) In programming, to place something on top of a stack or a pushdown list (pdl). 2. (n.) In terms of the web, jargon for push media.

push media (n.) Content sent to a user by a multicasting web server, as opposed to *pull media,* in which the user requests individual items. With push media, the user usually selects a channel that delivers a particular kind of content. Cable television is an example of push media. Pointcast and Marimba are widely used push systems.

P x 64 (n.) A conferencing standard introduced by the CCITT for compressed motion video with audio. It was devised for transfer over copper or fiber-optic phone lines. P x 64 encodes video at 30 frames per second (fps) in real time with synchronized audio for transmission at speeds of up to four megabits per second (Mbps). Pronounced "P times sixty-four."

Q

QA See *quality assurance.*

QAM See *quadrature amplitude modulation.*

QCIF See *Quarter CIF.*

QI See *Query Interface.*

QIC See *Quarter-Inch Committee.*

QPSK See *quadrature phase shift keying.*

QTVR See *QuickTime VR.*

quad See *quadruplex.*

quadrature amplitude modulation (QAM) (n.) A modulation process that incorporates both amplitude modulation (AM) and phase modulation to increase the number of bits per baud.

quadrature phase shift keying (QPSK) (n.) Frequency modulated transmission technique used in digital satellite transmission and in upstream signaling in hybrid fiber-coax (HFC) networks.

quadruplex (quad) (n.) Developed by Ampex, an industrial videotape format that offers broadcast quality. It has four video heads and uses two-inch wide videotape.

quad-speed (adj.) Describes CD-ROM drives with maximum data transfer rates of approximately 600 kilobytes per second (KBps), four times the rate at which first-generation CD-ROM drives operated.

quality assurance (QA) (n.) A discipline that addresses all business activities with the intention of improving procedures and outcomes and that submits production results to a stringent testing regimen.

quantization (n.) In video compression, a process that attempts to determine what information can be discarded safely without a significant loss in visual fidelity. Quantization uses DCT coefficients and provides many-to-one mapping. The quantization process is inherently lossy because of the many-to-one mapping process.

quantize (v.) In digitizing audio or video, to measure the amplitude of a sample at regular intervals to establish a representative numerical value to encode. Other steps in analog-to-digital (A/D) conversion are sampling and encoding.

quantum (n.) A small, indivisible piece of energy.

Quarter CIF (QCIF) (n.) Quarter Common

Intermediate Format; video frame specification in the ITU-T H.261 standard that calls for a resolution of 176 x 144 pixels. This is approximately one-fourth the size of CIF, and demands a proportionally smaller bandwidth for delivery.

Quarter-Inch Committee (QIC) (n.) Industry association that establishes standards for 0.25-inch wide tape backup units.

query 1. (v.) To request information from a database. 2. (n.) The request itself for particular information contained in a database.

Query Interface (QI) (n.) A database system that client programs can access in order to read or edit content.

queue (n.) In computing, a series of tasks or operations waiting to be performed.

QuickDraw (n.) A set of software routines that a Macintosh uses to display graphics.

QuickTime (n.) Developed by Apple Computer in 1991, a part of the system software architecture that seamlessly integrates audio, video, and animation across applications. QuickTime provides timing services to maintain synchronization between images and sound. Files in this format may be played by the MoviePlayer applet or by any application that can call a movie, as long as the QuickTime extension is in the system folder.

The format does not restrict the size of the window or the frame rate, but it does depend on the processing capabilities and the speed of the machine on which it plays back. With CinePak compression, QuickTime movies can be streamed from a 2X CD-ROM reader to a 320 x 240 pixel window at 12 to 15 frames per second (fps) on most machines. As is the case

with most digital audio-video players, the audio track will command the timing, and video frames will be dropped in order to maintain continuous, smooth sound delivery.

QuickTime video files can be captured with any AV Macintosh with built-in encoding capabilities, but the quality of this method of capture is much lower than that achieved with a dedicated encoder card, such as the VideoVision or the TARGA system. The tools available for manipulating QuickTime are available from Apple Computer. Adobe Premiere is the most widely used application for capturing and editing QuickTime files.

QuickTime version 3.0, introduced in 1998, offers cross-platform development and playback. It will handle many types of files, including MIDI, MPEG, virtual reality (VR), and animations. The ISO MPEG-4 working group has identified QuickTime as the media architecture of choice. CODECs from Sorenson, QDesign, QUALCOMM, and many others are included for video and audio compression. Media Player version 5.2 for Windows is an excellent way to view QuickTime.

QuickTime for Windows (n.) A version of QuickTime from Apple Computer that has been ported over to Windows. It plays QuickTime movies that have been specially processed, or "flattened," to remove their Macintosh binary headers. QuickTime movies have different brightness and contrast characteristics when viewed on an IBM-compatible machine as opposed to a Macintosh, because the two systems treat the gamma component of images differently. The QuickTime for Windows runtime player is distributed for free.

QuickTime VR (QTVR) (n.) QuickTime Virtual Reality; an extension of QuickTime version 2.0 and later versions. This extension from

Apple Computer allows playback of panoramic images in a VR environment through which users may navigate. The creation of QTVR files requires some advanced resources and the capacity to digitize photographs and to connect them seamlessly into a single landscape.

QWERTY (adj.) Describes a standard typewriter keyboard layout. *Q, W, E, R, T,* and *Y* are the first 6 keys on the left in the top row of letters. See figure.

QWERTY keyboard layout

257

R

RAD See *Rapid Application Development.*

radial (n.) A line drawn from the center of a disc to the edge.

radio button (n.) An interactive icon in the shape of a small circle with a dot in the center that represents a choice or a selection, usually found in a dialog box. Clicking on a radio button in a graphical user interface (GUI) selects one option and rejects all others. See figure.

radio buttons—lower case selected

radio frequency (RF) (n.) Electromagnetic waves in the bandwidth between the frequencies of audio and light, from about 500 kHz to 300 GHz. These waves are propagated in the air without a guide wire or a cable.

radio frequency ID circuit (n.) A type of integrated circuit (IC) that communicates using an integrated microwave transceiver.

radio frequency identification (RFID) (n.) The recognition of a specific wavelength in the radio frequency spectrum.

radio frequency interference (RFI) (n.) In the radio frequency (RF) spectrum, noise introduced by electromagnetic radiation. This noise causes undesirable effects in nearby electronic components that may be susceptible to disturbance, such as a sound card in a computer.

radiosity (n.) A method of simulating a light source for rendering three-dimensional images. Radiosity is more computationally intensive and more accurate than *ray tracing,* an alternative method.

radix (n.) In mathematics, the base of a numbering system. Binary numbers are radix 2. Decimal numbers are radix 10.

RAID See *redundant arrays of independent disks.*

rainbow series (n.) A set of technical manuals or specifications identified by the color of their covers or bindings. The names of types of CD-ROMs derive from the colors of the books containing their specifications. The series includes the Red, Yellow, Green, White, and Orange Books.

RAM See *random access memory*.

RAMDAC See *Random Access Memory Digital-to-Analog Converter*.

RAM disk (n.) Random access memory disk; a portion of internal dynamic memory used to emulate a virtual volume of storage space on a hard disk drive.

RAMP See *Remote Access Maintenance Protocol*.

random (adj.) Describes a condition that is unpredictable, arbitrary, or not organized by a recognizable scheme. These characteristics describe the output of a random number generator, for example.

random access (adj.) Describes a hardware delivery system that can leap to any indexed point in data files that reside in memory. Compare *linear*.

random access memory (RAM, pronounced "RAM") (n.) A memory storage chip installed in a computer. RAM holds information that a microprocessor can access rapidly. Generally, the operating system and the application programs are loaded into RAM. This part of a computer's memory can read (find and display) and write (record) information, and the user can update or amend it. RAM takes the form of a volatile integrated circuit (IC) containing Static RAM (SRAM) or Dynamic RAM (DRAM). In RAM, the order in which the microprocessor accesses different locations does not affect the speed of access.

Random Access Memory Digital-to-Analog Converter (RAMDAC, pronounced "RAM-dack") (n.) A combination of three fast DACs for RGB values and a Static RAM (SRAM) chip.

A graphics display adapter uses a RAMDAC to store the color palette and to generate the analog signals that drive a monitor. The DACs process the RGB values, and the SRAM serves as a color look-up table.

Rapid Application Development (RAD, pronounced "RAD") (n.) A software development tool that allows a programmer to build a user interface quickly, integrate media types, and create links between pieces of data. With the exception of Visual Basic (VB), these programs are best considered database development tools rather than multimedia design tools. Some of the common development systems are listed below:

- Delphi: A development tool from Borland based on Pascal. It compiles stand-alone machine language .exe and .dll files.

- PowerBuilder: A program developed by PowerSoft that applies its own scripting language, PowerScript, which is similar to BASIC.

- SQL Windows: A professional tool for database development from Gupta that can also handle multimedia.

- Visual Basic (VB): From Microsoft Corporation, a preferred programming tool for Windows applications. The tool makes it easy to build and reuse models with icons, buttons, and toolbars. In some cases, this program is a good choice for multimedia development in Windows because its products support OLE 2.0 and because operating system integration is automated. The program lacks a compiler, though.

RARE (Reseaux Associés pour la Recherche

Européenne) See *European Association of Research Networks.*

RARP See *Reverse Address Resolution Protocol.*

raster (n., adj.) 1. The area illuminated by the scanning beam of a display grid. A raster display device stores and displays data as horizontal rows on a uniform grid. 2. Bitmap data.

raster graphics (n.) Images composed of pixels arranged in rows and columns, as in a bitmap. Unlike vector graphics, each pixel is defined by data that describes its color and brightness. Compare *vector graphics.*

raster image processor (RIP) (n.) Software that converts vector data into a bitmap, typically for printing.

rasterize (v.) To convert vector data into a bitmapped image.

rave (v.) To speak at great length with evangelical commitment about a specific subject, particularly when addressing a listserv.

RAVE (n.) Developed by Apple Computer, the Application Programming Interface (API) for QuickDraw 3D. It incorporates the 3DMF file format for virtual reality modeling language (VRML) files and is intended to be multiplatform-compatible.

ray tracer (n.) In rendering an animation, a device used in modeling that sends hypothetical light beams across a scene and that calculates visual effects and reflections from objects in the scene. See figure.

RBOC See *Regional Bell Operating Company.*

RCA connector (n.) A common terminator on

projection in ray tracing

a cable used by most consumer audio and video equipment. The male connector is an inner pin encircled by a concentric ring. The female connector is a socket with a raised housing for the ring. A male RCA connector is also known as a *phono connector* or a *phono plug,* not to be confused with a *phone jack* or *plug,* which refers to a 0.25-inch pin with no ring around it. See figure.

male RCA connector

R-DAT See *rotating digital audio tape.*

RDBA See *Remote Database Access.*

RDBMS See *relational database management system.*

read (v.) In computer terminology, to transfer information from one storage medium to another medium or device. For example, data is read from a disk and written to a computer screen. Compare *write.*

reader (n.) Any device that identifies and transmits data, such as a CD-ROM player.

read-only memory (ROM) (n.) A computer storage medium that allows the user to recall and use information (read) but not to record or amend it (write).

real (adj.) Not simulated. Compare *virtual*.

RealAudio (n.) A client-server architecture for streaming realtime sound over the web. The RealAudio encoder compresses sound into RealAudio (.ra) files, which a special server streams. On the client side, a plug-in for a browser decodes the stream of data sent from the server, decompresses it, and sends it to the sound card. A 14.4-kilobyte-per-second (KBps) modem is adequate for sound reproduction, but the speed of the connection determines the quality of the sound produced, and faster connections yield much higher quality. Files may be encoded for playback at specific rates of transfer.

real estate (n.) 1. The space available for data on storage media. 2. The physical space on the desktop.

RealMedia (n.) A proprietary audio and video file format that is compressed for delivery via the web. The company RealNetworks, formerly called Progressive Networks, provides an encoder and a decoder, or player, for RealMedia files. They also provide the RealMedia server, which is required to deliver their media files.

real mode (n.) An operating mode of Intel 80x86 processors. Compare *protected mode*.

realtime (n., adj) The time during which a data processing event occurs. Data is received and processed so fast and the results are returned so quickly that the process seems instantaneous to the user. The term often refers to simulta-

neous digitization and compression of audio or video information. Compare *offline*.

realtime counter (n.) A unit that reads control track pulses and reports hours, minutes, seconds, and frames as a videotape machine records or plays.

Real-Time Operating System (RTOS) (n.) A CD-i operating system developed by Microware Corporation.

Real-Time Video (RTV) (n.) A low-level digital video–encoding scheme for desktop compression. RTV uses an Intel i750-based video card.

reassembly (n.) The process of reuniting a fragmented Internet Protocol (IP) packet before it is passed to the transport layer.

reboot (v.) To restart a computer without shutting off the power. Rebooting occurs when the Reset button is pressed or when the Restart option is chosen in software.

receiver (n.) 1. An electronic device designed to accept a signal that was transmitted or delivered by any means and then to decode it. Such equipment often receives and displays or reproduces broadcast audio or video signals. 2. The earpiece portion of a telephone headset that converts current into sound waves.

record 1. (n.) In a database, a group of related items, or fields, treated as a single unit of information. Pronounced "REK-erd." 2. (v.) To capture or encode an event on magnetic tape or in a digital format so that it can be preserved and reproduced later. Pronounced "ree-KORD."

rectifier (n.) An electronic component that converts alternating current (AC) into direct current (DC).

R

261

recursion (n.) In programming, a case in which a procedure calls itself. A functional programming language uses recursion at times when a procedural language would use iteration.

Recycle Bin (n.) In Microsoft Windows 95, 98, and NT, a receptacle represented by an icon. As with the trash can in the Mac OS, files to be deleted from a computer's storage system are placed in the Recycle Bin.

Red Book for PostScript (n.) 1. One of the four standard reference books about PostScript, along with the Blue Book, the Green Book, and the White Book. 2. A term that describes the audio-CD specification. 3. The 1984 standards issued by the ITU-T eighth plenary assembly, including the X.400 email specification, Group 1–4 fax standards, ISDN, and the V.x recommendations. Red Book for PostScript is part of the PostScript rainbow series.

Red Book standard (n.) The audio CD specification that Philips and Sony developed. The specification book defining the format for audio CDs originally had a red cover. In other books defining CD standards, many parameters are based on those in the Red Book.

red-green-blue (RGB) 1. (n.) A type of computer color display output signal consisting of separately adjustable red, green, and blue signals or components. Compare *composite video*, in which signals are combined prior to output. RGB monitors offer higher resolution than composite monitors. Digital RGB systems are available, but most computers use analog RGB video. 2. (adj.) Describes a type of color model in which colors are represented as the combination of red, green, and blue light. RGB color space is often represented as a square, with one corner black and the opposite corner white. See figures.

RGB color cube

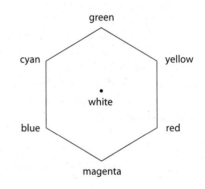

RGB hexagon.

redirector (n.) Software that intercepts requests for resources within a computer and analyzes them for remote access requirements. A redirector may assign a local disk identification letter to a logical disk on a Netware server.

reduced instruction set computing (RISC, pronounced "RISK") (n., adj.) A type of microprocessor with a simplified architecture that achieves high performance by reducing the range of instruction sets and executing them faster.

redundancy (n.) 1. Instances in which multiple interchangeable components perform a single function to minimize the effects of failures and errors. One common form of hardware redundancy is disk mirroring. Redundancy can also be used to detect and recover from errors in software. A common example is the cyclic redundancy check (CRC), which adds redundant data to a block in order to detect corruption during storage or transmission. 2. The process of digitizing or capturing the same data or descriptive information more than once. Copies of the same data are redundant. Compression routines throw out the redundant data.

redundant arrays of independent disks (RAID) (n.) An integrated collection of similar hard disk drives that function together to provide greater speed and integrity of data than a single drive. Originally, the *I* stood for *inexpensive*, referring to the 3.5-inch and 5.25-inch disks used for the first RAID systems. Drives are striped so that the writing of data may be synchronized between disks, and parity refers to the bits used for error correction. The following standard RAID specifications exist:

RAID 0	Nonredundant striped array
RAID 1	Mirrored arrays
RAID 2	Parallel array with error correction code (ECC)
RAID 3	Parallel array with parity
RAID 4	Striped array with parity
RAID 5	Striped array with rotating parity

Reed-Solomon Code (n.) A method of error correction named for Irving Reed and Gustave Solomon, who invented it in 1960.

reference level (n.) An established starting point for making relative measurements, most often of signal strength or power. The most common application is in audio engineering, in which the reference is in decibels per milliwatt (dBm).

referential integrity (n.) The consistency with which data possess properties in a relational database.

referrer (n.) The URL from which a web user is directed to another location.

reflected light (n.) In video production and photography, light that radiates or that is reflected from a surface or subject and that does not shine directly on the scene or the subject.

reflector (n.) A lighting accessory that spreads light and fills in shadows. It is usually made of white poster board, foamcore, or reflective metal.

refresh rate (n.) The number of times per second, or the frequency, at which a displayed image is scanned or renewed on a cathode-ray tube (CRT). In NTSC video, that rate is 60 times per second. On computer monitors, rates slower than 75 Hz can cause flicker and poor picture quality.

Regional Bell Operating Company (RBOC, pronounced "ARE-bock") (n.) One of the seven companies created when AT&T was dissolved. These companies are Ameritech, Bell Atlantic, BellSouth, NYNEX, Pacific Telesis, SBC Communications, and US West. GTE is not among this group but is the largest local exchange carrier (LEC) in the United States.

register (n.) 1. A small number of high-speed memory locations in the central processing unit (CPU) of a computer. Access to data in registers is faster than access to data in RAM. 2. An addressable location in a memory-mapped peripheral device.

R

regression (n.) A mathematical method in which an empirical function is derived from a set of experimental data.

regular expression (n.) An object or expression that describes a pattern of characters, or a text string. The Generalized Regular Expression Parser Unix utility searches a text file for a specific character string. In JavaScript, a regular expression is used to perform pattern matching.

relational database (n.) Developed by E. F. Codd, a type of database that allows data structures to be defined. The data is organized in tables, or collections of records, in which each record contains the same fields, or categories of information. The relationships between the data are defined. Certain fields are designated as keys, expediting searches. Records in different tables may be linked if they have a common field in each table. Oracle Database, FileMaker Pro, and Microsoft Access are examples.

relational database management system (RDBMS) (n.) Same as DBMS, since these databases are generally relational.

relay (n.) A type of switch that is opened or closed electronically to connect circuitry.

release (n.) A version of software made public. Prerelease versions are called *alpha* or *beta* test versions.

REM See *remark*.

remark (REM, pronounced "REHM") (n.) In programming code, a comment used to describe the purpose or the temporary status of a command.

Remote Access Maintenance Protocol

(RAMP) (n.) A protocol used in Internet applications.

remote bridge (n.) A router that connects physically dissimilar network segments across wide area network (WAN) links.

remote control (n., adj.) The ability to issue a command to an interactive program with an independent, electronic device. The device is operated from a distance and often employs infrared technology.

Remote Database Access (RDBA) (n.) The capacity to link a computer or terminal from a distance to a database system and read or update records.

Remote Method Invocation (RMI) (n.) A Java Application Programming Interface (API).

Remote Procedure Call (RPC) (n.) A widely used paradigm for client-server computing. A client sends a request to a remote system to execute a designated procedure using arguments supplied, and the result is returned to the client.

remote production unit (n.) A van or a mobile trailer that houses audio-video equipment for production at a site other than the studio.

removable cartridge (n.) An enclosed optical disc that can be ejected and inserted into any similar playback device. A SyQuest reader accepts a cartridge that typically holds between 44 and 270 megabytes (MB) of data. An Iomega Zip cartridge holds 100 MB of data, whereas a Jaz cartridge holds 1000 MB.

render (v.) 1. To calculate attributes of an image using geometric models as a basis, thereby producing a dimensional object. 2. In animation applications, to calculate the instructions that define a complex series of images.

repeater (n.) An amplifier needed at regular intervals to restore the power of an analog signal. Repeaters regenerate digital signals while removing spurious noise. Regeneration and retiming ensure that the signal is clearly transmitted. In a short run, a repeater simply propagates signals from one cable to another.

replicate (n.) A copy of a CD or of another disc pressed from a stamper disc. Pronounced "REP-li-kat."

replication (n.) 1. Mass reproduction of prerecorded discs or of media in general. Unlike duplication, the replication process periodically compares two copies of a database and updates both to reflect changes in them. 2. The ability of Lotus Notes to distribute document databases across telecommunications networks automatically. Lotus Notes supports a wide range of network protocols, including X.25 and TCP/IP.

report (n.) The output from a database. A report is organized according to specifications that were defined in response to a user's query.

repurpose (v.) To use content in a preexisting program to perform a function other than the one for which it was originally intended.

request (n.) In relation to the Internet, the GET (a page request) or the POST (a form submission) command placed in an HTML document. The request may instruct a Common Gateway Interface (CGI) script to access a database.

Request For Comments (RFC) (n.) A set of informational documents begun in 1969. RFCs state standards to be followed by those who develop software for the Internet. The World

Wide Web Consortium (W3C) approved all of the early RFCs. A comprehensive list of RFCs appears in the "Requests for Comments" appendix. The following RFCs are in common use:

- RFC 792 defines Internet Control Message Protocol (ICMP).

- RFC 822 defines the Internet standard format for electronic mail message headers. This format is also defined in STD 11. RFC 822 evolved from RFC 733.

- RFC 959 contains the official specifications for file transfer protocol (FTP).

- RFC 1661 defines Point-to-Point Protocol (PPP).

request for proposals (RFP) (n.) A formal bidding procedure in which vendors are encouraged to respond.

request for quotations (RFQ) (n.) A formal procedure through which an organization invites vendors' bids for equipment or services.

request for technology (RFT) (n.) A procedure that standardization bodies use to request technology that meets industry requirements.

request to send (RTS) (n.) A standard control signal that puts a modem in the originate mode, preparing it to send data.

Reseaux Associés pour la Recherche Européenne See *European Association of Research Networks.*

ResEdit See *Resource Editor.*

reserved memory (n.) The address range between 640 and 1024 kilobytes (KB) on an IBM-

265

compatible computer. MS-DOS reserves this memory for Basic Input/Output System (BIOS), video cards, and additional circuit boards.

resistance (n.) In an electrical circuit, the property of a conductor that inhibits the flow of current. Resistance is measured in ohms.

resolution (n.) 1. The number of pixels per a unit of area on a monitor screen or the dots per inch (dpi) in a printed graphic. A display with a finer grid has more pixels and a higher resolution; hence it can reproduce a more detailed image. 2. The size of a window used to display video or images, such as 640 x 480 pixels or 320 x 240 pixels. 3. The bit rate and the sample rate of a digital audio file, such as 16-bit, 44.1 KHz.

Resource Editor (ResEdit, pronounced "REZ-edit") (n.) A utility program for the Macintosh that allows a programmer to edit system resources, such as icons and dialog boxes.

resource fork (n.) One of the two branches in a Macintosh file. Reusable items, such as icons, fonts, dialog boxes, and menus are contained in a resource fork. Compare *data fork*. See also *Macintosh file system*.

Resource Interchange File Format (RIFF) (n.) Introduced by Microsoft and IBM in 1990, a cross-platform file format for images, audio, and other media types. A RIFF file can store multiple data types as distinct structures called *chunks*. See also *Media Control Interface*.

response-based (adj.) Describes a form of computer-based instruction that reacts to input and that causes a program to progress at a learner's individual rate.

restore (v.) 1. To copy an archived file from backup into local storage, where it can be readily accessed. 2. To return a window in a graphical user interface (GUI) to its previous dimensions after it has been resized, minimized, or maximized.

reticle (n.) A piece of glass with a chrome pattern for several die used in the photolithography process.

return code (n.) In relation to a request made on the Internet, a message that specifies whether the transfer was successful. For a list of failed return codes, see *client error* and *server error*. Successful return codes are as follows:

    200 = Success: OK.
    201 = Success: Created.
    202 = Success: Accepted.
    203 = Success: No Response.
    204 = Success: Partial Information.
    300 = Success: Redirected.
    301 = Success: Moved.
    302 = Success: Found.
    303 = Success: New Method.
    304 = Success: Not Modified.

reuse (v.) To apply code developed for one application program in another application. Object-oriented programming (OOP) offers reusability of code through inheritance and genericity. Class libraries with intelligent browsers and application generators are under development to help in this process. Polymorphic functional languages also support reusability while retaining the benefits of strong typing.

reverb (n.) A sound effect generated by a signal processor. When treated heavily with reverb, sounds appear to reverberate as though they were produced in a large room or concert hall. The degree of reverb applied by a processor may range from a slight amount to extreme, unrealistic proportions. Sound tracks to which effects have been applied are referred to as "wet," whereas tracks without effects are "dry."

Reverse Address Resolution Protocol (RARP) (n.) Defined in RFC 903, a protocol that provides the reverse function of Address Resolution Protocol (ARP). RARP maps a MAC address to an Internet address. RARP is primarily used by diskless nodes attempting to initialize and locate their Internet addresses.

reverse engineering (n.) The process of analyzing an existing software or hardware system, identifying its components, and recreating it.

revolutions per minute (rpm) (n.) A measurement of the speed at which an object spins.

RF See *radio frequency.*

RFC See *Request For Comments.*

RFI See *radio frequency interference.*

RFID See *radio frequency identification.*

RFP See *request for proposals.*

RFQ See *request for quotations.*

RFT See *request for technology.*

RGB See *red-green-blue.*

RG58 (n.) A 0.25-inch coaxial cable with low (52-ohm) impedance used for 10BASE2 Ethernet wiring. Also known as *cheapernet.*

RG62 (n.) A specification for ARCnet coaxial cable with 93-ohm impedance.

rheostat (n.) An electronic component that provides variable resistance.

ribbon cable (n.) A type of cable with multiple conductors that is as flat as a ribbon.

rib site (n.) With an on-demand, high-speed link to a backbone site, a computer that serves as a regional distribution point for third-party traffic in electronic mail and in Usenet news. Compare *backbone site.*

rich object (n.) In artificial intelligence (AI), an object that can have assertions made about it but that cannot be completely described or represented.

Rich Text Format (RTF) (n.) A format developed by Microsoft that defines text and that exchanges formatted text using normal alphanumeric symbols. The text includes embedded formatting information, such as italics or structural layout descriptors, along with characters. RTF is used for cross-platform applications when the characters and layout must be converted to a different word-processing application or file type.

RIFF See *Resource Interchange File Format.*

ring latency (n.) The time required for a signal to propagate once around a ring in a token ring or in an IEEE 802.5 network.

ring topology (n.) A network topology in which a series of repeaters are connected to one another with unidirectional transmission links. Connected in this way, they form a single, closed loop. Each station on the network connects to the network at a repeater.

RIP See *raster image processor* or *Routing Information Protocol.*

RISC See *reduced instruction set computing.*

RJ-11 (n.) A telephone jack with six connect-

R

ing wires that modems use when connecting to a leased line.

RLE See *run-length encoding.*

RLL See *Run-Length Limited.*

RLV (n.) Recordable laser videodisc developed by the Optical Disc Corporation. RLV is an outdated form of media used to record analog video and audio on a blank videodisc.

RMI See *Remote Method Invocation.*

RMS See *Root Mean Squared.*

roaming (n.) The use of a cellular phone to send and receive calls from locations outside a user's home calling area.

robot (n.) 1. A type of program that automatically retrieves a document anywhere on the web, along with those referenced in the web. Index-building robots retrieve a significant number of the references found in search engines. Also known as a *crawler* or a *spider.* 2. A program posing as an Internet Relay Chat (IRC) or a multiuser dungeon (MUD) user and usually performing a function.

robust (adj.) Describes a system with the ability to recover gracefully from exceptional inputs and adverse situations. A robust system is almost bulletproof.

Rock Ridge Format (n.) CD-recordable specifications for Unix that permit directory structures to be updated when new files are added to the disc. The specifications include the Rock Ridge Interchange Protocol Specification (RRIPS) and the System Use Sharing Protocol (SUSP). The SUSP extension to the ISO 9660 standard allows more than one file system ex-

tension to exist on a single CD-ROM. The RRIPS specification allows POSIX files and directories to be recorded on a CD-ROM without requiring modifications to files, such as renaming. Both of these specifications are extensions of the original ISO 9660 format for CD-ROM.

roll (n.) Lines of text or credits that typically move up the screen, often placed at the end of a video production. A roll is produced with a titler. See also *crawl.*

ROM See *read-only memory.*

root directory (n.) In MS-DOS, the top-most directory visible on a hard disk. All subdirectories are nested under this directory.

Root Mean Squared (RMS) (n.) 1. A formula used to measure the power of an audio amplifier. 2. A means of qualifying the capacity of loudspeakers.

rotating digital audio tape (R-DAT, pronounced "ARE-dat") (n.) The original name of the digital audio tape (DAT) format. Some early digital audio systems used stationary heads, as do analog tape decks. Machines with rotating heads, similar to the heads in a helical scan video recorder, became the standard.

rotational latency (n.) The time it takes for a sector on a disk to appear below the read/write head. Rotational latency is a component of access time.

rotational speed (n.) The speed at which a disk spins inside a drive, measured in revolutions per minute (rpm).

Rot-13 (n.) A form of encryption frequently used in Usenet postings. It transposes the letters *A* through *L* with the letters *M* through *Z*.

rough cut (n.) A working copy of an edited master tape.

round-trip time (RTT) (n.) The amount of delay on a network between the time a message is sent and the time the echo is returned.

route 1. (n.) A path taken by network traffic from the source to the destination. 2. (n.) A possible path from a particular host to another host or machine. 3. (v.) To send a message on a specific path to its destination.

router (n.) A protocol-dependent device that connects two or more networks at the network layer. It helps break down a large network into smaller subnetworks. Routers introduce longer delays and have lower throughput rates than bridges. Like a bridge, a router restricts local area network (LAN) traffic and passes data to a routed LAN only when it is intended for that LAN. A repeater, by contrast, indiscriminately passes along data, regardless of the intended destination. The term *router* is replacing the term *gateway*.

routing bridge (n.) A bridge in the media access control (MAC) layer that employs network-layer methods to determine the topology of a network.

Routing Information Protocol (RIP) (n.) 1. An Internet standard defined in RFC 1058, STD 34 and updated in RFC 1388. 2. A companion protocol to Internetwork Packet eXchange (IPX) for the exchange of routing information in a Novell network. RIP has been partly superseded by NetWare Link State Protocol (NLSP). This Novell protocol is not related to the Internet standard defined in RFC 1058.

routing protocol (n.) A method of distribut-

ing messages and data that uses a specific algorithm to define the path.

routing table (n.) A table stored in a router or any similar internetworking device that keeps track of routes to specific network destinations, sometimes using metrics associated with those routes.

routing update (n.) The message a router sends to indicate network accessibility and host information. Most often, routing updates are sent at regular intervals, especially after a change in network topology.

RPC See *Remote Procedure Call.*

rpm See *revolutions per minute.*

RRIPS See *Rock Ridge Format.*

RS (n.) Short for recommended standard; the Electronics Industries Association (EIA) has established many RS-x standards. Among those standards are the following:

- RS-170A is a recommended standard developed by the Electronics Industries Association (EIA) that specifies the parameters of color video signals for the NTSC format used in broadcast and in most consumer video products.

- RS-232 is a set of standards that specify three kinds of interfaces: mechanical, electrical, and functional. See figure on the following page.

- RS-232C is a serial interface standard developed by the Electronics Industries Association (EIA) for use in connecting computers and peripherals. The RS-232C port is a feature on many computing devices, and most equipment with an

R

signal designation		pin number		signal designation
secondary transmitted data	14		1	protected ground
DCE transmitter signal element timing	15		2	transmitted data
secondary received data	16		3	receive data
receiver signal element timing	17		4	request to send
	18		5	clear to send
secondary request to send	19		6	data set ready
data terminal ready	20		7	signal ground/common return
signal quality detector	21		8	received line signal detector
ring indicator	22		9	+ voltage
data signal rate selector	23		10	– voltage
DTE transmitter signal element timing	24		11	
	25		12	secondary received line signal detector
			13	secondary clear to send

RS-232 interface specifications

signal designation		pin number		signal designation
			1	shield
receive common	20		2	signaling rate indicator
	21		3	
send data	22		4	send data
send timing	23		5	send timing
receive data	24		6	receive data
request to send	25		7	request to send
receive timing	26		8	receive timing
clear to send	27		9	clear to send
terminal in service	28		10	local loopback
data mode	29		11	data mode
terminal ready	30		12	terminal ready
receiver ready	31		13	receiver ready
select standby	32		14	remote loopback
signal quality	33		15	incoming call
new signal	34		16	select frequency
terminal timing	35		17	terminal timing
standby/indicator	36		18	test mode
send common	37		19	signal ground

RS-449 interface specifications

RS-232C connector can be interfaced, as long as software drivers exist. This standard defines circuit functions and pin assignments. The physical connector comes in the traditional 25-pin version or in the newer 9-pin model. In data communications, this specification defines the interface between data terminal equipment (DTE) and data communications equipment (DCE) using serial binary data. This is the EIA equivalent of ITU-T standard V.24. The RS-232C electrical signal is unbalanced (± 5 volts to ± 12 volts), has polar non-return-to-zero (NRZ), and handles data transfer rates of up to 19.2 kilobits per second (Kbps).

• RS-232D is the Electronics Industries Association (EIA) equivalent of ITU-T standard V.28.

• RS-422 is the balanced version of RS-232, allowing longer runs and faster transmission. It operates in conjunction with RS-449, which specifies electrical characteristics of balanced circuits and their 37-pin connectors.

• RS-422A is a standard developed by the Electronics Industries Association (EIA) that defines the physical and functional features of a computer interface with communications equipment. A balanced line and a 40-pin connector are two of its features.

• RS-449 facilitates serial binary data interchange, usually in synchronous transmission modes. See figure.

• RS-530 is a standard developed by the Electronics Industries Association (EIA)

that defines a specification for the pinout of balanced interfaces, such as RS-422A with a DB-40 connector. RS-530 supersedes RS-449 and uses a 25-pin connector. It works with RS-232, but is not directly compatible.

RTF See *Rich Text Format.*

RTOS See *Real-Time Operating System.*

RTS See *request to send.*

RTT See *round-trip time.*

RTV See *Real-Time Video.*

rule of thirds (n.) An adage used in composing a scene. The premise is that a shot is most visually appealing if important events are placed at the intersection of imaginary vertical and horizontal lines that divide the screen into thirds, as in a tic-tac-toe board.

run-length encoding (RLE) (n.) A compression algorithm developed by Microsoft for eight-bit video. RLE replaces sequences, or runs, of consecutive repeated data with a single character and a descriptor for the length of the run. Long, frequent sequences of the same characters yield high compression ratios. This technique is particularly useful for encoding black-and-white images in which the data units would be single-bit pixels.

Run-Length Limited (RLL) (n.) A means of storing data on a hard disk. RLL increases the density of the data, creating more compact files.

runtime code (n.) Program code that allows playback or delivery of a program without requiring the parent application to be present.

R

Most multimedia authoring software tools give the developer the option of outputting a program with runtime code. In this format the program cannot be altered or reverse-engineered and requires less storage space than the parent application.

runtime license (n.) A type of license that permits the inclusion of runtime code in a replicated product.

S

safe zone (n.) The area that is safely within a border in the video frame, so that it does not disappear when viewed on a television screen. When a video signal is displayed on a television monitor, a significant portion of the outer frame is not visible. This could be as much as 20 percent of the frame, which "bleeds" off around the edges and disappears in overscan mode. See also *overscan*.

SALT See *Society for Applied Learning Technology*.

sampled sound (n.) A file containing data representing an event that has been digitally captured from an acoustic waveform rather than data resulting from electronic synthesis. An analog-to-digital converter is used to create an audio sample, which defines the frequency and amplitude of a sound.

sample rate (n.) The frequency at which bits of data are recorded in digitizing a sound. Normally, sound is sampled at 44.1 kHz. To reduce the amount of space required to store audio data, rates of 22.050 kHz and 11.025 kHz are used. These rates yield lower quality and are not advisable for high-fidelity music. When a sample encoded at a given bit rate is converted to a higher or a lower rate, some noise is introduced, but this is not nearly as serious as the artifacts generated in bit-rate conver-

sion from 16-bit to 8-bit audio.

sampling (n.) Measuring an analog signal periodically or obtaining the values of an analog function by regularly measuring the function. Sampling is a step in the process of converting an analog signal into a digital one. The other steps are quantizing and encoding. Sampling errors can cause aliasing effects and artifacts.

SAP See *Separate Audio Program*.

SAPI See *Scheduling Application Programming Interface* or *service access point identifier* or *Speech Application Programming Interface*.

SAS See *Statistical Analysis System*.

SASI See *Shugart Associates System Interface*.

satellite (n.) A receiver, a repeater, or a regenerator for microwave signals that is in geosynchronous orbit, typically 22 300 miles above the surface of Earth. The "footprint" at this distance is approximately one-third of the globe.

satellite transmission delay (n.) The time needed for a signal to travel from an Earth station to a satellite and to bounce back to a receiving station. For radio waves going at the speed of light (186 000 miles per second) to travel 44 600 miles, the delay is approximately a quarter of a second.

saturated color (n.) A bright color, especially red, that does not reproduce well on a video monitor because of its strong chroma component. It tends to saturate the screen with color or to bleed around the edges, producing a blurred image.

SB See *Sound Blaster.*

scalability (n.) A feature that allows content to be displayed at high resolutions on large monitors and at low resolutions on small monitors. Usually, scalable video or audio technologies allow the same data to be output over a range of quality levels, with better playback systems producing higher-quality products. A scalable font exists in a vector format and consists of a series of mathematical calculations that allow type to be resized without a loss of quality.

Scalable Processor Architecture (SPARC) (n.) An instruction set architecture that Sun Microsystems designed for its computers in 1985. SPARC implementations are based on RISC processors, usually contain 128 or 144 registers, and are pipelined for performance. Several different implementations of SPARC exist.

scalar 1. (n.) A single number, not a vector or a matrix of numbers. 2. (adj.) Describes a parallel processor that performs sequential operations that cannot be vectorized. See also *superscalar.*

scan 1. (v.) To convert a document or a graphic on paper or on film to a digital image format. 2. (n.) In relation to video terminology, the rapid journey of the scanning spot back and forth across the scan lines on the back side of a screen. 3. (n.) In laser disc technology, a mode of play in which the player skips over several disc tracks and displays occasional frames as it passes.

scan area (n.) The area to which the movement of the light source, the mirror, and the lens in a scanner is restricted.

scan contrast (n.) The range of values between white and black areas of a scanned image.

scan conversion (n.) The process of putting data into a grid format for display on a raster device. This is a necessary operation when converting from a computer's noninterlaced Video Graphics Array (VGA) format to an interlaced NTSC video source. Poor-quality scan conversion will cause annoying flicker when an NTSC monitor is used as the output from a computer video source.

scan lines (n.) The parallel lines on a video screen, from upper left to lower right, along which the scanner travels to pick up and lay down video information. NTSC systems use 525 scan lines to a screen; PAL systems use 625.

scanner (n.) 1. A hardware device that digitizes an optical image into an electronic image represented as binary data. This data can be used to create a computerized version of a photo or an illustration. A scanner can perform optical character recognition (OCR), converting printed documents to digital text files without requiring keyboard entry. 2. A lexical analyzer.

scanning frequency (n.) The number of horizontal or vertical sweeps across a video screen per second.

scanning spot (n.) In a cathode-ray tube (CRT), the beam generated by the electron gun that travels across the screen and paints a picture with red, green, and blue dots.

scan resolution (n.) The detail of an image as determined by the physical limitations of a scanner as well as by the software settings. Scan resolution is the number of dots per inch (dpi) that the scanner encodes. Higher resolutions create larger files and mean that a scanner must collect more information. It is important to scan at a resolution at least as high as that at which the image will be displayed. Screen resolution is typically only 72 dpi, whereas a standard for laser printing is 300 dpi. High-resolution film scanners can operate at levels above 2400 dpi.

scan threshold (n.) A user-defined setting on a scanner that instructs the detection circuitry to operate at a specified level of pixel brightness.

scene (n.) 1. Everything visible in a camera's viewfinder. 2. In videography, a sequence of related shots taken in a single location.

Scheduling Application Programming Interface (SAPI) (n.) Application Programming Interface (API) designed to support software that aids in time management and in arranging activities. The Microsoft SAPI works with its Schedule+ application.

SCMS See *Serial Copy Master System.*

score 1. (n.) The written notation that represents a musical composition. 2. (v.) To write a musical composition. 3. (n.) In Macromedia Director, either the representation of an animation sequence or a movie.

screen (n.) 1. The viewing area on a monitor, or any surface onto which images are projected.

2. A process used to produce gray levels. In the PostScript language, a screen may be defined by the shape of the spots on the screen, the size of the spots, and the screen angle. See figure.

a screen in PostScript

screen dump (n.) The process of saving the image that appears on a monitor as a graphics file or sending it to a printer.

screen saver (n.) A program that replaces the image displayed on a monitor with a shifting pattern that prevents a monitor from being etched by a still image. This program can be set to begin after a predetermined interval of inactivity and usually remains in effect until the mouse is moved or a key is pressed. Older monochrome monitors needed this type of protection, whereas newer color monitors are not at risk.

scrim (n.) Translucent material used in video production to defuse the intensity of light. It is placed over a lighting source to distribute the light for a scene more evenly. A scrim is usually made of silk, gauze, or lightweight screen.

script (v.) 1. To author in a high-level language by using statements in English that serve as commands. The original scripting language was HyperTalk, developed by Apple Computer.

2. (n.) A document that defines all the elements of a video or a film production, including dialog, camera position, lighting, and the set itself.

ScriptX (n.) Developed by the Kaleida alliance, an authoring and playback software system that provides cross-platform portability of multimedia software and that is a universal development tool.

scroll (v.) To cause text or graphics on the computer screen to move up or down, progressively revealing more data. Most word-processing programs allow the user to scroll with an upward or a downward arrow in a scroll bar on the side of a text field.

SCSI See *Small Computer System Interface.*

SCSI-1 See *Small Computer System Interface.*

SCSI-3 See *Small Computer System Interface.*

SCSI-2 See *Small Computer System Interface.*

SDH See *Synchronous Digital Hierarchy.*

SDK See *software developers kit.*

SDL See *Specification and Design Language.*

SDLC See *Synchronous Data Link Control.*

SDRAM See *Synchronous Dynamic RAM.*

SDSL See *Asymmetric Digital Subscriber Line.*

SDV See *Switched Digital Video.*

SEA See *self-extracting archive.*

search engine (n.) A database front end that allows a user to seek information on the Internet by keyword. Search engines may look for titles of documents, URLs, headers, or text.

search time (n.) The period required to locate specific data in a storage device.

SEC See *Single Edge Contact.*

SECAM See *Sequentiel Couleurs à Mémoire.*

secondary cache (n.) A cache between the primary cache and the main memory that is slower and larger than the primary cache. A secondary cache is typically external, accessed from the CPU.

sector (n.) On magnetic recording media, such as hard disks, each of the equal segments, or pie-shaped wedges, into which circular cylinders are logically divided. See figure.

sector layout

Secure Electronic Transaction (SET) (n.) A complex protocol for ensuring the privacy and integrity of information exchanged on the Internet.

Secure Sockets Layer (SSL) (n.) A protocol developed by Netscape and used by the HTTPS access method. SSL facilitates secure communication over the Internet. It is layered beneath application protocols (HTTP, SMTP, Telnet, FTP), and above the connection protocol (TCP/IP).

Secure Transfer Protocol (STP) (n.) A networking protocol that encrypts data.

seek time (n.) The average time required to locate specific data on a disk. It is often computed as the time necessary to move the read head to the correct track and the time needed for the disk to spin one-half of a rotation, the furthest distance from any given point on the disk.

SEG See *special effects generator.*

segment (n.) 1. In system architecture, a collection of pages in a memory management system. 2. In programming, a separate section of an executable program. 3. A portion of a video or an audio program with the first and last frames or the start and stop points identified, typically by time code. 4. An excerpt from a larger piece.

segue (n.) A transition between two scenes, events, or musical numbers in a medley. Pronounced "SEG-way."

self-diagnostics (n.) Procedures that a system uses to check its own operations and to identify errors, usually performed when power is turned on.

self-extracting archive (SEA) (n.) An executable file that automatically decompresses itself when it is run.

self-referential (adj.) Describes a data reduction technique based on redundancy within an encoded image. JPEG compression is self-referential. Intracoded frames, also known as *I-frames,* apply this concept in MPEG compression.

semiconductor (n.) 1. A material with limited conductivity. 2. An electronic component with circuitry that directs signals through gates and pathways based on the conductivity of the material. Transistors, diodes, and integrated circuits (ICs) that perform memory functions are fabricated from semiconductor materials.

sendmail (n.) The Berkeley Software Distribution (BSD) message transfer agent (MTA) that supports mail transport via TCP/IP using Simple Mail Transfer Protocol (SMTP). Sendmail is invoked via a mail user agent (MUA), such as the "mail" command.

Separate Audio Program (SAP) (n.) Audio signal that is delivered with a video program and that may be used as an alternative sound track.

sequence (n.) A progression of data, events, images, or sounds in a specified order. A *song* may be defined as a sequence of MIDI events.

sequencer (n.) 1. A computer or a controlling microprocessor that issues instructions to programmable musical instruments via MIDI. 2. The software program that enables a user to compose and edit music with a MIDI system.

Sequentiel Couleurs à Mémoire (SECAM, pronounced "SEE-cam") (n.) Patented by Henri de France in 1956, the French composite video standard adopted in Russia and in many Middle Eastern countries. The basis of operation is the sequential recording of primary colors in alternate lines. Specifications include a 50-Hz field frequency and 625 lines of image resolution. See also *National Televi-*

S

sion Standards Committee or *Phase Alternation Line.*

serial (adj.) Describes operations pertaining to a series or describes the sequential, time-based passage of data. Serial ports on computers process data one bit at a time in an orderly fashion as they pass information to or from input and output devices, such as modems and printers. The term *serial interface* implies that each bit is sent sequentially, as opposed to having groups of bits sent simultaneously in a parallel interface.

serial bus (n.) Physical interface that moves bits of data individually in a series, rather than in groups as a parallel bus does.

Serial Copy Master System (SCMS) (n.) A function on digital audio tape (DAT) consumer decks that discourages people from making multiple copies by adding data to the program of dubs that are not first-generation.

Serial Line Internet Protocol (SLIP) (n.) Defined in RFC 1055, software that transforms Internet Protocol (IP), which is typically used for Ethernet, so that it can be used on a serial line, such as a modem connected to an RS-232 serial port. SLIP appends a SLIP END character to a standard Internet datagram, allowing it to be distinguished as separate. The standard port configuration is eight data bits with no parity and with EIA or hardware flow control. No error detection is provided. Unlike Point-to-Point Protocol (PPP), a SLIP connection needs to have its IP address configuration set every time it is established.

serial port (n.) A connector on a computer in which a serial line connects peripherals that use a bitstream protocol. The usual configuration is a DB-25 connector carrying RS-232 signals. It is also known as a *comport* and is typically connected to a universal asynchronous receiver-transmitter (UART) integrated circuit (IC) that converts between serial and parallel formats.

serial VTR control (n.) Serial videotape recorder control; a computerized remote control of the functions of a VTR via a normal RS-232 or RS-422 cable connection.

serif (n.) In typography, a decorative flourish or a thin line at the top or the bottom of a letter. Fonts without serifs are called *sans serif.*

server (n.) 1. A software program that provides a service to a client. Server and client communicate via network hardware and protocols. The server may be a daemon, which constantly awaits requests from clients. Many server types are used on the Internet, including domain name system (DNS), Network File System (NFS), FTP, and Network Information Service (NIS). 2. A networked computer that provides a service for other computers connected to it. One example is a file server with a local disk; this server accommodates requests from remote clients to read and write files on that disk.

server error (n.) In relation to a request made on the Internet, an error that occurs at the server. Possible errors reported by a web server include the following:

- 500 = Internal Server Error. The server encountered an unexpected condition, which prevented it from fulfilling the request.

- 501 = Not Implemented. The server is not capable of supporting the request.

- 502 = Bad Gateway. While acting as a gateway or proxy, the server received an invalid response from the upstream server it accessed in attempting to fulfill the request.

- 503 = Service Unavailable. The server was unable to handle the request because of temporary overloading.

server-parsed HTML (SPML) (n.) Server-parsed Hypertext Markup Language; a special type of HTML file that includes server-specific commands.

server-side include (SSI) (n.) The capacity of an HTTP server to replace certain HTML tags in one HTML file with the contents of another file when the second file is sent from the server. See the appendix on HTML for more information.

service access point identifier (SAPI) (n.) The logical location where data-link layer services are provided to the network layer. Used as ISDN jargon.

service module (SM) (n.) A term sometimes used by the telephone company to describe the equipment that terminates a channel at the service point and connects a telephone line to a customer's router or some other interface.

service provider (n.) An entity that buys the services of a telecommunications supplier, advertises the service, and handles the calls.

servocontrol (n.) A device that converts weak mechanical force into greater force, which is a particularly useful function for a controlling mechanism that positions a lever, a gear, or a drive head.

session (n.) A CD-ROM recording event. If a single-session recording is closed out, no more data may be added to the disc or the index. A multisession CD-ROM XA drive will read multiple indexes, which are created when data is stored in more than one writing session on the same CD-ROM.

session layer (n.) The fifth layer in the Open Systems Interconnection (OSI) model. The session layer provides a means of communication and dialog control between end systems.

set (n.) A group of objects that share an identifiable characteristic. For every set, there is a predicate that is true only for those objects in the set.

SET See *Secure Electronic Transaction.*

set-top box (n.) Receiving equipment that sits on top of a television set and acts as an interface to a broadband network. It may be a simple device that translates cable television (CATV) frequencies, or it may be a complex digital device with signal processors that decode MPEG-2 satellite transmissions and demodulate them for viewing on an analog television set. It is expected that next-generation boxes will be addressable and capable of two-way communication.

SFX See *sound effects.*

SGML See *Standard Generalized Markup Language.*

SGRAM See *Synchronous Graphics RAM.*

shading (n.) In three-dimensional graphics, the gradation from light to dark, or the blending of colors on a surface. Flat shading is quickly computed but is of low quality. Gouraud shading provides better image quality but takes somewhat longer. Phong shading is of excellent quality but takes a long time to perform the neces-

279

sary calculations for each pixel.

shadow mask (n.) A method of construction for a display or a cathode-ray tube (CRT). The shadow mask is like a panel with very small holes situated behind the screen. The holes correspond to triad locations on the screen. The shadow mask guides the electron beams to strike one of the three phosphors in a triad. See figure.

shadow mask

shadow mask

shadow RAM (n.) Shadow random-access memory; a physical memory location in IBM-compatible computers where ROM code that is frequently accessed is stored in RAM to accelerate performance. The BIOS code that is normally executed in the slower ROM is copied, or "shadowed," in RAM to improve performance.

shallow binding (n.) A method of storing variable bindings. In this method, one can find the current value of a variable by looking at a known location rather than by searching an environment or an association list.

shared access (n.) In network technology, an access method that permits multiple stations to use the same transmission medium. Contended and explicit access are types of shared access. Compare *discrete access,* in which each station has to have a separate connection.

shared disc (n.) A CD-ROM or a laser disc cre-

ated through a joint production. A segment of the disc is allocated to each contributor.

shareware (n.) User-supported software program transferred or sold with the understanding that a fee will be paid to the program author if it meets the user's needs.

sharpen (v.) To enhance the distinction between darker and lighter pixels. Lines, edges, and other details in an image can be exaggerated through sharpening. Sharpening can enhance blemishes in the original, so it must be used judiciously. In the Adobe Photoshop program, the sharpen function appears as one of the filters with which a graphic selection may be processed.

shell (n.) The user interface. A shell is an external layer of a program that provides the user with controls and access to information. Common shells in the Unix environment are Bourne, tcsh, and Korn.

shielding (n.) A metallic foil or a braid that wraps conductors in a cable to reduce interference from magnetic fields.

Shift-click (v., n.) To hold down the Shift key while clicking the mouse. In most Macintosh and Microsoft Windows applications, this key combination allows the user to select a range of text between the original cursor position and the spot where the Shift-click takes place. It may be used to select multiple items on the desktop, as well.

Shockwave (n.) A plug-in for a web browser that allows the user to view files created with Macromedia Director. "Shocked" files may contain compressed audio, animations, and a high degree of interactivity.

short (n.) Any video or film that lasts less than

35 minutes.

shorthand (n.) A system of abbreviated communication, consistently used during "talk" sessions and in chat rooms. Examples:

/\/\/\	laughter
AFK	Away from keyboard
BCNU	Be seein' you
BRB	Be right back
BTW	By the way
CUL8R	See you later
ENQ?	Are you there?
FOAF	Friend of a friend
FYI	For your information
<g>	grin
IMHO	In my humble opinion
LTNS	Long time, no see
OIC	Oh, I see
OTOH	On the other hand
ROTFL	Rolling on the floor laughing
RTFM	Read the f****** manual
SEC	Wait a second
TIA	Thanks in advance
TMK	To my knowledge
TNX	Thanks
TTFN	Ta ta for now
WRT	With respect to

shot (n.) In production work, a continuous run with a film or a videotape recorder (VTR).

shovelware (n.) Software of little value that is added to a CD-ROM containing a primary application to fill up space in the package.

Shugart Associates System Interface (SASI, pronounced "SASS-y") (n.) The original incarnation of SCSI.

SI See *Système International d'Unités.*

sideband (n.) A narrow frequency located above or below the primary frequency in a tele-

communications signal.

SIF See *Source Image Format.*

SIG See *special interest group.*

SIGGRAPH (Pronounced "SEE-graf") (n.) Special interest group for computer graphics; an association of computer users who share an interest in graphics. SIGGRAPH is supported by the Association for Computing Machinery (ACM) and holds an annual conference that is well attended by designers, educators, and software-hardware developers in the field of graphics.

Signaling System 7 (SS7) (n.) Out-of-band (OOB) signaling system that uses high-speed, circuit-switched connections to process remote database interactions and provide fast call setup. SS7 makes enhanced telephony features available, such as call forwarding, caller ID, and call waiting. It plays an integral role in the deployment of ISDN. The SS7 protocol consists of the following four subprotocols:

1. Message Transfer Part (MTP), which provides functions for basic routing of signaling messages between signaling points.
2. Signaling Connection Control Part (SCCP), which provides additional routing and management functions for transfer of messages other than call setup between signaling points.
3. ISDN User Part (ISUP), which provides for transfer of call setup signaling information between signaling points.
4. Transaction Capabilities Application Part (TCAP), which provides for transfer of non-circuit-related information between signaling points.

signal switching point (SSP) (n.) A telephone company switch that recognizes Intelligent

S

Network calls and routes them according to information provided by a database.

signal-to-noise (S/N) (adj.) Describes the ratio between the strength of an audio or a video signal and the measurable amount of noise, or the undesirable interference, it has picked up in transfer. Higher S/N ratios mean higher-quality signals. Each generation of a tape dub has a lower S/N ratio. Digital media can achieve much higher S/N ratios than analog media can, and degradation does not occur in digital copies.

signal transfer point (STP) (n.) The packet switch in the Common Channel Interoffice Signaling (CCIS) system. The CCIS is a packet-switched telephone network that converts dialed digits into data, operating at 4.8 kilobits per second (Kbps).

signature (n.) 1. Information about the sender of an electronic mail message or a news posting appended at the end of an email message. A signature may include an ASCII logo or a memorable quote. 2. In programming, a means of separating subtyping and inheritance. The concept is similar to that of abstract base classes, but signatures have their own hierarchy and can be applied to compiled classes.

silicon (n.) A nonmetallic element used in the semiconductor industry as a substrate for multiple layers of material on which electrical circuits are created. Silicon begins as a crystal and grows to form a cylindrical "log," which is sliced into thin sections (typically 1/40 inch thick) to create bare wafers.

silicon-based life form (n.) Jargon for a very intelligent machine based on silicon chips. Compare *carbon-based life form*.

SIMD See *single instruction, multiple data*.

SIMM See *single in-line memory module*.

Simple Internet Protocol Plus (SIPP) (n.) A proposed standard for IP version 6 (IPv6), also known as IP Next Generation (IPng). One of the problems addressed by this new architecture is the need for more Internet addresses. IPv6 is defined in RFC 1752.

Simple Mail Transfer Protocol (SMTP) (n.) A server-to-server protocol used to transfer email between computers. SMTP is defined in RFC 821, STD 10. It is not the same protocol used to read messages sent through email.

Simple Management Protocol (SMP) (n.) A popular standard for network management.

Simple Network Management Protocol (SNMP) (n.) The Internet standard protocol used to manage nodes on an Internet Protocol (IP) network. SNMP is defined in RFC 1157, STD 15. SNMP version 2 (SNMP v2) is a revision of SNMP that improves security, performance, confidentiality, and communication between managers. The main components are defined in RFCs 1441 through 1452.

Simple Network Paging Protocol (SNPP) (n.) A standard for sending one-way and two-way wireless messages to pagers. SNPP is defined in RFC 1861. It creates a link between the Internet and a Telocator Alphanumeric Protocol (TAP) paging terminal.

simple profile (n.) Streams of MPEG that use only intracoded frames (I-frames) and predictive-coded frames (P-frames), employing less buffer memory for decoding. Coding with a simple profile is less efficient than coding with bidirectionally predictive frames (B-frames).

See also *MPEG frame type.*

simplex (n.) One-way transmission with the capacity either to send or to receive but not to do both at once.

simulated annealing (n.) A process based on successive update steps in which the length of each update step is proportional to an arbitrarily set parameter that is analogous to the role of a temperature. Simulated annealing may be applied to any minimization or learning process, and the steps may be either random or deterministic. As in the annealing of metals, the temperature is highest in the early stages of the process, which accelerates minimization or learning, and it is reduced for increased stability in later steps.

simulation (n.) The use of images and sound to represent a situation or an event somewhat realistically. The simulation mode is useful in training applications, enabling users to learn how to operate equipment. New techniques and technologies have evolved rapidly for simulating virtual reality (VR) with three-dimensional models, walk-throughs, and fly-bys.

single-attached (adj.) Connected to only one of the two rings of a Fiber Distributed Data Interface (FDDI) network. A host computer is typically connected in this fashion, whereas routers and concentrators are typically dual-attached.

Single Edge Contact (SEC) (n.) The housing cartridge for a Pentium II daughterboard that plugs into a card-edge processor slot on the motherboard. The standard Pentium II requires a 242-pin slot (Slot 1), while the Zeon fits in a 330-pin slot (Slot 2). Slot 1 is referred to as SEC-242, and Slot 2 is referred to as SEC-330.

single-ended (adj.) Describes an electrical connection with one hot wire and a second ground wire. In a *differential connection,* by contrast, a second hot wire carries an inverted version of the original signal.

single inheritance (n.) A way in which inheritance is resisted when a subclass may be derived from only one parent in an object-oriented language.

single in-line memory module (SIMM, pronounced "SIM") (n.) A high-density DRAM package with several plastic leaded chip carriers (PLCCs) connected to a single printed circuit board.

single in-line package (SIP) (n.) A form factor for a board-level component, such as a transistor whose connections all extend from one side.

single-instruction, multiple-data (SIMD) (n.) Parallel processing architecture in which one instruction operates on several pieces of data at once.

single large expensive disk (SLED) (n.) One high-capacity hard drive, as opposed to a redundant arrays of independent disks (RAID).

Single-Line Digital Subscriber Line (SDSL) (n.) See *Asymmetric Digital Subscriber Line.*

single-mode fiber (n.) A type of optical fiber that supports a single mode of light propagation above a cutoff wavelength. The core diameter is typically 5 to 10 mm, and transmission rates approach 100 GHz per kilometer.

SIP See *single in-line package.*

SIPP See *Simple Internet Protocol Plus.*

283

SIT See *StuffIt*.

site (n.) A web address or any Internet location where information can be viewed or accessed with a browser or a client application. A home page is usually the access point to a web site.

16-bit bus (n.) A type of data bus that can exchange 16 bits of data at a time with a microcomputer's processor or memory.

16-bit color (n.) A video monitor setting that allocates five bits of memory apiece to the red and the blue components of each pixel and six bits to the green component, providing up to 65 536 different colors at once.

16:9 (n.) An aspect ratio of the horizontal size of an image to the vertical size. The 16:9 ratio has been adopted for the high-definition television (HDTV) video format.

skinny DIP (Skinny dual in-line package) (n.) Jargon for a 24- or 28-position switch with a 0.3-inch row-to-row centerline.

skylight (n.) In videography, a clear glass filter that absorbs ultraviolet (UV) light and reduces haze. A skylight is often used as a lens protector.

slate (n.) A term derived from the movie industry, in which a slate board is held up to indicate the beginning of a new "take." In a recording studio, the slate usually consists of the engineer's voice, which identifies the take number, and an accompanying log sheet with the title, duration, and other particulars about the take.

slave (n.) 1. In computing, a secondary unit, such as a disk drive, that is controlled by the master device or system. 2. A videotape machine whose transport system is controlled by

a source deck or other master device.

SLED See *single large expensive disk*.

SLIP See *Serial Line Internet Protocol*.

slot mask (n.) A method of guiding electron beams in a picture. It is made of vertical wires that create the slots. The dot pitch in a slot mask is the space between the slots.

slow motion (n.) Display of frames in forward or in reverse at a slower-than-normal rate.

SM See *service module*.

Small Computer System Interface (SCSI, pronounced "SKUH-zee") (n.) An independent standard for a system-level interface between computers and such peripherals as hard disks, CD-ROMs, printers, and scanners. SCSI can connect a number of devices to a single controller on the computer's bus. All SCSI chains require termination at both ends, and devices on a SCSI chain must be set to different ID numbers. SCSI connections normally use single-ended drivers, as opposed to differential drivers. Single-ended SCSI can support up to six meters of cable, whereas differential SCSI can support up to 25 meters. Apple Computer established the SCSI interface in 1984 on the Macintosh computer. It was developed by Shugart Associates, which later became Seagate, so SCSI was originally called *Shugart Associates System Interface (SASI)* before it became an ANSI standard in 1986. The original standard is now called *SCSI-1* to distinguish it from SCSI-2 and SCSI-3, which include specifications for wide SCSI and fast SCSI, described in the paragraphs below.

- SCSI-1: Small Computer System Interface version 1; an eight-bit-wide parallel bus used to connect disk drives and all types of peripherals to an IBM-compatible PC or to a Macintosh. The origins of SCSI are found in the selector channel architecture designed by IBM for its System/360 computers. In 1981, Shugart Associates adapted it and called it the *Shugart Associates Systems Interface (SASI)*. By 1984 Apple Computer had incorporated it in the Macintosh. In 1986, ANSI released the first version of the SCSI standard. That original version is now called *SCSI-1*.

SCSI supports hard disk drives, CD-ROM drives, optical storage units, scanners, high-speed printers, and Group 4 fax machines. Up to eight devices can share the bus, including the host controller. Each device on the bus is manually assigned a SCSI ID number between 0 and 7 by means of a switch or jumper. The number of devices supported per bus is limited by the width of the data bus. A SCSI-1 chain may include eight devices, whereas a 16-bit-wide SCSI-2 or SCSI-3 bus may support up to 16 devices.

The SCSI adapter in the host PC is normally assigned SCSI ID 7, because the highest number wins a bus arbitration. Peripherals are usually assigned IDs starting at 0. Each end of a SCSI bus must be terminated with a resistor. Other devices on the SCSI bus must not be terminated.

Macintosh computers and peripherals are connected by either DB-25 or DB-50 SCSI connectors. IBM-compatible PCs use the RJ-21 Centronics-style 50-pin connector for SCSI-1 devices. To manage peripherals on a SCSI bus, Advanced SCSI Programming Interface (ASPI) software is used in the IBM PC environment. SCSI supports multiple host adapters on each bus, so that two computers may be con-

---

Types of SCSI Connectors

Connector End P=male; S=female	Description
RC-50 P/S	full-pitch Centronic 50-pin
DB-25 P/S	full-pitch D-Sub 25-pin
DB-50 P/S	full-pitch D-Sub 50-pin
RCII-50 P/S	Centronic half-pitch micro connector 50-pin
DBII-50 P/S	D-Sub half-pitch micro connector 50-pin
RC3-68 P/S	Centronic half-pitch micro connector 68-pin
DB3-68 P/S	D-Sub half-pitch micro connector 68-pin

---

nected to the same SCSI bus and can control the same peripheral.

SCSI data transfers may be either asynchronous or synchronous. In the asynchronous mode there is a handshake for each transferred byte, and the maximum data transfer rate is about two megabits per second (Mbps). In the synchronous mode data flows at a preset data rate, which is commonly five Mbps for SCSI-1 devices. The initiator and the target peripheral must support synchronous transfers at the same speed.

- SCSI-2: Small Computer System Interface version 2; enhancement to the SCSI-1 specification that delivers more compatibility among devices and faster data transfer rates. *Fast SCSI* is a subset of SCSI-2 and supports transfer rates of up to 10 megabits per second (Mbps), double the five-Mbps rate of SCSI-1 on an eight-bit-wide bus. The SCSI-2 specification defines five device types not covered by SCSI-1.

The original eight-bit-wide SCSI-1 bus is called *narrow SCSI*. The connectors for the

S

285

16-bit-wide bus differs from the SCSI-1 connector. A cable with 50-pin Micro-D-type connectors is specified for 16-bit transfers. For the 32-bit bus, or *wide SCSI,* a 68-pin P-type connector is specified. The SCSI-2 bus requires an odd parity bit for every eight data bits, whereas parity was optional in SCSI-1.

A fast, wide SCSI bus can support data transfer at up to 40 Mbps, although actual transfer rates from a disk drive are typically much lower, depending on the speed of the drive. SCSI-2 controllers support different speeds of transfer to each SCSI device on the bus, so both SCSI-1 and SCSI-2 devices can coexist. An extension of SCSI-2 called *ultra SCSI* doubles the transfer speed of fast SCSI to allow

SCSI connectors—68-pin to 50-pin conversion

transfer rates of 20 Mbps on an eight-bit connection and 40 Mbps on a 16-bit connection.

The following is a comparison of maximum theoretical data transfer rates for hard drive interfaces. Actual throughput is much slower than these maximum rates, depending on drive access times and other factors in each computer system.

Disk Interface	Maximum Transfer Rate
SCSI-1 (asynchronous)	2 Mbps
SCSI-1 (synchronous)	5 Mbps
SCSI-2 fast	10 Mbps
SCSI-2 16-bit-wide	10 Mbps
SCSI-2 fast and 16-bit-wide	20 Mbps
SCSI-2 32-bit-wide	20 Mbps
SCSI-2 fast and 32-bit-wide	40 Mbps

When SCSI-2 and SCSI-3 devices first connect asynchronously, they handshake in eight-bit narrow mode to ensure that data will transfer properly. The initiator and target then negotiate the maximum mutual capabilities.

- SCSI-3: Small Computer System Interface version 3; enhancement to SCSI-2 that supports up to 32 devices per bus with 16-bit transfers over a P-cable (using a 68-pin Micro-D-type connector). A subset of SCSI-3 called *fast-20* supports the transfer of data at up to 20 megabits per second (Mbps) over the original eight-bit "narrow" bus and up to 40 Mbps over a 16-bit-wide P-cable. Fast-20 controllers allow both fast and slow devices on the same bus. Because of the higher transfer rate, cables should not exceed 3 meters in length for single-ended SCSI buses, about half the distance allowed in SCSI-2 connections. For a differential bus the maximum length is 25 meters, which is the same as for SCSI-2. SCSI-2 has largely replaced SCSI-1, but SCSI-3 is not as prevalent.

SCSI-3 features a serial option using a six-pin connector. *Serial SCSI* supports various types of media, including fiber and twisted pairs for distances of up to a kilometer. The serial version offers a structured protocol model, faster data transfer, longer cables, and more device classes. It increases to 32 the number of devices that may share a bus. Embedding clock information in the serial data stream eliminates signal delay problems. SCSI-3 is a combination of separate standards defined by separate groups, as listed in the SCSI-3 table.

SCSI-3 Standards

Standard Number	Description
X3T9.2/9–10	SCSI-3 Parallel Interface
X3T9.2/91–11	SCSI-3 Interlocked Protocol
X3T9.2/91–13R2	SCSI-3 Generic Packetized Protocol (GPP)
X3T9.2/91–189	SCSI-3 Serial Bus Protocol (SBP)
X3T9.2/92–079	SCSI-3 Architecture Model
X3T9.2/92–103	SCSI-3 Fiber Channel Protocol (GPP & SBP)
X3T9.2/92–105	SCSI-3 Core Commands
X3T9.2/92–106	SCSI-3 Block Commands
X3T9.2/92–107	SCSI-3 Stream Commands
X3T9.2/92–108	SCSI-3 Graphic Commands
X3T9.2/92–109	SCSI-3 Medium Changer Commands
X3T9.2/92–141	SCSI-3 Queuing Model

small-office/home-office (soho) (adj.) Describes the market for a general level of features and sophistication in computers and peripherals.

Smalltalk (n.) An early object-oriented pro-gramming (OOP) system developed in 1972 by the Xerox PARC Software Concepts Group, led by Alan Kay. The system components are an interpreted language, a programming environment, and an object library. Innovations include a windowing system and a mouse. Smalltalk does not have multiple inheritance, so each class may have only one superclass.

smart card (n.) A device resembling a credit card with an embedded integrated circuit (IC) for storing data. Smart cards have been used to store medical and financial records, and a wide range of applications exist, including user profiles for network access worldwide.

SmartDrive (n.) Developed by Microsoft, a disk-caching program that speeds up disk access. A one-megabyte (MB) cache is usually adequate for most systems. At the prompt in DOS, one may type "SMARTDRV /S" to determine the size of the disk cache, to receive a report on cache hits, and to learn which drives are being cached. The hit-and-miss statistics help gauge the effectiveness of SmartDrive settings. A score in the high 80s shows that SmartDrive is well configured. A percentage below 80 indicates that the cache size should be increased. The SMARTDRV line in the autoexec.bat file may be edited to increase both the InitCacheSize and the WinCacheSize parameters. SmartDrive Monitor is an undocumented Windows program included with DOS 6.0 for managing the disk cache.

smart hub (n.) A concentrator for twisted-pair Ethernet or for ARCnets. Smart hub has management features that allow an administrator to configure a network and monitor performance.

SMDS See *switched multimegabit data service.*

SME See *subject matter expert.*

SMF See *Standard MIDI File.*

SMP See *Simple Management Protocol.* May also refer to *Symbolic Manipulation Program* or *symmetrical multiprocessing.*

SMPTE See *Society of Motion Picture and Television Engineers.*

SMR See *Specialized Mobile Radio.*

SMS See *System Management Server.*

SMTP See *Simple Mail Transfer Protocol.*

S/N See *signal-to-noise.*

SNA See *Systems Network Architecture.*

snail mail (n.) Letters sent via the U.S. postal service.

SND (n.) A Macintosh audio file format used for system sounds, as well as for recording and playback of audio.

sneakernet (n.) Jargon for transferring electronic information by physically carrying media from one machine to another. Depending on the type of media and the amount of data, using sneakernet may be more efficient than using a network.

sniffer (n.) A network monitoring tool that captures and decodes data packets to indicate protocol data. A scrap of JavaScript code that identifies the client program in use is called a *browser sniffer.*

SNMP See *Simple Network Management Protocol.*

SNPP See *Simple Network Paging Protocol.*

Society for Applied Learning Technology (SALT) (n.) An association of educators and instructional designers. SALT promotes technology in education.

Society of Motion Picture and Television Engineers (SMPTE) 1. (n.) A professional engineering society that works to develop standards for motion picture and television equipment. 2. (adj.) Describes the SMPTE time code standard implemented in professional video-editing systems. See also *time code.*

socket (n.) The means of creating a virtual connection between processes in a Unix system. Sockets provide the interface with network communication facilities. They can be of two types: the bidirectional stream or the fixed-length, destination-addressed datagram. A socket has a socket address, consisting of a port number and the local host's network address.

software (n.) The part of a computing system that is not hardware. A distinction may be made between system software and application software, or programs. *System software* typically includes an operating system that controls other programs; user environment software, such as a command line interpreter, a window system, and a desktop; tools for building other programs, such as assemblers, compilers, linkers, libraries, interpreters, cross-reference generators, and version control; debugging, profiling, and monitoring tools; and utility programs for sorting, printing, editing, and so forth. *Application programs* perform functions, such as accounting or designing. Such software includes both source code written by humans and executable machine code produced by assemblers or compilers. It does not usually include the data processed by programs, unless this is in a format such as multimedia that depends on the use of computers for its presentation.

software developers kit (SDK) (n.) Software that enables an application or a product to be integrated with systems, hardware, and other software.

software handshaking (n.) The transmission of data between two devices to establish their connection. It may involve sending Ctrl-S and Ctrl-Q characters to stop and to start transmission over an RS-232 connection.

software interrupt (n.) A suspension of processing caused by a machine language operation code rather than by a hardware event. It causes the processor to store the current state, store identifying information about the interrupt, and pass processor control to a first-level interrupt handler. A *trap* is similar, but it is caused by an unexpected software condition rather than by an intentional instruction.

soho See *small-office/home-office.*

Solaris (n.) Developed by Sun Microsystems, a common user environment that includes the Unix operating system and an X11-based window system. Solaris 2.x includes the SunOS 5.x version of Unix, OpenWindows 3.x, and tooltalk.

solid-state laser (n.) Light-emitting diode (LED) whose active medium is glass or crystal.

SONET See *Synchronous Optical Network.*

Sony 9-pin (n.) Standard connector used for serial machine control of professional videotape and audio tape transports. The term refers to the DB-9 connector or to the port on a device.

Sony/Philips Digital Interface Format (s/pdif, pronounced "SPID-if") (n.) A standard for interconnecting stereo digital audio devices, similar to the Audio Engineering Society/European Broadcast Union (AES/EBU) but with lower-grade wiring. The specification is referred to as *IEC 958 Type 11.*

SOP See *standard operating procedures.*

sort (v.) To arrange objects in a certain order. In a database the objects consist of one or more fields or members. One of the fields is the designated *sort key,* which means that the records will be ordered according to the values of that field.

Sound Blaster (SB) 1. (n.) Developed by Creative Labs, an audio card for IBM-compatible computers that has become a de facto standard in the industry. 2. (adj.) Describes compatibility with SB software drivers, setup instructions, and configuration parameters.

Sound Blaster AWE32 (n.) Sound Blaster Advanced WavEffect 32; common 16-bit sound card with the EMU8000 music synthesizer circuitry. The card features the Advanced Signal Processor, one megabyte (MB) of General MIDI samples, and 512 kilobytes (KB) of DRAM for additional samples. It supports CD-ROM drives by Creative Labs, Mitsumi, and Sony. It also supports General MIDI, Roland GS, and Sound Canvas MT-32 emulation.

sound card (n.) A circuit board added to the motherboard of a microcomputer. A sound card generates audio signals and provides output to headphones or to external speakers.

sound effects (SFX) (n.) Imported sounds, prerecorded and incorporated into a video sound track or an audio mix to enhance it.

S

sound pressure level (SPL) (n.) The amplitude of an audio waveform in the atmosphere.

Sound Recorder (n.) An applet, available in Microsoft Windows, that creates .wav audio files. The quality of the audio depends on the quality of the microphone used and the sampling circuitry on the installed sound card. To ensure the highest signal-to-noise (S/N) ratio, audio recordings should always be made by adjusting the input levels so that the meters reach, but do not exceed, peak levels. In digital recording, little headroom exists beyond the peak level, and input levels that are too hot will cause ugly distortion.

sound track (n.) The audio recording associated with a movie or a videotape production.

source code (n.) The text in which a computer program is written. It is then compiled into machine code which a processor can execute.

Source Image Format (SIF, pronounced "SIFF") (n.) A video parameter that specifies a resolution of 352 x 240 pixels at 30 Hz.

spam (v.) 1. To post undesirable messages to Usenet newsgroups or mailing lists. 2. To send unsolicited email indiscriminately to promote a product or a service, similar to junk mail in the U.S. postal service.

SPARC See *Scalable Processor Architecture.*

SPARCStation (n.) Scalable Processor Architecture Station; a workstation made by Sun Microsystems based on SPARC.

spatial resolution (n.) In graphic or video display, the number of lines or dots used to define an image. When it stands by itself, the word *resolution* means spatial resolution, rather than color-based or time-based resolution.

spawn (v.) To create a child process in a multitasking operating system.

s/pdif See *Sony/Philips Digital Interface Format.*

special effects generator (SEG) (n.) Any video signal processor that changes the way images appear on screen.

special interest group (SIG, pronounced "sig") (n.) A portion of the membership of a professional organization whose members have a particular interest in a certain topic or a narrow area of pursuit that is not addressed in general meetings of the organization. SIG members are self-selected, and they often meet outside of the regular program meetings of the parent organization.

Specialized Mobile Radio (SMR) (n.) A public telephone network service for private businesses. SMR uses mobile radiotelephones and base stations. It has been used successfully to dispatch truck and taxi fleets. Advances in digital technology make SMR a useful voice and data transmission technology because SMR signals reach approximately 25 times farther than cellular telephone signals.

Specification and Design Language (SDL) (n.) A specification and description of the behavior of telecommunications systems, defined by the ITU-T as Recommendation Z100. The area of application also includes process control and realtime applications. SDL provides a Graphic Representation (SDL/GR) and a textual Phrase Representation (SDL/PR), which are equivalent representations of the same semantics.

SPECint92 (n.) A benchmark derived from the results of a set of integer benchmarks.

SPECint92 is used to estimate the performance of integer code on a single-tasking computer.

spectrum (n.) A continuous range of frequencies.

speculative evaluation (n.) A process employed in parallel processing in which an evaluation is begun before it is needed. It can reduce overall program run time by making some results available earlier than they would be otherwise.

speculative execution (n.) A process that allows a superscalar processor to keep its functional units busy by executing instructions before they are needed. The Intel P6 uses speculative execution. See also *branch prediction*.

Speech Application Programming Interface (SAPI) (n.) A standard Microsoft API for speech synthesis and speech recognition in Windows 95. It allows developers to test speech software.

speech recognition See *voice recognition*.

speech synthesizer (n.) A device that produces human speech sounds from data in another form, such as a text file.

speech transmission index (STI) (n.) On a scale of 0 to 1.0, a measurement of how well a message is understood at the receiving end of a telecommunications link. A score of 1.0 is the best possible reception and clarity.

spider (n.) An automated agent or bot that searches the web for information. Search engines use a spider to locate and catalog new sites.

spike (n.) Abnormally high, brief voltage fluctuation that can occur on an ordinary electrical line providing power to a facility. Spikes can damage electrical circuits and components.

spindle synchronization (n.) A feature of some hard disk drives in which the rotational position of their spindles is synchronized. It is implemented in the RAID 3 format.

SPL See *sound pressure level*.

splice (v.) In relation to audio and video, to cut cleanly and bind together pieces of magnetic tape from different sources in order to achieve a seamless whole. Before digital media, splicing was the only way to edit audio and video content. Modern digital editing equipment allows the user to choose segments from various sources instantly, paste them together in memory, and change the result if it is not desirable. See figure.

splicing block for audio tape

spline (n.) A smooth curve that interpolates multiple points and that is defined by several other curves, or polynomials. The term originally described the flexible rod used in drafting to draw a curved line.

spline-based modeling (n.) The use of Bezier curves in three-dimensional modeling to bend shapes more smoothly and realistically.

split edit (n.) In postproduction, an edit of only the audio or video portion of a program, without changing the other element in the original source.

splitter (n.) A device that accepts one signal and provides multiple ports through which it may be accessed.

SPML See *server-parsed HTML.*

spool (n.) <u>S</u>imultaneous <u>p</u>eripheral <u>o</u>perations <u>online</u>; the temporary storage of data in a buffer to reduce delays in processing or printing.

spreadsheet (n.) A computer-generated worksheet consisting of columns and rows of numbers, letters, or other symbols. Formulas can be applied to a group of entries, and the results can be calculated automatically. Spreadsheets can be used for schedules, records of resources, accounting ledgers, balance sheets, grade books, and many other creative purposes.

sprite (n.) In Macromedia Director, a graphics element that can be manipulated on screen as an object.

SQL See *Structured Query Language.*

square-pixel digitizing (n.) Converting an image from a television signal, whose aspect ratio differs from that of a computer monitor, and correcting for distortion that would result from squeezing and cropping rectangular pixels. NTSC signals would be distorted up to 11 percent if corrections, or square pixels, were not interpolated from the rectangular pixels.

square wave (n.) A regular pulse with extremely fast rise and fall times. Each half of the wave cycle is either positive or negative, so it may be interpreted as a binary signal with on and off states.

squirt the bird (v.) Jargon meaning to direct a signal toward a telecommunications satellite.

SRAM See *Static RAM.*

SSI See *server-side include.*

SSL See *Secure Sockets Layer.*

SSP See *signal switching point.*

SS7 See *Signaling System 7.*

stack (n.) 1. In programming, a data structure for storing items that are intended to be accessed in last-in-first-out (LIFO) order. Most processors include support for stacks in their instruction set architectures. Stacks are commonly used to store subroutine arguments and return addresses. 2. In the Apple HyperCard program, a set of cards, or frames, with programmed HyperScripts.

stack overflow (n.) In programming, an error resulting from an attempt to push more items onto a stack than the allocated space allows.

stack pointer (n.) A variable that points to the top of a stack. If the stack is full, the pointer indicates the most recently pushed-on item. If the stack is empty, the pointer indicates the first empty location, which is where the next item will be placed.

stairstepping (n.) The uneven representation of diagonal lines or curves on a computer screen because pixels form only vertical and horizontal rows on a monitor at 72 dpi. Stairstepping, which manifests itself as jagged lines, can be corrected to a degree with antialiasing software.

stale pointer bug (n.) In programming, a class of subtle programming errors resulting from code that performs dynamic allocation of memory blocks. If several pointers address a block of storage and if that storage is freed or reallocated, it may lead to intermittent lossage.

The condition does not exist in higher-level languages with a garbage collector.

stamper (n.) A perfectly flat final mastering disc used to mold replicas.

stand-alone (adj.) 1. Describes a multimedia program that runs without needing the application that created it and that requires no other software support. 2. Describes equipment, such as an interactive kiosk, that is independent of a larger network.

standard (n.) A uniform protocol that defines communication between devices. Standards are established to reduce incompatibility between competitive technologies. They are often developed by a committee belonging to an industry association, such as the ISO. The Electronics Industries Association (EIA) sets RS standards. ANSI standards for data communications usually begin with the letter *X,* as in X3.4-1967, the ASCII code standard. The ITU-T, formerly known as the CCITT, publishes recommendations, such as the V.x series, rather than standards. These recommendations refer to data transfer over telephone lines.

Standard Generalized Markup Language (SGML) (n.) A generic markup language for representing documents. In SGML, information is treated separately from the manner in which it is presented. SGML is an ISO standard.

Standard MIDI File (SMF) (n.) Standard Musical Instrument Digital Interface File; the format universally accepted by musical applications for a stream of MIDI data in a file.

standard operating procedures (SOP, pronounced "ess-oh-PEE") (n.) Production processes that everyone follows in developing a multimedia project. This standardization allows more than one person to contribute to the production of graphics, audio, video and code. It also may specify such things as file name conventions and settings for production equipment.

standard tape interconnect (STI) (n.) A standard protocol for connecting tape formatters and controllers.

star coupler (n.) Passive device that distributes data from one or several input optical fibers to a greater number of output optical fibers.

start bit (n.) The initial bit of a transmitted character on a serial line. If the condition of a line is normally at logical 0 when no data is being transmitted, the start bit is at logical 1.

star topology (n.) A method of connecting devices in a local area network (LAN) that routes all communications through the central hub or the controller. See also *network topology.*

startup (n.) The mode in which a computer begins operation when it is switched on. The operating system, drivers, and selected applications are loaded on startup.

state (n.) The properties of an object that characterize its current condition.

Static RAM (SRAM, pronounced "ESS-ram") (n.) Static random-access memory; memory that retains a static value as long as power is supplied, unlike Dynamic RAM (DRAM), which must be refreshed regularly. In contrast to ROM, SRAM will lose its contents when the power is switched off. Usually faster than DRAM, SRAM is used where speed is critical, such as in cache memory applications.

station (n.) Data terminal equipment (DTE), such as a user device on a network node, that sends and receives messages on a data link.

Statistical Analysis System (SAS, pronounced "SASS") (n.) A statistical and matrix-handling language.

STD See *subscriber trunk dialing*.

STD (n.) A standard based on a Request For Comments (RFC) that has been adopted by the Internet Architecture Board (IAB). STD citations are listed here in order, with title, date issued, and RFC number.

- STD 01: Internet official protocol standards, 1998 (RFC 2400).
- STD 02: Assigned numbers, 1994 (RFC 1700).
- STD 03: Host requirements, 1989 (RFC 1122, RFC 1123).
- STD 04: Gateway requirements, 1987 (RFC 1009).
- STD 05: Internet Protocol, 1981 (RFC 0791, RFC 792, RFC 0919, RFC 0922, RFC 0950, RFC 1112).
- STD 06: User Datagram Protocol, 1980 (RFC 0768).
- STD 07: Transmission Control Protocol, 1981 (RFC 0793).
- STD 08: Telnet Protocol, 1983 (RFC 0854, RFC 0855).
- STD 09: File transfer protocol, 1985 (RFC 0959).
- STD 10: SMTP service extensions, 1995 (RFC 1869).
- STD 11: SMTP service extension for message size declaration, 1995 (RFC 1870).
- STD 12: Network Time Protocol, 1989 (RFC 1119).
- STD 13: Domain name system, 1987 (RFC 1034, RFC 1035).
- STD 14: Mail routing and the domain system, 1986 (RFC 0974).
- STD 15: Simple Network Management Protocol (SNMP), 1990 (RFC 1157).
- STD 16: Structure of management information, 1990 (RFC 1155, RFC 1212).
- STD 17: Management information base, 1991 (RFC 1213).
- STD 18: Exterior Gateway Protocol, 1984 (RFC 0904).
- STD 19: NetBIOS Service Protocols, 1987 (RFC 1001, RFC 1002).
- STD 20: Echo Protocol, 1983 (RFC 0862).
- STD 21: Discard Protocol, 1983 (RFC 0863).
- STD 22: Character Generator Protocol, 1983 (RFC 0864).
- STD 23: Quote of the Day Protocol, 1983 (RFC 0865).
- STD 24: Active Users Protocol, 1983 (RFC 0866).
- STD 25: Daytime Protocol, 1983 (RFC 0867).
- STD 26: Time Server Protocol, 1983 (RFC 0868).
- STD 27: Binary transmission Telnet option, 1983 (RFC 0856).
- STD 28: Echo Telnet option, 1983 (RFC 0857).
- STD 29: Suppress go ahead Telnet option, 1983 (RFC 0858).
- STD 30: Status Telnet option, 1983 (RFC 0859).
- STD 31: Timing mark Telnet option, 1983 (RFC 0860).
- STD 32: Extended options list Telnet option, 1983 (RFC 0861).
- STD 33: Trivial File Transfer Protocol, 1992 (RFC 1350).
- STD 34: Routing Information Protocol, 1988 (RFC 1058).
- STD 35: ISO transport service on top of the TCP version 3, 1978 (RFC 1006).

- STD 36: Transmission of IP and ARP over FDDI Networks, 1993 (RFC 1390).
- STD 37: Ethernet Address Resolution Protocol, 1982 (RFC 0826).
- STD 38: Reverse Address Resolution Protocol, 1984 (RFC 0903).
- STD 39: Interface Message Processor (under revision), 1981.
- STD 40: Host Access Protocol specification, 1993 (RFC 1221).
- STD 41: Transmission of IP datagrams over Ethernet networks, 1984 (RFC 0894).
- STD 42: Transmission of IP datagrams over experimental Ethernet networks, 1984 (RFC 0895).
- STD 43: Transmission of IP datagrams over IEEE 802 networks, 1993 (RFC 1042).
- STD 44: DCN (disconnect frame) Local-Network Protocols, 1993 (RFC 0891).
- STD 45: Internet Protocol on network system's HYPERchannel protocol specification, 1993 (RFC 1044).
- STD 46: Transmitting IP traffic over ARCnets, 1993 (RFC 1201).
- STD 47: Transmission of IP datagrams over serial lines: SLIP, 1993 (RFC 1055).
- STD 48: Transmission of IP datagrams over NetBIOS networks, 1993 (RFC 1088).
- STD 49: Transmission of 802.2 packets over IPX networks, 1993 (RFC 1132).
- STD 50: Definitions of managed objects for the Ethernet-like interface types, 1994 (RFC 1643).
- STD 51: Point-to-Point Protocol (PPP), 1994 (RFC 1661, RFC 1662).
- STD 52: Transmission of IP datagrams over SMDS, 1991 (RFC 1209).
- STD 53: Post Office Protocol (POP) version 3, 1996 (RFC 1939).
- STD 54: OSPF version 2, 1998 (RFC 2328).
- STD 55: Multiprotocol interconnect over frame relay, 1998 (RFC 2427).
- STD 56: RIP version 2, 1998 (RFC 2453).

step frame (n.) A function in video playback equipment that permits forward or reverse movement one frame at a time.

step time (n.) A method of recording discrete MIDI events one by one for later playback as a continuous stream, rather than recording in real time at a set tempo.

stereo (adj.) Describes sound emanating from two distinct sources, facilitating spatial placement of individual sounds in a panorama.

stereo chorusing See *chorus*.

STI See *speech transmission index* or *standard tape interconnect*.

still frame 1. (n.) A single frame of film or video displayed on a monitor as a static image. 2. (adj., still-frame) Describes graphical or textual information recorded on a single frame and intended to be displayed as a motionless image.

STM See *synchronous transfer mode*.

stop bit (n.) A control bit that signifies the end of an asynchronous character in data transmission. The stop bit is always the binary digit 0.

storyboard (n.) A sequence of graphic representations, often with dialog or captions, showing important scenes in a program. Used to plan a production, to visualize, and to present program ideas, a storyboard often consists of an artist's sketches in a form similar to that of a comic strip.

STP See *Secure Transfer Protocol* or *signal transfer point*. May also refer to *shielded twisted pair*.

S

stream (v.) To play sound or video in real time as the data is downloaded over the Internet. A plug-in to a web browser such as Netscape Navigator decompresses and plays the data as it is transferred over the World Wide Web to a computer. Streaming audio or video is an alternative to downloading an entire file, storing it on a local hard drive, and then playing it with a helper application. Streaming implies the execution of a decompression algorithm in real time. The quality of the streamed data is proportional to the speed of the Internet connection and to the power of the computer decoding the streamed file.

string (n.) In programming, an ordered series of data values, or bytes, which are usually printable characters. Larger character sets, such as Unicode (in which each character is represented by more than eight bits), are becoming more popular. Most programming languages differentiate between strings and numeric values.

stripe (v.) To record time code, usually SMPTE, on a channel of a videotape prior to editing. This procedure allows accurate access to individual frames.

structured language (n.) A programming language in which a program may be reduced to blocks or procedures that can be written without detailed knowledge of the inner workings of other blocks, thus allowing a top-down design approach.

Structured Query Language (SQL) (n.) A widely used programming language for defining, modifying, and accessing information in relational databases. SQL allows queries to be made from other programs.

STS See *synchronous transport signal.*

stub (n.) In programming, a dummy procedure used to link a program with a runtime library.

stub network (n.) A network that carries packets to and from local hosts exclusively. Typically, it does not carry traffic for other networks, although it may have paths to other networks.

StuffIt (SIT) (n.) A Macintosh compressed file format. StuffIt is used to reduce the size of a file before uploading it to a network or saving it on storage media.

stylus (n.) An input device shaped like a pen. A stylus is used to enter text, draw lines, or point to choices on a computer screen.

subassembly (n.) An individually replaceable component integrated with other components to form a system.

subclass (n.) In object-oriented programming (OOP), a class derived from a superclass by inheritance. A subclass contains all the features of the superclass, along with new features or redefined existing features.

subcode (n.) Control data included on a CD-ROM that defines track location and timing information. Text may also be stored in the subcode space.

subdirectory (n.) A data structure in the Microsoft DOS and Windows filing systems that represents a division of the root directory. A subdirectory may be further divided into numerous lower-level subdirectories to provide a means of managing data.

subject index (n.) An information resource in a networked computing environment with references to topics categorized by subject. Most subject indexes are arranged ontologically. Search engines differ in that they are based not on subjects but on relevance.

subject matter expert (SME, pronounced "SMEE") (n.) An authority on a particular subject who guides the development of content for a multimedia production or web site. It is the responsibility of the SME to ensure that technical details and facts related to the topic are accurate.

submenu (n.) A lower-level menu, or a series of choices, that the user reaches after selecting a main menu choice.

subnet (n.) A segment of a network that shares a network address with other portions of the network and that is identified by a subnet number.

subnet address (n.) The part of an Internet Protocol (IP) address that refers to a subnet. The host portion of an IP address is divided into the subnet part and the host part using an address (subnet) mask.

subnet bit mask (n.) A method of dividing an Internet Protocol (IP) network into smaller subnets, and identifying those subnets with some of the most significant bits from the host portion of the network address. An IP network address has 16 bits assigned as its network ID. If the complete network address is "129.4.0.0," the first 2 sets of eight bits in this dotted decimal format may be represented in binary as "10000001.00000100." The next set of eight bits is used to define the host address and the final eight bits define the station on the host. In a subnet bit mask, the alias "255," or "11111111" in binary, is used for the first 3 parts of the address, and the final eight bits may be designated locally as a number between 0 and 255.

Thus, "255.255.255.0" is used to define the upper 24 bits of the address, and the last eight bits are represented by a "0" in this case. The last eight bits may be used to identify a station on the host whose address is set to a number between 0 and 255.

subnetwork (n.) A small network linked with other networks by a router or a bridge.

subroutine (n.) In programming, a sequence of instructions that perform a particular task. Most programming languages allow subroutine code to be called from multiple places, including from within itself, in which case it is *recursive*. A function is similar to a *subroutine*, except that a function is primarily called to return a value.

subsample (v.) When capturing data, to discard portions of a signal for the purpose of reducing the amount of data that must be compressed. Most types of lossy compression perform this operation.

subscribe (v.) To request that one's address be added to a mail list or a newsgroup.

Subscriber Loop (n.) Circuit connecting the central office of a telephone company to the demarcation point on a customer's premises.

subscriber trunk dialing (STD) (n.) European method of measuring direct long-distance calls.

Subsplit (n.) Hybrid fiber-coax (HFC) networking term that defines an upstream channel between 5 and 50 MHz.

substrate (n.) In a CD-ROM or in another optical storage device, the molded plastic base on which data is encoded.

subtractive color (n.) Against a white back-

S

ground, the mixture of various intensities of the colors cyan, magenta, and yellow. Combinations of these colors can produce all visible colors.

superscalar (adj.) Describes a single processor that can execute two or more scalar operations in parallel, or simultaneously. Superscalar architectures, with the exception of those that are superpipelined, require multiple functional units that may or may not be identical.

supertrunk (n.) Television cable that carries multiple video signals between the facilities of a cable television (CATV) company.

Super-VHS (S-VHS) (n.) Super–video home system; an advancement of the VHS videotape format, featuring higher luminance and more lines of resolution.

Super Video Graphics Array (SVGA) (n.) A video standard established by the Video Electronics Standards Association (VESA). Updated versions allow resolutions of up to 1280 x 1024 pixels with 24-bit color.

supervisor mode (n.) The mode in which an operating system usually runs. It enables execution of all instructions, including privileged instructions. It may permit access to a reserved address space, to memory management hardware, or to peripherals that may not be accessible in user mode.

surface (n.) A three-dimensional space defined by the relationship between three variable coordinates: x, y, and z.

surface mount (n.) With reference to PC board assembly, a technique for high-density manufacturing using a variety of semiconductor packages.

surge protector (n.) A device used to monitor the level of electrical current between a power source and a computer or another electronic component. When the surge protector detects a surge of voltage beyond a certain limit, the circuit is shut down or the level is automatically reduced to prevent damage to the electronics.

surrogate travel (n.) A virtual reality (VR) system in which point-of-view (POV) travel is simulated, allowing the user to control the path taken through the environment.

Surround Video (n.) A technology developed by Microsoft for transforming panoramic images into graphics files. It permits users to view their surroundings in any direction from a fixed pivot point or points. Surround Video is conceptually similar to QuickTime VR from Apple Computer.

SUSP See *System Use Sharing Protocol.*

sustained transfer rate (n.) The number of bytes per second (Bps) a CD-ROM drive or another storage medium can deliver as it reads data objects larger than its internal buffer.

SVGA See *Super Video Graphics Array.*

S-VHS See *Super-VHS.*

S-video See *Y/C video.*

swap file (n.) In Microsoft Windows 3.1, a hidden system file located on a local hard disk in contiguous space. A swap file expands apparent internal RAM and may be permanent or temporary. Also known as *virtual memory.*

sweetening (n.) In video or film post-production, the development of an audio track with mixed elements, such as music, sound effects, and applause. In the process, the signal-to-noise (S/N) ratio is improved, and the general quality of the sound track is polished.

swim (n.) A form of drift in which a shadow image appears to move from the top to the bottom of a video screen. It is caused by noise in electronic signals or by noise generated locally in the display electronics.

switch (n.) 1. A device that opens or closes circuits or selects paths. In video production, a *switcher* is used to select the current signal source or the camera shot that becomes the output. 2. In MS-DOS, an argument to control the execution of a command. This argument usually involves a qualifying parameter, typically delimited by a / symbol.

Switched Digital Video (SDV) (n, adj.) Describes any digital video transmission received over a switched network.

Switched 56 (n.) Switched public data transmission service at 56 kilobits per second (Kbps).

switched line (n.) A telecommunications link that may follow a different physical path with each use of the service, as with the public telephone system.

switched multimegabit data service (SMDS) (n.) A "fast-packet" service that establishes high-speed connections between local area networks (LANs) through the public telephone network.

switched network (n.) Any network in which switching is used to set up a continuous pathway and to transmit messages directly from the sender to the recipient. Switching is typically

accomplished by disconnecting and reconnecting lines in different configurations to set up this continuous pathway.

Switched Telephone Network (n.) The direct dialing network of telephone lines that are generally used for dialed telephone calls. The term refers to any switching arrangement that does not require operator intervention.

symmetrical compression (n.) In audio-video encoding, an encoding technique that can produce decoded data identical to the data that existed before encoding.

sync See *synchronization.*

synchronization (sync) (n.) A part of a video signal, or a separate signal sent with the video, that carries timing information on each frame.

synchronized (adj.) Describes two or more events that are coordinated exactly in time. It is especially important that audio data and video images be synchronized when combined.

synchronous (adj.) Occurring at the same time or in real time, rather than being temporally separated. Having a conversation or a conference in real time is synchronous communication, whereas responding to an email message two hours after it was sent is asynchronous communication. In synchronous transmission, successive bits or events all move at a constant rate. The characters are spaced by time in a synchronous transmission, rather than by start and stop bits.

Synchronous Data Link Control (SDLC) (n.) The protocol used in the IBM Systems Network Architecture (SNA).

Synchronous Digital Hierarchy (SDH) (n.) A standard defined by the ITU-T that is techni-

S

cally consistent with Synchronous Optical Network (SONET).

Synchronous Dynamic RAM (SDRAM, Synchronous DRAM) (n.) A form of DRAM chip that adds a separate clock signal to the control signals, supporting burst access modes.

Synchronous Graphics RAM (SGRAM) (n.) A type of Synchronous DRAM chip used in graphics hardware. SGRAM is capable of burst operation, block write, and write per bit. This type of memory provides the high throughput required for three-dimensional rendering and full-motion video (FMV).

Synchronous Optical Network (SONET, pronounced "SAH-net") (n.) A broadband networking standard based on point-to-point optical fiber networks. The standard provides a high-bandwidth pipe to support services based on Asynchronous Transfer Mode (ATM). SONET establishes a digital hierarchical network with a consistent transport scheme. It has been optimized for fiber, in contrast to the plain old telephone system (POTS), which was designed for copper wires. SONET carries circuit-switched data in frames at speeds up to 48 gigabits per second (Gbps) in multiples of 51.84 megabits per second (Mbps). Each SONET frame is a two-dimensional table of bytes 9 rows high and 90 columns deep. Groups of frames are called *superframes*.

Data transfer rates at different levels of SONET are shown below:

OC Line	Rate	Capacity Level
OC-1	52 Mbps	28 DS-1 or 1 DS-3
OC-3	155 Mbps	84 DS-1 or 3 DS-3
OC-9	466 Mbps	252 DS-1 or 9 DS-3
OC-12	622 Mbps	336 DS-1 or 12 DS-3
OC-18	933 Mbps	504 DS-1 or 18 DS-3
OC-24	1.2 Gbps	672 DS-1 or 24 DS-3
OC-36	1.9 Gbps	1008 DS-1 or 36 DS-3
OC-48	2.5 Gbps	1344 DS-1 or 48 DS-3

synchronous transfer mode (STM) (n.) A method of transport and switching that relies on a fixed pattern of frames. This type of time-division multiplexing is used across the network interface for broadband ISDN.

synchronous transport signal (STS) (n.) The equivalent of a Synchronous Optical Network (SONET) optical carrier (OC), an electrical signal that is converted to an optical signal before transmission over optical fiber. An STS frame consists of the Synchronous Payload Envelope (SPE), Section Overhead (SOH), Line Overhead (LOH), Path Overhead (POH), and Payload. The SOH and LOH combined make up the Transport Overhead (TOH).

sync-locked (adj.) Describes the exact alignment of two signals. This occurs when the sync pulses of a videotape recorder (VTR) are locked with those of another videotape deck or camera.

syntax (n.) The conventions of a programming language that govern the formatting of an expression or a statement. If the expression follows a particular sequence and includes only acceptable characters, it is said to have proper syntax.

synthesized sound (n.) A type of sound consisting of waveforms created with mathematical formulas and produced by either analog or digital means. Such waveforms differ from ones sampled from acoustic sources.

synthesizer (n.) An instrument that creates sounds electronically. Controls on the instrument typically allow the user to change basic

Système International d'Unités

This table shows prefixes assigned in accordance with SI (Système International d'Unités).

Prefix	Exponent	Decimal Value
exa	10	1 000 000 000 000 000 000
peta	10	1 000 000 000 000 000
tera	10	1 000 000 000 000
giga	10	1 000 000 000
mega	10	1 000 000
kilo	10	1 000
hecto	10	100
deka	10	10
deci	10	.1
centi	10	.01
milli	10	.001
micro	10	.000 001
nano	10	.000 000 001
pico	10	.000 000 000 001
femto	10	.000 000 000 000 001

sound qualities, such as frequency, amplitude, and the envelope of each timbre. By definition, a synthesizer is not a sample player.

SyQuest (n.) Named after the company that manufactures it, a type of removable storage system that employs cartridges and that offers a high data transfer rate. Standard SyQuest cartridges hold 44, 88, 135, 200, or 270 megabytes (MB) of data on a 5.25-inch cartridge. A second-generation 3.5-inch cartridge holds 230 MB of data.

sysop See *system operator.*

system area (n.) The space on a CD-ROM located between the addresses 00:00:00 and 00:02:16. Data related to the operating system and error correction data are placed in the system area.

Système International d'Unités (SI) (n.) An international metric system introduced in France in 1960. It defines a quantity with a single unit and uses exponents to indicate powers of 10. These factors are applied to units such as Hertz, seconds, or meters. In computing and digital media, a quantity of bytes is expressed as a power of 2 rather than 10. Applying this distinction, the prefix *mega* means 1000 if it refers to Hertz, but it means 1024 if it refers to bytes. The table shows the SI prefix, the factor for each, and the decimal value. See table.

System Management Server (SMS) (n.) A tool developed by Microsoft for administering a Windows NT client-server network.

system operator (sysop, pronounced "SIS-op") (n.) The person who takes responsibility for managing a bulletin board system (BBS) or an email service.

System 7.5 (n.) A version of the Mac OS superseded by System 7.6 and ultimately replaced by System 8.0 in 1997.

S

System 7.x (n.) Any Mac OS later than System 7.0 and prior to System 8.

Systems Network Architecture (SNA) (n.) Proprietary IBM network design that preceded the OSI model. It was the first well-defined network architecture for online data processing systems, originally implemented for mainframe computing networks.

System Use Sharing Protocol (SUSP) (n.) An extension to the ISO 9660 standard. SUSP permits multiple file system extensions to exist on a single CD-ROM.

T

TA See *Terminal Adapter.*

table of contents (TOC, pronounced "tee-oh-SEE") (n.) The space on a CD-ROM where information is imprinted. The information is about the tracks on the disc, their starting locations, and the total length of the data on the disc.

TAC See *Terminal Access Controller.*

tach (n.) The mechanical, analog equivalent of a word clock. An electronic pulse that provides information about the speed and direction of tape in a video or audio device. No location or positional information is included.

tag (n.) A character or a string containing identifying information and connected to a piece of data, often at the beginning and the end. In HTML, a tag is placed before and after a text string to identify features or attributes of the data.

Tagged Image File Format (TIFF, pronounced "TIFF") (n.) Developed in 1986 by an industry group that included Aldus, Microsoft, and others, an image format used to store and exchange graphics on IBM-compatible and Macintosh platforms.

talk (n.) Network protocol that allows users on two or more remote computers to carry on a realtime dialog by typing their words on the screen for the other parties to see, as in a chat room.

talk mode (n.) A communication style that uses shorthand to save keystrokes. Talk mode is common in electronic mail and Usenet groups. Talk mode relies on the use of shorthand that often replaces commonly used expressions with the first letter of each word. For example, "IMHO" replaces "in my humble opinion." Writing "BYE?" (Are you ready to close the conversation?) is the standard way to end a talk-mode conversation. Typographical errors are not corrected by the typist in talk mode, unless severe confusion would result. Users type "xxx" and begin from a point prior to the error instead of making corrections to their text. See also *shorthand.*

tally light (n.) Indicator on the front of a camera that informs both the operator and the subject(s) that the camera is recording. The tally light is also visible in the viewfinder.

tap (n.) A connection to the main transmission line in a cable-based local area network (LAN).

TAP See *Telocator Alphanumeric Protocol.*

tape archive (TAR, pronounced "TAR") (n.)

A Unix command with numerous options that creates a single file archive of several smaller files. The file name extension in the Unix operating system is .tar.

tape storage (n.) A ribbon of magnetic recording media stored on a reel or a cassette. A tape can hold analog or digital data. Tape storage offers low cost per megabyte, but tape deteriorates over time. Another disadvantage is that accessing data from a tape is slow. The primary application in digital media is for archival backups, which are usually done overnight so that hard disk drives can be erased and used the next day to digitize new data.

tape transport (n.) The mechanical parts in a tape recorder that move the tape over the heads. See figure.

TAPI See *Telephony Application Programming Interface.*

TAR See *tape archive.*

TARGA See *Truevision Advanced Raster Graphics Adapter.*

TB See *terabyte.*

TBC See *time base corrector.*

TBK (n.) The file name extension for a file created by the multimedia authoring application ToolBook, developed by Asymmetrix.

TCM See *Trellis-coded modulation.*

TCP See *Transmission Control Protocol.*

TCP and UDP with Bigger Address (TUBA) (n.) A proposed standard for IP version 6

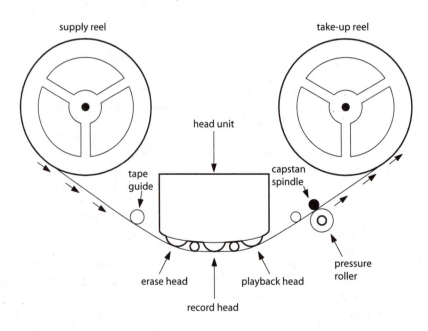

tape transport in a reel-to-reel recorder

(IPv6), also known as IP Next Generation (IPng). One of the problems addressed by this new architecture is the need for more Internet addresses. IPv6 is defined in RFC 1752.

TCP/IP See *Transmission Control Protocol/Internet Protocol.*

TDD See *Telecommunications Device for the Deaf.*

TDM See *time-division multiplexing.*

TDMA See *Time Division Multiple Access.*

TDR See *Time Domain Reflectometer.*

tear-off menu (n.) A small menu of frequently used tools represented by a box of icons in a graphical user interface (GUI). The menu may typically be repositioned on screen.

technology without an interesting name (TWAIN, pronounced "TWANE") (n.) The programming logic that allows graphics manipulation software to capture images from a scanner in a particular format that is readable by the software.

telco (n.) Abbreviation for *telephone company.*

telecine See *film chain.*

telecommunications (n.) The transfer of signals, sounds, and images over telephone or radio communications systems. Telecommunications includes passing information between voice systems and computer terminals over cable and wireless connections.

Telecommunications Act of 1996 (n.) Signed into law by Bill Clinton in February 1996, the reform of U.S. cable, telecommunications, and Internet laws. This act set terms for local exchange carrier (LEC) entry into long distance, deregulated cable rates, and attempted to criminalize the distribution of pornography on the Internet.

Telecommunications Device for the Deaf (TDD) (n.) A terminal device that deaf people use widely for text communication over telephone lines. The standard that most TDDs use is reportedly a survivor of Baudot code implemented asynchronously at 45.5 or 50 baud: 1 start bit, 5 data bits, and 1.5 stop bits. This standard is generally incompatible with standard PC modems. A typical TDD is about the size of a small laptop computer with a QWERTY keyboard and a small screen.

telecommute (v.) While working at home, to use telecommunications equipment to maintain contact with an office.

telecomputing (n.) Using a combination of telephone, television, cable, and computing technologies in a single system that is typically based in the home.

teleconference (n.) Set up by a telecommunications provider, a telephone call that enables more than two callers to participate in an *audioconference.* The use of video in a *videoconference* further allows participants at remote sites to see each other and to share visual data.

telephony (n.) With or without wiring, the transmission of electronic signals representing sounds or data to a remote location.

Telephony Application Programming Interface (TAPI) (n.) A Windows 95 Application Programming Interface (API) enabling hardware-independent access to telephone-based communication. TAPI covers a rather wide area of services, from initializing a modem and

T

305

placing a call to using voice mail or controlling a remote computer.

telephoto (n.) A camera lens with a long focal length and a narrow field of view. A telephoto is used to magnify objects that are far away.

teletext (n.) Computer-generated characters inserted into the vertical blanking interval (VBI) of a broadcast signal, normally during lines 18 to 21 of a one-way transmission.

television standards (n.) One of three standards for television signals used for both broadcast and videotape playback applications. The three formats are PAL, NTSC, and SECAM, and they have significant differences. One feature they all share is that each frame consists of two fields. PAL moves at 25 frames per second (fps) with 625 scan lines. It uses amplitude modulation (AM) at a channel bandwidth of 8 MHz. NTSC moves at 29.97 fps with 525 scan lines and uses AM at a channel bandwidth of 6 MHz. SECAM has the same frame rate and number of scan lines as PAL but uses frequency modulated (FM) subcarriers at a bandwidth of 8 MHz. In a few South American countries, hybrid formats known as *PAL-M* and *PAL-N* combine features of both NTSC and PAL. NTSC is the standard in most of Central America, whereas PAL is the standard in most western European countries. Here is a breakdown of which standards are used in various countries:

NTSC:	United States, Canada, Mexico, Japan, South Korea, the Philippines
PAL:	Great Britain, Germany, Spain, India, China, Australia
SECAM:	France, Hungary, Poland, Russia, Saudi Arabia, Egypt

Telnet (n.) The Internet standard protocol for remote terminal connection service. Telnet al-lows a user at one site to interact with a system at another site as if the user's terminal were directly connected to the host computer. Telnet is defined in RFC 854, STD 8, and is extended by other RFCs. National Center for Supercomputing Applications (NCSA) Telnet is the standard on the Macintosh platform.

Telocator Alphanumeric Protocol (TAP) (n.) A telecommunications protocol for submitting requests to a pager service. TAP is a half-duplex, ASCII-based protocol capable of submitting alphanumeric messages.

template (n.) A previously designed structure or shell into which data may be placed. A template gives graphic presentations a consistent appearance.

temporal redundancy (n.) The duplication of information found at earlier points in a stream of data or in a signal.

10BASE5 (Pronounced "ten-base-FIVE") (n.) Local area network (LAN) wiring that employs standard 50-ohm coaxial cable with BNC-style connectors. It supports the IEEE 802.3 Ethernet standard running at up to 10 Mbps over a maximum distance of 500 meters. Devices on a 10BASE5 network are typically connected to a router, a switch, or a hub.

10BASE-T (Pronounced "ten-base-TEE") (n.) Local area network (LAN) wiring that employs copper twisted-pair cable. It supports the IEEE 802.3 Ethernet standard running at up to 10 Mbps. Devices on a 10BASE-T network are typically connected to a router, a switch, or a hub.

10BASE2 (Pronounced "ten-base-TWO") (n.) Local area network (LAN) wiring that employs thin coaxial cable with BNC-style connectors.

It supports the IEEE 802.3 Ethernet standard running at up to 10 Mbps over a maximum distance of 200 meters. Devices on a 10BASE2 network are typically connected to a router, a switch, or a hub.

ter (n.) The third version of an original CCITT standard, as in V.27ter.

tera- Prefix meaning a trillion. In the decimal system, 1 000 000 000 000 is expressed as 10 to the 12th power. In the binary system, tera- is expressed as 2 to the 40th power, or 1 099 511 627 776.

terabyte (TB) (n.) Two to the 4th power eight-bit bytes, or more precisely 1 099 511 627 776 bytes.

terminal (n., adj.) 1. The hardware used in a computer-based information (CBI) system through which information passes. A terminal often takes the form of a remote workstation, such as a VT-100, with a visual display and keyboard connected to a central processing unit (CPU). A dumb terminal has no processing capability, whereas an intelligent terminal has its own processor. 2. Any point at which information can enter or exit a communication network.

Terminal Access Controller (TAC) (n.) Using the TACACS (Terminal Access Concentrator Access Control Server) protocol, which provides secure access to servers and data for LANs and telephone systems, a device that connects terminals to the Internet, typically with dialup modem connections.

Terminal Adapter (TA) (n.) A device that adapts ISDN Basic Rate Interface (BRI) channels to RS-232 and to other installed terminal equipment standards. TA connects to a computer or a router, replacing a modem.

terminal emulator (n.) Software that allows a networked computer to behave like a terminal, such as a VT-100. The computer presents itself as a terminal to the host computer and accepts the same escape sequences for functions.

terminate (v.) 1. To place an electrical load at the end of a circuit. 2. To install a connector at the end of a cable.

terminate and stay resident (TSR) (n.) In MS-DOS, a program that remains in memory once it has been loaded from a disk.

terminated line (n.) A circuit with resistance at the end point equal to the characteristic impedance of the line. The resistance ensures that no standing waves or reflections will be present when a signal enters near the end of the line.

terminator (n.) A resistor connected to the end of a cable that matches the impedance of the line in order to prevent reflections. Network wiring schemes and SCSI chains are examples of systems that require terminators.

tessellation (n.) Transformation of models that exist as coordinates in space into polygons.

texel (n.) Abbreviation for textured pixel.

text (n.) A string of data that consists of standard ASCII characters and no other information. A text file contains no binary data or formatting information.

tEXt (n.) One of the formats by which a Portable Network Graphics (PNG) file may be extended. It is a chunk of data semantically equivalent to the Unicode character set instead of Latin-1. This chunk contains:

Keyword:	1–79 bytes (character string)
Null separator:	1 byte
Compression flag:	1 byte
Compression method:	1 byte
Language tag:	0 or more bytes (character string)
Null separator:	1 byte
Translated keyword:	0 or more bytes
Null separator:	1 byte
Text:	0 or more bytes

The keyword is case-sensitive and it must contain only printable Latin-1 characters (33–126 and 161–255) and spaces (32), but no leading, trailing, or consecutive spaces.

text editor (n.) A utility program that manipulates text files, much as a word processor does. Unlike a word-processing application, a text editor does not embed control codes or escape sequences in the file for formatting. Programmers use text editors to write code or HTML documents.

text file (n.) A type of data file with characters that are printable letters, numbers, and symbols exclusively. The ASCII character set is most often used, and no invisible control characters are included. A text file could be created by a text editor and imported into a word processor, but it would not contain formatting information. See also *binary file* or *Rich Text Format*.

text-mode browser (n.) Universal client incapable of displaying graphics. A text-mode browser is useful on dumb terminals and on very slow computers. It offers many of the features available in a graphical browser. Lynx is a popular browser of this type.

texture (n.) A surface with varied intensities. It is often used as a region descriptor in image analysis and in computer vision. Texture may be described in statistical, structural, and spectral terms. A texture can be defined by the statistical properties of its gray levels. Structural descriptors characterize a texture as consisting of primitive textural elements (texels) that are regularly arranged on the surface. The Fourier spectrum may be used to describe the global periodicity of the gray levels of a surface by identifying high-energy peaks in the spectrum.

texture map (n.) The shading and surface features of a two-dimensional or three-dimensional object. In addition to being an image, a texture map can be a procedure calculated from formulas. See figures on the following page.

TFT See *thin film transistor*.

TFTP See *Trivial File Transfer Protocol*.

TGA (n.) Captured by a Truevision video card, a TARGA format with the file name extension .tga.

THD See *total harmonic distortion*.

thermal wax printer (n.) A color printer that creates an image by using heated pins to melt a thin coating of wax on a ribbon, transferring the wax onto the paper.

thin client (n.) In a system of networked computers, a client program that relies on the server for most of its system functions. Networked personal computers operate as "fat clients," depending on the server only for file storage and printing. The benefit of thin clients over fat ones is that maintenance tasks for thin clients are centralized on the server and need to be

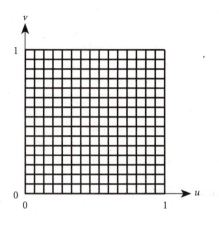

rectangular grid as a texture map

rectangular grid mapped onto a sphere

rectangular grid mapped onto a torus

done just once. In addition, thin clients have fewer hardware demands. Also called a *dumb terminal.*

Thin Ethernet (n.) A networking technology that uses thinner and cheaper coaxial cable than standard Ethernet does. Thin Ethernet adheres to the IEEE 802.3 standard. Transmission is at 10 megabits per second (Mbps) over a maximum distance of 200 meters, and cable ends are terminated with BNC connectors. Also called *cheapernet* or *10BASE2.*

thin film transistor (TFT) (n.) A miniature integrated circuit (IC) formed by thin layers of conductive material on an insulating substrate.

thrash (v.) To move about vigorously, accomplishing nothing. Overloaded paging systems waste much time thrashing, or moving data into and out of the core needlessly, as do systems with a cache conflict.

thread (n.) 1. A complete operation, a set of instructions, or a process executed by software that cannot be interrupted. 2. A series of interrelated messages sent over a network.

Threaded-Neill-Concelman (TNC) (n.) A threaded connector used with coaxial cables.

3-D Geometry File (3-DGF) (n.) A cross-platform format developed by Macromedia for exchanging three-dimensional geometric data.

3-DGF See *3-D Geometry File.*

3DO (n.) A manufacturer and marketer of an interactive multimedia player capable of high-resolution graphics and fast animation. The player reads specially formatted CDs and is designed to deliver games, movies, and educational applications. Pronounced "THREE-dee-OH."

three-finger salute (n.) The key combination Ctrl-Alt-Delete, which causes a Windows or MS-DOS operating system to reboot. Also known as a *warm boot.*

three-point lighting (n.) Also known as *Rembrandt lighting,* a common setup for lights in a video production or an animation scene. From the camera perspective, the key light is placed to the right, behind the camera, and is elevated at a distance. The second light is placed to the left, in a symmetrical relationship to the key light. Referred to as the *fill,* this second light is an omnidirectional or a point light at about half the intensity of the key. The third light is a back light, placed behind the subject and directly opposed to the fill light. A spotlight is generally used for the back light and has an intensity similar to that of the key light.

3/4-inch (adj.) Describes a videotape used in Sony U-matic video recorders. This format is used by some video professionals and in many television studios.

3:2 pulldown (n.) A method of converting film at 24 frames per second (fps) to interlaced video at 30 fps, with two fields per frame. The first two fields of video are derived from the first field of film. The next three fields of video are derived from the next frame of film. This process is repeated, alternating two video fields, then three video fields from each subsequent frame of film. This can cause noticeable flicker when the two fields in a single frame of interlaced video come from two different frames in the original film. See figure under *interfield frames.*

throughput (n.) The data processing capacity of a bus, or the rate at which it can pass data. It is most often expressed in bits per second (bps).

thumbnail (n.) Small version of a larger graphic image. A thumbnail is typically used to index a database of graphics or to preview an image that would take a great deal of space or time to draw at a larger resolution. An encapsulated PostScript file carries with it a TIFF thumbnail for previewing.

TIFF See *Tagged Image File Format.*

tilde (n.) ASCII character 126, ~. Pronounced "TIL-deh."

tiled windows (n.) In a graphical user interface (GUI), an arrangement of program windows in which the windows do not overlap.

tilt (v.) To pivot a video camera vertically, up or down, from a stationary position and height. A tilt follows movement, contrasts the size differences of two subjects, and may give the viewer a point-of-view (POV) sense of a subject's height.

timbre (n.) A musical term for the color of a tone, determined primarily by its overtone structure. The difference between an oboe and a flute sounding the same note is a difference in timbre. This is not to be confused with the pitch (frequency), the loudness (amplitude), or the shape (envelope) of a tone. Pronounced "TAM-bur."

time base corrector (TBC) (n.) A device that resets the timing portion of a video signal to the standard values for a given video format. A TBC cleans up the output of videotape players or computer video cards prior to broadcast. It can also synchronize two independent video signals.

time code (n.) Address code with time-referenced information that is recorded on a spare track of videotape or that is inserted in the vertical blanking interval (VBI) of a video signal. It is expressed as an eight-digit number that displays time in hours, minutes, seconds, and video frames in the format hh:mm:ss:ff.

time code generator (n.) A special type of signal generator that outputs SMPTE time code in the form of a regular pulse, which is typically recorded as an audio signal on an unused track of videotape.

time code reader (n.) An electronic device that reads and displays SMPTE time code. It is generally integrated in a professional-quality playback or recording deck.

Time Division Multiple Access (TDMA) (n.) A technique for transmitting digital wireless communications. By allocating unique time slots to each user on each channel, TDMA permits many users to access a single radio frequency (RF) channel sequentially without interference.

time-division multiplexing (TDM) (n.) A process in which multiple channels of information are mixed and transmitted over a single telecommunications link, with the channels taking turns using the link. A periodic synchronization signal is used so the receiver can distinguish between channels. TDM is inefficient when traffic is intermittent, because a time slot is allocated even when a channel has no data to transmit. Statistical TDM overcomes this problem. The portion of the bandwidth allocated to each user varies dynamically in the statistical model.

Time Domain Reflectometer (TDR) (n.) An electronic device used to locate short circuits and to track impedance characteristics in a data connection cable.

timeout (n.) A default action performed by a program when a predetermined period of time expires before a user enters data or offers input of any kind. This may result in initiating a screensaver or looping a sequence.

Time to Live (TTL) (n.) A field in an Internet Protocol (IP) header that tells how many more hops a given packet will make before it is discarded or returned.

title (n.) In electronic or digital publishing, a volume, a set of volumes, or a program on a CD-ROM.

titler (n.) In video post-production, a device that is used to generate characters for titles or captions that are overlaid on video frames.

titling (n.) The process of adding text to video to provide credits, to present captions, or to communicate printed information to the viewer.

TNC See *Threaded-Neill-Concelman.*

TOC See *table of contents.*

toggle 1. (v.) To switch between two applications or choices, such as on and off, with a single key or button. 2. (n.) Any two-position switch that may be mechanical or virtual.

token ring (n., adj.) A local area network (LAN) configured in a ring, around which a token (or a special signal) is passed between terminals over a single channel. The floating message, or the token, gives each terminal permission to transmit data. A Multistation Access Unit (MSAU) controls the passage of data around the ring at speeds of up to 16 megabits per second (Mbps). IBM developed this network structure, the IEEE 802.5 standard. See

311

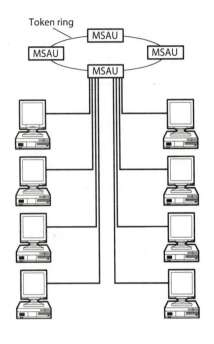

Token ring

MSAU
MSAU
MSAU
MSAU

token ring network

figure on the following page.

T1 (n., adj.) A digital carrier facility that transmits a DS-1 formatted digital signal at 1.544 megabits per second (Mbps). Two unshielded twisted-pair telephone lines are used to transport T1 signals, one pair for each direction. Some hybrid equipment operates at half the T1 rate in full-duplex mode, separating the sent and the received signals at each end with components. The transmitted signal consists of pulses a few hundred nanoseconds wide, each inverted with respect to the preceding one. At the sending end the strength of the signal is 1 volt, and at the receiving end the strength must be greater than 0.01 volts. This requires repeaters about every 6000 feet. The information is contained in the timing of the signals, not in the polarity. A process known as *bit stuff-*

ing is used so that the receiving apparatus will not lose track of the sending clock when a long sequence of bits of the same polarity is sent. Pronounced "TEE-one."

toolbar (n.) A collection of icons that activate program functions in a graphical user interface (GUI). In graphics programs, the tools may include a lasso selector, a text entry tool, and an eraser. Other tools determine the width and color of lines that are drawn.

torus (n.) A three-dimensional shape that resembles a donut and that is known as an *anchor ring*. For an example, see the B-spline figure.

total harmonic distortion (THD) (n.) A measure of performance in audio gear that monitors hum and other unwanted frequencies. THD is expressed as a percentage of noise compared with the total signal. Lower percentages are better.

touch screen (n., adj.) A display or a monitor serving as a control or input device that responds to a user's touch. Touch-screen systems employ a variety of technologies, such as plastic membranes, infrared grids, capacitance sensors, and acceleration detection devices.

tpi See *tracks per inch*.

TP/IX (n.) Internet protocol that changes TCP and User Datagram Protocol (UDP) headers into a 64-bit Internet Protocol (IP) address, a 32-bit port number, and a 64-bit sequence number. TP/IX is described in RFC 1475.

track (n.) 1. On an audio tape or a videotape, the physical area that contains an individual program or some control information. It could be compared to a lane on the freeway. 2. The process through which a recorded videotape plays back. A machine that "tracks" well has its heads properly aligned. Videotape tracks are recorded diagonally. 3. One of the adjacent bands of the data spiral on a compact disc. The tracks on a hard disk exist in the form of concentric circles rather than in a spiral shape.

trackball (n.) An alternative input device to a mouse. A trackball functions like an upside-down mouse and requires little desktop space. Spinning the ball causes the cursor on the screen to move.

tracking (n.) 1. The overall amount of space between characters in a line of text. This is different from kerning, which deals with the space between certain pairs of characters. 2. In video production, lateral camera movement that is aligned with moving subjects so that the background appears to move, not the subjects. 3. The alignment of audio or video playback and record heads in relation to the tape that moves over them.

track-relative time (n.) A method used to determine the start and stop times of audio segments on a mixed-mode disc.

tracks per inch (tpi) (n.) A measurement of the density of magnetic media. A DOS-formatted, high-density, 3.5-inch floppy disk holds 135 tpi.

traffic (n.) Over a period of time, the number of messages transmitted on a communications circuit.

transaction (n.) In reference to a database system, a unit of interaction that occurs individually and coherently.

transactional (adj.) Describes a retail kiosk where a customer can make a credit card purchase or conduct business.

transceiver (n.) A system that receives, ampli-

fies, and retransmits a signal without altering the original content significantly.

transcode (v.) To convert from one video or graphic format to another, as opposed to encoding, which refers to the original capture or digitization of images.

transducer (n.) Any device that converts one form of energy into another, such as a microphone that converts varying sound pressure levels into an analogous varied stream of voltage.

transfer rate (n.) The rate at which digital information is transferred to or from a storage medium or device. For example, a single-speed compact disc reader transfers data at approximately 150 kilobytes per second (KBps).

transistor (n.) A semiconductor with three terminals used for amplification. It was invented in 1947 at Bell Labs and remains the fundamental component of most electronic circuits. Transistors are miniaturized and combined with other components to create complex integrated circuits (ICs), such as logic gates, microprocessors, and memory. The two types are the bipolar transistor (also called the *junction transistor*) and the field-effect transistor (FET).

transistor-transistor logic (TTL) (n.) Bipolar integrated circuit (IC) logic that employs transistors with multiple emitters.

transit network (n.) Any network with paths to at least two other networks. It passes traffic between those networks and carries traffic for its own hosts.

transmission (n.) The electronic transfer of a signal or data from one location or device to another.

Transmission Control Protocol (TCP) (n.)

T

313

The transport layer protocol used for Ethernet and for the Internet, developed by the Defense Advanced Research Projects Agency (DARPA) and defined in RFC 793, STD 7. TCP is built on top of Internet Protocol (IP) and is usually combined with it. TCP adds reliable full-duplex communication, flow control, multiplexing, and process-to-process connections. Unlike the User Datagram Protocol (UDP), TCP is connection-oriented and stream-oriented.

Transmission Control Protocol/Internet Protocol (TCP/IP) (n.) The de facto standard Ethernet protocols for Internet communications. The Defense Advanced Research Projects Agency (DARPA) developed TCP for internetworking. It encompasses both network layer and transport layer protocols. IP is a packet-switching protocol, whereas TCP checks, tracks, and corrects transmission errors. Although TCP and IP specify two protocols at specific layers, the term *TCP/IP* is often used to refer to the entire protocol suite based on TCP and IP. That suite includes Telnet, FTP, User Datagram Protocol (UDP), and Realtime Transport Protocol (RTP).

transmission rate (n.) The speed at which data can be transferred across a communications medium under varying conditions.

transparency (n.) 1. The degree to which a computing system interferes with the process of user interaction with content. Intuitive software running on easy-to-use equipment makes technology transparent. 2. The property of a layer in a graphical composition that allows underlying layers to show through. An object with a transparent background allows lower layers to show clearly around the object in the foreground.

transponder (n.) A satellite communications device that can receive a signal, convert it to a new frequency, amplify it, and send it back to earth immediately. A transponder is normally contained within a retransmitting satellite.

transport layer (n.) The network entity responsible for end-to-end control of transmitted data in the OSI model.

transport protocol (n.) The protocol by which a service is delivered. Common ones are Simple Mail Transfer Protocol (SMTP), POP, and Unix-to-Unix CoPy (UUCP) for delivering Internet mail. For delivering news, Network News Transfer Protocol (NNTP) or UUCP is used.

tree (n.) A local area network (LAN) topology in the shape of a tree with only one route between network nodes.

Trellis-coded modulation (TCM) (n.) A technique employed by high-speed modems for detection and correction of data errors.

triad (n.) In an RGB display, a set of red, green, and blue phosphors arranged in a triangle. Three guns fire electron beams of different colors at the phosphors on the tube. The phosphors are excited by the beam, whose color matches theirs. The triad produces a single color, which is a combination of the colors of the three excited phosphors. See figure.

triad-phosphor dot pattern

tripod (n.) A camera mount with three legs

that provides stability and aids in moving the camera smoothly.

Trivial File Transfer Protocol (TFTP) (n.) A weak version of FTP that lacks authentication and other basic features. TFTP can be used to boot a networked machine.

Trojan horse (n.) Software that secretly conveys a means of access to the system on which it runs, allowing it to invade that system with a virus and make unauthorized changes to the configuration.

troubleshoot (v.) To test system components for continuity and proper performance and to identify faulty connections and parts. If a visual inspection does not indicate loose connections, voltage levels and logic circuits should be checked. If logic levels are improper, it could be the result of a malfunctioning integrated circuit (IC) or of noise caused by electromagnetic interference. Many systems are equipped with diagnostic test programs that may identify the cause of a problem. If all hardware components and connections have been tested and have passed inspection, the problem may be a bug in the software.

true color 1. (n.) A system in which color information belonging to an image is directly used to determine the output color, rather than serving as an index to a table of colors in a palette. 2. (adj.) Describes color systems with enough colors to create an image that looks natural to the human eye. It is typically defined as 24-bit color.

TrueType (n.) Developed by Apple Computer in 1991, a scalable font technology that is implemented in Microsoft Windows and in OS/2 operating systems, as well as in the Macintosh OS.

Truevision Advanced Raster Graphics Adapter (TARGA, pronounced "TAR-gah") (n.) 1. A 24-bit color image format that Truevision defined, originally for that company's line of TARGA videographics interface cards. Many other image-creation and image-editing programs have since used it as an exchange format. 2. A series of graphics cards produced by Truevision for microcomputers. The PC series was among the first to support full-color (24-bit) display.

trunk (n.) 1. In telecommunications, a telephone line, or a channel, between the telephone company's central office or switching center and another switching center or private branch exchange (PBX). 2. In cable television (CATV), part of a coaxial cable system that starts at the headend of a system and acts as the main distribution artery for CATV signals. The trunk cable connects with the distribution and feeder segments.

truth table (n.) A simple table that identifies all possible combinations of inputs and the corresponding outputs of such Boolean functions as AND, OR, NOT, NAND, NOR, IMPLIES, and XOR.

TSR See *terminate and stay resident.*

T3 (n.) A combination of 28 T1 lines with an aggregate data rate of 44.736 megabits per second (Mbps).

TTL See *Time to Live* or *transistor-transistor logic.*

TUBA See *TCP and UDP with Bigger Address.*

tunneling (n.) Encapsulation of one protocol within another. By using tunneling, data can be moved between administrative domains that use a protocol unsupported by the net-

T

work connecting the domains.

turnkey system (n.) An integrated hardware-software program that is ready to run without setup or engineering. The user simply turns a key to operate.

TWAIN See *technology without an interesting name.*

tweak (v.) Jargon meaning to change a value or setting slightly.

tween (v.) To create an interpolated image between two set images, or coordinates, in an animation or a graphics program. Tweening speeds up the creation of animated sequences by letting the user define only the key frame images and then instructing the computer to fill in the intervening pictures.

twisted pair (n.) In telecommunications, a standard cable made up of one or more pairs of copper wire twisted around one another to reduce induction and interference between the wires. See figure.

twisted-pair cable construction

2-D graphics (n.) Artwork and designs that exist in a single plane, or in two dimensions. Basic drawing applications are two-dimensional, and information is defined on an x-y plane.

two-phase commit (n.) Physically located on independent machines, a data notation method that ensures the success or the failure of each machine. If all statements succeed, an action is committed. If any one statement fails, all statements within the transaction revert to their original condition.

twos complement (n.) A system that represents negative numbers with binary data. Each bit of the number is inverted. Then 1 (000...00001) is added (ignoring overflow). Using all 1s to represent −1 avoids the two representations for 0 found in ones complement. This procedure simplifies the logic required for addition and subtraction but introduces complexity for negation. The examples below show the application of this concept.

$$000...00011 = +3$$
$$000...00010 = +2$$
$$000...00001 = +1$$
$$000...00000 = 0$$
$$111...11111 = -1$$
$$111...11110 = -2$$
$$111...11101 = -3$$

U

UART See *universal asynchronous receiver-transmitter.*

UAWG Consortium (n.) Universal ADSL Working Group Consortium; a group of network operators, computer companies, and telecommunications providers that developed a standard for splitterless ADSL, or ADSL Lite, referred to as G.lite by the International Telecommunications Union–Telecommunications Standardization Sector (ITU-T). See also *Asymmetric Digital Subscriber Line.*

UCS See *Universal Character Set.*

UDMA See *Ultra DMA.*

UDP See *User Datagram Protocol.*

UDTV See *ultra-high definition television.*

UHF See *ultra-high frequency.*

UI See *user interface.*

Ultimatte (n.) A brand name for a chroma key system used to overlay multiple video images. The Ultimatte system transfers the luminance (brightness) image of the dropout color, which enables the transfer of shadows to the composite image. Pronounced "UL-ti-mat."

Ultimedia (n.) The entire line of IBM multimedia tools and technologies. The IBM PS/2 Ultimedia model M57 SLC was IBM's first PS/2 machine with built-in multimedia capabilities. The Ultimedia line, dating from 1991, complies with Multimedia Personal Computer (MPC) specifications.

Ultra DMA (UDMA) (n.) Ultra direct memory access; advanced implementation of DMA that allows commands to transfer data at 33.3 megabits per second (Mbps). This is twice the original Burst DMA transfer rate of 16.6 Mbps, using the same standard 40-pin Integrated Drive Electronics (IDE) interface cable. To employ UDMA, the drive and the Basic Input/Output System (BIOS) must be compatible with the new standard, and device drivers must be loaded in the operating system. UDMA allows a host computer to send and retrieve data faster, particularly during sequential operations. It provides enhanced data integrity capabilities to the EIDE interface. It does this through improved timing margins and through the use of cyclic redundancy check (CRC), a data transfer error detection code. UDMA is endorsed by most industry hard drive manufacturers, including Fujitsu, IBM, Maxtor, Quantum, Seagate, Toshiba, and Western Digital.

ultra-high definition television (UDTV) (n.)

A proposed digital broadcast standard with higher resolution than high-definition television (HDTV). UDTV will provide approximately 3000 lines of resolution, as opposed to 1125 lines in HDTV. No standards have been established yet.

ultra-high frequency (UHF) (adj.) 1. Describes the radio frequency from 300 to 3000 MHz. 2. Describes the TV broadcast band occupied by UHF channels 14 through 83 in the United States, the range from 470 MHz to 890 MHz.

ultra SCSI (n.) A type of SCSI-2 bus that transfers data at 20 Mbps, referred to as *fast-20* by ANSI. Ultra wide SCSI transfers data at 40 Mbps. See also *Small Computer System Interface.*

ultraviolet (UV) (n.) Invisible electromagnetic radiation with wavelengths from 10 nanometers to 400 nanometers.

Ultrix (n.) A version of Unix implemented by Digital Equipment Corporation (DEC) for their RISC-based workstations.

U-matic (n., adj.) The trade name developed by Sony for 3/4-inch videotape recorders (VTRs) and videotape players.

UMB See *upper memory block.*

unbalanced (adj.) In audio and telecommunications, describes channels that carry a signal on one wire and use a second wire as a ground. Unbalanced wiring is less expensive than balanced configurations that carry the signal as a difference between two wires, and use a third wire as the ground. Unbalanced lines are more susceptible to spurious noise than are balanced lines.

underscan (v.) To limit the electron beam in a cathode-ray tube (CRT) to scan within the boundaries of the display. This reduces the normal size of a video image by as much as 20 percent. To ensure that the complete image is always visible within a display area, it is advisable to check the boundaries of an image in underscan mode. Computer monitors usually operate in underscan mode, but the underscanning feature is available only on professional-quality NTSC video monitors.

undo (v.) To void the user's last action in a graphical user interface (GUI). The Edit menu in most Microsoft programs offers the Undo function, which may also be invoked with the key combination Ctrl-Z.

unformatted capacity (n.) The amount of data that a storage device can hold without the information that makes it readable, such as the layout of tracks and the file allocation table.

Unicast (n.) Point-to-point, one-to-one transmission of data. Unicasting is the standard transmission method on the Internet. *Webcasting,* by contrast, is the process of broadcasting digital information to all parties tuned in to a channel through which data is pushed, or it is the process of sending software updates on request to multiple points.

Unicode (n.) A character coding scheme that uses 16 bits for each character, designed to extend the capabilities of ASCII, which uses seven bits. Nearly all letters and symbols in all languages can be represented in a standard way with Unicode. The first 128 characters of Unicode are identical to those in standard ASCII.

uniform resource locator (URL, pronounced "you-are-EL") (n.) A means of identifying an exact location on the Internet. A URL has four parts. In *http://hansenmedia.com/html/info/*

default.html, for example, there is the protocol type (*http://*), the DNS server name (*hansenmedia.com*), the subdirectory (*/html/info/*), and the file name (*default.html*).

Uniform Resource Name (URN, pronounced "you-are-EN") (n.) A naming scheme developed by the Internet Engineering Task Force (IETF) that provides for the resolution of names with greater persistence and reliability than is currently associated with URLs.

uninterruptible power supply (UPS) (n.) A device that can provide electrical power to a system if the normal power source fails. A UPS thereby prevents interrupted service.

unity gain (n.) In audio engineering, the condition in which input and output levels are equal, with no apparent amplification or attenuation.

universal asynchronous receiver-transmitter (UART or USART) (n.) An integrated circuit (IC) that converts between serial and parallel data formats. For example, a UART converts the parallel data from a computer into serial data for asynchronous transmission.

Universal Character Set (UCS) (n.) An ISO and International Electrotechnical Commission (IEC) standard listing of symbols established in 1993. The full name is the *Universal Multiple-Octet Coded Character Set.* The first part is the Architecture and Basic Multilingual Plane (BMP), based on Unicode and on an ISO draft for 16-bit character codes. Each plane consists of 256 x 256 locations. BMP is the initial plane, and others are supposed to follow. Java was the first programming language to define a character as 16 bits. Defined in ISO/IEC 10646, UCS includes the ASCII and Latin-1 subsets with their binary values unchanged.

universal client (n.) A program that runs on the client machine in a client-server network. A web browser is an example of a universal client. It is preferred by many over the term *browser.*

universal product code (UPC) (n.) The bar code used to identify items that are indexed in a retail store, implemented in the U.S. in 1973. It consists of a label with stripes of varied thickness that are read by an optical scanner. Information about the manufacturer and the product is encoded in the stripes. See also *bar code.*

Universal Resource Identifier (URI, pronounced "you-are-EYE") (n.) The term used for a short string, which is a name or address that references a file or a location on the Internet. It is used to identify a resource, such as a graphic file, that is embedded in an HTML document or the document itself. A uniform resource locator (URL) is a type of URI. A full definition of URI is contained in RFC 1630.

Universal Serial Bus (USB) (n.) An input/output (I/O) bus capable of data transfer at 12 megabytes per second (MBps) with up to 127 devices connected in a daisy chain. The USB specification was published in 1996 by a consortium of companies led by Intel Corporation, including Compaq, Digital Equipment Corporation, IBM, Microsoft, NEC Technologies, and Northern Telecom. In addition to a keyboard, a mouse, and a printer, a peripheral such as a CD-ROM drive or a modem may be connected to a single port on a PC. Typically, each device connected to a computer uses its own port. USB supports multiple isochronous data streams for multimedia applications. The USB specification supports self-identifying peripherals, a feature fully compatible with plug and play (PnP) systems. USB devices may be *hot plugged,* which means that power does not have to be turned off to connect or disconnect a peripheral. The operating system must support USB in order for it to function. Original versions of Windows 95 and Windows NT 4.0 do not support USB, but the OEM Service Release 2 (OSR-2) release of Windows 95 does. Windows 98 and Windows NT 5.0 fully support USB. It is expected that USB will become a primary means of connection in IBM-compatible PCs. Most major hardware, software, and telecommunications providers support USB.

Universal Time Coordinated (UTC) (n.) Another term for *Greenwich Mean Time*.

Unix (n.) Developed by Ken Thompson in 1969, the most popular general-purpose, multiuser operating system in the world. The coauthor is Dennis Ritchie, who created the C programming language. Unix became the first source-portable operating system in 1974 when it was implemented in C. Unix is the subject of an international standardization effort. It is a 32-bit system with excellent multitasking capabilities. Similar systems include Open Software Foundation (OSF), Version 7, Berkeley Software Distribution (BSD), Xenix, Ultrix, Linux, and GNU. *Unix* is a trademark, owned originally by AT&T, sold to Novell in 1993, and subsequently to Santa Cruz Operation, Inc. (SCO) in 1996. In 1993, Novell assigned the rights to the Unix name to X/Open Company Ltd., and they license it worldwide. For more information, go to *http://www.usenix.org*, or to *http://ww.eecs.nwu.edu/unix.html*.

Unix command (n.) A letter or combination of letters that may be entered at the command line to perform basic functions in Unix. See the appendix on Unix and Linux commands.

Unix-to-Unix CoPy (UUCP) (n.) A store-and-forward system. Primarily used in Unix systems, UUCP is also supported on other platforms, including VMS and personal computers. The term is commonly used to refer to the international network that employs UUCP to route email and news.

unshielded twisted pair (UTP) (n.) Standard networking cable under the Category 3 specification for network wiring.

unzip (v.) To use the PKUNZIP or WinZip program to extract files from a ZIP archive. Commonly used on MS-DOS or Windows systems, PKUNZIP is the companion to PKZIP, an archiving tool that creates ZIP archives. Both programs are from PKWare. Compare *zip*.

UPC See *universal product code*.

upgrade (n.) A recent release or version of a software program that includes more features or performs better than the previous one.

uplink (n.) A transmission system that sends signals to an orbiting satellite.

upload (v.) To send a file to a networked host or to another machine.

upper memory (n.) An area outside the first 640 kilobytes (KB) of conventional memory reserved for system software in MS-DOS. Programs cannot store information in upper memory. Upper memory blocks are typically used for terminate and stay resident (TSR) programs and device drivers.

upper memory block (UMB) (n.) In the MS-DOS operating system, 64 kilobytes (KB) of the expanded memory page frame above the first 640KB. The UMB can be used to store terminate and stay resident (TSR) programs or device drivers, leaving conventional memory free.

UPS See *uninterruptible power supply.*

upstream (adj.) In a two-way television network, describes the direction a signal travels from a receive site back to an origination site.

URI See *Universal Resource Identifier.*

URL See *uniform resource locator.*

URN See *Uniform Resource Name.*

USART See *universal asynchronous receiver-transmitter.*

USB See *Universal Serial Bus.*

Usenet (n.) Users' Network; running primarily on Unix machines, a massive bulletin board system (BBS) where people post and read messages and documents. A user needs a news reader in order to participate. Most Internet hosts subscribe to Usenet. Network News Transfer Protocol (NNTP) is the protocol commonly used to transfer news articles between a news server and a news reader. Usenet was started at Duke University in 1979 and is now the largest decentralized information utility.

user (n.) The operator of a computer program.

user address (n.) An individual's domain name or Internet Protocol (IP) address.

user agent (n.) The browser and platform used by a visitor to access a web server.

user authentication (n.) The act of checking for the user's name to allow access to a site or server. This is done automatically upon login by most servers.

user bits (n.) In terms of an 80-bit SMPTE time code word, undefined bits that are available for uses other than time code.

User Datagram Protocol (UDP) (n.) Connectionless protocol that adds reliability and multiplexing to Internet Protocol (IP). UDP is defined in RFC 768, STD 6 as an Internet standard transport layer protocol.

user-friendly (adj.) Describes a program or system designed for ease of operation.

user interface (UI) (n.) Software that facilitates communication with a computer. It may consist of a single line on which commands are entered, or it may consist of icons and menu bars in a graphical user interface (GUI).

user name (n.) In a host system that is accessible to multiple users, a unique identifier given to each user. Identification is required for accounting, security, login, and resource management. After typing in the user name, the user enters a password to access a service. A user name might be any string of alphanumeric characters. Typically, the name contains some combination of the first name, the last name, and initials of the individual user. Either system administrators or users may choose user names. They may serve as mailbox names in electronic mail addresses as well.

user session (n.) A period of activity for one user of a web site. A unique user is identified by the user's Internet Protocol (IP) address or domain name. By default, a user session is generally terminated when a user stays inactive for more than 30 minutes.

UTC See *Universal Time Coordinated.*

utility program (n.) Small application designed to support the operation of software and hardware. Examples of MS-DOS utilities are CHKDSK and DEFRAG.

UTP See *unshielded twisted pair.*

UUCP See *Unix-to-Unix CoPy.*

uuencode/uudecode (n.) A program that converts binary files into ASCII files for transmission and that decodes them upon reception. Pronounced "you-you-en-CODE-you-you-de-CODE."

UUNET (n.) A company that provides high-speed communications networks that carry Internet traffic, with links in the T1, T3, OC1, and OC3 ranges. These wide-bandwith networks are the backbones that carry Internet traffic around the world and meet at Network Access Points (NAPs). UUNET provides many Internet Service Providers (ISPs) with their connection to a backbone.

UV See *ultraviolet.*

V

validation (n.) The process of assessing and refining testing procedures and other components of an instructional design.

value (n.) In relation to color, the degree of lightness or darkness, or the intensity.

value-added reseller (VAR, pronounced "VAHR") (n.) A company that assembles systems, provides a package for customers, and offers service after the sale.

Van Jacobson compression (n.) Method of compressing TCP headers to decrease round-trip times with SLIP. Versions of SLIP implementing this type of compression are called *Compressed SLIP* or *C-SLIP*.

vaporware (n.) Software that has been announced but not released.

VAR See *value-added reseller*.

variable (n.) An object in a programming language that may assume different values, one at a time, of a prescribed data type. Compare *constant*.

variable-length coding (n.) In MPEG compression, the technique of assigning shorter identifiers, or code words, to more common events, and longer code words to less common events. Also known as *entropy coding*.

Variable Length Subnet Mask (VLSM) (n.) Implemented in the Open Shortest-Path First (OSPF) routing protocol, a means of dividing a single Internet Protocol (IP) block into smaller networks, or subnets, of different sizes.

varied repetition (n.) A technique used by instructional designers to present a segment of a lesson several times. The lesson has the same content each time but is presented in different ways.

VAX See *Virtual Address Extension*.

VAX/VMS See *Virtual Address Extension/Virtual Memory System*.

VB See *Visual Basic*.

VBI See *vertical blanking interval*.

VBX (n.) The file name extension for Visual Basic (VB).

VCL See *Visual Component Library*.

VCR See *videocassette recorder*.

VDT See *video display terminal*.

vector (n.) In graphics, a line or a movement

defined by its end points or by a defined position and one other point.

vector data (n.) Information that defines the characteristics of lines in a graphic.

vector graphics (n.) Images represented by mathematically defined shapes, such as lines, polygons, text, and groups of objects as opposed to bitmaps of these entities. Compare *raster graphics.*

vectorscope (n.) An instrument that tests a video signal and displays results as displacement in a circular pattern. The location of dots on the scope indicates the timing of various components of the test signal relative to signal reference points. A vectorscope is widely used to evaluate and adjust the color component of video signals.

Venn diagram (n.) A graphic representation of regions that represent parameters, or sets. Logical operations may be illustrated by the intersection, inclusion, or exclusion of regions in a Venn diagram. The overlapping circles in a Venn diagram represent a logical relationship between sets. See figure.

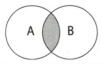

Venn diagram

VERONICA (Very Easy Rodent-Oriented Netwide Index to Computerized Archives) (n.) A search tool for the Internet.

vertical application (n.) An application program that provides functionality to a specific business process, such as accounting.

vertical blanking interval (VBI) (n.) In a video signal, the period during which picture information is suppressed and in which the scanning beam returns from the bottom of the picture to the top. Technically, the VBI consists of lines 1 through 21 of video field 1 and lines 263 through 284 of field 2 in the NTSC format. Frame numbers, flags, and closed captions are placed in this interval to maintain image stability and to provide access to a frame. A cable modem may use this space to send the equivalent of a 9600-bps signal during blanking interval. See also *horizontal blanking interval.*

vertical interval switching (n.) Alternating rapidly between two video signals during the vertical blanking interval (VBI) at the end of a scan, leaving no noticeable shift in the output signal.

vertical interval time code (VITC, pronounced "VIT-see") (n.) The insertion of SMPTE time code into the vertical blanking interval (VBI) between the two fields of a video frame. This method eliminates errors that may occur from tape stretch, which is a problem when longitudinal time code (LTC) is used. Unlike LTC, VITC can be read when a tape is paused. VITC appears as a row of dots on top of each video field and allows an operator to locate a specific frame.

vertical market (n.) A special group that requires products suited to its needs. The medical profession is a vertical market with unique information needs. By contrast, the markets for office management products are not highly differentiated.

Very Easy Rodent-Oriented Netwide Index to Computerized Archives See *VERONICA.*

Very High-Speed Digital Subscriber Line (VH-DSL) (n.) Variant of Asymmetric Digital Subscriber Line (ADSL) capable of delivering switched digital video over existing copper twisted pairs that are less than 3000 feet long. Also called *BDSL* (Broadband DSL) or *VDSL*.

very large-scale integration (VLSI) (n.) An integrated circuit (IC) that generally incorporates between 1000 and 9999 command processes, or logic gates, on a single silicon chip.

VESA See *Video Electronics Standards Association.*

VfW See *Video for Windows.*

VGA See *Video Graphics Array.*

VH-DSL See *Very High-Speed Digital Subscriber Line.*

VHS See *video home system.*

video (n.) The translation of moving images into electronic signals. The term *video* implies a stream of visual images displayed at a constant frame rate, usually with an audio track. The signals can be broadcast through the air via high-frequency carrier waves or distributed via closed-circuit cable. Video applications include commercial broadcasts, corporate communications, marketing, home entertainment, arcade games, security systems, and the moving picture component of multimedia programs.

video bandwidth (n.) Measured in MHz, the range of frequencies at which pixels may be processed by a monitor.

video black (n.) A portion of videotape with no images or sound recorded on it. Video black is used as a buffer between programs and is inserted before and after tape segments.

videocassette (n.) The case that holds magnetic tape used for videotape applications, most often in the VHS format.

videocassette recorder (VCR) (n.) A home videotaping device.

Video-CD (n.) Video–compact disc; a full-motion digital video format on CD-ROM using MPEG-1 video compression and incorporating a program control bar with controls similar to those of a VCR. Video-CD conforms to the White Book specification.

video clip (n.) A section of recorded video taken from a longer video recording.

video compression (n.) Data reduction in digital files that represent sequences of images. The reduction applies the concept that there are usually minor changes from one frame to the next. The differences in content between frames are encoded in the *interframe* coding technique, and content that is similar between frames is discarded. Another method of reducing file size in video compression is *intraframe* coding, in which data that defines an individual frame is reduced using discrete cosine transform (DCT). MPEG is a video compression format, as is the H.261 standard.

videoconference (n.) A meeting between participants at remote sites who can see and hear each other and share visual data in real time. Such a conference is possible when two or more locations are linked by fast telecommunications lines.

videodisc (n.) An optical laser disc, 9 or 12 inches in diameter, that stores data, text, still images, and full-motion video (FMV) in an analog format. The term *videodisc* refers to any platter from which video content can be decoded and displayed on a monitor, including a

Video-CD in the White Book format. A Video-CD contains video compressed using the MPEG-1 specification.

videodisc formats (n.) 1. Optical videodisc or laser disc. 2. CD-ROM formatted for either CD-i or Video-CD. 3. DVD, a specification introduced in 1995, and developed through the collaboration of Philips, Sony, Toshiba, and Panasonic.

video display (n.) Any cathode-ray tube (CRT) in the raster format that displays information from a video source. See also *monitor*.

video display terminal (VDT) (n.) A networked client with a keyboard and a screen. Workstations and dumb terminals are VDTs.

video driver (n.) The software interface between an application program and the video card hardware.

Video Electronics Standards Association (VESA, pronounced "VEE-sah") (n.) An industry trade group formed to codify the software interface for advanced video cards. The acronym is used to refer to the VESA local bus interface and to describe the slot on a computer that accepts a VESA card.

Video for Windows (VfW) (n.) Developed by Microsoft in 1992, a scalable digital video format that decodes digital video .avi files. It runs in all implementations of Microsoft Windows, including version 3.1, Windows NT, and Windows 95 and 98. This type of video file can be compressed by several popular CODECs, including Indeo and CinePak, making the files smaller and allowing them to stream at higher data rates.

video game (n.) Interactive game produced for a personal computer or for an arcade console,

generally distributed on a ROM cartridge or on a CD-ROM.

Video Graphics Array (VGA, pronounced "vee-gee-AY") (n.) A graphics display standard introduced in 1987 by IBM for PS/2 computers. The basic specification provides for 640 x 480 pixel resolution and 256 simultaneous colors. The standard has been expanded by graphics card manufacturers. See also *Super Video Graphics Array* and *Extended Graphics Adapter*.

video head (n.) A component in a videotape player over which the tape passes. The head reads, erases, or records the video signal.

video home system (VHS) (n.) A popular consumer 0.5-inch videotape format developed by Matsushita and JVC.

video-in-a-window (n.) The placement of a video clip on top of the background on a computer monitor. Video-in-a-window may be incorporated in the form of a quarter-screen box playing compressed digital video in one of the popular software CODECs, such as QuickTime or Video for Windows (VfW). It may also be input by means of a special video adapter card that can display an NTSC or a PAL signal on a Video Graphics Array (VGA) monitor.

video information system (VIS) (n.) Introduced by Tandy Corporation in 1992, a consumer multimedia player designed to plug into a home TV and to provide playback of interactive titles and standard audio CDs.

video object (n.) A file that contains a video clip.

video-on-demand (VOD) (n.) A system that allows users to select video programming from a broadband network. The system affords the user playback controls over a video.

video overlay (n.) The placement of computer-generated video over analog video, including letters produced by dedicated titling systems. A video overlay system requires a genlock to synchronize input signals.

videophone (n.) A telephone product used to transmit and receive compressed video and audio over existing telephone lines.

video RAM (VRAM, pronounced "VEE-ram") (n.) Video random-access memory; a special memory chip that is designed for video applications and that usually has a special port for video information. Other data travels through another port.

video reprocessing (n.) A common editing technique in which video from a computer source is keyed over existing video. See also *overlay*.

video server (n.) A networked storage device, typically a hard disk, an optical drive, or a CD-ROM jukebox, holding video data that is accessible online to delivery systems or workstations. A video server may perform decoding operations for its clients, or this may be performed at each workstation.

videotape (n.) Used to record moving pictures, a type of magnetic tape that can also record synchronized audio signals. See figure.

information on a videotape

videotape formats (n.) The analog tape standards used in recording video, informally differentiated by the width of the tape.

- 1-inch: Format used for professional broadcast-quality video recording and editing. This format is stored on open reels.

- 0.75-inch: Sony U-matic format. This format is stored in thick cassettes.

- 0.5-inch: Cassette-based format. VHS and Sony Betamax produce low-end consumer videotapes of this width. S-VHS and Super Beta produce higher-quality video in the 0.5-inch format.

- 8 mm: Consumer format that provides good-quality recording on small tape cassettes. This format is popular in handheld camcorders. An enhanced version called *Hi-8* has improved resolution and is comparable to S-VHS in quality. Hi-8 and S-VHS have 400 lines of resolution and S-video (Y/C video) separation, but the greater width of S-VHS tape makes it less prone to dropouts.

Many professionals prefer Sony Betacam SP for shooting and D-2 (digital composite) for editing masters. Professional studios use two digital formats: D-1 (digital component) by Sony and D-5 by Panasonic.

videotext (n.) A distribution system for information that uses screens of text as the primary content. Videotext services can be distributed through cable or broadcast television systems, or they can be sent over telephone lines to a computer that can construct the images on screen. The graphics are of relatively low resolution, and a proprietary decoder is required.

video user interface (VUI) (n.) Onscreen controls that allow a viewer to select channels or programs and control playback parameters.

videowall (n.) A rectangular configuration of monitors combined to form a large display. The monitors are generally controlled by a computer that distributes a single video image so that each tube contains one portion of the complete image.

viewer (n.) Software application that displays data in a specific format. A PowerPoint viewer displays presentations created with PowerPoint. If a viewer is installed, a file may be played without requiring the application that created the file.

viewfinder (n.) A small window on a camera through which the operator can see approximately what appears in the camera lens. Typically, the picture in a viewfinder is not framed exactly the way it will appear on film or video.

virtual (adj.) Describes an object, an entity, or a relationship that exists in software rather than in a tangible, physical condition. In computing, a virtual device could represent a hardware peripheral. The use of virtual devices helps programmers avoid hardware incompatibilities as actual configurations evolve. *Virtual* is a commonly used term for anything that exists but that has no concrete manifestation. An ensemble of samplers playing a MIDI score is called a *virtual orchestra*. Compare *real*.

virtual address (n.) The location of a device, such as a printer, belonging to a guest operating system. The virtual address is mapped to a physical device.

Virtual Address Extension (VAX, pronounced "VACKS") (n.) Released in 1978, a minicomputer design that was popular among programmers but that was replaced by powerful microcomputers 10 years later.

Virtual Address Extension/Virtual Memory System (VAX/VMS) (n.) A minicomputer and operating system (OS) developed by Digital Equipment Corporation (DEC). *OpenVMA*, a newer version of the OS, runs on the DEC Alpha and other types of processors.

virtual circuit (n.) A voice or data link that appears to the user to be a dedicated circuit, but which may be a temporary connection routed by whatever physical path is available at the time the connection is requested. A logical rather than a specific physical path over which a connection is made. A virtual circuit is a connection-oriented network service that does not rely on any particular routing pattern.

virtual device driver (VxD) (n.) A software agent in Microsoft Windows running as part of the kernel. A VxD has access to the memory of the kernel and of all running processes, as well as access to the hardware. VxDs written for Windows 3.x may generally be implemented in Windows 95.

virtual disk (n.) A conceptual drive rather than a physical drive. The user is not concerned with how the data is physically written. A virtual drive may span multiple physical drives, but it will appear to the user as only one drive.

Virtual Loadable Module (VLM) (n.) A term introduced by Novell for software modules that can be dynamically loaded to extend the functionality of the VLM Netware Requester for MS-DOS, which became standard beginning with Novell Netware 4.0.

virtual machine (n.) An abstract computing machine for which an interpreter exists. Virtual machines are used to implement portable executors for high-level languages. Java depends on the local installation of its virtual machine to function.

virtual memory (n.) The address space available to a process running in a system with a memory management unit (MMU). Hard disk space is used to virtually simulate internal RAM. Virtual memory may be much larger than the amount of physical RAM installed. The virtual address space is divided into pages. Paging allows the excess to be stored on disk and copied to RAM as required. This makes it possible to run programs whose code plus data size exceeds the amount of available RAM. A page is copied from disk to RAM when an attempt is made to access it and when it is not already present. This paging is performed automatically by collaboration between the CPU, the MMU, and the operating system.

Virtual Memory System (VMS) (n.) The proprietary operating system developed by Digital Equipment Corporation (DEC) for its VAX minicomputer.

Virtual Private Network (VPN) (n.) Technology that enables secure delivery of private data over the Internet by employing protected servers and encrypting data. VPN allows economical remote access to private data by eliminating the need for remote access hardware and systems.

virtual reality (VR) (n.) A realistic, computer-generated world in which users may participate by using data gloves and head-mounted graphic display units.

virtual reality modeling language (VRML) (n.) The standard for delivering virtual worlds on the Internet. VRML 1.0 was released in May 1995 as an adaptation of the Silicon Graphics

Open Inventor file format, which described static scenes. In December 1995 it was proposed that the next version of VRML incorporate programmable behaviors. The official VRML 2.0 specification was released in August 1996.

A stand-alone viewer or a plug-in for a browser is needed for viewing VRML. Netscape Navigator provides the Live3D plug-in as a standard component. The Cosmo Player from SGI is one of the more advanced tools.

A VRML file consists of text commands that a VRML viewer interprets and displays as an image. This image is called a *world* or a *scene*. Color, texture, lighting, sound, and motion are features of a virtual world. The text files that define a virtual world are similar to HTML files but have more complexity. A number of applications that render three-dimensional (3-D) models can export objects and scenes in the VRML format.

VRML files have "nodes" that define 3-D objects, such as cubes, spheres, and other shapes in a 3-D coordinate system. VRML adds dimensionality and advanced interactivity to HTML. A VRML viewer allows a user to navigate worlds, seeing 3-D objects from different perspectives. The mouse is used to provide perspective on the world and to move around in it. For example, a scene rotates around its center when the user clicks and drags the right mouse button in a circular direction.

There are several means of navigating in a VRML world. In Walk mode, the arrow keys move the cursor or an onscreen object up, down, right, or left in the scene. This can also be accomplished by clicking and dragging the mouse. In Fly mode, navigation functions are similar to those in a flight simulator. In Examine mode, the user may rotate the world around an object to change perspectives. In a VRML world, a user may visit predetermined points called *viewpoints*. It is possible to jump from one viewpoint to another in a virtual world, which is a valuable feature for a disoriented user. The user may adjust lighting and other details about the appearance of a world.

A VRML file is identifiable by its header, a necessary component of every legal file. An appropriate header would be *#VRML V2.0 utf8*. *#VRML* indicates the file type, *V2.0* indicates the version, and *utf8* identifies the character set to be used.

Utf8 allows the file to be written with non-ASCII characters, similar to Unicode, according to the ISO 10646 standard. HTML requires the use of special coded characters, or escape sequences, to represent non-ASCII characters. VRML does not require exclusively ASCII text, and the alphabet in any language can be used to create a VRML file. Comments may be inserted in a VRML file after the # character because the viewer ignores anything after that character on a line. The exception to this is the header, or the first line of the file.

Common terms have special definitions in the language of VRML. A *node* is a predefined word that describes something in a VRML scene. It is the VRML equivalent of a *tag* in HTML. A node is written with the first letter capitalized in every word. The VRML 2.0 specification defines both *Group* and *Leaf* nodes. A Group node can contain any number of Child nodes, but a Leaf node can include only specified nodes. Basic *field types* help define the characteristics of a node. Field types can be any kind of data, from integer numbers to color values.

Braces ({ }) are used to delimit the scope of the node in the same way that the angle brackets (< >) are used in HTML, but the name of a

node lies outside the brackets rather than inside. Unlike HTML tags, VRML nodes may be nested inside other nodes. All the parameters of a node are contained within a set of braces.

The basic building blocks of VRML are *primitives,* such as the Sphere, the Cone, the Box, and the Cylinder. These basic shapes render faster than complex ones. All geometry nodes must exist as the child of a Shape node, which has two fields: "appearance" and "geometry." Each object must be assigned a color because the default color for all objects is black. The Material node contains the color command, along with textures. The Transform node is a grouping node, used to locate and move objects. The Anchor node is also a grouping node, sending the browser to the URL identified in the link, which may be another VRML world.

The goal of the developers of VRML 2.0 is to provide a richer and more interactive user experience than is possible within the static boundaries of HTML or VRML 1.0. Static worlds are enhanced in VRML 2.0 with interaction, animation, scripting, and prototyping.

Version 2.0 of VRML adds many new nodes that were not available in version 1.0. Some of these allow the creation of *backdrops* for scenes with distant objects, as well as the *fog* effect. Another new node provides irregular "terrain" to replace flat planes and surfaces. Following terrain allows the user to travel up and down steps or ramps. Version 2.0 offers 3-D spatial Sound nodes. It is easier to optimize and parse files in VRML 2.0 than in VRML 1.0, thanks to a simplified "scene-graph" structure.

A user can directly interact with objects and creatures. New Sensor nodes set off events in specified areas of a world in response to objects. Collision detection defines the consistent behavior of solid objects.

Version 2.0 includes a number of animation tools called *Interpolators*. They allow the user to create predefined animations involving many features of a world. Interpolators can create objects such as flying birds, automatically opening doors, and objects that change color and morph from one shape to another. Interpolators can provide guided tours that move the user along a predefined path.

Virtual Telecommunications Access Method (VTAM) (n.) Programs designed to control communications between nodes and applications in Systems Network Architecture (SNA).

virus (n.) A self-replicating, destructive program.

VIS See *video information system.*

visible light (n.) Electromagnetic radiation in the spectrum between 400 nanometers and 700 nanometers that the unaided human eye can see.

Visual Basic (VB) (n.) A programming environment developed by Microsoft.

Visual Component Library (VCL) (n.) A library of objects for the Borland Delphi rapid application development software.

visualization (n.) In computer graphics, a technique that allows a computer to present graphic images or representations of phenomena that normally could not be viewed. Visualization is becoming an important tool in many science and engineering fields.

visual programming (n.) Creating programs in a language that supports visual interaction and allows the programmer to manipulate visual information.

VITC See *vertical interval time code.*

VLM See *Virtual Loadable Module.*

VLSI See *very large-scale integration.*

VLSM See *Variable Length Subnet Mask.*

VMS (n.) See *Virtual Memory System.*

VOD See *video-on-demand.*

voice-activated (adj.) Describes a program executed or controlled by the sound of a human voice.

voice channel (n.) In a telecommunications connection, the segment of the bandwidth allocated to transmitting voice messages.

voice coil (n.) An element present at both ends of a sound reinforcement system. In a microphone, the voice coil vibrates as sound waves strike it. In a loudspeaker, the wire coil connected to the cone causes the cone to vibrate.

voice-grade channel (n.) Signal path suitable for the transmission of speech, fax, analog, or digital data. A voice-grade channel has a frequency range of approximately 300 Hz to 3 kHz.

voice mail (n.) A system in which voice messages are recorded on a messaging system connected to a telephone private branch exchange (PBX). The addressee may access the messages after they are recorded.

voice-over (n., adj.) Narration for a video or movie in which the narrator does not appear on screen. A voice-over is recorded during postproduction.

voice recognition (n.) A system in which a

computer recognizes human speech and converts it into binary code or text files. Also known as *speech recognition.*

volatile (adj.) Describes a type of storage that requires constant electrical current to maintain data. The data is lost if the current is interrupted. RAM storage is volatile.

volatile storage (n.) A type of storage device in which data is lost if operating power is interrupted or if battery backup is not provided. An example of volatile storage is RAM.

voltage (n.) A quantity of electromotive force measured between two points in an electrical circuit. The voltage between two points may also be identified as the charge between those points (expressed in coulombs) divided by the capacitance (expressed in farads). The capacitance depends on the dielectric constant of the insulators present. Voltage is analogous to the pressure of water in a pipe, whereas current is analogous to the amount of water flowing over a unit of time.

volume (n.) A block of memory on a disk or a tape that may consume the entire medium or that may represent just a partition.

volume label (n.) The name a user assigns to a disk or a block of memory when it is formatted using MS-DOS.

voxel (n.) A volume element that is the three-dimensional (3-D) equivalent of a pixel. In other words, a voxel is the smallest region that may be defined discretely in a 3-D imaging system.

VPN See *Virtual Private Network.*

VR See *virtual reality.*

VRAM See *video RAM.*

VRML See *virtual reality modeling language.*

VTAM See *Virtual Telecommunications Access Method.*

VT-100 (n.) Built by Digital Equipment Corporation (DEC) in the early 1980s, a cathode-ray tube (CRT) video terminal whose control codes still form the basis of the X terminal set and of the ANSI and IBM PC standards. Most terminal emulators provide VT-100 compatibility.

VT-200 (n.) The Digital Equipment Corporation (DEC) video terminal that superseded the VT-100 series.

VUI See *video user interface.*

VU meter (n.) Volume unit meter; a measuring device used in audio recording and broadcasting to indicate amplitude levels relative to a standard. A VU is a form of decibel (dB) reference. It equals 1 milliwatt of power that meets with a 600-ohm load. VU meters are calibrated in order to indicate 0 dB as the maximum undistorted signal level, with a red zone for levels that exceed that point. See figure on the following page.

V.x (n.) A series of ITU-T standards for error correction, data compression, and testing for modem operations. The suffix *bis* indicates a second evolution, and the suffix *ter* a third evolution. Chronological developments are listed below:

- V.21: Modem protocol for 300-bit-per-second (bps), two-wire, full-duplex communications using frequency shift keying (FSK) modulation. All modern modems

VU meter

support both V.21 and a similar variant, Bell 103.

- V.22: Modem protocol that allows data rates of 1200 bps. V.22bis doubled this data rate.

- V.22bis: Modem protocol that allows a data rate of 2400 bps, twice that of V.22.

  V.23: Modem protocol that allows half-duplex (unidirectional) data transmission at 1200 bps.

- V.24: Standard defining interchange circuits between data terminal equipment (DTE) and data communications equipment (DCE). V.24 is the ITU-T equivalent of EIA standard RS-232C. V.24 recommends 12 modem carrier frequencies that do not interfere with Dual Tone Multi-Frequency (DTMF) or with other telephone control tones.

  Group A: 920 Hz, 1000 Hz, 1080 Hz, 1160 Hz
  Group B: 1320 Hz, 1400 Hz, 1480 Hz, 1560 Hz
  Group C: 1720 Hz, 1800 Hz, 1880 Hz, 1960 Hz

- V.25: Standard that allows an auto-answer

modem to determine the correct modulation standard to use.

- V.27: Protocol for duplex modems transmitting at 4800 bps with manual equalization over leased lines.

- V.27bis: Protocol for duplex modems transmitting at 2400/4800 bps with automatic equalization over leased lines.

- V.27ter: Protocol for duplex modems transmitting at 4800 bps over leased lines.

- V.28: Standard for double-current, unbalanced interchange circuits used in telecommunications.

- V.29: Protocol for duplex or half-duplex modems transmitting at 9600 bps point-to-point over four-wire leased telephone lines.

- V.32: Protocol for duplex modems transmitting at 4800 or 9600 bps with echo cancellation. Bidirectional data transmission is accomplished by subtracting what is sent from what is received.

- V.32bis: Extension of the V.32 modem protocol, allowing speeds of 7200, 12 000, and 14 400 bps. The modem will select the appropriate speed according to the current line conditions.

- V.32ter: Extension of the V.32bis modem protocol, allowing speeds of 19.2 kilobits per second (Kbps). Modem manufacturers extended V.32bis while waiting for V.34 to be developed.

- V.34: Standard modem serial line protocol for data signaling rates of up to 28 800 bps for use on the general switched telephone network and on leased point-to-point, two-wire, telephone-type circuits.

- V.35: Standard for data transmission at 48 Kbps over 60- to 108-kHz group band circuits. V.35 includes the 34-pin V.34 connector specifications normally implemented on a modular RJ-45 connector.

- V.42: Standard protocol with error correction between modems. V.42 includes Microcom Networking Protocol (MNP) up to Level 4.

- V.42bis: Extension of the V.42 standard modem protocol. V.42bis includes compression levels exceeding MNP-5.

- V.54: Standard that defines methods and devices for loop testing in modems.

- V.70: Standard modem protocol for Digital Simultaneous Voice and Data (DSVD).

- V.80: Defines the application interface for H.324 videoconferencing over modems.

- V.90: Standard modem protocol that incorporates the features of two competing formats, "X2" (3Com) and "K56flex" (Rockwell). It receives data at 56 kilobits per second (Kbps) and transmits at 33.6 Kbps.

VxD See *virtual device driver*.

W

WABI See *Windows Application Binary Interface.*

wafer (n.) A thin disk or a slice of silicon on which separate chips can be fabricated and cut into individual die.

WAIS See *Wide Area Information Servers.*

wait state (n.) A pause during which a processor waits one or more clock cycles until memory responds. A "zero wait state" system uses fast memory or a memory cache system to avoid wait states.

walk-through (n.) 1. A simulation that creates the effect of traveling through a computerized architectural model in which the viewer can interactively navigate a path. 2. In film and video production, a rehearsal without cameras.

WAN See *wide area network.*

Warez (n.) Jargon for software that is pirated and often distributed over bulletin board systems (BBSs). Pronounced "WAIRZ."

warm boot (v.) To restart a computer without turning off the power. In the Mac OS this is accomplished by selecting Restart from the Special menu. On an IBM-compatible ma-

chine it is done with the key combination Ctrl-Alt-Delete, which is known as a *three-finger salute.*

WATS See *wide area telephone service.*

WAV (n.) A Microsoft DOS and Windows file name extension, or a suffix, used to indicate a sound file. This type of file consists of a set of digitized samples representing waveforms. A sound card can realize these samples.

WAVE (n.) The preferred standard of multimedia sound for Microsoft and IBM. It is a RIFF file containing pulse code modulation (PCM) waveform audio data, and it is identified with the .wav extension.

waveform (n.) The regular variations in pressure that define a wave. A waveform may exist in any spectral range, but the term typically refers to audio and video waves. The frequency, amplitude, and all other parameters of a waveform may be digitized and stored in a wavetable as a sample.

waveform monitor (n.) A test instrument that displays a video signal graphed over a selected interval of time, rather than displaying a video picture. A waveform monitor measures video gain and sync pulses, as well as the frequency and amplitude of waves.

waveguide (n.) A conducting or dielectric device that can support and propagate one or more modes. The term generally refers to fiber-optic transmission media.

wavelength (n.) The distance between successive peaks of a regularly repeating waveform.

Wavelength Division Multiplexing (WDM) (n.) The combination of more than one light source and detector that operate at different wavelengths through the same fiber and that simultaneously transmit independent optical signals.

wavelet (n.) A waveform defined in both the frequency and the temporal domains. A Fourier transform converts a signal into a continuous series of sine waves, each with constant frequency and amplitude and with infinite duration. Most actual waves have a finite duration, however, and their frequencies change abruptly. Wavelet transforms convert a signal into a series of smaller waves, or wavelets. Signals processed by the wavelet transform are stored more efficiently than those processed by the Fourier transform. Actual waveforms with rough edges are better approximated by wavelet transforms.

wavetable (n.) A collection of digitized sound waves stored as samples in computer memory. A wavetable in a sound card holds the instrument sounds that a MIDI file uses to play music.

wavetable synthesis (n.) Audio signals that are based on digital samples of recorded sounds rather than on sounds that are artificially synthesized by a means such as frequency modulation (FM).

WDM See *Wavelength Division Multiplexing.*

web See *World Wide Web.*

web browser (n.) A universal client application used to read HTML files found on the World Wide Web. The two most widely used browsers are Netscape Navigator and MS Internet Explorer.

webcasting (n.) The act of broadcasting content, typically streaming media, from a web server. Webcasting works on a one-to-many principle, rather than the usual one-to-one principle that governs most Internet connections.

webmaster (n.) The person who maintains a World Wide Web server and its contents.

web page (n.) An HTML file that is identified by a URL and that a web browser can read. A web page may contain text, hypertext links to other locations, and images in the GIF and JPEG formats. Some servers can generate pages dynamically in response to a request by a Common Gateway Interface (CGI) script.

Web Request Broker (WRB) (n.) A multi-threaded HTTP server from Oracle Corporation that translates Oracle 7 database requests into HTML for delivery to the universal client.

web server (n.) A networked computer that responds to HTTP requests from remote clients by sending HTML documents. Multiple hostnames, known as *virtual servers,* may be mapped to the same computer. Apache and HTTPd are commonly used web servers.

web site (n.) A collection of HTML documents, known as *web pages,* that are delivered by a web server. The hostname portion of a URL identifies a web site.

WELL See *Whole Earth 'Lectronic Link.*

wet (n.) Refers to an audio track that has been treated with signal processing, particularly reverb. A wet track is processed with reverb, delay, or other effects, whereas a "dry" track has no effects.

what you see is what you get (WYSIWYG, pronounced "WIZZ-ee-wig") (n., adj.) A way of displaying graphics in some desktop publishing applications in which the screen reflects the exact way the printed page will appear.

Whetstone (n.) Program that simulates other arithmetic-intensive programs used in scientific computing to benchmark system performance. Whetstone tests do not perform input/output (I/O) or system calls. The units of measurement defining the speed at which a system performs floating-point operations are known as Whetstones.

white balance (n., adj.) An adjustment made to a camera or another video source so that a white object will produce the proper signal. Most consumer camcorders have automatic white-balance circuits. It is imperative to calibrate a video camera when light conditions change. This is often accomplished by recording a white page of paper full screen at the depth of the background. The camera then automatically corrects color as needed.

White Book standard (n.) 1. Developed by Philips and JVC in 1993, a specification for storing MPEG-1 video on a CD-ROM. The White Book standard is an extension of the Red Book standard for digital audio, the Yellow Book standard for CD-ROM, the Green Book standard for CD-i, and the Orange Book standard for CD-R. As with the other standards,

the name of the White Book standard describes the color of its cover. 2. The fourth book in Adobe's PostScript series, describing the format of Type 1 fonts. The other three official guides are known as the Blue Book, the Green Book, and the Red Book.

white flag (n.) In the transfer of film to videotape, a code used to mark a new full frame. Also known as *full-frame ID.*

white level (n.) The level of the brightest possible white value in a video signal. In most video formats, the white level equals the minimum voltage.

white pages (n.) Databases with basic information about Internet users, such as telephone numbers, email addresses, and street addresses. The white pages can be searched to gather information about individuals.

white paper (n.) A treatise defining a new technology or describing a process that is being implemented. White papers typically represent research, and they often project uses and applications of the topic under investigation.

whois (n.) An Internet directory service that locates information about networks and users on a remote server. Servers may respond to a TCP query or to the finger protocol. A list of whois servers appears at the FTP/gopher address *sipb.mit.edu.*

Whole Earth 'Lectronic Link (WELL) (n.) Popular online service based in Sausalito, California. The URL is *http://www.well.com.*

wide-angle (adj.) Describes a camera lens with a short focal length and a broad field of view.

Wide Area Information Servers (WAIS) (n.) A distributed information retrieval system that allows clients to retrieve documents by inputting keywords. A WAIS search returns a list of documents, prioritized according to the frequency with which the keyword occurs. Public domain versions are available, and a client can retrieve text or multimedia documents stored on a server. A relevance feedback mechanism allows the results of initial searches to improve future searches. The web and gopher are examples of other information retrieval systems. WAIS is supported by Apple Computer, Thinking Machines, and Dow Jones.

wide area network (WAN, pronounced "WAN") (n.) The integration of geographically distant or technologically incompatible local area networks (LANs). Technologies that contribute to the existence of these networks include Asynchronous Transfer Mode (ATM), ISDN, CCITT X.25, and frame relay. See also *local area network*.

wide area telephone service (WATS, pronounced "WAHTS") (n.) A long-distance toll service, inward or outward, offered at a discount by a telephone company.

wideband (n.) A data transmission system with a large bandwidth and with multiple-channel access.

widescreen TV (n.) Widescreen television; for high-definition television (HDTV) broadcast, a proposed ratio of 16:9, or 1.78:1, rather than the normal 4:3 aspect ratio for the screen. 16:9 is a ratio more similar to that of the film processors Cinemascope and Panavision, which exhibit aspect ratios in the range of 2.35:1. When the wider aspect ratio is shown on a standard screen, the result is called the *letterbox* effect.

wide SCSI (n.) Wide Small Computer System Interface; a form of SCSI-2 interface that allows a 16-bit bus and that supports transfer rates up to 20 megabytes per second (MBps), as does fast SCSI. The SCSI-2 version of wide SCSI that permits a 32-bit bus supports transfer rates up to 40 MBps. *Wide SCSI* generally refers to 16-bit-wide SCSI.

widow (n.) At the end of a paragraph, a short line of text or a partial word that is separated by a page or column break and that therefore appears on the next page or the next column.

wild (adj.) 1. Describes audio tracks that are recorded live in the field along with the video frames. 2. Describes audio tracks or sound effects that are not synchronized with a video track. Wild effects may be gathered and synchronized in postproduction. If an error is introduced in the sync signal during postproduction, audio tracks can become wild, or out of sync, by mistake.

wildcard See *global file specification*.

WIMP (n.) Windows, Icons, Menus, and Pointing device; a graphical user interface (GUI) invented at Xerox PARC, originally used by the Mac OS, and replicated by other systems.

Winchester disk (n.) A drive that consists of a stack of platters. The original development project for hard disk drives at IBM was called *Winchester*.

window (n.) 1. A defined area on a monitor designated for video or for other information. 2. The portion of a display in which a document or an application runs in a graphical user interface (GUI). An independent program will be displayed in its own window on the monitor. Several windows may be open at once in a multitasking environment.

window dub (n.) A videotape with a small window superimposed on each frame. The window displays positional information in time code as the tape plays. The window is called a *time code window.*

Windows See *Microsoft Windows.*

Windows Application Binary Interface (WABI, pronounced "WAH-bee") (n.) A Sun Microsystems software package that lets Microsoft Windows applications run in the X Window System. WABI 2.2 runs under Solaris on the SPARC, Intel, and PowerPC platforms. It translates USER.DLL, KERNEL.DLL, and GDI.DLL, the three core Windows libraries that redirect Windows calls to Solaris equivalents. For code other than core library calls, WABI either executes the instructions directly on the hardware, if it is Intel, or emulates them, either one instruction at a time or by translating a block of instructions and caching the result.

Windows for Workgroups 3.11 (n.) An upgrade to Windows 3.1. The upgrade added 32-bit file access, improved performance, and provided fax capability.

Windows Metafile (WMF) (n.) A format that stores an image as a series of Windows Graphical Device Interface (GDI) functions. The files, which are scalable drawings rather than bitmaps, require little storage space, display quickly on the screen, and are transportable among applications.

Windows 98 (Win98) (n.) Released in 1998, the version of the Microsoft Windows operating system for IBM-compatible computers that superseded Windows 95. It is not significantly different from Win95, but incorporates nu-

merous minor repairs and upgrades to the system. One notable advance is the FAT32 file system, which enables files on a hard disk to be stored in smaller blocks. The Internet Explorer browser is tightly integrated with this operating system.

Windows 95 (Win95) (n.) Released in August 1995, the version of the Microsoft Windows operating system for IBM-compatible computers that superseded Windows 3.1. Win95 is a complete operating system, not merely a graphical user interface (GUI) running on top of MS-DOS as Windows 3.1 is. Win95 provides 32-bit application support, preemptive multitasking, and threading. Networking is available in the form of TCP/IP, Internetwork Packet eXchange (IPX), SLIP, PPP, and Windows Sockets (Winsock).

Windows NT (n.) Windows New Technology; a 32-bit hardware-independent operating system from Microsoft that was originally designed for IBM-compatible workstations, servers, and corporate networks. Based on a microkernel, it has 32-bit addressing for up to 4 gigabytes (GB) of RAM. Windows NT features virtual hardware access to protect applications from crashing, installable file systems, and built-in networking. It offers multiprocessor support and high security.

Windows Sockets (Winsock) (n.) A specification conceived in 1991 for Microsoft Windows network software. Winsock defines how applications access network services, especially TCP/IP. Winsock provides a single Application Programming Interface (API) for which application developers may program. It is supported by Windows for Workgroups, Win32s, Windows 95, and Windows NT.

Windows 3.1 (n.) A version of Microsoft Windows with TrueType fonts and object linking and embedding (OLE). Windows 3.11 is the updated version.

WinG (Pronounced "win-GEE") (n.) A library of high-performance graphics routines that enhance the performance of Microsoft Windows. WinG adds halftone ability so that a system with an 8-bit palette can effectively present 24-bit color. The runtime library may be distributed without permission from Microsoft. It consists of WING.DLL for 16-bit systems and WING32.DLL for 32-bit implementations.

Win98 See *Windows 98.*

Win95 See *Windows 95.*

Winsock See *Windows Sockets.*

Win32 (n.) A 32-bit Application Programming Interface (API) that is supported by recent versions of Microsoft Windows and that incorporates features such as multiple threads and remote control of networked computers.

Win32s (n.) A software layer on top of Windows 3.1 that allows 32-bit applications to run.

WinToon (n.) Developed by Microsoft, an animation engine that runs in Windows 95. It efficiently layers a moving image in the foreground over a static background by minimizing the updates to redundant data from screen to screen.

WinZip (n.) The Microsoft Windows version of PKZIP, a compression utility.

wipe (n., v.) In video special effects, a transitional effect that erases an image by replacing it with another one.

wire frame model (n.) A three-dimensional representation of an object made with line segments. A wire frame model is created before an object is rendered.

wireless (adj.) Describes a network without a cable or a fiber-optic link between sending and receiving units. In a wireless network, telephone or data signals are transmitted via high-frequency waves.

wizard (n.) A help file with templates accessed through a dialog box. Wizards come bundled with Microsoft Windows applications.

WMF See *Windows Metafile.*

word clock (n.) A type of timing reference signal found in virtually all digital audio production equipment. The connector is typically a BNC type, and the signal consists of clock information running at the sample rate of the program material. This is the same as an AES/EBU null clock signal.

word wrap (n.) The capacity of a text editor or a word processor to send characters automatically to the next line when they reach the right margin. With word wrap, no line break or carriage return character is introduced.

workstation (n.) A monitor and a keyboard located on a network. Other devices may be connected to the network as well. A workstation may take the form of a dumb terminal connected to a server, or it could be a powerful networked computer.

World Wide Web (web, WWW) (n.) A distributed information retrieval system that operates over the Internet in a client-server environment. The web was developed by Tim Berners-Lee at the CERN High-Energy Physics Laboratories in Geneva, Switzerland. Hypertext links refer to HTML documents via a URL, which may refer to local or remote resources. These resources are accessible through FTP, gopher, Telnet, or news, as well as through the HTTP protocol used to transfer hypertext documents. A client program, or a browser, follows a link or sends a query to a server. The World Wide Web Consortium (W3C) is the primary standards body for the web.

World Wide Web Consortium (W3C) (n.) A group created at MIT in 1994. The W3C works with the global community to establish international standards for client and server protocols that enable Internet communications. Netscape Communications Corporation was a founding member. The director is Tim Berners-Lee, who is credited with creating the web.

worm (n.) Self-propagating, self-replicating computer program that spawns in a network environment. A 1982 issue of *ACM Communications* first identified network worms.

WORM See *write-once-read-many.*

WRB See *Web Request Broker.*

writable optical media (n.) A catchall phrase for any optical media on which a user can record data. Magneto-optical (MO) cartridges used in write-once-read-many (WORM) drives and CD-recordables (CD-Rs), or "one-offs," both fit in this category.

write (v.) To move data from one physical place to another or from one medium to another.

write-back (adj.) Describes a type of computer cache in which data is written to main memory only when it is forced out of the cache. Compare *write-through.*

write-once-read-many (WORM) (n.) Optical storage in which the laser physically and permanently alters the surface of a disk by burning pits in it. A WORM drive is excellent for long-term storage of important data, but the medium can be used only once; the data cannot be erased nor the space reclaimed. See also *CD-R* under *compact disc.*

write-through (adj.) Describes a type of computer cache in which data is written to main memory at the same time as it is written to the cache. Compare *write-back.*

W3C See *World Wide Web Consortium.*

WWW See *World Wide Web.*

WYSIWYG See *what you see is what you get.*

X–Z

X See *X Window System.*

XA See *extended architecture* or *CD-ROM extended architecture.*

Xanadu (n.) Utopian plan devised by Theodor Holm Nelson in the early 1970s. The plan was to integrate all the library collections in the world into a single system. The web embodies some of his principles, including the capacity for nonlinear exploration of textual and other information.

XAR See *extended attribute record.*

X BitMap (XBM) (n.) One of the approved graphics formats that may be used for placing images on the web.

XBM See *X BitMap.*

XCMD See *external command.*

XDR See *eXternal Data Representation.*

Xenix (n.) Developed by Microsoft in 1979, a Unix-like operating system for use on Intel processors. Santa Cruz Operation, Inc. (SCO) was contracted by Microsoft to continue to develop and market the product.

Xerox Corporation Palo Alto Research Center (Xerox PARC) (n.) The laboratories where many hardware and software innovations were developed from the early 1970s to the mid-1980s. Among them were the mouse, graphical user interfaces (GUIs), the laser printer, the local area network (LAN), and object-oriented programming (OOP).

Xerox Network System (XNS) (n.) An aging local area network (LAN) protocol developed by Xerox Corporation. Packet size is limited to 576 bytes in this system. It serves as the basis for the third and fourth layers of the Novell and the 3Com LAN protocols currently in use.

Xerox PARC See *Xerox Corporation Palo Alto Research Center.*

XFCN See *external functions.*

XGA See *Extended Graphics Adapter.*

XLR connector (n.) An audio connector used for most low-impedance microphones and for balanced lines between professional signal-processing equipment. Three wires are soldered to three pins inside the barrel of the connector. The ground wire or the shield is typically connected to pin 1. Pins 2 and 3 carry the same signal in equal strength, but with a reversed phase relationship. This allows for the cancellation of unwanted noise over long cables. The microphone lines used in most recording studios are 200-ohm balanced lines with the shield grounded only at the preamp end. If the shields are grounded at more than one point, a ground loop may be created, producing a 60-cycle hum. See figure.

male   female

XLR connectors

XML See *Extensible Markup Language.*

XModem (n.) Developed by Ward Christensen in the late 1970s, a common protocol for file transfer over serial lines connecting modems. XModem uses 128-byte packets with error detection and lets a receiving unit request retransmission of a corrupted packet from the sending unit. Sending and receiving programs can negotiate and establish the best rate of transfer that they can both support. Standard XModem specifies a one-second timeout during the reception of characters in the data block portion of a packet. Chuck Forsberg improved on XModem by developing YModem and ZModem.

XMS See *extended memory specification.*

Xn (n.) Any network-oriented windowed system based on TCP/IP. The most popular windowed system is X11.

XNS See *Xerox Network System.*

X/Open (n.) A consortium of computer manufacturers and software developers that promotes the design of portable Unix-based applications. Formed in 1984, X/Open is dedicated to reducing incompatibility between information systems. In 1996 X/Open consolidated with the Open Software Foundation to form the Open Group. For more information visit the web sites maintained by these organizations: *http://www.osf.org* and *http://opengroup.com.*

X PixMap (XPM) (n.) An approved graphics format for placing images on the web.

XPM See *X PixMap.*

X Series (n.) Referred to as X.n (pronounced "EX-dot-en"), a set of recommendations prepared by the ITU-T that defines interface features for data terminal equipment (DTE) and data communications equipment (DCE). The rules for connecting devices to the public switched telephone network (PSTN) and public data networks (PDNs) are set forth in the X Series. Some of the primary recommendations are described here:

- X.3: The ISO approved ITU-T standard specifying the basic functions and the user-selectable capabilities of a Packet Assembly/Disassembly (PAD) device in a public data network.

- X.21: A digital signal interface recommendation by the ITU-T. X.21 specifies data terminal equipment–data communications equipment (DTE-DCE) physical interface elements, data transfer up to 64 Kbps, alignment of call control characters and error-checking characters, elements of the call control phase for circuit-switched services, and test loops.

- X.25: A protocol suite for the data termi-

X
Y
Z

343

nal equipment–data communications equipment (DTE-DCE) interface in a packet-switched network, recommended by the ITU-T and approved by ISO. X.25 defines three levels: the physical level, the data link level, and the packet level. These levels are similar to the lower three layers of the Open Systems Interconnection (OSI) reference model. X.25 describes how data passes through public data communications networks worldwide. The three levels are further defined as follows:

Level 1: The physical and electrical characteristics of data terminal equipment (DTE) and data communications equipment (DCE). A duplex synchronous link is specified to provide a transmission path between terminal equipment and the network.

Level 2: The accessing protocol for public packet-switching networks with error correction.

Level 3: The procedures for constructing and controlling data packets that are passed between data terminals and circuit equipment.

- X.28: The ISO approved ITU-T standard that specifies how to control a Packet Assembly/Disassembly (PAD) device from character-mode DTE.

- X.29: The ISO approved ITU-T standard specifying procedures for the exchange of control information and user data between a Packet Assembly/Disassembly (PAD) device and remote packet-mode data terminal equipment (DTE). Character-mode DTEs are known as *X.29 terminals.*

- X.75: The ITU-T standard that specifies protocols for communication between two packet-switching data networks (PSDNs).

- X.400: The standard that defines how messages are exchanged between different email systems. It is a set of protocols that translate messages, but does not include the sender's name in messages sent.

- X.500: Defines the method by which different types of workstations may exchange email using a single consolidated directory.

X terminal (n.) A dedicated terminal that runs X-server software. X terminal is a standard architecture for Unix machines.

X3T10 (n.) The Advanced Technology Attachment (ATA) standards body.

X Window System (X) (n.) A windowed system often mistakenly called *X Windows.* A specification for device-independent windowing operations on bitmap display devices, it was originally developed by MIT's Project Athena. The server is the computer, or the X terminal, and the screen, the keyboard, the mouse, the server program, and the clients are application programs. Clients may run on the same computer as the server or on a different computer, and they communicate over Ethernet via TCP/IP protocols. X clients run on what is often considered a file server, but in X, the screen, the keyboard, and the mouse are served out to the applications. X is used on many Unix systems.

x-y coordinates (n.) Points on a plane divided horizontally by the x-axis and divided vertically by the y-axis. X-y coordinates are used to plot graphs and to identify locations on a two-dimensional display. Another plane may be added, providing a z-axis for three-dimensional models.

Yahoo! (Yet Another Hierarchically Officious Oracle!) (n.) One of the largest hierarchical indexes of content on the World Wide Web.

YCC format See *colorYCC*.

Y/C video (n.) A type of video signal used in the Hi-8 and the S-VHS videotape formats. It transmits luminance and color as separate components, avoiding the combination used in composite video and the resulting loss of picture quality. Also known as *S-video*.

Year 2000 (Y2K, pronounced "WIE-to-kay") (n., adj.) A situation that may cause problems in software systems at the turn of the century. Some programs, particularly those written many years ago, provided only the last two digits defining the year in a date. When the year *00* occurs, these programs may not continue to function properly.

Yellow Book standard (n.) The specification for standard CD-ROMs. Based on the Red Book audio standard, which preceded it, this standard defines two new modes: mode 1 and mode 2. It also establishes a third layer of error correction.

Yet Another Hierarchically Officious Oracle! See *Yahoo!*.

YMCK (n.) Abbreviation for yellow, magenta, cyan, and black. See also *CMYK*.

YModem (n.) A file transfer protocol used between modems. Chuck Forsberg developed it as the successor to XModem. He later developed ZModem to improve on YModem. Whereas XModem uses 128-byte packets, YModem can also use 1-kilobyte (KB) pack-

ets. YModem is a batch protocol, but YModem-G is a nonstop version with no error correction during transmission. File sizes are included in the YModem header when both binary and text files are sent. Files transferred via YModem should therefore preserve their exact length. File modification times may also be present in the YModem header. YModem can fall back to smaller packets when necessary, but there is no backward compatibility with XModem's error detection.

YModem-G (n.) A streaming version of YModem released in the early 1980s in which the transmitter sends packets to the receiver as rapidly as possible without waiting for acknowledgments. An error will cause the file transfer to abort completely.

Y2K See *Year 2000*.

YUV color system (n.) A method of defining video signals that separates the luminance (Y) and the chrominance (UV) components. Human vision is much more sensitive to variations in intensity than to variations in color. The YUV encoding process takes advantage of this phenomenon and provides a wider bandwidth for luminance information than for chrominance information. Individually, the letters *YUV* signify intensity, hue, and value.

zap (v.) Jargon meaning to fry a chip with static electricity.

z-buffer (n.) The memory allocated to holding the depth value of pixels.

zero insertion force (ZIF, pronounced "ZIFF") (adj.) Describes a type of socket used on a motherboard to allow the manual replacement of one processor chip with another.

zero level (n.) In audio production, a relative

X
Y
Z

level of intensity. *Analog zero* is a nominal decibel (dB) level near the top of a VU meter, and loud sounds are likely to exceed it during recording. *Digital zero,* which is the highest level that may be recorded without distortion, is an absolute limit. Depending on equipment settings, analog zero usually equals 18 dB below digital zero.

ZIF See *zero insertion force.*

zig-zag sequence (n.) A reordering of quantized DCT coefficients designed to facilitate entropy coding by placing low-frequency coefficients before high-frequency ones.

zip (v.) To compress a file using PKZIP or WinZip, an archiving program. The PKZIP program is commonly used on MS-DOS or Windows systems. The companion program is PKUNZIP. Compare *unzip.*

ZIP (n.) A file name extension for compressed files. Such files are commonly used on IBM-compatible computers.

Zip drive (n.) A cartridge drive developed by Iomega Corporation that reads and writes to removable 100-megabyte (MB) hard disks.

ZModem (n.) A file transfer protocol developed by Chuck Forsberg with error checking and crash recovery. Its transfer rate is similar to that of YModem-G. ZModem does not wait for acknowledgment after each block is sent but sends blocks in rapid succession, as the YModem-G protocol does. A ZModem transfer may be reconstructed at a later date, and the previously transferred information need not be present if a transmission is canceled or interrupted for any reason.

zone (n.) 1. A single network or domain name controlled by a specific authority. Individual zones, or domains, are delegated to individual Internet Service Providers (ISPs) by InterNIC, which controls the .com domain name system (DNS) zone. 2. In AppleTalk, a logical group of network devices.

zoom (v.) To enlarge or reduce the size of an image as it is displayed in a camera. This is done by changing the focal length of a zoom lens. Like optical systems, some digital systems give the user a zoom control, although digital zoom is not as high in resolution as is optical zoom.

zoom ratio (n.) The difference in magnification between the widest angle setting and the most extreme telephoto setting in a zoom lens. A 10:1 zoom ratio indicates that objects will appear 10 times closer at the extreme telephoto setting than they appear at the extreme wide-angle setting.

z-sorting (n.) In three-dimensional graphics, a method used to determine which pixels are shown. Z-sorting puts polygons in order from front to back and displays them in front. A more accurate method of sorting is z-buffering, in which the depth value of individual pixels is stored and the lowest value for each pixel is shown.

List of Appendices

These appendices are intended to provide readers with detailed information about topics related to digital media. The conventions and syntax used in current development languages, such as HTML, XML, and JavaScript, are provided as a reference for programmers.

I. Hypertext Markup Language (HTML)

This multipart appendix on HTML addresses many new features and functions of the language.

* **Basic Tutorial on HTML**
  Guidelines covering the primary elements and conventions, based on the original standard rendered by virtually all browsers.
* **New Features in HTML 4.0**
  Describes and shows examples of the new features in HTML 4.0 compared to version 3.2. Identifies obsolete and deprecated elements.
* **HTML Tags and Attributes**
  Explains the use of variables and identifies the attributes that may be specified for each element in HTML 4.0.
* **Cascading Style Sheets**
  Lists the commands that control layout in an HTML document and explains how variables are specified. Indicates how styles are rendered by browsers.
* **Server-Side Includes (SSI)**
  Explains how commands may be issued to a server, causing it to dynamically deliver content to an HTML page.
* **HTML Color Tables**
  An extensive list of colors and the corresponding code (hexadecimal triplet) used to specify each color.
* **HTML Coded Characters**
  A complete list of the ISO characters recognized by HTML and the escape sequences used to enter each nonstandard character.

II. JavaScript

An explanation of how JavaScript works. The syntax used for each Object is shown, along with a definition of its Properties, Methods, and Event Handlers. The Operators in JavaScript are also described.

III. Extensible Markup Language (XML)

This is the complete specification as approved by the World Wide Web Consortium (W3C).

IV. Unix/Linux Commands

Describes how to perform most common functions in the Unix or Linux operating system. A table of commands is included for quick reference, with a definition of the result of each command.

V. Standards Organizations

A description of the primary organizations that establish international standards and the work they do, along with contact information for each. Gives access information for the latest standards and specifications.

VI. Requests for Comment (RFC)

This selected list of the most important RFCs provides a historical perspective of Internet development. The title, author(s), date of submission, and status of each RFC is given.

VII. Copyright Issues

The issues surrounding copyrights are explained in lay terms. Discusses current laws related to ownership and protection of intellectual property of all kinds and ramifications for digital media and the Internet.

HTML

Basic Tutorial on HTML

HTML documents are plain-text (also known as ASCII) files that can be created using any text editor, such as Emacs or vi on a UNIX system, SimpleText on a Macintosh, or Notepad on an IBM-compatible machine. You can also use word-processing software if you save the document as "text only." In order to make HTML documents available to anyone with a web browser on the Internet, you will need to have them posted on a server. A webmaster at an educational institution, a corporation, or a commercial Internet Service Provider (ISP) will be able to assist you.

There are many WYSIWYG editors available to automate HTML development, and new tools for creating and managing entire sites. You may wish to try them after you learn some of the basics of HTML tagging. It is useful to know enough HTML to code a document before you become reliant on a WYSIWYG editor.

HTML Tags

An "element" is a fundamental component of the structure of a text document. Some examples of elements are heads, tables, paragraphs, and lists. HTML "tags" are used to mark the elements of a file for your browser. Elements may contain plain text, other elements, or both.

Tags identify the various elements in an HTML document. HTML tags consist of a left angle bracket (<), a tag name, and a right angle bracket (>). Tags are usually paired (e.g., <H1> and </H1>) to start and end the tag instruction. The end tag looks like the start tag except a slash (/) precedes the text within the brackets. Not all tags are supported by all web browsers. A browser usually ignores a tag that it does not support.

Some elements may include an "attribute," which is additional information included inside the start tag. For example, you can specify the alignment of images (top, middle, or bottom) by

---

This document is adapted from A Beginner's Guide to HTML, *which was created by the National Center for Supercomputing. It is printed with permission from the Board of Trustees of the University of Illinois. Source URL: http://www.ncsa.uiuc.edu/General/Internet/WWW/HTMLPrimer.html*

349

including the appropriate attribute with the image source HTML code. Tags that have optional attributes are noted below.

Note: HTML is not case-sensitive. <title> is equivalent to <TITLE> or <TiTlE>. There are a few exceptions noted in Escape Sequences section below.

A Minimal HTML Document

Every HTML document should contain certain standard HTML tags. Each document consists of head and body text. The head contains the title, and the body contains the actual text that is made up of paragraphs, lists, and other elements. Browsers expect specific information because they are programmed according to HTML and SGML specifications.

Required elements are shown in this sample document:

```
<html>
<head>
<TITLE>A Simple HTML Example</TITLE>
</head>
<body>
<H1>HTML is Easy To Learn</H1>
<P>Welcome to the world of HTML.
This is the first paragraph. While short, it is
still a paragraph!</P>
<P>And this is the second paragraph.</P>
</body>
</html>
```

The required elements are the <HTML>, <HEAD>, <TITLE>, and <BODY> tags, along with their corresponding end tags. Because you should include these tags in each file, you might want to create a template file with them. Some browsers will format your HTML file correctly even if these tags are not included, while other browsers will not.

To view a copy of the file that your browser reads to generate the information in your current window, select View Source (or the equivalent) from the browser menu. The file contents, along with all the HTML tags, are displayed in a new window.

This is an excellent way to discover how HTML is used and to learn tips and constructs. Of course, the HTML that you find might not be technically correct. Once you become familiar with HTML and check the many online and hard-copy references on the subject, you will learn to distinguish between "good" and "bad" HTML. You can save a source file with the HTML codes and use it as a template for one of your web pages, or you can modify the format to suit your purposes.

Markup Tags

HTML

This element tells your browser that the file contains HTML-coded information. The file extension .html also indicates that it is an HTML document. If you are restricted to 8.3 file names, use only .htm for your extension.

Head

The head element identifies the first part of your HTML-coded document. It contains the title, which is shown as part of your browser's window.

Title

The title element contains your document title and identifies its content in a global context. The title is displayed somewhere on the browser window (usually at the top), but not within the text area. The title is also displayed on someone's hot list or bookmark list, so choose something descriptive, unique, and relatively short. A title is also used during a WAIS search of a server.

For example, you might include a shortened title of a book with the chapter contents; for example, "NCSA Mosaic Guide (Windows): Installation." This tells the software name, the platform, and the chapter contents, which is more useful than calling the document Installation. Generally, titles should be restricted to 64 characters or fewer.

Body

The second part of your HTML document is the body, which contains the content of your document (displayed within the text area of your browser window). The tags explained below are used in the body of your HTML document.

Headings

HTML has six levels of headings, numbered 1 through 6, with 1 being the most prominent. Web browsers display headings in larger and/or bolder fonts than normal body text. The first heading in each document should be tagged <H1>.

The syntax of the heading element is: <Hn>Text of heading</Hn> where n is a number between one and six specifying the level of the heading.

Do not skip levels of headings in your document. For example, don't start with a level-one heading (<H1>) and follow it with a level-three (<H3>) heading.

Paragraphs

Unlike documents in most word processors, carriage returns in HTML files aren't significant. It doesn't matter how long your lines of text are, but it is best to restrict them to fewer than 72 characters in length. Word wrapping can occur at any point in your source file, and multiple spaces are collapsed into a single space by your browser.

351

In the example shown in the "Minimal HTML Document" section, the first paragraph is coded as

```
<P>Welcome to the world of HTML.
This is the first paragraph.
While short, it is
still a paragraph!</P>
```

In the source file there is a line break between the sentences. A web browser ignores this line break and starts a new paragraph only when it encounters another <P> tag.

Important: You must indicate paragraphs with <P> elements. A browser ignores any indentations or blank lines in the source text. Without <P> elements, the document becomes one large paragraph. (One exception is text tagged as "preformatted," which is explained below.) For example, the following would produce identical output to the "Minimal HTML" example:

```
<H1>Level-one heading</H1> <P>Welcome to the world of
HTML. This is the first paragraph. While short, it is
still a paragraph! </P>

<P>And this is the second paragraph.</P>
```

To preserve readability in HTML files, put headings on separate lines, use a blank line or two where it helps identify the start of a new section, and separate paragraphs with blank lines in addition to the <P> tags. These extra spaces help you when you edit your files, but your browser will ignore the extra spaces because it has its own set of rules on spacing that do not depend on the spaces you put in your source file.

Note: The </P> closing tag can be omitted because browsers understand that when they encounter a <P> tag, it implies that there is an end to the previous paragraph.

Using the <P> and </P> as a paragraph container means that you can center a paragraph by including the ALIGN=alignment attribute in your source file. The formatted version is below the tagged version.

```
<P ALIGN=CENTER>
This is a centered paragraph.</P>
```

This is a centered paragraph.

Lists

HTML supports unnumbered, numbered, and definition lists. You can nest lists, but use this feature sparingly because too many nested items can make a document difficult to follow.

Unnumbered Lists

To make an unnumbered, bulleted list:

1. Start with an opening list <UL> (for unnumbered list) tag.
2. Enter the <LI> (list item) tag followed by the individual item; no closing </LI> tag is needed.
3. End the entire list with a closing list </UL> tag.

Below is a sample three-item list:

```
<UL>
<LI> apples
<LI> bananas
<LI> grapefruit
</UL>
```

The output is:

- apples
- bananas
- grapefruit

The <LI> items can contain multiple paragraphs. Indicate the paragraphs with the <P> paragraph tags.

Numbered Lists

A numbered list (also called an ordered list, from which the tag name derives) is identical to an unnumbered list, except it uses <OL> instead of <UL>. The items are tagged using the same <LI> tag. The following HTML code:

```
<OL>
<LI> oranges
<LI> peaches
<LI> grapes
</OL>
```

produces this formatted output:

1. oranges
2. peaches
3. grapes

Definition Lists

A definition list (coded as <DL>) usually consists of alternating a definition term (coded as <DT>) and a definition (coded as <DD>). Web browsers generally format the definition on a new line.

The following is an example of a definition list:

```
<DL>
<DT> NCSA
<DD> NCSA, the National Center for Supercomputing Ap-
plications, is located on the campus of the University of
Illinois at Urbana-Champaign.
<DT> Cornell Theory Center
<DD> CTC is located on the campus of Cornell University
in Ithaca, New York.
</DL>
```

The output looks like:

NCSA
> NCSA, the National Center for Supercomputing Applications, is located on the campus of the University of Illinois at Urbana-Champaign.

Cornell Theory Center
> CTC is located on the campus of Cornell University in Ithaca, New York.

The <DT> and <DD> entries can contain multiple paragraphs (indicated by <P> paragraph tags), lists, or other definition information.

The COMPACT attribute can be used routinely in case your definition terms are short. If, for example, you are showing some computer options, the options may fit on the same line as the start of the definition.

```
<DL COMPACT>
<DT> -i
<DD>invokes NCSA Mosaic for Microsoft Windows using the
initialization file defined in the path
<DT> -k
<DD>invokes NCSA Mosaic for Microsoft Windows in kiosk
mode
</DL>
```

The output looks like:

-i   invokes NCSA Mosaic for Microsoft Windows using the initialization file defined in the path
-k   invokes NCSA Mosaic for Microsoft Windows in kiosk mode

Nested Lists

Lists can be nested. You can also have a number of paragraphs, each containing a nested list, in a single list item.

Here is a sample nested list:

```
<UL>
<LI> A few New England states:
    <UL>
    <LI> Vermont
    <LI> New Hampshire
    <LI> Maine
    </UL>
<LI> Two Midwestern states:
    <UL>
    <LI> Michigan
    <LI> Indiana
    </UL>
</UL>
```

The nested list is displayed as:

- A few New England states:
  - Vermont
  - New Hampshire
  - Maine
- Two Midwestern states:
  - Michigan
  - Indiana

Preformatted Text

Use the <PRE> tag (which stands for preformatted) to generate text in a fixed-width font. This tag also makes spaces, new lines, and tabs significant (multiple spaces are displayed as multiple spaces, and lines break in the same locations as in the source HTML file). This is useful for program listings, among other things. For example, the following lines:

```
<PRE>
  #!/bin/csh
  cd $SCR
  cfs get mysrc.f:mycfsdir/mysrc.f
  cfs get myinfile:mycfsdir/myinfile
  fc -02 -o mya.out mysrc.f
  mya.out
  cfs save myoutfile:mycfsdir/myoutfile
  rm *
</PRE>
```

display as:

```
#!/bin/csh
  cd $SCR
  cfs get mysrc.f:mycfsdir/mysrc.f
  cfs get myinfile:mycfsdir/myinfile
  fc -02 -o mya.out mysrc.f
  mya.out
  cfs save myoutfile:mycfsdir/myoutfile
  rm *
```

The <PRE> tag can be used with an optional WIDTH attribute that specifies the maximum number of characters for a line. WIDTH also signals your browser to choose an appropriate font and indentation for the text. Hyperlinks can be used within <PRE> sections. You should avoid using other HTML tags within <PRE> sections, however.

Note that because <, >, and & have special meanings in HTML, you must use their escape sequences (<, >, and &, respectively) to enter these characters. See the section on escape sequences for more information.

Extended Quotations

Use the <BLOCKQUOTE> tag to include lengthy quotations in a separate block on the screen. Most browsers change the margins for the quotation to separate it from surrounding text.

In the example:

```
<BLOCKQUOTE>
<P>Omit needless words.</P>
<P>Vigorous writing is concise. A sentence should contain no
unnecessary words, a paragraph no unnecessary sentences, for the
same reason that a drawing should have no unnecessary lines and a
machine no unnecessary parts.</P>
```

```
-William Strunk, Jr., 1918
</BLOCKQUOTE>
```

the result is:

> Omit needless words.
>
> Vigorous writing is concise. A sentence should contain no unnec-essary words, a paragraph no unnecessary sentences, for the same reason that a drawing should have no unnecessary lines and a ma-chine no unnecessary parts.
> -William Strunk, Jr., 1918

Addresses

The <ADDRESS> tag is generally used to specify the author of a document, a way to contact the author (e.g., an email address), and a revision date. It is usually the last item in a file.

For example, the last line of the online version of this guide is:

```
<ADDRESS>
A Beginner's Guide to HTML / NCSA /
pubs@ncsa.uiuc.edu / revised April 96
</ADDRESS>
```

The result is:

A Beginner's Guide to HTML / NCSA / pubs@ncsa.uiuc.edu / revised April 96

Note: <ADDRESS> is not used for postal addresses. See "Forced Line Breaks" below to learn how to format postal addresses.

Forced Line Breaks/Postal Addresses

The <BR> tag forces a line break with no extra (white) space between lines. Using <P> elements for short lines of text such as postal addresses results in unwanted additional white space. For example, with <BR>:

```
National Center for Supercomputing Applications<BR>
605 East Springfield Avenue<BR>
Champaign, Illinois 61820-5518<BR>
```

The output is:

National Center for Supercomputing Applications
605 East Springfield Avenue
Champaign, Illinois 61820-5518

Horizontal Rules

The <HR> tag produces a horizontal line the width of the browser window. A horizontal rule is useful when you are separating sections of your document. For example, many people add a rule at the end of their text and before the <ADDRESS> information.

You can vary a rule size (thickness) and width (the percentage of the window covered by the rule). Experiment with the settings until you are satisfied with the presentation. For example, to create a four-pixel-thick centered line half as wide as the window, use the tag <HR SIZE=4 WIDTH="50%">

Character Formatting

HTML has two styles for individual words or sentences: logical and physical. Logical styles tag text according to its meaning, while physical styles indicate the specific appearance of a section. For example, in the preceding sentence, the words "logical styles" might be tagged as a "definition." The same effect (formatting those words in italics) could be achieved with a different tag that tells your browser to "put these words in italics."

Note: Some browsers do not attach any style to the <DFN> tag, so you cannot be assured that all users would see the tagged phrase in italics.

Logical Versus Physical Styles

In the ideal SGML universe, content is divorced from presentation. Thus, SGML tags a level-one heading as a level-one heading, but it does not specify that the level-one heading should be, for instance, 24-point bold Times centered. The advantage of this approach (it's similar in concept to style sheets in many word processors) is that if you decide to change level-one headings to 20-point left-justified Helvetica, all you have to do is change the definition of the level-one heading in your web browser. Indeed, many browsers today let you define how you want the various HTML tags rendered onscreen.

Another advantage of logical tags is that they help enforce consistency in your documents. It's easier to tag something as <H1> than to remember that level-one headings are 24-point bold Times centered, for example. Consider the <STRONG> tag, which most browsers render in bold text. However, it is possible for a reader to prefer these sections to be displayed in red. Logical styles offer this flexibility.

Of course, if you want something to be displayed in italics, for example, and do not want a browser's setting to display it differently, use physical styles. Physical styles, therefore, offer consistency because something you tag a certain way will always be displayed that way for readers of your document.

Try to be consistent about which type of style you use. If you tag with physical styles, do so throughout a document. If you use logical styles, stick with them within a document. The version 4.0 release of HTML strongly advocates the use of Cascading Style Sheets (CSS) to apply styles in HTML documents.

Logical Styles

<DFN> for a word being defined. Typically displayed in italics.
(*NCSA Mosaic is a World Wide Web browser.*)

<EM> for emphasis. Typically displayed in italics.
(*Consultants cannot reset your password unless you call the help line.*)

<CITE> for titles of books, films, etc. Typically displayed in italics.
(*For Whom the Bell Tolls*)

<CODE> for computer code. Displayed in a fixed-width font.
```
(The <stdio.h> header file)
```

<KBD> for user keyboard entry. Typically displayed in plain fixed-width font.
```
(Enter passwd to change your password.)
```

<SAMP> for a sequence of literal characters. Displayed in a fixed-width font.
```
(Segmentation fault: Core dumped.)
```

<STRONG> for strong emphasis. Typically displayed in bold.
(**Note: Always check your links to see how text is displayed.***)*

<VAR> for a variable, where you will replace the variable with specific information. Typically displayed in italics.
(rm *filename* deletes the file.*)*

Physical Styles

<B>   bold text
<I>   italic text
<TT>   typewriter text (fixed-width font)

Escape Sequences (a.k.a. Character Entities)

Character entities have two functions:
1. Escaping special characters.
2. Displaying other characters not available in the plain ASCII character set (primarily characters with diacritical marks).

359

Three ASCII characters—the left angle bracket (<), the right angle bracket (>), and the ampersand (&)—have special meanings in HTML and therefore cannot be used "as is" in text. (The angle brackets are used to indicate the beginning and end of HTML tags, and the ampersand is used to indicate the beginning of an escape sequence.) Double quote marks may be used as-is, but a character entity may also be used (").

To use one of the three characters in an HTML document, you must enter its escape sequence instead:

<   escape sequence for <
>   escape sequence for >
&   escape sequence for &

Additional escape sequences support accented characters, such as:

ö   escape sequence for a lowercase o with an umlaut: ö

ñ   escape sequence for a lowercase n with a tilde: ñ

È escape sequence for an uppercase E with a grave accent: È

You can substitute other letters for the ö, ñ, and È shown above. Refer to the "HTML Coded Characters" section of this appendix for a complete list of special characters.

Note: Unlike the rest of HTML, the escape sequences are case sensitive. You cannot, for instance, use < instead of <.

Linking

The chief power of HTML comes from its ability to link text and/or an image to another document or section of a document. A browser highlights the identified text or image with color and/or underlines to indicate that it is a hypertext link (often shortened to hyperlink or link).

HTML's single hypertext-related tag is <A>, which stands for anchor. To include an anchor in your document:
1. Start the anchor with <A (include a space after the A).
2. Specify the document you're linking to by entering the parameter HREF="filename" followed by a closing right angle bracket (>).
3. Enter the text that will serve as the hypertext link in the current document.
4. Enter the ending anchor tag </A>. (No space is needed before the end anchor tag.)

Here is a sample hypertext reference in a file called US.html:

```
<A HREF="MaineStats.html">Maine</A>
```

This entry makes the word *Maine* the hyperlink to the document *MaineStats.html*, which is in the same directory as the first document.

Relative Path Names Versus Absolute Path Names

You can link to documents in other directories by specifying the relative path from the current document to the linked document. For example, a link to a file NYStats.html located in the subdirectory AtlanticStates would be:

```
<A HREF= "AtlanticStates/NYStats.html">New York</A>
```

These are called relative links because you specify the path to the linked file relative to the location of the current file. You can also use the absolute path name (the complete URL) of the file, but relative links are more efficient in accessing a server.

Path names use the standard Unix syntax. The Unix syntax for the parent directory (the directory that contains the current directory) is "..". (For more information consult a beginning UNIX reference text.)

If you were in the NYStats.html file and were referring to the original document US.html, your link would look like this:

```
<A HREF="../US.html">United States</A>
```

Generally, relative links should be used for the following reasons:

1. It is easier to move a group of documents to another location (because the relative path names will still be valid).
2. It is more efficient connecting to the server.
3. There is less to type.

However, use absolute path names when linking to documents that are not directly related. For example, consider a group of documents that comprise a user manual. Links within this group should be relative links. Links to other documents (perhaps a reference to related software) should use full path names. This way if you move the user manual to a different directory, none of the links would have to be updated.

URLs

The World Wide Web uses uniform resource locators (URLs) to specify location the of files on other servers. A URL includes the type of resource being accessed (e.g., web, gopher, WAIS), the address of the server, and the location of the file. The syntax is *scheme://host.domain [:port]/path/ filename* where *scheme* is one of the following types:

file
> A file on your local system.

ftp
>   A file on an anonymous FTP server.

http
>   A file on a World Wide Web server.

gopher
>   A file on a gopher server.

WAIS
>   A file on a WAIS server.

news
>   A Usenet newsgroup.

telnet
>   A connection to a Telnet-based service.

The *port* number can generally be omitted, unless it is specifically requested. For example, to include a link in your document to the NCSA primer (upon which this appendix is based), enter:

<A HREF="http://www.ncsa.uiuc.edu/General/Internet/WWW/HTMLPrimer.html">
NCSA's Beginner's Guide to HTML</A>

This entry makes the text *NCSA's Beginner's Guide to HTML* a hyperlink to your document.

Links to Specific Sections

Anchors can also be used to move a reader to a particular section in a document (either the same or a different document) rather than to the top, which is the default. This type of an anchor is commonly called a "named anchor" because to create the links, you insert HTML names within the document.

Internal hyperlinks are used to create a "table of contents" at the top of a long document. These hyperlinks move you from one location to another in the same document. You can also link to a specific section in another document.

Links Between Sections of Different Documents

Suppose you want to set a link from document A (documentA.html) to a specific section in another document (MaineStats.html).

Enter the HTML coding for a link to a named anchor:

```
documentA.html:

In addition to the many state parks, Maine is also home to
<a href="MaineStats.html#ANP">Acadia National Park</a>.
```

Think of the characters after the hash (#) mark as a tab within the MaineStats.html file. This tab tells your browser what should be displayed at the top of the window when the link is activated. In other words, the first line in your browser window should be the Acadia National Park heading.

Next, create the named anchor (in this example "ANP") in MaineStats.html:

```
<H2><A NAME="ANP">Acadia National Park</a></H2>
```

With both of these elements in place, you can bring a reader directly to the Acadia reference in MaineStats.html.

Note: You cannot make links to specific sections within a different document unless you have permission to edit the coded source of that document, or that document already contains in-document named anchors. For example, you could include named anchors to the NCSA online HTML guide in a document you are writing because there are named anchors in this guide. But if this document did not have named anchors, you could not make a link to a specific section because you cannot edit the original file on NCSA's server.

Links to Specific Sections Within the Current Document

The technique is the same except the file name is omitted. For example, to link to the ANP anchor from within MaineStats, enter:

```
...More information about <A HREF="#ANP">Acadia National
Park</a> is available elsewhere in this document.
```

Be sure to include the <A NAME=> tag where you want the link to jump to (<H2><A NAME="ANP">Acadia National Park</a></H2>).

Named anchors are useful when you think readers will print an entire document or when you have a lot of short information you want to place online in one file.

Mailto

You can make it easy for a reader to send email to a specific person or mail alias by including the mailto attribute in a hyperlink. The format is:

```
<A HREF="mailto:emailinfo@host">Name</a>
```

For example, enter:

```
<A HREF="mailto:brad@hansenmedia.com">Brad Hansen</a>
```

This creates a mail window configured to send email. You may put any valid Internet address in your mailto window.

Inline Images

Most web browsers can display inline images (images next to text) that are in X Bitmap (XBM), GIF, or JPEG format. Another image format recognized by current web browsers is the Portable Network Graphics (PNG) format. Each image takes time to process and slows down the initial display of a document. Carefully select your images and the number of images in a document.

To include an inline image, enter:

```
<IMG SRC=ImageName>
```

where *ImageName* is the URL of the image file.

The syntax for <IMG SRC> URLs is identical to that used in an anchor HREF. If the image file is a GIF file, then the file name part of *ImageName* must end with .gif. File names of X Bitmap images must end with .xbm; JPEG image files must end with .jpg or .jpeg; and Portable Network Graphic files must end with .png.

Image Size Attributes

Include two other attributes on <IMG> tags to tell your browser the size of the images it is downloading with the text. The HEIGHT and WIDTH attributes let the browser set aside the appropriate space (in pixels) for the images as it downloads the rest of the file. (Get the pixel size from your image-processing software, such as Adobe Photoshop.)

For example, to include a self-portrait image in a file along with the portrait's dimensions, enter:

```
<IMG SRC=SelfPortrait.gif HEIGHT=100 WIDTH=65>
```

Note: Some browsers use the HEIGHT and WIDTH attributes to stretch or shrink an image to fit into the allotted space when the image does not exactly match the attribute numbers. Not all browser developers think stretching/shrinking is a good idea. Do not assume your readers will have access to this feature. Check your dimensions and use the correct ones.

Aligning Images

You have some flexibility when displaying images. You can have images separated from text and aligned to the left, right, or center, or you can have an image aligned with text. Try several possibilities to see how your information looks best.

Aligning Text with an Image

By default, the bottom of an image is aligned with the baseline of the text that follows it. You can align images to the top or center of a paragraph using the ALIGN= attributes TOP and CENTER.

To align text with the top of the image, use the tag:

```
(<IMG SRC = "MyImage.gif" ALIGN=TOP>)
```

Note that the browser aligns only one line and then jumps to the bottom of the image for the rest of the text.

For text that is centered on the image, use the tag:

```
(<IMG SRC = "MyImage.gif" ALIGN=CENTER>)
```

Only one line of text is centered; the rest is below the image.

Images Without Text

To display an image without any associated text (e.g., your organization's logo), make it a separate paragraph. Use the paragraph ALIGN= attribute to center the image or adjust it to the right side of the window as shown on the following page:

```
<p ALIGN=CENTER>
<IMG SRC = "MyImage.gif">
</p>
```

The image is centered and the paragraph starts below it, left-justified.

Alternate Text for Images

Some World Wide Web browsers (primarily those that run on VT100 terminals) cannot display images. Some users turn off image loading if they have a slow connection, even if their software can display images. HTML provides a mechanism to tell readers what they are missing on your pages.

The ALT attribute lets you specify text to be displayed instead of an image. In the following example *UpArrow.gif* is the picture of an upward pointing arrow.

```
<IMG SRC="UpArrow.gif" ALT="Up">
```

With graphics-capable viewers that have image-loading turned on, the up arrow graphic is visible. With image-loading turned off, or with a VT100 browser, the word *Up* is shown in your window. It's a good idea to include alternate text for each image you use in your document as courtesy for your readers.

Background Graphics

Newer versions of web browsers can load an image and use it as a background when displaying a page. Some people like background images, and some don't. In general, if you want to include a background, make sure your text can be read easily when displayed on top of the image. Background images can be a texture or an object, such as a logo. You create the background image as you do any image.

However, you have to create only a small piece of the image. Using a tiling feature, a browser takes the image and repeats it across and down to fill your browser window. Basically, you generate one image, and the browser replicates it enough times to fill your window. This action is automatic when you use the background tag.

Below is the tag to include a background image included in the <BODY> statement as an attribute:

```
<BODY BACKGROUND="filename.gif">
```

Background Color

By default, browsers display text in black on a gray background. However, you can change both elements if you want. Some HTML authors select a background color and coordinate it with a change in the color of the text.

Always preview changes like this to make sure your pages are readable. (For example, many people find red text on a black background difficult to read.)

You change the color of text, links, visited links, and active links using attributes of the <BODY> tag. For example, enter:

```
<BODY BGCOLOR="#000000" TEXT="#FFFFFF" LINK="#9690CC">
```

This creates a window with a black background (BGCOLOR), white text (TEXT), and silvery hyperlinks (LINK).

The six-digit number and letter combinations represent colors by giving their RGB (red, green, blue) value. The six digits are three two-digit numbers in sequence, representing the amount of red, green, or blue as a hexadecimal value in the range 00-FF. For example, 000000 is black (no color at all), FF0000 is bright red, and FFFFFF is white (fully saturated with all three colors). These number and letter combinations are cryptic. The six-digit color codes that map specific colors in HTML 3.2 and later are provided in the "HTML Color Table" section at the end of this appendix.

External Images, Sounds, and Animation

You may want to have an image open as a separate document when a user activates a link on either a word or a smaller inline version of the image included in your document. This is called an external image, and it is useful if you do not wish to slow down the loading of the main document with large inline images.

To include a reference to an external image, enter:

```
<A HREF="MyImage.gif">link anchor</A>
```

You can also use a smaller image as a link to a larger image. Enter:

```
<A HREF="LargerImage.gif"><IMG SRC="SmallImage.gif"></A>
```

The reader sees the SmallImage.gif image and clicks it to open the LargerImage.gif file.

Use the same syntax for links to external animation and sounds. The only difference is the file extension of the linked file. For example, <A HREF="AdamsRib.mov">link anchor</A> specifies a link to a QuickTime movie. Some common file types and their extensions are:

File Type	Extension
ASCII text	.txt
HTML document	.htm (or .html)
GIF image	.gif
TIFF image	.tif (or .tiff)
X Bitmap image	.xbm
JPEG image	.jpg (or .jpeg)
PNG image	.png
PostScript file	.ps
AIFF sound file	.aif (or .aiff)
AU sound file	.au
WAV sound file	.wav
QuickTime movie	.mov
MPEG movie	.mpg (or .mpeg)

Keep in mind your intended audience's access to helper applications and plug-ins. For example, most Unix workstations cannot view QuickTime movies.

Tables

Before HTML tags for tables were finalized, authors had to format their tabular information carefully within <PRE> tags, counting spaces and previewing their output. Tables are useful for presenting tabular information, and they are a boon to creative HTML authors who use the table tags to present their regular web pages.

Think of your tabular information in light of the coding explained below. A table has heads where you explain what the columns/rows include, rows for information, and cells for each item. In the following table, the first column contains the header information, each row explains an HTML table tag, and each cell contains a paired tag or an explanation of the tag's function.

Table Elements

Element	Description
<TABLE>	Defines a table in HTML. If the BORDER attribute is present, your browser displays the table with a border.
<CAPTION>	Defines the caption for the title of the table. The default position of the title is centered at the top. The ALIGN=BOTTOM attribute can be used to position the caption below the table. *Note:* Any kind of markup tag can be used in the caption.
<TR>	Specifies a table row within a table. You may define default attributes for the entire row: ALIGN (LEFT, CENTER, RIGHT) and/or VALIGN (TOP, MIDDLE, BOTTOM). See Table Attributes at the end of this table for more information.
<TH>	Defines a table header cell. By default the text in this cell is bold and centered. Table header cells may contain other attributes to determine the characteristics of the cell and/or its contents. See Table Attributes at the end of this table for more information.
<TD>	Defines a table data cell. By default, the text in this cell is left-aligned and centered vertically. Table data cells may contain other attributes to determine the characteristics of the cell and/or its contents. See "Table Attributes" at the end of this table.

Table Attributes

Note: Attributes defined within <TH> ... </TH> or <TD> ... </TD> cells override the default alignment set in a <TR> ... </TR>. Attributes are listed below, along with their description.

ALIGN (LEFT, CENTER, RIGHT)
    Horizontal alignment of a cell.

VALIGN (TOP, MIDDLE, BOTTOM)
    Vertical alignment of a cell.

COLSPAN=n
    The number (n) of columns a cell spans.

ROWSPAN=n
    The number (n) of rows a cell spans.

NOWRAP
    Turn off word wrapping within a cell.

General Table Format

The general format of a table looks like this:

<TABLE>	<== start of table definition
<CAPTION> caption contents </CAPTION>	<== caption definition
<TR>	<== start of first row definition
<TH> cell contents </TH>	<== first cell in row 1 (a head)
<TH> cell contents </TH>	<== last cell in row 1 (a head)
</TR>	<== end of first row definition
<TR	<== start of second row definition
<TD> cell contents </TD>	<== first cell in row 2
<TD> cell contents </TD>	<== last cell in row 2
</TR>	<== end of second row definition
<TR>	<== start of last row definition
<TD> cell contents </TD>	<== first cell in last row
<TD> cell contents </TD>	<== last cell in last row
</TR>	<== end of last row definition
</TABLE	<== end of table definition

The <TABLE> and </TABLE> tags must surround the entire table definition. The first item inside the table, CAPTION, is optional. Then you can have any number of rows defined by the <TR> and </TR> tags. Within a row you can have any number of cells defined by the <TD>...</TD> or <TH>...</TH> tags. Each row of a table is formatted independently of the rows above and below it. This lets you easily display tables like the one above with a single cell, such as Table Attributes, spanning columns of the table.

Tables for Nontabular Information

Some HTML authors use tables to present nontabular information. For example, because links can be included in table cells, some authors use a table with no borders to create "one" image from separate images. Browsers that can display tables properly show the various images seamlessly, making the created image seem like an image map (one image with hyperlinked quadrants). Using table borders with images can create an impressive display as well.

Fill-out Forms

Web forms let you return information to a web server for some action. For example, suppose you collect names and email addresses so you can email information to people who request it. For each person who enters his or her name and address, you need some information to be sent and the respondent's particulars added to a database. This information is usually processed by a script or program written in Perl or another language that manipulates text, files, and information.

The forms are not hard to code. They follow the same constructs as other HTML tags. What can be difficult is the program or script that takes the data submitted in a form and processes it. Because of the need for specialized scripts to handle the incoming form information, fill-out forms are not discussed in this primer.

Troubleshooting

Avoid Overlapping Tags

Consider this example of HTML:

```
<B>This is an example of <DFN>overlapping</B> HTML
tags.</DFN>
```

The word *overlapping* is in both the <B> and <DFN> tags. A browser might be confused by this coding and might not display it the way you intend. The only way to know is to check each popular browser (a time-consuming proposition).

In general, avoid overlapping tags. Look at your tags and try pairing them up. Tags (with the obvious exceptions of elements whose end tags may be omitted, such as paragraphs) should be paired without an intervening tag in between. Look again at the example above. You cannot pair the bold tags without another tag in the middle (the first definition tag). Try matching your coding up like this to see if you have any problem areas that should be fixed before you release your files to a server.

Embed Only Anchors and Character Tags

HTML protocol allows you to embed links within other HTML tags:

```
<H1><A HREF="Destination.html">My heading</A></H1>
```

Do not embed HTML tags within an anchor:

```
<A HREF="Destination.html">
<H1>My heading</H1>
</A>
```

Although most browsers currently handle this second example, the official HTML specifications do not support this construct, and your file may not work with future browsers. Remember that browsers can be forgiving when displaying improperly coded files. However, that forgiveness may not continue in the next version of the software! When in doubt, code your files according to the HTML specification.

Character tags modify the appearance of the text within other elements:

```
<UL>
<LI><B>A bold list item</B>
<LI><I>An italic list item</I>
</UL>
```

Avoid embedding other types of HTML element tags. For example, you might be tempted to embed a heading within a list in order to make the font size larger:

```
<UL>
<LI><H1>A large heading</H1>
<LI><H2>Something slightly smaller</H2>
</UL>
```

Although some browsers handle this well, formatting of such coding is unpredictable because it is undefined. For compatibility with all browsers, avoid these kinds of constructs. Cascading Style Sheets (CSS) is the preferred method of defining style parameters in HTML documents.

What's the difference between embedding a <B> within a <LI> tag as opposed to embedding a <H1> within a <LI>? Within HTML the semantic meaning of <H1> is that it's the main heading of a document and that it should be followed by the content of the document. Therefore, it doesn't make sense to find a <H1> within a list.

Character formatting tags also are generally not additive. For example, you might expect that <B><I>some text</I></B> would produce bold-italic text. On some browsers it does; other browsers interpret only the innermost tag.

Final Steps

Validate your code. When you put a document on a web server, check the formatting and each link (including named anchors). Ideally, you will have someone else read through and comment on your files before you consider a document finished.

You can run your coded files through an HTML validation service that will tell you if your code conforms to accepted HTML. If you are not sure your coding conforms to HTML specifications, this can be a useful teaching tool. Fortunately, the service lets you select the level of conformance you want for your files (i.e., strict, level 2, level 3). If you want to use some codes that are not officially part of the HTML specifications, this latitude is helpful.

Dummy Images

When a <IMG SRC> tag points to an image that does not exist, a dummy image is substituted by your browser software. When this happens during your final review of your files, make sure that the referenced image does in fact exist, that the hyperlink has the correct information in the URL, and that the file permission is set appropriately (world-readable). Then check online again.

Update Your Files

If the contents of a file are static (such as a biography of George Washington), no updating should be needed. Time-sensitive documents should be changed often.

Updating is important when the file contains information such as a weekly schedule or a deadline for a program funding announcement. Remove out-of-date files or note why something that seems dated is still on a server (e.g., the program requirements remain the same for the next cycle so the file is still available as an interim reference).

Browsers Differ

Web browsers display HTML elements differently. Remember that not all codes used in HTML files are interpreted by all browsers. Any code a browser does not understand is usually ignored.

You could spend a lot of time making your file look perfect using your current browser. If you check that file using another browser, it may display quite differently. Hence, these words of advice: code your files using correct HTML. Leave the interpreting to the browsers and hope for the best.

Commenting Your Files

You might want to include comments in your HTML files. Comments in HTML are like comments in a computer program—the text you enter is not used by the browser in any formatting and is not directly viewable by the reader, just as computer program comments are not used and are not viewable. The comments are accessible if a reader views the source file, however.

Comments such as the name of the person updating a file, the software and version used in creating a file, or the date that a minor edit was made are the norm.

To include a comment, enter:

```
<!-- your comments here -->
```

You must include the exclamation mark and the hyphens as shown.

New Features in HTML 4.0

Version 4.0 of the Hypertext Markup Language (HTML) has a number of major improvements over the previous version 3.2. The new version includes the capacity to use Cascading Style Sheets (CSS) for precise formatting. The World Wide Web Consortium (W3C) recommends that developers move formatting information out of HTML text and use CSS whenever possible. Other new features are improvements to tables and forms, making them more flexible and more easily controlled. There are also new printing and multimedia features.

HTML 4.0 makes frames an official part of the specification, approving the <FRAME>, <FRAMESET>, and <IFRAME> elements. Supported by popular browsers since Netscape Navigator 2.0 and Internet Explorer 3.0, the HTML specification never defined them until version 4.0.

New characters previously not available in HTML have been included, making it a truly international language. In all previous versions of HTML, the basic character set implemented was Latin-1 (ISO 8859-1). Latin-1 is an 8-bit, single-byte-coded graphic character set capable of representing up to 256 characters. It contains letters for English, German, French, Spanish, and most Scandinavian languages. However, characters in the Greek, Hebrew, Arabic, and Cyrillic languages are not supported. Very little support is provided for scientific or mathematical symbols in Latin-1.

HTML 4.0 addresses these limitations by using the Universal Character Set (UCS). UCS is a character-by-character equivalent to Unicode 2.0, a character-encoding standard that uses a 16-bit set, thereby increasing the number of available characters to more than 65,000.

The remainder of this document details specific elements that have changed in HTML 4.0. Three elements are now obsolete, ten elements are deprecated (no longer supported), and more than fifteen new elements have been added.

Obsolete Elements

The three tags removed from the HTML specification are <XMP>, <PLAINTEXT>, and <LISTING>. These tags are to be replaced with <PRE> in all instances. Some browsers may continue to support these tags.

Deprecated Elements

These tags and attributes have been replaced by new HTML constructs. The W3C recommendation strongly urges that deprecated tags not be used, because they will eventually become obsolete in future browsers.

```
<APPLET>...</APPLET>
```

This tag allowed a Java applet to run. It should be replaced by the <OBJECT>...</OBJECT> tag.

`<ISINDEX>...</ISINDEX>`
This tag allowed a form to contain a basic string search. It should be replaced by the <INPUT> form element.

`<DIR>...</DIR>`
This tag was used to describe a directory list, which is identical to an unordered list. It should be replaced by a <UL>...</UL> list tag.

`<MENU>...</MENU>`
This tag was used to define a single-column menu list, which is identical to an unordered list. It should be replaced by a <UL>...</UL> list tag.

`<CENTER>...</CENTER>`
This tag was used to center either text or graphics. It should be replaced by a <DIV> tag, and the align attribute should be set to "center."

`<FONT>...</FONT>`
This tag was used to specify font face, size, and colors. Style sheets should be used for character formatting rather than HTML code.

`<BASEFONT>...</BASEFONT>`
This tag was used to set a base font size as a reference point for making the font larger or smaller. Style sheets should be used to set and reference relative font sizes.

`<STRIKE>...</STRIKE>` or `<S>...</S>`
These tags were used to create strikethrough characters. Style sheets should be used for all such character formatting.

`<U>...</U>`
These tags were used to underline characters. Style sheets should be used to create underlined text.

New Elements

The following is a brief description of new tags.

`<ABBR>...</ABBR>`
This tag identifies the abbreviated form of a term or phrase. Both a start tag and an end tag are required.

`<ACRONYM>...</ACRONYM>`
This tag identifies an acronym in a phrase of text. <ACRONYM> is similar in behavior to <EM> and <CODE>. Both a start tag and an end tag are required. Here is an example:

```
This document is about <ACRONYM>HTML</ACRONYM>, which
stands for Hypertext Markup Language. Version 4.0 should
be used to create documents for the <ACRONYM>WWW</ACRO-
NYM>.
<BUTTON>...</BUTTON>
```

This tag is used to create push buttons on forms that are similar to push buttons in most Windows applications. In its behavior, the <BUTTON> tag is like the "submit" and "reset" <INPUT> elements. The representation of a <BUTTON> has a 3-dimensional look, with beveled edges, and it appears to be depressed when a user clicks on it. Both a start tag and an end tag for <BUTTON> are required by HTML 4.0.

Here is an example:

```
<FORM action="http://hansenmedia.com/prog/newuser"
method="post">
Would you prefer to read these documents in German or
English?
<P>
  <INPUT type="radio" name="preference" value="Yes">
Yes<BR>
  <INPUT type="radio" name="preference" value="No">
No<BR>
<P>
  <BUTTON name="submit" value="submit" type="submit">
    Send</BUTTON>
  <BUTTON name="reset" type="reset">
Reset</BUTTON>
</FORM>
```

```
<COLGROUP>...</COLGROUP>
```
This tag allow tables to be formatted with groups of columns that share width and alignment properties, which are set by one or more of the new <COL> elements. If a <COLGROUP> is not specified and defined, HTML 4.0 formats a table with a single column group that contains all the columns. Both a start tag and an end tag are required by HTML 4.0 for <COLGROUP>. Here is an example of a table with one wide column and check box at the right side of each row.

```
<TABLE>
<COLGROUP span="8" width="20">
<COLGROUP span="1" width="0*">
<THEAD>
<TR>...
</TABLE>
```

<FIELDSET>...</FIELDSET>

This tag allows related form fields to be grouped, providing a way for information to be classified. When a group of form elements are enclosed in <FIELDSET> tags the browser groups the elements together. Both a start tag and an end tag are required by HTML 4.0. Here is an example of code with both the <FIELDSET> and <LEGEND> tags.

```
<HTML>
<HEAD>
<TITLE>Size of Research Report you would like</TITLE>
</HEAD>
<BODY>
Please select an option below indicating the length of
the report you are requesting.
<FORM action="..." method="post">
    <FIELDSET>
        <LEGEND align="top">Length of Report</LEGEND>
        Number of pages in the report:
        <SELECT NAME="Pages" SIZE="5">
        <OPTION VALUE="2 pages">2
        <OPTION VALUE="3 pages">3
        <OPTION VALUE="5 pages">5
        <OPTION VALUE="8 pages">8</SELECT>
        Number of words per page:
        <SELECT NAME="Words per Page" SIZE="5">
        <OPTION VALUE="150 words">150
        <OPTION VALUE="200 words">200
        <OPTION VALUE="250 words">250</SELECT>
    </FIELDSET>
</FORM>
</BODY>
</HTML>
```

<DEL>...</DEL> and <INS>...</INS>

These tags are used to identify portions of a document that have been edited since the previous version. <DEL>...</DEL> marks text that has been deleted. <INS>...</INS> is used to mark text that has been inserted. Both a start tag and an end tag are required by HTML 4.0 for <DEL> and <INS>.

Here is an example:

```
This is the new and improved online tutorial on HTML.
<INS>You have three options. You may begin the test,
practice, or exit.</INS> <DEL>You have two options. You
may begin the test or exit.</DEL>
```

`<LABEL>...</LABEL>`

This tag is used to specify the label text for a form field, and to identify parameters of form elements. Both a start tag and an end tag are required by HTML 4.0.

`<LEGEND>...</LEGEND>`

This tag is used in conjunction with <FIELDSET> to attach a label to a form grouping. Both a start tag and an end tag are required by HTML 4.0. See the <FIELDSET> example for usage.

`<NOFRAMES>...</NOFRAMES>`

This tag is used to specify alternate text if the browser is not able to display frames. Both a start tag and an end tag are required by HTML 4.0. Here is an example:

```
<NOFRAMES>This text is displayed by browsers unable to
render frames.</NOFRAMES>
```

`<NOSCRIPT>...</NOSCRIPT>`

This new tag is used to specify alternate text if the browser is not able to execute JavaScript. No text is rendered by the browser if JavaScript is supported. It should be placed within the HEAD tags. Both a start tag and an end tag are required by HTML 4.0. Here is an example:

```
<NOSCRIPT>This text is displayed by browsers unable to
process JavaScript.</NOSCRIPT>
```

`<OBJECT>...</OBJECT>`

This tag embeds an object on a page. The object could be an image, a document, a control, or an applet. Both a start tag and an end tag are required by HTML 4.0.

`<OPTGROUP>...</OPTGROUP>`

This tag groups menu options together in a SELECT, which is particularly useful for form accessibility. Both a start tag and an end tag are required by HTML 4.0.

`<PARAM>...</PARAM>`

This tag is used to pass additional parameters to a Java applet. A start tag is required, but an end tag is optional in HTML 4.0.

`<SPAN>...</SPAN>`

This tag is used to define a text container and apply style information to it, according to the conventions of Cascading Style Sheets (CSS). Both a start tag and an end tag are required by HTML 4.0. Here is an example:

```
<SPAN STYLE="color: red">This text is displayed in red.</
SPAN>
```

`<Q>...</Q>`
This tag functions in a way similar to the <BLOCKQUOTE> tag, but applies to short quoted sections that do not require paragraph breaks. Both a start tag and an end tag are required by HTML 4.0.

HTML 4.0 Tags and Attributes

This table lists alphabetically the HTML 4.0 tags approved by the World Wide Web Consortium (W3C). Most tags require an end tag to delimit the content between the start and end tag. If an end tag is optional, it is marked (O) in the following table. If an end tag is forbidden, it is marked (F). Some tags in version 4.0 are deprecated. This means that they may not be supported in future browser versions. Deprecated tags are marked (D) in the table, and they should be avoided.

Attributes that may be defined within the delimiters of a tag are listed under each tag. A tag may have any number of attributes in any order, providing they do not conflict with one another. If a variable is followed by ",—" in the table, multiple values may be used as long as they are separated by a comma. Some of the attributes that accept standard variables are listed here.

URL

URL stands for *uniform resource locator*. This may take several forms, as listed below:

directory
(http://www.hansenmedia.com/knowledgebase)

file
(http://www.hansenmedia.com/knowledgebase/definitions.htm)

specific location within a file
(http://www.hansenmedia.com/knowledgebase/definitions.htm#html4)
This URL refers to a local position within the current page without requiring a full path name.

Pixels

A measurement that defines the size of an area on the screen. It is expressed as a decimal number.

Color

Either a proper color name or a code that identifies the exact color to be used to define the background color, text color, and link colors. It consists of the # symbol followed by a six-digit hexadecimal triplet, with two digits for red, two for green, and two for blue. For example, magenta is #ff00ff, cyan is #00ffff, and gold is #d4a017. Colors are designated as shown below, where "#code" represents a hexadecimal triplet.

```
<body bgcolor="#code">   for background color
<body text="#code">      for color of text (all non-hyperlinked items)
<body link="#code">      for color of unvisited links
<body vlink="#code">     for color of visited links
<body alink="#code">     for color of active links (while being selected)
```

An example in HTML: <body bgcolor="#FFFF33" text="#000000" link="#FF00FF" vlink="#7F0000" alink="#7E587E">

Frame size

The size of a frame, which may be expressed in several ways. A number represents a measurement in pixels. A percentage is used to define a portion of the width of a page.

Alignment

Used to indicate the positioning of an image relative to surrounding text. It may also be used for positioning text on a page. Common options are left, right, center, and justified.

HTML Tag/Attributes		Function
<!>	(F)	Indicates a comment that will not be rendered on a page
<!DOCTYPE>	(F)	Header info that defines the file format
HTML		Contents are an HTML document
PUBLIC		Contents are a readable document
"standard"		Specifies the version of HTML used
		Usage: <!DOCTYPE HTML PUBLIC "-W3C HTML 4//EN">
</tag>		Ends the effect of the current tag (end tag)
<A >		Indicates an anchor (hypertext link)
HREF="URL">		Marks the beginning of a link to a document
NAME="#name">		Names the location on a page that becomes a target
REL="value,—"		The relationship of a link (jump to next target)
REV="value,—"		Reverses the relationship of a link (jump to previous link)
TARGET="value"		Displays contents of a URL in the named window
		Values: NAME, _BLANK, _PARENT, _SELF, _TOP
TITLE="text"		Provides a name for the page that is linked
<ABBR>		The abbreviated form of a term or phrase
<ACRONYM>		Identifies the content as an acronym
TITLE="text"		Displays text rather than the acronym
<ADDRESS>		Tightly formats text as a mailing address
<APPLET>		Instructs browser to execute a Java applet
ALIGN="alignment"		Aligns horizontally and vertically (LEFT, CENTER, RIGHT)
ALT="text"		Text that is displayed if that applet cannot be loaded
ARCHIVE=" value"		File name of an archive of multiple applets (extension .ZIP)

CODE=" *value,—*"		Java class code file that executes the applet
CODEBASE=" *value*"		Specifies the directory URL of the applet code
DOWNLOAD="*value*"		Specifies order in which images will be downloaded
HEIGHT="*pixels*"		Specifies the height of the display area in pixels
HSPACE="*pixels*"		Number of pixels spaced beside the applet displayed
MAYSCRIPT		Permits the browser to execute a JavaScript script
NAME="*text*"		Specifies a proper name for the applet
STYLE="*text*"		Specifies information about a style sheet (CSS)
TITLE="*text*"		Text to be displayed while applet is executing
VSPACE="*pixels*"		Number of pixels in the border above applet
WSPACE="*pixels*" or ="%"		Width of the display area

<AREA>	(F)	Describes the shape of a link on an image map
ALT="*text*"		Text displayed if image map cannot be rendered
COORDS="*values*"		The left, top, right, and bottom of the link area (required)
HREF="*URL*"		Location that is linked (required)
ID="*text*"		Refers to another location on the same page
NOHREF		This area is not a link
SHAPE="*value*"		Arranges image map values according to COORDS Values: RECT, CIRC, and POLY
TARGET="*text*"		Specifies window for display of named URL Values: _BLANK, _PARENT, _SELF, _ TOP

<B>	Indicates that text is to be bold

<BASE>	(F)	Specifies defaults for all URLs in a document
HREF="*URL*"		Absolute URL of home page (base for relative URLs)
TARGET="*text*"		Defines name or type of window for BASE HREF value Values: _BLANK, _PARENT, _SELF, _ TOP

<BASEFONT>	Changes default for fonts in document
COLOR="*text*"	Specifies the default font COLOR
NAME="*text*"	Specifies the default font NAME
SIZE="*number*"	Sets the default font SIZE between 0 and 7

<BIG>	Increases current font size by one

<BLOCKQUOTE>	Indents specified text on both sides

<BODY>	(O)	Indicates the beginning of page content
ALINK="*color*"		Sets the color of all active links
BACKGROUND="*URL*"		Sets an image as the page background (JPG, GIF, or PNG)
BGCOLOR="*color*"		Sets a color for the background of a page

LINK="*color*"		Sets the color of an unvisited link
TEXT="*color*"		Sets the default color of all text
VLINK="*color*"		Sets the visited link color
\<BR\>	(F)	Inserts a line break to start a new line of text
CLEAR=ALL		Instructs browser to clear text around a graphic or table
CLEAR=LEFT		Starts a new line below and left of image
CLEAR=NONE		Clears text without respect to margins
CLEAR=RIGHT		Starts a new line below and right of image
\<CAPTION\>		Sets placement for a caption above or below a table
ALIGN=BOTTOM		Places the caption below a table
ALIGN=TOP		Places the caption above a table (default)
\<CENTER\>	(D)	Centers text or an image across a page
		(Replaced by DIV align=center)
\<CITE\>		Italicizes text for all citations
\<CODE\>		Text is rendered in a mono-spaced font (program code)
		(*Note:* Does not override BASEFONT NAME)
\<COL\>	(F)	Specifies properties of columns in a table
ALIGN="*alignment*"		Specifies CENTER, LEFT, or RIGHT
SPAN="*number*"		Specifies number of columns defined by COL
\<COLGROUP\>		Specifies columns within a table cell
SPAN="*number*"		Specifies the number of consecutive columns in group
WIDTH="*pixels*" or "% "		Specifies width of columns inside a table cell
\<DD\>	(O)	Formats text as the definition of a term
\<DFN\>		"Defining instance," the first usage of a term or acronym
\<DIR\>		Formats text in a directory list, like a table of contents
\<DIV\>		Generic container, divides paragraphs of text
ALIGN="*alignment*"		Aligns text LEFT, RIGHT, or CENTER
\<DL\>		Formats a definition list
COMPACT		Reduces inter-item spacing in the list

<DT>		Defined term from a definition list, aligned left
<EM>		Emphasizes text (italic, usually)
<FIELDSET>		Groups elements together, facilitating form processing (LEGEND tag is used to create a caption for the FIELDSET)
CLASS="*text*"		Indicates the class attribute of the element
STYLE="*text*"		Specifies style sheet (CSS) information
TITLE="*text*"		The title of the FIELDSET container
<FONT>	(D)	Specifies font attributes
COLOR="*color*"		Changes the font color
SIZE="*number*"		Changes the font to size (0-7)
SIZE=+"*number*"		Increases font size (up to +6)
SIZE=-"*number*"		Decreases font size (down to -6)
<FORM>		Structures a data input form
ACTION="*URL*"		Location to which data is directed (cgi-bin)
ENCTYPE="*URL*"		Specifies MIME encoding type
METHOD="*protocol*"		Selects transfer protocol for submit (GET or POST)
ONRESET="*text*"		Specifies event when RESET button is clicked
ONSUBMIT="*text*"		Specifies event when SUBMIT button is clicked
TARGET="*text*"		Displays a window with the FORM results returned
		Values: _blank, _parent, _ self, _ top
<FRAME>	(F)	Sets the attributes for a frame, part of a FRAMESET
FRAMEBORDER="*value*"		Sets visible or invisible property of frame border
		Values: IE4 (1, 0); Navigator 4 (YES, NO)
MARGINHEIGHT="*pixels*"		Sets the space above and below an object in a frame
MARGINWIDTH="*pixels*"		Sets the space between an object and the sides of a frame
NAME="*frame*"		Assigns a name to the frame
NORESIZE		Prevents frame borders from being moved
SCROLLING="*value*"		Allows scroll bars within a frame (YES or NO)
SRC="*URL*"		Identifies contents to be places in the frame
<FRAMESET>		Specifies the region of the screen to display frames
BORDER="*pixels*"		Sets the width of frameset borders (default is 5)
COLS="*pixels*" or "%"		Sets the height of the frame columns
ROWS="*pixels*" or "%"		Sets the width of the frame rows
<H"*number*">		Sets the heading level for text (number 1-6)
ALIGN="*alignment*"		Controls the headline alignment
		Value: LEFT, CENTER, RIGHT

<HEAD>	(O)	The page header that defines document content
		Usage: <HEAD >
		<META CONTENT="MOZILLA">
		<TITLE> "This Home Page"</TITLE>
		</HEAD>

<HR>	(F)	Creates a horizontal rule line
ALIGN="*alignment*"		Positions the rule line on the page
NOSHADE		Solid line, not shaded (default is 3D shading)
SIZE="*pixels*"		Sets thickness (height) of the line in pixels
WIDTH="*pixels*" or "*%*"		Sets width of line in pixels or as a percentage of space

<HTML>	Identifies an HTML formatted document (required)
	Usage: <HTML >
	<BODY>
	<H2>This is a second level heading.</H2>
	<BODY>
	</HTML>

<I>	Renders text in italic font

<IFRAME>	Specifies an inline subwindow, or floating frame (IE4)
ALIGN="*alignment*"	Specifies the alignment of the IFRAME object
	Values: LEFT, CENTER, RIGHT, TOP, MIDDLE, BOTTOM
FRAMEBORDER="*value*"	Displays a 3D border around the IFRAME (default shows 3D)
	Values: 0 (show no 3D), 1 (show 3D border)
HEIGHT="*pixels*"	Specifies height of an IFRAME
MARGINHEIGHT="*pixels*"	Determines vertical space between an object and edge of the frame
MARGINWIDTH="*pixels*"	Determines horizontal space between text and the edge of the frame
SCROLLING="*value*"	Controls whether content may scroll (default is AUTO)
	Values: YES, NO, AUTO
SRC="*URL*"	Displays contents of the URL named
WIDTH="*pixels*"	Determines vertical dimensions of an IFRAME

<IMG>	(F)	Displays a graphical image
		Usage: <IMG SRC="THISFILE.GIF " >
		File types: GIF, JPG, PNG, XPM, XBM
ALIGN="*alignment*"		Positions the image in relation to text
		Values: BOTTOM, MIDDLE, LEFT, RIGHT, TOP
ALT="*text*"		Text that replaces a graphic that cannot be displayed

BORDER="*pixels*"		Identifies the thickness of a border around a graphic
		Default shows border; set to "0" to make invisible
HEIGHT="*pixels*"		Sets the vertical size of an image on a page
HSPACE="*pixels*"		Sets the horizontal space cleared around an image
ISMAP		The MAP is located on the server, or is server-side
SRC="*URL*"		Source location of URL or file to be displayed (required)
USEMAP="*URL*"		Specifies a client-side MAP, a file with the "#" prefix
VSPACE="*pixels*"		Clears vertical space above and below image
WIDTH="*pixels*" or "%"		Sets the width of an image horizontally
<INPUT>	(F)	Creates a form field, or input object (default is text)
ALIGN="*alignment*"		Positions an input field on a page (default is TOP)
		Values: BOTTOM, MIDDLE, LEFT, RIGHT, TOP
CHECKED		Sets a check box or radio button to TRUE
MAXLENGTH="*number*"		Sets maximum number of characters user may enter
NAME="*text*"		Gives the form field a name
ONBLUR="*text*"		When focus is removed from an object, JavaScript is executed
ONCHANGE="*text*"		When contents of a box are changed, JavaScript is executed
ONFOCUS="*text*"		When the form object receives focus, JavaScript is executed
ONSELECT="*text*"		When user selects contents of a text box, JavaScript is executed
SIZE="*number*"		Sets the size of a text box in characters
SRC="*URL*"		Identifies an image file for a button on a form
TYPE=CHECKBOX		A basic checkbox (yes/no) in the field
TYPE=FILE		Directs browser to upload the specified file
TYPE=HIDDEN		Field is not visible to the user
TYPE=IMAGE		A graphical form submission button
TYPE=PASSWORD		Text entry field in which text is not displayed
TYPE=RADIO		An option select field (radio button)
TYPE=RESET		A button that clears all fields
TYPE=SUBMIT		A form submission button
TYPE=TEXT		A standard text field with one line
		(*Note:* Although not part of the HTML 4.0 specification, TEXTAREA creates a standard text field with multiple lines in both Navigator 4.0 and IE 4.0)
VALUE="*text*"		Default value for a field (required by radio and checkboxes)
<INS>		Text that has been inserted (used for revisions)
<ISINDEX>	(F) (D)	Indicates that the document is a searchable index
ACTION="*text*"		Sends text to specified CGI program, followed by a question mark
PROMPT="*text*"		Substitutes specified text for the default prompt

<KBD>		Text appears in a bold mono-spaced font (keyboard style)
<LABEL>		Specifies label text for a form field

Usage: <FORM action="name" method="post">
      <LABEL for="uname">Your User Name: </LABEL>
      <INPUT type="text" id="username">
      </FORM>

ACCESSKEY="*text*"	Accelerator key that puts the insertion point in the labeled text box
CLASS="*text*"	Indicates that the subclass style sheet is used to render the LABEL
FOR="*text*"	Specifies a name for the control object
ID="*text*"	Specifies a unique value for the control element
LANG="*text*"	Indicates the language to be rendered by the browser (fr=French)
LANGUAGE="*text*"	Specifies scripting language used (default is JavaScript)
<LEGEND>	Prescribes a fieldset legend
ACCESSKEY="*text*"	Accelerator key that places focus on labeled control object
CLASS="*text*"	Indicates that the sub-class style sheet is used to render the LEGEND
ALIGN="*alignment*"	Positions specified LEGEND related to fieldset (default is LEFT)
CLASS="*text*"	Indicates that the sub-class style sheet is used to render the LEGEND
ID="*text*"	Specifies a unique value for the LEGEND
LANG="*text*"	Indicates the language to be rendered by the browser (fr=French)
LANGUAGE="*text*"	Specifies scripting language used (default is JavaScript)
STYLE="*text*"	Specifies the way a Cascading Style Sheet (CSS) is to be used
TITLE="*text*"	Indicates the title of the LEGEND
VALIGN="*alignment*"	Places LEGEND above or below fieldset (TOP or BOTTOM)
<LI>	The start of a new item on a list
TYPE=1	Arabic numbers (1, 2, 3) (Default)
TYPE=a	Lowercase letters (a, b, c)
TYPE=A	Uppercase letters (A, B, C)
TYPE=i	Lowercase Roman numerals (i, ii, iii, iv)
TYPE=I	Uppercase Roman numerals (I, II, III, IV)
TYPE="*value*"	Values: DISC, CIRCLE, SQUARE (shape of bullet symbol)
VALUE="*number*"	Sets the first number to be used in a sequence

<LINK>	(F)	Specifies a location in a document or a different document
		Must be used inside HEAD tags

HREF="*URL*"	Displays specified HTML document when user clicks on LINK
	(Required attribute; case sensitive to a browser)
REL="*value,—*"	Defines relationship of the link, or location of style sheet (CSS)
	Values: HOME, TOC, INDEX, GLOSSARY, COPYRIGHT, UP, NEXT, PREVIOUS, HELP (required attribute)
REV="*URL*"	Reverses relationship of a link; may be used to indicate author
TITLE="*URL*"	The title of the document named in the LINK
<MAP>	Defines the areas of a client-side image map that are links
	(AREA tag is required to specify hot spots on the map)
NAME="*name*"	The name of the map (required)
<MENU> (D)	Identifies the beginning of a menu list
COMPACT	Forces tighter lines in a MENU
<META>	Contains information defining a page
CONTENT="*text*"	The information contained (required)
HTTP-EQUIV="*value*"	Relates information with an HTTPd response field to the server
	Value: REFRESH (required attribute)
NAME="*text*"	The type of information contained in the CONTENT attribute
<NOFRAMES>	Specifies alternate text if browser cannot display frames
<NOSCRIPT>	Specifies alternate text if JavaScript cannot be executed
<OBJECT>	Embeds an object on a page
	OBJECT could be an image, control, applet, or document
ALIGN="*alignment*"	Positions the OBJECT in relation to text
	Values: BASELINE, TEXTBOTTOM, MIDDLE, TEXTMIDDLE, LEFT, RIGHT, CENTER, TEXTTOP,
BORDER="*pixels*"	Identifies the thickness of invisible border around OBJECT
	Default shows border; set to "0" to make invisible
CODEBASE="*URL*"	Specifies the URL in the programming code to reference (required)
DATA="*URL*"	Specifies the URL in the data to be accessed by OBJECT
DECLARE	Declares the OBJECT without instantiating it
HEIGHT="*pixels*"	Sets the vertical size of an OBJECT on a page (required)
HSPACE="*pixels*"	Sets the horizontal space cleared to the right or left of OBJECT

ID		Specifies a unique value that can be referenced elsewhere
SHAPES		Specifies that the OBJECT uses shaped hyperlinks
STANDBY="*text*"		Text to be displayed while OBJECT is loading
TYPE		Specifies MIME type to be used by OBJECT
USEMAP="*URL*"		Specifies a server-side MAP (filename and location)
VSPACE="*pixels*"		Clears vertical space above and below OBJECT
WIDTH="*pixels*" or "%"		Sets the width of the OBJECT horizontally
<OL>		An ordered list by number or letter
COMPACT		Reduces inter-item spacing in the list
START="*number*"		Specifies the first value to be used on the list
TYPE=1		Arabic numbers (1, 2, 3) (default)
TYPE=a		Lowercase letters (a, b, c)
TYPE=A		Uppercase letters (A, B, C)
TYPE=i		Lowercase Roman numerals (i, ii, iii, iv)
TYPE=I		Uppercase Roman numerals (I, II, III, IV)
<OPTGROUP>		Defines a group of options
DISABLED		Unavailable in this context
LABEL="*text*"		Specifies LABEL for hierarchical group
<OPTION>		Specifies a menu choice on a form
DISABLED		This choice may not be selected
SELECTED		The default choice in a list box
VALUE="*text*"		This text is sent to the server if option is chosen
<P>		A text paragraph
ALIGN="*alignment*"		Defines how text is aligned horizontally
		Values: CENTER, LEFT, RIGHT
<PARAM>	(F)	Passes parameters to a Java applet
<PRE>		Preformatted text with spaces and line returns
WIDTH="*number*"		Specifies the number of characters in each line
<Q>		A short inline quotation
<S>	(D)	Specified text displayed with a strike-through line
<SAMP>		Formats text samples in mono-spaced font (for code)
<SCRIPT>		Container for script statements
		Note: Hides script from browsers that cannot render scripts

LANGUAGE="*text*"		Specifies script language to use
SRC="*URL*"		Specifies the location of the script code

<SELECT>		A menu field or drop-down list box on a form
MULTIPLE		Allows more than one selection from a list
NAME="*text*"		The title for a list box
SIZE="*number*"		The number of items visible at once

<SMALL>   Instructs browser to use one size smaller than default font

<SPAN>		A generic language or style container
ALIGN="*alignment*"		Positions specified applet on a page (default is LEFT)
		Values: CENTER, LEFT, RIGHT, JUSTIFY
ID="*text*"		Specifies a unique value for element that can referenced elsewhere
STYLE="*text*"		Specifies the way a Cascading Style Sheet (CSS) is to be used

<STRIKE>	(D)	Display the text with a line through it (strike-through)

<STRONG>   Text is rendered with strong emphasis (typically bold)

<STYLE>		Names a style sheet (CSS) to be applied to the document
		Overrides linked style sheets and browser settings
TITLE="*text*"		Not rendered by browser (may be useful to author)
TYPE="*text*"		Specifies how a style sheet (CSS) is to be used
		Also defines MIME type to be used

<SUB>   Displays text in subscript

<SUP>   Displays text in superscript

<TABLE>		Formats a table on the page
ALIGN=*alignment*		Positions the entire table on the page
		Values: CENTER, LEFT, RIGHT
BORDER=*pixels*		Defines thickness of a border in pixels
CELLPADDING=*pixels*		Distance between the cell wall and contents
CELLSPACING=*pixels*		Distance between table cells
COLS"*number*"		Specifies the number of columns in the table
FRAME="*value*"		Determines appearance of outside table edge
		Values: ABOVE, BELOW, BORDER, BOX, HSIDES, LHS, RHS, VOID, VSIDES
RULES="*value*"		Specifies how interior borders appear in a table

	Values: GROUPS, COLS, NONE, ROWS
	"All" renders a rule on every row and column edge
	"ALL" renders a rule between every row and column
TITLE="*text*"	Specifies a title for the table
WIDTH="*pixels*" or "%"	Table width in pixels or as a percentage of available space
<TBODY>	Defines the table body and groups rows in a unit;
	Separates headers and footers with a horizontal rule
<TD>	Defines contents of a single table cell
ALIGN="*alignment*"	Horizontal positioning of text in cell
	Values: CENTER, LEFT, RIGHT
COLSPAN="*number*"	The number of cells spanned by a column
HEIGHT="*number*" or "%"	Cell height in pixels or as a percentage of table
NOWRAP	No line breaks allowed in the cell
ROWSPAN="*number*"	Number of table rows covered by the cell
VALIGN="*alignment*"	Vertical positioning of text inside a cell
	Values: BASELINE, TOP, MIDDLE, BOTTOM
WIDTH="*pixels*" or "%"	Cell width in pixels or as a percentage of the table
<TEXTAREA>	A text field with multiple lines in a form
COLS="*number*"	The width of the field, in characters (required)
NAME="*name*"	The name of the field (required)
ROWS="*number*"	The height of the field, in characters (required)
<TFOOT>	Renders a table footer, useful when printing multiple pages
<TH>	Renders a table header cell (bold text by default)
ALIGN="*alignment*"	Horizontal positioning of text in cell
	Values: CENTER, LEFT, RIGHT
COLSPAN="*number*"	The width of the table header in characters
HEIGHT="*pixels*" or "% "	Cell height in pixels or as a percentage of table
NOWRAP	No line breaks allowed in the cell
ROWSPAN="*number*"	Number of table rows covered by the cell
VALIGN="*alignment*"	Vertical positioning of text inside a cell
	Values: BASELINE, TOP, MIDDLE, BOTTOM
WIDTH="*pixels*" or "%"	Cell width in pixels or as a percentage of the table
<THEAD>	Renders a page header before body of table (on each printed page)
<TITLE>	Defines the title of the page shown in the title bar

390

\<TR\>		Defines a table row
ALIGN="*alignment*"		Horizontal positioning of text in cell
		Values: CENTER, LEFT, RIGHT
VALIGN="*alignment*"		Vertical positioning of text inside a cell
		Values: BASELINE, BOTTOM, MIDDLE, TOP
\<TT\>		Renders text in a fixed-width font (like a teletype)
		Same as SAMP or CODE designation
\<U\>	(D)	Renders text underlined
\<UL\>		Unordered list
TYPE"*value*"		Substitutes a symbol for the standard bullet
		Values: CIRCLE, DISC, SQUARE
\<VAR\>		Renders text in a small fixed-width font for program variables
CLASS="*text*"		Indicates the subclass to which element belongs
ID="*text*"		Specifies a unique value for the element
LANG="*text*"		Indicates the language to be rendered by the browser (fr=French)
LANGUAGE="*text*"		Specifies scripting language used (default is JavaScript)
STYLE="*text*"		Specifies the way a Cascading Style Sheet (CSS) is to be used
TITLE="*text*"		Title placed in the FIELDSET container
\<WBR\>		Allows a "word break," overriding a \<NOBR\> instruction

Cascading Style Sheets

Style Properties

Style properties specify individual characteristics of HTML elements. Styles dictate features of formatting and behaviors, such as the font size, the color of an object, and the distance from surrounding elements. A list of CSS properties is shown below, followed by a detailed description of each.

Color and Background Properties

- color
- background-color
- background-image
- background-repeat
- background-attachment
- background-position
- background

Font Properties

- font-family
- font-size
- font-weight
- font
- font-style
- font-variant

Text Properties

- text-align
- vertical-align
- text-indent
- line-height
- text-decoration
- text-transform
- letter-spacing
- word-spacing

Classification Properties

- display
- white-space
- list-style-type
- list-style-image
- list-style-position
- list-style

Box Properties

- width
- height
- float
- clear
- margin
- margin-top
- margin-right
- margin-bottom
- margin-left
- padding
- padding-top
- padding-right
- padding-bottom
- padding-left
- border
- border-top
- border-right
- border-bottom
- border-left
- border-width
- border-style
- border-color
- border-top-width
- border-right-width
- border-bottom-width
- border-left-width

Color and Background Properties

Color and background style properties control the color of text in an element and the background color or image displayed behind the element. Additional properties may be specified to control the position and appearance of a background image.

· color
· background-color
· background-image
· background-repeat
· background-attachment
· background-position
· background

Color, Background-Color

Values: red, #FF0000, FF0000, rgb(255,0,0), rgb(75%,0,50%)

The name of the color, the hexadecimal value of the color, the RGB (red, green, blue) values, or the RGB percentages may be used to specify a color. The value *transparent* is the default background-color value. Recognized color names are black, silver, gray, white, maroon, red, purple, fuchsia, green, lime, olive, yellow, navy, blue, teal, and aqua.

Background-Image

Values: url(images/graphic.gif)

The filename is used to identify the background image, along with the path to its location. If no background-image is desired, use the word *none*.

Background-Repeat

Values: repeat, no-repeat, repeat-x, repeat-y

The repeat instruction tiles the image behind the element being defined. Repeat-X tiles the image across the element horizontally. Repeat-Y tiles the image down the element vertically. No-Repeat displays the image once behind the element.

Background-Attachment

Values: fixed, scroll

Fixed keeps the background-image fixed in place as text scrolls through it. Scroll moves the image along with the text. The default is scroll.

Background-Position

Values:
      x, y, top, left, right, bottom, center

The position is always relative to the top-left corner of the element in which an image is positioned. The "x" is the horizontal position, and "y" is the vertical position of an image. Either value may be a percentage relative to the size of the element; a fixed amount such as "1in" (one inch); or one of the keywords that indicate a relative position.

Background

This property allows you to specify all the background properties in a single string. The following order must be used when specifying background properties:
background-color, background-image, background-repeat, background-attachment, background-position

Examples:

    H1 {background: url(images/picture.gif) no-repeat fixed left bottom}
    H2 {background: red}

Font Properties

Font properties control the font face, size, weight, and other variations of typeface.

· font-family
· font-size
· font-weight
· font
· font-style
· font-variant

Font-Family

Generic: serif, sans serif, monospace, fantasy, cursive
Specific: Palatino, Arial, Courier, Dingbats, Zapf Chancery. Any commonly available font may be specified by name.

Font-Size

Specific: pt (points), in (inches), cm (centimeter), px (pixels)
Relative: 150%, small, medium, large

Relative font sizes may be further qualified as follows:

xx-small	50% smaller than the x-small font
x-small	50% smaller than the small font
small	50% smaller than the medium font
medium	A medium-sized font, typically 10 point
large	50% larger than the medium font
x-large	50% larger than the large font
xx-large	50% larger than the x-large font
larger	50% larger than the parent element's font
smaller	50% smaller than the parent element's font

Font-Weight

Specific: normal, bold
Relative: bolder, lighter

The values of 100, 200, 300, 400, 500, 600, 700, 800, and 900 are used to indicate individual font weights, where 400 is "normal," and 700 is "bold." Additional weights, if available, will be displayed in the weight closest to the specified number.

Font

This property sets the font-weight, font-size, and font-family properties in a single string.
Examples:
    TD {font: bold 16pt Times}
    H1 {font: normal 20pt Arial}
    <H2 style="font: 16pt Palatino">Sample of Palatino Font</H2>

Font-Style

Values: normal, italic

If an italic variant of the current font is available, specifying "italic" will apply this property. If an italic variant is not available, the current font may appear in "oblique" or slanted style, rather than true italic.

Font-Variant

Values: normal, small-caps

If a small-caps variant of the current font is available, specifying "small-caps" will apply this property. If a small caps variant is not available, the current font will typically appear in upper case at the height of lower case letters.

Text Properties

These properties are used to control both text-level elements and block-level elements. Features affected are the relative horizontal and vertical position of block level elements; spacing between lines of text, between words, and between letters; text decoration; and text case.

- text-align
- vertical-align
- text-indent
- line-height
- text-decoration
- text-transform
- letter-spacing
- word-spacing

Text-Align

Values: left, center, right, justify

This property controls the horizontal alignment of paragraphs and other block-level elements.

Vertical-Align

Values: baseline, bottom, middle, text-bottom, text-top, top, sub, super

This property controls the position of both text and image elements related to adjoining elements.

Text-Indent

This property controls the first line of text in a paragraph. The length of the indent may be specified in an absolute value, such as ".50in" or a relative value, such as "10%."

Line-Height

This property controls the spacing of lines within a paragraph. It does not affect the space between paragraphs. The value may be set to an absolute number or to a percentage. Values such as "1.5" or "2" refer to multiples of the current line height. Set the line height to "2" to double space. To set the line height to 1 1/2 line spacing, use "1.5" or "150%."

Text-Decoration

Values: none, underline, overline, line-through, blink

This property controls the text formatting features listed.

Text-Transform

Values: capitalize, uppercase, lowercase, none

This property capitalizes the first letter of every word, dictates the case of all text, or displays text in the original capitalization.

Letter-Spacing and Word-Spacing

These properties control the space between individual letters or between words. Any recognized unit of measurement may be used to specify desired spacing, such as 4px, 3pt, 0.25in, or 2em.

Classification Properties

These properties control a number of behaviors, some of which are not obvious. The list-style properties have a noticeable affect.

- display
- white-space
- list-style-type
- list-style-image

- list-style-position
- list-style

Display

Values: block, inline, list-item, none

The display value "none" makes an element invisible, while leaving the display value empty (" ") allows an element to appear. An element is displayed when it is referred to as a "block" element, an "inline" element, or a "list-style" element. If an inappropriate value is specified it will be ignored and replaced by an acceptable value. The most commonly used display values are "none" and " ".

White-Space

Values: normal, pre, nowrap

This property controls the behavior of white space. Theoretically, the value of "normal" displays text in the normal fashion. The value "pre" allows more than one space in sequence to be displayed, rather than the normal collapsed status. The value of nowrap disables line wrapping in an element.

List-Style-Type

Values: none, disc, circle, square, decimal, lower-roman, upper-roman, lower-alpha, upper-alpha

The type of bullet is specified by this property. It controls lists that are not concurrently displaying a list image.

List-Style-Image

This property replaces the list bullet character with an image.
Examples:

    UL {list-style-image: url(images/newbullet.gif)}
    <UL style="list-style-image: url(newbullet.gif)">

If a value of "none" is specified, a list is displayed in the default list style.

List-Style-Position

Values: inside, outside

This property controls the relationship of a bullet to the text that follows. The value "inside" places the bullet character at the left-margin of the text, and wraps subsequent text to the same position. The value "outside" causes the bullet to appear to the left of any wrapped text.

List-Style

This property specifies two attributes at once. It controls either the list-style-type and the list-style-position, or the list-style-position and the list-style-image.

397

Box Properties

This group of properties controls block-level elements both individually and in relation to adjoining elements. Some of these properties control the entire element, such as height or width. Others control only one side of the element "box," such as margin-left or padding-bottom.

· width
· height
· float
· clear
· margin
· padding
· border
· border-width
· border-style
· border-color

Width and Height

Any recognized unit of measurement may be used to specify the height or width of an HTML object. The object will expand automatically to show all text contained in the box if the width or height assigned is too small.

Float

Values: left, right, none
Elements such as images and tables are instructed to "float" to the left or to the right of adjoining text. To wrap text on the right of an image, specify a float value of "left."

Clear

Values: left, right, both, none

This property works in conjunction with the float property. To prevent an element from being positioned next to a floating object, specify a value of "left" or "right" to prohibit floating objects to the left or right. Specify both to clear objects on both sides.

Margin

Values: margin-top, margin-right, margin-bottom, margin-left

This property controls the left, right, top and bottom margins around elements. The outer margins around an object may be controlled with any recognized unit of measurement.

Padding

Values: padding-top, padding-left, padding-bottom, padding-right

This property controls the distance between the element text and its box or container, in the same way that collapsing controls the space between text in a cell and the cell walls in a table. Padding refers to the inner margin. The amount of padding may be specified individually for each side of a text object in a box.

Border

This property sets uniform values for the border-style, border-width, and border-color properties. Border takes a maximum of three values. The first value specifies the border-width of all four borders. The second value specifies the border-style of all four borders. A third value specifies the color of all four borders.

Border-Width

Values: thin, medium, thick, 5px, .03in

This property controls the width of a border if one is used. One to four values may be specified. If a single value is specified it will be applied to every border. If two values are specified, the first value applies to the top and bottom border and the second value to the left and right sides. If three values are specified, the first value applies to the top border, the second value to the left and right borders, and the third value to the bottom border. If four values are specified, the values will apply respectively to the top, right, bottom and left sides. Any border may be individually specified by using the border-width-left, border-width-top, border-width-right, or border-width-bottom properties. Any recognized unit of measurement may be used to specify the border length.

Border-Style

Values: none, dotted, dashed, solid, double, groove, ridge, inset, outset

This property controls the type of border around an object, and what line style is used to draw the border. Any style other than "none" will cause a border line to appear around the element. This property applies only to block-level elements. If a single value is specified, the value affects all borders. If more than one value is specified, the values are applied to the sides in the same order as the border-width properties are applied.

Border-Color

Values: red, 00A0F7, #00FF00, rgb(255,0,0), rgb(0,100%,100%)

This property controls the color of a border if one is used. If a single value is specified, the value affects all sides of the object. If more than one value is specified, the values are applied to the sides in the same order as the border-width properties are applied.

Units in CSS1

Many style sheet properties accept a length descriptor. HTML supports two types of units: relative and absolute lengths.
Relative Units: em, ex, px

The height of the element's font relative to the output device is expressed in em, as in "0.5em." The height of the letter X relative to the output device is expressed in "ex," as in "0.75ex." Pixels relative to the output device are expressed in "px," as in "15px." Relative units allow web pages to scale better on different devices and clients.

Absolute units define specific distances.

Absolute Units: in, cm, mm, pt, pc

These represent inches, as in ".5in"; centimeters, as in "1cm"; millimeters, as in "15mm"; points (1/72 inch), as in "12pt"; and pica (1 pica = 12pt), as in "1pc."

Most lengths may also be expressed as percentages. Percentages are usually relative to the parent element. If a font size of 50% is specified, it conforms the element's font size to one half of the parent element's font size.

Support for CSS1

In the following table, IE 4.0 refers to Microsoft Internet Explorer version 4.0, and NC refers to Netscape Communicator. Yes or No indicates whether the browser supports the listed CSS1 property.

Color/Background Properties	IE 4.0	NC
color	Yes	Yes
background-color	Yes	Yes
background-image	Yes	Yes
background-repeat	No	Yes
background-attachment	No	Yes
background-position	No	No
background	Yes	Yes

Font Properties	IE 4.0	NC
font	Yes	Yes
font-family	Yes	Yes
font-size	Yes	Yes
font-style	Yes	Yes
font-variant	Yes	No
font-weight	Yes	Yes

Text Properties	IE 4.0	NC
letter-spacing	Yes	No
line-height	Yes	Yes
text-align	Yes	Yes
text-decoration	Yes	Yes

	IE 4.0	NC
text-indent	Yes	Yes
text-transform	Yes	Yes
vertical-align	Yes	No
word-spacing	No	No
Classification Properties	**IE 4.0**	**NC**
display	No	Yes
list-style-image	No	Yes
list-style-position	No	Yes
list-style-type	No	Yes
white-space	No	Yes
Box Properties	**IE 4.0**	**NC**
border	No	Yes
border-color	No	Yes
border-width	No	Yes
border-bottom	No	No
border-bottom-width	No	Yes
border-left	No	No
border-left-width	No	Yes
border-right	No	No
border-right-width	No	Yes
border-style	No	Yes
border-top	No	No
border-top-width	No	Yes
clear	No	Yes
float	No	Yes
height	Yes	Yes
margin	Yes	Yes
margin-bottom	No	Yes
margin-left	Yes	Yes
margin-right	Yes	Yes
margin-top	No	Yes
padding	No	Yes
padding-bottom	No	Yes
padding-left	No	No
padding-right	No	Yes
padding-top	No	Yes
width	Yes	Yes

Server-Side Includes

Server-Side Include (SSI) is a standard command that allows a web server to generate data and dynamically send it to an HTML document. It is commonly used to automate tasks, such as embedding information in a document as it is requested.

An SSI command begins with an HTML comment as follows:

```
<!--This is the format for a comment-->
```

A Server-Side Include command is embedded in the comment format with the following general syntax:

```
<!--#command tag="value"-->
```

This reference is not to an HTML tag, but rather to a tag that carries information used by the server to process the command. Each SSI command begins with a pound sign (#). Each tag, or parameter of a command, is followed by an equals sign (=) and an assigned value. The following example returns the date and the time that a file was last modified:

```
<!--#echo var="LAST_MODIFIED"-->
```

The syntax and meaning of each SSI command is shown here.

#echo

Returns the value of a variable. The five variables are:

```
DOCUMENT_NAME
DOCUMENT_URI
DATE_LOCAL
DATE_GMT
QUERY_STRING_UNESCAPED
```

Example:

```
Last modified: <EM><!--#echo var="LAST_MODIFIED"--></EM>
```

Yields the following:

```
Last modified: Tuesday, 24-Mar-99 16:41:36 EST
```

#include

Used to embed the contents of one file in another file.
Example:

```
<!--#include file="address.txt"-->
</BODY>
</HTML>
```

This script places the text of any file identified in the HTML document that requests it. All that is needed is a reference to the appropriate file instead of retyping that file's contents in a given location.

Another tag that may be used with #include is virtual=. The file= tag requires that the file must be in the same directory as the document. The virtual= tag allows access to any document that the server can find by relative reference.

Example:

```
<!--#include virtual="/directory/address.txt"-->
```

In this case, the address file can be placed in the site's root directory, and can be accessed from any file, even if it is located at another level in the directory tree.

#exec

May take either of two tags:

```
cmd=
cgi=
```

The command named in the cmd= tag will be executed using /bin/sh. If the tag is cgi=, the server looks in the specified cgi-bin directory. If the result of the script is a location tag, the server constructs a link to it. Otherwise, the result of the script is merged with the HTML file.

Administrators may disable #exec to prevent it from being used to compromise the security of a site.

#config

Three tags may be used:

```
errmsg=
sizefmt=
timefmt=
```

errmsg= determines what message is sent back to the client if an error occurs while parsing the document.

#sizefmt= specifies the formatting to be used when the size of a file is displayed. The options are bytes= or abbrev=.

#fsize= takes either the file= or the virtual= tags, and returns the size of the specified file as formatted by #config.

#flastmod= takes either the file= or the virtual= tags, and returns the last date modified.

timefmt= specifies the format to use when the server provides a date. The formatting string comes from Unix's strftime. The options are shown here:

%a	The abbreviated weekday
%A	The full weekday
%b	The abbreviated month name
%B	The full month name
%d	The day of the month as a decimal number
%D	The date in mm/dd/yy format
%e	The day of the month in two digits
%H	The hour of the 24-hour clock in two digits
%I	The hour of the 12-hour clock in two digits
%j	The day of the year as a decimal number
%m	The month of the year in two digits
%M	The minutes of the hour in two digits
%p	The local AM or PM string
%r	The 12-hour clock time in local HH:MM:SS AM/PM format
%S	The seconds of the minute in two digits
%T	The 24-hour clock time in HH:MM:SS format
%U	The week of the year in two digits (Sunday first)
%w	The day of the week in one digit
%W	The week of the year in two digits (Monday first)
%y	The year of the century in two digits
%Y	Year as a decimal number
%Z	The time zone name

Variables

Six environment variables are available (exclusive of the CGI variables):

LAST_MODIFIED	Reports the last time the current file was changed
DOCUMENT_NAME	Reports the document name

DOCUMENT_URI	Reports the full path relative to the document root
DATE_LOCAL	Reports the current local date and time
DATE_GMT	Reports the current Greenwich mean time in timefmt= format
QUERY_STRING_UNESCAPED	Reports the query string sent by the client, if any

Using Server-Side Includes

The SSIs must be enabled at the server level. They may be enabled for an entire site or for individual directories. They may be activated for all files or only for files with a special file extension, such as "shtml."

When the server receives a GET request from a client, it checks to see if the requested file ends in shtml. If it does, the server examines the file for SSIs because of the file extension. Directives are found and processed, and the entire document is sent back with content-type set to text/html if the following line was placed in the srm.conf file:

```
AddType text/html shtml
```

The server will parse a file only if the correct file extension is used.

Testing SSI

The following HTML document, named test.shtml, will test whether SSI is enabled on a server:

```
<HTML>
<HEAD>
<TITLE>Test for Server-Side Includes</TITLE>
</HEAD>
<BODY>
<P>
The date last modified<BR>
<!--#echo var="LAST_MODIFIED"-->
</BODY>
</HTML>
```

When accessed, the test.shtml page should produce the following output, depending on how the time format is configured:

```
The date last modified
Mon January 25 08:15:47 1999
```

SSIs are useful for implementing standard features on a site. Most sites have the same background on all pages, a copyright notice, and a link to the webmaster. The #include SSI can automate placing this type of information on every page.

405

Create the following template in a text editor for pages with included body and footer

```
<HTML>
<HEAD>
<TITLE>Template</TITLE>
</HEAD>
<!--#include virtual="body.inc"-->
<H1>Header</H1>
<P>
</P>
<!--#include virtual="footer.inc"-->
</BODY>
</HTML>
```

Save this file as template.shtml, or with the appropriate file extension for your server. Note that included files are named with the extension "inc" rather than "html." The included files contain HTML, but they are not complete legal documents. This is simply a way to reference the contents of the file.

The body.inc file might contain the following:

```
<BODY BACKGROUND="wallpaper.gif">
<A HREF="AboutUs.shtml"><IMG SRC="Images/logo.gif"
ALT="Logo" HEIGHT= 100 WIDTH=60>
```

The footer might contain copyright information and a link to the webmaster's email address. If that information changes, it only needs to be changed once in the "footer.inc" file.

Server-Side Includes are effectively used to automate a site and to provide information on the fly for visitors.

HTML Color Codes

Color Name	Code	Color Name	Code	Color Name	Code
AliceBlue	eff7ff	Cornsilk2	ece5c6	DimGray	463e41
AntiqueWhite	f9e8d2	Cornsilk3	c8c2a7	DodgerBlue	1589ff
AntiqueWhite1	feedd6	Cornsilk4	817a68	DodgerBlue2	157dec
AntiqueWhite2	ebdbc5	Cyan	00ffff	DodgerBlue3	1569c7
AntiqueWhite3	c8b9a6	Cyan1	57feff	DodgerBlue4	153e7e
AntiqueWhite4	817468	Cyan2	50ebec	Firebrick	800517
Aquamarine	43b7ba	Cyan3	46c7c7	Firebrick1	f62817
Aquamarine1	87fdce	Cyan4	307d7e	Firebrick2	e42217
Aquamarine2	7deabe	DarkGoldenrod	af7817	Firebrick3	c11b17
Aquamarine3	69c69f	DarkGoldenrod1	fbb117	FloralWhite	fff9ee
Aquamarine4	417c64	DarkGoldenrod2	e8a317	ForestGreen	4e9258
Azure	efffff	DarkGoldenrod3	c58917	Gainsboro	d8d9d7
Azure2	deecec	DarkGoldenrod4	7f5217	GhostWhite	f7f7ff
Azure3	bcc7c7	DarkGreen	254117	Gold	d4a017
Azure4	7a7d7d	DarkKhaki	b7ad59	Gold1	fdd017
Beige	f5f3d7	DarkOliveGreen	4a4117	Gold2	eac117
Bisque	fde0bc	DarkOliveGreen1	ccfb5d	Gold3	c7a317
Bisque2	ead0ae	DarkOliveGreen2	bce954	Gold4	806517
Bisque3	c7af92	DarkOliveGreen3	a0c544	Goldenrod	edda74
Bisque4	816e59	DarkOliveGreen4	667c26	Goldenrod1	fbb917
Black	000000	DarkOrange	f88017	Goldenrod2	e9ab17
BlanchedAlmond	fee8c6	DarkOrange1	f87217	Goldenrod3	c68e17
Blue	0000ff	DarkOrange2	e56717	Goldenrod4	805817
Blue1	1535ff	DarkOrange3	c35617	Gray	736f6e
Blue2	1531ec	DarkOrange4	7e3117	Gray0	150517
Blue3	1528c7	DarkOrchid	7d1b7e	Gray18	250517
Blue4	151b7e	DarkOrchid1	b041ff	Gray21	2b1b17
BlueViolet	7931df	DarkOrchid2	a23bec	Gray23	302217
Brown	980517	DarkOrchid3	8b31c7	Gray24	302226
Brown1	f63526	DarkOrchid4	571b7e	Gray25	342826
Brown2	e42d17	DarkSalmon	e18b6b	Gray26	34282c
Brown3	c22217	DarkSeaGreen	8bb381	Gray27	382d2c
Burlywood1	fcce8e	DarkSeaGreen1	c3fdb8	Gray28	3b3131
Burlywood2	eabe83	DarkSeaGreen2	b5eaaa	Gray29	3e3535
Burlywood3	c6a06d	DarkSeaGreen3	99c68e	Gray30	413839
Burlywood4	806341	DarkSeaGreen4	617c58	Gray31	41383c
CadetBlue	578693	DarkSlateBlue	2b3856	Gray32	463e3f
CadetBlue1	99f3ff	DarkSlateGray	25383c	Gray34	4a4344
CadetBlue2	8ee2ec	DarkSlateGray1	9afeff	Gray35	4c4646
CadetBlue3	77bfc7	DarkSlateGray2	8eebec	Gray36	4e4848
CadetBlue4	4c787e	DarkSlateGray3	78c7c7	Gray37	504a4b
Chartreuse	8afb17	DarkSlateGray4	4c7d7e	Gray38	544e4f
Chartreuse2	7fe817	DarkTurquoise	3b9c9c	Gray39	565051
Chartreuse3	6cc417	DarkViolet	842dce	Gray40	595454
Chartreuse4	437c17	DeepPink	f52887	Gray41	5c5858
Chocolate	c85a17	DeepPink2	e4287c	Gray42	5f5a59
Coral	f76541	DeepPink3	c12267	Gray43	625d5d
Coral2	e55b3c	DeepPink4	7d053f	Gray44	646060
Coral3	c34a2c	DeepSkyBlue	3bb9ff	Gray45	666362
Coral4	7e2817	DeepSkyBlue2	38acec	Gray46	696565
CornflowerBlue	151b8d	DeepSkyBlue3	3090c7	Gray47	6d6968
Cornsilk	fff7d7	DeepSkyBlue4	25587e	Gray48	6e6a6b

Color Name	Code	Color Name	Code	Color Name	Code
Gray49	726e6d	Green3	4cc417	LightPink3	c48189
Gray50	747170	Green4	347c17	LightPink4	7f4e52
Gray51	787473	GreenYellow	b1fb17	LightSalmon	f9966b
Gray52	7a7777	Honeydew	f0feee	LightSalmon2	e78a61
Gray53	7c7979	Honeydew2	deebdc	LightSalmon3	c47451
Gray54	807d7c	Honeydew3	bcc7b9	LightSalmon4	7f462c
Gray55	82807e	Honeydew4	7a7d74	LightSeaGreen	3ea99f
Gray56	858381	HotPink	f660ab	LightSkyBlue	82cafa
Gray57	878583	HotPink1	f665ab	LightSkyBlue2	a0cfec
Gray58	8b8987	HotPink2	e45e9d	LightSkyBlue3	87afc7
Gray59	8d8b89	HotPink3	c25283	LightSkyBlue4	566d7e
Gray60	8f8e8d	HotPink4	7d2252	LightSlateBlue	736aff
Gray61	939190	IndianRed	5e2217	LightSlateGray	6d7b8d
Gray62	959492	IndianRed1	f75d59	LightSteelBlue	728fce
Gray63	999795	IndianRed2	e55451	LightSteelBlue1	c6deff
Gray64	9a9998	IndianRed3	c24641	LightSteelBlue2	b7ceec
Gray65	9e9c9b	IndianRed4	7e2217	LightSteelBlue3	9aadc7
Gray66	a09f9d	Ivory	fffffee	LightSteelBlue4	646d7e
Gray67	a3a2a0	Ivory2	ececdc	LightYellow	fffedc
Gray68	a5a4a3	Ivory3	c9c7b9	LightYellow2	edebcb
Gray69	a9a8a6	Ivory4	817d74	LightYellow3	c9c7aa
Gray70	acaba9	Khaki	ada96e	LightYellow4	827d6b
Gray71	aeadac	Khaki1	fff380	LimeGreen	41a317
Gray72	b1b1af	Khaki2	ede275	Linen	f9eee2
Gray73	b3b3b1	Khaki3	c9be62	Magenta	ff00ff
Gray74	b7b6b4	Khaki4	827839	Magenta1	f43eff
Gray75	b9b8b6	Lavender	e3e4fa	Magenta2	e238ec
Gray76	bcbbba	LavenderBlush	fdeef4	Magenta3	c031c7
Gray77	bebebc	LavenderBlush2	ebdde2	Maroon	810541
Gray78	c1c1bf	LavenderBlush3	c8bbbe	Maroon1	f535aa
Gray79	c3c4c2	LavenderBlush4	817679	Maroon2	e3319d
Gray80	c7c7c5	LawnGreen	87f717	Maroon3	c12283
Gray81	cacac9	LemonChiffon	fff8c6	Maroon4	7d0552
Gray82	cccccb	LemonChiffon2	ece5b6	MediumAquamarine	348781
Gray83	d0cfcf	LemonChiffon3	c9c299	MediumBlue	152dc6
Gray84	d2d2d1	LemonChiffon4	827b60	MediumForestGreen	347235
Gray85	d5d5d4	LightBlue	addfff	MediumGoldenrod	ccb954
Gray86	d7d7d7	LightBlue1	bdedff	MediumOrchid	b048b5
Gray87	dbdbd9	LightBlue2	afdcec	MediumOrchid1	d462ff
Gray88	dddddc	LightBlue3	95b9c7	MediumOrchid2	c45aec
Gray89	e0e0e0	LightBlue4	5e767e	MediumOrchid3	a74ac7
Gray90	e2e3e1	LightCoral	e77471	MediumOrchid4	6a287e
Gray91	e5e6e4	LightCyan	e0ffff	MediumPurple	8467d7
Gray92	e8e9e8	LightCyan2	cfecec	MediumPurple1	9e7bff
Gray93	ebebea	LightCyan3	afc7c7	MediumPurple2	9172ec
Gray94	eeeeee	LightCyan4	717d7d	MediumPurple3	7a5dc7
Gray95	f0f1f0	LightGoldenrod	ecd872	MediumPurple4	4e387e
Gray96	f4f4f3	LightGoldenrod1	ffe87c	MediumSeaGreen	306754
Gray97	f6f6f5	LightGoldenrod2	ecd672	MediumSlateBlue	5e5a80
Gray98	f9f9fa	LightGoldenrod3	c8b560	MediumSpringGreen	348017
Gray99	fbfbfb	LightGoldenrod4	817339	MediumTurquoise	48cccd
Gray100	ffffff	LightGoldenrodYellow	faf8cc	MediumVioletRed	ca226b
Green	00ff00	LightPink	faafba	MidnightBlue	151b54
Green1	5ffb17	LightPink1	f9a7b0	MintCream	f5fff9
Green2	59e817	LightPink2	e799a3	MistyRose	fde1dd

Color Name	Code	Color Name	Code	Color Name	Code
MistyRose2	ead0cc	Pink3	c48793	SlateBlue2	6960ec
MistyRose3	c6afac	Pink4	7f525d	SlateBlue3	574ec7
MistyRose4	806f6c	Plum	b93b8f	SlateBlue4	342d7e
Moccasin	fde0ac	Plum1	f9b7ff	SlateGray	657383
NavajoWhite	fddaa3	Plum2	e6a9ec	SlateGray1	c2dfff
NavajoWhite2	eac995	Plum3	c38ec7	SlateGray2	b4cfec
NavajoWhite3	c7aa7d	Plum4	7e587e	SlateGray3	98afc7
NavajoWhite4	806a4b	PowderBlue	addce3	SlateGray4	616d7e
Navy	150567	Purple	8e35efr	Snow	fff9fa
OldLace	fcf3e2	Purple1	893bff	Snow2	ece7e6
OliveDrab	658017	Purple2	7f38ec	Snow3	c8c4c2
OliveDrab1	c3fb17	Purple3	6c2dc7	Snow4	817c7b
OliveDrab2	b5e917	Purple4	461b7e	SpringGreen	4aa02c
OliveDrab3	99c517	Red	ff0000	SpringGreen1	5efb6e
OliveDrab4	617c17	Red1	f62217	SpringGreen2	57e964
Orange	f87a17	Red2	e41b17	SpringGreen3	4cc552
Orange1	fa9b17	RosyBrown	b38481	SpringGreen4	347c2c
Orange2	e78e17	RosyBrown1	fbbbb9	SteelBlue	4863a0
Orange3	c57717	RosyBrown2	e8adaa	SteelBlue1	5cb3ff
Orange4	7f4817	RosyBrown3	c5908e	SteelBlue2	56a5ec
OrangeRed	f63817	RosyBrown4	7f5a58	SteelBlue3	488ac7
OrangeRed2	e43117	RoyalBlue	2b60de	SteelBlue4	2b547e
OrangeRed3	c22817	RoyalBlue1	306eff	Tan	d8af79
OrangeRed4	7e0517	RoyalBlue2	2b65ec	Tan1	fa9b3c
Orchid	e57ded	RoyalBlue3	2554c7	Tan2	e78e35
Orchid1	f67dfa	RoyalBlue4	15317e	Thistle	d2b9d3
Orchid2	e473e7	Salmon1	f88158	Thistle1	fcdfff
Orchid3	c160c3	Salmon2	e67451	Thistle2	e9cfec
Orchid4	7d387c	Salmon3	c36241	Thistle3	c6aec7
PaleGoldenrod	ede49e	Salmon4	7e3817	Thistle4	806d7e
PaleGreen	79d867	SandyBrown	ee9a4d	Tomato	f75431
PaleGreen1	a0fc8d	SeaGreen	4e8975	Tomato2	e54c2c
PaleGreen2	94e981	SeaGreen1	6afb92	Tomato3	c23e17
PaleGreen3	7dc56c	SeaGreen2	64e986	Turquoise	43c6db
PaleGreen4	4e7c41	SeaGreen3	54c571	Turquoise1	52f3ff
PaleTurquoise	aeebec	SeaGreen4	387c44	Turquoise2	4ee2ec
PaleTurquoise1	bcfeff	Seashell	fef3eb	Turquoise3	43bfc7
PaleTurquoise2	adebec	Seashell2	ebe2d9	Turquoise4	30787e
PaleTurquoise3	92c7c7	Seashell3	c8bfb6	Violet	8d38c9
PaleTurquoise4	5e7d7e	Seashell4	817873	VioletRed	e9358a
PaleVioletRed	d16587	Sienna	8a4117	VioletRed1	f6358a
PaleVioletRed1	f778a1	Sienna1	f87431	VioletRed2	e4317f
PaleVioletRed2	e56e94	Sienna2	e66c2c	VioletRed3	c12869
PaleVioletRed3	c25a7c	Sienna3	c35817	VioletRed4	7d0541
PaleVioletRed4	7e354d	Sienna4	7e3517	Wheat	f3daa9
PapayaWhip	feeccf	SkyBlue	6698ff	Wheat1	fee4b1
PeachPuff	fcd5b0	SkyBlue1	82caff	Wheat2	ebd3a3
PeachPuff2	eac5a3	SkyBlue2	79baec	Wheat3	c8b189
PeachPuff3	c6a688	SkyBlue3	659ec7	Wheat4	816f54
PeachPuff4	806752	SkyBlue4	41627e	Yellow	ffff00
Peru	c57726	SlateBlue	737ca1	Yellow1	fffc17
Pink	faafbe	SlateBlue1	7369ff	YellowGreen	52d017
Pink2	e7a1b0				

HTML Coded Characters

Code	Description	Code	Description
		Horizontal tab		Non-breaking Space
&#10:	Line feed	¡	Inverted exclamation
	Carriage Return	¢	Cent sign
 	Space	£	Pound sterling
!	Exclamation mark	¤	General currency sign
"	Quotation mark	¥	Yen sign
#	Number sign	¦	Broken vertical bar
$	Dollar sign	§	Section sign
%	Percent sign	¨	Umlaut (dieresis)
&	Ampersand	©	Copyright
'	Apostrophe	ª	Feminine ordinal
(	Left parenthesis	«	Left angle quote, guillemet left
)	Right parenthesis		
*	Asterisk	¬	Not sign
+	Plus sign	­	Soft hyphen
,	Comma	®	Registered trademark
-	Hyphen	¯	Macron accent
.	Period (fullstop)	°	Degree sign
/	Solidus (slash)	±	Plus or minus
0–9	Digits 0–9	²	Superscript two
:	Colon	³	Superscript three
;	Semi-colon	´	Acute accent
<	Less than	µ	Micro sign
=	Equals sign	¶	Paragraph sign
>	Greater than	·	Middle dot
?	Question mark	¸	Cedilla
@	Commercial at	¹	Superscript one
A–Z	Letters A–Z (upper case)	º	Masculine ordinal
[	Left square bracket	»	Right angle quote, guillemet right
\	Reverse solidus (backslash)		
]	Right square bracket	¼	Fraction one-fourth
^	Caret	½	Fraction one-half
_	Horizontal bar (underscore)	¾	Fraction three-fourths
`	Acute accent	¿	Inverted question mark
a–z	Letters a–z (lower case)	À	Capital A, grave accent
{	Left curly brace	Á	Capital A, acute accent
|	Vertical bar	Â	Capital A, circumflex accent
}	Right curly brace	Ã	Capital A, tilde
~	Tilde	Ä	Capital A, dieresis or umlaut mark

Code	Description	Code	Description
Å	Capital A, ring	ã	Small a, tilde
Æ	Capital AE diphthong (ligature)	ä	Small a, dieresis or umlaut mark
Ç	Capital C, cedilla	å	Small a, ring
È	Capital E, grave accent	æ	Small ae diphthong (ligature)
É	Capital E, acute accent	ç	Small c, cedilla
Ê	Capital E, circumflex accent	è	Small e, grave accent
Ë	Capital E, dieresis or umlaut mark	é	Small e, acute accent
Ì	Capital I, grave accent	ê	Small e, circumflex accent
Í	Capital I, acute accent	ë	Small e, dieresis or umlaut mark
Î	Capital I, circumflex accent	ì	Small i, grave accent
Ï	Capital I, dieresis or umlaut mark	í	Small i, acute accent
Ð	Capital Eth, Icelandic	î	Small i, circumflex accent
Ñ	Capital N, tilde	ï	Small i, dieresis or umlaut mark
Ò	Capital O, grave accent	ð	Small eth, Icelandic
Ó	Capital O, acute accent	ñ	Small n, tilde
Ô	Capital O, circumflex accent	ò	Small o, grave accent
Õ	Capital O, tilde	ó	Small o, acute accent
Ö	Capital O, dieresis or umlaut mark	ô	Small o, circumflex accent
×	Multiply sign	õ	Small o, tilde
Ø	Capital O, slash	ö	Small o, dieresis or umlaut mark
Ù	Capital U, grave accent	÷	Division sign
Ú	Capital U, acute accent	ø	Small o, slash
Û	Capital U, circumflex accent	ù	Small u, grave accent
Ü	Capital U, dieresis or umlaut mark	ú	Small u, acute accent
Ý	Capital Y, acute accent	û	Small u, circumflex accent
Þ	Capital Thorn, Icelandic	ü	Small u, dieresis or umlaut mark
ß	Small sharp s, German (sz ligature)	ý	Small y, acute accent
à	Small a, grave accent	þ	Small thorn, Icelandic
á	Small a, acute accent	ÿ	Small y, dieresis or umlaut mark
â	Small a, circumflex accent		

JavaScript Objects
and Operators

Overview

Netscape began developing a scripting language called LiveScript in 1994. It was renamed JavaScript in December 1995, when Netscape and Sun Microsystems agreed to partner in its development. It provides a method of introducing interactivity to HTML documents that is widely used. It runs in the browser on a client computer that can access a local Java Virtual Machine (JVM). A client-side program can be executed in response to user events, such as mouse clicks. JavaScript may also be used to directly control objects, such as the browser status bar and the browser display window. It provides interactivity between Java applets and plug-ins. JavaScript can verify that information has been entered into a form, interpret the entered text, and alert the user with an appropriate message dialog.

JavaScript objects are defined here, along with their properties, methods, and event handlers. Event handlers are expressions that JavaScript executes when specific types of events occur. Independent functions not connected with any particular object are also listed, as well as operators.

JavaScript is a reduced and redefined version of the Java programming language. JavaScript is case sensitive, as is Java. A dot (.) is placed between an object and its properties. An identifier is a name used in JavaScript for a variable or a function. The first letter of an identifier may be an ASCII letter, an underscore (_), or a dollar sign ($). It may not be a number. Braces ({ }) are placed around function definitions, if-then constructs, and repeat loops. Square brackets ([ ]) are placed around optional items, such as parameters. Optional items are shown in italic. The syntax for defining a function is as follows:

```
function functionName([parameters]) {
   [statement 1]
   [statement 2]
}
```

Certain words are reserved in JavaScript; they may not be used as identifiers (function names, variable names, or loop labels). The following words are part of the language syntax and are reserved: break, case, continue, default, delete, do, else, export, for, function, if, import, in, new, return, switch, this, typeof, var, void, while, and with.

An additional list of words is reserved by the version of JavaScript standardized by the European Computer Machinery Association (ECMA), known as ECMA-262. The following words are reserved for future expansion in this version of the language: catch, class, const, debugger, enum, extends, finally, super, throw, and try.

A variable is a name associated with a data value. A variable contains an associated value. This statement assigns the value 5 to a variable named x:

```
x = 5
```

This script adds 2 to x and assigns the result to the new variable sum:

```
sum = x + 2
```

Variables in JavaScript are untyped, which means that they can hold data of any kind. Before a variable can be used, it must be declared with the var keyword. A variable may be declared and initialized in the same statement, as in the following lines:

```
var x = 5;
var message = "hello world"
```

A JavaScript expression is any letter, number, array, function, variable, or phrase that the interpreter can evaluate. The expression true is a Boolean literal, the phrase "hello world" is a string literal, and the number 5 is a numeric literal. All are different types of expressions.

A JavaScript program is a collection of statements. Examples of statements are if, else if, switch, while, for, break, return, and with. A complete list of statements and their syntax is included at the end of this appendix. Statements are followed by semicolons (;).

An object in JavaScript is a compound data type that can represent multiple data values with a single unit. It is a collection of properties, and each property has a name and a value. An object is created with the new operator, followed by the name of a constructor function that initializes the object. The following example creates an object and establishes its properties. Note that the double slash is used to distinguish comments from actual code.

```
// Create an object and store a reference to it.
var book = new Object();

// Set a property in the object.
book.title = "The Dictionary of Computing and Digital
Media"

// Set another property in the object.
book.appendix.title = "JavaScript Objects and Operators"
```

A method is a JavaScript function that is invoked through an object. Functions are simply values stored in variables; these variables are properties of objects.

A method may be defined by the following procedure:

```
object.method = function;
```

The method may be invoked as follows, with the function surrounded by parentheses:

```
object.method(function);
```

Within the body of a method, the keyword "this" may be used to refer to the related object.

To make JavaScript respond dynamically to user input, event handlers are used. They may be defined as attributes of HTML objects. An event handler contains a piece of code to be executed when a particular event occurs, such as a mouse click. That code might send a message to the status bar or pop up an alert box containing text.

JavaScript can control most of the parts of a browser and responds to user actions such as form input and page navigation. All of the processing commands are written in a script that is embedded in an HTML document and carried out on the client side without reference back to a server.

A script is embedded in HTML with the <SCRIPT> element:

```
<SCRIPT>..(text of script goes here)..</SCRIPT>
```

The text of a script is placed between the <SCRIPT> tag and its end element. Attributes are specified in the following way:

```
<SCRIPT LANGUAGE="JavaScript">

text of a script

</SCRIPT>
```

When specifying the language, it is advisable to indicate which version of JavaScript is being used. JavaScript 1.0 is generally compatible with Netscape Navigator 2.0; JavaScript 1.1 is generally compatible with Navigator 3.0. Only the 4.0 version of Navigator will read all of the JavaScript 1.2 language. Some of the language in the first versions of JavaScript, 1.0 and 1.1, is implemented in Microsoft Internet Explorer version 3.0, but not consistently. In Internet Explorer 4.0 some, but not all, of the JavaScript 1.2 language is enabled. In 1997 the ECMA approved their expanded variation of JavaScript 1.1 (ECMA-262) which included international alphabets, and it is this version that is implemented in Internet Explorer 4.0.

In this document browser functionality is noted with N2 and N3 for the compatible versions of Navigator, and with IE3 for Internet Explorer 3.0. Navigator 4.0 is generally compatible with JavaScript 1.2. Navigator 4.0 is downward compatible and will read anything the earlier versions will read.

If the LANGUAGE attribute is not used, the SRC attribute may be used to identify a URL that will load the text of the script.

```
<SCRIPT LANGUAGE="language" SRC=url>
```

A user agent (browser) that is Java-enabled evaluates and stores the functions of each script it receives. The functions defined by the script are executed only when they are triggered by certain events within a page. Moving the cursor over an object or entering text into a text box may trigger the execution of a script.

The text of a script can be enclosed within comment elements to prevent browsers that are not capable of interpreting JavaScript from including it as text:

```
<SCRIPT LANGUAGE="JavaScript">

<!--"Hide script contents from incompatible browsers.

Complete text of JavaScript.

End hiding script contents."-->

</SCRIPT>
```

The following alphabetized list includes commonly used objects, properties, methods, and event handlers. It specifies which browsers are capable of handling them. Netscape Navigator 4.0 (N4) handles virtually all of them.

Objects

(with Properties, Methods, and Event Handlers)

anchor (N2, N3, IE3)

The target of a hypertext link.

Properties

name: A string value containing the name of an anchor. (not N2, N3)

applet (N3)

Represents a Java applet in a web page.

Properties

   name: A string value containing the NAME

area (N3)

Represents a clickable area in an image map.

Properties

   hash: An anchor name from a URL.

   host: The host and domain name part of a URL.

   hostname: The host, domain name, and port number of a URL.

   href: The complete URL.

   pathname: Just the path part of a URL, without host, domain, or port number.

   port: The port number of a URL.

   protocol: The protocol part of a URL, including the colon after it.

   search: The query part of a URL, which follows a question mark.

   target: The TARGET value of an AREA tag.

Methods

   getSelection: Returns the current selection value as a string.

Event Handlers

   onMouseOut: Specifies the script to be executed when a user moves the mouse outside the area defined.

   onMouseOver: Specifies the script to be executed when a user moves the mouse over the area defined.

   onDblClick: Specifies the script to be executed when a user double-clicks in the area. (not N2, N3, IE3, Macintosh)

Array (N3, IE3)

A new array is created with the command

arrayName = new Array(*arrayLength*)

Properties

   length: An integer defining the number of elements in an array.

   prototype: A way to add properties to an Array object.

Methods

   sort(): Sorts the elements of an array according to the function defined in parentheses, or alphabetically if no function is defined. (all browsers) join(): Converts all elements of an array to concatenated strings. (not IE3)

reverse(): Reverses the order of elements in an array. (not IE3)

concat(): Combines the elements of two arrays into a third. (not N2, N3, IE3)

pop(): Removes an element from the end of an array. (not N2, N3, IE3)

push(): Adds an element to the end of an array. (not N2, N3, IE3)

slice(): Returns a portion of an array, called a subarray. (not N2, N3, IE3)

button (N2, N3, IE3)

Represents a push button in an HTML form. It is a reflection of an INPUT element with a TYPE attribute of "button".

Properties

Inherits properties, methods, and event handlers from Input and HTMLElement.

name: The name of the button element.

value: The value of the button element.

type: The TYPE attribute of an INPUT tag. (not N2, IE3)

enabled: A Boolean value indicating a button's status. (not N2, N3)

form: Refers to the form object containing a button. (not N2, N3)

Methods

click(): Emulates the action of clicking on a button.

focus(): Gives a button focus.

Event Handlers

onClick: Specifies the script to be executed when the button is clicked.

onMouseDown: Specifies the script to be executed when a mouse button is pressed.

onMouseUp: Specifies the script to be executed when a mouse button is released.

onFocus: Specifies the script to be executed when a button is given focus. (not N2, N3)

checkbox (N2, N3, IE3)

Makes a checkbox in an HTML form available in JavaScript.

Properties

checked: A Boolean value indicating the status of a checkbox element.

defaultChecked: A Boolean value indicating that a checkbox element reflects the CHECKED attribute.

name: The name of the checkbox element.

value: The value of the checkbox element.

enabled: A Boolean value indicating whether the checkbox is enabled. (not N2, N3)

form: Refers to the form object containing the checkbox. (not N2, N3)

type: Indicates the TYPE attribute of the INPUT tag. (not N2, N3)

Methods

click(): Emulates the act of clicking the checkbox.

focus(): Gives the checkbox focus. (not N2, N3)

Event Handlers

onClick: Specifies the script to be executed when the checkbox is clicked.

onFocus: Specifies the script to be executed when focus is on the checkbox. (not N2, N3)

combo (N2, N3, IE3)

Represents a combo field in JavaScript.

Properties

listCount: The number of elements in a list.

listIndex: The index of the selected elements in a list.

multiSelect: A Boolean value that indicates whether a combo field is in multiselect mode.

name: The name of a combo field.

value: The value of a combo field.

enabled: A Boolean value indicating whether the combo box is enabled. (not N2, N3)

form: Refers to the form object containing the combo box. (not N2, N3)

Methods

click(): Emulates a click on the combo field.

clear(): Clears the contents of the combo field.

focus(): Gives the combo field focus.

addItem(*index*): Adds an item to the combo field just before the item at *index*.

removeItem(*index*): Removes the item at *index* from the combo field.

Event Handlers

onClick: Specifies the script to be executed when the mouse clicks on a combo field.

onFocus: Specifies the script to be executed when focus is given to a combo field.

Date (N2, N3, IE3)

Provides a way to use dates and times in JavaScript. Syntax for creating instances is as follows:

```
newObjectName = new Date(dateInfo)
```

If no *dateInfo* is specified, the new object returns the current date and time.

dateInfo may be used to specify a date and time in three ways:
1. *"month, day, year, hours;minutes;seconds"*
2. *"year, month, day"* (in integers)
3. *"year, month, day, hours, minutes, seconds"* (in integers)

Properties

prototype: Adds properties to a Date object. (not N2)

Methods

getTime(): Returns the time of the current Date object in milliseconds, with 00:00:00:00 set at 12:00 am, January 1, 1970.

getDate(): Returns an integer for the day of the month of the current Date (1–31).

getMonth(): Returns an integer for the month in the current Date object (0–11, beginning with January).

getDay(): Returns an integer for the day of the week of the current Date (0–6, beginning with Sunday).

getHours(): Returns an integer for the hour in the current Date object (0–23).

getMinutes(): Returns an integer for the minutes in the current Date object (0–59).

getSeconds(): Returns an integer for the seconds in the current Date object (0–59).

getYear(): Returns a two-digit integer for the year in the current Date object (for example, 68 for 1968).

getTimezoneOffset(): Returns an integer in minutes representing the difference between local time and Greenwich mean time (GMT).

toGMTString(): Returns the value of the current Date object in GMT in the form Day, DD MON YYYY HH;MM;SS GMT.

toLocalString(): Returns the value of the current Date object in local time.

UTC *(yearValue, monthValue, dateValue, hoursValue, minutesValue, secondsValue)*: Returns an integer number of milliseconds since 12:00 am, January 1, 1970, (00:00:00) in GMT.

parse*(dateString)*: Returns an integer number of milliseconds between 12:00 am, January 1, 1970, (00:00:00:00) and the date specified in *dateString*. (not IE3)

Other scripts that may be used to set date values, similar to those using the get command, are setDate*(dateValue)*, setHours*(hoursValue)*, setMinutes(*minutesValue*), setMonth(*month Value)*, setSeconds(*secondsValue)*, setTime*(timeValue)*, and setYear*(yearValue)*.

document (N2, N3, IE3)

Represents the attributes of the currently displayed HTML document. Its properties are derived from the BODY element.

Properties

alinkColor: The color of active links, defined as a hexadecimal triplet or a string.

anchors: An array of the anchor objects in the order they appear in an HTML document. anchors.length returns the number of anchors in a document.

bgColor: The background color of the document.

cookie: The current document's cookie values.

fgColor: The foreground color of the document.

forms: An array of form objects in the order in which the forms appear in an HTML file. forms.length returns the number of forms in the document.

lastModified: The last date on which the document was modified.

linkColor: The color of links, defined as a hexadecimal triplet or a string.

links: An array of the link objects in the order in which the hypertext links appear in an HTML document. links.length returns the number of links in a document.

location: The URL of the current document, expressed as document.URL. This property is deprecated.

referrer: The URL of the calling document.

title: The name of the current document.

vlinkColor: The color of followed links, defined as a hexadecimal triplet or a string.

applets: An array of the applet objects in the order in which they appear in the HTML document. applets.length returns the number of applets in the document. (not N2)

embeds: An array of the plugin objects in the order in which they appear in the HTML document. embeds.length returns the number of plug-ins in the document. (not N2, IE3)

images: An array of image objects in the order in which they appear in the HTML document. images.length returns the number of images in the document. (not N2, IE3)

URL: The URL of the current document. (not IE3)

Methods

close(): Closes the current output stream.

open(*mimeType*): Allows write() method and writeln() method to write to the document window. *mimeType* (optional) specifies a document type.

write(): Writes text and HTML to the specified document.

writeln(): Writes text and HTML to the specified document, and inserts a newline character.

clear(): Clears the document window. (not IE3)

captureEvents(): Specifies that a window with frames will capture all specified events. (not N2, N3, IE3)

releaseEvents(*eventType*): Forces the current window to release events which can then be passed to other objects. (not N2, N3, IE3)

routeEvent(*event*): Sends an event through the standard event hierarchy.

Event Handlers

onMouseDown: Specifies the script to be executed when a mouse button is pressed.

onMouseUp: Specifies the script to be executed when a mouse button is released.

onDblClick: Specifies the script to be executed when a mouse button is double clicked in a particular area. (not N2, N3, IE3, Macintosh)

onKeyUp: Specifies the script to be executed when a particular key is released. (not N2, N3, IE3)

onKeyDown: Specifies the script to be executed when a particular key is pressed. (not N2, N3, IE3)

onKeyPress: Specifies the script to be executed when a particular key is held down. (not N2, N3, IE3)

FileUpload (N3)

Represents a file upload element in an HTML form.

Properties

name: The name of the file upload element.

value: The field of a file upload element.

form (N2, N3, IE3)

Represents a single HTML form in JavaScript. It collects input from a user to send to a server.

Properties

action: The URL to which the form data is submitted. This is the form's ACTION attribute.

elements: An array of objects for each form element in sequential order.

encoding: The MIME encoding of the form as specified in the ENCTYPE attribute. This is the form's ENCTYPE attribute.

method: A method in which form data is submitted to a server. This is the form's METHOD attribute.

target: The name of the window that displays responses to form submissions. This is the form's TARGET attribute.

Methods

submit(): Submits form data to a server.

reset(): Resets a form. (not N2, IE3)

Event Handlers

onSubmit: Specifies the script to be executed when a form is submitted. The value true must be returned to enable the form to be submitted. If a false value is returned, the form is not submitted.

onReset: Specifies the script to be executed when a form is reset. (not N2, IE3)

frame (N2, N3, IE3)

Represents a frame window in JavaScript. Frames within a browser are instances of the Window object and do not exist separately.

Properties

frames: An array of objects for each frame in a window, sequentially ordered as they appear in the HTML source code.

parent: The name of the window containing the frame set.

self: An alternate name for the current window.

top: An alternate name for the topmost window.

window: An alternate name for the current window.

onBlur: Represents the onBlur event handler for a frame. The event handler may be changed by assigning new values to this property. (not N2)

onFocus: The onFocus event handler for the frame. The event handler may be changed by assigning new values to this property. (not N2)

Methods

alert(*message*): Displays *message* in a dialog box.

clearTimeout(*name*): Cancels the timeout identified by *name*.

close(): Closes the window.

confirm(*message*): Displays *message* in a dialog box with OK and Cancel buttons. The user determines the true or false status.

open(*url, name, features*): Opens *url* in the *name* window, or creates a new window with that name. *features* is a list of features for the new window. The feature list may contain name-value pairs as shown below:

```
width=pixels
height=pixels
status=[yes,no,1,0]
menubar=[yes,no,1,0]
```

```
scrollbars=[yes,no,1,0]
resizable=[yes,no,1,0]
toolbar=[yes,no,1,0]
location=[yes,no,1,0]
directories=[yes,no,1,0]
```

prompt(*message, response*): Displays *message* in a dialog box with the value of *response* in a text entry field. The user's response in the text entry field is returned.

setTimeout(*expression, time*): Evaluates *expression* after *time*.

blur(): Removes focus from the frame. (not N2)

focus(): Gives focus to the frame. (not N2)

clearInterval(*intervalID*): Cancels timeouts created with the setInterval method. (not N2, N3, IE3)

print(): Prints the contents of a frame or window. (not N2, N3, IE3)

setInterval(*expression, msec*): Evaluates *expression* after the duration specified by the *msec* parameter. (not N2, N3, IE3)

setInterval(*function, msec*): Calls a function after the duration specified by the *msec* parameter. (not N2, N3, IE3)

Event Handlers

onFocus: Specifies the JavaScript code to execute when the frame is given focus. (not N2)

onBlur: Specifies the script to be executed when focus is removed from the frame. (not N2)

onMove: Specifies the script to be executed when the frame is moved. (not N2, N3, IE3)

onResize: Specifies the script to be executed when the frame is resized. (not N2, N3, IE3)

Function (N3)

A means of indicating the JavaScript code that should be compiled as a function. *functionName* is used as a variable with a reference to the function.

Properties

arguments: An integer that represents the number of arguments in the function.

prototype: A means of adding properties to the Function object.

hidden (N2, N3, IE3)

Represents a hidden field in an HTML form. This invisible form element allows arbitrary data to be sent to a server when the form is submitted.

Properties

name: The name of a hidden element in the form of a string.

value: The value of a hidden text element in the form of a string.

type: The TYPE property of the INPUT tag. (not N2)

history (N2, N3)

Allows JavaScript to access the Navigator browser's history list. The contents of the list are not reflected in JavaScript for security.

Properties

length: The number of items in the history list, expressed as an integer.

Methods

back(): Refers to the previous document in the list.

forward(): Refers to the next document in the list.

go(*location*): Goes to the document in the history list specified by *location*, which may be a string or integer value. As an integer it indicates the relative position of the document in the list.

HTMLElement superclass (N4, IE4 only)

This is the superclass of all classes that represent HTML elements. Its objects, listed below, are used in various contexts in client-side JavaScript 1.2.

document.all[*i*]
document.anchors[*i*]
document.forms[*i*]
document.forms[*i*].elements[*j*]
document.images[*i*]
document.links[*i*]
document.*elementName*
document.*formName.elementName*

Properties

The following properties are implemented in Internet Explorer 4.0 only:

all[]: An array of all elements contained by an element.

children[]: All elements that are direct children of an element.

className: The value of the CLASS attribute.

document: Refers to the containing document object.

id: The value of the ID attribute.

innerHTML: The HTML text within an element.

innerText: The plain text within an element.

lang: The value of the LANG attribute.

offsetHeight: The height of an element.

offsetLeft: The x-coordinate of an element.

offsetParent: An element that contains offsetLeft and offsetTop.

offsetTop: The y-coordinate of an element.

offsetWidth: The width of an element.

outerHTML: The HTML text of an element, with start and end tags.

outerText: The plain text in a document, with start and end tags.

parentElement: An element that is the direct parent of this one.

sourceIndex: The index of an element in Document.all[].

style: The inline Cascading Style Sheet (CSS) attributes for an element.

tagName: The name of the HTML tag that created an element.

title: The value of the TITLE attribute.

Methods

The following methods are implemented in Internet Explorer 4.0 only:

contains(): Determines whether an element contains the one specified in ().

getAttribute(): Returns the value of a named attribute.

insertAdjacentHTML(): Inserts HTML text into the document nearest an element.

insertAdjacentText(): Inserts plain text into the document nearest an element.

removeAttribute(): Deletes an attribute and its value from an element.

scrollIntoView(): Scrolls the document so an element is visible in the window.

setAttribute(): Sets the value of an attribute of an element.

The following method is implemented in Navigator 4.0 only:

handleEvent(): Passes an event object to the appropriate event handler.

Event Handlers

onClick: Specifies the script to be executed when a mouse button is clicked.

onDblClick: Specifies the script to be executed when a mouse button is double clicked on an element.

onHelp: Specifies the script to be executed when a user requests help. (N4 only)

onKeyDown: Specifies the script to be executed when a particular key is pressed.

onKeyPress: Specifies the script to be executed when a particular key is held down.

onKeyUp: Specifies the script to be executed when a particular key is released.

onMouseDown: Specifies the script to be executed when a mouse button is pressed.

onMouseMove: Specifies the script to be executed when a mouse button is moved.

onMouseOut: Specifies the script to be executed when the mouse is moved off of an element.

onMouseOver: Specifies the script to be executed when the mouse is moved over an element.

onMouseUp: Specifies the script to be executed when a mouse button is released.

Image (N3)

Represents an image in an HTML document.

Properties

border: An integer representing the width of the border of an image in pixels.

complete: A Boolean value that indicates whether an image is done loading.

height: An integer representing the height of an image in pixels.

hspace: The HSPACE attribute of the IMG tag, expressed as an integer.

lowsrc: The URL of a low resolution version of an image.

name: The name of an Image object.

prototype: A means of adding properties to an Image object.

src: The URL of an image.

vspace: The VSPACE attribute of the IMG tag, expressed as an integer.

width: An integer representing the width of an image in pixels.

Event Handlers

onAbort: Specifies the script to be executed when an attempt to load an image is aborted. (not N2)

onError: Specifies the script to be executed when an error occurs during image loading. If this handler is set to *null*, the error message is suppressed. (not N2)

onLoad: Specifies the script to be executed when an image is completely loaded. (not N2)

onKeyDown: Specifies the script to be executed when a specific key is pressed. (not N2, N3, IE3)

onKeyUp: Specifies the script to be executed when a specific key is released. (not N2, N3, IE3)

onKeyPress: Specifies the script to be executed when a specific key is held down. (not N2, N3, IE3)

Layer (N4 only)

A means of embedding layers of content within a page. Layers allow dynamically positioned elements to be included in a dynamic HTML (DHTML) document.

Properties

above: Refers to a layer on top of the current layer.

background: Specifies the tiled background image of a layer.

below: Refers to a layer below the current layer.

bgColor: Sets the background color of a layer.

clip(*left, right, top, bottom, width, height*): Specifies the visible boundaries of the layer.

height: Specifies the height of a layer, expressed in pixels by an integer or by a percentage of the current layer.

ID: Names a layer for reference by other scripts. (Same as name.)

left: Specifies the horizontal position of the top-left corner of the layer, along with the top property.

page[*X, Y*]: Specifies the horizontal (X) or vertical (Y) position of the top-left corner of the layer relative to the overall enclosing document.

parentLayer: Specifies the layer object that contains the current layer.

siblingAbove: Specifies the layer object directly on top of the present one.

siblingBelow: Specifies the layer object directly under the present one.

SRC: Specifies the source URL of a layer's contents.

top: Specifies the y-coordinate of the top-left corner of the layer, along with the left property.

visibility: Specifies the visibility of the layer. The three variables are *show* (visible), *hidden* (not visible), and *inherit* (properties inherited from the parent layer).

width: Specifies the width of a layer or a boundary inside of which contents remain confined or wrap.

z-index: Specifies, with an integer, the stacking order (z-order) of a layer. Sets a layer's position within the overall rotational order if there are multiple layers.

Methods

captureEvents(): Specifies that a window with frames will capture all specified events.

handleEvent(): Dispatches an event to the appropriate handler.

load(*source, width*): Replaces the source with HTML (or JavaScript) from the file specified in *source*. Also passes a width value in pixels.

moveAbove(*layer*): Places the current layer above the *layer* identified in the stack.

moveBelow(*layer*): Places the current layer below the *layer* identified in the stack.

moveBy(*x, y*): Changes the position of the current layer by the pixel values specified.

moveTo(*x, y*): Changes the position of the current layer (within the containing layer) to the coordinates specified in pixels.

moveToAbsolute(*x, y*): Changes the position of the current layer (within a page) to the coordinates specified in pixels.

resizeBy(*width, height*): Changes the size of the current layer by the values specified in pixels.

resizeTo(*width, height*): Changes the size of the current layer to the values specified for width and height in pixels.

releaseEvents(*eventType*): Specifies that the current window should release events on input of *eventType*.

Event Handlers

onBlur: Specifies the script to be executed when the layer no longer has focus.

onFocus: Specifies the script to be executed when the layer gains focus.

onLoad: Specifies the script to be executed when the layer is loaded.

onMouseOut: Specifies the script to be executed when the mouse moves off the current layer. Properties that may be used include type, target, layer[n], page[n], and screen[n]. (not N2, N3, IE3)

onMouseOver: Specifies the script to be executed when the mouse enters the current layer. Properties that may be used include type, target, layer[n], page[n], and screen[n]. (not N2, N3, IE3)

link (N2, N3, IE3)

Represents a hypertext link in the body of an HTML document.

Properties

hash: The anchor name in a URL referenced (follows the hash mark #).

host: The host name and port number from a URL referenced.

hostname: The numerical IP address, or domain name, from the URL referenced.

href: The entire URL referenced. (The HREF attribute of the A element.)

pathname: The path portion of a URL referenced.

port: The port number from the URL referenced (ftp=21; WWW=80; Usenet news=119).

protocol: The protocol from the URL referenced, including the colon but not the slashes.

search: All information passed to a GET CGI-BIN call.

target: The name of a window or frame specified in the TARGET attribute.

text: The plain text between the <A> and </A> tags that created the object.

Event Handlers

onMouseUp: Specifies the script to be executed when the mouse button is released.

428

onClick: Specifies the script to be executed when a user clicks on a link.

onDblClick: Specifies the script to be executed when the mouse button is double clicked in a particular area. (not N2, N3, IE3, Macintosh)

moveMouse: Specifies the script to be executed when the mouse moves over a link. (not N2, N3)

onKeyUp: Specifies the script to be executed when a particular key is released. (not N2, N3, IE3)

onKeyDown: Specifies the script to be executed when a particular key is pressed. (not N2, N3, IE3)

onKeyPress: Specifies the script to be executed when a particular key is held down. (not N2, N3, IE3)

onMouseDown: Specifies the script to be executed when the mouse button is pressed. (not N2, N3, IE3)

onMouseOut: Specifies the script to be executed when the mouse cursor moves out of an object. In JavaScript 1.2, properties that may be used include type, target, layer[n], page[n], and screen[n]. (not N2, N3, IE3)

onMouseOver: Specifies the script to be executed when the mouse moves over a hypertext link. In JavaScript 1.2, properties that may be used include type, target, layer[n], page[n], and screen[n]. (not N2, N3, IE3)

location (N2, N3, IE3)

Reflects information about the current URL.

Properties

hash: The anchor name in the URL.

host: The host name and port number from the URL.

hostname: The numerical IP address, or domain name from the URL.

href: The entire URL.

pathname: The path portion of the URL.

port: The port number from the URL.

protocol: The protocol from the URL with the colon but not the slashes.

search: All information passed to a GET CGI-BIN call.

Methods

reload(): Reloads the current document. (not N2, IE3)

replace(*url*): Loads the *url* specified over the current entry in the history list; after this it is impossible to navigate back to the previous URL by using the Back button. (not N2, IE3)

Math (N2, N3, IE3)

Provides properties and methods for mathematical calculations.

Properties

E: Euler's constant (approximately 2.718282), which is used as the base for natural logarithms.

LN2: The natural logarithm of two (approximately 0.693147).

LN10: The natural logarithm of 10 (approximately 2.302585).

LOG10E: The base 10 logarithm of e (approximately 0.434294).

LOG2E: The base 2 logarithm of e (approximately 1.442695).

PI: The value of pi for calculating the circumference and area of a circle (approximately 3.14159).

SQRT1_2: The square root of one-half (approximately 0.7071).

SQRT2: The square root of two (approximately 1.4142).

Methods

abs(*number*): Returns the absolute value of *number* without consideration of its sign. abs(8) is equal to abs(-8).

acos(*number*): Returns the arc cosine of *number* in radians.

asin(*number*): Returns the arc sine of *number* in radians.

atan(*number*): Returns the arc tangent of *number* in radians.

atan2*(number1, number2)*: Returns the angle of the polar coordinate corresponding to the Cartesian coordinate *(number1,number2)*. (not IE3)

ceil*(number)*: Returns the smallest integer equal to or greater than *number*.

cos*(number)*: Returns the cosine of *number*.

exp*(number)*: Returns the value of e to the power of *number*.

floor(*number*): Returns the greatest integer equal to or less than *number*.

log*(number)*: Returns the natural logarithm (base e) of *number*.

max(*number1, number2*): Returns the greater of *number1* and *number2*.

min(*number1, number2*): Returns the smaller of *number1* and *number2*.

pow(*number1, number2*): Returns the value of *number1* to the power of *number2*.

random(): Returns a random number between zero and one.

round(*number*): Returns the closest integer to *number*, rounded off.

sin(*number*): Returns the sine of *number*, which is an angle expressed in radians.

sqrt(*number*): Returns the square root of *number*.

tan*(number)*: Returns the tangent of *number*, where *number* represents an angle in radians.

mimeType (N3)

Represents a MIME type supported by the client browser.

Properties

description: A description of the MIME type.

enabledPlugin: Refers to the plugin object that supports the MIME type.

suffixes: A list of file suffixes for the MIME type, separated by commas.

type: A string that indicates the MIME type itself, as in "video/mpeg".

navigator (N2, N3)

Provides information about the version of Navigator used by the client.

Properties

appCodeName: The code name of the client ("Mozilla" is used for Netscape Navigator).

appName: The name of the client ("Netscape" is used for Navigator).

appVersion(*platform; country*): The version number of the client's browser.

mimeTypes: Returns an array of the MIME types supported by the client browser. (not N2, IE3)

platform: Specifies the platform (Win32, MacPPC, Unix, etc.) for which Navigator was compiled on the client computer. (not N2, N3, IE3)

plugins: Returns an array of plug-ins in an HTML document in order of their appearance. (not N2, IE3)

userAgent: The complete value of the user-agent header sent in an HTTP request. The appCodeName and appVersion are contained in this header.

Methods

javaEnabled(): Indicates whether Java is enabled in a browser. (not N2, IE3)

preference(*preference.name,* setValue): Allows certain browser preferences to be set in signed scripts, as shown here:

autoupdate.enabled: Value (true/false) that sets whether autoinstall is enabled.

browser.enable_style_sheets: Value (true/false) that sets whether style sheets are enabled.

general.always_load_images: Value (true/false) that sets whether images are automatically loaded.

javascript.enabled: Value (true/false) that sets whether JavaScript is enabled.

network.cookie.cookieBehavior(*0, 1, 2*): Value that determines how cookies are handled, with three parameters. (*0* accepts all cookies; *1* accepts only those forwarded to the originating server; *2* denies all cookies.)

network.cookie.warnAboutCookies: Value (true/false) that sets whether the browser will warn the user before accepting cookies.

security.enable_java: Value (true/false) that sets whether Java is enabled.

option (N3)

Creates entries in a select list with the syntax shown here:

optionName = new Option(*optionText, optionValue, defaultSelected, selected*)
where

selectName.options[*index*] = *optionName*

Properties

defaultSelected: Specifies with a Boolean value whether an option is selected by default.

index: Specifies with an integer an option's index in the select list.

prototype: A means of adding properties to an Option object.

selected: Indicates with a Boolean value whether an option is currently selected.

text: The text displayed for an option.

value: The value sent to the server when a form is submitted.

password (N2, N3, IE3)

Represents a password text field from an HTML form in JavaScript.

Properties

defaultValue: The default value of the password element.

name: The name of the password element.

value: The value of the password element.

form: Refers to the form object containing the password field. (not N2, N3)

enabled: Indicates with a Boolean value if a password field is enabled. (not N2, N3)

Methods

focus(): Gives focus to the password field.

blur(): Removes focus from the password field.

select(): Selects the text in the password field.

Event Handlers

onBlur: Specifies the script to be executed when focus is removed from the password field. (not N2, N3)

onFocus: Specifies the script to be executed when focus is given to the password field. (not N2, N3)

plugin (N3)

Reflects a plug-in supported by the browser.

Properties

description: The description provided by the plug-in itself.

filename: The file name of the plug-in as it appears on the client's machine.

length: The number of MIME types supported by the plug-in, described as array elements of the plug-in object.

name: The name of the plug-in.

radio (N2, N3, IE3)

Represents a set of graphical radio buttons in an HTML form in JavaScript. Individual radio buttons in the set are accessed numerically in order, beginning with zero. Example: myButton[0], myButton[1], myButton[2] for three radio buttons.

Properties

checked: Indicates with a Boolean value whether a particular button is checked. Buttons may be selected or deselected with this property.

name: The name of a set of radio buttons.

value: The value of a specific radio button in a set.

defaultChecked: Indicates with a Boolean value whether a particular button reflects the CHECKED attribute. (not IE3)

length: Indicates with an integer the number of radio buttons in a set. (not IE3)

enabled: Indicates with a Boolean value whether a particular button is enabled. (not N2, N3)

form: Refers to the form object containing the radio button. (not N2, N3)

Methods

click(): The act of clicking a radio button.

focus(): Gives focus to a radio button. (not N2, N3)

Event Handlers

onClick: Specifies the script to be executed when a radio button is clicked.

onFocus: Specifies the script to be executed when a radio button is given focus. (not N2, N3)

RegExp (JavaScript 1.2, N4 only)

Represents a regular expression for pattern matching with strings. Properties identify a series of values that may be accessed in a search. Its arguments are pattern and attributes, constructed as follows: new RegExp(*pattern, attributes*)

Static Properties

$1,$2,$3,.. $9: Identifies the last nine substrings enclosed in parentheses that were matched.

input: The string to which a regular expression is compared.

lastMatch: Identifies the last matched characters.

lastParen: Identifies the last matched string that appeared in parentheses.

leftContext: Identifies the string just before the most recently matched regular expression.

multiline [*true, false*]: Determines whether a search continues beyond line breaks.

rightContext: Identifies the part of a string that continues beyond the most recently matched regular expression.

Flags

i: Ignore upper- and lowercase in search (optional).

g: Perform a global match in the search for a regular expression (optional).

gi: Perform a global match, ignoring case (optional).

Instance Properties

source: The pattern's text in a read-only version.

ignoreCase [*true, false*]: Sets the i (ignore case) flag value.

global [*true, false*]: Sets the g (global) flag value.

lastIndex: Indicates with an integer the index position at which to begin the next matching procedure.

Methods

compile: Defines a new pattern and attributes for a RegExp object, usually invoked at script startup.

exec(str): Executes the search for a regular expression matching the specified string (str).

test(str): Searches for a regular expression and the string specified (str).

reset (N2, N3, IE3)

Represents a reset button from an HTML form in JavaScript.

Properties

name: The name of the reset element.

value: The value of the reset element.

enabled: Indicates with a Boolean value whether the reset button is enabled. (not N2, N3)

form: Refers to the form object containing the reset button. (not N2, N3)

Methods

click(): The act of clicking the reset button.

focus(): Specifies the script to be executed when the reset button is given focus. (not N2, N3)

Event Handlers

onClick: Specifies the script to be executed when the reset button is clicked.

onFocus: Specifies the script to be executed when the reset button is given focus. (not N2, N3)

Screen (JavaScript 1.2 only, not N2, N3, IE3)

Specifies characteristics of the current screen.

Properties

availHeight: Specifies the height of the screen in pixels, after deducting display constraints defined by the OS.

availTop: Specifies the first available vertical pixel, after deducting display constraints defined by the OS.

availWidth: Specifies the width of the current screen in pixels, after deducting display constraints defined by the OS.

colorDepth: Specifies the bit depth, or number of colors for the current screen.

height: Specifies the height of the current screen in pixels.

pixelDepth: Specifies the resolution in bits per pixel of the current screen.

width: Specifies the width of the current screen in pixels.

select (N2, N3)

Represents a selection list from an HTML form in JavaScript.

Properties

length: Identifies with an integer the number of choices in a selection list.

name: The name of a selection list.

selectedIndex: The index of the currently selected option in a selection list.

options: An array that represents the choices in a selection list.

Properties of options include the following:

defaultSelected: Indicates with a Boolean value whether a particular option reflects the SELECTED attribute.

index: The index of an option.

length: The number of options in a selection list.

name: The name of the selection list.

selected: Indicates with a Boolean value whether a particular button is selected. Options may be selected or deselected with this property.

selectedIndex: Indicates with an integer the index of the currently selected option.

text: The text displayed in a selection list for a particular option.

value: The value for a specified option.

Methods

blur(): Takes focus away from a selection list. (not N2, N3)

focus(): Gives focus to a selection list. (not N2, N3)

Event Handlers

onBlur: The script code to be executed when focus is removed from a selection list.

onChange: The script to be executed when the selected option in a list changes.

onFocus: The script to be executed when focus is given to a selection list.

String (N2, N3, IE3)

Provides properties and methods for working with variables and string literals.

Properties

length: The number of characters in the string, expressed as an integer.

prototype: Means of adding properties to a String object. (not N2)

Methods

anchor(*name*): Returns a copy of the *name* string in the <A NAME=> format.

big(): Returns a copy of the specified string in the <BIG> format.

blink(): Returns a copy of the specified string in the <BLINK> format.

bold(): Returns a copy of the specified string in the <B> format.

charAt(*index*): Returns the character at the location in a string specified by *index*.

charCodeAt(*index*): Returns the encoded value of a character at the *index* position in a string.

fixed(): Returns a copy of the specified string in the <TT> format.

indexOf(*substring, start*): Returns the index of the first occurrence of *substring*, starting the search at *start*. By default, the search starts at the beginning of the string.

italics(): Returns a copy of the specified string in the <I> format.

lastIndexOf(*substring, start*): Returns the index of the first occurrence of *substring*, beginning at *start* and searching in reverse order. By default, the search starts at the end of the string.

436

link(*href*): Returns a copy of the *href* string in the <A HREF=> format.

match(*regexp*): Matches the regular expression specified, expressed as a variable or as a literal.

replace(*regexp, replacement*): Locates and replaces a regular expression with *replacement.*

search(*regexp*): Locates a regular expression and matches it to the specified string.

slice(*start, end*): Extracts a substring and derives a new string.

small(): Returns a copy of the specified string in the <SMALL> format.

strike(): Returns a copy of the specified string in the <STRIKE> format.

sub(): Returns a copy of the specified string in the <SUB> format.

sup(): Returns a copy of the specified string in the <SUP> format.

toLowerCase(): Returns a copy of the specified string with lowercase characters.

toUpperCase(): Returns a copy of the specified string with uppercase characters.

fontColor(*color*): Returns a copy of the *color* string in the <FONT COLOR=> format. (not IE3)

fontSize(*size*): Returns a copy of the *size* string in the <FONT SIZE=> format. (not IE3)

split(*delimiter*): Divides a string at every occurrence of *delimiter.* (not N2, IE3)

concat(*string2*): Combines two strings to make a new third one. (not N2, N3, IE3)

substring(*from, to*): Sets the number of characters within a string. Use *from* to specify the beginning point for the extraction process, ending at *to.* (not N2, N3, IE3)

submit (N2, N3, IE3)

Represents a submit button from an HTML form in JavaScript.

Properties

name: The name of the submit button element.

value: The value of the submit button element.

enabled: Indicates with a Boolean value whether the submit button is enabled. (not N2, N3)

form: Represents the form object containing a submit button. (not N2, N3)

type: The TYPE attribute of the INPUT tag. (not N2, IE3)

Methods

click(): Simulates clicking the submit button.

focus(): Gives focus to the submit button. (not N2, N3)

Event Handlers

onClick: Specifies the script to be executed when the submit button is clicked.

onFocus: Specifies the script to be executed when the submit button is given focus. (not N2, N3)

text (N2, N3, IE3)

Represents a text field from an HTML form in JavaScript.

Properties

defaultValue: The default value of the text element (VALUE attribute).

name: The name of the text field element.

value: The value of the text element.

enabled: Indicates with a Boolean value whether a text field is enabled. (not N2, N3)

form: Represents the form object containing a text field. (not N2, N3)

type: The TYPE attribute of the INPUT tag. (not N2, IE3)

Methods

focus(): Gives focus to the text field.

blur(): Removes focus from the text field.

select(): Selects text in the text field.

Event Handlers

onBlur: Specifies the script to be executed when focus is removed from a text field.

onChange: Specifies the script to be executed when text field content is changed.

onFocus: Specifies the script to be executed when the text field receives focus.

onSelect: Specifies the script to be executed when any text in the field is selected.

textarea (N2, N3, IE3)

Represents a multiline text field from an HTML form in JavaScript.

Properties

defaultValue: The default value of the textarea element (VALUE attribute).

name: The name of the textarea element.

value: The value of the textarea element.

enabled: Indicates with a Boolean value whether a textarea field is enabled. (not N2, N3)

form: Represents the form object containing a textarea field. (not N2, N3)

type: The TYPE attribute of the textarea INPUT tag. (not N2, IE3)

Methods

focus(): Gives focus to the textarea field.

blur(): Removes focus from the textarea field.

select(): Simulates selecting text in the textarea field.

Event Handlers

onBlur: Specifies the script to be executed when focus is removed from a textarea field.

onChange: Specifies the script to be executed when textarea field content is changed.

onFocus: Specifies the script to be executed when the textarea field receives focus.

onSelect: Specifies the script to be executed when any text in the textarea field is selected.

onKeyUp: Specifies the script to be executed when a specific key is released. (N4 only)

onKeyPress: Specifies the script to be executed when a specific key is held down by the user. (N4 only)

onKeyDown: Specifies the script to be executed when a specific key is pressed. (N4 only)

window (N2, N3, IE3)

The parent object for document, location, and history objects. This is the top-level object for an array of frames or a window. The Window is the "global object," and all expressions are evaluated in the context of the current window object.

Properties

defaultStatus: The default value displayed in the status bar.

frames: An array of objects representing each frame in the window, ordered as they appear in the HTML source code.

name: The name of a window or frame.

parent: The name of the window containing a frame set.

self: Another name for the current window.

status: Displays a message, consisting of assigned values, in the status bar.

statusbar=[*true,false,1,0*]: Controls whether the status bar in the target window is visible.

toolbar=[*true,false,1,0*]: Controls whether the toolbar in the target window is visible.

top: Another name for the top-most window.

window: Another name for the current window.

length: Indicates with an integer the number of frames in a parent window. (not IE3)

opener: The window object that contains the open() method used to open the current window. (not N2, IE3)

innerHeight(): Specifies the vertical size in pixels of the content area. (N4 only)

innerWidth(): Specifies the horizontal size in pixels of the content area. (N4 only)

pageXOffset: Specifies the current X position in pixels of the viewable window area. (N4 only)

pageYOffset: Specifies the current Y position in pixels of the viewable window area. (N4 only)

scrollbars [*visible=true,false*]: Controls whether scroll bars in the current window are visible. (N4 only)

Methods

alert(*message*): Causes a specified *message* to appear in a dialog box.

captureEvents():Specifies that a window with frames will capture all specified events. Used with enableExternalCapture.

clearTimeout(*name*): Cancels the timeout specified by *name*.

clearTimeout(*timeoutId*): Cancels the deferred execution of the *setTimeout* identified.

confirm(*question*): Displays a *question* in a dialog box, to which a user may respond "OK" or "Cancel." Returns true or false, depending on the button selected by the user.

length(): Specifies the number of frames in a window.

prompt(*message, response*): Shows *message* in a dialog box, along with a text entry field containing the default value of *response*. Returns a string with data keyed into a text entry field.

setTimeout(*code, delay*): Defers execution of *expression* until after *delay*, expressed in milliseconds.

stop(): Ends the current download. Simulates pressing the Stop button.

close(): Closes a specified window. (not IE3)

open(*url, name, features*): Opens the *url* specified in a window called *name*. A new window is created, if one does not exist by that name. The string argument "*features*" specifies parameters for the window that is opened. The following names and values may be specified. There are no spaces between values, but each is followed by a comma: (not IE3)
    alwaysLowered=[*yes,no,1,2*] (background window)
    alwaysRaised=[*yes,no,1,2*] (top-level window)
    directories=[*yes,no,1,0*]
    height=pixels
    location=[*yes,no,1,0*]
    menubar=[*yes,no,1,0*]
    resizable=[*yes,no,1,0*]
    scrollbars=[*yes,no,1,0*]
    status=[*yes,no,1,0*]
    toolbar=[*yes,no,1,0*]
    width=pixels

The following features pertain to Navigator 4.0 only:
    dependent[*yes,no,1,2*](on parent window)
    hotkeys=[*yes,no,1,2*]
    innerWidth=pixels
    innerHeight=pixels
    outerWidth=pixels
    outerHeight=pixels
    screenX=pixels
    screenY=pixels
    z-lock=[*yes,no,1,2*]

blur(): Removes focus from the window, in most cases sending it to the background. (not N2, IE3)

focus(): Gives keyboard focus to the top window, in most cases bringing it to the front. (not N2, IE3)

scrollTo(*x, y*): Scrolls the current window to the specified *x*- and *y*-coordinates. (not N2, IE3)

The following methods are new in JavaScript 1.2 and are implemented only in Navigator 4.0.

back(): Calls the previous URL visited, similar to activating the Back browser button.

clearInterval(*intervalID*): Eliminates timeouts created with the setInterval method.

disableExternalCapture(): Prevents a current window with frames from capturing events that occur in pages loaded from another location.

enableExternalCapture(): Allows a current window with frames to capture events that occur in pages loaded from another location.

event(): Describes the most recent event to occur in a window.

find([*string*], [*true, false*], [*true, false*]): Finds the *string* specified in the target window. The first Boolean true/false parameter specifies whether the search is case sensitive. The second true/false parameter specifies whether the search should be performed in reverse order.

forward(): Moves to the next URL listed, similar to activating the Forward browser button.

home(): Directs the browser to the user's home page.

moveBy(*x, y*): Repositions a window to the right (*x*) or down (*y*), according to the specified values.

movoTo(*x, y*): Positions the upper-left corner of a window at the specified location.

print(): Sends the contents of a frame or window to a printer. Simulates pressing the Print button.

releaseEvents(*eventType*): Rather than capturing events in the current window, allows them to be passed on to other objects.

resizeBy(*horizontal, vertical*): Beginning from the lower-right corner, resizes the window.

resizeTo(*outerWidth, outerHeight*): Applies the specified *outerWidth* and *outerHeight* properties to the window.

routeEvent(*event*): Sends an event through the normal hierarchy.

scrollBy(*horizontal, vertical*): Causes the viewing area of the current window to be scrolled by the number of pixels specified by the *horizontal* or *vertical* values.

scrollTo(*x, y*): Beginning at the upper-left corner of the current window, scrolls it to the position specified in the *x*- and *y*-coordinates.

setInterval(*expression, msec*): Evaluates the specified *expression* after the period identified by the *msec* parameter.

setInterval(*function, msec, args*): Continuously calls a *function* after the period specified by the *msec* parameter.

Event Handlers

onLoad: The script to be executed when the window or frame is done loading.

onUnload: The script to be executed when a user exits the document in a frame or window.

onBlur: The script to be executed when focus is removed from the window. (not N2, IE3)

onError: The script to be executed when a JavaScript error is returned while a document is loading. A JavaScript error message will not be displayed to the user if this event handler is set to null. (not N2, IE3)

onFocus: The script to be executed when the window receives focus. (not N2, IE3)

onResize: The script to be executed when the window is resized by a user. (not N2, IE3)

onMove: The script to be executed when the window is repositioned by a user. (N4 only)

onDragDrop: The script to be executed when an object is dropped into the window by a user. (N4 only)

Symbolic Operators

Arithmetic Operators (N2, N3, IE3)

+	Adds the operands on the left and on the right. (When used with strings rather than integers, it combines the operands into one string.)
-	When used as a binary operator, subtracts the right operand from the left operand.
-	Performs unary negation when placed immediately before an operand; converts an operand from positive to negative, and vice versa.
*	Multiplies two operands.
/	Divides the left operand by the right operand.
%	Returns the remainder of the left operand divided by the right operand.
++	Increases an operand by one (may be applied before or after an operand).
—	Decreases an operand by one (may be applied before or after an operand).

Assignment Operators (N2, N3, IE3)

These operators work with both numbers and strings. For example, with numbers the operator += performs addition and assignment. For strings it performs concatenation and assignment.

=	Assigns the value of the right operand to an expression. It causes the variable, element, or property a to refer to the value b.
	Example: a = b is equivalent to b

+= Adds the left and right operands, then assigns the total to the left operand. (When used with strings rather than integers, concatenation of the two operands is performed.)

> Example: a += b is equivalent to a = a + b

-= Subtracts the right operand from the left operand, then assigns the result to the left operand.

> Example: a -= b is equivalent to a = a - b

*= Multiplies two operands, then assigns the result to the left operand.

> Example: a *= b is equivalent to a = a * b

/= Divides the left operand by the right operand, then assigns the value to the left operand.

> Example: a /= b is equivalent to a = a / b

%= Divides the left operand by the right operand, then assigns the remainder to the left operand.

> Example: a %= b is equivalent to a = a % b

Bitwise Operators (N2, N3, IE3)

These operators treat their operands as binary numbers, convert them to integers with 32 bits, and return a JavaScript numerical value.

AND(&) Pairs corresponding bits, and returns one for each pair of ones. Returns zero for any other combination.

OR(|) Pairs corresponding bits, and returns one for each pair if either of the bits is a one. Returns zero if both bits are zero.

XOR(^) Pairs corresponding bits, and returns one for each pair where only one bit is a one. Returns zero for any other combination.

<< Shifts bits to the left by the number of bits indicated by the right operand. Bits shifted to the left are discarded, and zeros are shifted over from the right.

>> Shifts bits to the right by the number of bits indicated by the right operand. Bits shifted to the right are discarded. The bit furthest to the left is duplicated and shifted over from the left.

>>> Shifts bits to the right by the number of bits indicated by the right operand. Bits shifted to the right are discarded. Zeros are shifted over from the left.

Logical Operators

These operators perform Boolean algebra. They are particularly useful in complex comparisons that involve more than one variable, combined with if, while, and for statements.

&& (logical AND) Returns true when both operands are true, otherwise returns false.

|| (logical OR) Returns true if either operand is true. Returns false only when both operands are false.

! (logical NOT)   Returns true if the operand is false, and returns false if the operand is true. This unary operator precedes the operand.

Equality and Identity Operators (N2, N3, IE3)

==   Returns true if operands are equal (numbers, strings, or Boolean values) or if they refer to the same object (function, array, or object). This operator compares for equality without comparing type only in Internet Explorer 4.0.

!=   Returns true if operands are not equal or they refer to different objects.

===   Returns true only if operands are identical without comparing type.

!==   Returns true only if operands are not equal without comparing type.

Comparison Operators (N2, N3, IE3)

>   Returns true if the left operand is greater than the right operand.

<   Returns true if the left operand is less than the right operand.

>=   Returns true if the left operand is greater than or equal to the right operand.

<=   Returns true if the left operand is less than or equal to the right operand.

Conditional Operators

typeof: Returns the type of its single operand. Types that are returned are object, string, number, boolean, function, or undefined. (N3, IE3)

void: Discards its operand value or returns an undefined value. This unary operator may precede an expression with any value. (N3)

(? :): This is a ternary operator, which uses three operands. Returns value1 if the condition is true, otherwise returns value2.

Example: condition ? value1 : value2 (N2, N3, IE3)

Independent Functions

escape(*character*): Returns a string with *character* ASCII-encoded for transmission across networks to all computer platforms. NonASCII characters are encoded in the format %*xx*, where *xx* is two hexadecimal digits representing the character in ISO 8859 (Latin-1) coding. (N2, N3, IE3)

eval(*code*): Returns the result of evaluating an arithmetic expression, or executes the JavaScript statements represented by *code* and returns the value. (N2, N3, IE3)

isNaN(*value*): Evaluates *value* to determine whether it is NaN (not a number), and returns a Boolean value. (N2, N3, IE3)

parseFloat(*string*): Returns the value of *string* after converting it to a floating-point number. This function returns NaN (zero in MS Windows) when it encounters the first character that cannot be converted to a number. (N2, N3, IE3)

parseInt(*string, radix*): Returns the value of *string* after converting it to an integer in base *radix*. This function returns NaN (zero in MS Windows) when it encounters the first character that cannot be converted to an integer. (N2, N3, IE3)

unescape(*string*): Returns a character based on the ASCII encoding contained in *string*. It decodes a previously escaped string. (N2, N3, IE3)

Table of Operators

In this table, the first three columns on the left show the operators, types of operands, and operations performed. The associativity is shown in the next column (LTR = left to right, RTL = right to left). The order of precedence that each operator takes is shown in the last column on the right.

Operator	Type of Operand	Operation	Associativity	Precedence
(,)	Any	Multiple Evaluation	LTR	1
(=)	Variable, Any	Assignment	RTL	2
(+=, -=, *=, /=, %=, <<=, >>=, >>>=, &=, ^=, |=)	Variable, Any	Assignment with Operation	RTL	2
(? :)	Boolean, Any	Conditional (ternary)	RTL	3
(||)	Boolean	Logical OR	LTR	4
(&&)	Boolean	Logical AND	LTR	5
(|)	Integer	Bitwise OR	LTR	6
(^)	Integer	Bitwise XOR	LTR	7
(&)	Integer	Bitwise AND	LTR	8
(==, ! =)	Any	Checks for Equality/Identity	LTR	9
(<, <=, >, >=)	Numbers/Strings	Relational	LTR	10
(<<, >>, >>>)	Integer	Shift	LTR	11
(+, -)	Integer String (+ only)	Addition/Subtraction Concatenation	LTR	12
(*, /, %)	Integer	Multiply/Divide/Remainder	LTR	13
(++, —, -)	Integer	Increment/Decrement/Negate (unary)	RTL	14
(~)	Integer	Bitwise Complement (unary)		
(!)	Boolean	Logical Complement (unary)		
new	Constructor Call	Create New Object (unary)		
type of	Any	Return Data Type (unary)		
void	Any	Return Undefined Value (unary)		
([ ]) (( )) (.)	Array, Integer	Array Index	LTR	15
	Functions, Arguments	Function Calls		
	Object, Property	Property Access		

Statements

break: Exits from a for or a while loop and passes program control to the statement following the loop. (N2, N3)

case: Labels a statement within a switch statement. (JavaScript 1.2 only)

comment: Allows a programmer to comment on code. Comments are enclosed in a /* (start), */ (end) structure. (N2, N3)

continue: Continues iteration of a while or a for loop after the execution of the statements within the loop. (N2, N3) default: Labels the default statement within a switch statement. (JavaScript 1.2 only)

do/while: Sets up a continuous loop that executes statements and code until the condition evaluates to false. (JavaScript 1.2 only)

export(*expression*): In secure, signed scripts, it allows all of the properties, functions, and variables to be exported to another script. Used in conjunction with an import statement, it makes the *expression* variable or function accessible in other windows or execution contexts. (JavaScript 1.2 only)

for(*[expression]; [condition]; [increment];)*: Opens a for loop. Arguments initialize a variable (*expression*), create a condition to test for (*condition*), and specify incrementation. (N2, N3)

for/in: Introduces a variable to all the properties of an object and executes a block of code for each one, looping through the properties. (N2, N3)

function [name](*[arg1,... argn]*): Declares a function that event handlers or other processes may access. (N2, N3)

if/else: Conditionally executes code. Example: If (*expression*) *statement1* [else *statement2*]. Nested statements and functions will be executed depending on whether the condition described by *expression* is true or false. (N2, N3)

import (*variables*): In secure, signed scripts this statement allows all properties, functions, and variables to be imported from another script. Used in conjunction with the export statement, the named variables are imported. (JavaScript 1.2 only)

label(*identifier: statement*): Gives *statement* the name *identifier*. Creates a pointer to code located elsewhere in the script. The script is redirected to the labeled statement. (JavaScript 1.2 only)

return [*expression*]: Specifies an expression or value to be returned by a given function. (N2, N3)

switch (*expression*): Evaluates an expression and attempts to match it to a case or default pattern or label. If the expression matches the case, statements associated with the label are executed. (JavaScript 1.2 only)

this: A statement that refers to a specific object. For example, this.width = w passes a specified value to an object. (N2, N3)

var [*name*]: Declares and initializes the variable name. (N2, N3)

while (*expression*): A statement that constructs and begins a while loop. As long as a condition is true, the specified code is executed. (N2, N3)

with (*object*): A statement that sets the value for the default object and adds it to the front of a chain. (N2, N3)

Extensible Markup Language (XML) 1.0

Abstract

Extensible Markup Language (XML), a subset of SGML (Standard Generalized Markup Language), is completely described in this document. Its goal is to enable generic SGML to be served, received, and processed on the Web in the way that is now possible with HTML. XML has been designed for ease of implementation and for interoperability with both SGML and HTML.

Table of Contents

1. Introduction
    - 1.1   Origin and Goals
    - 1.2   Terminology
2. Documents
    - 2.1   Well-Formed XML Documents
    - 2.2   Characters
    - 2.3   Common Syntactic Constructs
    - 2.4   Character Data and Markup
    - 2.5   Comments
    - 2.6   Processing Instructions
    - 2.7   CDATA Sections
    - 2.8   Prolog and Document Type Declaration
    - 2.9   Standalone Document Declaration
    - 2.10 White Space Handling
    - 2.11 End-of-Line Handling
    - 2.12 Language Identification
3. Logical Structures
    - 3.1   Start-Tags, End-Tags, and Empty-Element Tags
    - 3.2   Element Type Declarations
        - 3.2.1   Element Content
        - 3.2.2   Mixed Content
    - 3.3   Attribute-List Declarations
        - 3.3.1   Attribute Types
        - 3.3.2   Attribute Defaults

447

        3.3.3   Attribute-Value Normalization
   3.4   Conditional Sections
4. Physical Structures
   4.1   Character and Entity References
   4.2   Entity Declarations
        4.2.1   Internal Entities
        4.2.2   External Entities
   4.3   Parsed Entities
        4.3.1   The Text Declaration
        4.3.2   Well-Formed Parsed Entities
        4.3.3   Character Encoding in Entities
   4.4   XML Processor Treatment of Entities and References
        4.4.1   Not Recognized
        4.4.2   Included
        4.4.3   Included If Validating
        4.4.4   Forbidden
        4.4.5   Included in Literal
        4.4.6   Notify
        4.4.7   Bypassed
        4.4.8   Included as PE
   4.5   Construction of Internal Entity Replacement Text
   4.6   Predefined Entities
   4.7   Notation Declarations
   4.8   Document Entity
5. Conformance
   5.1 Validating and Non-Validating Processors
   5.2 Using XML Processors
6. Notation

Appendices
  A. References
     A.1 Normative References
     A.2 Other References
  B. Character Classes
  C. XML and SGML (Non-Normative)
  D. Expansion of Entity and Character References (Non-Normative)
  E. Deterministic Content Models (Non-Normative)
  F. Autodetection of Character Encodings (Non-Normative)
  G. W3C XML Working Group (Non-Normative)

1. Introduction

Extensible Markup Language, abbreviated XML, describes a class of data objects called XML documents and partially describes the behavior of computer programs which process them. XML is an application profile or restricted form of SGML, the Standard Generalized Markup Language [ISO 8879]. By construction, XML documents are conforming SGML documents.

XML documents are made up of storage units called entities, which contain either parsed or unparsed data. Parsed data is made up of characters, some of which form character data, and some of which form markup. Markup encodes a description of the document's storage layout and logical structure. XML provides a mechanism to impose constraints on the storage layout and logical structure.

A software module called an XML processor is used to read XML documents and provide access to their content and structure. It is assumed that an XML processor is doing its work on behalf of another module, called the application. This specification describes the required behavior of an XML processor in terms of how it must read XML data and the information it must provide to the application.

1.1 Origin and Goals

XML was developed by an XML Working Group (originally known as the SGML Editorial Review Board) formed under the auspices of the World Wide Web Consortium (W3C) in 1996. It was chaired by Jon Bosak of Sun Microsystems with the active participation of an XML Special Interest Group (previously known as the SGML Working Group) also organized by the W3C. The membership of the XML Working Group is given in Appendix G. Dan Connolly served as the XML WG's contact with the W3C.

The design goals for XML are:
1. XML shall be straightforwardly usable over the Internet.
2. XML shall support a wide variety of applications.
3. XML shall be compatible with SGML.
4. It shall be easy to write programs that process XML documents.
5. The number of optional features in XML is to be kept to the absolute minimum, ideally zero.
6. XML documents should be human-legible and reasonably clear.
7. The XML design should be prepared quickly.
8. The design of XML shall be formal and concise.
9. XML documents shall be easy to create.
10. Terseness in XML markup is of minimal importance.

This specification, together with associated standards (Unicode and ISO/IEC 10646 for characters, Internet RFC 1766 for language identification tags, ISO 639 for language name codes, and ISO 3166 for country name codes), provides all the information necessary to understand XML Version 1.0 and construct computer programs to process it.

This version of the XML specification may be distributed freely, as long as all text and legal notices remain intact.

1.2 Terminology

The terminology used to describe XML documents is defined in the body of this specification. The terms defined in the following list are used in building those definitions and in describing the actions of an XML processor:

may   Conforming documents and XML processors are permitted to but need not behave as described.

must   Conforming documents and XML processors are required to behave as described; otherwise they are in error.

error   A violation of the rules of this specification; results are undefined. Conforming software may detect and report an error and may recover from it.

fatal error   An error which a conforming XML processor must detect and report to the application. After encountering a fatal error, the processor may continue processing the data to search for further errors and may report such errors to the application. In order to support correction of errors, the processor may make unprocessed data from the document (with intermingled character data and markup) available to the application. Once a fatal error is detected, however, the processor must not continue normal processing (i.e., it must not continue to pass character data and information about the document's logical structure to the application in the normal way).

at user option   Conforming software may or must (depending on the modal verb in the sentence) behave as described; if it does, it must provide users a means to enable or disable the behavior described.

validity constraint   A rule which applies to all valid XML documents. Violations of validity constraints are errors; they must, at user option, be reported by validating XML processors.

well-formedness constraint A rule which applies to all well-formed XML documents. Violations of well-formedness constraints are fatal errors.

match   (Of strings or names:) Two strings or names being compared must be identical. Characters with multiple possible representations in ISO/IEC 10646 (e.g. characters with both precomposed and base+diacritic forms) match only if they have the same representation in both strings. At user option, processors may normalize such characters to some canonical form. No case folding is performed. (Of strings and rules in the grammar:) A string matches a grammatical production if it belongs to the language generated by that production. (Of content and content models:) An element matches its declaration when it conforms in the fashion described in the constraint "Element Valid".

for compatibility   A feature of XML included solely to ensure that XML remains compatible with SGML.

for interoperability   A non-binding recommendation included to increase the chances that XML documents can be processed by the existing installed base of SGML processors which predate the WebSGML Adaptations Annex to ISO 8879.

2. Documents

A data object is an XML document if it is well-formed, as defined in this specification. A well-formed XML document may in addition be valid if it meets certain further constraints.

Each XML document has both a logical and a physical structure. Physically, the document is composed of units called entities. An entity may refer to other entities to cause their inclusion in the document. A document begins in a "root" or document entity. Logically, the document is composed of declarations, elements, comments, character references, and processing instructions, all of which are indicated in the document by explicit markup. The logical and physical structures must nest properly, as described in "4.3.2 Well-Formed Parsed Entities."

2.1 Well-Formed XML Documents

A textual object is a well-formed XML document if:
1. Taken as a whole, it matches the production labeled document.
2. It meets all the well-formedness constraints given in this specification.
3. Each of the parsed entities which is referenced directly or indirectly within the document is well-formed.

Document
```
[1] document ::= prolog element Misc*
```

Matching the document production implies that:
1. It contains one or more elements.
2. There is exactly one element, called the root, or document element, no part of which appears in the content of any other element. For all other elements, if the start-tag is in the content of another element, the end-tag is in the content of the same element. More simply stated, the elements, delimited by start- and end-tags, nest properly within each other.

As a consequence of this, for each non-root element C in the document, there is one other element P in the document such that C is in the content of P, but is not in the content of any other element that is in the content of P. P is referred to as the parent of C, and C as a child of P.

2.2 Characters

A parsed entity contains text, a sequence of characters, which may represent markup or character data. A character is an atomic unit of text as specified by ISO/IEC 10646 [ISO/IEC 10646]. Legal characters are tab, carriage return, line feed, and the legal graphic characters of Unicode and ISO/IEC 10646. The use of "compatibility characters", as defined in section 6.8 of [Unicode], is discouraged.

Character Range
```
[2] Char ::= #x9 | #xA | #xD | [#x20-#xD7FF]        /* any Unicode character,
                             | [#xE000-#xFFFD]           excluding the surrogate
                             | [#x10000-#x10FFFF]        blocks, FFFE, and FFFF.*/
```

The mechanism for encoding character code points into bit patterns may vary from entity to entity. All XML processors must accept the UTF-8 and UTF-16 encodings of 10646; the mechanisms for signaling which of the two is in use, or for bringing other encodings into play, are discussed later, in "4.3.3 Character Encoding in Entities."

2.3 Common Syntactic Constructs

This section defines some symbols used widely in the grammar.

S (white space) consists of one or more space (#x20) characters, carriage returns, line feeds, or tabs.

White Space
```
[3] S ::= (#x20 | #x9 | #xD | #xA)+
```

Characters are classified for convenience as letters, digits, or other characters. Letters consist of an alphabetic or syllabic base character possibly followed by one or more combining characters, or of an ideographic character. Full definitions of the specific characters in each class are given in "B. Character Classes."

A **Name** is a token beginning with a letter or one of a few punctuation characters, and continuing with letters, digits, hyphens, underscores, colons, or full stops, together known as name characters. Names beginning with the string "xml", or any string which would match (('X'|'x') ('M'|'m') ('L'|'l')), are reserved for standardization in this or future versions of this specification.

Note: The colon character within XML names is reserved for experimentation with name spaces. Its meaning is expected to be standardized at some future point, at which point those documents using the colon for experimental purposes may need to be updated. (There is no guarantee that any name-space mechanism adopted for XML will in fact use the colon as a name-space delimiter.) In practice, this means that authors should not use the colon in XML names except as part of name-space experiments, but that XML processors should accept the colon as a name character.

An **Nmtoken** (name token) is any mixture of name characters.

Names and Tokens

```
[4] NameChar ::= Letter ¦ Digit ¦ '.' ¦ '-' ¦ '_' ¦ ':' ¦ CombiningChar ¦ Extender
[5]     Name ::= (Letter ¦ '_' ¦ ':') (NameChar)*
[6]    Names ::= Name (S Name)*
[7]  Nmtoken ::= (NameChar)+
[8] Nmtokens ::= Nmtoken (S Nmtoken)*
```

Literal data is any quoted string not containing the quotation mark used as a delimiter for that string. Literals are used for specifying the content of internal entities (EntityValue), the values of attributes (AttValue), and external identifiers (SystemLiteral). Note that a SystemLiteral can be parsed without scanning for markup.

Literals

```
[9]   EntityValue ::= '"' ([^%&"] ¦ PEReference ¦ Reference)* '"'
                    ¦ "'" ([^%&'] ¦ PEReference ¦ Reference)* "'"
[10]     AttValue ::= '"' ([^<&"] ¦ Reference)* '"'
                    ¦ "'" ([^<&'] ¦ Reference)* "'"
[11] SystemLiteral ::= ('"' [^"]* '"') ¦ ("'" [^']* "'")
[12] PubidLiteral ::= '"' PubidChar* '"' ¦ "'" (PubidChar - "'")* "'"
[13]    PubidChar ::= #x20 ¦ #xD ¦ #xA ¦ [a-zA-Z0-9]
                    ¦ [-'()+,./:=?;!*#@$_%]
```

2.4 Character Data and Markup

Text consists of intermingled character data and markup. Markup takes the form of start-tags, end-tags, empty-element tags, entity references, character references, comments, CDATA section delimiters, document type declarations, and processing instructions.

All text that is not markup constitutes the character data of the document.

The ampersand character (&) and the left angle bracket (<) may appear in their literal form only when used as markup delimiters, or within a comment, a processing instruction, or a CDATA section. They are also legal within the literal entity value of an internal entity declaration; see "4.3.2 Well-Formed Parsed Entities". If they are needed elsewhere, they must be escaped using either numeric character references or the strings "&" and "<" respectively. The right angle bracket (>) may be represented using the string ">", and must, for compatibility, be escaped using ">" or a character reference when it appears in the string "]]>" in content, when that string is not marking the end of a CDATA section.

In the content of elements, character data is any string of characters which does not contain the start-delimiter of any markup. In a CDATA section, character data is any string of characters not including the CDATA-section-close delimiter, "]]>".

To allow attribute values to contain both single and double quotes, the apostrophe or single-quote character (') may be represented as "'", and the double-quote character (") as """.

Character Data
```
[14] CharData ::= [^<&]* - ([^<&]* ']]>' [^<&]*)
```

2.5 Comments

Comments may appear anywhere in a document outside other markup; in addition, they may appear within the document type declaration at places allowed by the grammar. They are not part of the document's character data; an XML processor may, but need not, make it possible for an application to retrieve the text of comments. For compatibility, the string "--" (double-hyphen) must not occur within comments.

Comments
```
[15] Comment ::= '<!--' ((Char - '-') ¦ ('-' (Char - '-')))* '-->'
```

An example of a comment:
```
<!-- declarations for <head> & <body> -->
```

2.6 Processing Instructions

Processing instructions (PIs) allow documents to contain instructions for applications.

Processing Instructions
```
[16]       PI ::= '<?' PITarget (S (Char* - (Char* '?>' Char*)))? '?>'
[17] PITarget ::= Name - (('X' ¦ 'x') ('M' ¦ 'm') ('L' ¦ 'l'))
```

PIs are not part of the document's character data, but must be passed through to the application. The PI begins with a target (PITarget) used to identify the application to which the instruction is directed. The target names "XML", "xml", and so on are reserved for standardization in this or future versions of this specification. The XML Notation mechanism may be used for formal declaration of PI targets.

2.7 CDATA Sections

CDATA sections may occur anywhere character data may occur; they are used to escape blocks of text containing characters which would otherwise be recognized as markup. CDATA sections begin with the string "<![CDATA[" and end with the string "]]>":

CDATA Sections

```
[18]    CDSect ::= CDStart CData CDEnd
[19]    CDStart ::= '<![CDATA['
[20]     CData ::= (Char* - (Char* ']]>' Char*))
[21]     CDEnd ::= ']]>'
```

Within a CDATA section, only the CDEnd string is recognized as markup, so that left angle brackets and ampersands may occur in their literal form; they need not (and cannot) be escaped using "<" and "&". CDATA sections cannot nest.

An example of a CDATA section, in which "<greeting>" and "</greeting>" are recognized as character data, not markup:

```
<![CDATA[<greeting>Hello, world!</greeting>]]>
```

2.8 Prolog and Document Type Declaration

XML documents may, and should, begin with an XML declaration which specifies the version of XML being used. For example, the following is a complete XML document, well-formed but not valid:

```
<?xml version="1.0"?>
<greeting>Hello, world!</greeting>
```

and so is this:

```
<greeting>Hello, world!</greeting>
```

The version number "1.0" should be used to indicate conformance to this version of this specification; it is an error for a document to use the value "1.0" if it does not conform to this version of this specification. It is the intent of the XML working group to give later versions of this specification numbers other than "1.0", but this intent does not indicate a commitment to produce any future versions of XML, nor if any are produced, to use any particular numbering scheme. Since future versions are not ruled out, this construct is provided as a means to allow the possibility of automatic version recognition, should it become necessary. Processors may signal an error if they receive documents labeled with versions they do not support.

The function of the markup in an XML document is to describe its storage and logical structure and to associate attribute-value pairs with its logical structures. XML provides a mechanism, the document type declaration, to define constraints on the logical structure and to support the use of predefined storage units. An XML document is valid if it has an associated document type declaration and if the document complies with the constraints expressed in it.

The document type declaration must appear before the first element in the document.

Prolog

```
[22]       prolog ::= XMLDecl? Misc* (doctypedecl Misc*)?
[23]      XMLDecl ::= '<?xml' VersionInfo EncodingDecl? SDDecl? S? '?>'
[24] VersionInfo ::= S 'version' Eq (' VersionNum ' | " VersionNum ")
[25]          Eq ::= S? '=' S?
[26]  VersionNum ::= ([a-zA-Z0-9_.:] | '-')+
[27]        Misc ::= Comment | PI | S
```

The XML document type declaration contains or points to markup declarations that provide a grammar for a class of documents. This grammar is known as a document type definition, or DTD. The document type declaration can point to an external subset (a special kind of external entity) containing markup declarations, or can contain the markup declarations directly in an internal subset, or can do both. The DTD for a document consists of both subsets taken together.

A markup declaration is an element type declaration, an attribute-list declaration, an entity declaration, or a notation declaration. These declarations may be contained in whole or in part within parameter entities, as described in the well-formedness and validity constraints below. For fuller information, see "4. Physical Structures."

Document Type Definition

```
[28]  doctypedecl ::= '<!DOCTYPE' S Name (S ExternalID)? S?  ('['  [ vc: Root Element Type ]
                      (markupdecl | PEReference | S)* ']' S?)?
                      '>'

[29]  markupdecl ::= elementdecl | AttlistDecl | EntityDecl        [ vc: Proper Declaration/PE
                      | NotationDecl | PI | Comment                  Nesting ]
                                                                   [ wfc: PEs in Internal
                                                                     Subset ]
```

The markup declarations may be made up in whole or in part of the replacement text of parameter entities. The productions later in this specification for individual nonterminals (elementdecl, AttlistDecl, and so on) describe the declarations after all the parameter entities have been included.

Validity Constraint: Root Element Type
The Name in the document type declaration must match the element type of the root element.

Validity Constraint: Proper Declaration/PE Nesting
Parameter-entity replacement text must be properly nested with markup declarations. That is to say, if either the first character or the last character of a markup declaration (markupdecl above) is contained in the replacement text for a parameter-entity reference, both must be contained in the same replacement text.

Well-Formedness Constraint: PEs in Internal Subset

In the internal DTD subset, parameter-entity references can occur only where markup declarations can occur, not within markup declarations. (This does not apply to references that occur in external parameter entities or to the external subset.)

Like the internal subset, the external subset and any external parameter entities referred to in the DTD must consist of a series of complete markup declarations of the types allowed by the nonterminal symbol markupdecl, interspersed with white space or parameter-entity references. However, portions of the contents of the external subset or of external parameter entities may conditionally be ignored by using the conditional section construct; this is not allowed in the internal subset.

External Subset

```
[30]     extSubset ::= TextDecl? extSubsetDecl
[31] extSubsetDecl ::= ( markupdecl | conditionalSect | PEReference | S )*
```

The external subset and external parameter entities also differ from the internal subset in that in them, parameter-entity references are permitted within markup declarations, not only between markup declarations.

An example of an XML document with a document type declaration:

```
<?xml version="1.0"?>
<!DOCTYPE greeting SYSTEM "hello.dtd">
<greeting>Hello, world!</greeting>
```

The system identifier "hello.dtd" gives the URI of a DTD for the document.

The declarations can also be given locally, as in this example:

```
<?xml version="1.0" encoding="UTF-8" ?>
<!DOCTYPE greeting [  <!ELEMENT greeting (#PCDATA)> ]>
<greeting>Hello, world!</greeting>
```

If both the external and internal subsets are used, the internal subset is considered to occur before the external subset. This has the effect that entity and attribute-list declarations in the internal subset take precedence over those in the external subset.

2.9 Standalone Document Declaration

Markup declarations can affect the content of the document, as passed from an XML processor to an application; examples are attribute defaults and entity declarations. The standalone document declaration, which may appear as a component of the XML declaration, signals whether or not there are such declarations which appear external to the document entity.

Standalone Document Declaration

```
[32] SDDecl ::= S 'standalone' Eq "'" ('yes' | 'no')
                "'"
              | S 'standalone' Eq '"' ('yes' | 'no') [ vc: Standalone Document
                '"'                                           Declaration ]
```

In a standalone document declaration, the value "yes" indicates that there are no markup declarations external to the document entity (either in the DTD external subset, or in an external parameter entity referenced from the internal subset) which affect the information passed from the XML processor to the application. The value "no" indicates that there are or may be such external markup declarations. Note that the standalone document declaration only denotes the presence of external declarations; the presence, in a document, of references to external entities, when those entities are internally declared, does not change its standalone status.

If there are no external markup declarations, the standalone document declaration has no meaning. If there are external markup declarations but there is no standalone document declaration, the value "no" is assumed.

Any XML document for which standalone="no" holds can be converted algorithmically to a standalone document, which may be desirable for some network delivery applications.

Validity Constraint: Standalone Document Declaration

The standalone document declaration must have the value "no" if any external markup declarations contain declarations of:

- attributes with default values, if elements to which these attributes apply appear in the document without specifications of values for these attributes, or
- entities (other than amp, lt, gt, apos, quot), if references to those entities appear in the document, or
- attributes with values subject to normalization, where the attribute appears in the document with a value which will change as a result of normalization, or
- element types with element content, if white space occurs directly within any instance of those types.

An example XML declaration with a standalone document declaration:

```
<?xml version="1.0" standalone='yes'?>
```

2.10 White Space Handling

In editing XML documents, it is often convenient to use "white space" (spaces, tabs, and blank lines, denoted by the nonterminal S in this specification) to set apart the markup for greater readability. Such white space is typically not intended for inclusion in the delivered version of the document. On the other hand, "significant" white space that should be preserved in the delivered version is common, for example in poetry and source code.

An XML processor must always pass all characters in a document that are not markup through to the application. A validating XML processor must also inform the application which of these characters constitute white space appearing in element content.

A special attribute named xml:space may be attached to an element to signal an intention that in that element, white space should be preserved by applications. In valid documents, this attribute, like any other, must be declared if it is used. When declared, it must be given as an enumerated type whose only possible values are "default" and "preserve". For example:

```
<!ATTLIST poem   xml:space (default|preserve) 'preserve'>
```

The value "default" signals that applications' default white-space processing modes are acceptable for this element; the value "preserve" indicates the intent that applications preserve all the white space. This declared intent is considered to apply to all elements within the content of the element where it is specified, unless overriden with another instance of the xml:space attribute.

The root element of any document is considered to have signaled no intentions as regards application space handling, unless it provides a value for this attribute or the attribute is declared with a default value.

2.11 End-of-Line Handling

XML parsed entities are often stored in computer files which, for editing convenience, are organized into lines. These lines are typically separated by some combination of the characters carriage-return (#xD) and line-feed (#xA).

To simplify the tasks of applications, wherever an external parsed entity or the literal entity value of an internal parsed entity contains either the literal two-character sequence "#xD#xA" or a standalone literal #xD, an XML processor must pass to the application the single character #xA. (This behavior can conveniently be produced by normalizing all line breaks to #xA on input, before parsing.)

2.12 Language Identification

In document processing, it is often useful to identify the natural or formal language in which the content is written. A special attribute named xml:lang may be inserted in documents to specify the language used in the contents and attribute values of any element in an XML document. In valid documents, this attribute, like any other, must be declared if it is used. The values of the attribute are language identifiers as defined by [IETF RFC 1766], "Tags for the Identification of Languages":

Language Identification

```
[33] LanguageID ::= Langcode ('-' Subcode)*
[34]   Langcode ::= ISO639Code | IanaCode | UserCode
[35] ISO639Code ::= ([a-z] | [A-Z]) ([a-z] | [A-Z])
[36]   IanaCode ::= ('i' | 'I') '-' ([a-z] | [A-Z])+
[37]   UserCode ::= ('x' | 'X') '-' ([a-z] | [A-Z])+
[38]    Subcode ::= ([a-z] | [A-Z])+
```

The Langcode may be any of the following:

- a two-letter language code as defined by [ISO 639], "Codes for the representation of names of languages."
- a language identifier registered with the Internet Assigned Numbers Authority [IANA]; these begin with the prefix "i-" (or "I-").
- a language identifier assigned by the user, or agreed on between parties in private use; these must begin with the prefix "x-" or "X-" in order to ensure that they do not conflict with names later standardized or registered with IANA.

There may be any number of Subcode segments; if the first subcode segment exists and the Subcode consists of two letters, then it must be a country code from [ISO 3166], "Codes for the representation of names of countries." If the first subcode consists of more than two letters, it must be a subcode for the language in question registered with IANA, unless the Langcode begins with the prefix "x-" or "X-".

It is customary to give the language code in lower case, and the country code (if any) in upper case. Note that these values, unlike other names in XML documents, are case insensitive.

For example:

```
<p xml:lang="en">The quick brown fox jumps over the lazy dog.</p>
<p xml:lang="en-GB">What colour is it?</p>
<p xml:lang="en-US">What color is it?</p>
<sp who="Faust" desc='leise' xml:lang="de">
  <l>Habe nun, ach! Philosophie,</l>
  <l>Juristerei, und Medizin</l>
  <l>und leider auch Theologie</l>
  <l>durchaus studiert mit heißem Bemüh'n.</l>
  </sp>
```

The intent declared with xml:lang is considered to apply to all attributes and content of the element where it is specified, unless overridden with an instance of xml:lang on another element within that content.

A simple declaration for xml:lang might take the form

```
xml:lang  NMTOKEN  #IMPLIED
```

but specific default values may also be given, if appropriate. In a collection of French poems for English students, with glosses and notes in English, the xml:lang attribute might be declared this way:

```
<!ATTLIST poem   xml:lang NMTOKEN 'fr'>
<!ATTLIST gloss  xml:lang NMTOKEN 'en'>
<!ATTLIST note   xml:lang NMTOKEN 'en'>
```

3. Logical Structures

Each XML document contains one or more elements, the boundaries of which are either delimited by start-tags and end-tags, or, for empty elements, by an empty-element tag. Each element has a type, identified by name, sometimes called its "generic identifier" (GI), and may have a set of attribute specifications. Each attribute specification has a name and a value.

Element

```
[39] element ::= EmptyElemTag
     | STag content ETag [ WFC: Element Type Match ] [ VC: Element Valid ]
```

This specification does not constrain the semantics, use, or (beyond syntax) names of the element types and attributes, except that names beginning with a match to (('X'|'x')('M'|'m')('L'|'l')) are reserved for standardization in this or future versions of this specification.

Well-Formedness Constraint: Element Type Match

The Name in an element's end-tag must match the element type in the start-tag.

Validity Constraint: Element Valid

An element is valid if there is a declaration matching elementdecl where the Name matches the element type, and one of the following holds:

1. The declaration matches EMPTY and the element has no content.
2. The declaration matches children and the sequence of child elements belongs to the language generated by the regular expression in the content model, with optional white space (characters matching the nonterminal S) between each pair of child elements.
3. The declaration matches Mixed and the content consists of character data and child elements whose types match names in the content model.
4. The declaration matches ANY, and the types of any child elements have been declared.

3.1 Start-Tags, End-Tags, and Empty-Element Tags

The beginning of every non-empty XML element is marked by a start-tag.

Start-tag

```
[40]     STag ::= '<' Name (S Attribute)*      [ WFC: Unique Att Spec ] S? '>'
[41] Attribute ::= Name Eq AttValue            [ VC: Attribute Value Type ]
                                               [ WFC: No External Entity References ]
                                               [ WFC: No < in Attribute Values ]
```

The Name in the start- and end-tags gives the element's type. The Name-AttValue pairs are referred to as the attribute specifications of the element, with the Name in each pair referred to as the attribute name and the content of the AttValue (the text between the ' or " delimiters) as the attribute value.

Well-Formedness Constraint: Unique Att Spec
No attribute name may appear more than once in the same start-tag or empty-element tag.

Validity Constraint: Attribute Value Type
The attribute must have been declared; the value must be of the type declared for it. (For attribute types, see "3.3 Attribute-List Declarations.")

Well-Formedness Constraint: No External Entity References
Attribute values cannot contain direct or indirect entity references to external entities.

Well-Formedness Constraint: No < in Attribute Values
The replacement text of any entity referred to directly or indirectly in an attribute value (other than "<") must not contain a <.

An example of a start-tag:
```
<termdef id="dt-dog" term="dog">
```

The end of every element that begins with a start-tag must be marked by an end-tag containing a name that echoes the element's type as given in the start-tag:

End-tag
```
[42] ETag ::= '</' Name S? '>'
```

An example of an end-tag:
```
</termdef>
```

The text between the start-tag and end-tag is called the element's content:

Content of Elements
```
[43] content ::= (element | CharData | Reference | CDSect | PI | Comment)*
```

If an element is empty, it must be represented either by a start-tag immediately followed by an end-tag or by an empty-element tag. An empty-element tag takes a special form:

Tags for Empty Elements
```
[44] EmptyElemTag ::= '<' Name (S Attribute)* S? [ WFC: Unique Att '/>' Spec ]
```

Empty-element tags may be used for any element which has no content, whether or not it is declared using the keyword EMPTY. For interoperability, the empty-element tag must be used, and can only be used, for elements which are declared EMPTY.

Examples of empty elements:
```
<IMG align="left"
 src="http://www.w3.org/Icons/WWW/w3c_home" />
<br></br>
<br/>
```

3.2 Element Type Declarations

The element structure of an XML document may, for validation purposes, be constrained using element type and attribute-list declarations. An element type declaration constrains the element's content.

Element type declarations often constrain which element types can appear as children of the element. At user option, an XML processor may issue a warning when a declaration mentions an element type for which no declaration is provided, but this is not an error.

An element type declaration takes the form:

Element Type Declaration
```
[45] elementdecl ::= '<!ELEMENT' S Name S contentspec S? [ VC: Unique Element Type
                     '>'                                        Declaration ]
[46] contentspec ::= 'EMPTY' | 'ANY' | Mixed | children
```

where the Name gives the element type being declared.

Validity Constraint: Unique Element Type Declaration
No element type may be declared more than once.

Examples of element type declarations:
```
<!ELEMENT br EMPTY>
<!ELEMENT p (#PCDATA|emph)* >
<!ELEMENT %name.para; %content.para; >
<!ELEMENT container ANY>
```

3.2.1 Element Content

An element type has element content when elements of that type must contain only child elements (no character data), optionally separated by white space (characters matching the nonterminal S). In this case, the constraint includes a content model, a simple grammar governing the allowed types of the child elements and the order in which they are allowed to appear. The grammar is built on content particles (cps), which consist of names, choice lists of content particles, or sequence lists of content particles:

Element-content Models

```
[47] children ::= (choice | seq) ('?' | '*' | '+')?
[48]       cp ::= (Name | choice | seq) ('?' | '*' | '+')?
[49]   choice ::= '(' S? cp ( S? '|' S? cp )* S? ')'          [ VC: Proper Group/PE Nesting ]
[50]      seq ::= '(' S? cp ( S? ',' S? cp )* S? ')'          [ VC: Proper Group/PE Nesting ]
```

where each Name is the type of an element which may appear as a child. Any content particle in a choice list may appear in the element content at the location where the choice list appears in the grammar; content particles occurring in a sequence list must each appear in the element content in the order given in the list. The optional character following a name or list governs whether the element or the content particles in the list may occur one or more (+), zero or more (*), or zero or one times (?). The absence of such an operator means that the element or content particle must appear exactly once. This syntax and meaning are identical to those used in the productions in this specification.

The content of an element matches a content model if and only if it is possible to trace out a path through the content model, obeying the sequence, choice, and repetition operators and matching each element in the content against an element type in the content model. For compatibility, it is an error if an element in the document can match more than one occurrence of an element type in the content model. For more information, see "E. Deterministic Content Models."

Validity Constraint: Proper Group/PE Nesting
Parameter-entity replacement text must be properly nested with parenthetized groups. That is to say, if either of the opening or closing parentheses in a choice, seq, or Mixed construct is contained in the replacement text for a parameter entity, both must be contained in the same replacement text. For interoperability, if a parameter-entity reference appears in a choice, seq, or Mixed construct, its replacement text should not be empty, and neither the first nor last non-blank character of the replacement text should be a connector (| or ,).

Examples of element-content models:
```
<!ELEMENT spec (front, body, back?)>
<!ELEMENT div1 (head, (p | list | note)*, div2*)>
<!ELEMENT dictionary-body (%div.mix; | %dict.mix;)*>
```

3.2.2 Mixed Content

An element type has mixed content when elements of that type may contain character data, optionally interspersed with child elements. In this case, the types of the child elements may be constrained, but not their order or their number of occurrences:

Mixed-content Declaration

```
[51] Mixed ::= '(' S? '#PCDATA' (S? '|' S? Name)* S? ')*'
             | '(' S? '#PCDATA' S? ')'                        [ VC: Proper Group/PE Nesting ]
                                                              [ VC: No Duplicate Types ]
```

where the Names give the types of elements that may appear as children.

Validity Constraint: No Duplicate Types
The same name must not appear more than once in a single mixed-content declaration.

Examples of mixed content declarations:
```
<!ELEMENT p (#PCDATA|a|ul|b|i|em)*>
<!ELEMENT p (#PCDATA | %font; | %phrase; | %special; | %form;)* >
<!ELEMENT b (#PCDATA)>
```

3.3 Attribute-List Declarations

Attributes are used to associate name-value pairs with elements. Attribute specifications may appear only within start-tags and empty-element tags; thus, the productions used to recognize them appear in "3.1 Start-Tags, End-Tags, and Empty-Element Tags." Attribute-list declarations may be used:

- To define the set of attributes pertaining to a given element type.
- To establish type constraints for these attributes.
- To provide default values for attributes.

Attribute-list declarations specify the name, data type, and default value (if any) of each attribute associated with a given element type:

Attribute-list Declaration
```
[52] AttlistDecl ::= '<!ATTLIST' S Name AttDef* S? '>'
[53]      AttDef ::= S Name S AttType S DefaultDecl
```

The Name in the AttlistDecl rule is the type of an element. At user option, an XML processor may issue a warning if attributes are declared for an element type not itself declared, but this is not an error. The Name in the AttDef rule is the name of the attribute.

When more than one AttlistDecl is provided for a given element type, the contents of all those provided are merged. When more than one definition is provided for the same attribute of a given element type, the first declaration is binding and later declarations are ignored. For interoperability, writers of DTDs may choose to provide at most one attribute-list declaration for a given element type, at most one attribute definition for a given attribute name, and at least one attribute definition in each attribute-list declaration. For interoperability, an XML processor may at user option issue a warning when more than one attribute-list declaration is provided for a given element type, or more than one attribute definition is provided for a given attribute, but this is not an error.

3.3.1 Attribute Types

XML attribute types are of three kinds: a string type, a set of tokenized types, and enumerated types. The string type may take any literal string as a value; the tokenized types have varying lexical and semantic constraints, as noted:

Attribute Types

```
[54]        AttType ::= StringType | TokenizedType
                                   | EnumeratedType
[55]     StringType ::= 'CDATA'
[56] TokenizedType ::= 'ID'                          [VC: ID ]
                                                     [VC: One ID per Element Type ]
                                                     [VC: ID Attribute Default ]
                     | 'IDREF'                       [VC: IDREF ]
                     | 'IDREFS'                      [VC: IDREF ]
                     | 'ENTITY'                      [VC: Entity Name ]
                     | 'ENTITIES'                    [VC: Entity Name ]
                     | 'NMTOKEN'                     [VC: Name Token ]
                     | 'NMTOKENS'                    [VC: Name Token ]
```

Validity Constraint: ID
Values of type ID must match the Name production. A name must not appear more than once in an XML document as a value of this type; i.e., ID values must uniquely identify the elements which bear them.

Validity Constraint: One ID per Element Type
No element type may have more than one ID attribute specified.

Validity Constraint: ID Attribute Default
An ID attribute must have a declared default of #IMPLIED or #REQUIRED.

Validity Constraint: IDREF
Values of type IDREF must match the Name production, and values of type IDREFS must match Names; each Name must match the value of an ID attribute on some element in the XML document; i.e. IDREF values must match the value of some ID attribute.

Validity Constraint: Entity Name
Values of type ENTITY must match the Name production, values of type ENTITIES must match Names; each Name must match the name of an unparsed entity declared in the DTD.

Validity Constraint: Name Token
Values of type NMTOKEN must match the Nmtoken production; values of type NMTOKENS must match Nmtokens.

Enumerated attributes can take one of a list of values provided in the declaration. There are two kinds of enumerated types:

Enumerated Attribute Types

```
[57] EnumeratedType ::= NotationType | Enumeration
[58]   NotationType ::= 'NOTATION' S '(' S? Name (S? '|' S? Name)*   [ VC: Notation Attributes ]
                        S? ')'
[59]    Enumeration ::= '(' S? Nmtoken (S? '|' S? Nmtoken)* S?       [ VC: Enumeration ]
                        ')'
```

A NOTATION attribute identifies a notation, declared in the DTD with associated system and/or public identifiers, to be used in interpreting the element to which the attribute is attached.

Validity Constraint: Notation Attributes
Values of this type must match one of the notation names included in the declaration; all notation names in the declaration must be declared.

Validity Constraint: Enumeration
Values of this type must match one of the Nmtoken tokens in the declaration.

For interoperability, the same Nmtoken should not occur more than once in the enumerated attribute types of a single element type.

3.3.2 Attribute Defaults

An attribute declaration provides information on whether the attribute's presence is required, and if not, how an XML processor should react if a declared attribute is absent in a document.

Attribute Defaults

```
[60] DefaultDecl ::= '#REQUIRED' | '#IMPLIED'
                     | (('#FIXED' S)? AttValue)   [ VC: Required Attribute ]
                                                  [ VC: Attribute Default Legal ]
                                                  [ WFC: No < in Attribute Values ]
                                                  [ VC: Fixed Attribute Default ]
```

In an attribute declaration, #REQUIRED means that the attribute must always be provided, #IMPLIED that no default value is provided. If the declaration is neither #REQUIRED nor #IMPLIED, then the AttValue value contains the declared default value; the #FIXED keyword states that the attribute must always have the default value. If a default value is declared, when an XML processor encounters an omitted attribute, it is to behave as though the attribute were present with the declared default value.

Validity Constraint: Required Attribute
If the default declaration is the keyword #REQUIRED, then the attribute must be specified for all elements of the type in the attribute-list declaration.

Validity Constraint: Attribute Default Legal

The declared default value must meet the lexical constraints of the declared attribute type.

Validity Constraint: Fixed Attribute Default

If an attribute has a default value declared with the #FIXED keyword, instances of that attribute must match the default value.

Examples of attribute-list declarations:

```
<!ATTLIST termdef
          id      ID       #REQUIRED
          name    CDATA    #IMPLIED>
<!ATTLIST list
          type    (bullets|ordered|glossary)   "ordered">
<!ATTLIST form
          method  CDATA    #FIXED "POST">
```

3.3.3 Attribute-Value Normalization

Before the value of an attribute is passed to the application or checked for validity, the XML processor must normalize it as follows:

- a character reference is processed by appending the referenced character to the attribute value
- an entity reference is processed by recursively processing the replacement text of the entity
- a whitespace character (#x20, #xD, #xA, #x9) is processed by appending #x20 to the normalized value, except that only a single #x20 is appended for a "#xD#xA" sequence that is part of an external parsed entity or the literal entity value of an internal parsed entity
- other characters are processed by appending them to the normalized value

If the declared value is not CDATA, then the XML processor must further process the normalized attribute value by discarding any leading and trailing space (#x20) characters, and by replacing sequences of space (#x20) characters by a single space (#x20) character.

All attributes for which no declaration has been read should be treated by a non-validating parser as if declared CDATA.

3.4 Conditional Sections

Conditional sections are portions of the document type declaration external subset which are included in, or excluded from, the logical structure of the DTD based on the keyword which governs them.

Conditional Section

```
[61]    conditionalSect ::= includeSect | ignoreSect
[62]         includeSect ::= '<![' S? 'INCLUDE' S? '[' extSubsetDecl ']]>'
[63]          ignoreSect ::= '<![' S? 'IGNORE' S? '[' ignoreSectContents* ']]>'
[64] ignoreSectContents ::= Ignore ('<![' ignoreSectContents ']]>' Ignore)*
[65]              Ignore ::= Char* - (Char* ('<![' | ']]>') Char*)
```

Like the internal and external DTD subsets, a conditional section may contain one or more complete declarations, comments, processing instructions, or nested conditional sections, intermingled with white space.

If the keyword of the conditional section is INCLUDE, then the contents of the conditional section are part of the DTD. If the keyword of the conditional section is IGNORE, then the contents of the conditional section are not logically part of the DTD. Note that for reliable parsing, the contents of even ignored conditional sections must be read in order to detect nested conditional sections and ensure that the end of the outermost (ignored) conditional section is properly detected. If a conditional section with a keyword of INCLUDE occurs within a larger conditional section with a keyword of IGNORE, both the outer and the inner conditional sections are ignored.

If the keyword of the conditional section is a parameter-entity reference, the parameter entity must be replaced by its content before the processor decides whether to include or ignore the conditional section.

An example:

```
<!ENTITY % draft 'INCLUDE' >
<!ENTITY % final 'IGNORE' >
<![%draft;[
<!ELEMENT book (comments*, title, body, supplements?)>
]]>
<![%final;[
<!ELEMENT book (title, body, supplements?)>
]]>
```

4. Physical Structures

An XML document may consist of one or many storage units. These are called entities; they all have content and are all (except for the document entity, see below, and the external DTD subset) identified by name. Each XML document has one entity called the document entity, which serves as the starting point for the XML processor and may contain the whole document.

Entities may be either parsed or unparsed. A parsed entity's contents are referred to as its replacement text; this text is considered an integral part of the document.

An unparsed entity is a resource whose contents may or may not be text, and if text, may not be XML. Each unparsed entity has an associated notation, identified by name. Beyond a require-

ment that an XML processor make the identifiers for the entity and notation available to the ·
application, XML places no constraints on the contents of unparsed entities.

Parsed entities are invoked by name using entity references; unparsed entities by name, given in
the value of ENTITY or ENTITIES attributes.

General entities are entities for use within the document content. In this specification, general
entities are sometimes referred to with the unqualified term entity when this leads to no ambigu-
ity. Parameter entities are parsed entities for use within the DTD. These two types of entities use
different forms of reference and are recognized in different contexts. Furthermore, they occupy
different namespaces; a parameter entity and a general entity with the same name are two distinct entities.

4.1 Character and Entity References

A character reference refers to a specific character in the ISO/IEC 10646 character set, for example one not directly accessible from available input
devices.

Character Reference
```
[66] CharRef ::=  '&#' [0-9]+ ';'
                 | '&#x' [0-9a-fA-F]+ ';' [ WFC: Legal Character ]
```

Well-Formedness Constraint: Legal Character
Characters referred to using character references must match the production for Char.

If the character reference begins with "&#x", the digits and letters up to the terminating ; provide
a hexadecimal representation of the character's code point in ISO/IEC 10646. If it begins just
with "&#", the digits up to the terminating ; provide a decimal representation of the character's
code point.

An entity reference refers to the content of a named entity. References to parsed general entities
use ampersand (&) and semicolon (;) as delimiters. Parameter-entity references use percent-sign
(%) and semicolon (;) as delimiters.

Entity Reference
```
[67]   Reference ::= EntityRef | CharRef
[68]   EntityRef ::= '&' Name ';'        [ WFC: Entity Declared ]
                                         [ VC: Entity Declared ]
                                         [ WFC: Parsed Entity ]
                                         [ WFC: No Recursion ]
[69] PEReference ::= '%' Name ';'        [ VC: Entity Declared ]
                                         [ WFC: No Recursion ]
                                         [ WFC: In DTD ]
```

Well-Formedness Constraint: Entity Declared

In a document without any DTD, a document with only an internal DTD subset which contains no parameter entity references, or a document with "standalone='yes'", the Name given in the entity reference must match that in an entity declaration, except that well-formed documents need not declare any of the following entities: amp, lt, gt, apos, quot. The declaration of a parameter entity must precede any reference to it. Similarly, the declaration of a general entity must precede any reference to it which appears in a default value in an attribute-list declaration. Note that if entities are declared in the external subset or in external parameter entities, a non-validating processor is not obligated to read and process their declarations; for such documents, the rule that an entity must be declared is a well-formedness constraint only if standalone='yes'.

Validity Constraint: Entity Declared

In a document with an external subset or external parameter entities with "standalone='no'", the Name given in the entity reference must match that in an entity declaration. For interoperability, valid documents should declare the entities amp, lt, gt, apos, quot, in the form specified in "4.6 Predefined Entities." The declaration of a parameter entity must precede any reference to it. Similarly, the declaration of a general entity must precede any reference to it which appears in a default value in an attribute-list declaration.

Well-Formedness Constraint: Parsed Entity

An entity reference must not contain the name of an unparsed entity.

Unparsed entities may be referred to only in attribute values declared to be of type ENTITY or ENTITIES.

Well-Formedness Constraint: No Recursion

A parsed entity must not contain a recursive reference to itself, either directly or indirectly.

Well-Formedness Constraint: In DTD

Parameter-entity references may only appear in the DTD.

Examples of character and entity references:

```
Type <key>less-than</key> (&#x3C;) to save options.
This document was prepared on &docdate; and
is classified &security-level;.
```

Example of a parameter-entity reference:

```
<!-- declare the parameter entity "ISOLat2"... -->
<!ENTITY % ISOLat2
        SYSTEM "http://www.xml.com/iso/isolat2-xml.entities" >
<!-- ... now reference it. -->
%ISOLat2;
```

4.2 Entity Declarations

Entities are declared thus:

Entity Declaration
```
[70] EntityDecl ::= GEDecl
                   | PEDecl
[71]     GEDecl ::= '<!ENTITY' S Name S EntityDef S? '>'
[72]     PEDecl ::= '<!ENTITY' S '%' S Name S PEDef S? '>'
[73]  EntityDef ::= EntityValue | (ExternalID NDataDecl?)
[74]      PEDef ::= EntityValue | ExternalID
```

The Name identifies the entity in an entity reference or, in the case of an unparsed entity, in the value of an ENTITY or ENTITIES attribute. If the same entity is declared more than once, the first declaration encountered is binding; at user option, an XML processor may issue a warning if entities are declared multiple times.

4.2.1 Internal Entities

If the entity definition is an EntityValue, the defined entity is called an internal entity. There is no separate physical storage object, and the content of the entity is given in the declaration. Note that some processing of entity and character references in the literal entity value may be required to produce the correct replacement text: see "4.5 Construction of Internal Entity Replacement Text."

An internal entity is a parsed entity.

Example of an internal entity declaration:
```
<!ENTITY Pub-Status "This is a pre-release of the specification.">
```

4.2.2 External Entities

If the entity is not internal, it is an external entity, declared as follows:

External Entity Declaration
```
[75] ExternalID ::= 'SYSTEM' S SystemLiteral
                  | 'PUBLIC' S PubidLiteral S SystemLiteral
[76] NDataDecl ::= S 'NDATA' S Name                    [ VC: Notation Declared ]
```

If the NDataDecl is present, this is a general unparsed entity; otherwise it is a parsed entity.

Validity Constraint: Notation Declared
The Name must match the declared name of a notation.

The SystemLiteral is called the entity's system identifier. It is a URI, which may be used to retrieve the entity. Note that the hash mark (#) and fragment identifier frequently used with URIs are not, formally, part of the URI itself; an XML processor may signal an error if a fragment identifier is given as part of a system identifier. Unless otherwise provided by information outside the scope of this specification (e.g. a special XML element type defined by a particular DTD, or a processing instruction defined by a particular application specification), relative URIs are relative to the location of the resource within which the entity declaration occurs. A URI might thus be relative to the document entity, to the entity containing the external DTD subset, or to some other external parameter entity.

An XML processor should handle a non-ASCII character in a URI by representing the character in UTF-8 as one or more bytes, and then escaping these bytes with the URI escaping mechanism (i.e., by converting each byte to %HH, where HH is the hexadecimal notation of the byte value).

In addition to a system identifier, an external identifier may include a public identifier. An XML processor attempting to retrieve the entity's content may use the public identifier to try to generate an alternative URI. If the processor is unable to do so, it must use the URI specified in the system literal. Before a match is attempted, all strings of white space in the public identifier must be normalized to single space characters (#x20), and leading and trailing white space must be removed.

Examples of external entity declarations:

```
<!ENTITY open-hatch
        SYSTEM "http://www.textuality.com/boilerplate/OpenHatch.xml">
<!ENTITY open-hatch
        PUBLIC "-//Textuality//TEXT Standard open-hatch boilerplate//EN"
        "http://www.textuality.com/boilerplate/OpenHatch.xml">
<!ENTITY hatch-pic
        SYSTEM "../grafix/OpenHatch.gif"
        NDATA gif >
```

4.3 Parsed Entities

4.3.1 The Text Declaration

External parsed entities may each begin with a text declaration.

Text Declaration

```
[77] TextDecl ::= '<?xml' VersionInfo? EncodingDecl S? '?>'
```

The text declaration must be provided literally, not by reference to a parsed entity. No text declaration may appear at any position other than the beginning of an external parsed entity.

4.3.2 Well-Formed Parsed Entities

The document entity is well-formed if it matches the production labeled document. An external general parsed entity is well formed if it matches the production labeled extParsedEnt. An external parameter entity is well-formed if it matches the production labeled extPE.

Well-Formed External Parsed Entity

```
[78] extParsedEnt ::= TextDecl? content
[79]        extPE ::= TextDecl? extSubsetDecl
```

An internal general parsed entity is well-formed if its replacement text matches the production labeled content. All internal parameter entities are well-formed by definition.

A consequence of well-formedness in entities is that the logical and physical structures in an XML document are properly nested; no start-tag, end-tag, empty-element tag, element, comment, processing instruction, character reference, or entity reference can begin in one entity and end in another.

4.3.3 Character Encoding in Entities

Each external parsed entity in an XML document may use a different encoding for its characters. All XML processors must be able to read entities in either UTF-8 or UTF-16.

Entities encoded in UTF-16 must begin with the Byte Order Mark described by ISO/IEC 10646 Annex E and Unicode Appendix B (the ZERO WIDTH NO-BREAK SPACE character, #xFEFF). This is an encoding signature, not part of either the markup or the character data of the XML document. XML processors must be able to use this character to differentiate between UTF-8 and UTF-16 encoded documents.

Although an XML processor is required to read only entities in the UTF-8 and UTF-16 encodings, it is recognized that other encodings are used around the world, and it may be desired for XML processors to read entities that use them. Parsed entities which are stored in an encoding other than UTF-8 or UTF-16 must begin with a text declaration containing an encoding declaration:

Encoding Declaration

```
[80] EncodingDecl ::= S 'encoding' Eq ('"' EncName '"'
                      | "'" EncName "'" )
[81]      EncName ::= [A-Za-z] ([A-Za-z0-9._] | '-')*     /* Encoding name contains
                                                       only Latin characters */
```

In the document entity, the encoding declaration is part of the XML declaration. The EncName is the name of the encoding used.

In an encoding declaration, the values "UTF-8", "UTF-16", "ISO-10646-UCS-2", and "ISO-10646-UCS-4" should be used for the various encodings and transformations of Unicode / ISO/IEC 10646, the values "ISO-8859-1", "ISO-8859-2", ... "ISO-8859-9" should be used for the parts of ISO 8859, and the values "ISO-2022-JP", "Shift_JIS", and "EUC-JP" should be used for the various encoded forms of JIS X-0208-1997. XML processors may recognize other encodings; it is recommended that character encodings registered (as charsets) with the Internet Assigned Numbers Authority [IANA], other than those just listed, should be referred to using their registered names. Note that these registered names are defined to be case-insensitive, so processors wishing to match against them should do so in a case-insensitive way.

In the absence of information provided by an external transport protocol (e.g. HTTP or MIME), it is an error for an entity including an encoding declaration to be presented to the XML processor in an encoding other than that named in the declaration, for an encoding declaration to occur other than at the beginning of an external entity, or for an entity which begins with neither a Byte Order Mark nor an encoding declaration to use an encoding other than UTF-8. Note that since ASCII is a subset of UTF-8, ordinary ASCII entities do not strictly need an encoding declaration.

It is a fatal error when an XML processor encounters an entity with an encoding that it is unable to process.

Examples of encoding declarations:

```
<?xml encoding='UTF-8'?>
<?xml encoding='EUC-JP'?>
```

4.4 XML Processor Treatment of Entities and References

The table below summarizes the contexts in which character references, entity references, and invocations of unparsed entities might appear and the required behavior of an XML processor in each case. The labels in the leftmost column describe the recognition context:

| | Entity Type | | | | |
	Parameter	Internal	External General	Unparsed Parsed General	Character
reference in content	not recognized	included	included if validating	forbidden	included
reference in attribute value	not recognized	included in literal	forbidden	forbidden	included
occurs as attribute value	not recognized	forbidden	forbidden	notify	not recognized
reference in entity value	included in literal	bypassed	bypassed	forbidden	included
reference in	included as PE	forbidden	forbidden	forbidden	forbidden

Reference in Content
as a reference anywhere after the start-tag and before the end-tag of an element; corresponds to the nonterminal content.

Reference in Attribute Value
as a reference within either the value of an attribute in a start-tag, or a default value in an attribute declaration; corresponds to the nonterminal AttValue.

Occurs as Attribute Value
as a Name, not a reference, appearing either as the value of an attribute which has been declared as type ENTITY, or as one of the space-separated tokens in the value of an attribute which has been declared as type ENTITIES.

Reference in Entity Value
as a reference within a parameter or internal entity's literal entity value in the entity's declaration; corresponds to the nonterminal EntityValue.

Reference in DTD
as a reference within either the internal or external subsets of the DTD, but outside of an EntityValue or AttValue.

4.4.1 Not Recognized

Outside the DTD, the % character has no special significance; thus, what would be parameter entity references in the DTD are not recognized as markup in content. Similarly, the names of unparsed entities are not recognized except when they appear in the value of an appropriately declared attribute.

4.4.2 Included

An entity is included when its replacement text is retrieved and processed, in place of the reference itself, as though it were part of the document at the location the reference was recognized. The replacement text may contain both character data and (except for parameter entities) markup, which must be recognized in the usual way, except that the replacement text of entities used to escape markup delimiters (the entities amp, lt, gt, apos, quot) is always treated as data. (The string "AT&T;" expands to "AT&T;" and the remaining ampersand is not recognized as an entity-reference delimiter.) A character reference is included when the indicated character is processed in place of the reference itself.

4.4.3 Included If Validating

When an XML processor recognizes a reference to a parsed entity, in order to validate the document, the processor must include its replacement text. If the entity is external, and the processor is not attempting to validate the XML document, the processor may, but need not, include the entity's replacement text. If a non-validating parser does not include the replacement text, it must inform the application that it recognized, but did not read, the entity.

This rule is based on the recognition that the automatic inclusion provided by the SGML and XML entity mechanism, primarily designed to support modularity in authoring, is not necessarily appropriate for other applications, in particular document browsing. Browsers, for example, when encountering an external parsed entity reference, might choose to provide a visual indication of the entity's presence and retrieve it for display only on demand.

4.4.4 Forbidden

The following are forbidden, and constitute fatal errors:
- the appearance of a reference to an unparsed entity.
- the appearance of any character or general-entity reference in the DTD except within an EntityValue or AttValue.
- a reference to an external entity in an attribute value.

4.4.5 Included in Literal

When an entity reference appears in an attribute value, or a parameter entity reference appears in a literal entity value, its replacement text is processed in place of the reference itself as though it were part of the document at the location the reference was recognized, except that a single or double quote character in the replacement text is always treated as a normal data character and will not terminate the literal. For example, this is well-formed:

```
<!ENTITY % YN '"Yes"' >
<!ENTITY WhatHeSaid "He said &YN;" >
```

while this is not:

```
<!ENTITY EndAttr "27'" >
<element attribute='a-&EndAttr;'>
```

4.4.6 Notify

When the name of an unparsed entity appears as a token in the value of an attribute of declared type ENTITY or ENTITIES, a validating processor must inform the application of the system and public (if any) identifiers for both the entity and its associated notation.

4.4.7 Bypassed

When a general entity reference appears in the EntityValue in an entity declaration, it is bypassed and left as is.

4.4.8 Included as PE

Just as with external parsed entities, parameter entities need only be included if validating. When a parameter-entity reference is recognized in the DTD and included, its replacement text is enlarged by the attachment of one leading and one following space (#x20) character; the intent is to constrain the replacement text of parameter entities to contain an integral number of grammatical tokens in the DTD.

4.5 Construction of Internal Entity Replacement Text

In discussing the treatment of internal entities, it is useful to distinguish two forms of the entity's value. The literal entity value is the quoted string actually present in the entity declaration, corresponding to the non-terminal EntityValue. The replacement text is the content of the entity, after replacement of character references and parameter-entity references.

The literal entity value as given in an internal entity declaration (EntityValue) may contain character, parameter-entity, and general-entity references. Such references must be contained entirely within the literal entity value. The actual replacement text that is included as described above must contain the replacement text of any parameter entities referred to, and must contain the character referred to, in place of any character references in the literal entity value; however, general-entity references must be left as-is, unexpanded. For example, given the following declarations:

```
<!ENTITY % pub    "&#xc9;ditions Gallimard" >
<!ENTITY   rights "All rights reserved" >
<!ENTITY   book   "La Peste: Albert Camus,
&#xA9; 1947 %pub;. &rights;" >
```

then the replacement text for the entity "book" is:

```
La Peste: Albert Camus,
© 1947 Éditions Gallimard. &rights;
```

The general-entity reference "&rights;" would be expanded should the reference "&book;" appear in the document's content or an attribute value.

These simple rules may have complex interactions; for a detailed discussion of a difficult example, see "D. Expansion of Entity and Character References."

4.6 Predefined Entities

Entity and character references can both be used to escape the left angle bracket, ampersand, and other delimiters. A set of general entities (amp, lt, gt, apos, quot) is specified for this purpose. Numeric character references may also be used; they are expanded immediately when recognized and must be treated as character data, so the numeric character references "<" and "&" may be used to escape < and & when they occur in character data.

All XML processors must recognize these entities whether they are declared or not. For interoperability, valid XML documents should declare these entities, like any others, before using them. If the entities in question are declared, they must be declared as internal entities whose replacement text is the single character being escaped or a character reference to that character, as shown below:

```
<!ENTITY lt    "&#38;#60;">
<!ENTITY gt    "&#62;">
<!ENTITY amp   "&#38;#38;">
<!ENTITY apos  "&#39;">
<!ENTITY quot  "&#34;">
```

Note that the < and & characters in the declarations of "lt" and "amp" are doubly escaped to meet the requirement that entity replacement be well-formed.

4.7 Notation Declarations

Notations identify by name the format of unparsed entities, the format of elements which bear a notation attribute, or the application to which a processing instruction is addressed.

Notation declarations provide a name for the notation, for use in entity and attribute-list declarations and in attribute specifications, and an external identifier for the notation which may allow an XML processor or its client application to locate a helper application capable of processing data in the given notation.

Notation Declarations

```
[82] NotationDecl ::= '<!NOTATION' S Name S (ExternalID |  PublicID) S?  '>'
[83]     PublicID ::= 'PUBLIC' S PubidLiteral
```

XML processors must provide applications with the name and external identifier(s) of any notation declared and referred to in an attribute value, attribute definition, or entity declaration. They may additionally resolve the external identifier into the system identifier, file name, or other information needed to allow the application to call a processor for data in the notation described. (It is not an error, however, for XML documents to declare and refer to notations for which notation-specific applications are not available on the system where the XML processor or application is running.)

4.8 Document Entity

The document entity serves as the root of the entity tree and a starting-point for an XML processor. This specification does not specify how the document entity is to be located by an XML processor; unlike other entities, the document entity has no name and might well appear on a processor input stream without any identification at all.

5. Conformance

5.1 Validating and Non-Validating Processors

Conforming XML processors fall into two classes: validating and non-validating.

Validating and non-validating processors alike must report violations of this specification's well-formedness constraints in the content of the document entity and any other parsed entities that they read.

Validating processors must report violations of the constraints expressed by the declarations in the DTD, and failures to fulfill the validity constraints given in this specification. To accomplish this, validating XML processors must read and process the entire DTD and all external parsed entities referenced in the document.

Non-validating processors are required to check only the document entity, including the entire internal DTD subset, for well-formedness. While they are not required to check the document for validity, they are required to process all the declarations they read in the internal DTD subset and in any parameter entity that they read, up to the first reference to a parameter entity that they do not read; that is to say, they must use the information in those declarations to normalize attribute values, include the replacement text of internal entities, and supply default attribute values. They must not process entity declarations or attribute-list declarations encountered after a reference to a parameter entity that is not read, since the entity may have contained overriding declarations.

5.2 Using XML Processors

The behavior of a validating XML processor is highly predictable; it must read every piece of a document and report all well-formedness and validity violations. Less is required of a non-validating processor; it need not read any part of the document other than the document entity. This has two effects that may be important to users of XML processors:

- Certain well-formedness errors, specifically those that require reading external entities, may not be detected by a non-validating processor. Examples include the constraints entitled Entity Declared, Parsed Entity, and No Recursion, as well as some of the cases described as forbidden in "4.4 XML Processor Treatment of Entities and References."
- The information passed from the processor to the application may vary, depending on whether the processor reads parameter and external entities. For example, a non-validating processor may not normalize attribute values, include the replacement text of internal entities, or supply default attribute values, where doing so depends on having read declarations in external or parameter entities.

For maximum reliability in interoperating between different XML processors, applications which use non-validating processors should not rely on any behaviors not required of such processors. Applications which require facilities such as the use of default attributes or internal entities which are declared in external entities should use validating XML processors.

6. Notation

The formal grammar of XML is given in this specification using a simple Extended Backus-Naur Form (EBNF) notation. Each rule in the grammar defines one symbol, in the form

```
symbol ::= expression
```

Symbols are written with an initial capital letter if they are defined by a regular expression, or with an initial lower case letter otherwise. Literal strings are quoted.

Within the expression on the right-hand side of a rule, the following expressions are used to match strings of one or more characters:

#xN

where N is a hexadecimal integer, the expression matches the character in ISO/IEC 10646 whose canonical (UCS-4) code value, when interpreted as an unsigned binary number, has the value indicated. The number of leading zeros in the #xN form is insignificant; the number of leading zeros in the corresponding code value is governed by the character encoding in use and is not significant for XML.

[a-zA-Z], [#xN-#xN]

matches any character with a value in the range(s) indicated (inclusive).

[^a-z], [^#xN-#xN]

matches any character with a value outside the range indicated.

[^abc], [^#xN#xN#xN]

matches any character with a value not among the characters given. "string" matches a literal string matching that given inside the double quotes. 'string' matches a literal string matching that given inside the single quotes.

These symbols may be combined to match more complex patterns as follows, where A and B represent simple expressions:

(expression)

expression is treated as a unit and may be combined as described in this list:

A?	matches A or nothing; optional A.
A B	matches A followed by B.
A | B	matches A or B but not both.
A - B	matches any string that matches A but does not match B.
A+	matches one or more occurrences of A.
A*	matches zero or more occurrences of A.

Other notations used in the productions are:

/* ... */

comment.

[wfc: ...]

well-formedness constraint; this identifies by name a constraint on well-formed documents associated with a production.

[vc: ...]
validity constraint; this identifies by name a constraint on valid documents associated with a production.

Appendices

A. References

A.1 Normative References

Alvestrand, H., ed. *RFC 1766: Tags for the Identification of Languages.* Internet Engineering Task Force, 1995.

International Organization for Standardization. *ISO 639 (E): Codes for the Representation of Names of Languages.* Geneva: ISO, 1988.

International Organization for Standardization. *ISO 3166-1 (E): Codes for the Representation of Names of Countries and Their Subdivisions—Part 1: Country Codes.* Geneva: ISO, 1997.

International Organization for Standardization/International Electrotechnical Commission. *ISO/IEC 10646 (E): Information Technology—Universal Multiple-Octet Coded Character Set (UCS)—Part 1: Architecture and Basic Multilingual Plane,* plus amendments 1–7. Geneva: ISO/IEC, 1993.

Simonsen, Keld et al., eds. *Official Names for Character Sets.* Internet Assigned Numbers Authority. See *ftp://ftp.isi.edu/in-notes/iana/assignments/character-sets.*

Unicode Consortium. *The Unicode Standard, Version 2.0.* Reading, MA: Addison-Wesley Developers Press, 1996.

A.2 Other References

Aho, Alfred V., Ravi Sethi, and Jeffrey D. Ullman. *Compilers: Principles, Techniques, and Tools.* Reading, MA: Addison-Wesley, 1986. Report correction, 1988.

Berners-Lee, T., L. Masinter, and M. McCahill, eds. *RFC 1738: Uniform Resource Locators (URL).* Internet Engineering Task Force, 1994.

Berners-Lee, T., R. Fielding, and L. Masinter. *Uniform Resource Identifiers (URI): Generic Syntax and Semantics.* 1997. In progress; see updates to RFC 1738.

Brüggemann-Klein, Anne. "Regular Expressions into Finite Automata." *Theoretical Computer Science* 120: 197–213, 1993. Extended abstract in *Latin:* 97–98, 1992.

Brüggemann-Klein, Anne, and Derick Wood. *Deterministic Regular Languages.* Freiburg, Germany: University of Freiburg, 1991.

Clark, James. *Comparison of SGML and XML.* See *http://www.w3.org/TR/NOTE-sgml-xml-971215.*

Fielding, R., ed. *RFC 1808: Relative Uniform Resource Locators.* Internet Engineering Task Force, 1995.

International Organization for Standardization. *ISO 8879 (E): Information Processing—Text and Office Systems—Standard Generalized Markup Language (SGML).* Geneva: ISO, 1986.

International Organization for Standardization/International Electrotechnical Commission. *ISO/IEC 10744 (E): Information Technology—Hypermedia/Time-based Structuring Language (HyTime).* Geneva: ISO/IEC, 1992. Extended Facilities Annex, 1996.

Moats, R., ed. *RFC 2141: URN Syntax.* Internet Engineering Task Force, 1997.

B. Character Classes

Following the characteristics defined in the Unicode standard, characters are classed as *base characters* (among others, these contain the alphabetic characters of the Latin alphabet, without diacritics), *ideographic* characters, and *combining* characters (among others, this class contains most diacritics); these classes combine to form the class of letters. Digits and extenders are also distinguished.

Characters

```
[84]        Letter ::= BaseChar | Ideographic
[85]        BaseChar ::=  [#x0041-#x005A] | [#x0061-#x007A]
                        | [#x00C0-#x00D6] | [#x00D8-#x00F6]
                        | [#x00F8-#x00FF] | [#x0100-#x0131]
                        | [#x0134-#x013E] | [#x0141-#x0148]
                        | [#x014A-#x017E] | [#x0180-#x01C3]
                        | [#x01CD-#x01F0] | [#x01F4-#x01F5]
                        | [#x01FA-#x0217] | [#x0250-#x02A8]
                        | [#x02BB-#x02C1] | #x0386 | [#x0388-#x038A]
                        | #x038C | [#x038E-#x03A1] | [#x03A3-#x03CE]
                        | [#x03D0-#x03D6] | #x03DA | #x03DC | #x03DE
                        | #x03E0 | [#x03E2-#x03F3] | [#x0401-#x040C]
                        | [#x040E-#x044F] | [#x0451-#x045C]
                        | [#x045E-#x0481] | [#x0490-#x04C4]
                        | [#x04C7-#x04C8] | [#x04CB-#x04CC]
                        | [#x04D0-#x04EB] | [#x04EE-#x04F5]
                        | [#x04F8-#x04F9] | [#x0531-#x0556] | #x0559
                        | [#x0561-#x0586] | [#x05D0-#x05EA]
                        | [#x05F0-#x05F2] | [#x0621-#x063A]
                        | [#x0641-#x064A] | [#x0671-#x06B7]
                        | [#x06BA-#x06BE] | [#x06C0-#x06CE]
                        | [#x06D0-#x06D3] | #x06D5 | [#x06E5-#x06E6]
```

```
|  [#x0905-#x0939]  |  #x093D  |  [#x0958-#x0961]
|  [#x0985-#x098C]  |  [#x098F-#x0990]
|  [#x0993-#x09A8]  |  [#x09AA-#x09B0]  |  #x09B2
|  [#x09B6-#x09B9]  |  [#x09DC-#x09DD]
|  [#x09DF-#x09E1]  |  [#x09F0-#x09F1]
|  [#x0A05-#x0A0A]  |  [#x0A0F-#x0A10]
|  [#x0A13-#x0A28]  |  [#x0A2A-#x0A30]
|  [#x0A32-#x0A33]  |  [#x0A35-#x0A36]
|  [#x0A38-#x0A39]  |  [#x0A59-#x0A5C]  |  #x0A5E
|  [#x0A72-#x0A74]  |  [#x0A85-#x0A8B]  |  #x0A8D
|  [#x0A8F-#x0A91]  |  [#x0A93-#x0AA8]
|  [#x0AAA-#x0AB0]  |  [#x0AB2-#x0AB3]
|  [#x0AB5-#x0AB9]  |  #x0ABD  |  #x0AE0
|  [#x0B05-#x0B0C]  |  [#x0B0F-#x0B10]
|  [#x0B13-#x0B28]  |  [#x0B2A-#x0B30]
|  [#x0B32-#x0B33]  |  [#x0B36-#x0B39]  |  #x0B3D
|  [#x0B5C-#x0B5D]  |  [#x0B5F-#x0B61]
|  [#x0B85-#x0B8A]  |  [#x0B8E-#x0B90]
|  [#x0B92-#x0B95]  |  [#x0B99-#x0B9A]  |  #x0B9C
|  [#x0B9E-#x0B9F]  |  [#x0BA3-#x0BA4]
|  [#x0BA8-#x0BAA]  |  [#x0BAE-#x0BB5]
|  [#x0BB7-#x0BB9]  |  [#x0C05-#x0C0C]
|  [#x0C0E-#x0C10]  |  [#x0C12-#x0C28]
|  [#x0C2A-#x0C33]  |  [#x0C35-#x0C39]
|  [#x0C60-#x0C61]  |  [#x0C85-#x0C8C]
|  [#x0C8E-#x0C90]  |  [#x0C92-#x0CA8]
|  [#x0CAA-#x0CB3]  |  [#x0CB5-#x0CB9]  |  #x0CDE
|  [#x0CE0-#x0CE1]  |  [#x0D05-#x0D0C]
|  [#x0D0E-#x0D10]  |  [#x0D12-#x0D28]
|  [#x0D2A-#x0D39]  |  [#x0D60-#x0D61]
|  [#x0E01-#x0E2E]  |  #x0E30  |  [#x0E32-#x0E33]
|  [#x0E40-#x0E45]  |  [#x0E81-#x0E82]  |  #x0E84
|  [#x0E87-#x0E88]  |  #x0E8A  |  #x0E8D
|  [#x0E94-#x0E97]  |  [#x0E99-#x0E9F]
|  [#x0EA1-#x0EA3]  |  #x0EA5  |  #x0EA7
|  [#x0EAA-#x0EAB]  |  [#x0EAD-#x0EAE]  |  #x0EB0
|  [#x0EB2-#x0EB3]  |  #x0EBD  |  [#x0EC0-#x0EC4]
|  [#x0F40-#x0F47]  |  [#x0F49-#x0F69]
|  [#x10A0-#x10C5]  |  [#x10D0-#x10F6]  |  #x1100
|  [#x1102-#x1103]  |  [#x1105-#x1107]  |  #x1109
|  [#x110B-#x110C]  |  [#x110E-#x1112]  |  #x113C
|  #x113E  |  #x1140  |  #x114C  |  #x114E  |  #x1150
|  [#x1154-#x1155]  |  #x1159  |  [#x115F-#x1161]
|  #x1163  |  #x1165  |  #x1167  |  #x1169
```

```
                         | [#x116D-#x116E] | [#x1172-#x1173] | #x1175
                         | #x119E | #x11A8 | #x11AB | [#x11AE-#x11AF]
                         | [#x11B7-#x11B8] | #x11BA | [#x11BC-#x11C2]
                         | #x11EB | #x11F0 | #x11F9 | [#x1E00-#x1E9B]
                         | [#x1EA0-#x1EF9] | [#x1F00-#x1F15]
                         | [#x1F18-#x1F1D] | [#x1F20-#x1F45]
                         | [#x1F48-#x1F4D] | [#x1F50-#x1F57] | #x1F59
                         | #x1F5B | #x1F5D | [#x1F5F-#x1F7D]
                         | [#x1F80-#x1FB4] | [#x1FB6-#x1FBC] | #x1FBE
                         | [#x1FC2-#x1FC4] | [#x1FC6-#x1FCC]
                         | [#x1FD0-#x1FD3] | [#x1FD6-#x1FDB]
                         | [#x1FE0-#x1FEC] | [#x1FF2-#x1FF4]
                         | [#x1FF6-#x1FFC] | #x2126 | [#x212A-#x212B]
                         | #x212E | [#x2180-#x2182] | [#x3041-#x3094]
                         | [#x30A1-#x30FA] | [#x3105-#x312C]
                         | [#xAC00-#xD7A3]
[86]    Ideographic ::= [#x4E00-#x9FA5] | #x3007 | [#x3021-#x3029]
[87] CombiningChar ::= [#x0300-#x0345] | [#x0360-#x0361]
                         | [#x0483-#x0486] | [#x0591-#x05A1]
                         | [#x05A3-#x05B9] | [#x05BB-#x05BD] | #x05BF
                         | [#x05C1-#x05C2] | #x05C4 | [#x064B-#x0652]
                         | #x0670 | [#x06D6-#x06DC] | [#x06DD-#x06DF]
                         | [#x06E0-#x06E4] | [#x06E7-#x06E8]
                         | [#x06EA-#x06ED] | [#x0901-#x0903] | #x093C
                         | [#x093E-#x094C] | #x094D | [#x0951-#x0954]
                         | [#x0962-#x0963] | [#x0981-#x0983] | #x09BC
                         | #x09BE | #x09BF | [#x09C0-#x09C4]
                         | [#x09C7-#x09C8] | [#x09CB-#x09CD] | #x09D7
                         | [#x09E2-#x09E3] | #x0A02 | #x0A3C | #x0A3E
                         | #x0A3F | [#x0A40-#x0A42] | [#x0A47-#x0A48]
                         | [#x0A4B-#x0A4D] | [#x0A70-#x0A71]
                         | [#x0A81-#x0A83] | #x0ABC | [#x0ABE-#x0AC5]
                         | [#x0AC7-#x0AC9] | [#x0ACB-#x0ACD]
                         | [#x0B01-#x0B03] | #x0B3C | [#x0B3E-#x0B43]
                         | [#x0B47-#x0B48] | [#x0B4B-#x0B4D]
                         | [#x0B56-#x0B57] | [#x0B82-#x0B83]
                         | [#x0BBE-#x0BC2] | [#x0BC6-#x0BC8]
                         | [#x0BCA-#x0BCD] | #x0BD7 | [#x0C01-#x0C03]
                         | [#x0C3E-#x0C44] | [#x0C46-#x0C48]
                         | [#x0C4A-#x0C4D] | [#x0C55-#x0C56]
                         | [#x0C82-#x0C83] | [#x0CBE-#x0CC4]
                         | [#x0CC6-#x0CC8] | [#x0CCA-#x0CCD]
```

```
              | [#x0CD5-#x0CD6] | [#x0D02-#x0D03]
              | [#x0D3E-#x0D43] | [#x0D46-#x0D48]
              | [#x0D4A-#x0D4D] | #x0D57 | #x0E31
              | [#x0E34-#x0E3A] | [#x0E47-#x0E4E] | #x0EB1
              | [#x0EB4-#x0EB9] | [#x0EBB-#x0EBC]
              | [#x0EC8-#x0ECD] | [#x0F18-#x0F19] | #x0F35
              | #x0F37 | #x0F39 | #x0F3E | #x0F3F
              | [#x0F71-#x0F84] | [#x0F86-#x0F8B]
              | [#x0F90-#x0F95] | #x0F97 | [#x0F99-#x0FAD]
              | [#x0FB1-#x0FB7] | #x0FB9 | [#x20D0-#x20DC]
              | #x20E1 | [#x302A-#x302F] | #x3099 | #x309A
[88]    Digit ::= [#x0030-#x0039] | [#x0660-#x0669]
              | [#x06F0-#x06F9] | [#x0966-#x096F]
              | [#x09E6-#x09EF] | [#x0A66-#x0A6F]
              | [#x0AE6-#x0AEF] | [#x0B66-#x0B6F]
              | [#x0BE7-#x0BEF] | [#x0C66-#x0C6F]
              | [#x0CE6-#x0CEF] | [#x0D66-#x0D6F]
              | [#x0E50-#x0E59] | [#x0ED0-#x0ED9]
              | [#x0F20-#x0F29]
[89]    Extender ::=  #x00B7 | #x02D0 | #x02D1 | #x0387 | #x0640
              | #x0E46 | #x0EC6 | #x3005 | [#x3031-#x3035]
              | [#x309D-#x309E] | [#x30FC-#x30FE]
```

The character classes defined here can be derived from the Unicode character database as follows:

- Name start characters must have one of the categories Ll, Lu, Lo, Lt, Nl.
- Name characters other than Name-start characters must have one of the categories Mc, Me, Mn, Lm, or Nd.
- Characters in the compatibility area (i.e. with character code greater than #xF900 and less than #xFFFE) are not allowed in XML names.
- Characters which have a font or compatibility decomposition (i.e. those with a "compatibility formatting tag" in field 5 of the database— marked by field 5 beginning with a "<") are not allowed.
- The following characters are treated as name-start characters rather than name characters, because the property file classifies them as Alphabetic: [#x02BB-#x02C1], #x0559, #x06E5, #x06E6.
- Characters #x20DD-#x20E0 are excluded (in accordance with Unicode, section 5.14).
- Character #x00B7 is classified as an extender, because the property list so identifies it.
- Character #x0387 is added as a name character, because #x00B7 is its canonical equivalent.
- Characters ':' and '_' are allowed as name-start characters.
- Characters '-' and '.' are allowed as name characters.

C. XML and SGML (Non-Normative)

XML is designed to be a subset of SGML, in that every valid XML document should also be a conformant SGML document. For a detailed comparison of the additional restrictions that XML places on documents beyond those of SGML, see [Clark].

D. Expansion of Entity and Character References (Non-Normative)

This appendix contains some examples illustrating the sequence of entity- and character-reference recognition and expansion, as specified in "4.4 XML Processor Treatment of Entities and References."

If the DTD contains the declaration

```
<!ENTITY example "<p>An ampersand (&#38;#38;) may be escaped
numerically (&#38;#38;#38;) or with a general entity
(&amp;amp;).</p>" >
```

then the XML processor will recognize the character references when it parses the entity declaration, and resolve them before storing the following string as the value of the entity "example":

```
<p>An ampersand (&#38;) may be escaped
numerically (&#38;#38;) or with a general entity
(&amp;amp;).</p>
```

A reference in the document to "&example;" will cause the text to be reparsed, at which time the start- and end-tags of the "p" element will be recognized and the three references will be recognized and expanded, resulting in a "p" element with the following content (all data, no delimiters or markup):

```
An ampersand (&) may be escaped numerically (&#38;) or with a general entity
(&amp;).
```

A more complex example will illustrate the rules and their effects fully. In the following example, the line numbers are solely for reference.

```
1 <?xml version='1.0'?>
2 <!DOCTYPE test [
3 <!ELEMENT test (#PCDATA) >
4 <!ENTITY % xx '&#37;zz;'>
5 <!ENTITY % zz '&#60;!ENTITY tricky "error-prone" >' >
6 %xx;
7 ]>
8 <test>This sample shows a &tricky; method.</test>
```

This produces the following:

- in line 4, the reference to character 37 is expanded immediately, and the parameter entity "xx" is stored in the symbol table with the value "%zz;". Since the replacement text is not rescanned, the reference to parameter entity "zz" is not recognized. (And it would be an error if it were, since "zz" is not yet declared.)
- in line 5, the character reference "<" is expanded immediately and the parameter entity "zz" is stored with the replacement text "<!ENTITY tricky "error-prone" >", which is a well-formed entity declaration.
- in line 6, the reference to "xx" is recognized, and the replacement text of "xx" (namely "%zz;") is parsed. The reference to "zz" is recognized in its turn, and its replacement text ("<!ENTITY tricky "error-prone" >") is parsed. The general entity "tricky" has now been declared, with the replacement text "error-prone".
- in line 8, the reference to the general entity "tricky" is recognized, and it is expanded, so the full content of the "test" element is the self-describing (and ungrammatical) string This sample shows a error-prone method.

E. Deterministic Content Models (Non-Normative)

For compatibility, it is required that content models in element type declarations be deterministic.

SGML requires deterministic content models (it calls them "unambiguous"); XML processors built using SGM L systems may flag non-deterministic content models as errors.

For example, the content model ((b, c) | (b, d)) is non-deterministic, because given an initial b the parser cannot know which b in the model is being matched without looking ahead to see which element follows the b. In this case, the two references to b can be collapsed into a single reference, making the model read (b, (c | d)). An initial b now clearly matches only a single name in the content model. The parser doesn't need to look ahead to see what follows; either c or d would be accepted.

More formally: a finite state automaton may be constructed from the content model using the standard algorithms, e.g. algorithm 3.5 in section 3.9 of Aho, Sethi, and Ullman [Aho/Ullman]. In many such algorithms, a follow set is constructed for each position in the regular expression (i.e., each leaf node in the syntax tree for the regular expression); if any position has a follow set in which more than one following position is labeled with the same element type name, then the content model is in error and may be reported as an error.

Algorithms exist which allow many but not all non-deterministic content models to be reduced automatically to equivalent deterministic models; see Brüggemann-Klein 1991 [Brüggemann-Klein].

F. Autodetection of Character Encodings (Non-Normative)

The XML encoding declaration functions as an internal label on each entity, indicating which character encoding is in use. Before an XML processor can read the internal label, however, it apparently has to know what character encoding is in use—which is what the internal label is trying to indicate. In the general case, this is a hopeless situation. It is not entirely hopeless in XML, however, because XML limits the general case in two ways: each implementation is assumed to support only a finite set of character encodings, and the XML encoding declaration is restricted in position and content in order to make it feasible to autodetect the character encoding in use in each entity in normal cases. Also, in many cases other sources of information are available in addition to the XML data stream itself. Two cases may be distinguished, depending on whether the XML entity is presented to the processor without, or with, any accompanying (external) information. We consider the first case first.

Because each XML entity not in UTF-8 or UTF-16 format must begin with an XML encoding declaration, in which the first characters must be '<?xml', any conforming processor can detect, after two to four octets of input, which of the following cases apply. In reading this list, it may help to know that in UCS-4, '<' is "#x0000003C" and '?' is "#x0000003F", and the Byte Order Mark required of UTF-16 data streams is "#xFEFF".

- 00 00 00 3C: UCS-4, big-endian machine (1234 order)
- 3C 00 00 00: UCS-4, little-endian machine (4321 order)
- 00 00 3C 00: UCS-4, unusual octet order (2143)
- 00 3C 00 00: UCS-4, unusual octet order (3412)
- FE FF: UTF-16, big-endian
- FF FE: UTF-16, little-endian
- 00 3C 00 3F: UTF-16, big-endian, no Byte Order Mark (and thus, strictly speaking, in error)
- 3C 00 3F 00: UTF-16, little-endian, no Byte Order Mark (and thus, strictly speaking, in error)
- 3C 3F 78 6D: UTF-8, ISO 646, ASCII, some part of ISO 8859, Shift-JIS, EUC, or any other 7-bit, 8-bit, or mixed-width encoding which ensures that the characters of ASCII have their normal positions, width, and values; the actual encoding declaration must be read to detect which of these applies, but since all of these encodings use the same bit patterns for the ASCII characters, the encoding declaration itself may be read reliably
- 4C 6F A7 94: EBCDIC (in some flavor; the full encoding declaration must be read to tell which code page is in use)
- other: UTF-8 without an encoding declaration, or else the data stream is corrupt, fragmentary, or enclosed in a wrapper of some kind

This level of autodetection is enough to read the XML encoding declaration and parse the character-encoding identifier, which is still necessary to distinguish the individual members of each family of encodings (e.g. to tell UTF-8 from 8859, and the parts of 8859 from each other, or to distinguish the specific EBCDIC code page in use, and so on).

Because the contents of the encoding declaration are restricted to ASCII characters, a processor can reliably read the entire encoding declaration as soon as it has detected which family of encodings is in use. Since in practice, all widely used character encodings fall into one of the categories above, the XML encoding declaration allows reasonably reliable in-band labeling of character encodings, even when external sources of information at the operating-system or transport-protocol level are unreliable.

Once the processor has detected the character encoding in use, it can act appropriately, whether by invoking a separate input routine for each case, or by calling the proper conversion function on each character of input.

Like any self-labeling system, the XML encoding declaration will not work if any software changes the entity's character set or encoding without updating the encoding declaration. Implementors of character-encoding routines should be careful to ensure the accuracy of the internal and external information used to label the entity.

The second possible case occurs when the XML entity is accompanied by encoding information, as in some file systems and some network protocols. When multiple sources of information are available, their relative priority and the preferred method of handling conflict should be specified as part of the higher-level protocol used to deliver XML. Rules for the relative priority of the internal label and the MIME-type label in an external header, for example, should be part of the RFC document defining the text/xml and application/xml MIME types. In the interests of interoperability, however, the following rules are recommended.

- If an XML entity is in a file, the Byte-Order Mark and encoding-declaration PI are used (if present) to determine the character encoding. All other heuristics and sources of information are solely for error recovery.
- If an XML entity is delivered with a MIME type of text/xml, then the charset parameter on the MIME type determines the character encoding method; all other heuristics and sources of information are solely for error recovery.
- If an XML entity is delivered with a MIME type of application/xml, then the Byte-Order Mark and encoding-declaration PI are used (if present) to determine the character encoding. All other heuristics and sources of information are solely for error recovery.

These rules apply only in the absence of protocol-level documentation; in particular, when the MIME types text/xml and application/xml are defined, the recommendations of the relevant RFC will supersede these rules.

G. W3C XML Working Group (Non-Normative)

This specification was prepared and approved for publication by the W3C XML Working Group (WG). WG approval of this specification does not necessarily imply that all WG members voted for its approval. The current and former members of the XML WG are:

Jon Bosak, Sun (Chair); James Clark (Technical Lead); Tim Bray, Textuality and Netscape (XML Co-editor); Jean Paoli, Microsoft (XML Co-editor); C. M. Sperberg-McQueen, U. of Ill. (XML Co-editor); Dan Connolly, W3C (W3C Liaison); Paula Angerstein, Texcel; Steve DeRose, INSO; Dave Hollander, HP; Eliot Kimber, ISOGEN; Eve Maler, ArborText; Tom Magliery, NCSA; Murray Maloney, Muzmo and Grif; Makoto Murata, Fuji Xerox Information Systems; Joel Nava, Adobe; Conleth O'Connell, Vignette; Peter Sharpe, SoftQuad; John Tigue, DataChannel

Editors:
> Tim Bray (Textuality and Netscape) <tbray@textuality.com>
> Jean Paoli (Microsoft) <jeanpa@microsoft.com>
> C. M. Sperberg-McQueen (University of Illinois at Chicago)
> <cmsmcq@uic.edu>

This specification uses the term URI, which is defined by [Berners-Lee et al.], a work in progress expected to update [IETF RFC1738] and [IETF RFC1808].

> Extensible Markup Language (XML) 1.0
> W3C Recommendation February 10, 1998
> REC-xml-19980210

Status of This Document

This document has been reviewed by W3C Members and other interested parties and has been endorsed by the Director as a W3C Recommendation. It is a stable document and may be used as reference material or cited as a normative reference from another document. W3C's role in making the Recommendation is to draw attention to the specification and to promote its widespread deployment. This enhances the functionality and interoperability of the Web.

This document specifies a syntax created by subsetting an existing, widely used international text processing standard (Standard Generalized Markup Language, ISO 8879:1986(E) as amended and corrected) for use on the World Wide Web. It is a product of the W3C XML Activity, details of which can be found at http://www.w3.org/XML. A list of current W3C Recommendations and other technical documents can be found at http://www.w3.org/TR.

The list of known errors in this specification is available at http://www.w3.org/XML/xml-19980210-errata. Please report errors in this document to xml-editor@w3.org.

Unix/Linux Operating System Commands

There are many different flavors of Unix. Linux is a popular variant that is freely distributed. This is a general description of how to get around in most Unix systems. The availability of the commands listed here depends on the system you are using. To get online help from any Unix system, type "man programname" for local documentation on the program you specify.

Several conventions are followed in this document. Unix is case sensitive. If a capital letter is shown in a command, it is required. An empty set of angle brackets (<>) represents the <return> or <enter> key. A set of brackets with a label inside (<label>) represents the key with that label. Single quotation marks are used to indicate variable characters and file names. The single quotation marks are not to be typed in the shell window. Parentheses are used to set off instructions and are not to be included in the commands. Brackets around a [path] are not typed, but indicate that the path to a file or directory must be included in the command.

Many Unix commands are *base commands* that can be followed by a series of *switches*, or modifiers, with no space between them. Most Unix shells require a dash before the switches. The format is as follows:

```
command -switch1switch2
```

Passwords, Ownership, Permissions

As a multitasking, multiuser operating system, Unix requires a security system. The three methods of security employed by Unix are individual passwords for users, file ownership by users, and permissions granted by file owners.

Passwords

```
passwd
```
Changes a user's password at any time. The system asks for the old password, then the new one, then a confirmation of the new password. A password should be 6-8 characters long, with at least one numeric character. Non-alphanumeric characters are acceptable.

Ownership

```
chown
```
The creator of a file is automatically the owner. Change ownership with the chown command, as follows:

```
chown newowner 'fname' <>
```

Permissions

`chmod`

> Used by a file owner to change permissions. This command uses modes to set permissions: r (read), w (write), and x (execute). Multiple permissions may be set with one chmod command by adding together modes to give o (owner), u (user group), or a (all) permissions.

File Manipulation

File names in any of the following commands may include wildcards. The ? allows any one character, whereas * allows no character or any number of characters. All Unix switches can be combined; thus, "ls -al" would produce an expanded listing including any hidden files.

`ls`

> Lists the files in the current directory; if followed by 'fname' it indicates whether that file exists.
> `-l`   Shows expanded listing, identifying files and directories.
> `-d`   Lists directories only.
> `-a`   Includes hidden files.

`cat 'fname'`

> Displays the content of 'fname' on the screen, with scrolling. Multiple files can be displayed by concatenating.

`cat 'fname1' > > 'fname2'`

> Appends (concatenates) 'fname1' at the end of 'fname2.'

`more 'fname'`

> Displays 'fname' one screen at a time; subsequent screens are displayed by pressing <spacebar>, subsequent lines with <>. Press q to end the display. Paging backward is not possible on most systems.

`diff 'fname1' 'fname2'`

> Compares two files and displays the differences. Lines from 1 are preceded by <, and lines from 2 are preceded by >.

Copying, Moving, and Deleting Files

`cp [path]/'fname1' [path]/'fname2'`
> Copies 1 to 2. If no path is specified, the current directory is used.

`mv [path]/'fname1' [path]/'fname2'`
> Changes the name of the file from 1 to 2.

> With both cp and mv, Unix will overwrite any existing files named 'fname2' without warning.

`rm [path]/'fname'`
> Removes (deletes) 'fname.' Concatenation is possible; wildcards may be used. Unix does not allow recovery of deleted files.

`-i`
> Requires confirmation for each specific file deleted.

Compressing, Backing Up, and Restoring Files

Compressing a file in Unix typically applies the Ziv-Lempel algorithm. Related files can be combined and compressed as one file using the tar utility.

`compress 'fname'`
> Encodes 'fname,' reduces its size, and adds the extension .Z.
> `-v`   The percentage of the compression will be listed upon completion.

`uncompress 'fname'`
> Restores 'fname.Z' to its unencoded state.

`gzip 'fname'`
> Encodes 'fname' using a different compression algorithm and adds the extension .gz.

`gunzip 'fname'`
> Restores 'fname.gz' to its unencoded state.

`tar -cvf 'fname1.tar' [path] /'fname2' 'fname3'`
> Copies 'fname2' and 'fname3' to the archive 'fname1.tar.'
> `-c`   Specifies a new archive.
> `-v`   Displays a list of the files being archived (verbose mode).
> `-f`   Creates the archive as a file.

`tar -xvf [path]/ 'fname.tar'`
> Restores files from an archive file and displays a list of them on the screen.
> `-x`   Restores files from an archive file.

Directory Manipulation

`mkdir [path] 'dirname'`
> Creates the directory 'dirname' in the location specified by [path]. If [path] is not given, 'dirname' is created in the current directory.

`cd [path] 'dirname'`
> Changes to the directory 'dirname' at the location [path].

> Type "$home" at the beginning of [path] to start at the root directory; $home as 'dirname' returns the user to the home directory.

`cd`
> Returns the user to the home directory on most systems, or moves one directory up the tree.

`pwd`
> Displays the path of the working directory.

`rmdir [path] 'dirname'`
Removes the specified directory, but only if it is empty.

`rm -r 'dirname'`
Removes the specified directory and its contents recursively through all subdirectories.

On most systems, the rm command does not ask for confirmation unless the -i switch is set.

Monitoring the System and Disk Usage

The following commands allow a user to check whether a process is running in the background and to shut down a program without waiting for it to finish.

`ps -a`
Provides a list of current processes. -ef gives more details than -a.

`top -i #`
Lists the running processes and the percentage of cpu usage by each, updating the list every # seconds. Press q to end the display.

`kill [PID]`
Kills the process with the given process identification.

`kill -HUP [PID]`
Causes the process specified to reread its configuration file, allowing it to be restarted with different parameters.

To check the available disk space:

`df -k`
Displays a list of directories, their sizes, and the percentage of the disk in use. The -k option displays the size in kilobytes rather than blocks.

`du -k [path]`
Provides a listing of the files in the directory specified by [path] and their sizes.

`dtree`
Displays the directory structure.

Using Unix Mail

Reading and Processing Received Mail in Unix

The following are command-line options for sending mail:

`mail`
Invokes the mail client. If mail has been received, headers are displayed.

p
>   Displays the current message. To make a message current, enter its number.

+
>   Displays the next message.

− (dash)
>   Displays the previous message.

M
>   Displays the current message, page by page.

d
>   Deletes the current message. To delete a specific message, add its number.

u
>   Restores (undeletes) the most recently deleted message.

s 'fname'
>   Saves the current message as 'fname' with headers.

w 'fname'
>   Saves the current message with no headers.

Sending Mail

In compose mode Mail will prompt for a subject. Type a subject and press <>; then type the message.

~v :
>   Switches to vi to compose the message (see the Editors section below).

<Ctrl>C
>   Aborts composition without sending the mail.

. (period)
>   Alone on a line, the . command terminates composition and sends the mail.

~r 'fname'
>   Incorporates 'fname' in the current message, at the current cursor position.

r
>   Replies to the current message; enters compose mode.

q
>   Quits Mail (the command x may also be used).

Editors

The most common Unix text editor is vi. It is a line editor, meaning that its functions normally are executed line by line or word by word. It operates in either command or insert mode. Some editing functions may be carried out from command mode.

496

Starting vi

`vi 'fname'`
> If 'fname' does not already exist, it will be created. A number of files may be loaded simultaneously by concatenating file names. Move to the next file by typing "n."

Command Mode

`: (colon)`
> Type a colon (:) to enter command mode. Then type a command and press <>.

`:q`
> Leaves vi.

`:q!`
> Leaves without saving the file buffer.

`:w 'fname'`
> Writes the current file to a disk as 'fname'; if a file of that name already exists, it will be overwritten.

`:lnumber1, lnumber2 w 'fname'`
> Writes the portion of the current file that lies between lnumber1 and lnumber2 to 'fname.'

`:x`
> Saves the file and quits (:wq may also be used).

Moving Around in a File

The following commands are not prefaced with a colon. They are used to move the cursor within a file for viewing or to reach the point where editing is to begin.

`- (dash) or <up arrow>`
> Move up one line.

`<> or <down arrow>`
> Move down one line.

`<backspace> or <left arrow>`
> Move left one character.

`<spacebar> or <right arrow>`
> Move right one character.

`$`
> Move to the end of the line.

`^`
> Move to the beginning of the line.

`H`
> Move to the top of the screen.

L
> Move to the bottom of the screen.

M
> Move to the middle of the screen.

`<Ctrl>D`
> Move down half a page.

`<Ctrl> U`
> Move up half a page.

`<Ctrl> F`
> Move down a whole page.

`<Ctrl> B`
> Move up a whole page.

`'lnumber' G`
> Go to a specific line (:set nu displays line numbers).

G
> Go to the end of the file.

`/'text'`
> Search forward for 'text' in a file.

`?'text'`
> Search backward for 'text' in a file.

n
> Continue the search for the next instance of 'text' (when using /'text' and ?'text').

N
> Go back to the previous instance of 'text.'

Editing in Command Mode

Editing commands that can be used without entering insert mode:

x
> Delete the character under the cursor; nx (n = a number) deletes n characters.

dd
> Delete the current line; ndd deletes n lines.

p
> Enter the most recently deleted text after the cursor; p pastes in front of the cursor.

yy
> Copy the line to the buffer (yank).

`O <esc>`
> Insert a blank line above the cursor.

`o <esc>`
> Insert a blank line below the cursor.

`r 'newchar'`
> Replace the character at the cursor with 'newchar.'

`R 'newchars'`
> Replace multiple characters.

`:r 'fname'`
> Insert the file 'fname' in the current file at the cursor.

> *Note:* All replace commands put vi in insert mode; type <esc> to return to command mode.

`u`
> Undo the most recent change.

`. (period)`
> Repeat the last command.

Editing in Insert Mode

In insert mode vi behaves like a standard ASCII text editor. After entering insert mode, vi remains in insert mode until <esc> is pressed; commands that belong to command mode are not executed. Typed characters are entered as text.

`i :`
> Enter insert mode; text fills to the left of the cursor.

`a :`
> Enter insert mode; text fills to the right of the cursor.

`I :`
> Insert text at the beginning of the line.

`A :`
> Insert text at the end of the line.

`<Esc> :`
> Exit insert mode.

Networking

Networking capabilities are built into the Unix operating system. Telnet provides remote command capabilities, and FTP allows the transfer of files between machines. All networking activities require a daemon program running on the server and a client program running on the remote computer.

Telnet

The telnet protocol allows remote computers to log in and execute standard Unix commands on a Unix server. The server may be accessed from a PC or Macintosh computer running a telnet client. From a Unix command line, type "telnet machinename" to begin using telnet.

After the client connects to the daemon on the server, the daemon will ask for a username and password. Once authenticated, the user can execute all standard Unix commands. To end a telnet session, type "exit" at the command line.

FTP

File transfer protocol allows machines to pass files back and forth. Upon the opening of an FTP connection, the prompt is ftp>, not the standard %. If the remote machine supports anonymous FTP, you can enter the word "anonymous" in response to the request for your name and enter your email address as the password.

Other than commands for transferring files, only three commands work under an FTP connection: ls lists directories, pwd gives the path name of the working directory, and cd allows you to change directories.

These commands function only on the host system when a user is logged in. To begin an FTP session, open the desired local directory where data will be transferred.

Individual files are transferred with the put or the get command. To transfer 'filename' from the local machine to the host, type:

```
put 'filename'
```

To retrieve 'filename' from the host and store it on the local machine, type:

```
get 'filename'
```

The FTP daemon alerts the user when a file transfer is completed.

Transferring multiple files is accomplished with the mget and mput commands. These commands will accept arguments consisting of either a list of file names or a generic name using wildcards to specify a group of files. The daemon asks before transferring each file when a group of files are sent together. Enter a "y" to send a file or an "n" to skip over a file in the group. The following command transfers the three specified files one after another from the local machine to the host:

```
mput filename1 filename2 filename3
```

The following command retrieves all files beginning with the characters filenam and seeks confirmation before each file is transferred.

```
mget filenam*
```

Binary or ASCII File Transfers

The FTP program on the server must be set to binary file transfer mode to transfer compressed files. Because binary mode works for both ASCII and executable files, it is the preferred default setting. Enter "ascii" or "binary" at the FTP prompt to select the type of files to be transferred.

To terminate an FTP session and shut down the client, enter the command "bye" or "quit." Enter the command "close" to terminate the current connection and leave the client running. Initiate a new connection by typing "open machinename."

Getting Help

The "man" pages in Unix provide an online help system. To get detailed help on any command, type "man" followed by the command. For help on chmod, enter the following at a shell prompt:

```
man chmod
```

The online documentation for chmod will be formatted and displayed, and the more command may be used to page forward.

List of Unix/Linux Commands

Command	Function	Command	Function
addbib	Create or extend a bibliographic database.	cpio	Copy file archives in and out of an archive file.
alias	Create short nicknames for long commands.	cpp	Start the C language preprocessor.
apropos	Locate commands by keyword lookup.	csh	Start a shell (command interpreter) with a C-like syntax and interactive features.
ar	Create library archives and add or extract files.	ctags	Create a tags file for use with ex and vi.
at, batch	Execute a command at a specified time.	date	Display or set the date.
		dbx	Start a source-level debugger.
awk	Start a pattern scanning and processing language.	deroff	Remove nroff, troff, tbl, and eqn constructs.
banner	Display a string in large letters.	df	Report the free disk space on file systems.
basename	Display portions of path names and file names.	diff	Display line-by-line differences between pairs of text files.
biff	Give notice of incoming mail messages.	dtree	Display the directory structure.
bin-mail, binmail	Start a mail-processing program.	du	Display the number of disk blocks used per directory or file.
cal	Display a calendar.		
calendar	Start a simple reminder service.	echo	Echo arguments to the standard output.
cat	Concatenate and display.	ed, red	Start a basic line editor.
cb	Start a simple C program beautifier.	enscript	Print a text file in a special way.
cc	Start a C compiler.	eqn, neqn, checkeq	Typeset mathematics.
cd, chdir	Change the working directory.		
checknr	Check nroff and troff input files and report possible errors.	error	Insert compiler error messages at the responsible source-file lines.
chgrp	Change the group ownership of a file.	ex, edit, e	Start a line editor.
chmod	Change the permissions mode of a file.	exit	Exit the current shell (may log you out).
chown	Change the ownership of a file or directory to another user.	expand, unexpand	Expand Tab characters to Space characters, and vice versa.
clear	Clear the screen.	expr	Evaluate an argument as a logical, arithmetic, or string expression.
cmp	Perform a byte-by-byte comparison of two files.	file	Determine the type of a file by examining its contents.
colcrt	Filter nroff output for a terminal lacking overstrike capability.	find	Find files by name, or by other characteristics.
comm	Display lines in common, and lines not in common, between two sorted lists.	finger	Display information about users.
compress	Compress files.	fmt, fmt_mail	Start a simple text and mail-message formatter.
cp	Copy or duplicate a file.		

Command	Function	Command	Function
fold	Fold long lines for display on an output device of a given width.	nawk	Start the pattern scanning and processing language.
ftp	Start a file transfer program.	nice	Run a command at low priority.
gcore	Get core images of the running processes.	nm	Print a symbol name list.
gprof	Display call-graph profile data.	nroff	Format documents for display or for a line-printer.
grep	Search a file or files for a regular expression or a string.	od	Make an octal, decimal, hexadecimal, or ascii dump.
groups	Display a user's group memberships.		
gzip	Compress a file and add the extension .gz.	passwd, chfn, chsh	Change local or Network Information System (NIS) password.
gunzip	Restores a compressed file to its unencoded state.	paste	Join corresponding lines of several files or subsequent lines of one file.
hashmake, hashcheck	Report spelling errors.	pr	Prepare file(s) for printing.
head	Display the first few lines of a text file.	printenv	Display the environment variables currently set.
history	Show the name of the current host system.	prof	Display profile data.
		ps	Display the status of current processes.
imake	Open the C preprocessor interface to the make utility.	ptx	Generate a permutated index.
indent	Indent and format a C program source file.	pwd	Display the path name of the current working directory.
install	Install files.	quota	Display a user's disk quota and usage.
join	Apply this relational database operator.	ranlib	Convert archives to random libraries.
kill	Terminate a process.	rcp	Copy remote files.
last	Show the last logins by a user or terminal.	rcs	Change RCS (revision history) file attributes.
ld, ld.so	Open the link editor, or dynamic link editor.	rcsdiff	Compare RCS revisions.
leave	Remind user when to leave.	rev	Reverse the order of characters in each line.
less	Show one page at a time (opposite of more).	rlogin	Remote log in to another machine (see telnet).
lex	Start a lexical analysis program generator.	rm, rmdir	Remove (unlink) a file or directory.
lint	Start a C program verifier.	roffbib	Format and print a bibliographic database.
ln	Make hard or symbolic links to files.	rsh	Open a remote shell.
login	Log in to the system.		
look	Find words in the system dictionary or lines in a sorted list.	rup, ruptime	Show the host status of local machines.
lookbib	Find references in a bibliographic database.	rusers	Show who's logged in on local machines.
		rwall	Write to all users over a network.
lorder	Find an ordering relation for an object library.	rwho	Show who's logged in on local machines.
lp, cancel	Send/cancel requests to a printer.	sccs	Open the front end for the Source Code Control System (SCCS)
lpq	Display the queue of printer jobs.	sccs-admin, admin	Create and administer SCCS history files.
lpr	Send a job to the printer.		
lprm	Remove jobs from the printer queue.	sccs-cdc, cdc	Change the delta commentary of an SCCS delta.
ls	List the contents of a directory.		
mail, Mail	Read or send mail messages.	sccs-comb, comb	Combine SCCS deltas.
make	Maintain, update, and regenerate related programs and files.	sccs-delta, delta	Make a delta to an SCCS file.
		sccs-get, get	Retrieve a version of an SCCS file.
man	Display Unix reference manual pages; get help on a command.	sccs-help, help	Ask for help regarding SCCS error or warning messages.
mesg	Permit or deny messages on the terminal.		
mkdir, md	Make a directory.	sccs-prs, prs	Display selected portions of an SCCS history.
mkstr	Create an error message file by massaging C source files.	sccs-prt, prt	Display delta table information from an SCCS file.
more, page	Display a text file one page at a time.		
mv	Move or rename files.	sccs-rmdel, rmdel	Remove a delta from an SCCS file.

Command	Function	Command	Function
sccs-sact, sact	Show the editing-activity status of an SCCS file.	ul	Underline.
		uncompress	Expand compressed files.
sccs-sccsdiff, sccsdiff	Compare two versions of an SCCS file.	unifdef	Resolve and remove ifdef'd lines from cpp input.
sccs-unget, unget	Undo a previous get of an SCCS file.	uniq	Remove or report adjacent duplicate lines.
sccs-val, val	Validate an SCCS file.	units	Start the conversion program.
script	Make a typescript of a terminal session.	uptime	Show how long the system has been up.
sed	Start a stream editor.	users	Display a compact list of users logged in.
sh	Open the shell, a standard Unix system command interpreter.	uucp, uulog, uuname	Copy from system to system.
size	Display the size of an object file.	uudecode	Decode the ASCII representation of a binary file.
sleep	Suspend execution for a specified interval.	uuencode	Encode a binary file.
sort	Sort and collate lines.	uusend	Send a file to a remote host.
sortbib	Sort a bibliographic database.	uux	Perform remote system command execution.
spell, spellin	Report spelling errors.		
split	Split a file into pieces.	vacation	Reply to mail automatically.
strings	Find printable strings in an object file or in a binary file.	vgrind	Grind nice program listings.
		vi, view, vedit	Start the visual display editor based on ex.
strip	Remove symbols and relocation bits from an object file.	vtroff	Troff to a raster plotter.
stty	Set or alter the options for a terminal.	w	Show who is logged in and what they are doing.
su	Super-user; temporarily switch to a different user ID.	wait	Wait for a process to finish.
symorder	Rearrange a list of symbols.	wall	Write to all users logged in.
tabs	Set tab stops on a terminal.	wc	Display a count of lines, words, and characters.
tail	Display the last part of a file.		
talk	Talk to another user.	what	Extract SCCS-version information from a file.
tar	Create tape archives, and add or extract files.	whatis	Display a one-line summary of a keyword.
tbl	Format tables for nroff or troff.		
tee	Replicate the standard output.	whereis	Locate the binary, source, and manual page files for a command.
telnet	Open a connection to a remote system using Telnet protocol.	which	Locate a command; display its path name or alias.
test	Return true or false according to a conditional expression.	who	Show who is logged in on the system.
tftp	Open a trivial file transfer program.	whoami	Display the effective current user name.
time	Time a command.	write	Write a message to another user.
touch	Update the access and modification times of a file.	xargs	Construct the arguments list(s) and execute a command.
troff	Typeset or format documents.	xstr	Extract strings from C programs to implement shared strings.
true, false	Provide truth values.		
tsort	Perform a topological sort.	yacc	Start yet another compiler-compiler, a parsing program generator
tty	Display the name of the terminal.		
ue	Start the Full Screen Text Editor Version 3.9e.	yes	Be repetitively affirmative.
		zcat	Display compressed files.

Standards Organizations

As more individuals engage in creating and distributing multimedia products, the need for standardization regarding protocols, file types, compression techniques, and a host of other issues becomes increasingly critical. Much is at stake in the establishment and adoption of standards for hardware manufacturers, software developers, multimedia producers, and for end-users. This appendix is an introduction to the organizations that make recommendations which ultimately determine how we create, deliver, and use digital media.

The International Organization for Standardization (ISO) in Geneva is the head of all national standardization bodies. "ISO" means "equal" in Greek, and is pronounced "EYE-soh." The name of the organization is a play on words rather than an acronym.

Along with the International Electrotechnical Commission (IEC), the ISO coordinates national standards activities worldwide. Results of their work are published as ISO standards. Among them are standards for electrical connectors, computer protocols, file formats, and programming languages. The ISO/IEC Joint Technical Committee 1 (JTC 1) deals with information technology. The following is a list of ISO Technical Committees that address issues related to computing and multimedia:

ISO/IEC JTC 1	Information technology.
ISO/IEC JTC 1/WG 3	Open electronic data interchange.
ISO/IEC JTC 1/SC 1	Vocabulary.
ISO/IEC JTC 1/SC 6	Telecommunications, exchanges between systems.
ISO/IEC JTC 1/SC 7	Software engineering.
ISO/IEC JTC 1/SC 21	Information retrieval, transfer and management for OSI.
ISO/IEC JTC 1/SC 23	Optical disc cartridges for information interchange.
ISO/IEC JTC 1/SC 24	Computer graphics and image processing.
ISO/IEC JTC 1/SC 25	Interconnection of information technology equipment.
ISO/IEC JTC 1/SC 29	Coded representation of pictures, audio, and multimedia.
ISO TC 42	Photography.
ISO TC 43	Acoustics.
ISO TC 130	Graphic technology.
ISO TC 171	Document and image recording methods, storage, and use.

The accepted procedure for developing and approving international standards is specified in the 1989 revision of the ISO/IEC directives. It is an involved process with numerous activities and critical milestones. Procedures in which committees engage include five stages of development that lead to approval and publication.

1. The Proposal Stage: Members cast ballots on the creation of a new standards project.
2. The Preparatory Stage: A project leader manages the development of a working draft.
3. The Committee Stage: Consensus is achieved on a Committee Draft (CD).
4. The Approval Stage: National bodies vote on a Draft International Standard (DIS).
5. The Publication Stage: ISO publishes the International Standard (IS).

ISO standard documents are copyrighted by ISO and are not freely available as public domain documents. Other international standardization organizations (ITU and IETF) offer their documents on the Internet freely, or send out paper versions at no charge. By a liaison contribution from ISO/IEC JTC 1/SC 6 to the Internet Architecture Board (IAB), some of the OSI standards are available as PostScript files via FTP from *merit.edu* in the directory *pub/is*.

Standards documents may be obtained directly from ISO at:

ISO Sales
Case Postale 56
CH-1211 Geneve 20
Switzerland
site: www.iso.ch
email: sales@isocs.iso.ch
phone: 41 22 749 0222

The *ISO Bulletin* contains information about current standardization activities and articles about various standards. It lists all the ISO standards published or withdrawn, the DISs circulated, and the CDs registered. An annual ISO Catalogue, which lists all ISO standards in force and other ISO publications, is also available.

The following is a selected, partial listing of a few of ISO standards documents that apply to computers, telecommunications, and multimedia:

ISO 646	Seven-bit ASCII with national variants (ECMA-6).
ISO 2022	ESC sequences for switching between various character sets (ECMA-35).
ISO 2382	Information technology—Vocabulary.
ISO 3166	Codes for the representation of names of countries. This standard defines a two-letter, a three-letter and a numeric code for each country. US/USA/840=United States, FR/FRA/250=France, DE/DEU/276=Germany. The two-letter codes are Internet top-level domain names.
ISO 8632	Computer Graphics Metafile (CGM). This standard defines a file format for two-dimensional vector graphics. Part 1 defines the elements (lines, filled polygons, text, colors) that appear in a CGM and the other parts

define three different encodings for these graphic elements: character encoding, binary encoding, and clear text encoding. This standard format can store resolution-independent graphics. The main difference between CGM and PostScript is that PostScript is a full programming language while CGM is just a simple list of graphical elements, which makes CGM suitable for re-editing.

ISO 8879	Standard Generalized Markup Language (SGML), a format for storing documents.
ISO 9127	User documentation and cover information for software packages.
ISO 9541	Font and character information interchange.
ISO 9592	Programmer's Hierarchical Interactive Graphics interface (PHIGS).
ISO 9593	PHIGS Language Bindings (Fortran, Pascal, Ada, C).
ISO 9636	Graphical device interfaces.
ISO 9660	CD-ROM volume and file structure (ECMA-119).
ISO 9899	The C programming language.
ISO 9945	Unix-style system calls and shell commands (POSIX).
ISO 10646	A 32-bit character set called UCS containing nearly all known characters.
ISO 10744	HyTime hypertext/multimedia extension to SGML.
ISO 10918	Still image data compression standard (JPEG).
ISO 11172	Digital video/audio compression and encoding (MPEG-1).
ISO 12083	Standardized SGML document type definitions for books, tables, and formulas.
ISO 13818	Digital video/audio compression and encoding (MPEG-2).

Another active organization whose work is becoming increasingly important as the need for global networks grows is the International Telecommunications Union (ITU), a United Nations agency that recommends standards for telecommunications. One of its previous bodies was the International Telephone and Telegraph Consultative Committee (CCITT), which is now called ITU-T (Telecommunications Standardization Sector). A group from the CCITT/ITU-T meets every few years and compiles a list of questions about possible improvements in international electronic communication. Experts from different countries meet in study groups to develop recommendations which are adopted and published.

Relevant to computing are the ITU-T V series of recommendations on modems (V.32 and V.42) and the X series on data networks and OSI (X.25 and X.400). In telecommunications the "I" and Q series define ISDN. The Z series defines specification and programming languages (SDL and CHILL). The T series relates to text communication (facsimile and video text), and the H series addresses digital sound and video encoding standards.

The names of committees have evolved in recent years. The former International Radio Consultative Committee (CCIR) and the International Frequency Registration Board (IFRB) are now together called ITU-R (Radiocommunication Sector). Previously known as the Telecommunications Development Bureau (BDT), this organization is now referred to as ITU-D.

ITU publishes many ISO computer and telecommunication-related standards under a different cover. Its recommendations and a free ITU List of Publications are available from:

International Telecommunications Union
General Secretariat—Sales Section
Place des Nations
CH-1211 Geneve 20
Switzerland
site: www.itu.int
email: helpdesk@itu.ch
phone: 41 22 7305111
fax: 41 22 73051

The following is a short list of ITU-T/CCITT recommendations that apply to multimedia and networked communications:

H.261	Video telephony standard.
V.21	Duplex 300 bps modem modulation.
V.22	Duplex 1200 bps modem modulation.
V.22bis	Duplex 2400 bps modem modulation.
V.32	Duplex modem modulation up to 9600 bps.
V.32bis	Duplex modem modulation up to 14 400 bps.
V.34	Duplex modem modulation up to 28 800 bps.
V.42	HDLC based error correction protocol for modems.
V.42bis	Lempel-Ziv-based data compression algorithm for HDLC protocols.
V.90	Duplex modem modulation up to 56 000 bps.
X.25	An interface to a public or private packet data network.
X.3/ X.28/ X.29	Specifies connection of asynchronous ASCII terminals to X.25 networks.

The European Computer Manufacturers Association (ECMA) has been a forum for data processing experts since 1961. This group has prepared and submitted agreements for standardization to ISO, ITU, and other standards organizations. One example is the ECMA-262 standard, a version of JavaScript equivalent to Netscape's JavaScript version 1.1, using unicode characters rather than ASCII. ECMA standards are free and may be ordered from:

European Computer Manufacturers Association
114 Rue du Rhone
CH-1204 Geneva
Switzerland
site: www.ecma.ch
e-mail: helpdesk@ecma.ch
phone: 41 22 7353634
fax: 41 22 7865231

Internet standards have been developed to promote protocol-based interoperability. There are two primary areas of responsibility under which these standards are developed. The first is strategic concerns, which are handled by the Internet Society (ISOC) and the Internet Architecture Board (IAB). The second is technical development, which is handled by the Internet Engineering Task Force (IETF) and the Internet Research Task Force (IRTF).

The ISOC is a non-profit professional society with open membership. The IAB is approved by the ISOC, as is the formal documentation of the Internet standards process. The IAB oversees the architecture and growth of the Internet and it approves members to the Internet Engineering Steering Group (IESG). Working groups belonging to the IETF define specific Internet standards by consensus. Anyone may participate in the working groups, since much work is conducted by electronic mail. The IETF meets three times per year, and the documents it produces are freely available. Internet standards are published as the online Request For Comments (RFC) series. The World Wide Web consortium maintains an up to date Internet site located at *w3c.org* with all current and historical recommendations, proposals, and drafts.

The Institute of Electrical and Electronics Engineers (IEEE) also publishes standards. The URL for the IEEE Computer Society is *www.computer.org*. Publications may be ordered by email from the IEEE Computer Society Press at *cs.books@compmail.com*.

The European Telecommunication Standards Institute (ETSI), an organization that addresses European standards for telecommunications, may be contacted at:

ETSI
F-06921 Sophia Antipolis Cedex
France
phone: 33 92 94 42 00
fax: 33 93 65 47 16

The Conference of European Posts and Telecommunications Administrations (CEPT), an agency that coordinates efforts in Europe, may be contacted at:

CEPT Liaison Office
Seilerstrasse 22
CH-3008 Bern
Switzerland
phone: 41 31 62 20 81
fax: 41 31 62 20 78

Two sources for standards in the United States are listed below:

Phillips Business Information
1201 Seven Locks Road
Potomac, MD 20854
phone: 1 301 424 3338 or 800 777 5006
fax: 1 301 309 3847

Document Center
1504 Industry Way, Unit 9
Belmont, CA 94002
phone: 1 415 591 7600
fax: 1 415 591 7617

Many standards documents are available on the Internet. Here are a few web sites that provide information on standards:

http://www.ietf.org	Internet Engineering Task Force
http://www.databeam.com	Standards Watch
http://www.x3.org	National Committee for IT Standards
http://www.opengroup.org	X/Open
http://www.nist.gov	Government Archives (/msid)

The following table shows FTP sites where information may be accessed. The address must be preceded by *ftp://*.

FTP Address	Directory	Content
cs.ucl.ac.uk	/src	ISODE, PP, OSIMIS
"	/osi-ds	Internet X.500 documents
"	/ietf-osi-oda	Internet ODA documents
aun.uninett.no	/ietf/mhs-ds	X.500 based routing drafts
ftp.ifi.uio.no	/pub/SGML	SGML/HyTime related
dkuug.dk	/i18n	internationalization standards
ftp.ripe.net	/ietf	Internet documents
merit.edu	/pub/iso	some ISO standards (CLNP, etc.)
osi.ncsl.nist.gov	/*	GOSIP information
unicode.org	/pub	Unicode/ISO 10646 material
sunsite.unc.edu	/pub	Unix-Sun related
ftp.dstc.edu.au	/pub/arch/RM-ODP	Open Distributed Processing

A few standards bodies located in individual countries are listed below with street address, telephone number, and facsimile number. There are approximately 100 individual national standards bodies. Contact information is listed on the following pages for the standards bodies identified by acronym as well as for other bodies.

AFNOR	Association française de normalisation	France
ANSI	American National Standards Institute	United States
BIS	Bureau of Indian Standards	India
BSI	British Standards Institution	United Kingdom
DIN	Deutsches Institut fur Normung	Germany
DS	Dansk Standardiseringsraad	Denmark
NNI	Nederlands Normalisatie-instituut	Netherlands
NSF	Norges Standardiseringsforbund	Norway
SAA	Standards Association of Australia	Australia
SCC	Standards Council of Canada	Canada
UNI	Ente Nazionale Italiano di Unificazione	Italy

Australia
Standards Association of Australia
P.O. Box 1055
Strathfield-N.S.W. 2135
phone: 61 2 746 47 00
fax: 61 2 746 84 50

Canada
Standards Council of Canada
45 O'Connor Street, Suite 1200
Ottawa, Ontario
K1P 6N7
phone: 1 613 238 32 22
fax: 1 613 995 45 64

China
China State Bureau of Technical Supervision
4, Zhi Chun Road
Haidian District
P.O. Box 8010
Beijing
phone: 86 1 202 58 35
fax: 86 1 203 10 10

Denmark
Dansk Standardiseringsraad
Baunegaardsvej 73
DK-2900 HELLERUP
phone: 45 39 77 01 01
fax: 45 39 77 02 02
email: ds@itc.dk

France
Association française de normalisation
Tour Europe
Cedex 7
F-92049 PARIS LA DÉFENSE
phone: 331 42 91 55 55
fax: 331 42 91 56 56

Germany
DIN, Deutsches Institut fur Normung
Burggrafenstrasse 6
D-10787 BERLIN
phone: 49 30 26 01 0
fax: 49 30 26 01 12 31

India
Bureau of Indian Standards
Manak Bhavan
9 Bahadur Shah Zafar Marg
New Dehli 110002
phone: 91 11 331 79 91
fax: 91 11 331 40 62

Israel
Standards Institution of Israel
42 Chaim Levanon Street
Tel Aviv 69977
phone: 972 3 646 51 54
fax: 972 3 641 96 83

Italy
Ente Nazionale Italiano di Unificazione
Via Battistotti Sassi 11
I-20133 MILANO
phone: 39 2 70 02 41
fax: 39 2 70 10 61 06

Japan
Japanese Industrial Standards Committee
c/o Standards Department Agency of
    Industrial Science and Technology
Ministry of International Trade and Industry
1-3-1, Kasumigaseki, Chiyoda-ku
Tokyo 100
phone: 81 3 35 01 92 95/6
fax: 81 3 35 80 14 18

Mexico
Dirección General de Normas
Calle Puente de Tecamachalco No. 6
Lomas de Tecamachalco
Sección Fuentes
Naucalpan de Juárez
53 950 Mexico
phone: 52 5 520 84 94
fax: 52 5 540 51 53

Netherlands
Nederlands Normalisatie-Instituut
Kalfjeslaan 2
P.O. Box 5059
2600 GB Delft
phone: 31 15 69 03 90
fax: 31 15 69 01 90

Norway
Norges Standardiseringsforbund
Postboks 7020 Homansbyen
N-0306 Oslo 3
phone: 47 2 46 60 94
fax: 47 2 46 44 57

Poland
Polish Committee for Standardization,
    Measures, and Quality Control
UI. Elektoralna 2
00-139 Warszawa
phone: 48 22 20 54 34
fax: 48 22 20 83 78

Russian Federation
State Committee for Standardization,
    Metrology, and Certification
Leninsky Prospekt 9
Moskva 117049
phone: 7 095 236 40 44
fax: 7 095 236 82 09

Spain
Asociación Española de
    Normalización y Certificación
Calle Fernández de la Hoz, 52
E-28010 Madrid
phone: 34 1 310 48 51
fax: 34 1 310 49 76

Sweden
SIS—Standardiseringskommissionen
  i Sverige
Box 3295
S-103 66 Stockholm
phone: 46 8 613 52 00
fax: 46 8 11 70 35

Switzerland
Swiss Association for Standardization
Mülebachstr 54
CH-8008 Zurich
phone: 41 1 254 54 54
fax: 41 1 254 54 74

United Kingdom
British Standards Institution
2 Park Street
GB-London W1A 2BS
phone: 44 71 629 90 00
fax: 44 71 629 05 06

United States
American National Standards Institute
11 West 42nd Street, 13th floor
New York 10036
phone: 1 212 642 4900
fax: 1 212 398 0023

Requests for Comment

This is a selected listing of the Request For Comments (RFC) documents processed by the Internet Engineering Task Force (IETF). Listed chronologically, each RFC number is followed by the name of the creator(s), and the date created. Additional information states whether it supersedes an earlier document or has become obsolete. The status of the RFC is also identified; in addition to Standards, Proposed Standards, and Draft Standards, the status may be Experimental, Informational, Best Current Practice, or Historic.

0717   Assigned Network Numbers. J. Postel. 7/76. (Historic)

0739   Assigned numbers. J. Postel. 11/77. (Obsoletes RFC 0503, RFC 0604) (Obsoleted by RFC 0750) (Historic)

0750   Assigned numbers. J. Postel. 9/78. (Obsoletes RFC 0739) (Obsoleted by RFC 0755) (Historic)

0755   Assigned numbers. J. Postel. 5/79. (Obsoletes RFC 0750) (Obsoleted by RFC 0758) (Historic)

0758   Assigned numbers. J. Postel. 8/79. (Obsoletes RFC 0755) (Obsoleted by RFC 0762) (Historic)

0759   Internet Message Protocol. J. Postel. 8/80. (Historic)

0768   User Datagram Protocol. J. Postel. 8/80. (Standard)

0776   Assigned numbers. J. Postel. 1/81. (Obsoletes RFC 0770) (Obsoleted by RFC 0790) (Historic)

0778   DCNET Internet Clock Service. D.L. Mills. 4/81. (Historic)

0790   Assigned numbers. J. Postel. 9/81. (Obsoletes RFC 0776) (Obsoleted by RFC 0820) (Historic)

0791   Internet Protocol. J. Postel. 9/81. (Obsoletes RFC 0760) (Standard)

0792   Internet Control Message Protocol. J. Postel. 9/81. (Obsoletes RFC 0777) (Updated by RFC 0950) (Standard)

0793   Transmission Control Protocol. J. Postel. 9/81. (Standard)

0800   Request For Comments summary notes: 700–799. J. Postel, J. Vernon. 11/82. (Informational)

0818   Remote User Telnet service. J. Postel. 11/82. (Historic)

0820   Assigned numbers. J. Postel. 8/82. (Obsoletes RFC 0790) (Obsoleted by RFC 0870) (Historic)

0821   Simple Mail Transfer Protocol. J. Postel. 8/82. (Obsoletes RFC 0788) (Also STD 0010) (Standard)

0822   Standard for the format of ARPA Internet text messages. D. Crocker. 8/82. (Obsoletes RFC 0733) (Updated by RFC 1123, RFC 1138, RFC 1148, RFC 1327, RFC 2156) (Also STD 0011) (Standard)

0826   Ethernet Address Resolution Protocol: Converting network protocol addresses to 48-bit Ethernet addresses for transmission on Ethernet hardware. D.C. Plummer. 11/82. (Standard)

0840   Official protocols. J. Postel. 4/83. (Obsoleted by RFC 0880) (Historic)

0854   Telnet Protocol specification. J. Postel, J.K. Reynolds. 5/83. (Obsoletes RFC 0764) (Standard)

0855   Telnet Option specifications. J. Postel, J.K. Reynolds. 5/83. (Standard)

0862   Echo Protocol. J. Postel. 5/83. (Standard)

0863   Discard Protocol. J. Postel. 5/83. (Standard)

0865   Quote of the Day Protocol. J. Postel. 5/83. (Standard)

0866   Active users. J. Postel. 5/83. (Standard)

0867   Daytime Protocol. J. Postel. 5/83. (Standard)

0868   Time Protocol. J. Postel, K. Harrenstien. 5/83. (Standard)

0869   Host Monitoring Protocol. R. Hinden. 12/83. (Historic)

0891   DCN local-network protocols. D.L. Mills. 12/83. (Standard)

0894   Standard for the transmission of IP datagrams over Ethernet networks. C. Hornig. 4/84. (Standard)

0895   Standard for the transmission of IP datagrams over experimental Ethernet networks. J. Postel. 4/84. (Standard)

0899   Request For Comments summary notes: 800–899. J. Postel, A. Westine. 5/84. (Informational)

0903   Reverse Address Resolution Protocol. R. Finlayson, T. Mann, J.C. Mogul, M. Theimer. 6/84. (Standard)

0904   Exterior Gateway Protocol formal specification. D.L. Mills. 4/84. (Updates RFC 0827, RFC 0888) (Historic)

0907   Host Access Protocol Specification. Bolt Beranek and Newman Laboratories. 7/84. (Updated by RFC 1221) (Standard)

0913   Simple File Transfer Protocol. M. Lottor. 9/84. (Historic)

0914   Thinwire protocol for connecting personal computers to the Internet. D.J. Farber, G. Delp, T.M. Conte. 9/84. (Historic)

0916   Reliable Asynchronous Transfer Protocol (RATP). G.G. Finn. 10/84. (Historic)

0919   Broadcasting Internet Datagrams. J.C. Mogul. 10/84. (Standard)

0922   Broadcasting Internet datagrams in the presence of subnets. J.C. Mogul. 10/84. (Standard)

0929   Proposed Host-Front End Protocol. J. Lilienkamp, R. Mandell, M.A. Padlipsky. 10/84. (Historic)

0937   Post Office Protocol, Version 2. M. Butler, J. Postel, D. Chase, J. Goldberger, J.K. Reynolds. 2/85. (Obsoletes RFC 0918) (Historic)

0950   Internet Standard Subnetting Procedure. J.C. Mogul, J. Postel. 8/85. (Updates RFC 0792) (Standard)

0953   Hostname Server. K. Harrenstien, M.K. Stahl, E.J. Feinler. 10/85. (Obsoletes RFC 0811) (Historic)

0954   NICNAME/WHOIS. K. Harrenstien, M.K. Stahl, E.J. Feinler. 10/85. (Obsoletes RFC 0812) (Draft standard)

0959   File Transfer Protocol. J. Postel, J.K. Reynolds. 10/85. (Obsoletes RFC 0765) (Updated by RFC 2228) (Standard)

0974   Mail routing and the domain system. C. Partridge. 1/86. (Standard)

0977   Network News Transfer Protocol. B. Kantor, P. Lapsley. 2/86. (Proposed standard)

1001   Protocol standard for a NetBIOS service on a TCP/UDP transport: Concepts and methods. NetBIOS Working Group, Defense Advanced Research Projects Agency, Internet Activities Board, End-to-End Services Task Force. 3/87. (Standard)

1002   Protocol standard for a NetBIOS service on a TCP/UDP transport: Detailed specifications. NetBIOS Working Group. Defense Advanced Research Projects Agency, Internet Activities Board, End-to-End Services Task Force. 3/87. (Standard)

1006   ISO transport services on top of TCP, Version 3. M.T. Rose, D.E. Cass. 5/87. (Obsoletes RFC 0983) (Standard)

1009   Requirements for Internet gateways. R.T. Braden, J. Postel. 6/87. (Obsoletes RFC 0985) (Obsoleted by RFC 1812) (Historic)

1034   Domain names: Concepts and facilities. P.V. Mockapetris. 11/87. (Obsoletes RFC 0973, RFC 0882, RFC 0883) (Obsoleted by RFC 1065, RFC 2308) (Updated by RFC 1101, RFC 1183, RFC 1348, RFC 1876, RFC 1982, RFC 2065, RFC 2181) (Standard)

1035   Domain names: Implementation and specification. P.V. Mockapetris. 11/87. (Obsoletes RFC 0882, RFC 0883, RFC 0973) (Updated by RFC 1101, RFC 1183, RFC 1348, RFC 1876, RFC 1982, RFC 1995, RFC 1996, RFC 2065, RFC 2181, RFC 2136, RFC 2137, RFC 2308) (Standard)

1042   Standard for the transmission of IP datagrams over IEEE 802 networks. J. Postel, J.K. Reynolds. 2/88. (Obsoletes RFC 0948) (Standard)

1044   Internet Protocol on Network System's HYPERchannel: Protocol specification. K. Hardwick, J. Lekashman. 2/88. (Standard)

1049   Content-type header field for Internet messages. M.A. Sirbu. 3/88. (Standard)

1050   RPC: Remote Procedure Call Protocol specification. Inc. Sun Microsystems. 4/88. (Obsoleted by RFC 1057) (Historic)

1055   Nonstandard for transmission of IP datagrams over serial lines: SLIP. J.L. Romkey. 6/88. (Standard)

1056   PCMAIL: A distributed mail system for personal computers. M.L. Lambert. 6/88. (Obsoletes RFC 0993) (Informational)

1058   Routing Information Protocol. C.L. Hedrick. 6/88. (Updated by RFC 1388, RFC 1723) (Historic)

1083   IAB official protocol standards. Defense Advanced Research Projects Agency, Internet Activities Board. 12/88. (Obsoleted by RFC 1100, RFC 1250, RFC 2200, RFC 2300, STD 0001, RFC 2400) (Historic)

1088   Standard for the transmission of IP datagrams over NetBIOS networks. L.J. McLaughlin. 2/89. (Standard)

1094   NFS: Network File System Protocol specification. Sun Microsystems. 3/89. (Also RFC 1813) (Informational)

1099   Request for Comments Summary: RFC Numbers 1000–1099. J. Reynolds. 12/91. (Informational)

1100   IAB official protocol standards. Defense Advanced Research Projects Agency, Internet Activities Board. 4/89. (Obsoletes RFC 1083) (Obsoleted by RFC 1130, RFC 1250, RFC 2200, RFC 2300, STD 0001, RFC 2400) (Historic)

1112   Host extensions for IP multicasting. S.E. Deering. 8/89. (Obsoletes RFC 0988, RFC 1054) (Updated by RFC 2236) (Standard)

1119   Network Time Protocol, Version 2 specification and implementation. D.L. Mills. 9/89. (Obsoletes RFC 0958, RFC 1059) (Obsoleted by RFC 1305) (Standard)

1122   Requirements for Internet hosts: Communication layers. R.T. Braden. 10/89. (Standard)

1123   Requirements for Internet hosts: Application and support. R.T. Braden. 10/89. (Updates RFC 0822) (Updated by RFC 2181) (Standard)

1132   Standard for the transmission of 802.2 packets over IPX networks. L.J. McLaughlin. 11/89. (Standard)

1137   Mapping between Full RFC 822 and RFC 822 with Restricted Encoding. S. Kille. 12/89. (Updates RFC 0976) (Historic)

1140   IAB official protocol standards. Defense Advanced Research Projects Agency, Internet Activities Board. 5/90. (Obsoletes RFC 1130) (Obsoleted by RFC 1200, RFC 1250, RFC 2200, RFC 2300, STD 0001, RFC 2400) (Historic)

1155   Structure and identification of management information for TCP/IP-based internets. M.T. Rose, K. McCloghrie. 5/90. (Obsoletes RFC 1065) (Also STD 0016) (Standard)

1157   Simple Network Management Protocol (SNMP). J.D. Case, M. Fedor, M.L. Schoffstall, C. Davin. 5/90. (Obsoletes RFC 1098) (Standard)

1158   Management Information Base for network management of TCP/IP-based internets: MIB-II. M.T. Rose. 5/90. (Obsoleted by RFC 1213, STD 0017) (Draft standard)

1163   Border Gateway Protocol (BGP). K. Lougheed, Y. Rekhter. 6/90. (Obsoletes RFC 1105) (Obsoleted by RFC 1267) (Historic)

1164   Application of the Border Gateway Protocol in the Internet. J.C. Honig, D. Katz, M. Mathis, Y. Rekhter, J.Y. Yu. 6/90. (Obsoleted by RFC 1268) (Historic)

1171   Point-to-Point Protocol for the transmission of multi-protocol datagrams over Point-to-Point links. D. Perkins. 7/90. (Obsoletes RFC 1134) (Obsoleted by RFC 1331) (Draft standard)

1184   Telnet Linemode Option. D.A. Borman. 10/90. (Obsoletes RFC 1116) (Draft standard)

1188   Proposed standard for the transmission of IP datagrams over FDDI networks. D. Katz. 10/90. (Obsoletes RFC 1103) (Draft standard)

1189   Common Management Information Services and Protocols for the Internet (CMOT and CMIP). U.S. Warrier, L. Besaw, L. LaBarre, B.D. Handspicker. 10/90. (Obsoletes RFC 1095) (Historic)

1191   Path MTU discovery. J.C. Mogul, S.E. Deering. 11/90. (Obsoletes RFC 1063) (Draft standard)

1194   Finger User Information Protocol. D.P. Zimmerman. 11/90. (Obsoletes RFC 0742) (Obsoleted by RFC 1288, RFC 1196) (Draft standard)

1200   IAB official protocol standards. Defense Advanced Research Projects Agency, Internet Activities Board. 4/91. (Obsoletes RFC 1140) (Obsoleted by RFC 1250, RFC 2200, RFC 2300, STD 0001, RFC 2400) (Historic)

1201   Transmitting IP traffic over ARCNET networks. D. Provan. 2/91. (Obsoletes RFC 1051) (Standard)

1203   Interactive Mail Access Protocol, Version 3. J. Rice. 2/91. (Obsoletes RFC 1064) (Historic)

1209   Transmission of IP datagrams over the SMDS Service. D.M. Piscitello, J. Lawrence. 3/91. (Standard)

1212   Concise MIB definitions. M.T. Rose, K. McCloghrie. 3/91. (Standard)

1213   Management Information Base for network management of TCP/IP-based internets: MIB-II. K. McCloghrie, M.T. Rose. 3/91. (Obsoletes RFC 1158) (Updated by RFC 2011, RFC 2012, RFC 2013) (Standard)

1214   OSI internet management: Management Information Base. L. LaBarre. 4/91. (Historic)

1230   IEEE 802.4 token bus MIB. K. McCloghrie, R. Fox. 5/91. (Updated by RFC 1239) (Historic)

1231   IEEE 802.5 token ring MIB. K. McCloghrie, R. Fox, E. Decker. 5/91. (Obsoleted by RFC 1743, RFC 1748) (Updated by RFC 1239) (Proposed standard)

1239   Reassignment of experimental MIBs to standard MIBs. J.K. Reynolds. 6/91. (Updates RFC 1229, RFC 1230, RFC 1231, RFC 1232, RFC 1233) (Proposed standard)

1240   OSI connectionless transport services on top of UDP, Version 1. C. Shue, W. Haggerty, K. Dobbins. 6/91. (Proposed standard)

1243   AppleTalk Management Information Base. S. Waldbusser. 7/91. (Obsoleted by RFC 1742) (Proposed standard)

1247   OSPF Version 2. J. Moy. 7/91. (Obsoletes RFC 1131) (Obsoleted by RFC 1583) (Also RFC 1246, RFC 1245) (Draft standard)

1253   OSPF Version 2 Management Information Base. F. Baker, R. Coltun. 8/91. (Obsoletes RFC 1252) (Obsoleted by RFC 1850) (Also RFC 1247, RFC 1245, RFC 1246) (Proposed standard)

1267   Border Gateway Protocol, Version 3 (BGP-3). K. Lougheed, Y. Rekhter. 10/91. (Obsoletes RFC 1163) (Historic)

1268   Application of the Border Gateway Protocol in the Internet. Y. Rekhter, P. Gross. 10/91. (Obsoletes RFC 1164) (Obsoleted by RFC 1655) (Historic)

1280   IAB OFFICIAL PROTOCOL STANDARDS. J. Postel. 3/92. (Obsoleted by RFC 2200, RFC 2300, STD 0001, RFC 2400) (Historic)

1288   The Finger User Information Protocol. D. Zimmerman. 12/91. (Obsoletes RFC 1196, RFC 1194, RFC 0742) (Draft standard)

1293   Inverse Address Resolution Protocol. T. Bradley, C. Brown. 1/92. (Obsoleted by RFC 2390) (Proposed standard)

1294   Multiprotocol interconnect over frame relay. T. Bradley, C. Brown, A. Malis. 1/92. (Obsoleted by RFC 1490, RFC 2427, STD 0055) (Proposed standard)

1305   Network Time Protocol (Version 3) Specification, Implementation. David L. Mills. 3/92. (Obsoletes RFC 0958, RFC 1059, RFC 1119) (Draft standard)

1314   A file format for the exchange of images in the Internet. A. Katz, D. Cohen. 4/92. (Proposed standard)

1315   Management Information Base for frame relay DTEs. C. Brown, F. Baker, C. Carvalho. 4/92. (Obsoleted by RFC 2115) (Proposed standard)

1323   TCP Extensions for high performance. V. Jacobson, R. Braden, D. Borman. 5/92. (Obsoletes RFC 1072, RFC 1185) (Proposed standard)

1334   PPP Authentication Protocols. B. Lloyd, W. Simpson. 10/92. (Obsoleted by RFC 1994) (Proposed standard)

1340   Assigned numbers. J. Reynolds, J. Postel. 7/92. (Obsoletes RFC 1060) (Obsoleted by RFC 1700) (Historic)

1341   MIME (Multipurpose Internet Mail Extensions): Mechanisms for specifying and describing the format of Internet message bodies. N. Borenstein, N. Freed. 6/92. (Obsoleted by RFC 1521) (Proposed standard)

1342   Representation of non-ASCII text in Internet message headers. K. Moore. 6/92. (Obsoleted by RFC 1522) (Informational)

1350   TFTP Protocol, Revision 2. K. Sollins. 7/92. (Obsoletes RFC 0784) (Updated by RFC 1782, RFC 1783, RFC 1784, RFC 1785, RFC 2347, RFC 2348, RFC 2349) (Also STD 0033) (Standard)

1352   SNMP security protocols. J. Galvin, K. McCloghrie, J. Davin. 7/92. (Proposed standard)

1356   Multiprotocol interconnect on X.25 and ISDN in packet mode. A. Malis, D. Robinson, R. Ullmann. 8/92. (Obsoletes RFC 0877) (Draft standard)

1360   IAB official protocol standards. J. Postel. 9/92. (Obsoleted by RFC 1410, RFC 2200, RFC 2300, STD 0001, RFC 2400) (Also RFC 1280) (Historic)

1374   IP and ARP on HIPPI. J. Renwick, A. Nicholson. 10/92. (Proposed standard)

1377   The PPP OSI Network Layer Control Protocol (OSINLCP). D. Katz. 11/92. (Proposed standard)

1378   PPP AppleTalk Control Protocol (ATCP). B. Parker. 11/92. (Proposed standard)

1381   SNMP MIB Extension for X.25 LAPB. D. Throop, F. Baker. 11/92. (Proposed standard)

1389   RIP Version 2 MIB extensions. G. Malkin, F. Baker. 1/93. (Obsoleted by RFC 1724) (Proposed standard)

1390   Transmission of IP and ARP over FDDI networks. D. Katz. 1/93. (Standard)

1398   Definitions of managed objects for the Ethernet-like interface types. F. Kastenholz. 1/93. (Obsoletes RFC 1284) (Obsoleted by RFC 1643, STD 0050, RFC 1623) (Draft standard)

1408   Telnet environment option. D. Borman, Editor. 1/93. (Updated by RFC 1571) (Historic)

1410   IAB official protocol standards. J. Postel, Editor. 3/93. (Obsoletes RFC 1360) (Obsoleted by RFC 1500, RFC 2200, RFC 2300, STD 0001, RFC 2400) (Historic)

1413   Identification Protocol. M. St. Johns. 1/93. (Obsoletes RFC 931) (Proposed standard)

1418   SNMP over OSI. M. Rose. 3/93. (Obsoletes RFC 1161, RFC 1283) (Proposed standard)

1419   NMP over AppleTalk. G. Minshall, M. Ritter. 3/93. (Proposed standard)

1444   Conformance statements for version 2 of the Simple Network Management Protocol (SNMPv2). J. Case, K. McCloghrie, M. Rose, S. Waldbusser. 4/93. (Obsoleted by RFC 1904) (Proposed standard)

1459   Internet Relay Chat Protocol. J. Oikarinen, D. Reed. 5/93. (Experimental)

1460   Post Office Protocol, Version 3. M. Rose. 6/93. (Obsoletes RFC 1225) (Obsoleted by RFC 1725) (Draft standard)

1461   SNMP MIB extension for Multiprotocol Interconnect over X.25. D. Throop. 5/93. (Proposed standard)

1469   IP Multicast over token ring local area networks. T. Pusateri. 6/93. (Proposed standard)

1490   Multiprotocol interconnect over frame relay. T. Bradley, C. Brown, A. Malis. 7/93. (Obsoletes RFC 1294) (Obsoleted by RFC 2427, STD 0055) (Draft standard)

1495   Mapping between X.400 and RFC 822 Message Bodies. H. Alvestrand, S. Kille, R. Miles, M. Rose, S. Thompson. 8/93. (Obsoletes RFC 987, RFC 1026, RFC 1138, RFC 1148, RFC 1327) (Obsoleted by RFC 2156) (Proposed standard)

1497   BOOTP Vendor Information Extensions. J. Reynolds. 8/93. (Obsoletes RFC 1395, RFC 1084, RFC 1048) (Obsoleted by RFC 1533) (Updates RFC 951, RFC 0951) (Draft standard)

1499   Request For Comments summary notes: 1400-1499. J. Elliott. 1/97. (Informational)

1500   Internet official protocol standards. J. Postel. 8/93. (Obsoletes RFC 1410) (Obsoleted by RFC 1540, RFC 2200, RFC 2300, STD 0001, RFC 2400) (Historic)

1502   X.400 Use of Extended Character Sets. H. Alvestrand. 8/93. (Proposed standard)

1507   DASS: Distributed Authentication Security Service. C. Kaufman. 9/93. (Proposed standard)

1508   Generic Security Service Application Programming Interface. J. Linn. 9/93. (Obsoleted by RFC 2078) (Proposed standard)

1512   FDDI Management Information Base. J. Case, A. Rijsinghani. 9/93. (Updates RFC 1285) (Proposed standard)

1513   Token ring extensions to the remote network monitoring MIB. S. Waldbusser. 9/93. (Updates 1271) (Proposed standard)

1515   Definitions of managed objects for IEEE 802.3 medium attachment units (MAUs). D. McMaster, K. McCloghrie, S. Roberts. 9/93. (Proposed standard)

1516   Definitions of managed objects for IEEE 802.3 repeater devices. D. McMaster, K. McCloghrie. 9/93. (Obsoletes RFC 1368) (Obsoleted by RFC 2108) (Draft standard)

1521   MIME (Multipurpose Internet Mail Extensions) Part One: Mechanisms for Specifying and Describing the Format of Internet Message Bodies. N. Borenstein, N. Freed. 9/93. (Obsoletes RFC 1341) (Obsoleted by RFC 2045, RFC 2046, RFC 2047, RFC 2048, RFC 2049, BCP0013) (Updated by RFC 1590) (Draft standard)

1522   MIME (Multipurpose Internet Mail Extensions) Part Two: message header extensions for non-ASCII text. K. Moore. 9/93. (Obsoletes RFC 1342) (Obsoleted by RFC 2045, RFC 2046, RFC 2047, RFC 2048, RFC 2049, BCP0013) (Draft standard)

1523   The text/enriched MIME content-type. N. Borenstein. 9/93. (Obsoleted by RFC 1563, RFC 1896) (Informational)

1524   A user agent configuration mechanism for multimedia mail format Information. N. Borenstein. 9/93. (Informational)

1533   DHCP options and BOOTP vendor extensions. S. Alexander, R. Droms. 10/93. (Obsoletes RFC 1497, RFC 1395, RFC 1084, RFC 1048) (Obsoleted by RFC 2132) (Proposed standard)

1534   Interoperation between DHCP and BOOTP. R. Droms. 10/93. (Draft standard)

1540   Internet official protocol standards. J. Postel. 10/93. (Obsoletes RFC 1500) (Obsoleted by RFC 1600, RFC 2200, RFC 2300, STD 0001, RFC 2400) (Historic)

1541   Dynamic Host Configuration Protocol. R. Droms. 10/93. (Obsoletes RFC 1531) (Obsoleted by RFC 2131) (Proposed standard)

1542   Clarifications and extensions for the bootstrap protocol. W. Wimer. 10/93. (Obsoletes RFC 1532) (Updates RFC 0951) (Draft standard)

1548   Point-to-Point Protocol (PPP). W. Simpson. 12/93. (Obsoletes RFC 1331) (Obsoleted by RFC 1661) (Updated by RFC 1570) (Draft standard)

1552   PPP Internetworking Packet Exchange Control Protocol (IPXCP). W. Simpson. 12/93. (Proposed standard)

1559   DECnet Phase IV MIB extensions. J. Saperia. 12/93. (Obsoletes RFC 1289) (Draft standard)

1575   An echo function for CLNP (ISO 8473). S. Hares, C. Wittbrodt. 2/94. (Obsoletes RFC 1139) (Draft standard)

1577   Classical IP and ARP over ATM. M. Laubach. 1/94. (Obsoleted by RFC 2225) (Proposed standard)

1582   Extensions to RIP to support demand circuits. G. Meyer. 2/94. (Proposed standard)

1584   Multicast extensions to OSPF. J. Moy. 3/94. (Proposed standard)

1598   PPP in X.25. W. Simpson. 3/94. (Proposed standard)

1610   Internet official protocol standards. J. Postel. 7/94. (Obsoletes RFC 1600) (Obsoleted by RFC 1720, RFC 2200, RFC 2300, STD 0001, RFC 2400) (Historic)

1618   PPP over ISDN. W. Simpson. 5/94. (Proposed standard)

1619   PPP over SONET/SDH. W. Simpson. 5/94. (Proposed standard)

1623   Definitions of Managed Objects for the Ethernet-like Interface Types. F. Kastenholz. 5/94. (Obsoletes RFC 1398) (Obsoleted by RFC 1643, STD 0050) (Also STD 0050) (Standard)

1629   Guidelines for OSI NSAP allocation in the Internet. R. Colella, R. Callon, E. Gardner, Y. Rekhter. 5/94. (Obsoletes RFC 1237) (Draft standard)

1638   PPP Bridging Control Protocol (BCP). F. Baker, R. Bowen. 6/94. (Obsoletes RFC 1220) (Proposed standard)

1643   Definitions of managed objects for the Ethernet-like interface types. F. Kastenholz. 7/94. (Obsoletes RFC 1623, RFC 1398) (Also STD 0050) (Standard)

1651   SMTP service extensions. Klensin, N. Freed, M. Rose, E. Stefferud, D. Crocker. 7/94. (Obsoletes RFC 1425) (Obsoleted by RFC 1869, STD 0010) (Draft standard)

1652   SMTP service extension for eight-bit-MIME transport. J. Klensin, N. Freed, M. Rose, E. Stefferud, D. Crocker. 7/94. (Obsoletes RFC 1426) (Draft standard)

1653   SMTP service extension for message size declaration. J. Klensin, N. Freed, K. Moore. 7/94. (Obsoletes RFC 1427) (Obsoleted by RFC 1870, STD 0011) (Also STD 0011) (Draft standard)

1661   Point-to-Point Protocol (PPP). W. Simpson, Editor. 7/94. (Obsoletes RFC 1548) (Updated by RFC 2153) (Also STD 0051) (Standard)

1694   Definitions of Managed Objects for SMDS Interfaces using SMIv2. T. Brown, K. Tesink. 8/94. (Obsoletes RFC 1304) (Draft standard)

1700   Assigned numbers. J. Reynolds, J. Postel. 10/94. (Obsoletes RFC 1340) (Also STD 0002) (Standard)

1720   Internet official protocol standards. J. Postel. 11/94. (Obsoletes RFC 1610) (Obsoleted by RFC 1780, STD 0001, RFC 1880, RFC 1920, RFC 2200, RFC 2300, RFC 2400) (Also STD 0001) (Historic)

1722   RIP, Version 2: Protocol applicability statement. G. Malkin. 11/94. (Draft standard)

1723   RIP, Version 2: Carrying additional information. G. Malkin. 11/94. (Obsoletes RFC 1388) (Obsoleted by RFC 2453) (Updates RFC 1058) (Updated by RFC 2453, STD 0056) (Draft standard)

1724   RIP, Version 2: MIB extensions. G. Malkin, F. Baker. 11/94. (Obsoletes RFC 1389) (Draft standard)

1725   Post Office Protocol, Version 3. J. Myers, M. Rose. 11/94. (Obsoletes RFC 1460) (Obsoleted by RFC 1939, STD 0053) (Draft standard)

1730   Internet Message Access Protocol, Version 4. M. Crispin. 12/94. (Obsoleted by RFC 2060, RFC 2061) (Proposed standard)

1738   Uniform resource locators (URL). T. Berners-Lee, L. Masinter, M. McCahill. 12/94. (Updated by RFC 1808, RFC 2368) (Proposed standard)

1740   MIME encapsulation of Macintosh files: MacMIME. P. Faltstrom, D. Crocker, E. Fair. 12/94. (Proposed standard)

1748   IEEE 802.5 MIB using SMIv2. K. McCloghrie, E. Decker. 12/94. (Obsoletes RFC 1743, RFC 1231) (Updated by RFC 1749) (Draft standard)

1757   Remote network monitoring management information base. S. Waldbusser. 2/95. (Obsoletes RFC 1271) (Draft standard)

1771   Border Gateway Protocol, Version 4 (BGP-4). Y. Rekhter, T. Li. 3/95. (Obsoletes RFC 1654) (Draft standard)

1772   Application of the Border Gateway Protocol in the Internet. Y. Rekhter, P. Gross. 3/95. (Obsoletes RFC 1655) (Draft standard)

1777   Lightweight Directory Access Protocol. W. Yeong, T. Howes, S. Kille. 3/95. (Obsoletes RFC 1487) (Draft standard)

1778   String representation of standard attribute syntaxes. T. Howes, S. Kille, W. Yeong, C. Robbins. 3/95. (Obsoletes RFC 1488) (Draft standard)

1779   A String Representation of Distinguished Names. S. Kille. 3/95. (Obsoletes RFC 1485) (Draft standard)

1800   Internet official protocol standards. J. Postel. 7/95. (Obsoletes RFC 1780) (Obsoleted by RFC 1880, STD 0001, RFC 1920, RFC 2200, RFC 2300, RFC 2400) (Also STD 0001) (Historic)

1808   Relative uniform resource locators. R. Fielding. 6/95. (Updates RFC 1738) (Updated by RFC 2368) (Proposed standard)

1812   Requirements for IP Version 4 routers. F. Baker. 6/95. (Obsoletes RFC 1716, RFC 1009) (Proposed standard)

1831   RPC: Remote Procedure Call protocol specification, Version 2. R. Srinivasan. 8/95. (Proposed standard)

1832   XDR: External Data Representation Standard. R. Srinivasan. 8/95. (Draft standard)

1850   OSPF Version 2 Management Information Base. F. Baker, R. Coltun. 11/95. (Obsoletes RFC 1253) (Draft standard)

1864   The content-MD5 header field. J. Myers, M. Rose. 10/95. (Obsoletes RFC 1544) (Draft standard)

1866   Hypertext Markup Language: 2.0. T. Berners-Lee, D. Connolly. 11/95. (Proposed standard)

1869   SMTP service extensions. J. Klensin, N. Freed, M. Rose, E. Stefferud, D. Crocker. 11/95. (Obsoletes RFC 1651) (Also STD 0010) (Standard)

1870   SMTP service extension for message size declaration. J. Klensin, N. Freed, K. Moore. 11/95. (Obsoletes RFC 1653) (Also STD 0010) (Standard)

1886   DNS Extensions to support IP version 6. S. Thomson, C. Huitema. 12/95. (Proposed standard)

1889   RTP: A transport protocol for realtime applications. Audio-Video Transport Working Group, H. Schulzrinne, S. Casner, R. Frederick, V. Jacobson. 1/96. (Proposed standard)

1890   RTP profile for audio and video conferences with minimal control. Audio-Video Transport Working Group, H. Schulzrinne. 1/96. (Proposed standard)

1902 Structure of management information for Version 2 of the Simple Network Management Protocol (SNMPv2). SNMPv2 Working Group, J. Case, K. McCloghrie, M. Rose, S. Waldbusser. 1/96. (Obsoletes RFC 1442) (Draft standard)

1903 Textual conventions for Version 2 of the Simple Network Management Protocol (SNMPv2). SNMPv2 Working Group, J. Case, K. McCloghrie, M. Rose, S. Waldbusser. 1/96. (Obsoletes RFC 1443) (Draft standard)

1904 Conformance statements for Version 2 of the Simple Network Management Protocol (SNMPv2). SNMPv2 Working Group, J. Case, K. McCloghrie, M. Rose, S. Waldbusser. 1/96. (Obsoletes RFC 1444) (Draft standard)

1905 Protocol operations for Version 2 of the Simple Network Management Protocol (SNMPv2). SNMPv2 Working Group, J. Case, K. McCloghrie, M. Rose, S. Waldbusser. 1/96. (Obsoletes RFC 1448) (Draft standard)

1906 Transport mappings for Version 2 of the Simple Network Management Protocol (SNMPv2). SNMPv2 Working Group, J. Case, K. McCloghrie, M. Rose, S. Waldbusser. 1/96. (Obsoletes RFC 1449) (Draft standard)

1907 Management information base for Version 2 of the Simple Network Management Protocol (SNMPv2). SNMPv2 Working Group, J. Case, K. McCloghrie, M. Rose, S. Waldbusser. 1/96. (Obsoletes RFC 1450) (Draft standard)

1908 Coexistence between Version 1 and Version 2 of the Internet-standard network management framework. SNMPv2 Working Group, J. Case, K. McCloghrie, M. Rose, S. Waldbusser. 1/96. (Obsoletes RFC 1452) (Draft standard)

1920 Internet Official Protocol Standards. J. Postel. 3/96. (Obsoletes RFC 1780, RFC 1720, RFC 1800, RFC 1880) (Obsoleted by RFC 2000, RFC 2200, RFC 2300, RFC 2109, STD 0001, RFC 2400) (Also STD 0001) (Historic)

1932 IP over ATM: A Framework Document. R. Cole, D. Shur,, C. Villamizar. 4/96. (Informational)

1939 Post Office Protocol, Version 3. J. Myers, M. Rose. 5/96. (Obsoletes RFC 1725) (Updated by RFC 1957, RFC 2449) (Also STD 0053) (Standard)

1942 HTML tables. D. Raggett. 5/96. (Experimental)

1945 Hypertext Transfer Protocol: HTTP/1.0. T. Berners-Lee, R. Fielding, H. Frystyk. 5/96. (Informational)

1962 PPP Compression Control Protocol (CCP). D. Rand. 6/96. (Updated by RFC 2153) (Proposed standard)

1968 PPP Encryption Control Protocol (ECP). G. Meyer. 6/96. (Proposed standard)

1973 PPP in frame relay. W. Simpson. 6/96. (Proposed standard)

1980 A proposed extension to HTML: Client-side image maps. J. Seidman. 8/96. (Informational)

1989 PPP link quality monitoring. W. Simpson. 8/96. (Obsoletes RFC 1333) (Draft standard)

1990   PPP Multilink Protocol (MP). K. Sklower, B. Lloyd, G. McGregor, D. Carr, T. Coradetti. 8/96. (Obsoletes RFC 1717) (Draft standard)

1994   PPP Challenge Handshake Authentication Protocol (CHAP). W. Simpson. 8/96. (Obsoletes RFC 1334) (Draft standard)

2000   Internet official protocol standards. J. Postel, Editor. 2/97. (Obsoletes RFC 1920, RFC 1880, RFC 1800, RFC 1780, RFC 1720, RFC 1610, RFC 1600, RFC 1540, RFC 1500, RFC 1410, RFC 1360, RFC 1280, RFC 1250, RFC 1200, RFC 1140, RFC 1130, RFC 1100, RFC 1083) (Obsoleted by RFC 2200, STD 0001, RFC 2300, RFC 2400) (Also STD 0001) (Historic)

2015   MIME security with Pretty Good Privacy (PGP). M. Elkins. 10/96. (Proposed standard)

2017   Definition of the URL MIME external-body access-type. N. Freed, K. Moore, A. Cargille. 10/96. (Proposed standard)

2020   IEEE 802.12 interface MIB. J. Flick. 10/96. (Proposed standard)

2023   IP Version 6 over PPP. D. Haskin, E. Allen. 10/96. (Proposed standard)

2026   The Internet Standards Process, Revision 3. S. Bradner. 10/96. (Obsoletes RFC 1602) (Also BCP0009) (Best current practice)

2032   RTP Payload Format for H.261 Video Streams. T. Turletti, C. Huitema. 10/96. (Proposed standard)

2038   RTP payload format for MPEG1/MPEG2 video. D. Hoffman, G. Fernando, V. Goyal. 10/96. (Obsoleted by RFC 2250) (Proposed standard)

2043   PPP SNA Control Protocol (SNACP). A. Fuqua. 10/96. (Proposed standard)

2045   Multipurpose Internet mail extensions (MIME) Part One: Format of Internet message bodies. N. Freed, N. Borenstein. 11/96. (Obsoletes RFC 1521, RFC 1522, RFC 1590) (Updated by RFC 2184, RFC 2231) (Draft standard)

2046   Multipurpose Internet mail extensions (MIME) Part Two: Media types. N. Freed, N. Borenstein. 11/96. (Obsoletes RFC 1521, RFC 1522, RFC 1590) (Draft standard)

2047   Multipurpose Internet mail extensions (MIME) Part Three: Message header extensions for non-ASCII text. K. Moore. 11/96. (Obsoletes RFC 1521, RFC 1522, RFC 1590) (Updated by RFC 2184, RFC 2231) (Draft standard)

2048   Multipurpose Internet mail extensions (MIME) Part Four: Registration procedures. N. Freed, J. Klensin, J. Postel. 11/96. (Obsoletes RFC 1521, RFC 1522, RFC 1590) (Also BCP0013) (Best current practice)

2049   Multipurpose Internet Mail Extensions (MIME) Part Five: Conformance criteria and examples. N. Freed, N. Borenstein. 11/96. (Obsoletes RFC 1521, RFC 1522, RFC 1590) (Draft standard)

2050   Internet registry IP allocation guidelines. K. Hubbard, M. Kosters, D. Conrad, D. Karrenberg, J. Postel. 11/96. (Also BCP0012) (Best current practice)

2060   Internet Message Access Protocol, Version 4, Revision 1. M. Crispin. 12/96. (Obsoletes RFC 1730) (Proposed standard)

2062 Internet Message Access Protocol: Obsolete syntax. M. Crispin. 12/96. (Proposed standard)

2065 Domain name system security extensions. D. Eastlake 3rd, C. Kaufman. 1/97. (Updates RFC 1034, RFC 1035) (Proposed standard)

2067 IP over HIPPI. J. Renwick. 1/97. (Draft standard)

2068 Hypertext Transfer Protocol: HTTP/1.1. R. Fielding, J. Gettys, J. Mogul, H. Frystyk, T. Berners-Lee. 1/97. (Proposed standard)

2070 Internationalization of the Hypertext Markup Language. F. Yergeau, G. Nicol, G. Adams, M. Duerst. 1/97. (Proposed standard)

2077 Model primary content type for multipurpose Internet mail extensions. S. Nelson, C. Parks, Mitra. 1/97. (Proposed standard)

2080 RIPng for IPv6. G. Malkin, R. Minnear. 1/97. (Proposed standard)

2083 PNG (Portable Network Graphics) specification. T. Boutell. 1/97. (Informational)

2086 IMAP4 ACL extension. J. Myers. 1/97. (Proposed standard)

2087 IMAP4 QUOTA extension. J. Myers. 1/97. (Proposed standard)

2090 TFTP Multicast Option. A. Emberson. 2/97. (Experimental)

2096 IP Forwarding Table MIB. F. Baker. 1/97. (Obsoletes RFC 1354) (Proposed standard)

2097 The PPP NetBIOS Frames Control Protocol (NBFCP). G. Pall. 1/97. (Proposed standard)

2099 Request for Comments summary RFC Numbers 2000–2099. J. Elliott. 3/97. (Informational)

2100 The naming of hosts. J. Ashworth. 4/97. (Informational)

2110 MIME email encapsulation of aggregate documents, such as HTML (MHTML). J. Palme, A. Hopmann. 3/97. (Proposed standard)

2115 Management information base for frame relay DTEs using SMIv2. C. Brown, F. Baker. 9/97. (Obsoletes RFC 1315) (Draft standard)

2118 Microsoft point-to-point compression (MPPC) Protocol. G. Pall. 3/97. (Informational)

2119 Keywords for use in RFCs to indicate requirement levels. S. Bradner. 3/97. (Also BCP0014) (Best current practice)

2131 Dynamic Host Configuration Protocol. R. Droms. 3/97. (Obsoletes RFC 1541) (Draft standard)

2132 DHCP options and BOOTP vendor extensions. S. Alexander, R. Droms. 3/97. (Obsoletes RFC 1533) (Draft standard)

2141 URN syntax. R. Moats. 5/97. (Proposed standard)

2156 Mime Internet X.400 Enhanced Relay (MIXER): Mapping between X.400 and RFC 822/ MIME. S. Kille. 1/98. (Obsoletes RFC 0987, RFC 1026, RFC 1138, RFC 1148, RFC 1327, RFC 1495) (Updates RFC 0822) (Proposed standard)

2157 Mapping between X.400 and RFC 822/MIME message bodies. H. Alvestrand. 1/98. (Proposed standard)

2160 Carrying PostScript in X.400 and MIME. H. Alvestrand. 1/98. (Proposed standard)

2181 Clarifications to the DNS specification. R. Elz, R. Bush. 7/97. (Updates RFC 1034, RFC 1035, RFC 1123) (Proposed standard)

2190 RTP payload format for H.263 Video Streams. C. Zhu. 9/97. (Proposed standard)

2192 IMAP URL scheme. C. Newman. 9/97. (Proposed standard)

2193 IMAP4 mailbox referrals. M. Gahrns. 9/97. (Proposed standard)

2196 Site security handbook. B. Fraser. 9/97. (Obsoletes RFC 1244) (Also FYI0008) (Informational)

2197 SMTP service extension for command pipelining. N. Freed. 9/97. (Obsoletes RFC 1854) (Draft standard)

2198 RTP payload for redundant audio data. C. Perkins, I. Kouvelas, O. Hodson, V. Hardman, M. Handley, J.C. Bolot, A. Vega-Garcia, S. Fosse-Parisis. 9/97. (Proposed standard)

2199 Request for Comments Summary notes: 2100–2199. A. Ramos. 1/98. (Informational)

2200 Internet Official Protocol Standards. J. Postel. 6/97. (Obsoletes RFC 2000, RFC 1920, RFC 1880, RFC 1800, RFC 1780, RFC 1720, RFC 1610, RFC 1600, RFC 1540, RFC 1500, RFC 1410, RFC 1360, RFC 1280, RFC 1250, RFC 1200, RFC 1140, RFC 1130, RFC 1100, RFC 1083) (Obsoleted by RFC 2300, RFC 2400, STD 0001) (Also STD 0001) (Standard)

2205 Resource ReSerVation Protocol (RSVP), Version 1 Functional Specification. R. Braden, Ed., L. Zhang, S. Berson, S. Herzog, S. Jamin. 9/97. (Proposed standard)

2209 Resource ReSerVation Protocol (RSVP), Version 1: Message processing rules. R. Braden, L. Zhang. 9/97. (Informational)

2212 Specification of guaranteed quality of service. S. Shenker, C. Partridge, R. Guerin. 9/97. (Proposed standard)

2215 General characterization parameters for integrated service network elements. S. Shenker, J. Wroclawski. 9/97. (Proposed standard)

2219 Use of DNS aliases for network services. M. Hamilton, R. Wright. 10/97. (Also BCP0017) (Best current practice)

2225 Classical IP and ARP over ATM. M. Laubach, J. Halpern. 4/98. (Obsoletes RFC 1626, RFC 1577) (Proposed standard)

2228 FTP security extensions. M. Horowitz, S. Lunt. 10/97. (Updates RFC 0959) (Proposed standard)

2231 MIME parameter value and encoded word extensions: Character sets, languages, and continuations. N. Freed, K. Moore. 11/97. (Obsoletes RFC 2184) (Updates RFC 2045, RFC 2047 RFC 2183) (Proposed standard)

2239   Definitions of managed objects for IEEE 802.3 medium attachment units (MAUs) using SMIv2. K. de Graaf, D. Romascanu, D. McMaster, K. McCloghrie, S. Roberts. 11/97. (Proposed standard)

2250   RTP payload format for MPEG1/MPEG2 video. D. Hoffman, G. Fernando, V. Goyal, M. Civanlar. 1/98. (Obsoletes RFC 2038) (Proposed standard)

2251   Lightweight Directory Access Protocol, Version 3. M. Wahl, T. Howes, S. Kille. 12/97. (Proposed standard)

2255   LDAP URL format. T. Howes, M. Smith. 12/97. (Proposed standard)

2266   Definitions of managed objects for IEEE 802.12 repeater devices. J. Flick. 1/98. (Proposed standard)

2272   Message processing and dispatching for Simple Network Management Protocol (SNMP). J. Case, D. Harrington, R. Presuhn, B. Wijnen. 1/98. (Obsoletes RFC 2262) (Proposed standard)

2273   SNMPv3 applications. D. Levi, P. Meyer, B. Stewart. 1/98. (Obsoletes RFC 2263) (Proposed standard)

2275   View-based Access Control Model (VACM) for the Simple Network Management Protocol (SNMP). B. Wijnen, R. Presuhn, K. McCloghrie. 1/98. (Obsoletes RFC 2265) (Proposed standard)

2277   IETF policy on character sets and languages. H. Alvestrand. 1/98. (Also BCP0018) (Best current practice)

2278   IANA charset registration procedures. N. Freed, J. Postel. 1/98. (Also BCP0019) (Best current practice)

2279   UTF-8, a transformation format of ISO 10646. F. Yergeau. 1/98. (Obsoletes RFC 2044) (Proposed standard)

2283   Multiprotocol extensions for BGP-4. T. Bates, R. Chandra, D. Katz, Y. Rekhter. 2/98. (Proposed standard)

2284   PPP Extensible Authentication Protocol (EAP). L. Blunk, J. Vollbrecht. 3/98. (Proposed standard)

2289   A one-time password system. N. Haller, C. Metz, P. Nesser, M. Straw. 2/98. (Obsoletes RFC 1938) (Draft standard)

2300   Internet Official Protocol Standards. J. Postel. 5/98. (Obsoletes RFC 2200, RFC 2000, RFC 1920, RFC 1880, RFC 1800, RFC 1780, RFC 1720, RFC 1610, RFC 1600, RFC 1540, RFC 1500, RFC 1410, RFC 1360, RFC 1280, RFC 1250, RFC 1200, RFC 1140, RFC 1130, RFC 1100, RFC 1083) (Obsoleted by RFC 2400, STD 0001) (Also STD 0001) (STANDARDS TRACK)

2301   File format for Internet fax. L. McIntyre, S. Zilles, R. Buckley, D. Venable, G. Parsons, J. Rafferty. 3/98. (Proposed standard)

2302	Tagged Image File Format (TIFF)—image/TIFF MIME sub-type registration. G. Parsons, J. Rafferty, S. Zilles. 3/98. (Proposed standard)
2303	Minimal PSTN address format in Internet mail. C. Allocchio. 3/98. (Proposed standard)
2304	Minimal fax address format in Internet mail. C. Allocchio. 3/98. (Proposed standard)
2306	Tagged Image File Format (TIFF): F profile for facsimile. G. Parsons, J. Rafferty. 3/98. (Informational)
2308	Negative caching of DNS queries (DNS NCACHE). M. Andrews. 3/98. (Obsoletes RFC 1034) (Updates RFC 1034, RFC 1035) (Proposed standard)
2311	S/MIME, Version 2: Message specification. S. Dusse, P. Hoffman, B. Ramsdell, L. Lundblade, L. Repka. 3/98. (Informational)
2326	Real Time Streaming Protocol (RTSP). H. Schulzrinne, A. Rao, R. Lanphier. 4/98. (Proposed standard)
2328	OSPF Version 2. J. Moy. 4/98. (Obsoletes RFC 2178) (Also STD 0054) (Standard)
2331	ATM signaling support for IP over ATM: UNI Signaling 4.0 Update. M. Maher. 4/98. (Proposed standard)
2332	NBMA Next Hop Resolution Protocol (NHRP). J. Luciani, D. Katz, D. Piscitello, B. Cole, N. Doraswamy. 4/98. (Proposed standard)
2334	Server Cache Synchronization Protocol (SCSP). J. Luciani, G. Armitage, J. Halpern, N. Doraswamy. 4/98. (Proposed standard)
2347	TFTP option extension. G. Malkin, A. Harkin. 5/98. (Obsoletes RFC 1782) (Updates RFC 1350) (Draft standard)
2348	TFTP blocksize option. G. Malkin, A. Harkin. 5/98. (Obsoletes RFC 1783) (Updates RFC 1350) (Draft standard)
2349	TFTP timeout interval and transfer size options. G. Malkin, A. Harkin. 5/98. (Obsoletes RFC 1784) (Updates RFC 1350) (Draft standard)
2357	IETF criteria for evaluating reliable multicast transport and application protocols. A. Mankin, A. Romanow, S. Bradner, V. Paxson. 6/98. (Obsoletes RFC 1650) (Informational)
2358	Definitions of managed objects for Ethernet-like interface types. J. Flick, J. Johnson. 6/98. (Obsoletes RFC 1650) (Proposed standard)
2360	Guide for Internet standards writers. G. Scott. 6/98. (Also BCP0022) (Best current practice)
2361	WAVE and AVI Codec registries. E. Fleischman. 6/98. (Informational)
2368	The mailto URL scheme. P. Hoffman, L. Masinter, J. Zawinski. 7/98. (Updates RFC 1738, RFC 1808) (Proposed standard)

2371   Transaction Internet Protocol, Version 3. J. Lyon, K. Evans, J. Klein. 7/98. (Proposed standard)

2373   IP Version 6 addressing architecture. R. Hinden, S. Deering. 7/98. (Obsoletes RFC 1884) (Proposed standard)

2374   IPv6 aggregatable global unicast address format. R. Hinden, M. O'Dell, S. Deering. 7/98. (Obsoletes RFC 2073) (Proposed standard)

2380   RSVP over ATM implementation requirements. L. Berger. 8/98. (Proposed standard)

2384   POP URL scheme. R. Gellens. 8/98. (Proposed standard)

2387   The MIME multipart/related content-type. E. Levinson. 8/98. (Obsoletes RFC 2112) (Proposed standard)

2388   Returning values from forms: multipart/form-data. L. Masinter. 8/98. (Proposed standard)

2389   Feature negotiation mechanism for File Transfer Protocol. P. Hethmon, R. Elz. 8/98. (Also RFC 0959) (Proposed standard)

2390   Inverse Address Resolution Protocol. T. Bradley, C. Brown, A. Malis. 8/98. (Obsoletes RFC 1293) (Draft standard)

2392   Content-ID and message-ID uniform resource locators. E. Levinson. 8/98. (Obsoletes RFC 2111) (Proposed standard)

2393   IP Payload Compression Protocol (IPComp). A. Shacham, R. Monsour, R. Pereira, M. Thomas. 12/98. (Proposed standard)

2396   Uniform resource identifiers (URI): Generic syntax. T. Berners-Lee, R. Fielding, L. Masinter. 8/98. (Draft standard)

2397   The "data" URL scheme. L. Masinter. 8/98. (Proposed standard)

2400   Internet official protocol standards. J. Postel, J. Reynolds. 9/98. (Obsoletes RFC 2300, RFC 2200, RFC 2000, RFC 1920, RFC 1880, RFC 1800, RFC 1780, RFC 1720, RFC 1610, RFC 1600, RFC 1540, RFC 1500, RFC 1410, RFC 1360, RFC 1280, RFC 1250, RFC 1200, RFC 1140, RFC 1130, RFC 1100, RFC 1083) (Also STD 0001) (Standard)

2401   Security architecture for Internet Protocol. S. Kent, R. Atkinson. 11/98. (Obsoletes RFC 1825) (Proposed standard)

2406   IP Encapsulating Security Payload (ESP). S. Kent, R. Atkinson. 11/98. (Obsoletes RFC 1827) (Proposed standard)

2409   Internet Key Exchange (IKE). D. Harkins, D. Carrel. 11/98. (Proposed standard)

2418   IETF Working Group Guidelines and Procedures. S. Bradner. 9/98. (Obsoletes RFC 1603) (Also BCP0025) (Best current practice)

2419   PPP DES Encryption Protocol, Version 2 (DESE-bis). K. Sklower, G. Meyer. 9/98. (Obsoletes RFC 1969) (Proposed standard)

2420   PPP Triple-DES Encryption Protocol (3DESE). H. Kummert. 9/98. (Proposed standard)

2421   Voice Profile for Internet Mail, Version 2. G. Vaudreuil, G. Parsons. 9/98. (Obsoletes RFC 1911) (Proposed standard)

2422   Toll quality voice: 32-kbit/s ADPCM MIME sub-type registration. G. Vaudreuil, G. Parsons. 9/98. (Obsoletes RFC 1911) (Proposed standard)

2423   VPIM voice message MIME sub-type registration. G. Vaudreuil, G. Parsons. 9/98. (Obsoletes RFC 1911) (Proposed standard)

2424   Content duration MIME header definition. G. Vaudreuil, G. Parsons. 9/98. (Proposed standard)

2425   A MIME content-type for directory information. T. Howes, M. Smith, F. Dawson. 9/98. (Proposed standard)

2427   Multiprotocol interconnect over frame relay. C. Brown, A. Malis. 9/98. (Obsoletes RFC 1490, RFC 1294) (Standard)

2428   FTP extensions for IPv6 and NATs. M. Allman, S. Ostermann, C. Metz. 9/98. (Proposed standard)

2429   RTP payload format for the 1998 version of ITU-T, Rec. H.263 Video (H.263+). C. Bormann, L. Cline, G. Deisher, T. Gardos, C. Maciocco, D. Newell, J. Ott, G. Sullivan, S. Wenger, C. Zhu. 10/98. (Proposed standard)

2434   Guidelines for writing an IANA considerations section in RFCs. T. Narten, H. Alvestrand. 10/98. (Also BCP0026) (Best current practice)

2435   RTP payload format for JPEG-compressed video. L. Berc, W. Fenner, R. Frederick, S. McCanne, P. Stewart. 10/98. (Obsoletes RFC 2035) (Proposed standard)

2440   Open PGP message format. J. Callas, L. Donnerhacke, H. Finney, R. Thayer. 11/98. (Proposed standard)

2444   The one-time-Password SASL mechanism. C. Newman. 10/98. (Updates RFC 2222) (Proposed standard)

2445   Internet calendaring and ccheduling core object specification (iCalendar). F. Dawson, D. Stenerson. 11/98. (Proposed standard)

2449   POP3 extension mechanism. R. Gellens, C. Newman, L. Lundblade. 11/98. (Updates RFC 1939) (Proposed standard)

2452   IP, Version 6 management information base for Transmission Control Protocol. M. Daniele. 12/98. (Proposed standard)

2453   RIP, Version 2. G. Malkin. 11/98. (Obsoletes RFC 1388, RFC 1723) (Updates RFC 1723, RFC 1388) (Also STD 0056) (Standard)

2454   IP Version 6 management information base for User Datagram Protocol. M. Daniele. 12/98. (Proposed standard)

2460   Internet Protocol, Version 6 (IPv6) specification. S. Deering, R. Hinden. 12/98. (Obsoletes RFC 1883) (Draft standard)

2462   IPv6 stateless address autoconfiguration. S. Thomson, T. Narten. 12/98. (Obsoletes RFC 1971) (Draft standard)

2463   Internet Control Message Protocol (ICMPv6) for Internet Protocol, Version 6 (IPv6) Specification. A. Conta, S. Deering. 12/98. (Obsoletes RFC 1885) (Draft standard)

2464   Transmission of IPv6 packets over Ethernet networks. M. Crawford. 12/98. (Obsoletes RFC 1972) (Proposed standard)

2467   Transmission of IPv6 packets over FDDI networks. M. Crawford. 12/98. (Obsoletes RFC 2019) (Proposed standard)

2470   Transmission of IPv6 packets over Token Ring Networks. M. Crawford, T. Narten, S. Thomas. 12/98. (Proposed standard)

2472   IP, Version 6 over PPP. D. Haskin, E. Allen. 12/98. (Obsoletes RFC 2023) (Proposed standard)

2473   Generic packet tunneling in IPv6 Specification. 12/98. (Proposed standard)

Copyright Issues

Ownership

The act of digitizing pictures, sounds, words, and other concrete forms of expression is commonplace. The proliferation of scanners and capture cards makes the acquisition of graphics and audio available to anyone with a computer. Yet multimedia producers must be especially careful about how the assets they digitize are used and distributed. A photograph is the property of the camera operator; each song belongs to its composer; text is owned by the writer; a graphic belongs to the artist; a sound is the property of the person who creates or samples it. Original work in any of these forms may not be copied and resold without express permission from the copyright holder, and it is the responsibility of the person who would digitize and use an asset to locate and secure permission from the owner.

A copyright provides ownership of intellectual property in which the author secures certain exclusive rights to an original work for a limited time. Copyright law is authorized by Article 1, Section 8 of the Constitution. The clause gives Congress the power "to promote science . . . by securing for limited times to authors . . . the exclusive right to their writings." Copyright protects the author's original expression only. It does not extend to ideas or facts presented in a copyrighted work. It does not include previously existing material that an author has incorporated into a new work.

Recognized Copyrights in the United States

Copyright should not be confused with personality rights, such as the right of privacy, which are used to protect the name, voice, or persona of an individual. Things that are created by people are referred to as intellectual property since they are products of the mind. A work must be original to be copyrighted, and this means that it was created by the author. The work need not be different from everything preceding it, but it must embody creativity and it must be the "expression of an author." Only nonutilitarian aspects of a work are protected by copyright. If something is both a work of authorship and a useful article, copyright will not protect the useful aspects. It must exist in a fixed, tangible medium of expression. An idea is not protectable, but the expression of an idea is. In the United States, copyright includes the following rights:

1. *Reproductive Right:* The right to make copies of a work.
2. *Adaptive Right:* The right to produce derivative works based on a copyrighted work.

3. *Distribution Right:* The right to distribute copies of a work. (This includes importation right, the right to prevent unauthorized importation of a work.)
4. *Performance Right:* The right to perform a copyrighted work in public. (The performance right does not ordinarily apply to sound recordings, but a limited performance right prohibiting only digital performances of sound recordings was added in 1995.)
5. *Display Right:* The right to display a copyrighted work in public. (These rights apply to musical, dramatic, literary, choreographic, film, and video programs only. They do not apply to audio recordings or architectural designs.)

In addition to the rights that are part of copyright, United States law also provides for an author's rights in certain works of visual art such as signed and numbered limited edition paintings, photographs, or sculptures. These rights are technically not part of copyright, because they belong only to the author of the work, do not survive the author, and cannot be bought or sold (although they may be waived by contract). The two rights of an author are the rights of attribution and integrity:

Attribution Right: The right of the author to claim authorship of a work, and the right to prevent being incorrectly identified as the author of a work.

Integrity Right: The right to prevent intentional distortion or destruction of a work and to prevent others from attributing a distorted version of the work to the author.

Not all rights last for the same period of time. Typically, a copyright endures for the life of the author plus 70 years; an author's rights, on the other hand, endure only for the life of the author. A series of restrictions on rights are found in Sections 107 through 120 of the copyright law.

Fair Use

The "fair use" doctrine allows the courts to avoid rigid application of copyright statutes when this would inhibit creativity. Fair use originated "for criticism, comment, news reporting, teaching, . . . scholarship, or research . . . the distinction between 'fair use' and infringement may be unclear and not easily defined. There is no specific number of words, lines, or notes that may be taken safely without permission. Acknowledging the source of the copyrighted material does not substitute for obtaining permission."

The 1961 Report of the Register of Copyrights on the General Revision of the United States Copyright Law provides the following examples of fair use:
1. Reproduction by a teacher or student of a part of a work to illustrate a lesson.
2. Summary of an address or article with short quotations in a news report.
3. Quotation of short passages in a scholarly or technical work for illustration or clarification of the author's observations.
4. Quotation of excerpts in a review or criticism for purposes of illustration or comment.
5. Reproduction by a library of a portion of a work to replace a missing or damaged section.
6. Incidental reproduction in a newsreel or broadcast of a work that appears embedded in the scene of an event being reported.

Assuming that a piece of media (text, audio, graphic, or video) is the exclusive property of its creator, questions arise regarding conditions under which a portion of the piece may be used legally without specific license from the author. Permission is not required to make "fair use" of a copyrighted work. Four factors are used to determine whether a proposed use of a copyrighted work is a fair use:

1. "The purpose and character of the use." A nonprofit educational use is more likely to be deemed a fair use than a commercial use.
2. "The nature of the copyrighted work." Copying factual material is more likely to be considered a fair use than copying the same amount of artistic or fictional material.
3. "The amount and substantiality of the portion used in relation to the work as a whole." A small percentage or a limited amount is more likely to be allowable than a large part.
4. "The effect of the use upon the potential market or upon the value of a copyrighted work." No reduced earning capacity for the copyright holder should result from fair use.

The Consortium of College and University Media Centers (CCUMC) Fair Access Working Committee has made recommendations addressing the extent to which multimedia content may be used by instructors and students in an educational setting. More information may be found online at *http://www.indiana.edu/~ccumc/copyright.html*. The following guidelines are extracted from the Working Committee's recommendations:

1. Educators may use portions of lawfully acquired copyrighted works in producing and using their own multimedia programs as teaching tools in support of an identified curriculum in face-to-face instruction. Similar use is permitted for remote instruction over an institution's electronic network, provided there are technological limitations on access to the network programs (a password or PIN) and on the total number of students enrolled.
2. Related to motion media, up to 10% or three minutes, whichever is less, in the aggregate of a copyrighted motion media work may be reproduced or otherwise incorporated as part of a multimedia program produced by an educator or student for educational purposes.
3. Related to text material, up to 10% or 1000 words may be incorporated; less than 250 words in the case of a poem, but no more than one poem by a single poet or five poems from an anthology may be used.
4. Related to music, up to 10% of an individual composition, or up to 10% of a musical recording, may be used for educational purposes. No more than 30 seconds of an individual copyrighted composition may be used in any case.
5. The reproduction of no more than five photographs and illustrations copyrighted by a single artist may be used in any one program. Not more than 10% or 15 images, whichever is less, may be used from a published collective work.
6. In any case where commercial reproduction and distribution will occur, licenses must be obtained.
7. Educators and students must obtain permission for all copyrighted works incorporated in programs that are distributed over uncontrolled electronic networks, for productions that are replicated beyond one copy, and in cases where institutions collaborate.
8. Citations and credit must be attributed to all sources of copyrighted works incorporated in multimedia programs, including those prepared under fair use. In the case of images

used in remote instruction, the copyright notice, date, and name must appear onscreen with the image.

Public Domain

A work in the public domain may be used by anyone for any purpose. Here are some of the ways in which a work may be deemed to be in the public domain:

1. The term of copyright has expired.
2. The work was created by the United States government and cannot be copyrighted.
3. The work is a title, a name, or a short phrase or slogan, and although it could be considered a trademark, it may not be copyrighted.
4. The copyright is forfeited. The copyright is forfeited in works published without notice prior to a change in the law that eliminated the notice requirement (March 1, 1988, the effective date of the Berne Convention Implementation Act).
5. The copyright has been abandoned. A direct statement or overt act dedicating the work to public domain is required by the copyright holder (a statement that anyone may reproduce, perform, or display the work without restrictions). Posting a work on a computer network does not constitute abandonment.

If there are any restrictions declared by the author on the use of a work, it is not public domain. It is copyrighted, and restrictions are essentially limitations. For example, the restriction that a work may only be given away for free is a limitation using the distribution right. Once a work is in the public domain, whether by expiration or dedication by the copyright holder, it cannot be restored except under certain conditions provided by the General Agreement on Tariffs and Trade (GATT) in 1994.

Failure to assert copyright against an infringer does not place a work in the public domain. At most, it might prevent the copyright owner from recovering from that infringer, if, for example, a statute of limitations has expired or if the infringer has relied on the copyright owner's failure to sue.

Replication of Audio Recordings

The Audio Home Recording Act (AHRA) was passed in October 1992. It added 10 sections to the United States Copyright Act, one of which provided an alternative to the fair use analysis for musical recordings. It states:

> No action may be brought under this title alleging infringement of copyright based on the manufacture, importation, or distribution of a digital audio recording device, a digital audio recording medium, an analog recording device, or an analog recording medium, or based on the noncommercial use by a consumer of such a device or medium for making digital musical recordings or analog musical recordings.

This means consumers cannot be sued for making analog or digital audio copies for private noncommercial use. It applies to music only, not to recordings of spoken words. The AHRA provided that a royalty payment (the "DAT tax") be paid for each sale of digital audio tape to compensate composers for profits lost due to these copies.

The right to prevent the unauthorized fixation and trafficking in sound recordings and music videos was added to copyright law in 1994. "Rights in Unfixed Works," as they are called, resulted from GATT.

All Rights Reserved

According to the 1911 Buenos Aires Convention on Literary and Artistic Copyrights, once copyright was obtained for a work in one signatory country, the other signatories offered protection without requiring registration, if a notice reserving rights was stated. The notice that complied with Buenos Aires was "All Rights Reserved." The "All Rights Reserved" notice no longer serves a useful purpose since the Buenos Aires Convention is not relevant today, having been superseded by other copyright treaties, such as the Universal Copyright Convention and the Berne Convention.

An official copyright notice includes the letter "C" in a circle or the word "Copyright," the year of initial publication, and the name of the copyright owner. If a copyright notice is included on a work to which the defendant in an infringement suit had access, the offender may not plead "innocent infringement." It is wise to include a notice on all published copies of a work.

Duration of Copyright

The duration of a copyright depends on whether the work was created before or after January 1, 1978, the effective date of the Copyright Act of 1976. This act was amended by the Copyright Term Extension Act, which became law in October 1998. The amended law extends the term of most copyrights by 20 years. The Extension Act includes the following provisions:

1. Extends the duration of copyright in a work created on or after January 1, 1978, to the life of the author and 70 years (previously 50 years) after the author's death, and applies the same extension to joint works.
2. Extends the duration of copyright in anonymous works or works made for hire on or after January 1, 1978, to 95 years (previously 75 years) from the year of the first publication, or 120 years (previously 100 years) from the year of creation, whichever expires first
3. Prohibits the annulment or limitation of rights or remedies under state laws with respect to sound recordings fixed before February 15, 1972, until February 15, 2067 (previously 2047).
4. Extends from December 31, 2027, to December 31, 2047, the duration of copyright in works published on or before December 31, 2002.
5. Extends the duration of copyrights in their renewal term at the time of the effective date of this Act to 95 years from the date such copyrights were originally secured.

The law permits an author to terminate a transfer or a license of a renewal (executed before January 1, 1978) of a copyright (other than a work made for hire) subsisting in its renewal term on the effective date of this Act, for which the termination right has not been exercised, and has expired, by such date. Allows termination of a transfer or license grant at any time during the five years beginning at the end of 75 years from the date the copyright was originally secured. Copyrights are not renewable. Attribution and integrity rights endure only for the lifetime of the author.

During the last 20 years of any term of copyright of a published work, the law allows a library or archive to reproduce, distribute, display, or perform in digital form a copy or phonorecord of such work for purposes of preservation, scholarship, or research after determining that none of the following conditions apply:
1. The work is subject to normal commercial exploitation.
2. A copy or phonorecord of the work can be obtained at a reasonable price.
3. The copyright owner or its agent provides notice that either of such conditions applies.

The law declares that the distribution of phonorecords before January 1, 1978, shall not constitute publication of the musical work for purposes of copyright infringement under the Copyright Act of 1909.

Copyright and the Internet

Usenet postings and email messages are copyrighted. They are "original works fixed in a tangible medium of expression." Only a clear declaration by the author would place a work into public domain. The two doctrines that allow copying are fair use and implied license. If the use was not commercial in nature, the posting was not an artistic or dramatic work, a short quotation was made for criticism and comment, and there was no impact on any market for the posting, it would probably qualify as fair use. Quoting of private email messages that met such criteria would also qualify. However, disseminating some email messages could lead to liability unrelated to copyright if the message were defamatory, an invasion of privacy, or a trade secret.

If a clearly visible limitation on the right to copy or quote is stated in the posting or message, it would be difficult to defend against infringement. On the other hand, implied license might be assumed for email messages posted to a public mailing list without stated limitations.

Postings and email messages are not usually registered with the Copyright Office. Registration is a requirement in order for a copyright owner to recover statutory damages and attorney fees. Therefore, if a copyright owner were to sue for infringement of an email or posting, he or she would probably be limited to collecting actual damages caused by the infringement (i.e., an actual monetary loss or a profit to the infringer that resulted from the infringement). Because those damages are so negligible, it would be of little benefit to sue, even if the copying of an email or posting were an infringement.

Digital Millennium Copyright Act

Effective October 1998, this law has numerous provisions for multimedia producers worldwide and impacts those who provide Internet services. The main provisions of this Act are:
1. Implements the terms of the World Intellectual Property Organization (WIPO) Copyright Treaties (Title I).

2. Prohibits circumvention of technological measures that control access to copyrighted works (copy protection schemes) (Title I).
3. Limits liability to online service providers (Title II).
4. Provides exemptions for use of diagnostic computer programs (Title III).
5. Makes other miscellaneous changes (Title IV).
6. Provides two years of protection for certain designs for useful articles (Title V).

The WIPO Copyright Treaties Implementation Act (Title I) grants copyright protection to:
1. Sound recordings that were first fixed in a treaty party (a country other than the United States that is a party to international copyright agreements).
2. Pictorial, graphic, or sculptural works incorporated in a building or an architectural work embodied in a building located in the United States or a treaty party.

Section 103 of the Act prohibits two things. The first is circumvention of technological protection measures that control access to protected works. The second is manufacturing or distributing technology designed to circumvent measures that control access to or protect rights of copyright owners. There are two exemptions to these prohibitions. The first is for nonprofit libraries, archives, or educational institutions that gain access to a commercially exploited copyrighted work solely to make a good faith determination of whether to acquire such work, subject to certain conditions. The second exemption is for law enforcement and intelligence activities.

The law defines "copyright management information" as the title and name of author and copyright owner conveyed in connection with copies or phonorecords of a work or performances or displays. The law recognizes digital forms of this information as valid. It prescribes criminal penalties for violations committed for commercial advantage or financial gain. It makes criminal penalties inapplicable to nonprofit libraries, archives, and educational institutions. It also imposes a statute of limitations on criminal proceedings.

The Online Copyright Infringement Liability Limitation Act (Title II) amends federal copyright law to exempt an online material provider from liability for direct infringement, based solely on the intermediate storage and transmission of material through such provider's system or network, if:
1. The transmission was initiated by another person.
2. The storage and transmission is carried out through an automatic process.
3. No copy of such material is maintained in a manner ordinarily accessible to anyone other than the intended recipients and no copy is maintained any longer than necessary.

The law exempts such a provider from liability if the provider is not aware of facts or circumstances from which infringing activity is apparent and if there is no financial benefit directly attributable to the infringing activity. It further exempts a provider from any claim based on disabling online access to material in response to knowledge or information that such material is infringing, whether or not such material is in fact an infringement. The law also makes liable for damages any person who misrepresents that online material is an infringement.

The law provides that it is not a copyright infringement for the owner or lessee of a machine to make a copy of a computer program solely by activating a machine that lawfully contains an authorized copy of the program exclusively for maintenance or repair of that machine, provided:

1. The new copy is used in no other manner and is destroyed immediately after the maintenance or repair.
2. Any program that is not necessary for machine activation is not accessed or used other than to make such new copy by activation of the machine.

Differences Between Copyright and Patent

The primary differences between a copyright and a patent in the United States are as follows:

1. The subject matter protected: A copyright covers "works of authorship" (literary, dramatic, musical, pictorial, graphic, audio-video, sound recordings, and the like). A patent covers an invention or a useful new feature of a product or process.
2. The requirement for protection: To be copyrighted, a work must be original and fixed in a tangible medium of expression. A patented invention must be new and useful. A patent is not automatic; it must be issued by the United States Patent and Trademark Office.
3. When protection begins: Copyright protection currently begins when a work is created. Patent protection begins when a patent is issued.
4. Duration of protection: Copyright protection typically lasts for 50 years beyond the author's death. Patents filed after June 8, 1995, in the United States have a term of 20 years from the filing date. Patents in effect on that date have a term of 20 years, or 17 years from the date of issue, whichever is longer.
5. Infringement: If a person other than the copyright owner independently comes up with a similar work, there is no infringement. A patent confers a monopoly that prevents others from selling the patented invention, although a person may independently reinvent a patented invention.

Another significant difference is the cost. A copyright is free. A patent is costly and the patent application process is much more complex. A copyright protects an author's rights inherent in a work. A patent provides ownership to an inventor in exchange for publicly sharing the details and specifications of an invention.

Copyright and Employment

The company for which an employee works may own the copyrights to his or her work by applying either the assignment or the work-made-for-hire doctrine:

Assignment: Many companies automatically acquire a blanket assignment of copyright for any works created on the job starting at time of hiring.

Work made for hire: A work qualifies as a work made for hire if it was prepared by an employee within the scope of employment or if it was specially commissioned and the parties agreed in writing that it was to be considered a work for hire.

Infringement and Penalties

Infringement is considered a civil matter (a tort). It may also be a federal crime in certain circumstances. If it is willful and committed for commercial advantage or financial gain, it is subject to criminal prosecution. In cases of offending reproduction or distribution rights of 10 or more copies with a value of more than $2500 during any 180-day period, the offense is a felony. The statute of limitation for copyright infringement for both civil suits and criminal prosecutions is three years.

The United States government may be sued for copyright infringement. Whether a state may be sued is unclear. The Eleventh Amendment says that a state cannot be sued in federal court. The Copyright Act expressly states, however, that a state can be sued for copyright infringement. Until 1996, it was generally thought that the clause in the Copyright Act did indeed make a state liable for its infringements. However, a 1996 case involving an Indian tribe suing a state on an issue completely unrelated to copyright put some important restrictions on the ability of Congress to abrogate a state's immunity. As a result, there is considerable uncertainty today as to whether a state may be sued for copyright infringement.

Works of the United States government are generally considered to be in the public domain. For purposes of copyright law, the United States Postal Service, the District of Columbia, Puerto Rico, and organized territories of the United States are not considered to be part of the United States government.

If an independent contractor working for the government produces a work, it may be copyrighted, and nothing prevents that contractor from assigning the copyright to the government. Unlike federal government works, those credited to state governments are subject to copyright.

Securing Copyright on an Original Story or Song

In the United States and most other countries, a work is automatically copyrighted when it is created. The following statement is from Section 102 of the Copyright Act:

> Copyright protection subsists . . . in original works of authorship fixed in any tangible medium of expression, now known or later developed, from which they can be perceived, reproduced, or otherwise communicated, either directly or with the aid of a machine or device.

A work is "fixed" in a tangible medium of expression when its embodiment in a copy or phonorecord, by or under the authority of the author, is sufficiently permanent or stable to permit it to be perceived, reproduced, or otherwise communicated for a period of more than transitory duration.

It is not necessary to register a work with the Copyright Office or to provide a copyright notice on the work. However, it is wise to register a work and to include a copyright notice for purposes of defending it against infringement.

How to Register a Copyright with the United States Copyright Office

Forms for registering are available from the Copyright Office at its online address: *http://lcweb.loc.gov/copyright/forms.html*. They are in the Adobe Acrobat (.pdf) format. A copyright may be registered by filing the appropriate form with a $20 payment for registration and two copies of the work. A Copyright Office Information Package includes the appropriate forms and instructions for filing. For information, contact the United States Copyright Office at (202) 707–3000, or call (202) 707–6737 to order forms. Packages are available for the following types of media:

> *Computer programs:* Form TX, Package 113
>
> *Photographs:* Form VA, Package 107
>
> *Motion pictures and video recordings:* Form PA, Package 110
>
> *Games:* Form TX, Package 108
>
> *Drawings, prints, and visual artworks:* Form VA, Package 115
>
> *Music (sheet or lyrics):* Form PA, Package 105
>
> *Music (sound recordings):* Form SR, Package 121
>
> *Dramatic scripts, plays, and screenplays:* Form PA, Package 119
>
> *Books, manuscripts, and nondramatic literature:* Form TX, Package 109

Protecting Rights with Specific Licenses

Creators of multimedia who have ownership in content may need to consider ways to protect their interests. A licensing contract is ambiguous if the rights granted are not specific. A licensee grants an implied negative covenant to the licensor not to use the ungranted portion of the copyright to the detriment of the licensee. There are four steps that parties may take to clarify contractual license agreements:

1. Specify the rights that are granted and those that are not. One right that many multimedia producers may wish to retain is the Right to Reuse Art, or to make a number of copies to show as portfolio samples. The wording in a contract might be as follows: . . . Nothing in this Contract deprives the Licensor of the right to copy or display the Artwork otherwise exclusively licensed hereunder to the extent (1) the Artwork is not sold, (2) it is used solely for the purposes of promoting the Licensor's work in a portfolio, and (3) the Licensee shall have continuing nonexclusive rights to the Artwork.

2. The Reservation of Rights clause may be included in a license contract to avoid granting more rights than intended. It could be stated in the following terms: . . . This Contract is a complete statement of the rights granted related to the Artwork that is licensed. All rights and licenses of any kind, including copyrights and rights that might otherwise be implied that are not expressly granted in this Contract are reserved exclusively by the Licensor.

3. Multimedia producers may wish to include a Merger clause in their licenses. Such a clause is intended to prevent a court from considering previous verbal agreements (or anything else) that may modify the terms of a contract. An example might read as follows: . . . This contract sets forth the entire agreement of the parties relating to its subject matter and merges and supersedes all prior discussions or understandings of any kind, written or oral. The terms of this contract may not be changed, modified, canceled, or terminated except by a written document signed by all parties to this contract that explicitly refers to this contract.

4. Producers and developers may choose to specify that the publisher of their work maintain accurate records related to royalties, and that an accountant be permitted to inspect the books on which royalties are based annually. This is a Standard Audit clause.

As they apply to interactive digital media, copyright laws are being defined and tested on a case-by-case basis. Precedents are being set at a time when new forms of art, and indeed the media and forms of communication by which they are fixed and transmitted, are evolving at an accelerated pace. Still, the age-old concepts of fairness and granting credit where it is due will guide decisions as they always have.

Copyright Information on the Internet

The Copyright Act is available on the World Wide Web at:
www.law.cornell.edu/usc/17/overview.html

The 1971 Paris Text of the Berne Convention is also at the Cornell site:
www.law.cornell.edu/treaties/berne/overview.html

The Multilaterals Project, which provides copies of both the Berne Convention and the Universal Copyright Convention, is available at Tufts:
www.tufts.edu/fletcher/multilaterals.html

The Coalition for Networked Information (CNI) sponsors CNI-Copyright, an Internet mailing list devoted to copyright issues. The FTP site is:
ftp://ftp.cni.org/CNI/forums/cni-copyright

Some Usenet newsgroups that address copyright issues are:
misc.legal, misc.legal.computing, misc.legal.moderated, and *comp.software.licensing*